SCIENCE EXPLORER

SCIENCE EXPLORER

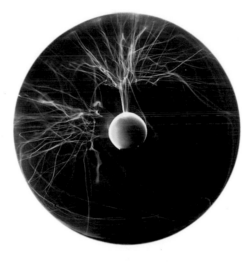

Written by

DAVID BURNIE

JACK CHALLONER

CHRISTOPHER COOPER

PETER LAFFERTY

DR ANN NEWMARK

STEVE PARKER

A Dorling Kindersley Book

LONDON, NEW YORK,
MELBOURNE, MUNICH, AND DELHI

The Eyewitness Guides were conceived by Dorling Kindersley Limited
and Editions Gallimard

Published in the United States by
DK Publishing, Inc.
375 Hudson Street
New York, NY10014

04 05 10 9 8 7 6 5 4 3 2 1

A catalog record for this book is available from the Library of Congress

ISBN 0-7566-0430-3

Reproduced in Singapore by Colourscan
Printed and bound in Hong Kong by Toppan

See our complete product line at
www.dk.com

Contents

ENERGY

LIGHT

MATTER

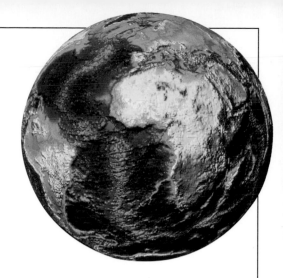

CHEMISTRY

ELECTRICITY

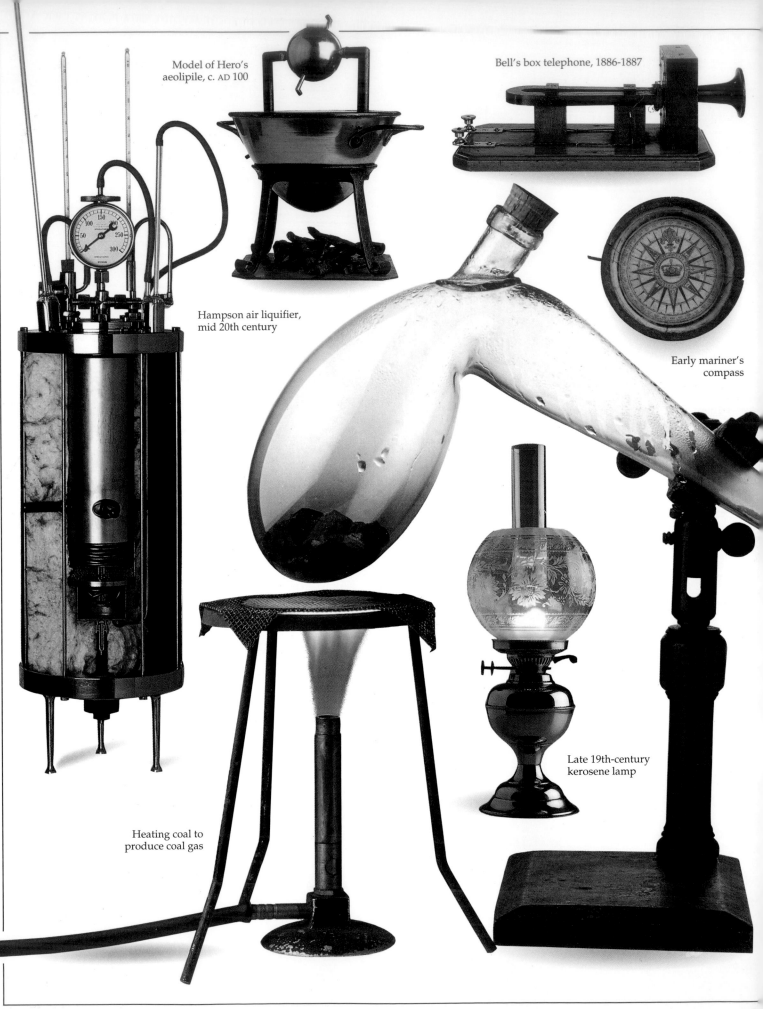

Model of Hero's aeolipile, c. AD 100

Bell's box telephone, 1886-1887

Hampson air liquifier, mid 20th century

Early mariner's compass

Late 19th-century kerosene lamp

Heating coal to produce coal gas

ENERGY

Late 19th-century
burning lens

Late 19th-century apparatus
to show that heat causes
expansion in solids

Model of a Greek ship of 800 BC

Model of an early
20th-century tram

L.C.C.

Model of a Pelton wheel,
late 19th century

Melting ice in
a hot liquid

What is energy?

THE FAITHFUL SUN
The Sun is the supplier of nearly all the energy on Earth. The energy from the Sun travels through the 93 million miles (150 million km) of space to the Earth as electromagnetic radiation, a form of energy that includes light, X-rays, and radio waves.

WITHOUT ENERGY, there would be nothing. There would be no Sun, no wind, no rivers, and no life at all. Energy is everywhere, and energy changing from one form to another is behind everything that happens. Energy, defined as the ability to make things happen, cannot be created. Nor can it be destroyed. Plants and animals harness energy from nature to help them grow and survive. The most intelligent of animals, human beings, have developed many ways of using the available energy to improve their lives. Ancient people used energy from fire, and they developed tools to use energy from their muscles more effectively. But ancient people did not understand the role of energy in their lives. Such an understanding of energy has really developed only over the past few hundred years.

AN ENERGETIC FROG
This frog needs energy to jump. Because anything that moves has energy, energy is needed to start the frog moving. The frog obtains the energy it needs from food. When the frog lands, it will lose the energy of its movement. But the energy will still exist as heat in its body and in the surrounding soil, air, and water.

A BRIGHT SPARK
On a hot and humid day, electrical energy builds up as electric charges separate in the clouds. When the separation is large enough, there is enough energy to spark from the cloud down to the ground in an impressive display. The electrical energy becomes heat energy, light energy, and the sound energy of thunder.

ENERGY UNDERGROUND
The energy released by this geyser did not come from the Sun. It comes from the heat of molten rock in the Earth and heat generated by friction and pressure as the rocks deep underground push against each other. In some places, people use the heat energy generated in this way as an alternative to fossil fuels for heating homes or generating electricity.

SEETHING VOLCANO
Huge amounts of energy are released in a large volcanic eruption. This painting of the eruption of Mount Vesuvius in Italy shows molten lava, smoke, poisonous gas, and ashes being blown into the air. In AD 79, the volcano erupted, covering the towns of Herculaneum and Pompeii with debris.

CARNIVOROUS PLANT
Animals need to obtain
their energy by eating other
living things. But most plants
can store energy directly from the Sun
by a process called photosynthesis. When
sunlight falls on a plant, it causes chemical
reactions which result in energy being stored in
chemicals within the plant. Some plants, such as this
Venus fly trap, supplement their energy by attracting
insects – they digest the insects, making use of the
energy and chemicals stored in the insect's body.

ENERGY FROM THE WIND
Energy is needed to make these trees bend over. As the Sun
heats the Earth, it does so unevenly, because some parts of
the Earth heat up more quickly than others. This causes
differences in air pressure, and high-pressure air moves to
equalize with lower-pressure air, creating winds. So the
energy from wind is really energy from the Sun.

ENERGY IN RUNNING WATER
As the Sun's energy warms the seas
and rivers, some of the water evaporates,
and it rises high into the atmosphere
where it condenses to form clouds. The
water droplets in the clouds gather
and fall back to Earth as raindrops.
The rain gathers into fast-moving
streams. The energy of
running water comes
originally from the Sun.

Muscle energy

IN ANCIENT TIMES, PEOPLE USED THE ENERGY of their own muscles to do work such as gathering food and building shelter. To make this muscle energy even more useful, and to use it efficiently, early people invented simple tools. The first tools were made of wood and stone, but once smelting was developed metal tools became available. Another source of muscle power was found in animals - one large animal, such as an ox, can be up to seven times more powerful than one human. Animals were used on their own for transporting people and goods, but they were also used together with simple tools and machines to perform more complex tasks, such as plowing fields and pumping water for irrigation. By making more use of this kind of muscle energy, people had more time to develop other skills and activities.

Wall painting from the tomb of the Pharaoh Rekmire showing an Egyptian bow drill in use

Bow

INUIT ENERGY SAVER
One of the earliest types of tool is the bow drill. Bow drills were used in many cultures for jobs as varied as starting fires and drilling holes. This Inuit bow drill was probably made for drilling holes in bones and wood. Bow drills are made from a central pole, which is held firmly in place but can rotate, and a bow that quickly rotates the central pole. This action transfers the human muscle energy to the tip of the central pole, where the work is being done.

Leather string makes the pole rotate

Central pole

Metal tip

PLOWING THE SOIL
A plow is a tool used to break up soil to prepare it for sowing seeds. This model, showing a man driving a plow pulled by a pair of oxen, was found buried deep in an Egyptian tomb of c. 2000 BC. It shows that people have used plows for thousands of years. In fact, the first plows were used around 4000 BC in Mesopotamia. Originally, they were pushed entirely by people, but later people learned to make plows more efficient by using animals that pulled a plow as it was pushed into the soil by a person.

Person applies muscle energy to the plow

The tip of the plow breaks the soil

Plow is pushed into soil

SADDLE STONE GRINDER
Grinding grain was one of the major activities of early peoples. Many machines have been used to supply the energy for this task, including windmills and water wheels (pp. 18-19), steam engines (pp. 28-29), and electric motors. The earliest method involved placing the grain on a stone, called a saddle stone because of its shape, and crushing the grains with another stone, which was often called a rubber. This Egyptian limestone figure of c. 2310 BC was found in a tomb. It shows a female servant grinding grain and suggests that this was a common activity as long as 4,000 years ago.

Soil

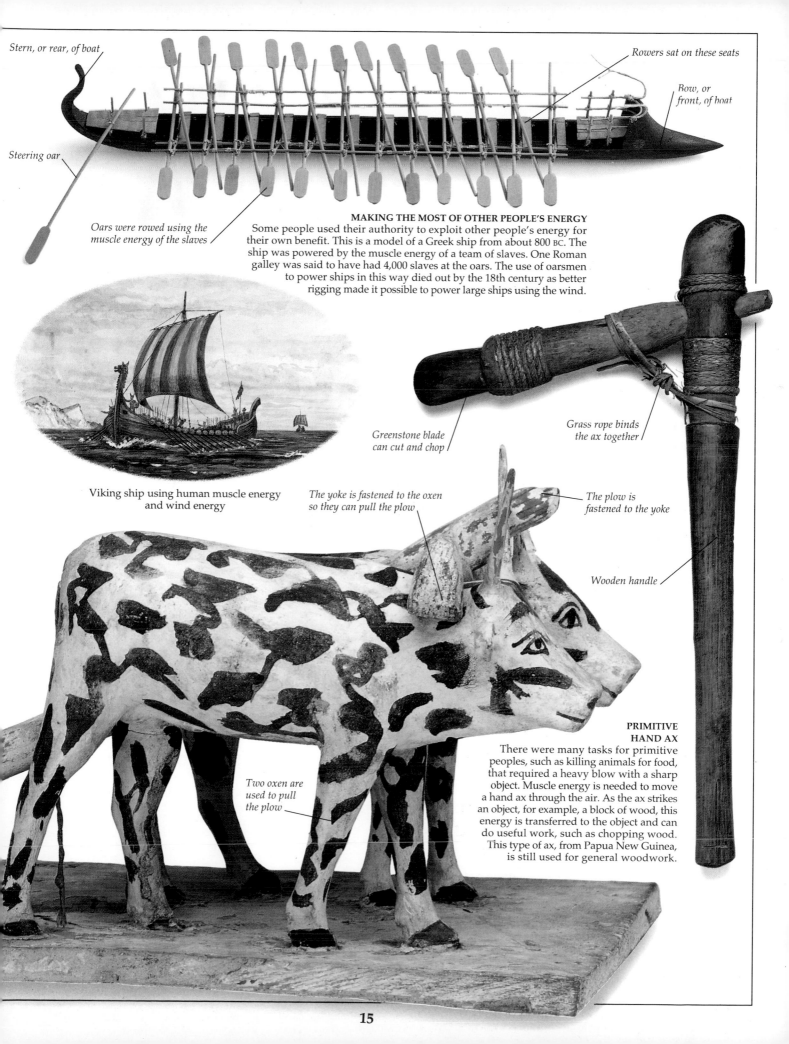

Stern, or rear, of boat

Rowers sat on these seats

Bow, or front, of boat

Steering oar

Oars were rowed using the muscle energy of the slaves

MAKING THE MOST OF OTHER PEOPLE'S ENERGY

Some people used their authority to exploit other people's energy for their own benefit. This is a model of a Greek ship from about 800 BC. The ship was powered by the muscle energy of a team of slaves. One Roman galley was said to have had 4,000 slaves at the oars. The use of oarsmen to power ships in this way died out by the 18th century as better rigging made it possible to power large ships using the wind.

Viking ship using human muscle energy and wind energy

Greenstone blade can cut and chop

Grass rope binds the ax together

The yoke is fastened to the oxen so they can pull the plow

The plow is fastened to the yoke

Wooden handle

PRIMITIVE HAND AX

There were many tasks for primitive peoples, such as killing animals for food, that required a heavy blow with a sharp object. Muscle energy is needed to move a hand ax through the air. As the ax strikes an object, for example, a block of wood, this energy is transferred to the object and can do useful work, such as chopping wood. This type of ax, from Papua New Guinea, is still used for general woodwork.

Two oxen are used to pull the plow

Energy from fire

MYTHS ABOUT FIRE

The energy released by burning fuels was an extremely important resource for early people. But even though fire was used every day, they did not understand what it really was. To them, fire was magic. Throughout the world, different cultures had different ideas to explain where fire came from. Some said it was given by the gods. This statue is of Xuihtecuhtli, the Aztec Lord of Fire. His image was placed in the hearth of every Aztec home.

HUMAN BEINGS HAVE USED FIRE for thousands of years, though the date of the discovery or first use of fire is unknown. It is known, however, that late Stone Age cave dwellers kept their caves warm with fires which, it seems, were kept alight continuously for months or years. Since then, people have learned to use the energy of fire in many ways, from cooking food and lighting their homes, to smelting ore, firing pottery, and making glass. Most of the energy from fire is heat energy that is released when a fuel is burned. The first fuel was wood, but charcoal, which is produced by heating wood without air, burns with a hotter flame. Burning charcoal and using bellows to increase the supply of air causes the charcoal to burn hotter, making it possible to extract metals from their ores. The metal atoms in metal ores are usually bound tightly to oxygen atoms, and energy from fire is needed to separate them into oxygen plus the pure metal. Although most of the energy of fire is heat, energy in the form of light and sound is also released. This is why fire can be seen, felt, and heard.

FIRE FOR COOKING

There is evidence from caves in China that fire was first used in cooking as long ago as 500,000 years. The heat energy from fire can be used to change food in many ways. It can make meat more tender, and it can make food safer to eat by killing harmful bacteria. Also, the heat of a fire can help combine ingredients into new substances, as it does when dough is baked into bread.

SMELTING THE ORE

Ores are rocks that contain metals, but not in a pure state. Energy is needed to extract, or "smelt," metals from their ores. The metal atoms are tightly combined with atoms of other elements, such as oxygen. The energy that fire supplies breaks the metal from its bonds with the other elements. The first metals to be smelted were copper and tin, which people later learned to combine to make bronze. All metals need a high temperature to be smelted, and the use of bellows helps to reach this by increasing the supply of air to the fire. This is a model of a primitive hearth from the Sudan in Africa. A hearth like this one can reach temperatures of around 1650° F (900° C). In some parts of Central Africa, smelting hearths are still used.

Sticks operate the bellows

Bellows increase the supply of air to the fire

Charcoal is the fuel for the fire

Metal ore is placed in the fire

Smelted metal is left at the bottom of the fire

Upper level is cooler

Ceramic pots held the batch for melting

Containers for cooling glass slowly

Blowpipe was inserted through one of these windows

Wood fire is burned at the bottom of the furnace

GLASSMAKER'S FURNACE

Fire is an essential element in making glass. The main ingredient of glass is sand, which is mixed with other ingredients to form the "batch." The batch is melted by the heat from fire; and when it is cooled the glass is formed. A fire raged at the bottom of this 16th-century furnace, and the batch was melted in the large ceramic pots. A glass blower could then reach through one of the windows and pick up some of the molten mixture on the end of a "blowpipe," which was then used to blow the glass into the desired shape. A mold could also be used to help achieve this. Glass was first made as long ago as 4000 BC, and there is evidence to show that it was blown in this way during the 1st century BC.

ROMAN CENTRAL HEATING

Fire has been used to heat homes for many thousands of years. The ancient Greeks were the first to use central heating, but the Romans improved on it with a sophisticated heating system called a "hypocaust." It heated the rooms of public baths and some houses. A fire was lit and tended by a slave, and the hot air from the fire moved around in ducts under the floors, eventually escaping through a chimney. This potentially dangerous use of fire in the home may have been one of the reasons the Romans were also the first to have organized fire fighters.

Roman glass bottles, c. AD 3-4

Bellows are made of leather and clay

Energy from wind and water

ANCIENT PEOPLE COULD SEE that there was tremendous force in the natural motion of wind and water. Although they had no scientific understanding of energy, they realized they could harness these natural forces to do some heavy work. Early civilizations used "mechanical energy" to do work like lifting, grinding grain, building, and transporting people and goods. This mechanical energy could be obtained from wind or moving water. Wind and water flow are the most visible examples of natural energy on the Earth, but that energy originally comes from the Sun (pp. 54-55). The wind that turns the sails of a windmill and fills the sails of a sailing boat is caused by the Sun heating the Earth. The rain that falls from the sky was once ocean, lake, or river water that evaporated back into the atmosphere because of the Sun's energy.

ENERGY FOR THE DAILY GRIND
Horizontal water wheels like this are called "Greek" or "Norse" wheels. This wheel was used to grind grain into flour. Grain was placed into the top of the funnel-shaped container, called a hopper, and fell down between the millstones. The top millstone was turned by the water wheel underneath, and the grain was crushed to make flour, which fell down into the trough below. Horizontal wheels like this need fast-moving water to be effective.

Water power

Water wheels were used for irrigation as long ago as 600 BC, but water power was first used for grinding corn around 100 BC in various parts of the world. The type of water wheel used depended on how fast the stream or river flowed. The use of water power has since developed in many different ways, and it is still an important alternative to fossil fuels.

Gears transfer mechanical energy to different parts of the mill

Belts are attached to pulleys

Reels hold the cotton

USING WATER IN INDUSTRY
Until the invention of the steam engine, water power was heavily used in industry. This model shows a cotton mill that was built at the end of the 18th century. Water flowed underneath the mill, turning the water wheel. The movement of the water was a reliable and free source of energy. It powered the machines in the mill through gears and pulleys. To make use of water, such mills had to be built near rivers. Steam engines, in contrast, could be used anywhere – one of the main reasons steam power took over in industry.

The wheel moves in the direction of the water flow

Water falls into the water wheel

Undershot water wheel

Belts transmit the power from the water wheel to the machines

OVERSHOT WHEEL
Overshot water wheels are used where water falls from a great height, having potential energy, but it is slow moving, having little kinetic energy. The water pulls one side of the wheel around with it as the water falls.

Slow-moving water source

UNDERSHOT WHEEL
These water wheels are used in fast-moving water which has a lot of kinetic energy (pp. 22-23). The water passes under the wheel and pushes blades, which turn the wheel. This could be connected to heavy machinery in factories.

The wheel moves in the direction of the water flow

Fast-moving water source

Wind power

One of the earliest forms of power that people learned to use, wind was used to move boats with cloth sails as long ago as 3500 BC. On land, the first windmills seem to have been used in Persia around AD 700. The sails turned horizontally and were connected directly to grindstones used to grind grain. Wind power is also used for irrigating dry land and draining wet land. The wind is used as an alternative energy source to generate electricity.

The vanes turn at a constant speed, even if the wind speed changes

Large gear wheel transmits power to the grindstone

This mechanism allows each sail or vane to twist automatically away from the wind, if the wind is too strong

Top cap houses the machinery that takes the motion of the sails and converts it into the mechanical energy of the grindstone

Fantail regulates the movement of the top cap

Mast holds the sail

Square sail captures the wind

Large hopper directs the grain onto the grindstone

Top cap turns automatically, so the sails face the wind if the fantail turns

Oars are used to steer the boat

Animal carvings decorate covered seats

Grindstone grinds the corn

Balcony

GRINDING CORN
This is a model of a windmill built at the beginning of the 19th century in the UK. Like most European mills, it has vertical (rather than horizontal) sails or vanes. They turn around as some of the horizontal motion of the wind is changed to a rotational motion of the sails. Their motion is transferred by gears and pulleys to a grindstone, which grinds grain into flour. To make use of as much of the energy of the wind as possible, the "top cap" of the windmill automatically turns around to face into the wind if the wind changes direction. Wind power is of great importance in places prone to flooding, like Holland, where it has been used for pumping water to drain the land. In 1341, a bishop in Holland even tried to claim legally all of the wind that blew through his town.

SAILING BOATS
Most modern sailboats have triangular sails that can be moved to catch the most wind energy. This is a model of an Egyptian ship from around 1300 BC that used square sails, which can efficiently use the energy of the wind only if they have the wind behind them. By 200 BC, ships in the Mediterranean used sails that could be moved to make use of the wind's energy, even if it was not blowing directly behind the sails.

Living quarters for the miller

Early 19th-century windmill

LISTENING TO THE WIND
The Greek engineer Hero of Alexandria (pp. 34-35) designed this musical organ which was powered by the wind. Sound is a form of energy that travels from the source to our ears by the vibration of air molecules. Hero used the energy of the wind to push a piston in the organ back and forth. The piston pushed air through the organ pipes, which vibrated the air around them, making the sound. Hero's design for this organ is very similar to the design of the modern pipe organ.

Potential energy

The hands turn slowly with the release of energy from the falling weight

AN EGG THAT IS RELEASED from some height on to a hard surface will fall, and it will probably break. Before the egg is released, it has the "potential" to fall. People know that an egg released from a height will fall, and most people also realize that the higher and the heavier the egg, the greater the chance that it will break. But where does the egg's potential to fall come from? Someone may have lifted it up, working against gravity and using the energy in their muscles from the food they have eaten to do so. Potential energy is stored whenever something moves in the opposite direction to a force acting on it. So, stretching an elastic band stores energy because the molecules of the elastic are moved apart, working against the forces between the molecules that are pulling them together. There are many forms of potential energy, and many forms of energy that it can become. But the total amount of energy always stays the same.

HUYGENS'S CLOCK
Dutch scientist Christian Huygens (1629-1695) was the inventor of the pendulum clock, which he first devised by attaching a pendulum to the gears of a mechanical clock. The regular swing of the pendulum made the clock run much more precisely than before. This is a model of a clock Huygens made in 1673. The energy to drive the hands of this clock against friction comes from the falling of the lead weight, which releases a fraction of the weight's potential energy with each tick. The clock stops when the weight reaches its lowest position. The energy, or "work," of the person who raises the weight is stored in the weight as potential energy, which is released as the weight descends.

POTENTIAL ENERGY AT WAR
These Roman soldiers are storing their muscle energy in a catapult. When the catapult is released, the potential energy the soldiers contributed is released. The catapult will shoot a missile forward toward the enemy, using all of its stored potential energy.

Small weight acts as a counterbalance, keeping the string tight

Lead weight loses potential energy as it descends

WINDING UP THE CLOCK
Inside a mechanical clock is a coiled piece of metal called a "mainspring." The mainspring stores the muscle energy of the person who winds up the clock. The clock can run for a few days by releasing the potential energy stored in the mainspring. This clock mechanism transforms this energy into the movement of the hands, the sound of the ticking, and a small amount of heat. Many other types of clock, such as water clocks or candle clocks, rely on the steady release of some form of potential energy to keep time. Many scientists used to think the Universe was like a huge clockwork machine, gradually winding down as time passes.

Key is used to transfer energy from the muscles to the clock

Gearing inside the clock mechanism controls the release of the energy

The pendulum is kept swinging by the energy of the falling weight

GRANDFATHER CLOCK
A "grandfather clock" is a large clock that is housed in a freestanding case. This one has three dials, all driven by the energy of the falling weights.

STUDYING IMPACT

Although it was not until the mid-19th century that people really understood potential energy, it was the subject of many experiments carried out during the century before. In this experiment Dutch scientist Willem s'Gravesande (pp. 22-23) studied potential energy by dropping balls of various weights on to soft clay. He found that the impact the balls made in the clay depended on the weight of the balls and the height from which the balls fell. In other words, the potential of the balls to make an impact was greater from a greater height. S'Gravesande also experimented with energy stored in springs, and he built machines to measure and demonstrate the properties of moving objects.

Metal ball

ENERGY IN A MATCH HEAD

A match stores potential energy in the chemicals that form the match head. Many chemicals, or mixtures of chemicals, undergo reactions in which they may give out energy. When a match is rubbed against a scratchy surface, the molecules in the head of the match are rearranged. The molecules react by igniting, causing energy to be released in the form of heat and light.

Chemicals in the match head store potential energy

Scratchy surface against which the match is rubbed

When the match is struck, it ignites

Soft clay records the impact of the ball

The size of the dent can now be measured

The ball has used its potential energy to make the dent

1 POTENTIAL ENERGY

The metal ball is suspended over some soft clay. The ball has been weighed beforehand, and now its height over the clay is measured. In order to release the potential energy stored in the ball, the string must be cut.

2 THE ENERGY OF IMPACT

The impact in the clay shows the amount of kinetic energy of the ball as it hit the clay. The kinetic energy of an object increases as it accelerates. If the ball had twice the weight, it would have had twice the impact.

GALILEO GALILEI

One of the first modern physicists was Galileo Galilei (1564-1642), an Italian scholar. He experimented with objects falling and rolling down slopes. Although he could not have known about energy, he seemed to have a natural grasp of the idea of potential energy. This was truly remarkable because, at the time, everyone else followed the ideas of Aristotle (pp. 22-23), who thought that objects moved because it was "in their nature to do so." By combining careful experimentation and brilliant reasoning, Galileo showed that this view was incorrect. Objects fall not just because they are heavy, but because they are given potential energy – perhaps by someone lifting them. Without Galileo, it may have taken much longer to realize this.

The barrel has potential energy

To make use of its potential energy, the barrel must be pushed over the "hill"

The barrel has used its supply of potential energy

POTENTIAL HILL

Energy is needed to move any object against the force of gravity, which tries to pull the object down. To get a barrel to the top of a hill, muscle energy must be applied to move the barrel. When the barrel rolls down the hill, it gradually loses its potential energy until it reaches its lowest potential energy at the bottom of the slope. Natural processes act in the same way, always finding their lowest energy. Notice the shape of the hill: it has a bump over which the barrel must be pushed before its potential energy can be released. Many chemical reactions, like the burning of matches (see top), also have a potential energy "hill" – they must be given energy to start, but then they continue of their own accord. For matches, the energy to get over the hill is supplied by the heat produced when the matches are struck.

21

The energy of movement

EVERYTHING THAT MOVES HAS ENERGY called "kinetic" energy. The faster an object moves, and the more mass it has, the more kinetic energy it has. In 1686, the German mathematician Gottfried Wilhelm Leibniz (1646-1716) introduced the term *vis viva*, meaning living force, which was very close to the idea of kinetic energy that was worked out in the 1800s. The *vis viva* of an object depended on its mass and speed. Scientists noticed that this energy seemed to be "conserved" – a moving ball could transfer its energy to a stationary one. However, when a moving object hits a soft material, such as sand, it is obvious that the energy is not conserved because the sand seems to absorb the movement. This puzzle remained unsolved until it was shown that moving objects have energy that can be changed into other forms (pp. 30-31). Thus when a moving object hits sand the energy is not lost, but changed into a form such as heat. All forms of energy are either kinetic or potential energy.

WHAT THE GREEKS THOUGHT
The Greek philosopher Aristotle (384-322 BC) thought that things move towards their "natural place" because of their nature. A stone is heavy, so it will fall. It is in a bird's nature to fly. Because these ideas seemed correct, no one tested them to find out whether they were true. Indeed, it was nearly 2,000 years later (p. 330) that people started experimenting with objects in motion and challenging Aristotle's view.

Moving hammer has a lot of kinetic energy

Two objects of the same mass

SAME MASS, DIFFERENT SPEEDS *(left and above)*
Two objects of the same mass traveling at different speeds have different amounts of kinetic energy. A ball with twice the speed will have four times the kinetic energy. Kinetic energy depends on the square of the speed (four is two squared). A ball with ten times the speed will have 100 times the kinetic energy.

The kinetic energy of the hammer is transferred to the nail

HAMMERING THE NAIL
The head of a hammer has a good deal of kinetic energy as it strikes a nail. Once the hammer comes to a stop it has lost all of its kinetic energy. But the energy has not disappeared. It has been transferred to the atoms and molecules of the nail, the wood, the air, and even the hammer. This random kinetic energy is heat.

SAME SPEED, DIFFERENT MASSES *(above)*
Two objects with different masses traveling at the same speed have different amounts of kinetic energy. An object with twice the mass will have twice the kinetic energy. The mass of an object is the amount of matter it is made of, and mass is directly related to weight, which is the force of gravity pulling on an object.

Two objects of different masses

The energy the nail gains is transferred to the wood

SCIENTISTS IN CONFLICT
Through the 18th century, there was a great deal of argument about Leibniz's idea of *vis viva*. One person involved in this controversy was Gabrielle de Breteuil, Marquise du Châtelet (c. 1700-1749). Many scientists rejected the idea of *vis viva*, but the Marquise was convinced that Leibniz was right. In 1740 she wrote a book that convinced many others that the *vis viva* idea was correct.

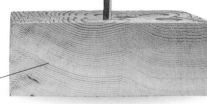

STUDYING *VIS VIVA*

Dutch scientist Willem s'Gravesande (1688-1742) built several machines to experiment with motion. He also made machines that calculated how compressed springs can make things move as they are released. It seemed that the *vis viva* was somehow stored up in the spring. It is now known that potential energy stored in an object, such as a spring, becomes kinetic energy as it makes an object move.

Balls are suspended from pegs

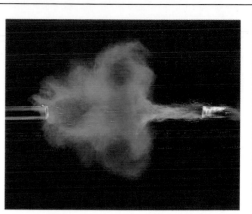

FIRING A BULLET

Whenever something is made to move, it is given kinetic energy. When a bullet is fired, the energy for the movement of the bullet comes from the explosion of gunpowder in the barrel. The explosion produces mainly heat energy. This is transferred to the air in the gun barrel, which rapidly expands as it is heated, giving its kinetic energy to the bullet. The bullet is pushed at high speed, and the energy of the bullet is then transferred to the object the bullet hits.

EXPERIMENTING WITH COLLISIONS

This replica of one of s'Gravesande's machines has two balls. One ball is made to swing from a particular distance from the middle of the apparatus and collide with the other, stationary, ball. The masses of the balls and the distances that they swing are measured. S'Gravesande used this information to calculate how much *vis viva* the moving ball had at the time of collision. Although Leibniz believed that the total amount of *vis viva* stayed the same, the balls eventually came to a stop. Leibniz suggested that the motion was not lost, but became motion inside the ball. We now know that this motion is heat.

Pegs mark the positions of the strings

Scale allows distance of ball from the center of the machine to be measured

Stationary ball is hit by moving ball

Ball is released from a particular distance

Imponderable fluids

MOST SCIENTISTS of the 18th century believed that matter is made of particles. Many of them thought that effects such as light, heat, magnetism, and electricity were also made of particles. These "effects" were known to travel from place to place. Scientists thought that to do this, the particles had to flow like fluid, be weightless (experiments to weigh heat and electricity were unsuccessful), and be able to penetrate objects. Each phenomenon was thought to be carried by different fluids, which were called "imponderable fluids," so they would be completely separate. The greatest interest was in heat and electricity; further study of these effects contributed to the downfall of this theory. By the middle of the 19th century the idea of imponderable fluids was proven to be incorrect.

Hand is placed on top of glass globe to produce a glow

ELECTRICAL FLUID
At the beginning of the 18th century, Francis Hauksbee (c. 1666-1713) was in London, UK, investigating the effects of electricity. He made a machine with a glass globe from which most of the air was removed. When the globe was rotated and a hand was placed on top of the globe, electricity was produced, often giving a strange glow. Hauksbee thought the glow was caused by electrical fluid. Using this machine, he also observed that threads hung around or inside the globe were stiffened by the electricity, as if a fluid were escaping from them.

Hauksbee's drawing shows that the threads become stiff as electrical fluid escapes

Turning the handle rotates the glass globe

A large wheel rotates the globe very quickly even when the handle is turned very slowly

SCIENTIFIC INVESTIGATOR
Isaac Newton (1642-1727) (p. 94) investigated the behavior of the natural world, but he did not try to explain why things behave as they do. However, he did seem to favor the idea that light is made up of particles of "fire." Although he died before the imponderable fluid theory became popular, Newton continued to have a huge influence on scientists, and many of his ideas were said to be in favor of imponderable fluids.

Hauksbee's "Barometric Light Experiment"

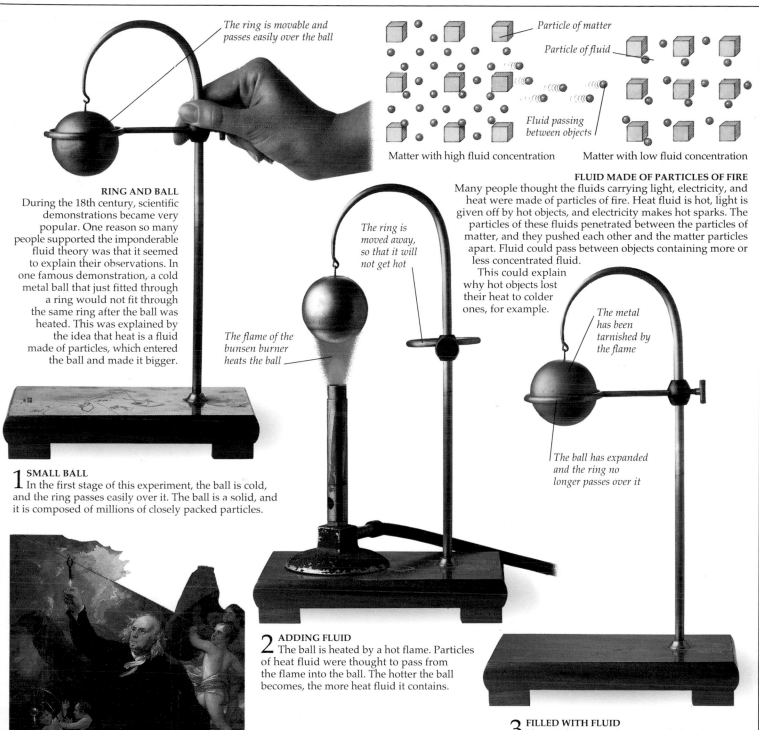

The ring is movable and passes easily over the ball

Particle of matter

Particle of fluid

Fluid passing between objects

Matter with high fluid concentration | Matter with low fluid concentration

RING AND BALL
During the 18th century, scientific demonstrations became very popular. One reason so many people supported the imponderable fluid theory was that it seemed to explain their observations. In one famous demonstration, a cold metal ball that just fitted through a ring would not fit through the same ring after the ball was heated. This was explained by the idea that heat is a fluid made of particles, which entered the ball and made it bigger.

The ring is moved away, so that it will not get hot

The flame of the bunsen burner heats the ball

FLUID MADE OF PARTICLES OF FIRE
Many people thought the fluids carrying light, electricity, and heat were made of particles of fire. Heat fluid is hot, light is given off by hot objects, and electricity makes hot sparks. The particles of these fluids penetrated between the particles of matter, and they pushed each other and the matter particles apart. Fluid could pass between objects containing more or less concentrated fluid.
   This could explain why hot objects lost their heat to colder ones, for example.

The metal has been tarnished by the flame

The ball has expanded and the ring no longer passes over it

1 SMALL BALL
In the first stage of this experiment, the ball is cold, and the ring passes easily over it. The ball is a solid, and it is composed of millions of closely packed particles.

ELECTRICAL FLUID
American scientist Benjamin Franklin (1706-1790) is famous for demonstrating that lightning is electrical. He flew a kite in a thunderstorm and observed what happened when a lightning bolt struck the kite. The lightning was conducted to the ground, behaving just like sparks made in his laboratory. Franklin showed that lightning is caused by electricity, but he mistakenly thought it was carried by a fluid.

2 ADDING FLUID
The ball is heated by a hot flame. Particles of heat fluid were thought to pass from the flame into the ball. The hotter the ball becomes, the more heat fluid it contains.

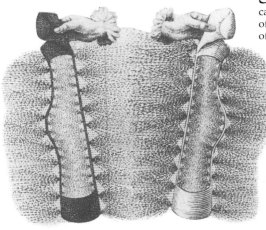

3 FILLED WITH FLUID
The ball has expanded so much that the ring cannot pass over it. It was thought that particles of the metal were pushed apart as particles of heat fluid were crammed between them.

ELECTRIFIED SOCKS
Many observations were made about the effects of electricity. People could make it, store it, and pass sparks of it between objects. In 1758 Robert Symmer (c. 1707-1763) noticed that his silk socks behaved in a strange way as he took them off. They produced sparks and would often fill out, like a wind sock in a strong wind. The socks seemed to be filled with electrical fluid that produced sparks as it passed from his leg to the socks. These effects are actually caused by static electricity, an imbalance of electrical charge between the body and the socks.

Heat energy

FORGING WITH FIRE
Fire has been used by humans for thousands of years to provide light, warmth, and the heat needed for cooking and smelting. Forging is the art of heating metal in fire and then hammering it into shapes, such as horseshoes.

DURING THE 17TH AND 18TH CENTURIES there was disagreement about the actual nature of heat. Some people thought heat was a fluid, called "caloric," that passed from hot to cold. Others thought heat was the motion of the particles that make up matter. Joseph Black (1728-1799), a Scottish chemist who followed the caloric theory of heat, believed that "temperature" was the concentration of caloric in an object, and founded a new science called "calorimetry." But a series of experiments involving friction demonstrated that heat could be generated from muscle energy. This put an end to the caloric theory. Heat was finally shown to be a form of energy by the experiments of James Joule (pp. 30-31). Thermodynamics (pp. 32-33) - the study of heat as energy - was born. It is now known that heat is simply the kinetic energy of the countless moving atoms and molecules of matter. The hotter something is, the faster its atoms and molecules move.

This side shows Fahrenheit

This side shows Celsius

The alcohol inside the tube expands as its molecules move more quickly

HEAT FROM CHEMICALS
When chemical reactions take place there is often a rise or fall in temperature, as heat energy is released or taken in. Some reactions need an energy input in order to take place. Others give out energy, as when water is added to calcium oxide, or quicklime. As the molecules of the two substances rearrange to form a new substance, calcium hydroxide, they release chemical potential energy which had been stored between them. The released energy makes the atoms and molecules move more quickly, so the temperature rises.

Cold water

The calcium oxide and water are mixed together in this vessel

Steam condenses on the inside of the flask

MEASURING TEMPERATURE
The temperature of any substance is directly related to the average kinetic energy of the atoms or molecules of which it is made. Although the lowest temperature on this thermometer is -4° F (-20° C), the lowest possible temperature (called absolute zero) is about -459° F (-273° C). This temperature occurs only when atoms and molecules have no kinetic energy, or motion, at all. Fahrenheit (F) and Celsius (C) are the most commonly used scales of temperature.

Calcium oxide, also known as quicklime

Enough energy is released to boil some of the water

The lid prevents too much heat from escaping through the top

Ice is packed into these two spaces

STUDYING HEAT
Joseph Black (p.149) thought that heat capacity was the amount of heat a substance could hold. It is actually a measure of how much energy is needed to raise the temperature of a substance by a particular amount. More heat is needed to raise the temperature of 2.2 lbs (1 kg) of water by 1.8° F (1° C) than to do the same to 2.2 lbs of iron, for example.

The hot object is placed in the basket

A CAPACITY FOR MELTING ICE
This is a cutaway of an "ice calorimeter" that belonged to the French scientists Antoine Lavoisier (1743-1794) and Pierre-Simon Laplace (1749-1827). With this apparatus, the amount of heat given out by a heated object as it cooled is measured. A warm object is placed in the basket, and ice is packed around it. The temperature of the ice remains at freezing as it melts with heat from the hot object. The object cools down to the same temperature as the ice, then the melted ice is let out of the calorimeter at the bottom to be weighed. This shows the capacity for heat of the object.

GENERATING HEAT BY FRICTION
Benjamin Thompson (1753-1814) was born in Massachusetts and was given the title Count Rumford after working for the Bavarian government. While watching the boring of cannon barrels in a Munich weapons factory, he noticed that huge amounts of heat were generated by friction between the cutting tools and the metal gun barrels. If heat were a fluid, it would have been used up very quickly, but the heat generated by friction continued to be released as long as the barrels were drilled. In the 1790s Count Rumford concluded that heat must be a form of motion.

Melted ice runs out through this pipe

THE LINK BETWEEN FRICTION AND HEAT
When things are rubbed, they become hot. The 19th-century equipment shown here demonstrates that there is a link between mechanical "work" (kinetic energy, pp. 22-23) and heat. Water in the small copper tube heats up from the friction that occurs between the revolving copper tube and the wood as the handle is turned. The more it is turned, the hotter the water becomes – it could even be boiled.

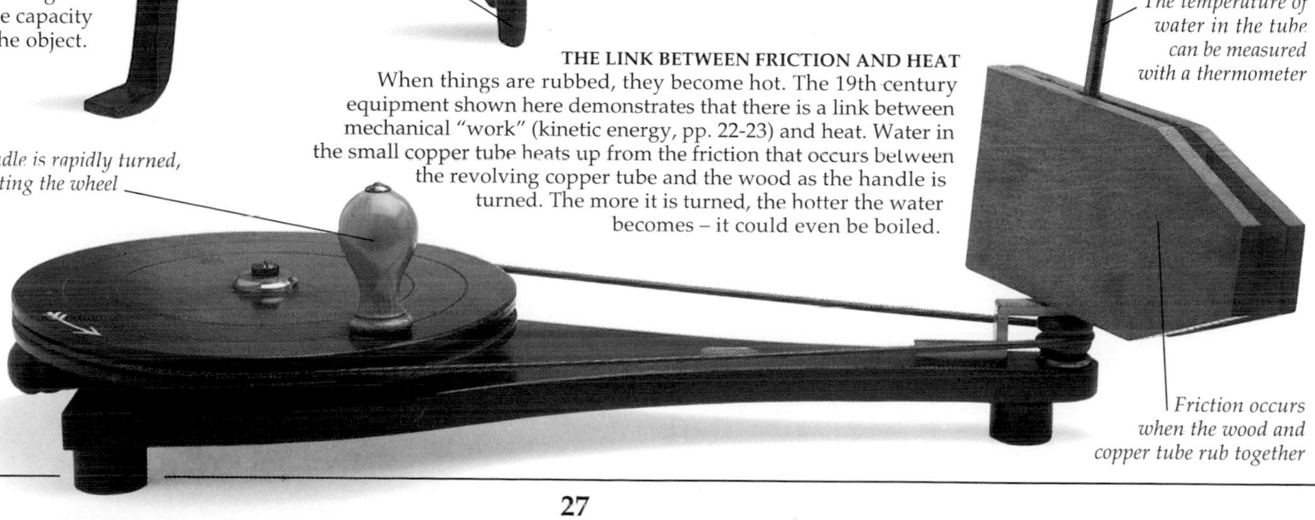

The temperature of water in the tube can be measured with a thermometer

Handle is rapidly turned, rotating the wheel

Friction occurs when the wood and copper tube rub together

Electromagnetism

ELECTRICITY AND MAGNETISM have been known for about 3,000 years. It was noticed long ago that when some materials are rubbed, they can attract or repel other objects. Quite separately, people noticed that some natural materials seemed to have unusual powers that attracted objects with iron in them. During the 18th century, experimenters were familiar with most of the ways electricity and magnetism behave. But the two were seen as separate. Each one was thought to be carried by a "fluid" (pp. 24-25) that passed between materials, causing the attractions and repulsions people had observed. In the first half of the 19th century, an amazing discovery was made: electricity can make magnetism, and magnetism can make electricity. The discoveries of electromagnetism were very important to an understanding of energy. If these two "natural forces" could change from one to the other, maybe other "forces of nature" could do so, too. The stage was set for the development of the Law of Conservation of Energy.

MICHAEL FARADAY
One of the most important figures in the development of an understanding of electromagnetism was Englishman Michael Faraday (1791-1867). He explored the relationship between electricity and magnetism by careful and inspired experimentation at the Royal Institution in London, UK.

Magnetism

The strange, invisible forces of magnetism had puzzled people from the time magnetic rocks were discovered. What makes a compass needle move? How does a magnet know when a nearby object contains iron? Even when magnetism began to be studied in experiments, there seemed to be no connection between this "natural force" and the other "forces of nature," as they were called, such as light, gravity, heat, and electricity.

The pins are pulled to the stone by a magnetic force

LEADING THE WAY
Early people found that magnetic rocks like this would always point in the same direction if suspended on a string, making them useful to travelers for finding directions. They were named "lodestones," meaning "leading stones."

MAGNETIC COMPASS
The Earth acts as a huge magnet, for reasons which are still not fully understood. Because compasses contain magnets that are able to move freely, they respond to the Earth's magnetic field. This is an early mariners's compass. The magnet is beneath the card.

Spheres made of magnetite, a magnetic iron ore

Compass needle

Magnetic model of the Earth

Bar magnets

EXPERIMENTER'S BOX
This beautiful box from the 18th century is full of objects used to experiment with magnetism. It shows that people were fascinated by the effects of magnetism and tried to find out more about them. The first person to describe fully the various effects of magnetism was Dr. William Gilbert (1544-1603) in his book *De Magnete*. He also tried to explain the attraction of the planets to the Sun in terms of magnetism.

Electricity

Although electricity was known to the ancient Greeks, the scientific study of electricity was only really begun in the 16th century by William Gilbert. He discovered, for example, that objects "charged" with electricity either attracted (pulled) or repelled (pushed away) other "charged" objects. Electricity was studied with great interest. Many theories were put forward to explain it and how it caused objects to move and even made sparks. Scientists soon began to search for a connection between these effects and other "forces of nature."

Each coil has a total length of about 70 ft (21 m) and is wound in layers, each separated from the next by cotton cloth

AMBER ATTRACTION
Electricity seems to have been discovered in ancient Greece, probably when someone rubbed a piece of amber and noticed that it picked up light objects such as feathers. The word "electricity" is from the Greek word for amber, *elektron*. Many other things can be given static, or stationary, electricity by rubbing them. Static electricity has "potential energy."

ELECTRICITY AND MAGNETISM
This iron ring with two coils wound around it is a replica of one used by Michael Faraday in 1831, in one of his most famous experiments. Faraday discovered that although the coils were not actually connected to each other, electricity was produced in one coil every time the electric current through the other one changed. Hans Christian Oersted had already discovered that an electric current (moving electricity) produced a magnetic effect around it (see below). Faraday realized that the "induction" of electricity in the second coil could be explained only by the presence of such a magnetic effect in the iron core. Experiments of this type paved the way for an understanding of energy. Electricity and magnetism had always been two separate things, but now it was becoming clear that they could be converted, one to the other.

TORSION BALANCE
This piece of equipment was developed by Charles Augustin de Coulomb (1738-1806) to investigate the forces between electrical charges. The metal bar in the middle is hung on a long, thin metal wire that twists if the bar turns. Static electricity was introduced into the apparatus at the two brass knobs outside the glass. The two metal spheres inside the glass also became charged (because the parts inside the glass were made of metal, through which electricity can easily pass), and attracted or repelled each other, according to the type and amount of charge introduced. Coulomb worked out the size of the forces involved from the amount the bar twisted as the spheres were pulled and pushed.

Charged objects were brought near this knob

Long, thin metal wire

Charged objects, such as amber, were brought near this knob

This sphere is fixed

Coils of copper wire

The bar is free to turn

The jar contained a chemical called ammonium chloride

When wires are connected to the two terminals, electricity is released

Wires from a battery connect to both terminals

Compass needle is magnetic

When the current flows, the needle is at right angles to the apparatus, but when there is no current, the needle points north

OERSTED'S NEEDLE
This apparatus demonstrates a discovery made in 1820 by Hans Christian Oersted (1777-1851). When an electric current flowed above and below the compass needle, the needle swung across the wire. This seemed to show that the current was producing a magnetic effect. Energy in the form of electric current changes into magnetic energy, which makes the magnetic needle move.

The scale shows how much the bar turns

EARLY BATTERY
The Leclanché cell is an early example of what is commonly called a battery. The cell provided a supply of current, or moving, electricity, which could be used by scientists in their experiments. Most batteries used today are actually Leclanché cells, tightly cased in metal rather than a glass jar.

The porous pot contained a mixture of carbon and manganese dioxide

The conservation of energy

By THE 1840s IT HAD BECOME APPARENT that the "forces of nature," which had been thought of as separate "imponderable fluids" (pp. 24-25), could be transformed into each other. For example, the work of Oersted and Faraday (pp. 28-29) showed that electricity and magnetism can change from one to the other. Mechanical "work," such as lifting a weight, can be converted to heat by friction (pp. 26-28). It was the painstaking work of the amateur scientist James Joule (1818-1889) that began to prove that "energy," as it became known, can not be created or destroyed, it can only change in form. This idea is known as the conservation of energy.

NATURAL FORCES
In 1847, Greman scientist Hermann von Helmholtz (1821-1894) became the first person to explain the conservation of energy clearly. He said that all natural forces are either "living" or "tensional" and can be converted into one another. The word energy did not take on its current scientific meaning until the mid-19th century.

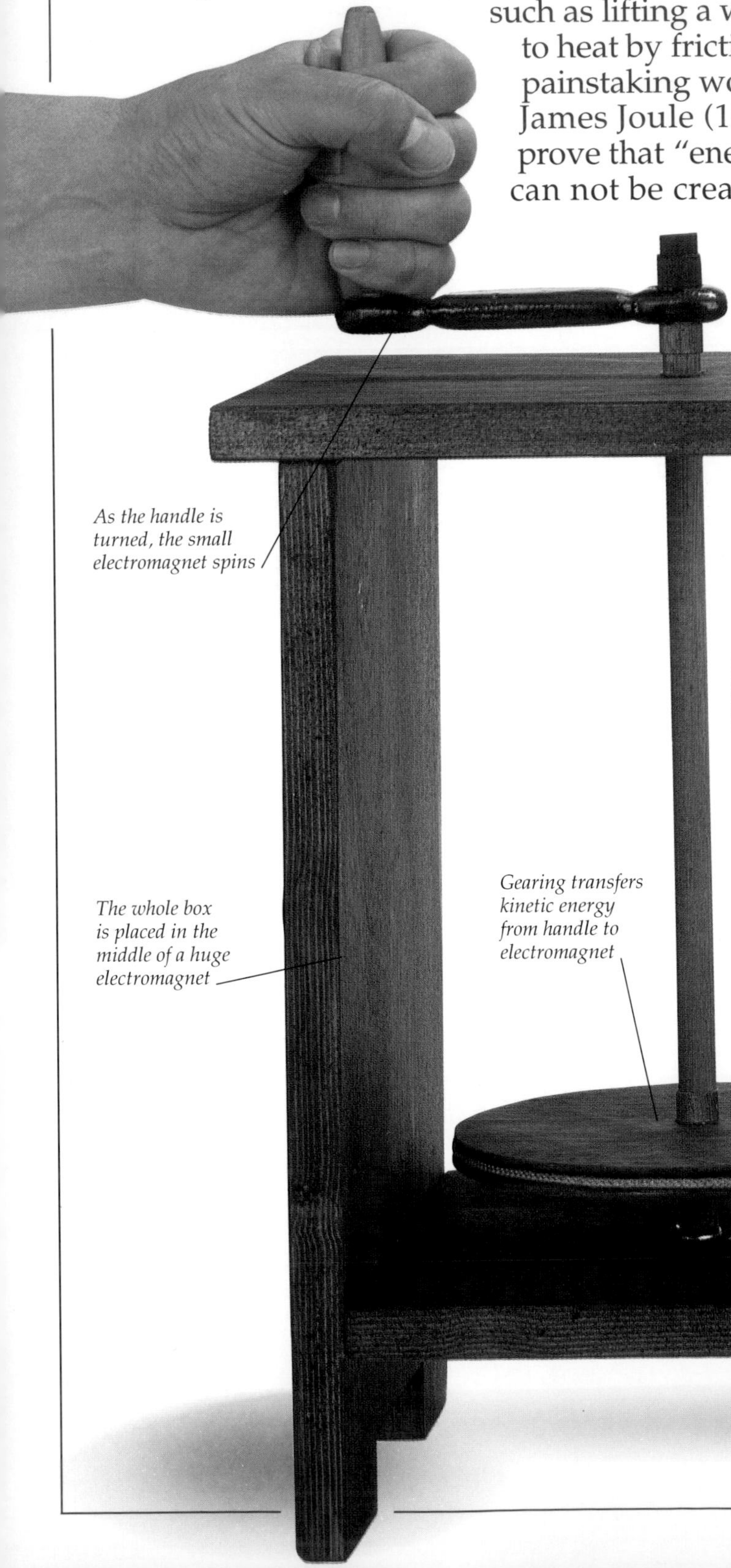

As the handle is turned, the small electromagnet spins

The whole box is placed in the middle of a huge electromagnet

Gearing transfers kinetic energy from handle to electromagnet

JAMES PRESCOTT JOULE
The son of a wealthy English brewer, Joule converted a room in his father's house into a laboratory. In 1838 he began his measurements of heat given out by varoius processes. He even spent much of his honeymoon studying a waterfall, trying to show that heat was produced as the water splashed into the pool at the bottom. The unit of energy, the joule was named after him.

JOULE'S REVOLVING ELECTROMAGNET
In the early part of the 1840s Joule wanted to show that the electrical energy generated by mechanical energy in a dynamo can produce another form of energy, heat. He built a small revolving electromagnet, which was turned rapidly between the poles of another electromagnet that surrounded the box shown here. He enclosed the revolving electromagnet in a glass tube full of water and measured the temperature of the water before and after the experiment to within $\frac{1}{30}$ of a degree Fahrenheit ($\frac{1}{50}$ Celsius). As the electromagnet spun it generated an electric current that could be measured by a sensitive meter. Joule found that the current warmed the water. The amount of heat produced was always directly related to the electric current, which was in turn directly related to the amount of mechanical work used to turn the handle.

HEATING BY STIRRING

Joule knew that the heat produced in his revolving electromagnet came from the muscle energy that was used to turn its handle. So he wanted to find the relationship between this mechanical "work" and heat. Joule's most famous experiment, in which no electric current was involved, did just that. The apparatus consisted of a brass paddlewheel that stirred water in a copper vessel. The paddlewheel was turned by falling weights. As the weights fell, they possessed mechanical, or kinetic, energy. Joule let the weights fall many times. The weights turned the paddlewheel and stirred the water as they fell. Each time the temperature of the water rose by an amount that depended on how far the weights fell. This showed that the kinetic energy of the weights as they fell now existed as heat energy in the water.

Handle allows the weights to be lifted

Ropes are attached over pulleys to weights

A very sensitive thermometer is placed in this hole

Vanes break up the flow of the water in the vessel

Copper vessel holds water

Metal spindle is oiled to reduce heat energy loss through friction

A paddle inside the vessel is turned by these pulley wheels

Pulley wheels of different sizes allow the paddle to be turned at different speeds

Water is held in this vessel

The amount of heat energy absorbed by the apparatus can be taken into account, making the experiment very accurate

THE MECHANICAL EQUIVALENT OF HEAT

This apparatus, made in 1884, is similar to Joule's paddle-wheel apparatus, but it gave a more accurate figure for the "mechanical equivalent of heat." The amount of heat energy needed to raise the temperature of 2.2 lb (1 kg) of water by 1.8° F (1° C) is one kilocalorie, or about 4,000 joules. This is the same amount of mechanical energy needed to lift a 4-ton weight by 4 inches (10 cm).

Iron bound by ribbon of oiled silk

Glass cylinder is filled with water and corked during the experiment

The electromagnet's core is made of six strips of iron, separated by oiled paper

Foil with slit interrupts electromagnetic currents

Silk-covered copper wire is wrapped around the iron core

Wooden sticks are wrapped in varnished flannel to produce a layer of air in the apparatus

Wires to meter

Wire dips into mercury to make a connection to a meter

Muscles use chemical energy from food to produce mechanical energy

Light passes through pinhole

Chemicals on photographic plate record light

Bulb converts electricity to light

Dynamo produces electricity for bulb

CONVERTING FORMS OF ENERGY

Joule's experiments proved that when one form of energy is converted into another, no energy is destroyed. For example, food (a source of chemical potential energy) is used to make muscles work. The muscle energy is used to turn the handle of a dynamo, and this energy is converted to electrical energy. This electrical energy is then converted into the heat and light produced by a light bulb, and next some of the light energy is captured on a photographic plate. Thus, some of the original chemical potential energy becomes chemical potential energy again. The total amount of energy in this scenario remains the same – it is the amount that was provided at the outset by the chemical potential energy from the food.

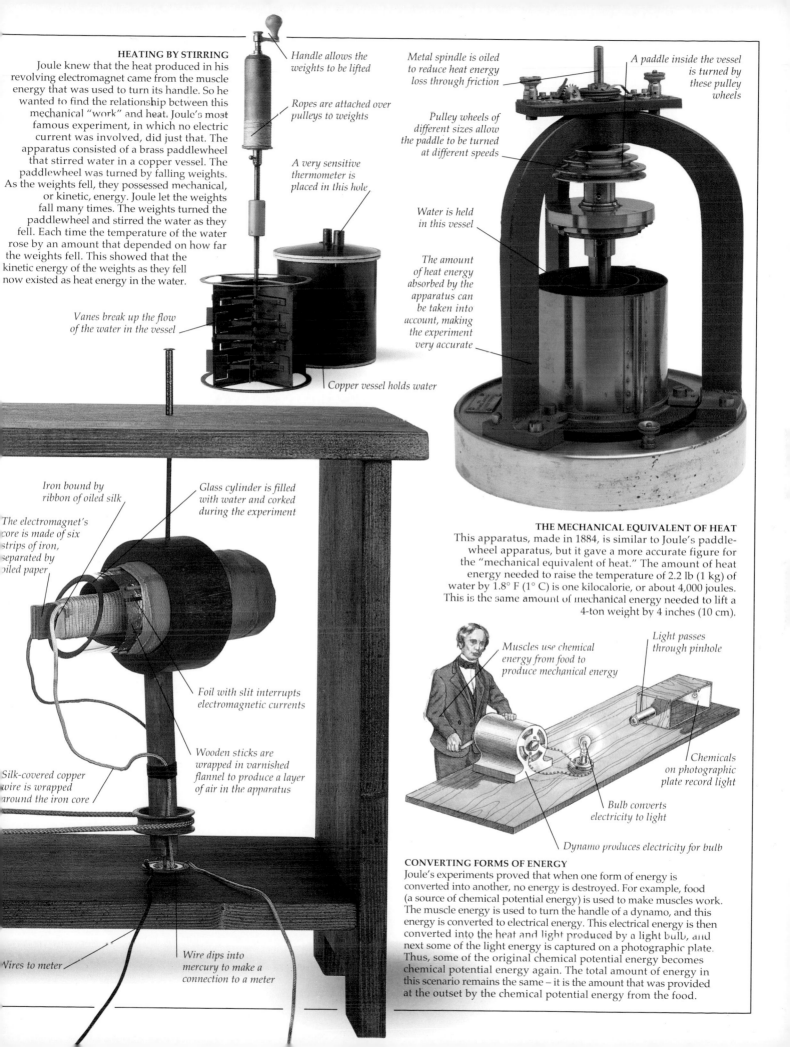

Thermodynamics

HEAT BEHAVES IN A PREDICTABLE WAY. For example, when ice is placed in hot water, it melts. Heat – and other forms of energy – acts as if it obeys "laws" that restrict its behavior, and the study of heat as a form of energy is called thermodynamics. The "laws of thermodynamics" were worked out during the mid 19th century. The "law of conservation of energy" says that energy cannot be created or destroyed, but can only change from one form to another. This is the first law of thermodynamics. Any form of energy can be converted entirely into heat. But when heat energy is changed into other forms, it can never do so entirely. Some of it always remains as heat, and temperatures always even out. This is the second law of thermodynamics. The behavior of heat energy can be explained by the fact that it is the motion of particles of matter – atoms and molecules. The temperature of matter is the average energy of all its particles. Conduction, the transfer of heat between matter in contact, happens because the particles of a hot object transfer some of their energy to those of a cooler object.

COOL BOTTLE
This bottle from the Sudan was designed to keep drinks cold on hot days. To work, the bottle itself must be wet. Water on the side of the bottle evaporates, and this requires energy. The energy is supplied by the bottle and its contents in the form of heat. As they lose heat, they become cooler. This is what happens to a person when they are wet on a hot day and is why they feel cold.

FOREVER IN MOTION
No machine can ever be 100 percent efficient because a certain amount of energy will always be lost as heat. This means that there can be no such thing as a perpetual motion machine, which would work forever and never run out of energy, but many people still try to make one. This attempt was built in 1747. Iron balls fell on to a large wheel and turned the wheel around to operate the diagonal screw. The screw would then lift the balls up to repeat the process perpetually. But in practice the machine did not work because it would eventually slow down to a halt as its energy was lost as heat.

AN INTELLIGENT BOTTLE?
A variation of the vacuum flask invented by Dewar (above right) was mass-produced in the early 20th century and sold under the trade name Thermos. Because they keep hot drinks hot and cold drinks cold, they are useful for picnics, as this 1940s advertisement shows. The flasks cannot tell the difference between temperatures, but their internal vacuum stops conduction, so the temperature of the liquid does not change.

Liquid is put into flask through top opening

Top of the flask is closed to prevent convection

STOPPING THE ESCAPE OF HEAT
The vacuum flask, or Dewar flask, was invented by the Scottish physicist James Dewar (1842-1923). This is one of Dewar's experimental flasks that has been cut away to reveal the inside. The flask contains a partial vacuum between its walls that greatly reduces conduction, the transfer of heat energy between matter in contact. A perfect vacuum contains no matter, so it does not conduct heat. Heat energy can become radiation and can pass between particles, even in a vacuum, but the vacuum flask has silvered walls that reflect radiated heat. The flask is closed to maintain the vacuum and prevent convection, the transfer of heat by air circulation.

Air is taken out through this tube to create a vacuum

Vacuum between the inner and outer walls prevents conduction

Liquid is kept inside

Silvered walls reflect radiated hea

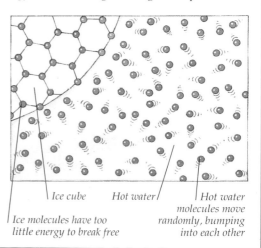

HOW TO MAKE AIR LIQUID

Air is a mixture of gases. If gases are cooled enough, they become liquids. One way of doing this is by forcing them to expand suddenly. This is what happens in a Hampson Air Liquifier. Air is pumped in at the top under pressure. It is forced through the tiny nozzle at the bottom, and as it leaves the nozzle it expands into an almost empty space. This expansion requires energy, which has to come from within the gas, so the gas cools. The cooling effect is large enough to make some of the air change to a liquid form. The rest of the air is pumped around again to repeat the process.

Water pipe

Thermometers measure the temperature of the cooling water

Air is pumped in here

Dial gives measurement of pressure

Insulation prevents heat from outside warming the liquid gas

Pipe brings cold air back to the top

Water circulates here

Pipes carry water to cool the pressurized gas, which heats up as it is pressurized

Pressurized air is forced through nozzle

Liquid collects here

Liquid is drained off here

The glass cover prevents breezes from turning the vanes

Vanes turn when electromagnetic radiation falls on them

One side of each aluminum vane is coated with mica, which absorbs more of the radiation

Gas molecules travel at many hundreds of mph (km/h)

TURNING THE VANES

There are millions and millions of air molecules inside the glass cover of this Crookes's radiometer. They are all moving around randomly, bouncing into each other, the vanes, and the glass. One side of each vane gets hotter than the other side because it is coated with mica, which absorbs more electromagnetic radiation, such as light, than aluminum, which is reflective. This warms the surrounding air, which further increases the speed of the molecules. They bump into the vane more often on the warm side, pushing it around.

FREEZING HOT

When ice is placed into a hot liquid, the ice will melt and become liquid, and the liquid will cool. But why does the liquid not solidify to become ice? Because heat energy passes from hot to cold, eventually evening out. This is the second law of thermodynamics. As the ice cubes in the glass melt with the heat energy from the hot water, the water cools. This will continue until the mixture is at the same temperature throughout. It is possible to make heat energy pass from cold objects to hot, but to do so energy needs to be supplied; for example, in a refrigerator, where it is supplied by the energy used in running the refrigeration process.

PARTICLES OF ICE AND LIQUID

Thinking of matter in terms of its particles helps to explain why ice cubes melt in hot water. The water molecules that make up an ice cube have less kinetic energy than those of the hot water, and merely vibrate around a fixed position. Hot water molecules have more kinetic energy and move around randomly. Sometimes they bump into molecules at the edge of the ice cube and transfer some of their kinetic energy to them. This transfer of kinetic energy then continues until the energy is shared between all the molecules in the mixture. The molecules in the ice are given enough kinetic energy to break free of each other, and they become liquid water. The hot water molecules slow down as they lose some of their energy, which means that they will become cooler. Eventually, the whole mixture will become the same temperature.

Ice cube *Hot water* *Hot water molecules move randomly, bumping into each other*

Ice molecules have too little energy to break free

33

Steam energy

WHEN STEAM CONDENSES, or turns back into water, it suddenly occupies a much smaller space than before. If a piston is put between the condensing steam and the air, it will be moved as the air pushes down to fill the space. By connecting the piston to a pump, the energy of the air can be used to pump water from flooded mines. Before the steam engine, flooding in coal mines had been tackled using pumps driven by animals or water wheels. The first practical steam engine was put into operation in 1712 by English inventor Thomas Newcomen (1663-1729). His engines were very successful, but the design was greatly improved by James Watt of Scotland. Watt made the steam engine more efficient and designed it to produce circular motion, which could drive many machines other than pumps.

Large tank contains water

Wooden beam rocks as the piston moved up and down

Chain is connected to the piston

Rod controls taps

Cylinder contains a piston that moves up and down

Water is sprayed into the cylinder to condense the steam

Taps allow steam and water into and out of cylinder

Coal is put through this spout onto a grate inside

The burned coal falls onto this tray

MINERS FRIEND
Thomas Savery (1650-1715) patented the design for this steam pump in 1698. The pump was intended to clear water from flooded mines, but the pipes carrying the steam often burst.

As the steam excapes here, the ball rotates

The steam is forced through the pipes and into the ball

Water is placed in the boiler and heated

A fire provides the heat energy to boil water in the boiler

HERO'S AEOLIPILE
This is a model of an aeolipile, invented by a Greek engineer, Hero of Alexandria (c. AD 100). It was a forerunner of Parsons's steam turbine (pp. 38-39). Water in the boiler gained heat energy from a fire underneath. As the water boiled, steam was formed and forced out through the holes in the arms of the ball. The ball turned as a "reaction" to the escape of steam, so this is a "reaction turbine." The machine was not powerful enough to do any useful work.

EXPERIMENTS WITH STEAM
Willem s'Gravesande (pp. 22-23) used this small copper sphere in his experiments with gases. The sphere contained water, which was heated to boiling point over a fire. The sphere was then fixed to the wheels, and a hole in the sphere was opened. The force of the escaping steam pushed the sphere forward.

A ROYAL DEMONSTRATION
This small steam engine was made by or for John Theophilus Desaguliers (1683-1744) around 1740 to demonstrate the principles of the "atmospheric" steam engine to the British royal family. An atmospheric engine creates a near vacuum, usually beneath a piston, so that the air pressure on the other side can push the piston. This is the same way that a drinking straw works, except that instead of sucking air out to create the vacuum, steam from a boiler is "condensed" to form water in a cylinder, leaving mostly empty space. The air above the piston pushes with the force of atmospheric pressure. The energy is actually transferred to the piston from the millions of air molecules that hit the top of the piston each second. This model used steam energy to pump water from a bucket on the floor to the box halfway up.

SPRAYING COLD WATER

Thomas Newcomen's steam engine (see right) was an atmospheric engine that pumped water from the bottom of a mine at the rate of 440 gal (2,000 L) per minute. The steam condensed inside the cylinder when cold water was sprayed into it. This was inefficient, because heat was wasted as the cylinder cooled. James Watt improved this by making the steam condense away from the cylinder, so the cylinder was kept hot.

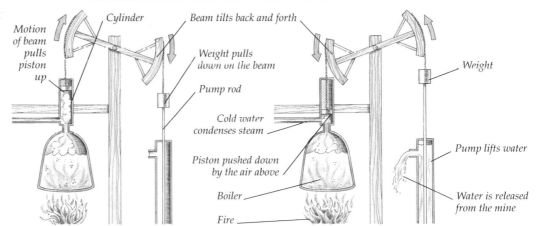

Motion of beam pulls piston up

Cylinder

Beam tilts back and forth

Weight pulls down on the beam

Pump rod

Cold water condenses steam

Piston pushed down by the air above

Boiler

Fire

Weight

Pump lifts water

Water is released from the mine

1 THE PISTON RISES
Atmospheric steam engines work on a simple principle. First, the weight of the pump rod pulls down on the beam, lifting the piston. This fills the cylinder with steam from the boiler.

2 THE PISTON FALLS
Cold water is sprayed into the cylinder. The steam loses heat energy, changing back into water. The air above the piston now pushes it down. The beam tilts and works the pump.

Water is pulled up from the bucket and flows out of this tap

Chain is connected to the rods of the pumps

The rods of the pump are heavy and pull the piston back up the cylinder

Water is taken up from a bucket that is placed at the bottom of this pipe

STEAM IN THE FACTORY
The steam engine had a huge impact on industry. Once engines could produce circular motion, they could take over from water wheels (pp. 18-19) to provide energy in factories. Factories could then run more powerful machines, and they no longer needed to be built by a river. The steam engine in this cotton mill was in another room, and its energy was transmitted to the machinery by pulleys and belts.

Exhaust escapes from this pipe

Exhaust gases from the boiler go past the cylinder and the boiler, helping to keep them hot

Coal goes into hatch

Cylinder stays hot inside the boiler, so wastes less energy

Crank is connected to the piston, and turns the wheels of the steam engine

Handle for the driver

Richard Trevithick

Footplate for the driver

Boiler is made from 1½-in (38-mm) thick metal

Model of Trevithick's London locomotive, *Catch Me Who Can*

HIGH-PRESSURE STEAM
Until 1800, all steam engines were atmospheric engines, because the boilers could not withstand steam at pressures much higher than that of the atmosphere. The first person to use high-pressure steam was Englishman Richard Trevithick (1771-1833), who built the first locomotive in 1804. Similar work was done in the US by Oliver Evans (1755-1819). High-pressure engines, like this Trevithick locomotive, used more coal and were more powerful than atmospheric engines. This allowed steam to be used for transport.

Energy for transport

MOVING PEOPLE AND GOODS from place to place is a vital part of any civilization. The earliest ways of getting around made use of animals (pp. 14-15) and wind (pp. 18-19) as energy sources. Toward the end of the 18th century, the first canals were built – with horses providing the energy to drag barges along canals. But everyday travel on land was still slow and awkward. At the beginning of the 19th century, the steam engine became powerful enough to be given wheels and take its energy source of coal with it. The railway age had begun, and soon trains were carrying passengers and freight in many countries. By the end of the 19th century, the internal combustion engine had been invented. It made use of the energy released by rapidly burning fuel inside its cylinders, making motor vehicles possible. As technology improved in the 20th century, other forms of transportation appeared, such as streetcars and aircraft.

ONE HORSEPOWER

The horse has always been an important source of energy for transportation. Assyrian horse-drawn chariots like this were very fast and used in races and for hunting. Groups of horses were used for transport in many other ways. Stagecoaches often used 12 horses to pull them. In 1783 James Watt defined the power of one horse as a unit of power, the "horsepower."

Steering wheel

Horizontal cylinder

Passenger seat

Driver's seat

Oak frame

Brake

The engine ran on gasoline

Belts transmit energy to the wheels

ENERGY CARRIAGE

The internal combustion engine is compact and powerful enough for its energy source – usually gasoline – to be carried with it. This is a model of a motor carriage made in 1875 by Siegfried Marcus, an Austrian engineer. The car had a top speed of about 4 mph (6 km/h). Although it worked remarkably well for its time, Marcus did not realize the potential of his motor car. It was another 11 years before the first real motor car appeared on the market. It was made by Karl Benz (1844-1929) of Germany.

FOUR-CYLINDER ENGINE

This engine from a 1920s Austin Seven motor car is cut away to show inside one of the cylinders. The engine has four cylinders, each containing a piston that moves up and down about 2,400 times per minute. The piston's motion can be described by four movements, or strokes. First, the piston moves down, and gasoline vapor is sucked into the cylinder from the carburetor. Then, the piston moves up again to compress the vapor at the top of the cylinder. This is the "compression stroke." Next, a spark from the spark plug causes the gasoline vapor to explode, forcing the piston down the cylinder again. This supplies the energy for the car. Finally, the piston moves back up, pushing the used fuel out to the exhaust pipe. This "four-stroke cycle" has been used in most motor vehicles made since 1876.

MOVING STEAM ENGINES

Locomotives took over from stagecoaches and canals when people began to realize that they were faster and more powerful. The first passenger railroad opened in 1830 in the UK. There was much opposition to the railroads, mainly from the owners of canals and stagecoach companies. Many people were afraid of the railroads because they thought it was dangerous to travel at speeds greater than 12 mph (20 km/h).

OTTO'S ENGINE

In 1876 Nikolaus Otto of Germany became the first person to build and sell a four-stroke engine – on which most later engines have been based. He called it the "Silent Otto" because it ran so quietly. One of the main features of the four-stroke engine is the "compression stroke." More energy is released if the fuel is a vapor under pressure. The idea was first developed by a Frenchman, Alphonse Beau de Rochas (1815-1891), but it was Otto who made it a success.

Pulley wheel is connected to the dynamo

Camshaft sprocket connects crankshaft to camshaft

INNOVATIVE DEVELOPMENTS IN CITY TRANSPORT

This is a model of a streetcar that was part of a transport service run in London, UK, in the early 1900s. The first streetcars appeared in New York City in 1832. They were horse-drawn, but soon other energy sources were tried – first steam, then electricity. The first electric streetcars were introduced in Berlin, Germany, in 1881. They used electric rails in the road, which could be dangerous. As an alternative, overhead cables were developed. Electricity with high potential energy (pp. 20-21) was supplied through the wires, powering an electric motor in the car that turned the wheels. Streetcars, like trains, must stay on rails. In a crowded city street this could be a problem, so streetcars were soon replaced in most places by other forms of transportation, such as buses. However, streetcars can help prevent traffic jams and are appearing in some cities again. Streetcars have the added advantage of being less polluting than other forms of transport.

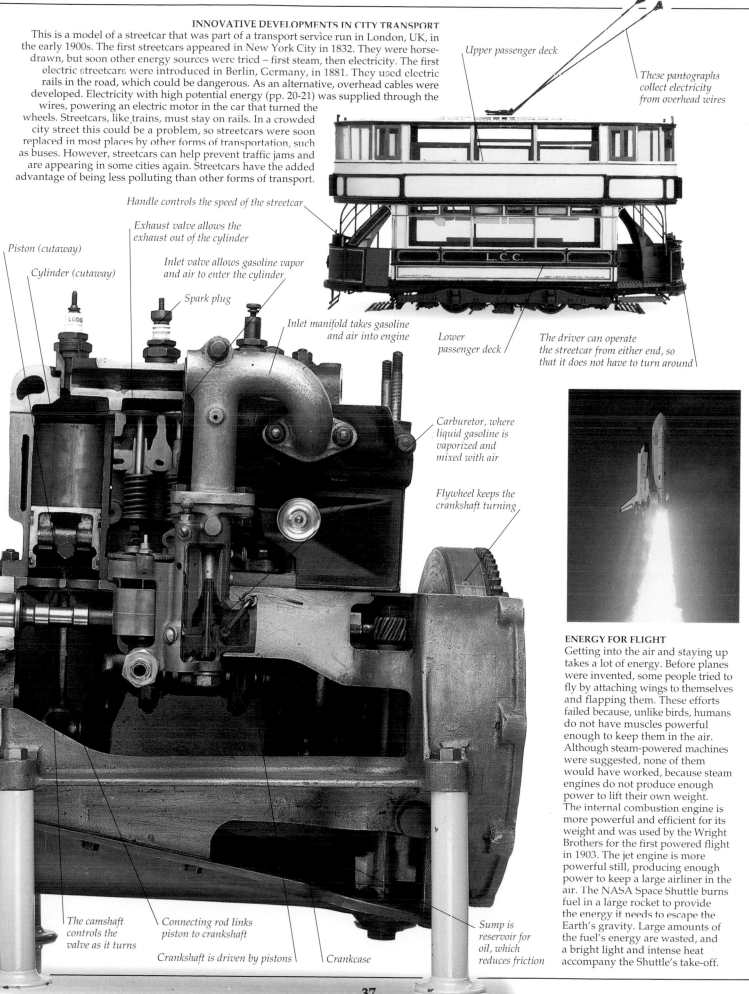

Upper passenger deck

These pantographs collect electricity from overhead wires

Handle controls the speed of the streetcar

Exhaust valve allows the exhaust out of the cylinder

Piston (cutaway)

Cylinder (cutaway)

Inlet valve allows gasoline vapor and air to enter the cylinder

Spark plug

Inlet manifold takes gasoline and air into engine

Lower passenger deck

The driver can operate the streetcar from either end, so that it does not have to turn around

Carburetor, where liquid gasoline is vaporized and mixed with air

Flywheel keeps the crankshaft turning

The camshaft controls the valve as it turns

Connecting rod links piston to crankshaft

Crankshaft is driven by pistons

Crankcase

Sump is reservoir for oil, which reduces friction

ENERGY FOR FLIGHT
Getting into the air and staying up takes a lot of energy. Before planes were invented, some people tried to fly by attaching wings to themselves and flapping them. These efforts failed because, unlike birds, humans do not have muscles powerful enough to keep them in the air. Although steam-powered machines were suggested, none of them would have worked, because steam engines do not produce enough power to lift their own weight. The internal combustion engine is more powerful and efficient for its weight and was used by the Wright Brothers for the first powered flight in 1903. The jet engine is more powerful still, producing enough power to keep a large airliner in the air. The NASA Space Shuttle burns fuel in a large rocket to provide the energy it needs to escape the Earth's gravity. Large amounts of the fuel's energy are wasted, and a bright light and intense heat accompany the Shuttle's take-off.

Generating electricity

GRAMME DYNAMO

A dynamo is a machine that turns mechanical energy (pp. 14-15) into electrical energy. Zénobe Théophile Gramme (1826-1901) of Belgium invented the first practical dynamo in 1870. This one produced "direct current," or DC. Direct-current electricity cannot be distributed over large distances, so this dynamo supplied electricity only on a small scale. The coils in the middle of the dynamo were turned at high speed by a steam engine, and the two large coils produced a magnetic field around them. This generated the electricity.

Electricity is the most convenient form of energy to use in the home and in many parts of industry. But electricity must be produced, or generated. There are many ways to generate a voltage, or electrical potential energy (pp. 20-21), but the best way is to use electromagnetism (pp. 28-29). Michael Faraday visualized a magnet's energy as a "field." When metal moves through a "magnetic field," a voltage is produced. Using this effect, various "magnetoelectric" machines were developed, and by the end of the 19th century steam engines and water turbines were turning large generators to make electricity for homes, offices, and factories. One very important invention that enabled electricity to be generated on a large scale was the steam turbine. It was much faster and more efficient than the steam engines that had been used before. Steam turbines are still used to drive most generators.

Sir Charles Parsons

STEAM TURBINE GENERATOR

Until the invention of the steam turbine in 1884, dynamos and generators were powered by traditional steam engines. But these were inefficient and could not turn fast enough to produce electricity on a large scale. The steam turbine was developed by the Irish engineer Sir Charles Parsons (1854-1931). The steam turbine here made use of the energy of high-pressure steam at 400° F (200° C) to drive the generator. The turbine turned 4,800 times every minute, and yet it ran so smoothly that it did not have to be bolted down. It generated 100,000 joules of electrical energy every second (100kW).

Wires through which electricity leaves the generator

The governor keeps the machine turning at the correct speed

The generator

Parsons's steam turbine, built in 1889

Powerful magnets turn inside these coils

EARLY POWER STATION

By 1882, American inventor Thomas Edison was operating a power plant in New York City. The use of electricity soon spread to much of the world. This is a model of a power station built at Deptford, in London, UK. It began generating electricity in 1889, and it was capable of supplying electrical energy at a rate of over one million joules every second. It was designed by Sebastian Ziani de Ferranti (1864-1930), an engineer living in London. It was the largest and most powerful power station of its time and provided energy for half of London. It was powered by a huge steam engine. All large power stations since the beginning of the 20th century have run on either steam turbines or water turbines. As electricity came to be supplied on a large scale, its energy could be used in an ever-increasing number of ways, in industry and in the home.

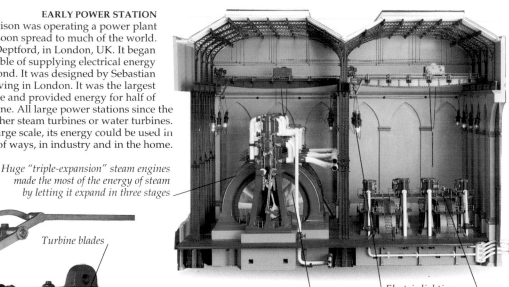

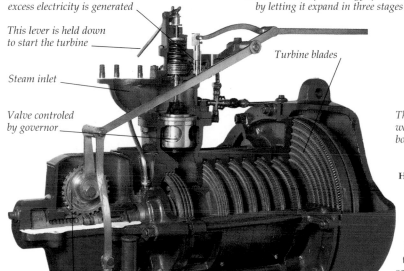

Steam is allowed in here to slow the turbine when excess electricity is generated

This lever is held down to start the turbine

Steam inlet

Valve controled by governor

Huge "triple-expansion" steam engines made the most of the energy of steam by letting it expand in three stages

Turbine blades

This wheel rotates rapidly to prevent the valve from seizing up

The steam to drive the engines was produced by burning coal in boilers in another part of the station

Electric lighting

Notice how small a person is, compared to the generators

HOW THE STEAM TURBINE WORKS

Steam entered at the top of Parsons's steam turbine and forced its way down, past the valve. It found its way into the axle of the turbine blades and then pushed its way out, turning the blades as it did so. As the steam finished in one blade, it went to the next. Each blade is slightly bigger than the next – this is because to get the energy from the steam, the steam must be allowed to expand. For the same reason, the steam outlet is bigger than the steam inlet.

Steam inlet

Inside the turbine are rows of turbine blades

Steam outlet

Tray catches drips of oil

PYLONS AND TRANSFORMERS

To distribute electrical energy over large distances, it is transformed, or changed, to a high voltage (usually between 132,000 and 400,000 volts) before being transformed back to smaller voltages (between 110 and 240 volts). There are transformers at each end of the line – at the power station and at local "substations." Alternating current is used because direct current cannot be transformed and does not travel well. The system for distributing electricity was devised by an Eastern European-born American electrical engineer, Nikola Tesla (1856-1943). Pylons carrying overhead cables are the most common way of distributing electricity, because digging power lines underground can be expensive. The large cooling towers are a familiar sight at power stations. They cool the water that is used to condense the steam that leaves the turbines, turning the steam back into water.

Energy in the home

FOR THOUSANDS OF YEARS people have used energy to cook their food and to provide heat and light in their homes. This energy was usually obtained from fire by burning wood, oil, or candles. During the 19th century, coal gas began to be used in millions of homes in many countries. Later, powerful electrical generators were built to supply electricity to homes. Electricity is more convenient than gas as a source of energy in the home because it can be used for jobs other than heating, lighting, and cooking. It provides the energy for an ever-increasing variety of appliances such as hair driers, microwave ovens, and televisions.

Glass chimney

Etched glass shade makes the light from the lamp more diffuse, or spread out

THE WARM GLOW OF KEROSENE

Kerosene is a part of the mixture that makes up crude oil, but it can also be made from coal or wood. Kerosene lamps have a wick that slowly absorbs the fuel, and the amount of light given out can be controlled by lowering or raising the wick. The wick burns away by only a small amount. With heat, the kerosene turns into a vapor and burns strongly around the wick. The burning vapor gives out intense light because it is so hot. Kerosene lamps such as this were used a great deal during the late 19th century because they gave good, controllable light. The glass chimney was an important invention, because it increased the draft around the wick, making the flame burn more brightly.

Knob to raise or lower wick

Holes allow fresh air to the wick

Kerosene burns with a smokeless flame

FIREWOOD FOR THE WINTER

The people in this medieval picture are using energy from fire to help them cook and keep warm in the winter. Outside the cottage, people are chopping and gathering firewood. As the wood burns, it releases heat and light. The glow of the flames can just be seen, and a woman and baby are sitting in front of the hearth to keep warm.

Fuel is kept in this container

COOKING WITH SPIRITS

Denatured alcohol, or spirits, was used as a fuel in this portable stove invented in 1850. The fuel was held in the closed container above the cage, which held a wick. When the wick was lit, it heated the fuel above it. The heat vaporized the fuel, which escaped under pressure through the nozzle. As it escaped, the fuel was ignited by the second wick, and this produced a flame that roared into the chamber, above which a pot or pan of food was placed.

Cooking pot is placed on ring

Flame roars through opening

Fuel escapes through nozzle, which faces second wick when in use

Kerosene is kept in brass tank reservoir

No 1510
SOYER'S
MAGIC STOVE
No 2306

Second wick ignites vaporized fuel

Wick is lit to heat fuel

BLOWING HOT AND COLD

A fan is just what is needed on a hot day. The blades of an electric fan are turned by an electric motor, but the blades of this unusual gas-powered fan of 1904 are turned in quite a different way. Gas is burned in two cylinders at the base of the fan, like the cylinders of an internal combustion engine in a car. There is a piston in each of the cylinders that is pushed up as the gas explodes. The pistons are connected to the axle at the center of the fan blades, and the blades are made to turn as the pistons move up and down. Because this fan burns gas, the cooling effect it has is only slightly greater than the heat it produces.

Fan blades turn, creating a cooling breeze

Fan moves as the pistons move up and down

Rod connects piston to fan blades

Axle

Top of cylinder

Piston is inside here

Gas is let in through this pipe

Heavy cast-iron body ensures stability

ENERGY FOR BATHTIME

Hot water has not always been available in the home because heat is needed to raise the temperature of the water. Without inventions such as water heaters, like this 1925 gas-burning model, bath water must be heated on stoves or fires, or people must bathe in cold water.

BOILING THE KETTLE

Electric kettles heat water by passing electricity through a heating element. This one was made in the 1920s and has a heating element in its base, away from the water.

Wicker handle

Lid

Spout

Kettle is made of brass

Heating element is inside the base of the kettle

Electrical connections are made to these two terminals

ENERGY FOR ENTERTAINMENT

The introduction of electricity into the homes of millions of people across the world has increased the number of ways that energy is used. This television is hooked up to a satellite dish that can detect signals sent via satellite from anywhere in the world. The light and sound that make up the action of a television picture are coded into a radio wave and sent to a satellite far above the Earth's surface. The satellites then amplify the signal and send it back to Earth, to be detected by satellite dishes and decoded into a television picture. The first event to have satellite coverage was the 1964 Olympic Games in Tokyo.

COOKING WITH RADIATION

Microwave ovens cook food by focusing intense electromagnetic radiation onto food placed inside. The microwave radiation is matched to the frequency that makes hydrogen atoms, such as those in water, vibrate, so the water inside the food heats up.

Measuring energy

THERE ARE MANY SITUATIONS in which there is a need to know how much energy is being changed from one form to another. For example, a company that generates electricity needs a way to find out how much electrical energy is used by each of its customers. In most scientific experiments there is some form of energy measurement. A meter is an instrument that measures energy, and the standard unit of energy is the joule (J), named after James Joule. But energy can be measured in many different units. A Calorie is defined as the amount of heat energy needed to raise the temperature of 2.2 lb (1 kg) of water by 1.8°F (1°C). Power is simply the rate at which the energy is changed. The watt (W) is the unit of power and is named after James Watt (p.288).

One W means 1 J of energy being changed each second. So, a 1,000 W (1 kW) electrical appliance changes 1,000 J (1 kJ) of electrical energy into the same amount of heat energy each second. If the appliance was left on for one hour, it would use 3,600 kJ, or 1 kilowatt-hour (1 kWh) of electrical energy.

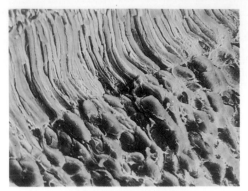

NATURAL ENERGY METERS
Human and animal brains receive signals from specialized nerve endings, which measure energy, or changes in energy. This picture shows the light-sensitive receptors of the eye, which measure the light energy that enters the eye. There are nerves that are sensitive to heat and pressure in the skin, to light in the eyes, and to vibrations in the ears. Without these energy sensors, humans and animals would have no way of sensing the world around them.

MOVING NEEDLE METER
Electricity is the most commonly used form of energy, and there are many ways of measuring it. When working with electric circuits, it is usually important to know how much electricity is being supplied (current), and how much energy each unit of electricity is able to supply (voltage). Most meters to measure electricity work by changing a little of the electrical energy into magnetism, and making the resulting magnetic force move a needle on a dial. This meter from the late 1800s was one of the first to measure current and voltage reliably.

Cutaway of electric current meter, or ammeter (side view)

Top view of an electric current meter, or ammeter

Coil produces a magnetic force which depends on the current flowing

Wires can be connected to these terminals

Electricity passes through these coils and produces magnetism

Moveable weight

Small magnet is turned by the magnetism from the coils, causing the needle to move

Glass protects the needle from damage and from air currents, which can affect the measurement

Wires are connected to these terminals to complete the circuit

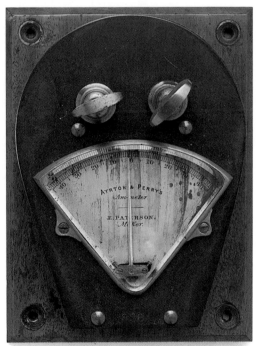

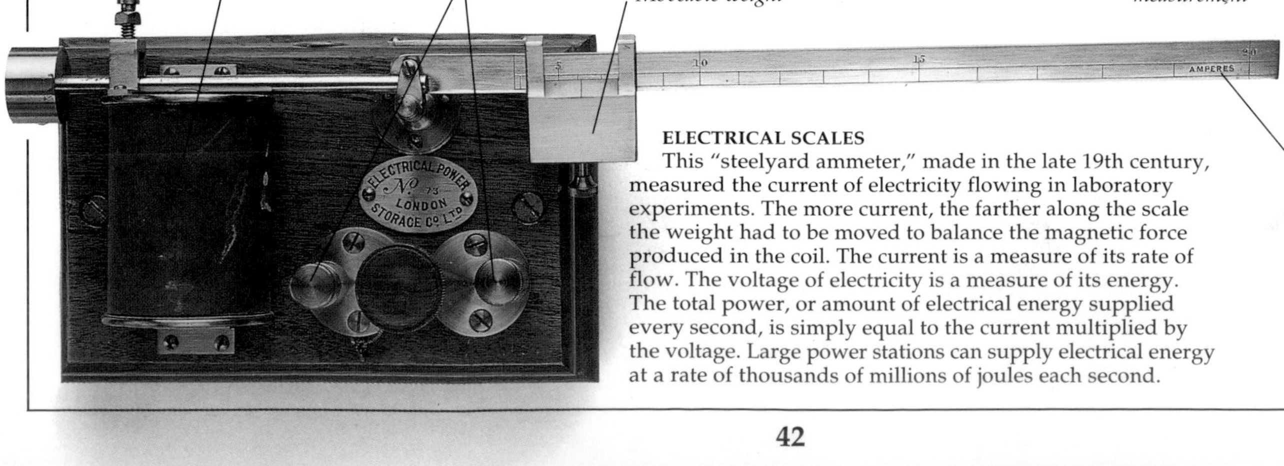

Scale

ELECTRICAL SCALES
This "steelyard ammeter," made in the late 19th century, measured the current of electricity flowing in laboratory experiments. The more current, the farther along the scale the weight had to be moved to balance the magnetic force produced in the coil. The current is a measure of its rate of flow. The voltage of electricity is a measure of its energy. The total power, or amount of electrical energy supplied every second, is simply equal to the current multiplied by the voltage. Large power stations can supply electrical energy at a rate of thousands of millions of joules each second.

BURNING FUEL

Different fuels can release different amounts of chemical energy as heat. This is denatured alcohol, which is often used as a fuel for small stoves. (pp. 40-41) Denatured alcohol, butane, propane, and paraffin are all common domestic fuels. Gasoline, another common fuel, is used mainly in car engines (pp. 36-37). 1.76 pints (1 l) of gasoline will release about 40 million J when burned completely. Depending on how it is burned, most of this will become heat immediately. This makes it a very convenient fuel to burn in engines.

ONE JOULE OF ENERGY

The international unit of energy is the joule. An apple weighing about 3.5 oz (100g) lifted 39 in (1 m) is given 1 joule (1 J) of potential energy. If it is dropped through the same distance, that 1 J of potential energy will be changed to 1J of kinetic energy as it falls, and then to 1J of heat and sound energy as it hits the ground. A 60-W light bulb changes 60 J of electrical energy into light and heat every second. That is enough energy to lift 60 apples 39 in (1m). The Sun radiates 39,000 million million J of energy into space every second.

THERMAL ENERGY

The molecules of any substance are in constant motion, so they possess kinetic energy. The temperature of a substance is related to the average kinetic energy of all of the particles of which it is made. A thermometer is an energy measuring device. The jam in this jar is at a temperature of 152°F (67°C). Each of the molecules of the jam has a tiny amount of kinetic energy. There are so many molecules that the total heat energy, or thermal energy, of the jam is about 58,000 J.

DRIVING A CAR

All the energy that a car uses to accelerate and keep moving comes from the gasoline or diesel fuel it burns in its engine. A typical "fuel-efficient" car will use about 1.3 gal (6 l) of fuel on a 60-mile (100-km) journey. This means that about 240 million J of energy is obtained from the fuel. Only about one-third of the energy obtained from the fuel turns the wheels. Some cars can produce 100 "horsepower." One horsepower is about 746 W (746 J/sec), which is approximately the power that a horse can develop in pulling a load.

A MESSAGE IN SMOKE

Before the invention of the telegraph, long-distance communication was very difficult. Smoke signals were one way to get a message beyond shouting distance, but they were useful for communicating only in clear daylight. They were used in many parts of the world, including China, Australia, and North America. At night, when smoke signals could not be seen, the light of fires was used to send messages. There were many other methods of long-distance communication that did not rely on electricity, such as beating logs and drums, or signaling with flags.

Energy for communication

Aʟʟ ꜰᴏʀᴍꜱ ᴏꜰ ᴄᴏᴍᴍᴜɴɪᴄᴀᴛɪᴏɴ require energy – both to create a message and to send it. A person waving to another, for example, needs energy for moving his or her hand, then light energy transmits the image of the wave to the other person. Because of this need for energy, communicating over large distances was difficult before the use of electricity, which made communication much faster and easier. The first large-scale form of communication to use electricity was the telegraph. One of the first successful telegraphs was constructed in 1837. It consisted of compass needles that turned as a current flowed through a wire. Over the next century many more electrical machines were developed to aid communication. In the 1880s the telephone was invented, and its use quickly spread across the world. By the early 20th century, radio waves were being used to communicate over large distances. Since the 1930s, radio communication has become part of everyday life, and satellites have made worldwide communication faster and easier.

Insulated handle is pressed to send messages

When contact is made, the instrument is ready to receive

Wire connects from here to electromagnet to receive incoming messages

Wire connects from here to receiving station

Wire connects from here to a battery

Morse Key No. 1

MORSE AND HIS CODE

Samuel Morse (1791-1872) was an American artist and scientist who made important contributions to communications. In 1838, he put the Morse code into operation to send messages over long distances via the telegraph. The Morse code is still used today. The letters of the alphabet are each represented by a combination of short and long electrical pulses, called "dots" and "dashes," which are produced on transmitting machines. These pulses can be received in a number of ways. One of the most common is that they activate a sounder, a machine that converts the electrical pulse into long or short beeps. This is Morse Key No. 1, which is simply a switch that sends a dot or a dash when the handle is pressed. This one was used by the Post Office Telegraph service in the UK.

Samuel Morse

Each key represents a letter and another symbol

Space key

TAPPING OUT A MESSAGE

In the 1850s, the Hughes Telegraph was used a great deal, mainly in France. It was invented by David Hughes of Kentucky. The printing wheel, which has the letters of the alphabet, prints a letter on to the printing paper when one of the 28 keys is pressed. In the same motion, electrical contact is made, and a pulse of electrical energy is sent down the telegraph line to an identical machine, which prints the same message.

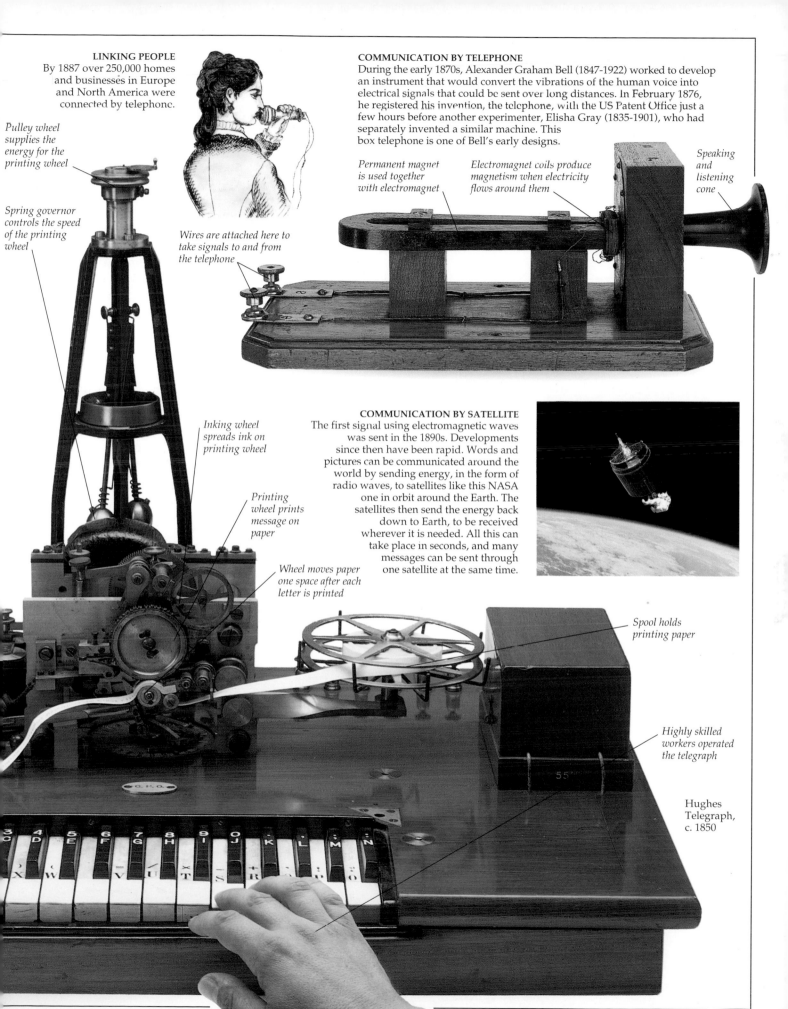

LINKING PEOPLE
By 1887 over 250,000 homes and businesses in Europe and North America were connected by telephone.

Pulley wheel supplies the energy for the printing wheel

Spring governor controls the speed of the printing wheel

Wires are attached here to take signals to and from the telephone

Inking wheel spreads ink on printing wheel

Printing wheel prints message on paper

Wheel moves paper one space after each letter is printed

COMMUNICATION BY TELEPHONE
During the early 1870s, Alexander Graham Bell (1847-1922) worked to develop an instrument that would convert the vibrations of the human voice into electrical signals that could be sent over long distances. In February 1876, he registered his invention, the telephone, with the US Patent Office just a few hours before another experimenter, Elisha Gray (1835-1901), who had separately invented a similar machine. This box telephone is one of Bell's early designs.

Permanent magnet is used together with electromagnet

Electromagnet coils produce magnetism when electricity flows around them

Speaking and listening cone

COMMUNICATION BY SATELLITE
The first signal using electromagnetic waves was sent in the 1890s. Developments since then have been rapid. Words and pictures can be communicated around the world by sending energy, in the form of radio waves, to satellites like this NASA one in orbit around the Earth. The satellites then send the energy back down to Earth, to be received wherever it is needed. All this can take place in seconds, and many messages can be sent through one satellite at the same time.

Spool holds printing paper

Highly skilled workers operated the telegraph

Hughes Telegraph, c. 1850

Energy in waves

WHEN A PENDULUM SWINGS back and forth, or oscillates, it has a fixed amount of energy, which changes between potential energy at each end of its swing and kinetic energy at the center. The rate of oscillation is the frequency. An oscillating object can pass some or all of its energy onto other objects by a wave motion. For example, when water is forced to oscillate, the energy of the oscillation is spread out to the surrounding water by a wave as each water molecule affects its nearest neighbors. Sound travels in a similar way. In the 1860s, James Clerk Maxwell (1831-1879) found that light waves are traveling oscillations of electromagnetic energy. He also predicted the existence of other electromagnetic waves, which were later demonstrated by Heinrich Hertz (1857-1894).

WATER RIPPLES
The energy of a falling drop of water spreads out as a wave.

Peak of wave

Trough of wave

The distance from peak to peak is called the wavelength

Energy is transferred along the wave

THE ANATOMY OF A WAVE
A cross section of a water wave shows its structure. The peaks and troughs occur where water is displaced above or below the normal water level. The height of a peak is called the amplitude of the wave. Amplitude is reduced as the wave travels outward and the energy is spread over larger and larger circles. The water moves up and down, but not along with the wave – only the energy moves outward.

LIGHT WAVE EXPERIMENT
Bright and dark patterns caused by interference

This colorful demonstration, known as Newton's rings, suggests that light is a wave motion. This is because the colors are produced by "interference," an effect common to all waves. Two layers of glass are held together with screws, and both pieces reflect light from their surfaces. When two light waves combine, their peaks and troughs reinforce each other in some places and cancel each other out in others. When water waves interfere, the water can become choppy. In the same way, light interference causes bright and dark areas in this experiment.

Screws adjust distance between two layers of glass

Prongs vibrate 440 times each second

ELECTROMAGNETIC RADIATION
James Clerk Maxwell was a brilliant mathematician and physicist whose work on electromagnetism followed that of Michael Faraday (pp.28-29). He put Faraday's discoveries into mathematical form, and his calculations suggested that light is an oscillation of energy between electricity and magnetism. His calculations also suggested that other types of electromagnetic waves exist with frequencies higher and lower than that of light. In 1888, the German physicist Heinrich Hertz (p. 48) produced and detected lower-frequency electromagnetic waves in his laboratory, confirming Maxwell's ideas. These are now known as radio waves and are just part of the electromagnetic spectrum that Maxwell had predicted (see also p.108).

Invisible sound wave has a frequency of 440 hertz

Tuning fork produces sound waves as it oscillates

Microphone detects sound waves and converts them into electrical energy

Wires carry electricity to oscilloscope

Screen is coated with phosphorus, which glows when hit by electrons

Shape of sound wave is traced by an oscillating beam of electrons in the oscilloscope

RADIO WAVES FOR COMMUNICATION

Italian scientist Guglielmo Marconi (1874-1937) was the pioneer of radio communication (p. 307). He realized that the electromagnetic waves Hertz had discovered could be used to transmit information. On December 11, 1901, Marconi transmitted a signal from Cornwall, UK, to Newfoundland, a distance of about 2,000 miles (3,300 km). Radio soon proved to be a very effective method of communication. Since then, the energy of electromagnetic radiation has been used to carry huge amounts of information, including television pictures.

ENERGY THROUGH THE AIRWAVES

The logo of the RKO broadcasting company shows a radio transmitter sending out its radio waves in every direction.

TRACING THE ENERGY OF SOUND WAVES

When a tuning fork is struck, it oscillates at a definite frequency and disturbs the air at the same frequency. The energy of the disturbance spreads through the air as a sound wave, part of which meets the microphone. In the microphone, the energy of the sound makes a coil of wire oscillate, again at the same frequency. A magnet sits in the middle of the coil of wire, and a small electric current is generated in the coil. Because the coil is moved back and forth, the current changes direction with the same frequency, passing as a wave down the wires to the oscilloscope. The oscilloscope, an instrument commonly used for testing electric circuits, displays the oscillating current on its screen.

PULSE DURATION
1 2 3

SWEEP SPEED
1 2 3

SWITCH ON 30 Secs BEFORE MAINS H.T.

PULSE AMPLITUDE

ASTIGMATISM

TIME
10

FOCUS

BRIGHTNESS

X SHIFT

Y SHIFT

OFF

H.T.

ON

4 K.V.

E.H.T.

8 K.V.

Energy in packets

MANY EXPERIMENTS WITH LIGHT and other forms of electromagnetic radiation (pp. 46-47) suggest that its energy is carried by waves. Electromagnetic waves were discovered mathematically by James Clerk Maxwell, and in the 1880s the experiments of Heinrich Hertz (1857-1894) seemed to prove Maxwell's ideas correct. However, one of Hertz's experiments led him to discover a curious phenomenon now known as the photoelectric effect. It could not be explained by Maxwell's ideas. As well as behaving as a wave, like ripples on a lake, light is made up of particles called photons. Each photon is a packet of energy. This was explained in 1905 by Albert Einstein (pp. 50-51). Other forms of energy come in definite amounts in a similar way, and energy is said to be "quantized." The discovery that energy is quantized dramatically changed our understanding of the Universe.

HERTZ AND HIS EXPERIMENTS
Between 1885 and 1889, the German physicist Heinrich Hertz carried out a series of experiments that confirmed the existence of Maxwell's electromagnetic radiation. During these famous experiments, Hertz noticed that the radiation he had made affected the electrodes in his apparatus in a surprising way (see below). On investigation, this effect could be explained fully only by the fact that the radiation occurs in definite packets (see also p. 306).

Air is pumped from sealed glass container

Electromagnetic radiation of known frequencies is allowed into the apparatus through this hole

Electricity is connected to this terminal

Electrodes

Electrons are thrown out from atoms in the electrode by the extra energy

DISLODGING ELECTRICITY
Hertz used this equipment to investigate the photoelectric effect. Electricity jumped across the gap at the center. When the gap was enlarged, the electricity stopped, but when electromagnetic radiation fell on the electrodes, the electricity once again jumped the gap. The radiation had dislodged some of the electricity. If the radiation was a continuous wave, all of its frequencies would have this effect, if they were intense enough. But the effect occurred only for radiation above a particular value. This is because the energy comes in packets, each with a definite energy, depending on the frequency of the radiation.

Electricity needs more energy to jump the gap

Ultraviolet light

Meter measures whether any electricity has jumped

Battery

SHEDDING LIGHT ON THE EXPERIMENT
During the experiment, electricity, with potential energy, is produced by a battery. When the gap is too large, the potential energy is not enough for the electricity to jump the gap. But when ultraviolet light falls on the negative electrode, the electricity is given extra energy. The energy comes in separate bundles called quanta. A quantum of electromagnetic radiation, such as ultraviolet light, is called a photon.

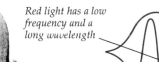

Red light has a low frequency and a long wavelength

Envelope of waves

Blue light has a higher frequency than red light, so its waves are more tightly packed

A PHOTON OF RED LIGHT
A photon does not really look like anything, but many people find it useful to think of it as a packet of waves because electromagnetic radiation behaves as waves and particles. The energy of a photon depends only on its frequency.

A PHOTON OF BLUE LIGHT
The frequency of blue light is higher than that of red light, so a blue wave packet would contain more tightly packed waves. The energy of a photon of blue light is about 0.0000000000000000005 joules; about twice as much as a photon of red light.

LIGHT SPECTRUM
Visible light is just a small portion of the complete spectrum of electromagnetic radiation. All such radiation is identical, except that the photons differ in the energy they carry. Photons of X-rays carry much more energy than those of visible light, and photons of radio waves have much less energy than those of visible light. Prisms separate electromagnetic radiation according to the amount of energy and can be used to analyze the radiation from a hot object.

Visible light is made of a spectrum of colors

PLANCK AND ENERGY LEVELS
In the 1890s, Max Planck (see also p. 110) was studying the problem of radiation given off by hot objects. This had been a problem for some time because Maxwell's theory of electromagnetic waves could not explain the radiation from hot objects. In 1900, Planck made a bold suggestion. Instead of being allowed any amount of energy as they vibrated, the atoms of matter could have only particular values of energy. So, instead of losing energy continuously as they cool, atoms jump from one energy of vibration down to the next, giving out a definite amount of energy each time. This energy must come in separate packets, or photons. In 1905, Einstein developed this idea to explain the photoelectric effect.

LIGHT FROM SHOOTING STARS
Although they look white, these very hot shooting stars are actually giving off the whole spectrum of visible light, and more. The amount of each frequency present depends on the temperature of the shooting star. This can be explained only by the fact that the radiation comes in packets. The energy of each packet depends on its frequency.

Light-sensitive metal, such as selenium, is exposed to light

Photographer calculates exposure times from the meter reading

Scheelite in natural light

Ammeter built into light meter registers electric current

SHINING ROCKS
Many substances, such as this scheelite, fluoresce under ultraviolet light. This happens when photons of radiation with higher frequency (so higher energy) than visible light fall on them. This gives their atoms more energy. The atoms release this energy again, often in the form of lower-energy photons. These lower-energy photons are often those of visible light. This is one way substances can be made to glow in the dark.

A HELP TO PHOTOGRAPHERS
Light meters, such as this early model, became available in the 1930s. They use the photoelectric effect to measure the intensity of light. The metals in the meter are specially chosen because they are light sensitive, or affected by visible light. Photons of light hit the metal atoms and give up all their energy to electrons, dislodging them from the metal atoms. The electrons can then be measured by a meter that detects current. The brighter the light, the more electrons dislodged, and the greater the current.

Scheelite in ultraviolet light

Mass energy

By THE END OF THE 19TH CENTURY, scientists thought that energy was well understood. In 1905, Albert Einstein (1879-1955) challenged the accepted view of the world. During that year he wrote three very important articles. One of these explained the photoelectric effect, and one involved heat energy. The most famous article discussed his Special Theory of Relativity, in which he concentrated on the fact that the speed of light is fixed. He came up with some startling conclusions. One of these is that energy has mass and that mass is therefore a form of energy. Einstein's celebrated equation, $E=mc^2$, describes this mass-energy idea mathematically. The E stands for a change in energy, c is the speed of light, and m is the corresponding mass. According to this idea, when 1 ton is lifted through 3.2 ft (1 m), it gains 0.000000000004 oz (0.0000000001 g). This change in mass is so small that it becomes measurable only when huge amounts of energy are involved, such as in nuclear reactions.

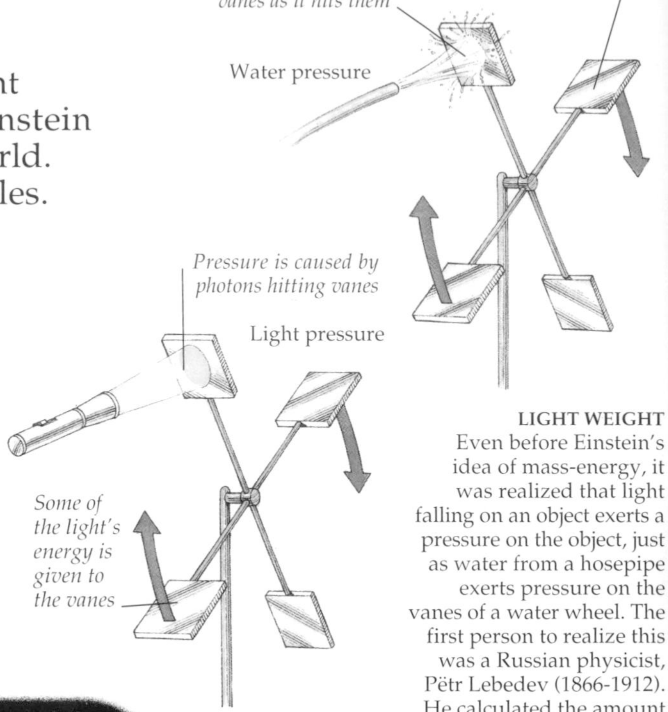

Some of the water's kinetic energy is given to the vanes

Water presses on vanes as it hits them

Water pressure

Pressure is caused by photons hitting vanes

Light pressure

Some of the light's energy is given to the vanes

LIGHT WEIGHT
Even before Einstein's idea of mass-energy, it was realized that light falling on an object exerts a pressure on the object, just as water from a hosepipe exerts pressure on the vanes of a water wheel. The first person to realize this was a Russian physicist, Pëtr Lebedev (1866-1912). He calculated the amount of pressure that light exerted and found that it depended on the speed of light and the amount of energy the light carried. This fits in with Einstein's equation $E=mc^2$. Because light has mass, it must be affected by gravity. Of course, light exerts so little pressure that its effect would not be noticed in day-to-day life.

Pëtr Lebedev

HEAT HAS MASS
During the 18th century, when natural forces such as heat were thought to be carried by fluids many experiments were carried out to discover whether heat has mass. Scientists of that time found that heat has no mass. They were wrong, but it is not surprising that they came to this conclusion. The amount of mass gained by an object as it gains heat energy is tiny – far too small to be measured even by the most accurate scales. The demonstration shown here is exaggerated to help explain that energy has mass.

Weights are at the same temperature

Masses of the weights are equal, so they balance

1 BALANCED MASSES
These scales are balanced, showing that the masses of the two metal weights are equal. The weights are at the same temperature, so they have the same amount of heat energy, and their atoms and molecules have the same average speed.

EINSTEIN AND RELATIVITY

German physicist Albert Einstein was born the year that James Maxwell Clerk (pp. 46-47) died. Although he did not do well in school, Einstein was a genius who was to change the face of science. Before Einstein, energy was energy and mass was mass. But Einstein's Special Theory of Relativity, first published in his article "On the Electrodynamics of Moving Bodies," suggested that energy and mass are directly linked. The truth of Einstein's insight has since been proved many times. He won a Nobel Prize in 1921 for his services to physics.

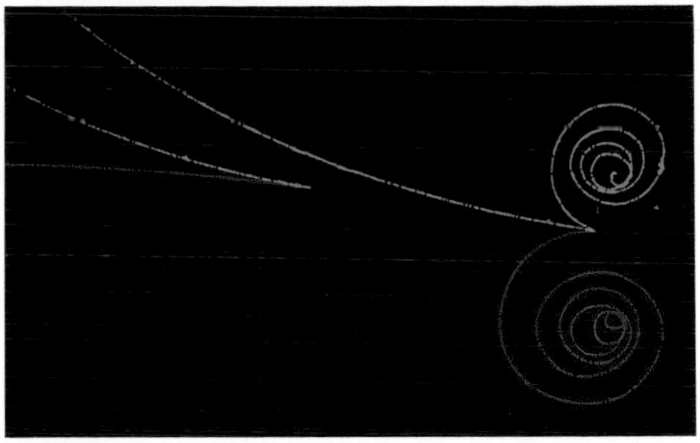

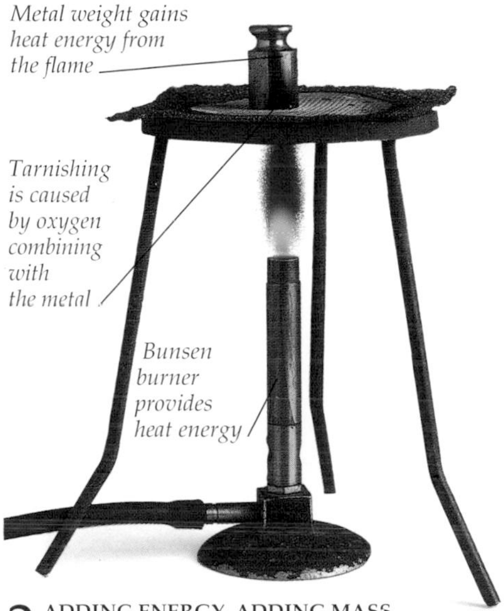

Metal weight gains heat energy from the flame

Tarnishing is caused by oxygen combining with the metal

Bunsen burner provides heat energy

MAKING MATTER

This colorful picture shows the trails left by tiny particles in the reaction chamber of a large particle accelerator, a machine used to produce nuclear reactions. Energy, in the form of two photons of electromagnetic radiation, enters at the right-hand side. Each one suddenly becomes matter in the form of an electron (green) and a positron (red). The electrons and positrons are electrically charged and spiral in the chamber's strong magnetic field. The long green line is another electron that has been knocked off an atom.

2 ADDING ENERGY, ADDING MASS

One of the metal weights from the scales is taken away and heated by a Bunsen burner. As the metal weight heats up, it gains heat energy. This increases the average speed of its atoms and molecules. It also increases the metal weight's mass, because energy has mass.

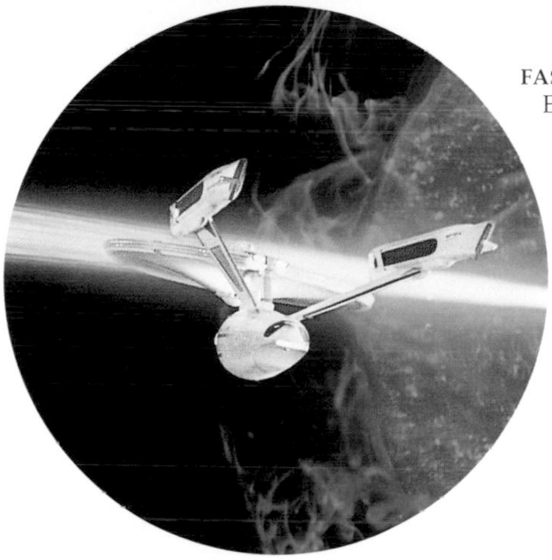

FASTER THAN THE SPEED OF LIGHT

Ever since the discovery that light travels at 186,000 miles/sec (300,000 km/sec), people have dreamed of traveling at the same speed or faster. In the television series, "Star Trek," the *Starship Enterprise* frequently travels faster than the speed of light. This is not really possible, because the speed of light is the speed limit in the Universe. The faster an object travels, the more kinetic energy, and mass, it gains. At light speed, an object would become so heavy that an infinite amount of energy would be needed to move it.

Cool weight is unchanged

3 ENERGY IMBALANCE

When the metal weight is placed back on to the scale, it no longer balances with the other weight. This is because it contains extra energy in the form of heat. In this demonstration the scales have been tipped to suggest an increase in mass, although in reality the increase is so small it could not be detected in this way.

Metal weight that was heated has gained heat energy, so it has also gained mass

Scales no longer balance

Energy from the nucleus

FERMI'S REACTION
On December 2, 1942 the first artificial nuclear chain reaction was produced by a team of scientists led by the brilliant Italian physicist Enrico Fermi (1901-1954). The successful experiment took place in a squash court at the University of Chicago. A chain reaction works a bit like lighting a match. The heat from the friction of striking the match allows some of the atoms to burn, releasing more heat, which keeps the reaction going.

From THE EARLY 1900s ON, scientists knew that the atoms that make up matter consist of tiny nuclei surrounded by electrons. The nucleus was found to be made up of tightly packed particles, which were named protons and neutrons. Electrons are held in the atom by electromagnetism (pp. 28-29), but the forces that hold the nucleus together are far greater. Those forces are the key to nuclear power. There are two main ways by which this energy can be released: fission and fusion. In each case, a reaction occurs in the nuclei of atoms, and the matter left after the reaction has a little less mass than before. The "lost" mass is changed into energy, some of which is released as high-energy electromagnetic radiation. The rest becomes heat, which can be used to heat, which can be used to destroy things, in nuclear weapons, or to generate electricity, in nuclear reactors.

BALANCING THE REACTIONS
It is possible to measure the masses of the particles involved in a nuclear reaction. One common fission reaction involves a nucleus of uranium splitting into nuclei of barium and krypton. The reaction begins when one neutron bombards the uranium. During the reaction three neutrons are released. When the mass of the uranium nucleus before the reaction is compared to the mass of the barium and krypton afterward, it is found that some mass has disappeared. The missing mass has been converted into energy. In this example the mass lost is less than one thousandth of the mass present at the beginning of the reaction, and it is converted into just $\frac{1}{30,000,000,000,000}$ joule (J) for each atom of uranium. However, atoms are so small that if 2.2 lbs (1 kg) of uranium was completely "fissioned" in this way, more than 10 million million J of energy would be released.

Incoming neutron moves towards unstable nucleus

Large, unstable nucleus

Two smaller, stable nuclei are created

Three free neutrons

NUCLEAR FISSION
The nuclei of atoms are made up of protons and neutrons. All nuclei are unstable to a certain degree. In general, the bigger a nucleus, the more unstable it is. If a neutron hits an unstable nucleus, the nucleus is split into two smaller, more stable nuclei. These smaller nuclei need fewer neutrons to make them stable, and two or three neutrons are usually released. These neutrons can cause other nuclei to break up, and can start a chain reaction. The energy needed to hold all of the particles together in the new nuclei is less than that required in the original nucleus, and the "spare" energy is released, mostly as heat.

HOW BIG IS A NUCLEUS?
There are a staggering 10,000 million million million molecules of sugar in this cube. Each molecule consists of 24 atoms. But most of an atom, and of the sugar cube, is empty space. This is because the nucleus of an atom takes up only one 1,000-million-millionth of the space of the atom. If a nucleus were the size of a sugar cube, an atom would be about 0.6 miles (1 km) across.

Two different versions, or "isotopes," of hydrogen nucleus

Nucleus of helium has two protons

Free neutron

NUCLEAR FUSION
At very high temperatures, small nuclei can be fused together to make larger ones. This is what happens at the heart of stars such as the Sun. If the new nucleus needs less energy to hold it together than the old ones, energy will be released and mass will be "lost." The most common fusion reaction is the one that builds a nucleus of helium from nuclei of hydrogen. This reaction has been carried out in special fusion reactors, and many people hope that it will be the energy source of the future. It would be clean, safe, and there would be no radioactive waste.

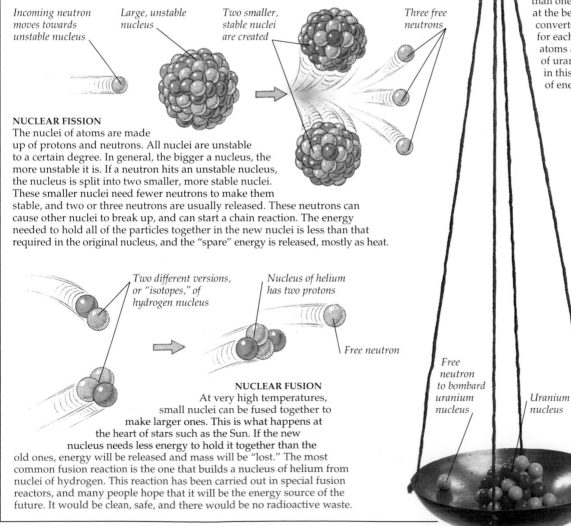

Free neutron to bombard uranium nucleus

Uranium nucleus

TESTING THE HYDROGEN BOMB AT BIKINI

In 1939 the great physicist Albert Einstein sent a letter to President Franklin D. Roosevelt. Einstein suggested that a nuclear chain reaction could be used to generate electricity, or to make a bomb. Einstein thought that a bomb would never actually be used, but instead would act as a "deterrent" in World War II. However, Einstein's suggestions were investigated, and since then many countries have acquired nuclear weapons. This explosion of a hydrogen bomb was a test carried out on the Bikini atoll in the Pacific Ocean in 1956. Hydrogen bombs use uncontrolled nuclear fusion to release huge amounts of energy. Atom bombs use nuclear fission.

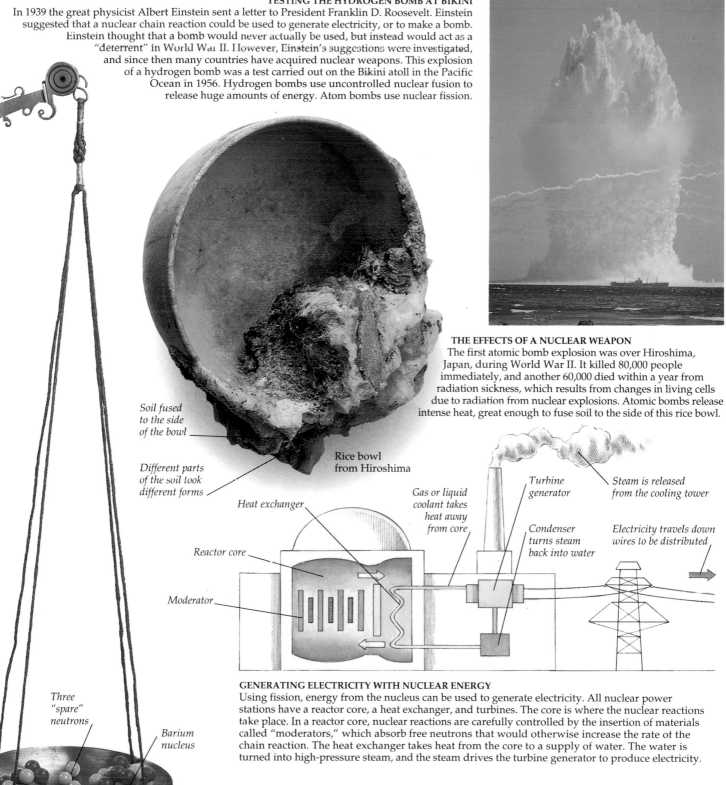

Soil fused to the side of the bowl

Different parts of the soil took different forms

Rice bowl from Hiroshima

THE EFFECTS OF A NUCLEAR WEAPON

The first atomic bomb explosion was over Hiroshima, Japan, during World War II. It killed 80,000 people immediately, and another 60,000 died within a year from radiation sickness, which results from changes in living cells due to radiation from nuclear explosions. Atomic bombs release intense heat, great enough to fuse soil to the side of this rice bowl.

Steam is released from the cooling tower

Turbine generator

Gas or liquid coolant takes heat away from core

Condenser turns steam back into water

Electricity travels down wires to be distributed

Heat exchanger

Reactor core

Moderator

GENERATING ELECTRICITY WITH NUCLEAR ENERGY

Using fission, energy from the nucleus can be used to generate electricity. All nuclear power stations have a reactor core, a heat exchanger, and turbines. The core is where the nuclear reactions take place. In a reactor core, nuclear reactions are carefully controlled by the insertion of materials called "moderators," which absorb free neutrons that would otherwise increase the rate of the chain reaction. The heat exchanger takes heat from the core to a supply of water. The water is turned into high-pressure steam, and the steam drives the turbine generator to produce electricity.

Three "spare" neutrons

Barium nucleus

Krypton nucleus

Mass has been lost in the reaction, so the right-hand pan weighs less than the left-hand pan

THE IDEAL ENERGY SOURCE?

Nuclear power stations release no dangerous fumes during normal operation. However, after fission occurs, the "spent" fuel stays dangerously radioactive for thousands of years and must be buried deep underground or at sea. At this nuclear waste dump in Washington State, a Geiger counter is being used to monitor the radiation being released. Another problem with nuclear power is the danger of accidents. These can have devastating effects, like the disasters at Chernobyl, in the Ukraine, Three Mile Island, Pennsylvania, and Windscale, UK.

Energy from the Sun

THE SUN HAS ALWAYS BEEN of great importance to people by providing heat and light. But early people could not have known the importance of the Sun as the provider of practically all the energy the Earth receives. Without the energy that reaches the Earth through space, there would be no plant or animal life on the planet. The energy of most alternative energy sources, such as wind energy, originally comes from the Sun. It is also the Sun's energy, stored in plants millions of years ago, that is released when fossil fuels (pp. 60-61) are burned. The Earth receives only a tiny fraction of the huge amount of energy released by the Sun. This energy comes from fusion reactions deep at its center. The Sun emits such vast amounts of energy, which has mass, that it is getting lighter by millions of tons every second.

BASKING IN THE SUN
Reptiles like this sand lizard are coldblooded. This means they cannot regulate their body temperature. Many coldblooded creatures react to changes in temperature by becoming more or less active. This shows how important the Sun's heating effect is to such animals. The sand lizard relies on the energy it gets directly from the Sun, to warm its body.

Lens focuses the sunlight

Lens faces the Sun

Metal stand for lens

FREE ELECTRICITY FROM THE SUN
When light hits the special chemicals in a solar cell, electrical potential energy, or voltage, is produced. A cell like this one from the communications satellite *Telstar* will produce only a small voltage, but a large number of cells wired together provides all the energy needed to receive and transmit signals from and to the Earth. It is possible to use solar cells on Earth as an alternative source of energy (pp. 64-65) but they are better suited to provide the smaller amounts of energy needed by small spacecraft.

Cells contain crystals of silicon, which convert solar energy into electricity

SUNLIGHT AND SUN HEAT
A convex lens, such as this burning lens, can focus sunlight to a point, causing paper to burn. The Sun radiates a range of frequencies in addition to visible light. Infrared is electromagnetic radiation just outside the visible range. Although it cannot be seen by human eyes, its effects can often be felt as heat. The frequencies of infrared radiation match those that start atoms and molecules vibrating. This means they heat up, and their heat can be enough to start a reaction. Burning lenses were often used by chemists to help reactions to occur.

Paper is scorched where sunlight shines

A FUSION OF IDEAS
In 1938, the German physicist Hans Bethe (b. 1906) first suggested that nuclear fusion might be what provides the energy of stars such as the Sun. He was correct, but a better understanding of the processes involved has been the result of work by many great scientists. Bethe was rewarded for his discoveries in 1967 with the Nobel Prize for Physics.

LOOKING INSIDE THE SUN

The Sun is made up of a number of layers. The conditions in each layer are very different. At the very center is the intensely hot core, where most of the energy of the Sun is produced. The energy is released by fusion. For fusion to take place, a very high temperature is required. The temperature in the core of the Sun is known to be about 27,000,000° F (15,000,000° C). The diameter of the Sun is about 3 billion times the width of this book, and its own gravity crams everything together at its center, causing huge pressures that result in heat being generated. Once started, the fusion reactions themselves release heat, which helps them to keep going. The energy released at the core travels outward from atom to atom, first by radiation and then by convection, until it reaches the part of the Sun that is visible, the photosphere. Outside the photosphere is the chromosphere, which is something like an atmosphere. It takes thousands of years for energy to travel from the core to the photosphere.

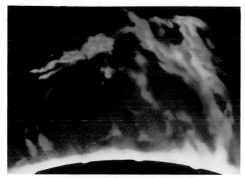

A PROMINENT FEATURE

Often about one-third of the diameter of the Sun, huge eruptions of hot gases like this are called solar prominences. They seem to be linked with sunspots and the Sun's magnetic energy. Sunspots are slightly cooler areas on the surface of the Sun and are seen as darker patches. Prominences often arc between two sunspots. During a solar eclipse, as the Moon passes between the Sun and the Earth, large prominences become visible to the eye.

Energy is released at core

Radiation zone, where energy is radiated from atom to atom

Convection zone, where heat energy rises away from the Sun's center

Chromosphere is a layer of hot gases surrounding the photosphere

Sunspots move around the photosphere and seem to come and go in a cycle of about 11 years

Solar prominence arcs from one sunspot to another

Photosphere is the visible surface of the Sun

Photosynthesis

WHEN ENERGY from the Sun falls on plant leaves, it can be stored as chemical potential energy in plants. This is photosynthesis - the process by which light energy is taken into plant cells and stored as it separates oxygen from water. The discovery of photosynthesis was gradual. Toward the end of the 18th century, Joseph Priestley (1733-1804), an English chemist, studied the gases involved in burning. He discovered that plants change the quality of the air around them. They do this by taking in what is now known as carbon dioxide and giving out what is now known as oxygen. In 1779 the Dutch scientist Jan Ingenhousz (1730-1799) discovered that this happens only when a plant is exposed to light. By the end of the 19th century, photosynthesis was understood in terms of energy. It is a process vitally important to life on Earth. Without photosynthesis, there would be no food for animals or humans. Photosynthesis in plants living millions of years ago converted solar energy into the chemical energy available when fossil fuels are burned.

MAKING SUGAR
In 1864, a German chemist called Julius Sachs (1832-1897) discovered which chemicals are involved in photosynthesis. He found that carbon dioxide taken in by plants is combined with hydrogen from water, which is made of oxygen and hydrogen. The energy for this reaction comes from light falling on the plant. The hydrogen and carbon dioxide join to form glucose, a type of sugar that is the food for the plant. Some of the glucose is made into starch, which is a good energy store. The oxygen that is separated from the water is released by the plant.

The carbon dioxide in the jar is gradually replaced by oxygen

Plant cells in the leaves take in carbon dioxide and give out oxygen

Water stops the gases from escaping

Gas jar filled with carbon dioxide

Candle will not burn in the carbon dioxide

PRIESTLEY'S EXPERIMENT
In the 1770s, Joseph Priestley (p. 256) was investigating gases. At that time, it was believed that burning involved the release of a substance named "phlogiston." When a candle burned, for example, it was thought to be releasing "phlogisticated air." This was a gas that did not allow anything to burn in it and was poisonous to animals. Priestley was surprised to discover that if a plant was placed in the gas, it could "de-phlogisticate" the air, making it breathable again. Priestley discovered the two gases that are now known as carbon dioxide and oxygen.

1 PHLOGISTICATED AIR
Burning will not occur in carbon dioxide gas, and the gas can be deadly if breathed. Priestley obtained samples of the gas (he called it "phlogisticated" air) by burning a small candle in a jar and by collecting the gas as a by-product from the brewery next door to his home. It is now known that carbon dioxide is also released as a result of respiration, the reverse of photosynthesis.

Water trough

2 PHOTOSYNTHESIS IN ACTION
Priestley left plants in jars full of carbon dioxide. Although he did not know it, the plants were photosynthesizing and taking in the carbon dioxide they needed to make the chemicals necessary to survive and grow. During photosynthesis the plants gave out oxygen gas, which then filled the jars. Priestley experimented with the gas and realized that it had very different properties from the carbon dioxide gas.

Small candle used to fill a jar with carbon dioxide, and to test the gas in a jar

WHAT HAPPENS INSIDE A PLANT CELL

All the complex chemical reactions involved in photosynthesis take place inside the cells of plants in parts called chloroplasts. Chloroplasts contain special chemicals, such as chlorophyll, that absorb energy from light. In a split second the energy passes quickly through the chloroplast as tiny currents of electricity, separating atoms of oxygen from water molecules and joining together the hydrogen and the carbon dioxide to form glucose. The glucose is then transported around the plant to wherever it is needed, by a network of tubes called the phloem.

Chloroplasts in green plants contain chlorophyll

Nucleus controls the activities of the cell

Endoplasmic reticulum transports nutrients within the cell

Green plant leaf

Vacuole stores sap

Cell wall

Ivy leaves

Green leaves contain a large proportion of chlorophyll

Pink leaves contain a mixture of pigments, including xanthophyll and Beta-carotene

Coleus leaves

GREEN LEAVES AND PINK LEAVES

Inside the chloroplasts in plant cells, there are special chemicals that absorb the light falling on the plant. These chemicals absorb only particular colors of light, reflecting all other colors. The most common of these chemicals is chlorophyll, which reflects green light, giving most plants a green color. However, the mixture of chemicals inside chloroplasts can vary, and some plants have differently colored leaves as a result. These other chemicals work in the same way as chlorophyll. During autumn, the chlorophyll in the leaves of green leafy trees is broken down, revealing the colors of the other chemicals present in the leaves.

3 BURNING PLANT GAS (below)

Priestley found that candles burn very well in the gas produced by the plants. Of course, oxygen is used up in burning, so the candles eventually would be extinguished once again. However, if a plant was placed in the jar once this had happened, it would replace the carbon dioxide with oxygen. In photosynthesis, energy is taken in by the plant and oxygen is released. In burning, oxygen is used up and energy is released.

Oxygen is combined with carbon, present in the wax, to produce carbon dioxide

The candle burns well in the oxygen, releasing energy as heat and light

The mouse breathes in the oxygen that was produced by the green plant

REACHING FOR THE LIGHT

Light is vital to all plants, so plants need to be exposed to as much of it as possible. This is why plants bend towards light. There is a huge variety of plants which photosynthesize. Each has developed its own way of guaranteeing a share of the incoming sunlight. For example, the giant redwood trees of North America can grow to a height of more than 350 feet (100 m). Other plants have evolved to grow in desert or tundra conditions, using the light energy available in places where most other plants would not survive.

4 BREATHING PLANT GAS

Priestley also found that the gas produced by the plants was breathable. When he placed an animal, such as a mouse, in a bell jar that contained oxygen, it was able to breathe normally. Like humans, animals need to breathe oxygen in order to burn food within the body to obtain energy.

Energy from food

SPINACH FOR ENERGY
Popeye, a cartoon character created in the 1930s, becomes incredibly strong when he eats spinach. He was originally intended to promote healthy eating for children. Spinach contains not only energy but also vitamins and minerals, which are other essential parts of food.

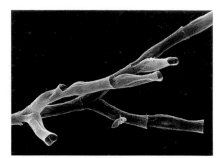

FEEDING THEMSELEVES
All organisms that make their own food – like these phytoplankton – are called autotrophic, meaning self-feeding. Most autotrophic organisms are plants, which take energy from sunlight by photosynthesis.

ALL LIVING THINGS need energy for a variety of activities, such as growing, moving, and keeping warm. Some, such as plants, capture energy - usually from sunlight - and store it as chemical potential energy. Other living things that cannot capture energy in this way have to make use of the energy stored elsewhere. They get this energy by feeding on other animals or plants. Humans eat plants and animals to obtain the energy they need. The food that humans eat is burned, or oxidized, inside the body during digestion. In a similar way, fossil fuels, such as coal and oil, are oxidized when they are ignited. Oxygen from the air combines with a substance that is burned. When fossil fuels burn, they release heat and light in flames. When food is burned in the body, chemical energy is released. Different types of food store and release different amounts of energy. Fat, for example, is a more concentrated energy store than sugar.

Food energy values

When food is burned in an animal's body, the chemical potential energy stored within it is released. Different foods release different amounts of energy. The amount of energy released by foods is usually measured in kilocalories (kcal) or joules (J) - 1 kcal is equal to about 4,200 J, and is also called a Calorie. There are three groups of energy, giving chemicals in food. They are carbohydrates, fats, and proteins.

ENERGY FROM FRUIT
Fruit such as these grapes contains natural sugars that provide energy. Each grape provides about 1 kcal. If more sugar is eaten than the body needs, the sugar is converted into fat, a good store of food energy, so that it can be used another time.

ENERGY FROM SUGAR
In the middle of the 19th century, French physiologist Claude Bernard discovered how large carbohydrate molecules are converted to smaller molecules of glucose in the liver. Food containing carbohydrates must first be broken down into glucose, a type of sugar, before its energy can be obtained. The glucose is carried from the liver around the bloodstream and combined with oxygen, releasing energy in a process called "aerobic respiration." In this process, glucose and oxygen become water and carbon dioxide. This is the reverse of photosynthesis, in which glucose is made from water and carbon dioxide, and energy is taken in by a plant.

ENERGY FROM POTATOES
This potato contains a lot of starch, which stores the energy that a new plant needs to begin growing. Starch molecules must be broken down in the body into simple sugar molecules before their energy can be released.

Grapes contain 60 Calories per 3½ oz (100 g)

Potatoes contain about 90 Calories per 3½ oz (100 g)

Grain contains about 300 Calories per 3½ oz (100 g)

ENERGY FROM SEEDS
Seeds, such as these sunflower seeds, contain most of their energy in fats. Many seeds can be eaten whole, and many types are also crushed to release fats in the form of oils, which can be used in cooking.

Sunflower seeds contain about 330 Calories per 3½ oz (100 g)

ENERGY FROM MEAT
Meat is a good source of energy, and much of its energy is stored in fat. But meat is not a very efficient energy source. For example, only a small amount of the energy taken in by a living chicken can be obtained by someone who eats it.

Roast chicken contains about 300 Calories per 3½ oz (100 g)

ENERGY FROM GRAIN
Grain is a good source of energy because it is a direct store of the energy of photosynthesis. This type of wheat is grown to be fed to animals, such as cattle. Other types are often ground into flour for human consumption in products such as bread.

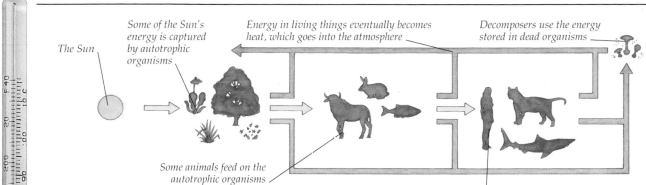

The Sun

Some of the Sun's energy is captured by autotrophic organisms

Energy in living things eventually becomes heat, which goes into the atmosphere

Decomposers use the energy stored in dead organisms

Some animals feed on the autotrophic organisms

Some animals feed on other animals

Test tube holds water

Clamp holds test tube

Thermometer registers the heat energy that the burning peanut has transferred to the water

Water heats as peanut burns

Flame leaves a layer of soot on the test tube

Burning peanut

ENERGY IN A FOOD CHAIN

Because energy cannot be created or destroyed, the energy in food is easily traced back to its source, the Sun. When the Sun's energy falls on autotrophic organisms, some of it is stored in fats, proteins, and carbohydrates in their bodies. When these organisms are eaten, some of the energy they contain is passed on to the animals that eat them. Some of this energy, in turn, is passed on to meat-eating animals when they eat the animals from the previous stage. At each stage of the food chain, some energy escapes as the heat produced by living things.

ENERGY FOR LIFE

All of the energy needed to move this athlete is provided by the food he has eaten. Once food has been processed in the stomach and intestines, it is transported around the body in the blood, to carry out the processes of life. Energy is used in many ways in the body, for instance, to send messages through nerves to the muscles to make the muscles work and to keep warm.

TOO MUCH ENERGY

The amount of energy a person needs each day depends on how active they are. If a person takes in more fats and carbohydrates than they need, they will be stored in the body so that their energy can be used in the future. Excess carbohydrates are converted to fats in the liver, and they are stored with excess fats beneath the skin.

BURNING A PEANUT

This simple experiment shows the amount of energy available in one peanut. The heat energy released by the burning peanut warms the water in the test tube. If the amount of water is known and the temperature rise is measured using the thermometer, the energy supplied to the water can be calculated. The result of this experiment will not be very accurate because much of the heat escapes to the air, or heats the test tube. A more accurate result can be obtained using an enclosed container, so that no heat is lost to the air. This is what happens in a bomb calorimeter (see right).

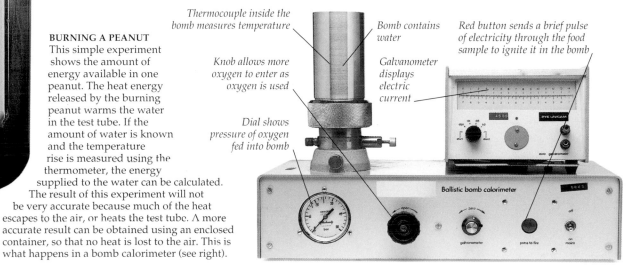

Thermocouple inside the bomb measures temperature

Knob allows more oxygen to enter as oxygen is used

Dial shows pressure of oxygen fed into bomb

Bomb contains water

Galvanometer displays electric current

Red button sends a brief pulse of electricity through the food sample to ignite it in the bomb

Ballistic bomb calorimeter

BURNING FOOD IN A BOMB CALORIMETER

Food energy values were first measured using calorimeters like this one. Food is placed in a metal container called the bomb (top left). The food is then ignited by passing electricity through it. As the food burns, it releases energy, and this warms the water passing around it. The rise in temperature can then be measured and converted into kilocalories or joules. Food scientists can also learn how much energy is available from a particular food by measuring how much carbohydrate, protein, and fat the food contains, because the energy values of these food groups are well known.

Fossil fuels

COAL, OIL, AND NATURAL GAS are called fossil fuels. They were formed by the action of bacteria and the pressure of the Earth on the remains of tiny organisms that lived millions of years ago. The energy originally came from the Sun and was stored as chemical potential energy by photosynthesis. Coal was the first fossil fuel to be used on a large scale. Raw coal can be burned to provide heat. When coal is heated in a closed vessel without burning, it produces a gas that can be used as fuel. This "coal gas" gave a convenient supply of energy to homes during the 19th century and part of the 20th. "Natural gas" is similar to coal gas. It is often found near oil, which is the fossil fuel that dominates the 20th century. From oil comes gasoline and other fuels, which can be burned to release their fossil energy. Once burned, fossil fuels cannot be used again, and the gases released by burning fossil fuels can pollute the Earth. For these reasons, it is important to use fossil fuels efficiently.

COLLECTING OIL
In some places oil seeps from rocks called "oil shale." This type of oil is "crude oil," and it has been collected at its source and used for centuries. The oil was once commonly used for lighting, but it was never ideal because when it burns it becomes smelly and smoky.

Steam condenses on the glass vessel

MAKING COAL GAS
Coal is a mixture of many different substances. When it is heated, it breaks down into those substances. In this glass vessel, coal is being heated and is releasing coal gas. This gas is being burned at the open end of the vessel. Coal gas is made mainly of hydrogen and methane – the other substances that make up coal remain as solids or thick liquids. Both of these gases burn well, combining with oxygen in the air. As they burn, they release energy that originally came from the Sun. The energy is released as heat and light in the flame. This is why coal gas was used mainly for heating and lighting in streets, homes, and factories.

Lumps of coal are heated, but not burned

Filter prevents the flames from coming into contact with the glass vessel

Bunsen burner flame provides heat energy

Clamp holds the glass vessel away from the flame so it does not overheat

ANCIENT FOREST
About 300 million years ago much of the Earth was covered with swamps and forests, full of plants. These plants were a natural store of chemical energy from photosynthesis. When the plants died, some of them were buried. Under the right conditions they slowly turned into coal over millions of years.

HOW OIL AND GAS ARE FORMED

Oil has been used on a large scale only since it was first drilled in Pennsylvania in 1859. Natural gas – made mainly of methane – has replaced coal gas because it is more convenient and the same volume releases more energy. Oil and natural gas are usually found together.

1 SUN AND SEA
Like coal, the story of the formation of oil and gas begins millions of years ago when the Sun's energy was stored in tiny marine organisms, such as algae and plankton. Instead of decaying in the usual way when they died, they were buried in layers of sediment, such as sand and salt.

Sea

Millions of tiny marine organisms

Older layers of sediment

Lower layer of rock

2 BACTERIAL ACTION
Over millions of years the chemicals that made up the organisms were converted into oil and natural gas as bacteria and the pressure of more layers of sediment broke them down. The pressure of the moving rocks of the Earth caused the layers to be "folded" or broken. The oil and natural gas often collected in the resulting shapes.

Marine organisms are buried in layers of sediment

New layers are constantly being formed

Layers of rock and sediment are folded by huge pressures as the Earth shifts

3 RISING ENERGY
Oil and natural gas are less dense than water, so they can rise through "permeable" rocks, which are not solid. They then collect underneath an "impermeable," or solid, layer of rock called a caprock. By studying rock formations, the site of oil and natural gas can be predicted with great accuracy.

Natural gas rig

Oil rig

Natural gas site

Oil site

Both fuels collect under caprock

Gas and oil have seeped up through layers of permeable rock

When the coal gas is lit, a flame is produced

Coal gas travels down the neck of the vessel

Simple crane hoists basket in and out

HOW TO FIND THE CALORIFIC VALUE

It is often necessary to find out how much energy is available in fossil fuels. For example, engineers need to know the "energy content" - or calorific value - of a fuel that powers an engine. A calorimeter can be used to discover the calorific value of a given fuel. The gas calorimeter shown here was designed by the British scientist Charles Boys (1855-1944). A steady supply of gas is burned inside, and this heats a steady supply of water. By measuring the temperature rise in the water, the calorific value of the burning gas can be calculated. Thirty-four cubic feet (1 cubic m) of coal gas releases about 19 million joules. The same volume of natural gas releases about twice as much energy.

Small microscope allows accurate readings to be taken

Thermometer measures the temperature of water leaving calorimeter

Thermometer measures the temperature of water entering calorimeter

Water flows in through this tap

Water flows out of this tap

Gas enters the apparatus through this tap

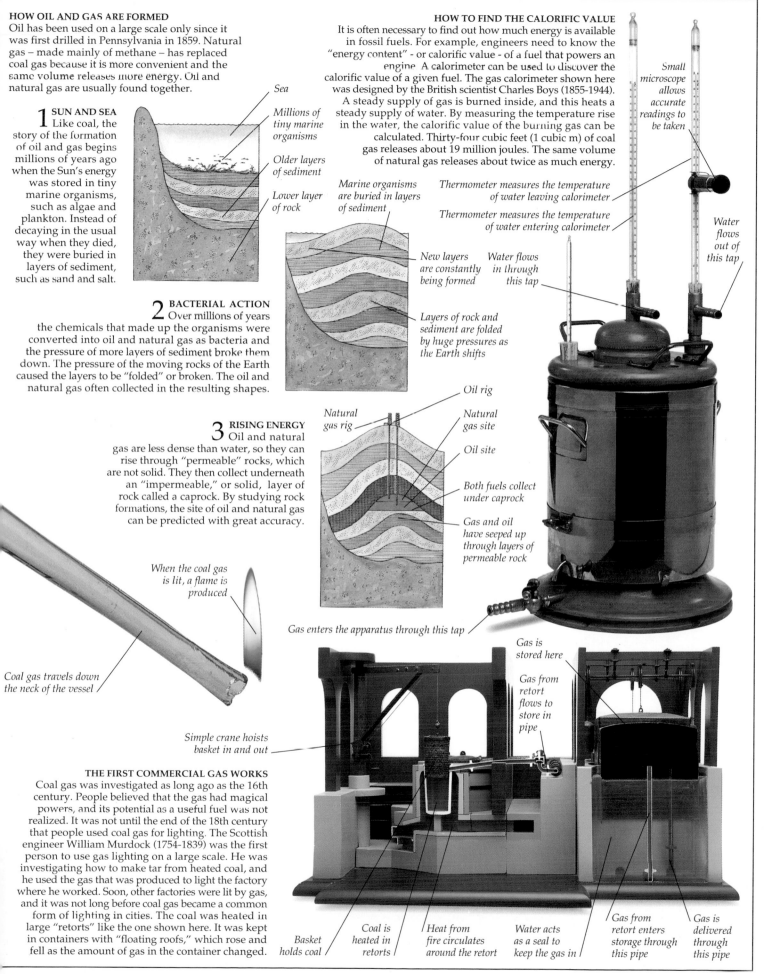

Gas is stored here

Gas from retort flows to store in pipe

THE FIRST COMMERCIAL GAS WORKS

Coal gas was investigated as long ago as the 16th century. People believed that the gas had magical powers, and its potential as a useful fuel was not realized. It was not until the end of the 18th century that people used coal gas for lighting. The Scottish engineer William Murdock (1754-1839) was the first person to use gas lighting on a large scale. He was investigating how to make tar from heated coal, and he used the gas that was produced to light the factory where he worked. Soon, other factories were lit by gas, and it was not long before coal gas became a common form of lighting in cities. The coal was heated in large "retorts" like the one shown here. It was kept in containers with "floating roofs," which rose and fell as the amount of gas in the container changed.

Basket holds coal

Coal is heated in retorts

Heat from fire circulates around the retort

Water acts as a seal to keep the gas in

Gas from retort enters storage through this pipe

Gas is delivered through this pipe

Energy on a global scale

DURING THE 20TH CENTURY, energy has become much more easily available. Most of the energy comes from the burning of fossil fuels. When burned, fossil fuels release substances such as carbon dioxide and smoke into the air. Such substances are not harmful in small amounts, but the demand for energy is so great that millions of tons are released each year. This causes air pollution, which has a worldwide effect. It is not known exactly how much fossil fuel is left for people to use, but it is known that the supply will not last forever. The developed nations of the world use fossil fuels at an incredible rate, mostly for transportation and to generate electricity. Nuclear power is being used in increasing amounts to help satisfy the huge demand for energy. The nuclear fuels could last many hundreds of years, even if the demand increases. However, nuclear power creates problems, because nuclear fission leaves radioactive waste. It can also be the cause of harmful accidents.

TERMITES AND METHANE
Many animals, such as termites, make methane gas in their digestive systems. Although termites are small, there are so many of them that the methane they produce affects the quality of the air on a global scale. In a similar way, the use of energy by the human race is causing changes in the air, often by pollution, with gases such as carbon dioxide.

NUCLEAR DISASTER
On April 26, 1986, a nuclear reactor in a power station at Chernobyl, in the Ukraine (bottom right quarter), caught fire. It released huge amounts of radioactivity, which has harmful and long-term effects on all life. This map of the globe shows one way in which the huge demand for energy can have global effects. The pink areas on the map received radioactive contamination as winds carried the effects of the disaster around the globe.

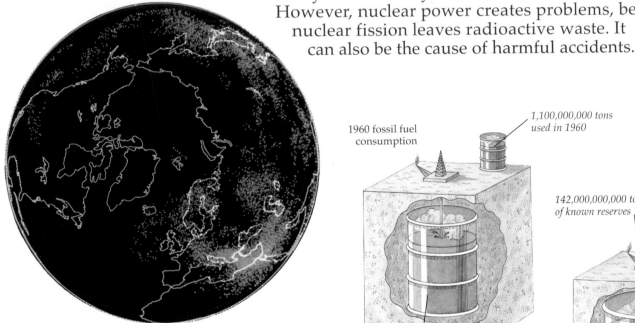

1960 fossil fuel consumption

1,100,000,000 tons used in 1960

41,000,000,000 tons of known reserves

1990 fossil fuel consumption

3,000,000,000 tons used in 1990

142,000,000,000 tons of known reserves

FOSSIL FUELS IN RESERVE
Each year, more oil and natural gas are found and brought up from underground to be burned to release energy. But just how long will the reserves of oil and gas last? In 1960, 40 billion tons of oil and gas were known to exist underground. At the rate they were being used that year across the world, the reserve was estimated to last about 40 years. By 1990, much more oil and gas had been discovered, but the rate at which it was used had also increased. As with the 1960 figures, the 1990 reserve was estimated to last for about 40 years.

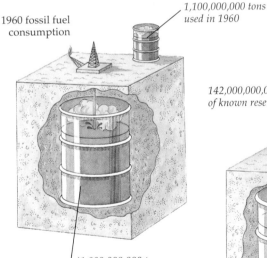

THE RETURN OF MUSCLE POWER
These police officers in Seattle use bicycles rather than cars to get around their beat in the center of the city. Not only does this save energy and decrease pollution, but the officers are also able to get from place to place more quickly than in the cars that clog the city streets. By cycling, walking, and using public transport such as buses, the amount of fuel used for transport can be vastly reduced.

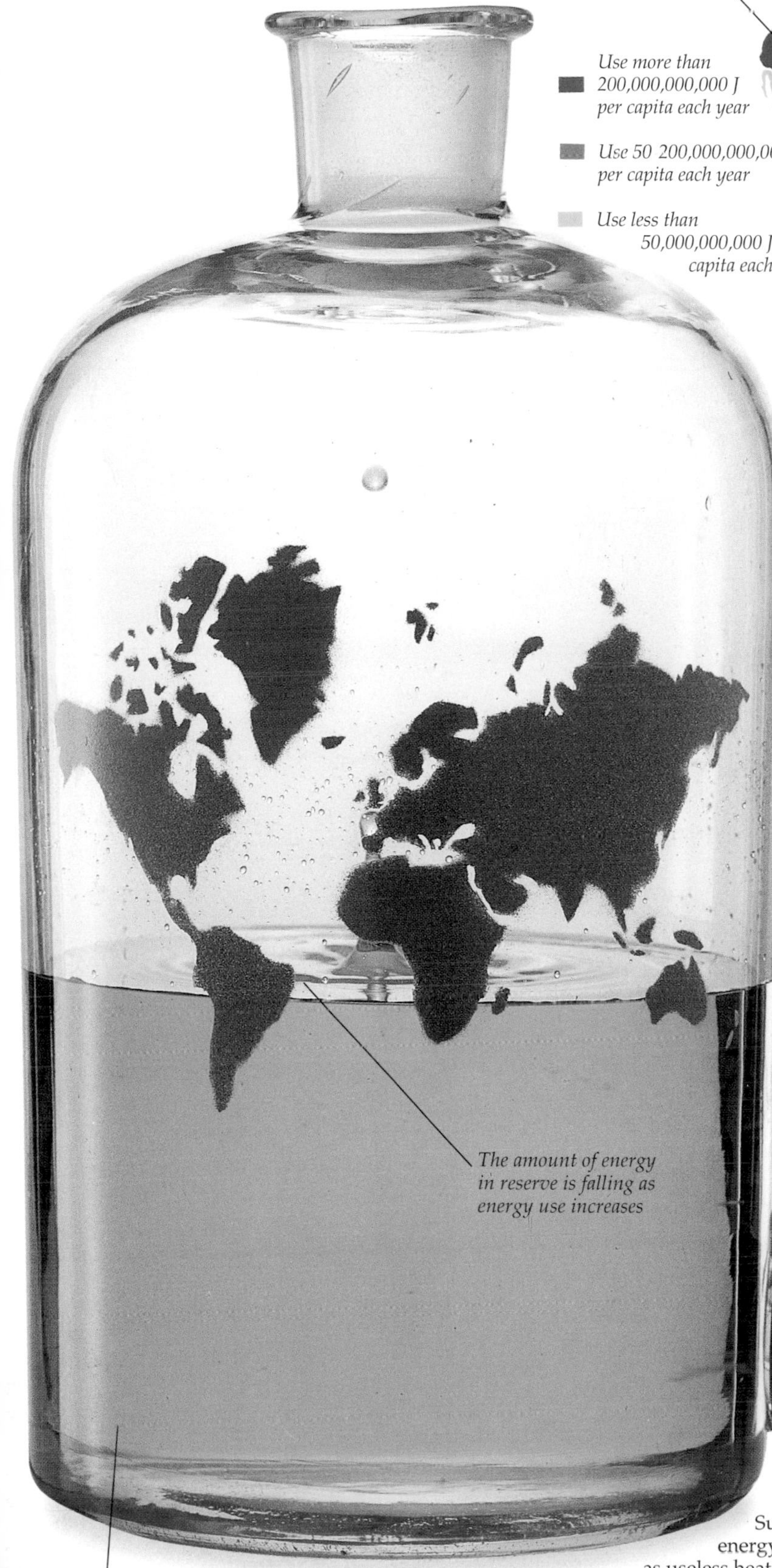

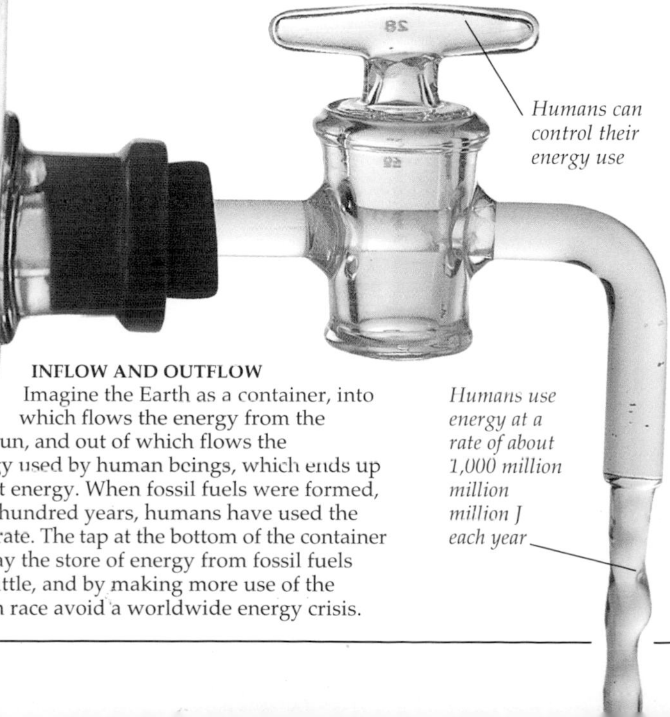

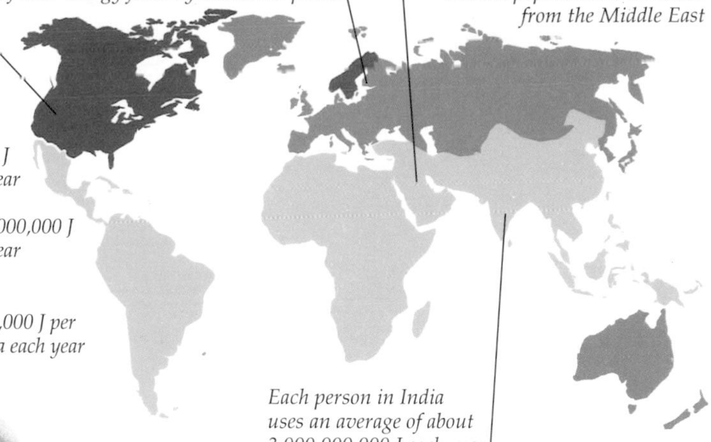

The Sun's energy comes to the Earth at a nearly constant rate

The US uses about one-third of the total available energy but has only one-twentieth of the Earth's population

Some Scandinavian countries obtain much of their energy from hydroelectric power

Most of the fossil fuels used by the world's population is obtained from the Middle East

■ Use more than 200,000,000,000 J per capita each year

■ Use 50 200,000,000,000 J per capita each year

□ Use less than 50,000,000,000 J per capita each year

Each person in India uses an average of about 3,000,000,000 J each year

HOW MUCH ENERGY PEOPLE USE
This map shows the differences in energy use between the developed and the less-developed countries of the world. In developed countries, energy is obtained mainly from fossil fuels. In many less-developed countries, people still depend on muscle energy for their needs. Because people in developed countries have more vehicles and electrical appliances, they use more energy than people living in the less-developed countries.

THE LIVING EARTH
In 1979, the British scientist James Lovelock put forward the idea that the Earth and all life on it is one huge living organism. He named the organism Gaia, after the Greek Earth goddess. This picture shows Lovelock with a statue of the goddess Gaia. He suggested that Gaia is responsible for keeping the conditions in the sea and on the land right for Gaia to carry on living. Now that the population of Earth and its energy use have grown so large, humans can affect land, sea, and air in ways that throw Gaia off balance.

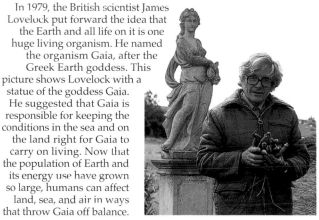

The amount of energy in reserve is falling as energy use increases

Humans can control their energy use

INFLOW AND OUTFLOW
Imagine the Earth as a container, into which flows the energy from the Sun, and out of which flows the energy used by human beings, which ends up as useless heat energy. When fossil fuels were formed, the container was full. For the past few hundred years, humans have used the energy from fossil fuels at an incredible rate. The tap at the bottom of the container is being opened more and more. One day the store of energy from fossil fuels will run out. Only by closing the tap a little, and by making more use of the Sun's energy flowing in, will the human race avoid a worldwide energy crisis.

Earth's store of energy is mostly fossil fuels

Humans use energy at a rate of about 1,000 million million million J each year

Alternative energy

THE DEMAND FOR ENERGY in the past hundred years has been incredible. There are problems with using fossil fuels on as large a scale as they are used at present. These problems can be dealt with in two ways. First, people can make better use of the energy fossil fuels supply by being less wasteful. Second, people can use energy from alternative sources. One alternative to fossil fuels is nuclear energy, but this has problems of its own. Solar, hydroelectric, and geothermal energy are all examples of energy sources that are renewable, or that will not run out, unlike fossil fuels.

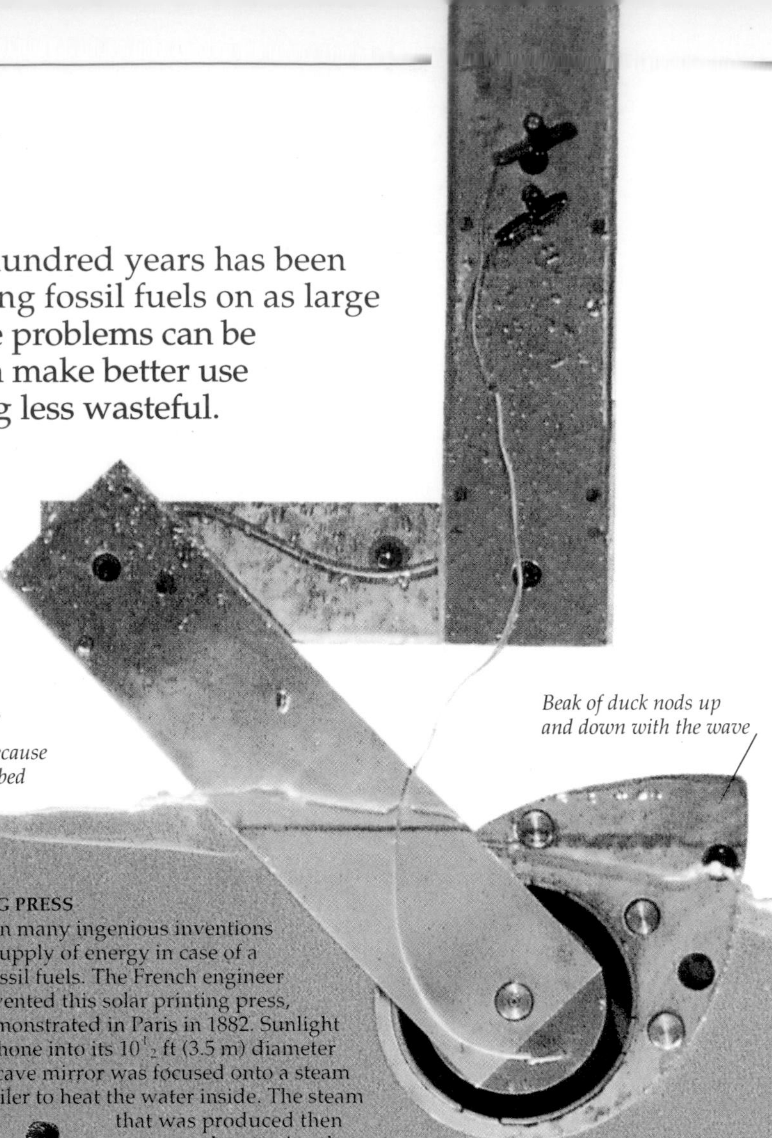

Behind the duck, the water is calm, because the energy of the wave has been absorbed

Beak of duck nods up and down with the wave

SOLAR PRINTING PRESS
There have been many ingenious inventions to provide a supply of energy in case of a shortage of fossil fuels. The French engineer Abel Pifre invented this solar printing press, which he demonstrated in Paris in 1882. Sunlight that shone into its $10\frac{1}{2}$ ft (3.5 m) diameter concave mirror was focused onto a steam boiler to heat the water inside. The steam that was produced then powered an engine that in turn provided the energy for the printing press. On the day of Pifre's demonstration, his press printed more than 2,000 copies of a special publication that he called the *Soleil-Journal*, or *Sun Journal*.

Nozzle through which jet of water flows

Pairs of buckets stop the water, taking most of its kinetic energy

Pelton wheel, also known as the jet-splitting double-bucket turbine (below and right)

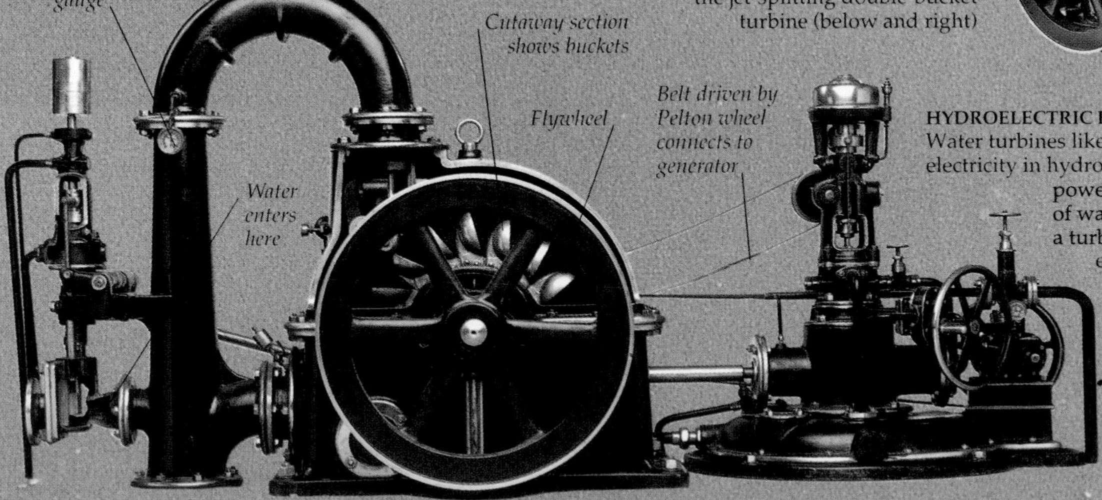

Water-pressure gauge

Cutaway section shows buckets

Flywheel

Water enters here

Belt driven by Pelton wheel connects to generator

HYDROELECTRIC ENERGY
Water turbines like this Pelton wheel are used to produce electricity in hydroelectric power stations. Hydroelectric power is created when the potential energy of water held in a reservoir above a turbine is changed to kinetic energy as the water is released through a nozzle. The water turns a turbine, which is connected to a generator. The rate at which electrical energy is produced depends on how fast the water flows and how far above the turbine the reservoir is. The Pelton wheel was designed by the American mining engineer Lester Pelton (1829-1908).

DUCKS IN THE WATER

As the Sun warms the Earth, it creates wind. The wind's kinetic energy can be changed into electrical energy with the use of wind turbines, which are a development of windmills. However, some of the wind's energy disturbs the surface of the sea and causes waves, just as blowing over a puddle makes ripples. The waves take some of the wind's kinetic energy, and this energy can be used to generate electricity. One of the most successful ways of doing this is to use Salter Ducks, designed in the 1970s by the British engineer Stephen Salter. Rows of Salter Ducks in the sea absorb much of the energy carried by the waves, and nod up and down as waves hit them. This motion drives pumps that push a liquid through a generator to generate electricity.

USING SALTER DUCKS

Salter Ducks (above right) can be used in oceans, seas, and large lakes. They are attached together and floated in a line so that their pointed "beaks" face incoming waves. Salter Ducks are very efficient, harnessing over one-third of the energy of the waves. Despite this, long lines of them would be needed to generate electricity in quantities large enough to be useful. The design is fairly complex, which means that it may not be practical to use them on a large scale.

Crest of wave

The water moves about a fixed point but does not move along with the wave

WOOD CHIP GAS

Biomass is the name for plants whose energy is made use of by human beings. For instance, logs used for wood-burning stoves are biomass. Small chips of wood can also be used as biomass. The chips are loaded into a tank, where they will be made to produce a gas. This gas is then burned to release its energy. The wood could be used as a fuel itself, but the gas is easier to transport than wood. All the energy stored in the wood chips comes from the Sun and is stored by photosynthesis.

PONDS THAT COLLECT ENERGY

Solar energy, or energy from the Sun, can be used directly in many ways. These solar ponds in Israel are an unusual example. The ponds contain a mixture of chemicals that store the Sun's energy. During the winter, this energy is then used to generate cheap electricity. But solar energy can also be used in countries that are not as hot and sunny as Israel. For instance, buildings all over the world use solar collectors to heat water, and solar cells can be used anywhere to operate simple machines like calculators.

ENERGY FROM HOT ROCKS

This power station in Iceland uses geothermal energy, which is heat energy from beneath the surface of the Earth, to produce hot water and steam. The steam drives turbines that generate nearly 3,000,000 J of electrical energy per second, and the hot water is piped to homes. Much of the heat energy comes from molten rocks underground.

Making the most of energy

DURING THE PAST 100 YEARS, the world demand for energy has grown enormously. Supplying energy in such huge amounts has caused many problems, such as the limited quantity of fossil fuels available today. Renewable sources of energy can be used as alternatives to fossil fuels, but much more work needs to be done before they can take over. There is one obvious course of action: using less energy. By making the most of the many types of energy that are available, fossil fuels will last longer and alternative energy sources will be further developed. There are many ways of making the most of energy. For example, the energy that public transportation, such as buses and trains, uses is spread between many passengers and can reduce traffic jams in busy cities. Engines designed to be more efficient use less energy to do the same job as other, inefficient, engines. Combined heat and power stations heat water for nearby homes by using heat that would otherwise be wasted. Everyone can help to ensure that energy is used wisely so that there will be plenty left to use in the future.

MAKING THE MOST OF A ROCKING CHAIR
One way to make the most of energy is to use energy that would otherwise be wasted. This "New Domestic Motor," invented in 1873, made use of "the latent feminine energy." It allowed three jobs to be done at once. As the worker rocked in the rocking chair, sewing or doing other handiwork, a system of levers, weights, and pulleys was set in motion. This rocked a baby and churned butter at the same time.

SAME LIGHT, LESS ENERGY
These two light bulbs give out the same amount of light, yet one of them uses much less electrical energy than the other. The meters below show how much electricity is being used each second by the bulbs. The traditional incandescent bulb on the left has a thin, coiled filament that becomes white hot when electricity passes through it. Much of the electricity it uses becomes heat and is wasted. The compact fluorescent bulb (right) has no filament, and much more of the electricity it uses becomes light. A huge amount of energy would be saved if everyone used efficient lighting. Energy can also be saved if lights that are not needed are switched off.

Bulbs produce the same amount of light

60-watt bulb

18-watt bulb

Incandescent bulb uses over twice the electricity per second as the fluorescent bulb

Fluorescent bulb uses much less energy per second than the incandescent bulb

Cable carries electricity

THE SUN CAN HELP

In most countries the Sun is not reliable or powerful enough to provide all the energy a household needs. However, the Sun's energy can be used to supplement other energy sources. Solar collectors like this one, fitted to the roof, can use the Sun's energy to heat water for household use. If the Sun is not intense enough on a particular day, then a gas or electric boiler is used, but on sunnier days the solar collector can supply the needs of a household. The electricity or gas is used only when necessary, and so less energy is wasted.

Pipes hold water for heating

Mineral wool insulates the water pipes

Two layers of metal foil reflect radiant energy back onto water pipes

Light aluminum frame

Transparent film allows radiation from the Sun to be converted into energy

INSULATING THE HOME

Most homes do not use energy efficiently. Heat is lost through windows, walls, and the roof. This means that more energy is needed to keep the house warm. There are many things that can be done to a house to improve its energy efficiency, such as double glazing, draftproofing, and insulating ceilings, walls, floors, and hot-water boilers. Lagging the attic insulates the roof, keeping the house warm in winter and cool in summer. Most modern homes, like this one, are insulated while they are being built, but it is also possible to add insulation to an older home.

SECOND TIME AROUND

This pile of used plastic is waiting to be recycled, rather than being thrown away. To recycle this plastic, it must be heated so that it melts and can be molded into a new shape. Glass can be recycled in a similar way. Recycling is an important way of making the most of energy, because less energy is needed to make things out of recycled materials than if manufacturers start with raw materials. Many people throw things away when they are no longer needed, but this is a waste of the energy that was put into making them, and can cause pollution. Buying fewer unnecessary goods and re-using items are other important ways to be energy efficient.

NEWSPAPER LOGS

Using things again, whether for the same purpose or for something else, can help avoid wasting energy. A good deal of energy can be obtained from many materials by burning them. Some countries burn much of their trash in power stations and use the heat that is released to make steam to power electricity generators. A similar thing can be done on a smaller scale. These logs are made from old newspapers, which are often thrown away after they have been read. Logs like these burn for up to two hours, providing a cheap way to heat a home. Another way paper can be used again is to make it into recycled paper.

Newspapers are soaked in water and placed into this machine to compress them

Compressed and dried newspaper logs

The origins and destiny of energy

THE UNIVERSE IS TRULY VAST. The Earth is part of the solar system, centered around the Sun. The Sun is one tiny part of a collection of 100,000 million stars in a galaxy called the Milky Way. This is just one of a huge group of galaxies. There are millions upon millions of other galaxies, separated by enormous distances of almost empty space. In that space is the light and other radiation given off by countless stars like the Sun. All of the radiation and all of the matter that make up the Universe are forms of energy. At the centers of stars, matter is constantly being lost, but an equivalent amount of energy is always released as a result.

Energy condenses into matter

AN OPEN AND SHUT UNIVERSE
According to Hindu myths, many Universes are created by the god Vishnu when he opens and shuts his eyes. As he opens his eyes, he dreams, and his dream is a new Universe. After many millions of years, he shuts his eyes and that Universe ends. Some scientists believe that the Universe may one day collapse on itself, to be re-born in a new Big Bang. This could repeat forever, with a different Universe resulting each time, just as Vishnu's dreams would each have been different.

The Universe is not infinitely large, but it seems to have begun with a "Big Bang," in which a fixed amount of energy came from nothing. Some scientists say that this fixed amount of energy is available for only a fixed amount of time, and that one day the Universe will be squashed out of existence in a "Big Crunch."

THE BIG BANG
Observations of the stars and galaxies that make up the Universe suggest that they are all moving apart. This means that the very space of which the Universe is made is expanding – stretching like the rubber skin of some huge balloon. If this is true then at some time, about 15,000 million years ago, all of space and time must have come out of nothing in a huge explosion that is now called the Big Bang.

1 SINGLE POINT OF ENERGY
According to the Big Bang theory, all space and time were created at a single point far smaller than an atom. That point must have contained all the energy of the Universe, and because all of space was so small, it must have been incredibly hot. At such high temperatures the forces we know today, such as gravity, would have been very different. There would have been no matter – only heat energy would have existed.

2 A SUDDEN INFLATION OF SPACE
Just after the moment of creation, space and time itself began to expand at an incredible rate. This was not an explosion in space, but an inflation of space. It is thought that the reason for the inflation was that at such high energies, gravity may become a push rather than a pull force.

3 FORMING MATTER
At the end of the very rapid inflation, the Universe became cooler, and the particles that make up matter began to form out of some of the energy. Just as water vapor condenses to form water droplets as it cools, so matter was formed from "condensed" energy as the Universe cooled.

Robert Wilson (left) and Arno Penzias after winning the 1978 Nobel Prize for their discovery

ECHOES OF THE BIG BANG
In 1964 two American physicists, Robert Wilson and Arno Penzias, detected electromagnetic radiation, which exactly fitted the predictions of the Big Bang theory. The total amount of energy in the Universe is fixed, and it cannot be destroyed. Much of the energy took the form of matter in the early Universe, but some of it still remains as a "record" of the Big Bang. This record is the radiation that Wilson and Penzias detected.

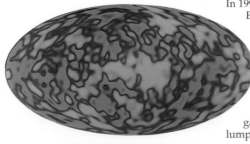

EXPLORING THE RIPPLES
In 1992 the American COBE (Cosmic Background Explorer) satellite gathered information about the radiation that fills space. When information from the whole sky was put together and enhanced by a computer, it showed that the Universe is not quite the same in every direction. The patches on the picture show that space in the early Universe was not even but contained irregular "ripples," around which energy in the form of matter gathered. This seems to explain why matter is lumped together in some places and not in others.

The Universe continues
to expand

The Universe appears to be flat
but may actually be curved

Between galaxies is
mostly empty space

Galaxies form from
condensing matter

4 **A LUMPY UNIVERSE**
If the Universe was perfectly
smooth as it expanded, it would not
be "lumpy" as it is observed to be. The
young Universe was very slightly irregular,
and gravity pulled together the newly formed
matter into galaxies, which give space its "lumpiness."

5 **CURVED SPACE AND THE END OF TIME**
According to the theory of the Big Bang, the Universe
continues to expand, and this fits with the observation that galaxies
are moving apart. If this theory is correct, space should be "curved" like
the surface of an inflating balloon. From the Earth, space seems to be "flat,"
but it could be very slightly curved, hardly noticeable to us because of the expansion.

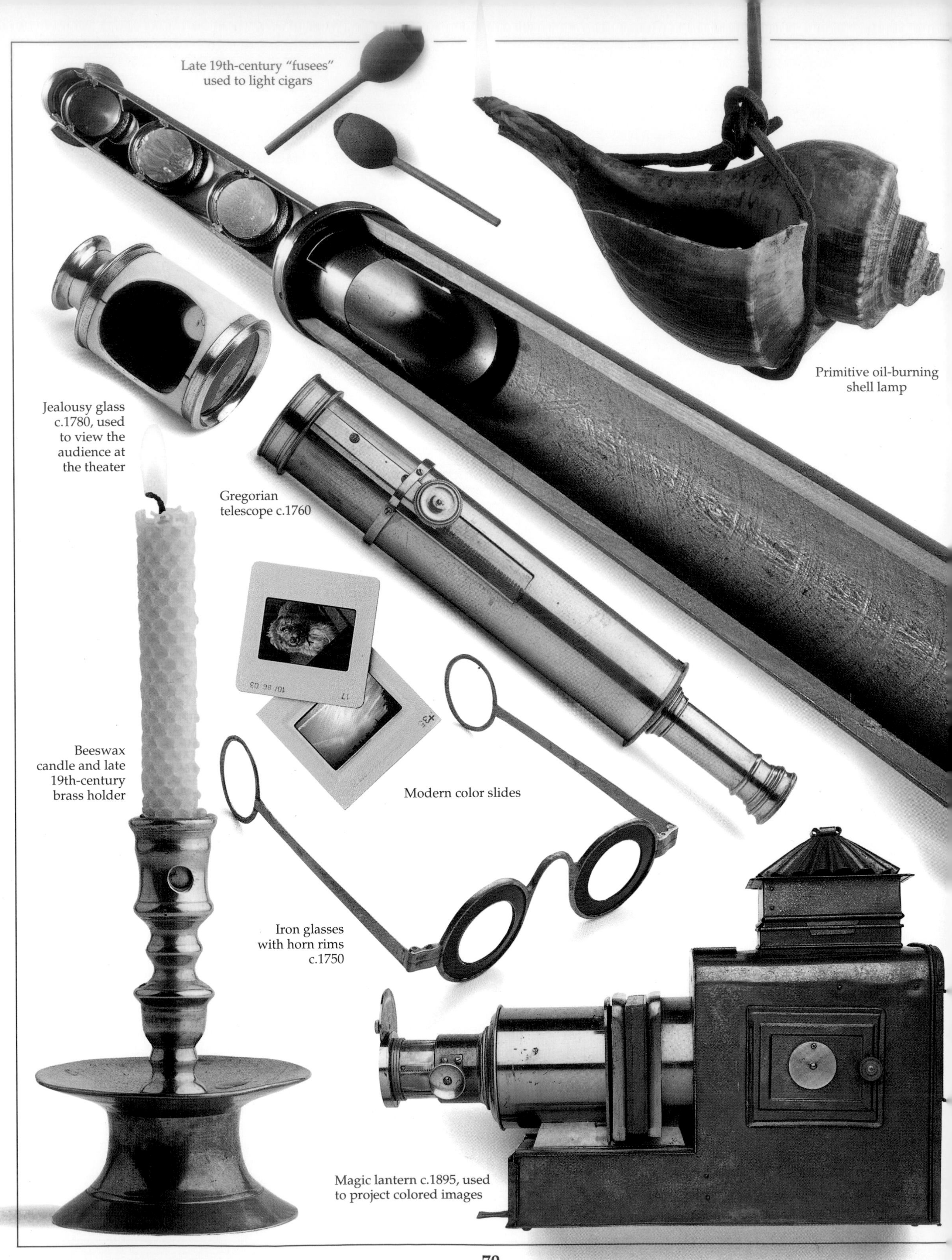

Late 19th-century "fusees" used to light cigars

Primitive oil-burning shell lamp

Jealousy glass c.1780, used to view the audience at the theater

Gregorian telescope c.1760

Modern color slides

Beeswax candle and late 19th-century brass holder

Iron glasses with horn rims c.1750

Magic lantern c.1895, used to project colored images

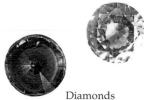
Diamonds
(front and back)

Compact disc

LIGHT

Geissler tube used
for lighting

Reflecting cat's eye

Barton's button c.1830

Cutaway refracting telescope

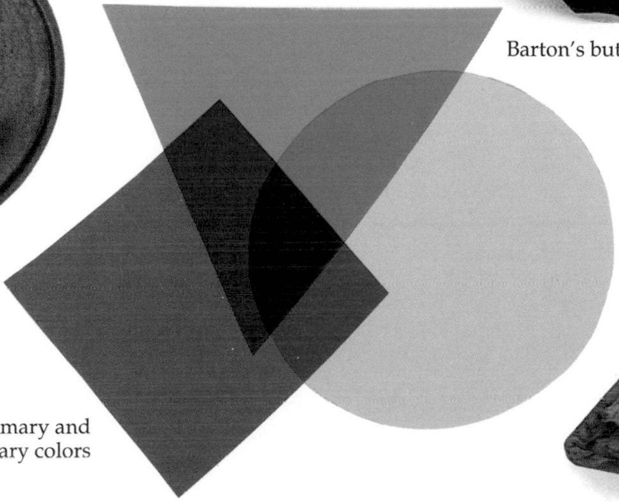

Primary and
secondary colors

Coronet Midget
camera c.1934

Light, myth, and magic

IMAGINE WHAT WOULD happen to the earth if tomorrow the sun did not rise. Within hours it would become as cold as winter. After a few days ponds and rivers would begin to freeze, and plants and animals would start to die. Soon, oil would turn solid, and engines would not work. Power station generators would come to a standstill. There would be no way to transport food to stores, or to bring it home. Unless fuel could be found to make a fire, there would be no light or heat.

But could this ever happen? With current knowledge of the solar system, it is certain that the answer is no. But in the past people could not be so certain. They had no clear idea of how the sun produced light or why it moved through the sky. By worshiping the sun as a god, they guarded against it going out.

FROM HEAT TO LIGHT
Lightning is produced when an electric spark makes air so hot that it glows. In nature most forms of light are brought about by heat.

LURING LIGHT
The eerie "Will o' the wisp" is a naturally occurring flame that can occur over marshy ground. The flame's fuel is methane, a gas produced by rotting plants. The methane bubbles rise to the surface together with phosphine, a gas from the rotting remains of animals. Phosphine ignites when it meets air, lighting the methane. The quickly moving flame is almost impossible to follow.

Replica of an Inca sun mask

LIVELY LIGHT
Legends and folklore are full of spirits, apparitions, and sea monsters that glow in the dark. Many of these "sightings" are probably due to plants and animals that can make their own light. Living things, like this planktonic fish, use these lights to confuse their enemies, find a mate, or lure food toward them.

LIGHT FROM ABOVE
In the far North and South, the night sky sometimes lights up with beautiful curtains of light known as "auroras." They occur when tiny electrically charged particles from the sun collide with atoms in the earth's atmosphere. The earth's magnetic field draws the particles toward the North and South Poles. The name "aurora" is the Latin word for "dawn."

THE SPLENDOR OF THE SUN
This golden mask is a replica of one made by the Incas in Ecuador. The Incas worshiped the sun and believed that their rulers were the sun's living descendants.

THE SUN IN STONE
This stone face once stared out from a great pyramid built in the 16th century by the Aztecs of Mexico. It stood in the Aztec capital city, Tenochtitlan, which was built on islands in Lake Texcoco. It is a "calendar stone," showing the sun god Tonatiuh surrounded by symbols of the universe and the days of the year. The triangle pointing outward represents the sun's rays. Such stones were used not only as calendars, but also to help predict when solar eclipses would occur.

THE SUN IN ANCIENT EGYPT
This scene is from the throne of the Egyptian pharaoh Tutankhamen, who lived about 1350 BC. Tutankhamen's father-in-law swept away all the traditional gods and replaced them with one – Aton, the sun god. When Tutankhamen came to the throne he restored the old gods, but Aton remained the most important.

FACING THE LIGHT
In ancient times people did not know about photosynthesis – the process by which plants use light. But they could see that plants needed light because leaves and flowers grow so that they face the light, and they often turn to follow the sun's changing position through the day. The sunflower was used in sun worship in Central and South America. It gets its English name from its sunlike face. In French, it is called "tournesol," meaning "turn towards the sun."

IMPERIAL SUN
This sun symbol is found at the City Palace, Jaipur, India. It is thought to be the imperial symbol of the family of the 18th-century warrior-astronomer Maharajah Jai Singh, whose leader was known as the "Sun of the Hindus." In 1728 he began building a complex outdoor observatory, the Jantar Mantar, which is still in use in Jaipur. It contains a massive sundial.

Making light

At some time in the distant past, humans learned how to harness fire. At first, fire was something they had to find and collect. They would light piles of branches from bushfires and keep them blazing for as long as they could. If the flames went out, the search for new fire had to begin again. Later, people discovered ways to make fires themselves. By striking stones together, or rubbing wood against wood, they could make sparks or generate enough heat to set fire to dry tinder. Once they had mastered this, they could have light and heat whenever they wanted.

LIGHT FROM FLAMES
Light is a form of energy. When a fire is lit, chemical energy is released. The burning fuel emits gases, and the chemical energy heats the gas atoms, making them glow, or incandesce. A flame's color tells how much energy is being released, and how hot the flame is. A dull yellow flame is cooler than a bright blue one – but will still burn anything that is too close.

FIRE FROM ABOVE
According to the legends of ancient Greece, the god Zeus prevented humans from having fire. However, Prometheus stole some fire from the mountain home of the gods and brought it down into the world. The "bringing of fire" stills happens today at the beginning of the Olympic Games, when a burning flame is carried from Greece to the place where the games are to be held.

TARRED TORCHES
Poles topped with burning tar or rags cast a bright yellow light. These flaming torches could be carried from place to place or fastened to walls. Roman cities used torches as street lighting over 2,000 years ago.

Pyrites

Flint

STRIKING A LIGHT
Flint and iron pyrites are two minerals that give off sparks if they are hit with something hard. They were probably the first pieces of firemaking equipment to be used by our ancestors. To produce a flame, the sparks had to land on tinder – a dry, light material, such as wood dust, feathery plant seeds, or fungus. In later years, flint and iron pyrites were both used to ignite gunpowder in "flintlock" rifles. Older cigarette lighters also use artificial "flints" to make sparks.

FIRE PLOUGH AND HEARTH
Rubbing your hands together makes them become warm. This is because friction caused by rubbing gives rise to heat. With hands, the rise in temperature is small. But if a stick is rubbed very quickly against another piece of wood, it can become hot enough to make tinder catch fire. In this Aboriginal fire plough and hearth from Australia, the stick, or "plough," is pushed along the groove towards the "hearth." Hot pieces of the stick jump on to the tinder placed in the hearth to make a flame.

Plough

Hearth

GUIDING LIGHT
The Pharos of Alexandria was the first recorded full-scale lighthouse. It was over 260 ft (80 m) high, and it used the light of burning wood to guide ships into harbor. It was completed in 280 BC, but was eventually toppled by an earthquake.

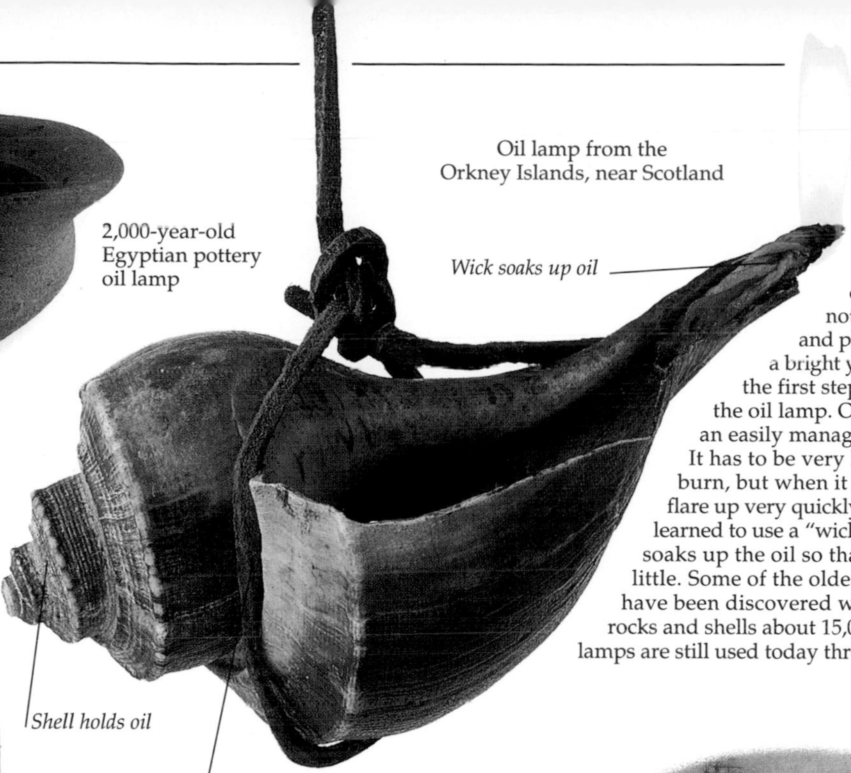

Oil lamp from the
Orkney Islands, near Scotland

2,000-year-old
Egyptian pottery
oil lamp

Wick soaks up oil

LIGHT FROM OIL

In the earliest days of fire, humans noticed that animal fat and plant oils burned with a bright yellow light. This was the first step in the invention of the oil lamp. Oil, on its own, is not an easily manageable source of light. It has to be very hot before it will burn, but when it is hot it will often flare up very quickly. Eventually, people learned to use a "wick" – something that soaks up the oil so that it burns little by little. Some of the oldest oil lamps that have been discovered were made out of rocks and shells about 15,000 years ago. Oil lamps are still used today throughout the world.

Shell holds oil

Leather is used to suspend the lamp

THE SEARCH FOR OIL

Before gas lighting was invented, there was a great demand for animal oil. Oil came mainly from the fat of sea animals – whales, seals, and even penguins – which was boiled down in huge vats to make "tallow."

Beeswax
candle

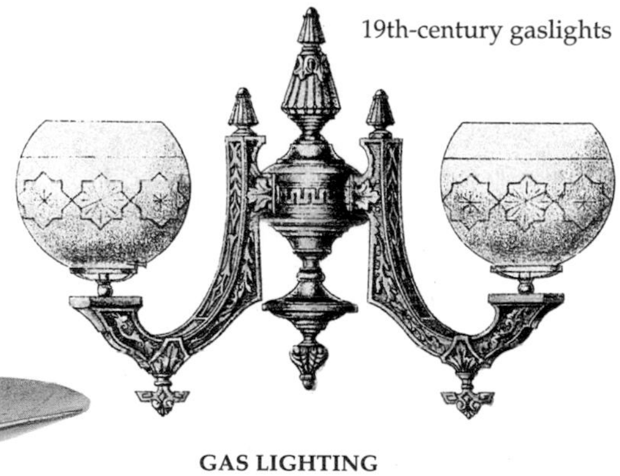

19th-century gaslights

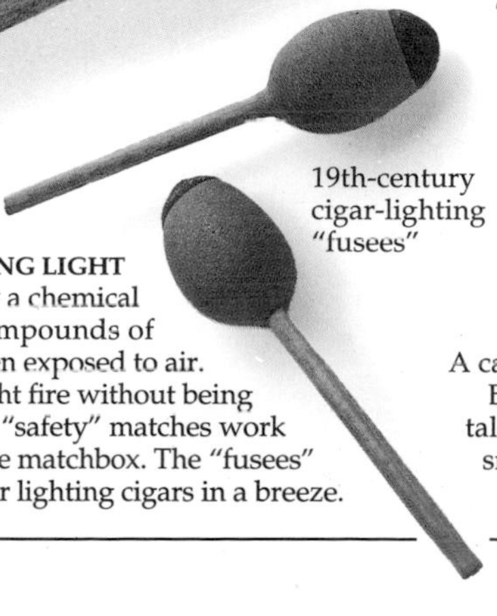

GAS LIGHTING

During the 19th century, gas lighting became widespread in towns and cities. At first, gaslights were simply jets of burning gas. Later, their brightness was increased by using a "mantle." This is a fine net of chemically treated fabric that fits over the gas jet. The heat of the gas flame causes the mantle to give off a bright light.

19th-century
cigar-lighting
"fusees"

TRAVELING LIGHT

Matches create a flame by a chemical reaction. Most use compounds of phosphorus, which catch fire when exposed to air. Early matches sometimes caught fire without being struck at all, but more modern "safety" matches work only when struck against the matchbox. The "fusees" shown here were designed for lighting cigars in a breeze.

SOLID OIL LAMP

A candle is simply an oil lamp with solid oil. Before the 1800s candles were made of tallow or beeswax. They produced a lot of smoke but not much light. Today, most candles are made of paraffin wax.

Shadows

Since ancient times, people have known that light travels in straight lines. This can be seen by looking at the beam of light from a film projector. The beam is made up of many "rays" of light. Although the rays spread out in the shape of a fan, each individual ray travels in a straight line from the projector to the screen. If somebody stands up and blocks part of the beam, some of the light rays will not reach the screen, while the light rays in the rest of the beam carry on as before. The result is an area without light – a shadow.

STRAIGHT SUNBEAMS
Sunbeams show that light travels in straight lines. Sunbeams can be seen only if dust, as in this old barn, or droplets of moisture in the air scatter some of their light. The scattered light travels outward in straight lines, and some of it reaches the eyes, so that the beam can be seen.

Pointer

The pointer's shadow touches a curved line that indicates the time

TIME FROM THE SUN
The sun always moves across the sky at a steady rate, so if a stick is pushed vertically into the ground, the time of day can be told by seeing where its shadow lies. This is the principle of the sundial. Simple sundials were used in Egypt at least 3,000 years ago. This unusual column sundial was made in Germany in about 1550. The time is shown both on the column and on the vertical faces beneath it.

Compass used to set the sundial in the correct direction

Dial marked with hours

SHARP SHADOWS
Light rays fan out from a candle in straight lines to cast a shadow of anything that blocks their path. Etienne de Silhouette (1709-1767), a French government minister, used this principle to make shadow portraits that were much cheaper than paintings. Today, the name silhouette is used to describe any black shape seen against the light.

Sun — *Light rays from sun* — *Moon* — *Umbra (sun fully hidden)*

Penumbra (sun partly hidden) — *Earth*

SHADOWS IN SPACE
During an eclipse of the sun, the moon comes between the earth and the sun and its shadow moves across the earth. In the middle of the shadow, the "umbra," all the sun's light is blocked. Around this is the "penumbra," where only part of the sun's light is blocked. Anyone in the path of the umbra sees a "total" eclipse, in which the sun disappears. People in the path of the penumbra see a "partial" eclipse. To them, part of the sun is always visible.

Leonardo da Vinci

STUDYING SHADOWS
The great Italian artist and engineer Leonardo da Vinci (1452-1519) investigated almost every branch of science, including the study of light. This sketch from one of his many notebooks shows light travelling outward from a pair of candles and casting shadows on either side of an object. Beneath the drawing are some of da Vinci's notes, written in the back-to-front "mirror writing" that he often used.
Da Vinci applied his findings as a scientist to his works of art. In many of his paintings he used deep shadows to build up an image.

PREDICTING AN ECLIPSE
When Christopher Columbus landed on Jamaica in 1504 he could not persuade the native Indians to give him enough supplies. Columbus knew that an eclipse of the moon was about to occur, so he "commanded" the moon to go dark. The Indians were so astonished by his "powers" that they gave him the help he needed.

STUDYING LIGHT

The German mathematician and astronomer Johannes Kepler (1571-1630) is remembered chiefly for his discovery that the planets move in elliptical orbits. But Kepler was also interested in the study of light. In 1604 he published a book called *Astronomiae pars Optica* which explained, with the help of a number of experiments, how light traveled in straight lines, how it cast shadows, and how it bent when it moved from one substance to another. Kepler also realized why people with long or short sight cannot see clearly (see also p. 339).

Flat silhouette puppets

Decorative wooden theater

Light source is placed behind this screen

PLAYING WITH SHADOWS

In a shadow theater like the one above, flat puppets cast their shadows on to a screen. The shadows are sharp because the puppets and the screen are kept close together. If the puppets move too far back, their shadows become blurred. This can be seen by using a table lamp. If an object is held near the table, its shadow will be sharp. If the object is then moved towards the lamp, the shadow will become blurred.

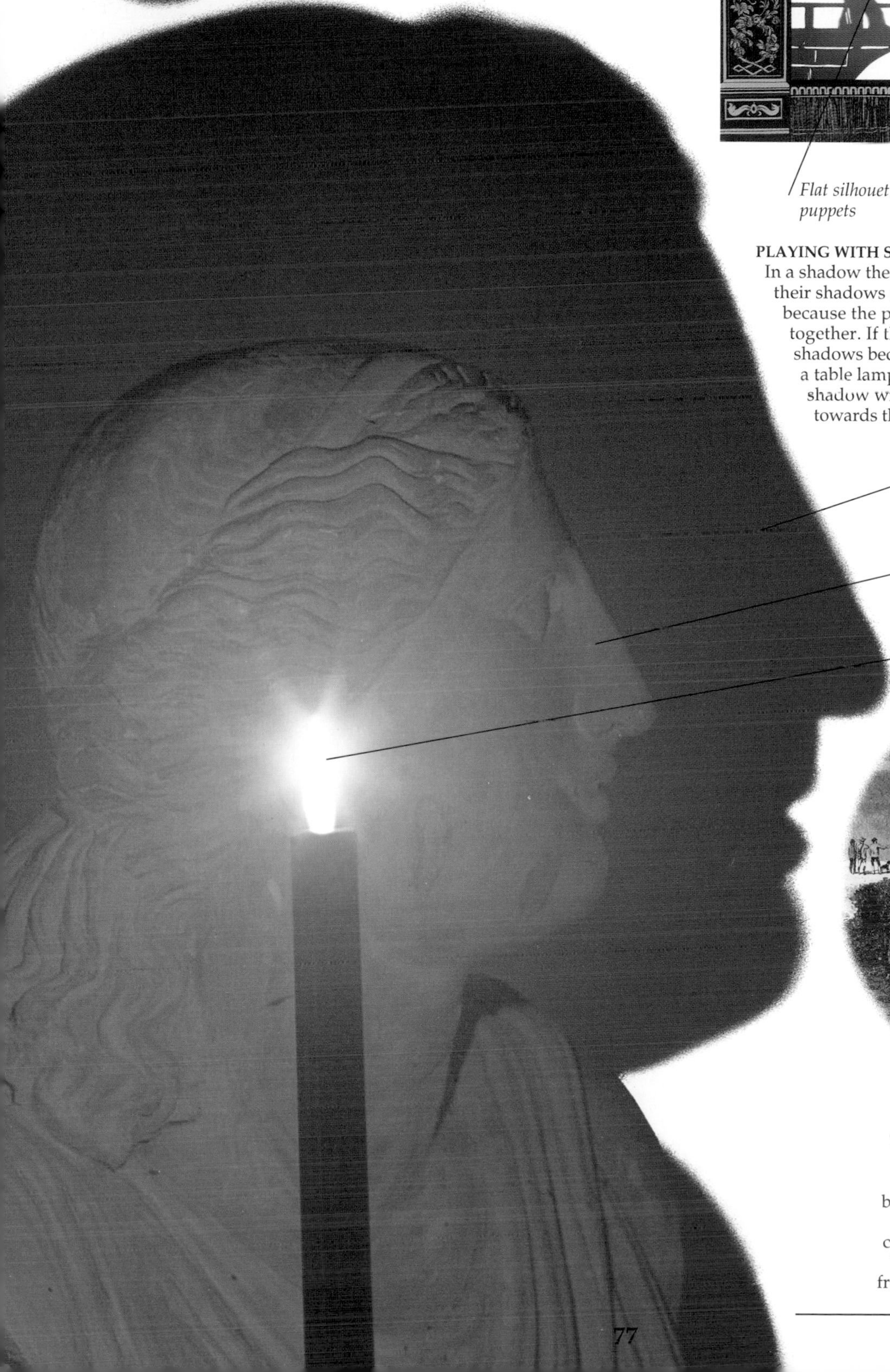

The shadow is sharp because the source of light is small

Object blocks the path of light and casts a shadow

Flame from the candle

THE SPECTER OF THE BROCKEN

The "Brockenspekter" is a phenomenon that occurs in high mountains when a climber's shadow falls on the clouds because the sun is in a low position behind the climber. If the conditions are right, colored rings are seen around the shadow. This unusual trick of light gets its name from the Brocken, a mountain in Germany.

Reflecting light

WHEN A RAY of light hits a mirror it is reflected, meaning that it bounces back. This can be seen by looking at the surface of a pool of water, just as people would have done long ago. As long as the water's surface is smooth, light is reflected in an orderly way and there is a clear image. But if the water becomes ruffled by the wind, light is reflected in many different directions. Instead of a clear image, there is now a jumble of scattered light. It is known that the ancient Greek mathematician Euclid understood how light is reflected. As long ago as 300 BC, he investigated how reflection takes place, and so did a number of Greek scientists who followed him. But it was not until the 1100s that the Arab scientist Alhazen pieced together the law that describes exactly what happens to a ray of light when it strikes a surface and then bounces off it.

MIRRORED IN WATER
The surface of still water makes a natural mirror. According to Greek mythology, a youth called Narcissus fell in love with his own reflection in a pool of water. When he tried to reach the reflection, he fell into the water and drowned.

EARLY MIRROR
This Egyptian bronze mirror was made in about 1300 BC. The bronze was highly polished to give a clear reflection. Glass mirrors date back many centuries, but mirrors of clear glass first appeared in Venice in about AD 1300. Like today's mirrors, they were backed by a very thin layer of metal, which reflected light.

CURVED AND FLAT SURFACES (*below and right*)
The kind of reflection that is seen in a mirror depends on its shape and how far away things are. Here are reflections from flat, or "plane," concave, and convex surfaces.

REFLECTIONS AND IMAGES
Reflection always involves two rays – an incoming, or "incident," ray and an outgoing, or "reflected," ray. The law of reflection states that the two rays are at identical angles but on opposite sides of the "normal" – an imaginary line at right angles to the mirror, through the point where the rays meet. When an object is viewed in a mirror, the eyes take in light rays that have been reflected. But the brain assumes that the light rays have reached the eyes in straight lines. The brain works backward along the light paths and perceives an image behind the mirror. This "virtual" image does not really exist because it does not actually produce light. The other kind of image, one that produces light, is known as a "real" image. A real image can be thrown onto a screen, but a virtual image cannot.

Plane mirror

Object *Incident ray* *Virtual image*

Reflected ray

Path of light perceived by the brain

Mirror

Eye

Concave mirrors make objects look smaller and upside-down, unless they are very close

CONCAVE MIRRORS
When parallel light rays strike a concave mirror, which is curved inward, they are reflected in so that they come together, or converge. What is seen in a concave mirror depends on its distance from the object being reflected. If the inside of a spoon is held close to the eye, a magnified, upright view of the eye will be seen. If the spoon is moved away, a miniature, upside-down view of the whole face will be seen.

Concave mirror

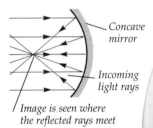

Concave mirror

Incoming light rays

Image is seen where the reflected rays meet

Concave spoon

GHOSTLY APPEARANCE
If viewed from certain angles, glass on its own can act as a mirror. In the past this was used to create "ghosts" on stage. The ghost was actually an actor under the stage. An angled plane of glass reflected light from the ghost towards the audience. They would see the ghost, but not the glass.

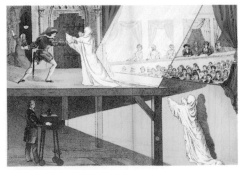

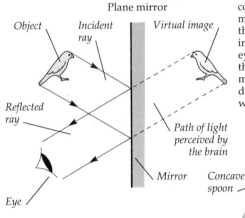

Because the apple is so close to this concave bowl, a large, upright image is formed

Concave bowl

CONVEX MIRRORS

A convex mirror bulges outward. When parallel light rays strike the mirror, they are reflected so that they spread out, or diverge. When someone looks into a convex mirror, their brain traces back along the rays as if they were coming from behind the mirror. A small, upright "virtual" image of anything reflected in the mirror is seen. Because convex mirrors give a wide view, they are used in cars. They make things look small, so drivers must remember that things in a rearview mirror may be closer than they seem.

Convex mirror

Incoming light ray

Reflected light ray

Virtual image is seen behind the mirror

Convex mirror

Convex cup

Upright images are formed of all the objects in a wide area

The cylindrical mirror reflects a perfectly shaped image

CHANGING SHAPE

This painting of a butterfly looks strange and distorted. But when it is reflected in a cylindrical mirror, it becomes perfectly shaped. Paintings like this are examples of "anamorphic" toys, which were very popular in the 18th and 19th centuries. Anamorphic artists worked by looking at the mirror, rather than the paper.

Anamorphic butterfly, 1870

Concave–convex dish

Cut diamonds

Front view sparkles

Rear view is dark

BOUNCING BACK

A cut diamond is designed to reflect most of the light that falls on its front. Some of the light is reflected by the outside of the diamond's upper faces and some by the inside of the lower faces. This is why a diamond sparkles when viewed from the front but is dull when seen from behind.

Observer looks here

Plane mirror set at 45° gives a sideways view

Distorted images are formed by the changing curves of this surface

False front

The flat part of the plate is a plane mirror that forms a clear image of anything reflected in it

PLANE MIRRORS

A flat, or "plane," mirror reflects objects without distorting them. Although the image is the right way up, it is back-to-front or left-right reversed. Police cars and ambulances often have back-to-front signs, which look the right way around when seen in a car mirror.

Plane mirror

Incoming light ray

Plane mirror

Reflected light ray

SEEING SIDEWAYS

This polemoscope, or "jealousy glass," was made in 1780. It was designed to make it look as though the person using it was looking forward, but in fact it contains a plane mirror that gives a sideways view. Jealousy glasses were used in theaters by people who wanted to keep a close eye on the audience rather than the entertainment.

Bending light

WHEN LIGHT PASSES FROM ONE SUBSTANCE to another it is bent, or "refracted." One way to see refraction is to put something in a glass of water. Its shape will seem to change because the light rays bend as they leave the water and enter the air. People have known about refraction for a long time. Early scientists realized that it was a precise effect and tried to make a mathematical law to show how much bending occured. The Egyptian geographer Ptolemy (AD 90-168) probably devised the first "law of refraction." It worked in some cases, but was unreliable. Alhazen (pp. 78) investigated refraction but could not predict how far light would bend. The problem was solved in 1621 by Willebrord Snell, and his law is still known as "Snell's Law."

WISHFUL THINKING
Ptolemy carried out several experiments to investigate how far light was bent. He devised a law to explain the amount of refraction, but even his own results did not always agree with his law.

Light ray

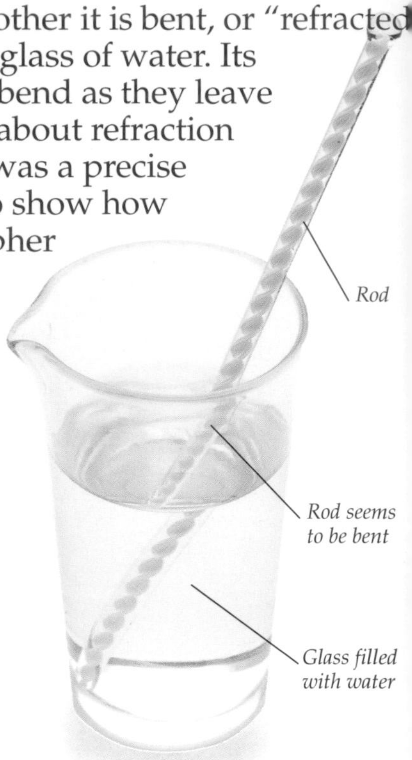

Rod

Rod seems to be bent

Glass filled with water

Ray of light is bent as it leaves the air and enters the left face of the block

Clear glass block

Light inside the block travels in a straight line

BENT BUT UNBROKEN
This glass rod seems to be made of separate parts all at different angles. This happens because light from different parts of the rod passes through different combinations of water, glass, and air. Each time it moves from one substance to another, it is bent.

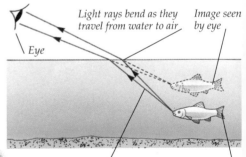

Light rays bend as they travel from water to air

Image seen by eye

Eye

Light from object

Actual position of object

HOW DEEP IS IT?
When an object is seen in water, the light rays from it are bent as they travel from water to air. The eyes follow the rays back as though they had traveled in straight lines, so a "virtual" image is seen. This image is not as deep as the object.

As it leaves the block and enters the air, the light is bent back again

SNELL'S LAW OF REFRACTION
In this experiment a beam of light is bent as it enters and leaves a clear glass block. When the beam hits the block, it turns more steeply toward it – the beam shown here becomes more horizontal. When it leaves the block, it is bent again in the opposite direction. The amount of bending is very precise. If the beam enters or leaves the block head-on, it will not be bent at all. If it enters or leaves at any other angle, it will be bent, and the bending increases as the beam gets further from the head-on position. In 1621 the Dutch mathematician and astronomer Willebrord Snell found there was a characteristic ratio between a beam's "angle of incidence" (its angle before bending) and its "angle of refraction" (its angle after bending). His law shows that every substance has a characteristic bending power – its "refractive index." The more a substance bends light, the larger its refractive index.

WILLEBRORD SNELL
Willebrord Snell (1580-1626) discovered one of the most important laws concerning light. He also pioneered triangulation, a way to measure distances by using the angles between different points.

BENDING BY AIR
Light rays can sometimes be bent without passing from one substance to another. In air this happens when light travels through layers that are at different temperatures. Cold air is more dense and heavier than warm air, so it acts like a different substance. The results can be spectacular, as this old engraving shows.

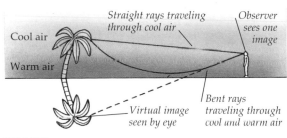

Straight rays traveling through cool air

Observer sees one image

Cool air

Warm air

Bent rays traveling through cool and warm air

Virtual image seen by eye

MIRAGES
A mirage occurs when a layer of warm air next to the ground is trapped by cooler air above. Light is bent toward the horizontal line of vision and eventually it is made to travel upward by total internal reflection. The mirage is an upside-down "virtual" image.

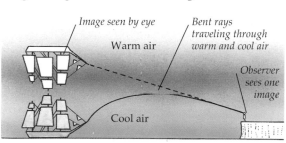

Image seen by eye

Bent rays traveling through warm and cool air

Warm air

Observer sees one image

Cool air

LOOMING
In this form of mirage, warm air lies over a layer of cold air. The light rays traveling from cold to warm air are bent toward the horizontal line of vision and eventually reflected downward. As a result, an object seems to "loom" above its real position.

SCHLIEREN PHOTOGRAPHY
Air at different temperatures bends light by different amounts. Schlieren photography is a way of making these differences easy to see. It works by blocking some of the light coming from the object, so that the bent light becomes more visible. Above is a Schlieren photograph of a candle. It shows layers of air at different temperatures around the flame.

Candlelight is focused as it travels through the sphere

CONCENTRATING LIGHT
These water-filled spheres are known as lacemaker's condensers. They were made in the early 19th century and were used by lacemakers to help them see their work. When light travels through the glass spheres, it is bent in a way that makes it fall on a small area of the lace. The condenser concentrates, or "focuses," the light.

Each condenser focuses light on a different area

HOW THE CONDENSER WORKS
When light rays travel through a curved surface, some rays are bent more than others. A lacemaker's condenser focuses the rays so that they meet in a small area. The condenser acts like a convex lens.

Light focused on embroidery

Looking through lenses

I**F YOU LOOK** through a window, everything beyond it seems about the same as it would without the window there. But if you look through a glass of water, what you see is very different. The view is distorted, and it may be reversed. The reason for this is that the glass of water acts like a lens; it bends the light rays that pass through it. There are two main types of lens. A convex, or converging, lens curves outward, and makes light bend inward. A concave lens is just the opposite: it curves inward, and makes light bend outward. If parallel rays of light strike a convex lens head-on, they are bent so that they all pass through one place – the "principal focus." The distance from the principal focus to the center of the lens is called the "focal distance." The shorter this distance, the more powerful the lens.

LATIN LENTILS
The word "lens" comes from the Latin name for lentils. A lentil seed is flat and round, and its sides bulge outward – just like a convex lens.

EYEGLASSES
Eyeglasses have been used in the West for at least 700 years. The earliest had convex lenses, and they were worn by farsighted people, to help them focus on nearby objects. Later, concave lenses were made for people with nearsightedness, or myopia. In 1784 Benjamin Franklin invented "bifocals" – glasses with lenses split into two parts, each with a different focal length.

Concave lens

Object

Eye

Diverging rays

Concave lens

Diminished, "virtual" image

SPEADING OUT
When rays of light pass through a concave lens, the lens bends them so that they diverge, or spread apart. But the eye sees light as though it travels in straight lines, so the light seems to come from a "virtual" image, which is diminished, or smaller than the object.

Convex upper lens for seeing distant objects

Concave lower lens for seeing at close quarters

English bifocal glasses, 1885

Glass contact lenses (actual size), made in about 1930

Horn lens holder

Lens

Decorative ribbons were attached here

Mixed lens

Diminished inner image

CONTACT LENSES
A contact lens does the same job as an eyeglass lens, but it sits on the surface of the eye. The first contact lenses were made in 1887, using glass. They were large, thick, and probably very uncomfortable. Today, contact lenses are much smaller and made out of plastic. One advantage of contact lenses is that, unlike eyeglasses, they allow clear vision across the whole of the eye's field of view.

Iron-framed glasses, 1750

Magnified outer image

Object

Eye

Aspheric lens

MIXED LENSES
Optical instruments sometimes need lenses that bend light in unusual ways. This "aspheric" lens is two types in one: it is convex near its edges, but concave at the center. Lenses like this are used in rangefinders and weapons systems.

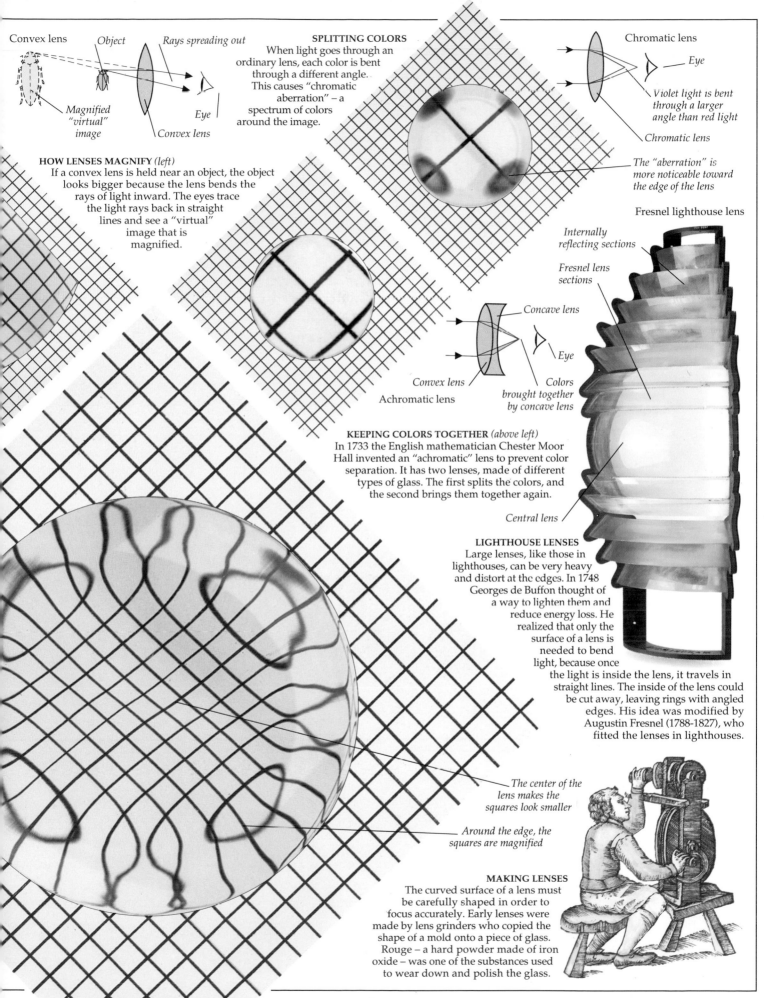

Convex lens   Object   Rays spreading out

Magnified
"virtual"
image

Eye

Convex lens

HOW LENSES MAGNIFY (left)
If a convex lens is held near an object, the object looks bigger because the lens bends the rays of light inward. The eyes trace the light rays back in straight lines and see a "virtual" image that is magnified.

SPLITTING COLORS
When light goes through an ordinary lens, each color is bent through a different angle. This causes "chromatic aberration" – a spectrum of colors around the image.

Chromatic lens

Eye

Violet light is bent
through a larger
angle than red light

Chromatic lens

The "aberration" is
more noticeable toward
the edge of the lens

Fresnel lighthouse lens

Internally
reflecting sections

Fresnel lens
sections

Concave lens

Eye

Convex lens

Colors
brought together
by concave lens

Achromatic lens

KEEPING COLORS TOGETHER (above left)
In 1733 the English mathematician Chester Moor Hall invented an "achromatic" lens to prevent color separation. It has two lenses, made of different types of glass. The first splits the colors, and the second brings them together again.

Central lens

LIGHTHOUSE LENSES
Large lenses, like those in lighthouses, can be very heavy and distort at the edges. In 1748 Georges de Buffon thought of a way to lighten them and reduce energy loss. He realized that only the surface of a lens is needed to bend light, because once the light is inside the lens, it travels in straight lines. The inside of the lens could be cut away, leaving rings with angled edges. His idea was modified by Augustin Fresnel (1788-1827), who fitted the lenses in lighthouses.

The center of the
lens makes the
squares look smaller

Around the edge, the
squares are magnified

MAKING LENSES
The curved surface of a lens must be carefully shaped in order to focus accurately. Early lenses were made by lens grinders who copied the shape of a mold onto a piece of glass. Rouge – a hard powder made of iron oxide – was one of the substances used to wear down and polish the glass.

Seeing light images

How exactly do the eyes work? Until about AD 1000 it was widely believed that the eyes gave out light, and that the light somehow formed a picture. People thought that if a hand was put in front of them, there would be no image because the light would not be able to come out. But in about 1020, the Arab scientist Alhazen correctly suggested that things work the other way around – that the eyes take in light, rather than give it out. During the following centuries, doctors and scientists made detailed studies of the eye's structure. They learned that the eye's lens throws an image onto a living screen, called the retina. Thanks to the invention of the microscope, it is now known that the retina is packed with light-sensitive cells that send messages through the optic nerve to the brain.

MAKING AN IMAGE
In the 17th century the French philosopher and mathematician René Descartes explained how the eye forms an image on the retina. This is one of his drawings. Instead of myths or magic, he used simple physical principles to find out what happens to light once it enters the eyeball.

The eyeball is surrounded by the sclera – a hard, white, protective layer

Muscles linking eye and eye socket

Pupil

Cornea

Blood vessels

Optic nerve

Bone at bottom of eye socket

INSIDE AN EYE
This model human eye, made in France in about 1870, shows the different parts that make up this complicated and sensitive organ. The eye sits inside a bony cup called the eye socket. It is crisscrossed by tiny blood vessels that keep it supplied with oxygen. Pairs of muscles link the eye to the eye socket. When a muscle contracts, the eye swivels in its socket. At the back of the eye is the optic nerve, which takes electrical signals to the brain. At the front is the cornea, a clear protective layer. Behind the cornea is the pupil, an opening that lets in light.

The pupil is smallest in bright light

The iris is made up of a ring of muscle that controls the size of the pupil

OPENING UP
The eye must work well both in bright noon sunshine and in deep shade. Beneath its outer surface is the iris, a mechanism that helps it cope with hugely varying amounts of light. The iris gives the eye its color, and it closes up the pupil in bright light and opens it wide in dim light.

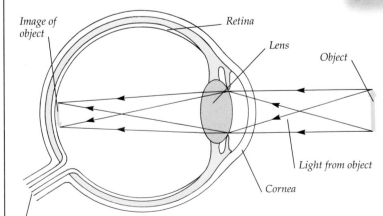

Image of object

Retina

Lens

Object

Light from object

Cornea

Optic nerve

HOW THE EYE FORMS IMAGES
The eye forms an image the same way as a camera. Light travels through the lens and is focused on the retina, which is full of light-sensitive nerve endings. When light strikes them they transmit signals through the optic nerve to the brain. The retinal image is upside-down, but, partly because it is that way from birth, the brain properly analyzes the signal.

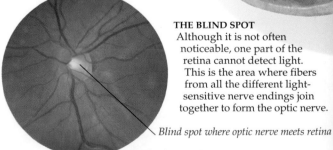

THE BLIND SPOT
Although it is not often noticeable, one part of the retina cannot detect light. This is the area where fibers from all the different light-sensitive nerve endings join together to form the optic nerve.

Blind spot where optic nerve meets retina

Back of an eyeball

Sliding object to test *focusing ability of the eye*

Eyepiece

Handle

MEASURING UP THE EYES
This "optometer," made in the 19th century, was a simple instrument that measured the eye's refraction. By doing this, an optician could select lenses to correct defects of vision. A modern optometrist will examine the eyes in many different ways. Tests establish the shapes of the eyes and characteristics of their lenses. The tests will also show if some colors are seen better than others.

LONG AND SHORT SIGHT
This 14th-century monk is wearing spectacles to correct an eye condition that is common in older people – farsightedness, or presbyopia. In this defect of vision, the lens does not bend light from nearby objects enough. The rays meet the retina before they have been brought into focus, and the result is a blurred image. Nearsightedness, or myopia, occurs when the lens bends light from distant objects too much, and the rays meet before they hit the retina. A third kind of defect, called astigmatism, results in part of the image being blurred. It is caused by the cornea not being the right shape.

Lens

The spaces between the lens, the iris, and the cornea are filled with a clear fluid

Ciliary muscles contract to make the lens thicker and relax to make it thinner

THE LENS REVEALED
In this model eye, the iris hinges away to show the lens beneath. The lens is made of a substance like hard jelly, and its shape is changed by tiny muscles. When the eye looks at any object, the muscles pull the lens, making it flatter. This changes the focal length, and the object is brought into focus on the retina.

Tiny blood vessels and nerves run over the surfaces of the eye

These glands make tears to keep the eye's surface moist

COMPOUND EYES
The human eye has a single lens and screen of light-sensitive nerve endings. Many insects have "compound" eyes, which are divided into hundreds or thousands of compartments. Each compartment is an individual eye with its own lens. On their own, these eyes cannot see much detail, but the insect's brain adds their signals together to build up an image. The compound eyes of this horsefly cover most of its head. Their brilliant colors are due to an effect called interference.

Bringing things closer

UNAIDED VIEW
Seen with the naked eye, the moon looks very small. This is because light rays from its edges reach the eye close together.

NO ONE KNOWS who first discovered that a pair of lenses could be used to make distant objects look closer. According to one story, the breakthrough was made accidentally in 1608 by Hans Lippershey, a Dutch spectacle-maker, or his assistant. However, at least two other people, including Zacharias Janssen, also claimed the discovery as theirs. What is certain is that Lippershey was quick to see the value of the "telescope," as it later became known. He applied to the Dutch government for a patent, hoping to prevent anyone else from making and selling his invention. But his request was turned down. Within just a few months, telescopes were being made and demonstrated all over Europe.

SKY WATCHER
Galileo Galilei (1564-1642) was an Italian astronomer and mathematician. Observations that he made using his own telescopes challenged beliefs of the time about the movements of the planets.

Galileo's telescope (replica)

Sliding tube for focusing

Eyepiece

Objective lens

Refracting telescopes

The first telescopes were all "refractors." Refracting telescopes use lenses to make light bend. A simple refractor has two lenses – a large objective lens with a long focal length at the end of the telescope, and a smaller eyepiece lens with a short focal length into which the observer looks. The objective lens gathers the light rays from a distant object and then bends them to form an upside-down "real" image. Light rays from this image pass through the eyepiece lens, and are bent again so that they become parallel. Because the eye cannot tell that the light has been bent, the distant object looks bigger.

Refracting telescope

Real image

Eyepiece lens bends the light rays

Observer

Eye traces back along light rays to see magnified object

18th-century refracting telescope (model)

Sliding tube for focusing

Eyepiece lens turns the image the right side up

GALILEO'S TELESCOPE *(above)*
In 1609 news reached Galileo of the telescopes that were being made in Holland, and he immediately set to work building his own. This is a replica of one of the earliest that he made. It contains two lenses – a convex objective lens, and a smaller concave eyepiece lens (in other telescopes the eyepiece lens is often convex). Galileo's early telescopes magnified up to 30 times, and he used them to look at the moon, the planets, and the stars. He discovered four of the moons that orbit Jupiter. He also found out that the Milky Way is made up of millions of stars that are invisible to the naked eye.

INSIDE A REFRACTING TELESCOPE
This replica of a refracting telescope follows a design that was popular during the 18th century. It has a three-lens eyepiece, and all its lenses are chromatic – so the image would have been blurred by fringes of color.

Light from distant object

Objective lens

GATHERING MORE LIGHT
To produce images of distant stars, a telescope must gather as much light as possible. This is done by increasing the diameter of the lenses or mirrors. Large lenses are more difficult to make than large mirrors, so the world's biggest optical telescopes are all reflectors. This large reflector *(right)* was made in 1789 by the astronomer William Herschel. Its main mirror was about 4 feet (120 cm) across.

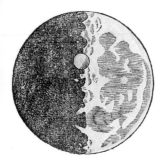

THE MOON BY GALILEO
In beautiful ink sketches that were published in his book *Sidereus Nuncius*, Galileo illustrated the rugged surface of the moon as he saw it through his telescope. Before he did so, many people – including scientists – thought that the moon was as smooth as a mirror.

THE MOON TODAY
Modern telescopes show the surface of the moon in great detail, with its mountain ranges and waterless "seas."

Sliding lens shield

Objective lens

Objective mirror

Secondary mirror

Observer looks here

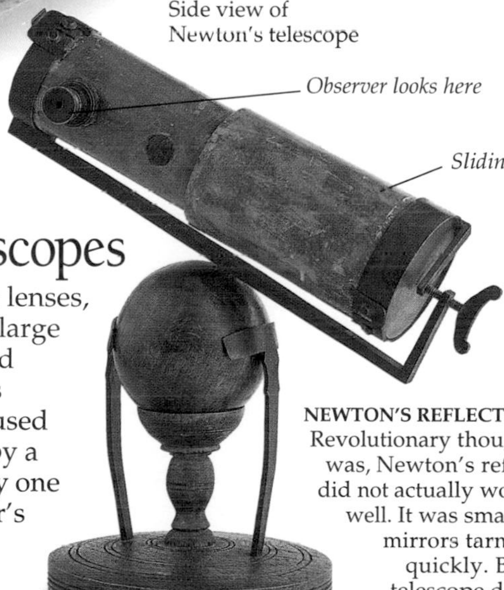

Side view of Newton's telescope

Observer looks here

Sliding focus

Wooden ball mounting allows telescope to swivel

Reflecting telescopes

Before the invention of achromatic lenses, color dispersion was a problem with large refractors. In 1668 Isaac Newton designed a "reflecting" telescope that avoided this problem. Instead of relying on lenses, it used mirrors. The incoming light is gathered by a large, curved mirror, and then reflected by one or more smaller mirrors into the observer's eye. Two ways of viewing the image are by looking through a hole in the objective mirror, as in a "Cassegrain" reflector, or by looking through the side of the telescope, as in a "Newtonian" reflector. Because mirrors do not disperse colors, the image is sharper.

NEWTON'S REFLECTOR
Revolutionary though it was, Newton's reflector did not actually work very well. It was small, and its mirrors tarnished very quickly. But Newton's telescope did prove that mirrors could be used to magnify. It was the forerunner of the giant reflectors that are used in observatories today.

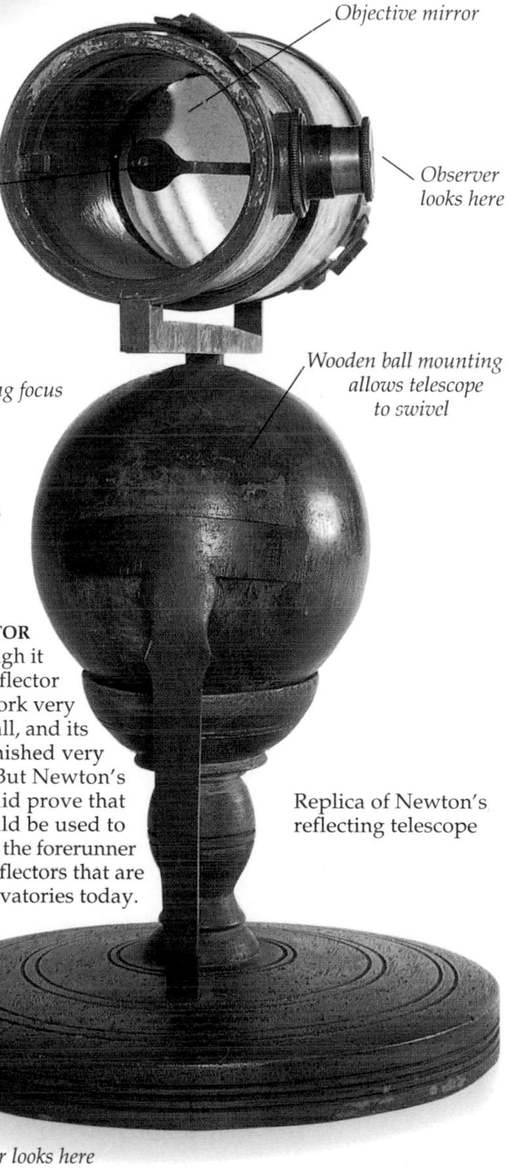

Replica of Newton's reflecting telescope

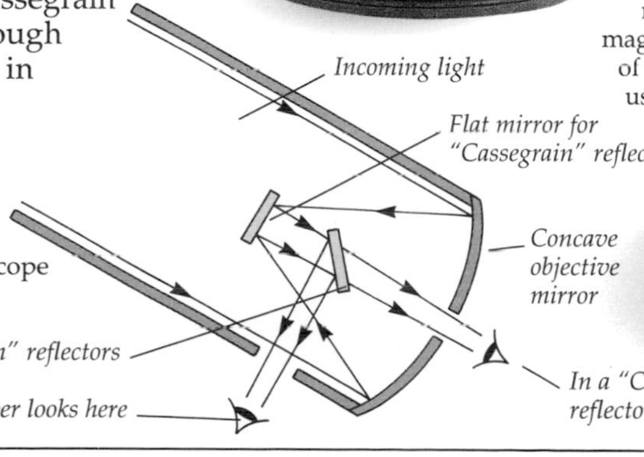

Reflecting telescope

Incoming light

Flat mirror for "Cassegrain" reflectors

Concave objective mirror

Flat secondary mirror for "Newtonian" reflectors

In a "Newtonian" reflector the observer looks here

In a "Cassegrain" reflector the observer looks here

Making things bigger

SECRET LIVES
This drawing shows a life-size animal (upper right) and how Anton van Leeuwenhoek saw it using his single-lens microscope (left).

I**N** 1665 **AN** Englishman named Robert Hooke published a remarkable book called *Micrographia*, which contained detailed descriptions and drawings of "minute bodies," from flies to fleas. With the help of a recent invention, the microscope, Hooke showed things that once had been invisible. Two types were in use – the "simple" microscope, which had just one lens, and the "compound" microscope, which had two lenses or more. Hooke used a compound microscope. In contrast, Anton van Leeuwenhoek, another pioneer of microscopy, used simple microscopes with very good lenses. He made each lens himself, and his great care was rewarded with exceptional results. He made detailed studies of many tiny "animalcules," and was the first person ever to see bacteria.

Leeuwenhoek's microscope (actual size)

Screw for focusing

Pin for holding specimen

Lens held between two plates

Using Leeuwenhoek's microscope

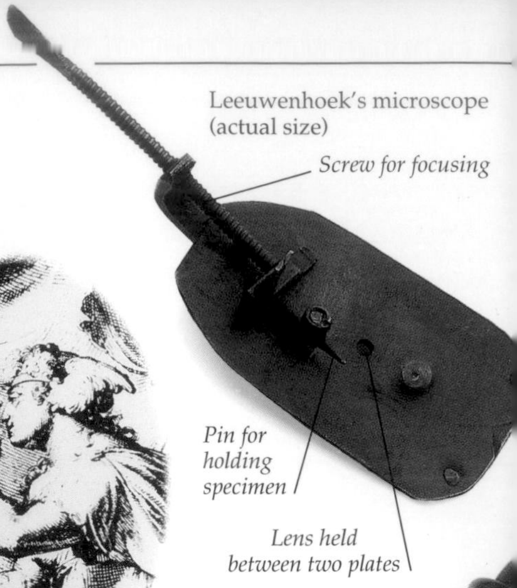

LEEUWENHOEK'S MICROSCOPE
The microscope used by Anton van Leeuwenhoek (1632-1723) was a tiny instrument made of metal. Its single lens was about $^1/_{25}$ in (1 mm) thick, and it had such a short focal length that the microscope had to be held very close to the eye. The lens was fixed between two flat metal plates. The object to be viewed was placed on a pin, and this was moved by a system of screws to bring it into focus. Leeuwenhoek actually made many hundreds of simple microscopes of various designs. Their magnifying power varied from about 70 times to more than 250 times.

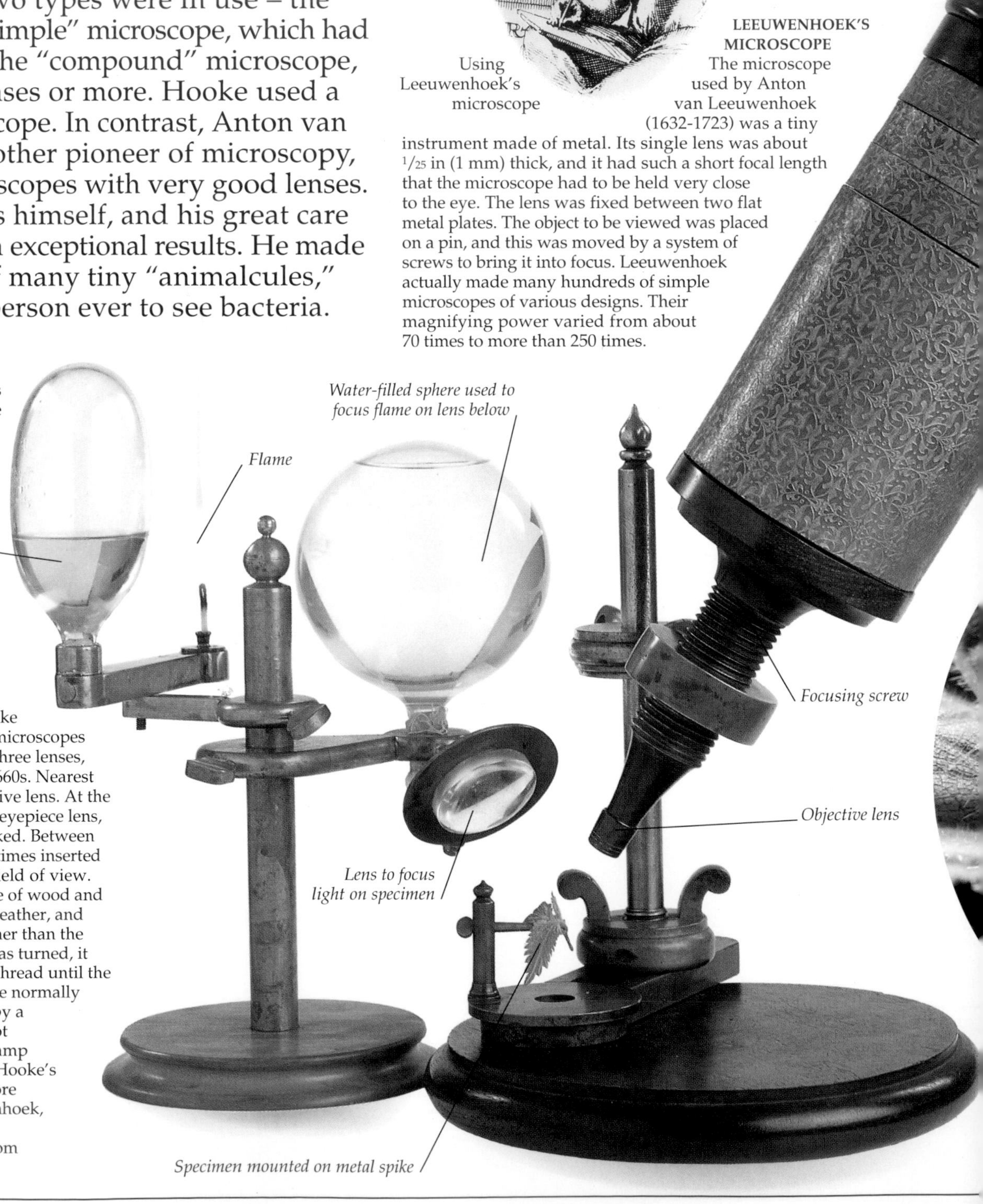

Replica of Hooke's compound microscope

Water-filled sphere used to focus flame on lens below

Flame

Oil reservoir

Focusing screw

HOOKE'S MICROSCOPE
The compound microscope was invented in about 1590 by Zacharias Janssen. Robert Hooke (1635-1703) made compound microscopes containing two or sometimes three lenses, which he began using in the 1660s. Nearest to the specimen was the objective lens. At the top of the microscope was the eyepiece lens, through which the viewer looked. Between these two lenses, Hooke sometimes inserted a "field lens" to increase the field of view. Hooke's microscope was made of wood and pasteboard covered with fine leather, and was focused by moving it, rather than the specimen. If the microscope was turned, it moved up and down a screw thread until the specimen could be seen. Hooke normally worked with his microscope by a sunlit window. If there was not enough light, he used the oil lamp that is shown here. Although Hooke's microscope was larger and more complex than that of Leeuwenhoek, chromatic aberration (p. 83) prevented Hooke's version from producing such clear images.

Objective lens

Lens to focus light on specimen

Specimen mounted on metal spike

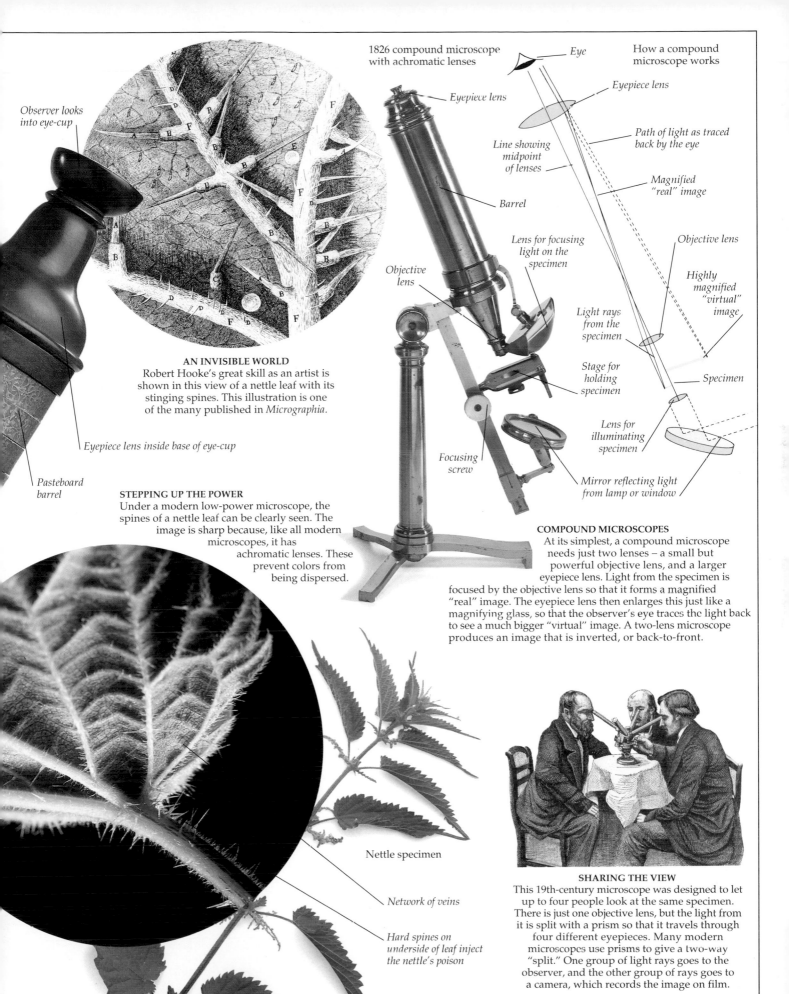

Observer looks into eye-cup

1826 compound microscope with achromatic lenses

Eyepiece lens

Line showing midpoint of lenses

Objective lens

Barrel

Lens for focusing light on the specimen

Stage for holding specimen

Focusing screw

Lens for illuminating specimen

Mirror reflecting light from lamp or window

How a compound microscope works

Eye

Eyepiece lens

Path of light as traced back by the eye

Magnified "real" image

Objective lens

Highly magnified "virtual" image

Light rays from the specimen

Specimen

AN INVISIBLE WORLD
Robert Hooke's great skill as an artist is
shown in this view of a nettle leaf with its
stinging spines. This illustration is one
of the many published in *Micrographia*.

Eyepiece lens inside base of eye-cup

Pasteboard barrel

STEPPING UP THE POWER
Under a modern low-power microscope, the
spines of a nettle leaf can be clearly seen. The
image is sharp because, like all modern
microscopes, it has
achromatic lenses. These
prevent colors from
being dispersed.

COMPOUND MICROSCOPES
At its simplest, a compound microscope
needs just two lenses – a small but
powerful objective lens, and a larger
eyepiece lens. Light from the specimen is
focused by the objective lens so that it forms a magnified
"real" image. The eyepiece lens then enlarges this just like a
magnifying glass, so that the observer's eye traces the light back
to see a much bigger "virtual" image. A two-lens microscope
produces an image that is inverted, or back-to-front.

Nettle specimen

Network of veins

Hard spines on underside of leaf inject the nettle's poison

SHARING THE VIEW
This 19th-century microscope was designed to let
up to four people look at the same specimen.
There is just one objective lens, but the light from
it is split with a prism so that it travels through
four different eyepieces. Many modern
microscopes use prisms to give a two-way
"split." One group of light rays goes to the
observer, and the other group of rays goes to
a camera, which records the image on film.

Recording light

NEARLY A THOUSAND years ago the Arab scientist Alhazen explained how the sun's image could be produced in a darkened room. The light was made to pass through a small hole in one wall, so that it formed an image on a wall opposite. The *camera obscura*, which is Latin for "darkened room," became a popular curiosity used for seeing the sun and for looking at streets and landscapes. By the 1660s portable camera obscuras had been designed that had lenses, paper screens, and even focusing mechanisms. In fact, they had all the makings of modern cameras – except that they had no way to "record" the images that they formed. More than 150 years passed before Joseph Niepce discovered a method to record light, and true photography was born.

EARLIEST SURVIVING PHOTOGRAPH
In 1822 Joseph Niepce (1765-1833) focused this view from his window onto a sheet of pewter coated with light-sensitive bitumen. After eight hours he rinsed it with lavender oil and white petroleum. The bitumen washed away, except where light had fallen on it; the remaining bitumen made a photograph.

William Fox Talbot

Negatives and positives

Almost simultaneously, practical photography was invented by Willam Fox Talbot and Louis Daguerre, but Daguerre's method of making photographs is not the one that is in use today. Instead, modern cameras use the technique that was pioneered in the early 1830s by Talbot (1800-1877). He soaked paper in silver chloride, a chemical that darkens when exposed to light. When he let light fall on the paper, it produced a "negative" image. By using the same process to copy the negative, he could then make an unlimited number of "positive" prints.

Talbot's camera (front view)

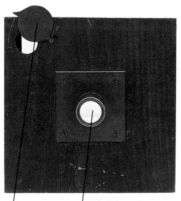

Fixed-focus lens

Viewfinder with flap to shut off light

Using Fox Talbot's experimental camera of 1835

Upside-down image thrown on screen

PAPER NEGATIVE
William Fox Talbot made this tiny negative in August 1835. It shows a window of his home, Lacock Abbey, in England. The light-sensitive paper was exposed for half an hour.

FORMING AN IMAGE
During his first attempts at photography, William Fox Talbot made a camera out of a large box. This is an experimental version of one that he made in 1835. The box had a single lens, which created an upside-down image. Fox Talbot positioned light-sensitive paper at the back of the box and let some light fall on it for more than an hour. But the results were disappointing. Not enough light fell on the paper to expose it properly, so the image had very little detail. Talbot got around this problem by making much smaller cameras, just over 2 ½ in (6 cm) square. With these cameras the lens was very close to the paper, so the light falling on the paper was more intense. With one of these tiny cameras, Talbot made his famous negative shown on the left.

THE DAGUERROTYPE

In the early 1830s Louis Daguerre (1789-1851) formed a partnership with Joseph Niepce, who had taken the world's first photograph. He experimented with ways to record images on plates of copper. He coated the plates with silver and then exposed them to iodine to make them sensitive to light. At first, Daguerre had little luck. However, one day he accidentally discovered that mercury vapor would "develop" an image on a plate, even if it had been exposed for as little as 15 minutes. He later found out how to "fix" the image, so that the silver no longer reacted to light and the picture became permanent. "Daguerrotypes" were immensely popular, and the Daguerrotype camera was the first to be sold to the public.

A ground-glass screen at the rear of the camera was used to check the focusing

The image was focused by sliding the rear of the camera in or out

A shutter in front of the lens was moved aside to make the exposure

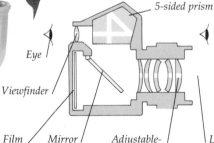

Light rays pass through the lens, and cross over

GHOSTLY FIGURES

Early cameras needed a lot of light, so exposures took minutes or even hours. If anything moved during this time, it showed up as faint images known as "ghosting." Modern cameras avoid this problem by having much shorter exposure times.

Light rays spread out from the object in all directions

Focusing the SLR camera

Taking the picture

5-sided prism

Eye

Viewfinder

Film / Mirror / Adjustable-focus lenses

Light entering camera

Mirror swings up to let light reach the film

Viewfinder

Film was placed here

Lens

MIDGET CAMERAS

These tiny cameras were made in 1934 out of Bakelite, the earliest form of plastic. They used tiny rolls of film, and both have a fixed-focus lens and a separate viewfinder. Each one is only a little bigger than a matchbox.

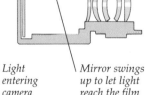

SLR CAMERA

In a single-lens reflex (SLR) camera, the same group of lenses is used for checking the focus and for producing the picture. When an image is viewed through the camera, light passes through the lenses and is reflected upward by a mirror onto a focusing screen made of ground glass. A prism sends light out of the viewfinder by total internal reflection, so the image can be seen on the screen. When you press the shutter, the mirror quickly swings upward, so that light can reach the film.

Projecting pictures

W HEN A PICTURE IS TAKEN with a camera the lens gathers and focuses light to produce a small upside-down image on the film. Imagine what would happen if the film were replaced with a small light source. The light rays would then move in exactly the opposite direction. The same lens would produce a large image outside the camera that could be focused on a screen. The camera would now be a projector. Projectors produce still images, but if the images change very quickly – more than about 15 times a second – the eyes and brain cannot keep up with them. Instead of seeing lots of separate pictures, "persistence of vision" makes the pictures seem to merge together. When this happens only the changes within each still image (like an arm moving) are noticed. In the 1880s and 1890s a number of people, including the French brothers Auguste and Louis Lumière, used this principle to make moving pictures. They devised cameras that could take pictures in quick succession and projectors that could show them at the same speed. The result was the illusion of movement – or motion pictures.

MAGIC MOMENTS
During the 19th century "magic lantern" shows were a very popular form of entertainment, and they attracted large audiences. This lantern could make images that "dissolved" from one to another.

OIL-FIRED LANTERN
This "magic lantern" was built about 1895. It used a three-wick oil lamp to shine a powerful beam through glass slides. At the beginning of a lantern show, the projectionist would light the lamp and then push it into position at the back of the lantern. Inside, a concave mirror behind the lamp reflected the light forward, and this was bent inward by a set of condenser lenses so that it passed through the picture on the slide. The light then traveled through a projection lens, which could be moved backward or forward to focus an image on the screen. Once the show was under way, the lanternist had to be careful not to touch the top of the lantern, because it became very hot.

"New Pattern Helioscopic Lantern," c.1895, viewed from above

Focusing wheel for projection lens

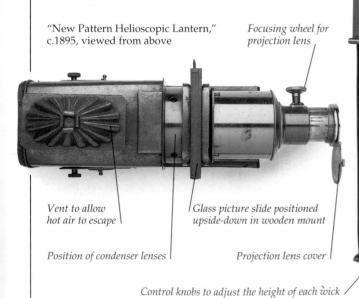

Vent to allow hot air to escape

Glass picture slide positioned upside-down in wooden mount

Position of condenser lenses

Projection lens cover

Control knobs to adjust the height of each wick

Viewing window for inspecting oil lamp

PICTURES ON THE MOVE

The praxinoscope was a simple scientific toy that made still pictures come to life. It did not project light – instead, it reflected it. The lamp was surrounded by a ring of pictures, showing something in different stages of movement. The pictures faced inward, and opposite each one was a mirror. By turning a handle, the ring of pictures could be made to turn. If the ring was turned fast enough, the separate reflections in each mirror would seem to merge, until they began to move. The praxinoscope shown here was designed in about 1879.

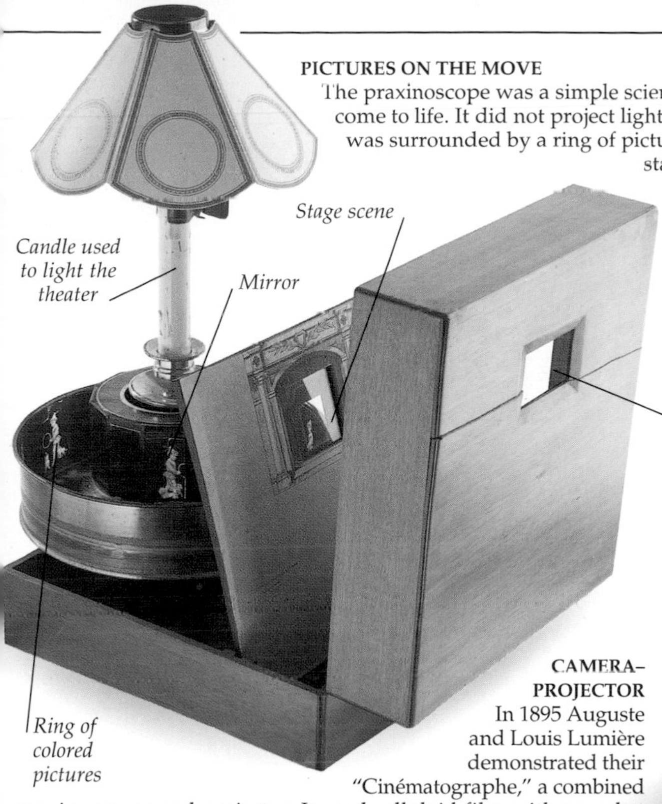

Candle used to light the theater

Stage scene

Mirror

Viewing hole

Ring of colored pictures

CAMERA– PROJECTOR

In 1895 Auguste and Louis Lumière demonstrated their "Cinématographe," a combined movie camera and projector. It used celluloid film with sprocket holes along each edge, which a claw pulled to move the film along. This "Biokam," made four years later, was a camera and projector that worked in the same way. It was wound by a hand-crank and was designed to photograph or project pictures at a rate of 16 per second – fast enough to give an illusion of movement.

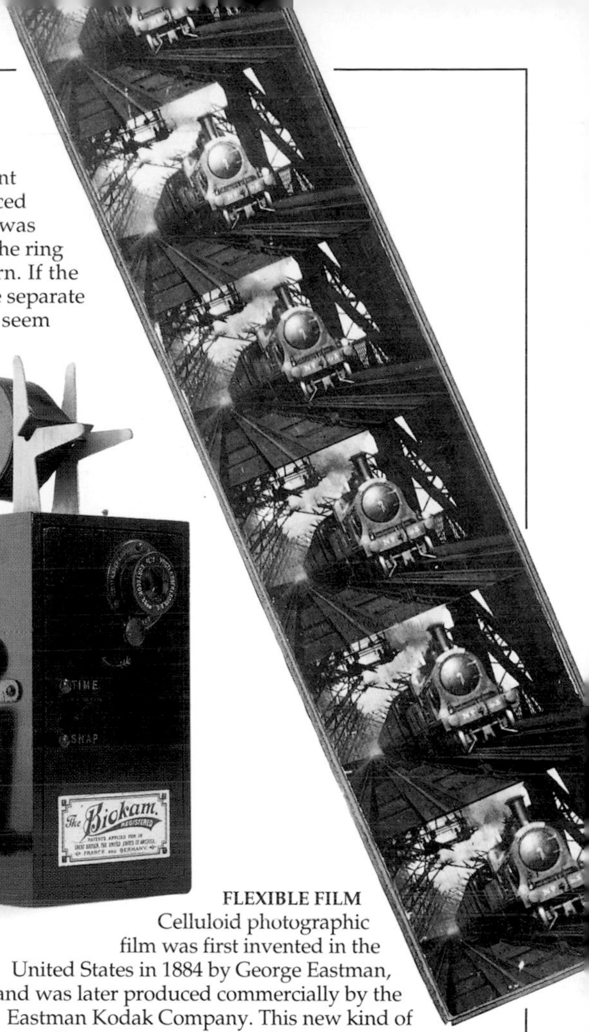

FLEXIBLE FILM

Celluloid photographic film was first invented in the United States in 1884 by George Eastman, and was later produced commercially by the Eastman Kodak Company. This new kind of film was strong but flexible enough to be wound into a roll. Within a decade, celluloid film was being used to make moving pictures. This scene of an approaching steam train was made in 1898.

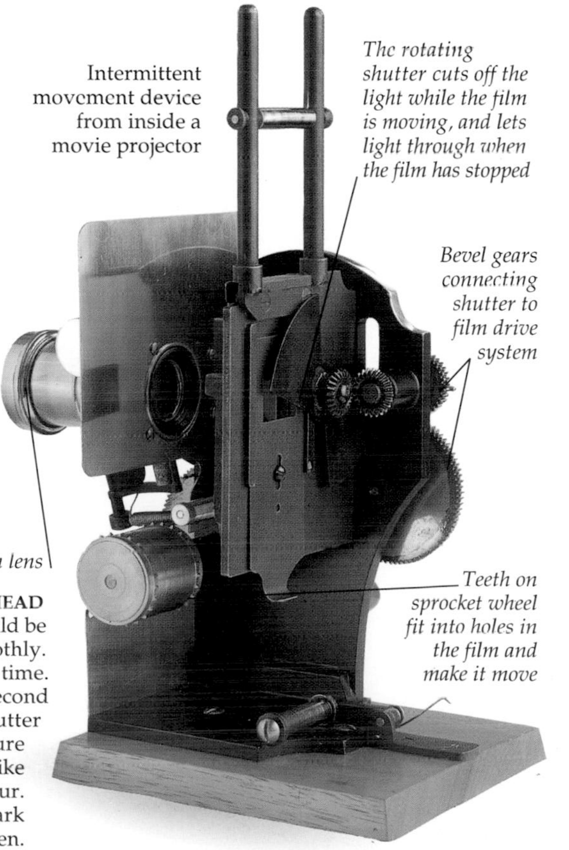

The projected image

Intermittent movement device from inside a movie projector

The rotating shutter cuts off the light while the film is moving, and lets light through when the film has stopped

Bevel gears connecting shutter to film drive system

Projection lens

JUMPING AHEAD

If a movie projector were slowed down, it would be easy to see that the film does not move smoothly. Instead, it jumps forward one picture at a time. Each picture is held still for a fraction of a second while it is projected on to the screen. A shutter then closes off the light, and the next picture jumps into position. If the film did not jump like this, all the viewer would see would be a blur. As long as the film moves quickly, the dark intervals between the pictures cannot be seen.

Teeth on sprocket wheel fit into holes in the film and make it move

Sliding mechanism to focus the image

Glass slide in wooden mount

Splitting light

IN 1665 A GREAT PLAGUE RAGED through Britain. The famous University of Cambridge was closed, but a young student named Isaac Newton continued his studies there and at home. This period of intense work was to turn him into the greatest figure that science had yet known. Newton experimented with a prism to see how it made light bend, and he noticed that a prism seemed to bend light of different colors by different amounts. He decided to investigate what happened when daylight passed through a prism and was thrown on to a screen. To begin with he worked with light shining through a round hole in his shutters. This produced a stretched image of the Sun, with a blue top edge and a red lower edge. But when the light went through a narrow slit before reaching the prism, the result was spectacular. Now, instead of mainly white light, he saw a multicolored band called a spectrum. Through this experiment and others, Newton concluded that white light is a mixture of many colors. His prism refracted, or bent, the colors by different amounts, making them spread out, or "disperse," so that they could be seen.

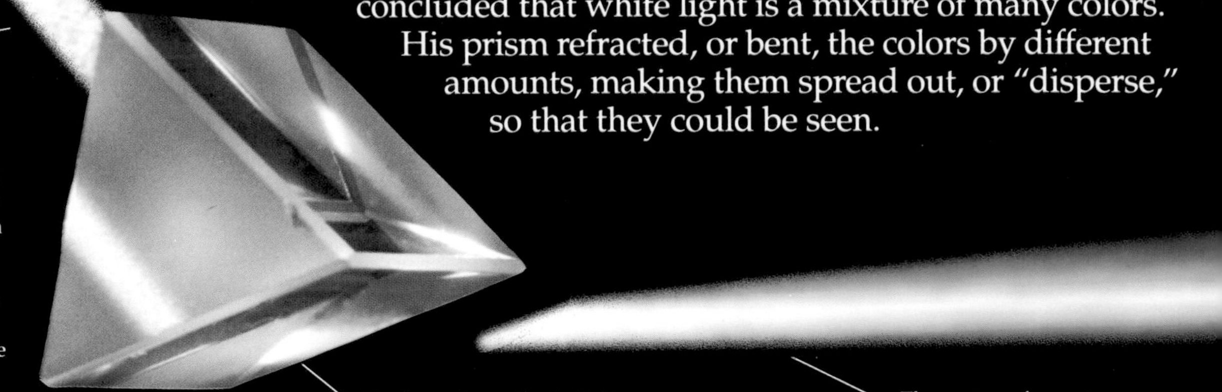

Newton let a beam of sunlight through a small hole in the shutter of his window

NEWTON'S PRISM EXPERIMENTS
"In a very dark Chamber, at a round hole . . . made in the Shut of a Window, I placed a glass Prism . . . ." So begins one chapter in Newton's *Opticks*, a book that describes his experiments with light and color. Newton did more than just split white light into a spectrum. He also combined it again, and he investigated the different colors that his prisms produced. In his crucial experiment (shown here), white light is split by one prism, so that it forms a spectrum. The spectrum falls on a screen with a small slit, so that light of just one color can pass through. This light then passes through another prism, which bends it by a particular angle but fails to split it into many colors. Newton learned from this that the colors were in the white light – they were not produced by the prism.

The first prism splits the light into a spectrum of colors

The spectrum fans out and meets a screen

ISAAC NEWTON
The work of Isaac Newton (1642-1727) dominated physics for nearly two centuries. He published two of the most important scientific books ever written: *Principia* (1687), which explained his laws of motion and theory of gravitation; and *Opticks* (1704), which investigated light. In 1703 he became President of the Royal Society, a distinguished scientific "club" formed in 1662. An independent, brilliant thinker, Newton was not an easy man to get along with.

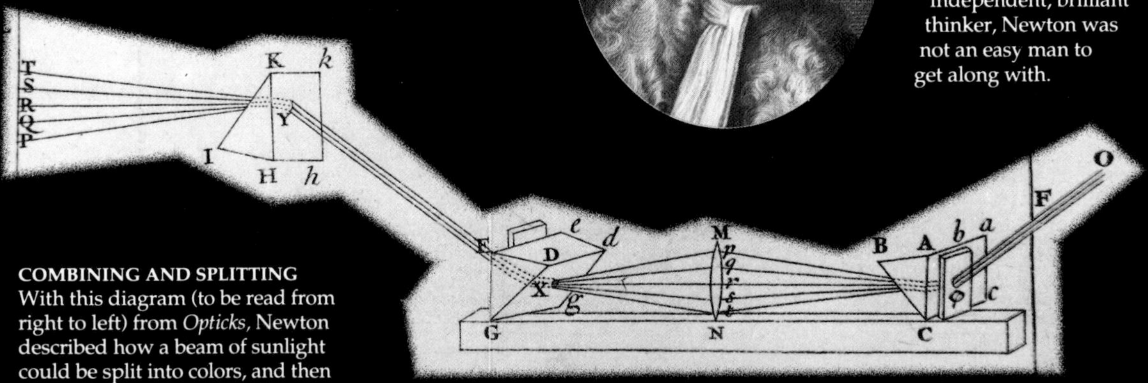

COMBINING AND SPLITTING
With this diagram (to be read from right to left) from *Opticks*, Newton described how a beam of sunlight could be split into colors, and then recombined to form white light once more. He did this by passing light ("O") through a prism and then a lens. The lens made the different colors converge on a second prism. This second prism spread the converging light rays so that they became parallel, forming a beam of white light. In this experiment, Newton used a third prism ("Y") to split the beam of white light again. This light was made to fall on a screen. He found that if he cut out or "intercepted" any of the colored light that hit the lens, this color would disappear from the spectrum on the screen.

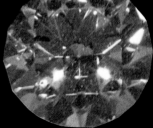

SPARKLING GEMS
A cut diamond acts like a collection of prisms. When light passes through the diamond, the colors are dispersed and then reflected back out. The angle of each facet, or side of the gem, is specially calculated to give the diamond its "fire."

COLORS IN THE SKY

Newton wrote about the way rainbows are colored in his book *Opticks*. He knew that refraction was involved, and that it must occur when sunlight passes through raindrops. However, Newton was not the first to suggest this. The French philosopher René Descartes was the first person to reveal the mysteries of the rainbow. But as Newton's illustration shows, he was able to work out precisely how light from the Sun is split, and how it can form not just one rainbow, but sometimes two.

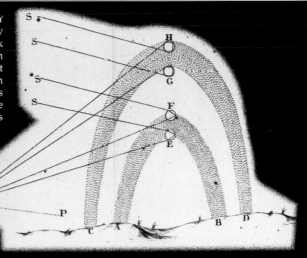

THE RAINBOW IN HISTORY

According to the Bible, the rainbow is a sign in the sky showing that the great flood will not be repeated. An old legend says that by digging at the foot of a rainbow, a pot of gold can be found. But however hard it is searched for, the foot can never be reached. This is because rainbows always move with the observer.

Red light is unchanged by passing through the prism

A narrow slit in the screen lets only light of a single color pass through

Red light passes through the slit

The red light meets a second prism, which refracts the light through an angle that can be measured

Red light that was not refracted because it "grazed," or did not pass through, the prism

PRIMARY RAINBOW

In a primary rainbow white light is reflected just once as it travels through a raindrop. The colors are dispersed as they enter and leave the drop. The colors seen depend on the position of the drop in the sky. Red light is seen from raindrops at an angle of 42° to the line of the horizon, and blue light is seen from those at 40°. All other colors are seen from drops between these two angles.

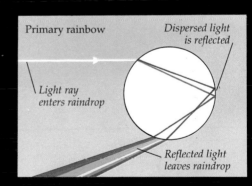

Primary rainbow

Dispersed light is reflected

Light ray enters raindrop

Reflected light leaves raindrop

DOUBLE BOWS

Rainbows are formed when sunlight shines through water droplets. The droplets reflect and refract the light rays, making their colors disperse into a spectrum. In a "primary" rainbow, colors are seen from light rays that enter each droplet from the top. In a "secondary" rainbow, colors are seen from rays entering droplets from the bottom. Secondary rainbows appear only when the sunlight is bright, and when the water droplets are uniformly spread out.

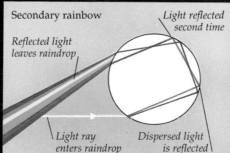

Secondary rainbow

Light reflected second time

Reflected light leaves raindrop

Light ray enters raindrop

Dispersed light is reflected

SECONDARY RAINBOW

A secondary rainbow forms outside a primary one. Light is reflected twice by each raindrop and emerges at a steeper angle to the ground. The order of the colors is reversed. (This is why a secondary rainbow seems like a reflection.) In a secondary rainbow, red light is seen from raindrops that are at an angle of 50° to the line of the horizon, and blue light from drops at an angle of 54°.

Adding light

W HEN A GREEN LIGHT AND A RED LIGHT are shone together on a wall, what color is seen? The answer isn't greenish-red or even reddish-green, but an entirely new color: yellow. If a third color – blue – is then added, the color changes again. Instead of greenish-reddish-blue, white light appears. When Isaac Newton conducted his splitting-light experiments, he made white light out of all the colors of the spectrum. But the experiment with colored lights on these two pages shows that the whole spectrum is not needed to make white light. In fact, just red, green, and blue can be added together to produce white. In various combinations, they will also make almost any other color. For this reason, they are known as the "additive primary colors."

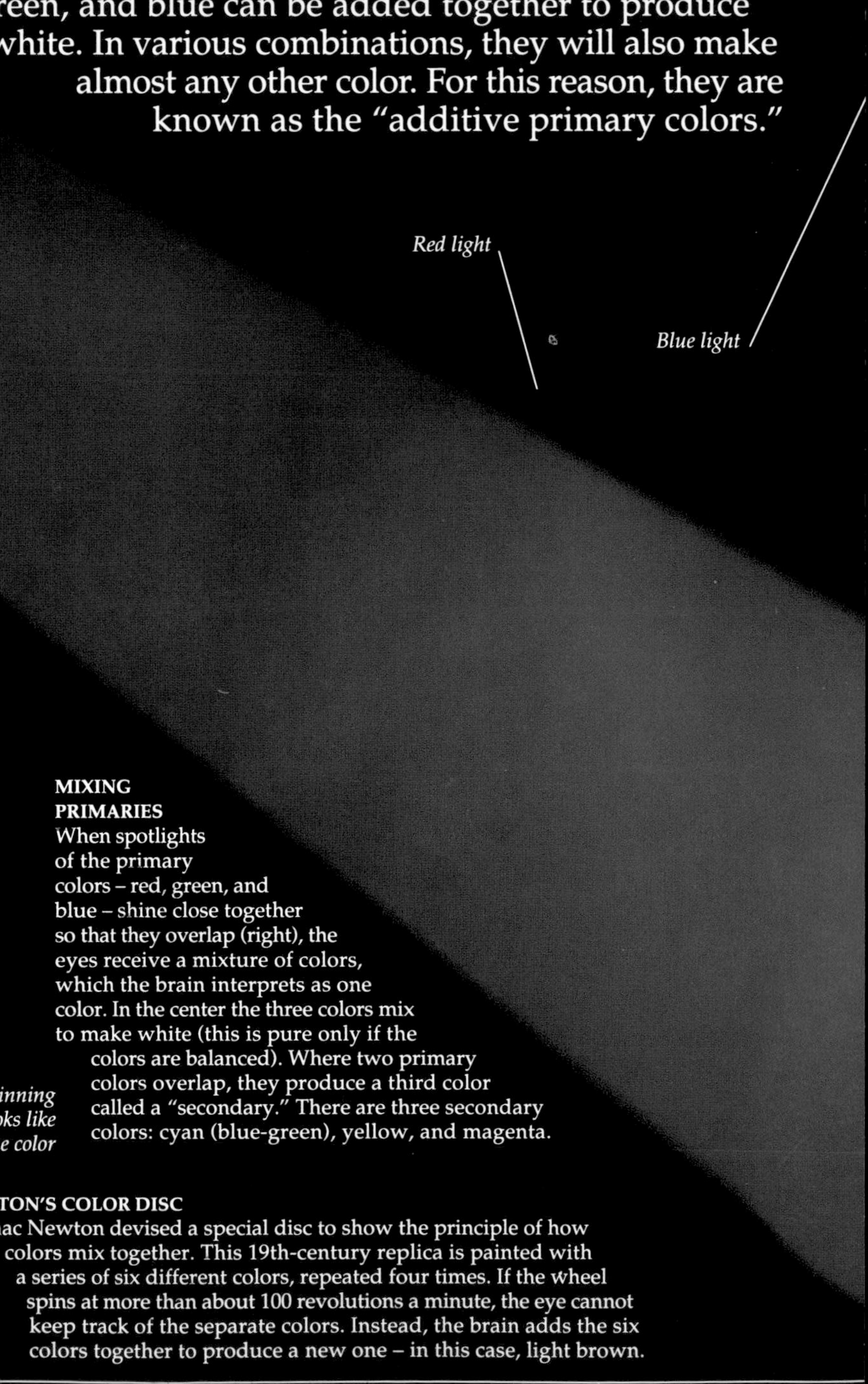

SPINNING COLORS
This 19th-century spinning top was based on the same principle as Newton's color wheel (below). When the top spun, its colors added together, and one color was seen.

When the wheel is still, the individual colors can be seen

Red light

Blue light

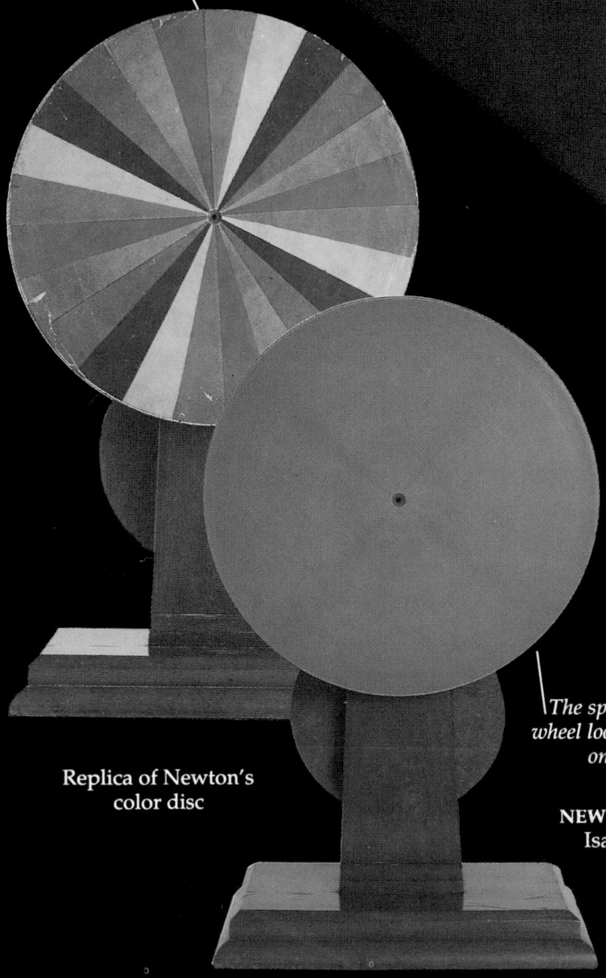

Replica of Newton's color disc

The spinning wheel looks like one color

MIXING PRIMARIES
When spotlights of the primary colors – red, green, and blue – shine close together so that they overlap (right), the eyes receive a mixture of colors, which the brain interprets as one color. In the center the three colors mix to make white (this is pure only if the colors are balanced). Where two primary colors overlap, they produce a third color called a "secondary." There are three secondary colors: cyan (blue-green), yellow, and magenta.

NEWTON'S COLOR DISC
Isaac Newton devised a special disc to show the principle of how colors mix together. This 19th-century replica is painted with a series of six different colors, repeated four times. If the wheel spins at more than about 100 revolutions a minute, the eye cannot keep track of the separate colors. Instead, the brain adds the six colors together to produce a new one – in this case, light brown.

PAINTING WITH DOTS

"Pointillism" is a style of painting, which was made famous by Impressionist artists such as Georges Seurat (1859-1891). Pointillists created their pictures by painting countless tiny dots of different colors. If a Pointillist painting is looked at closely, each individual colored dot can be seen. If viewed from farther away, the dots add together to give areas of a single color.

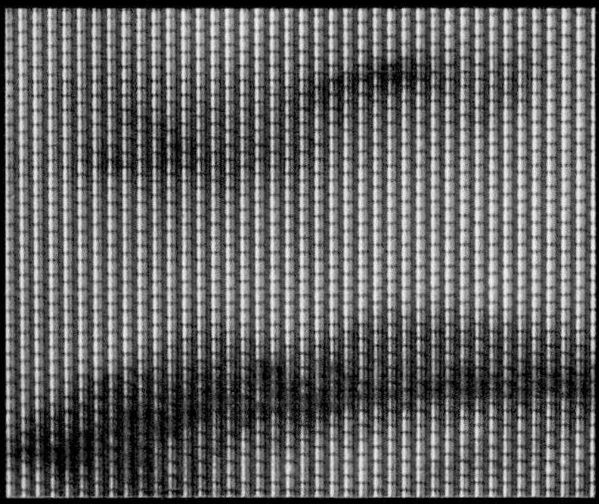

Green light

COLOR ON THE SCREEN

A color television picture is made up of tiny strips of red, green, and blue light. From the normal viewing distance, the colors from neighboring strips add together. The screen cannot produce pure colors such as yellow, but it can suggest yellow by lighting up neighboring green and red strips.

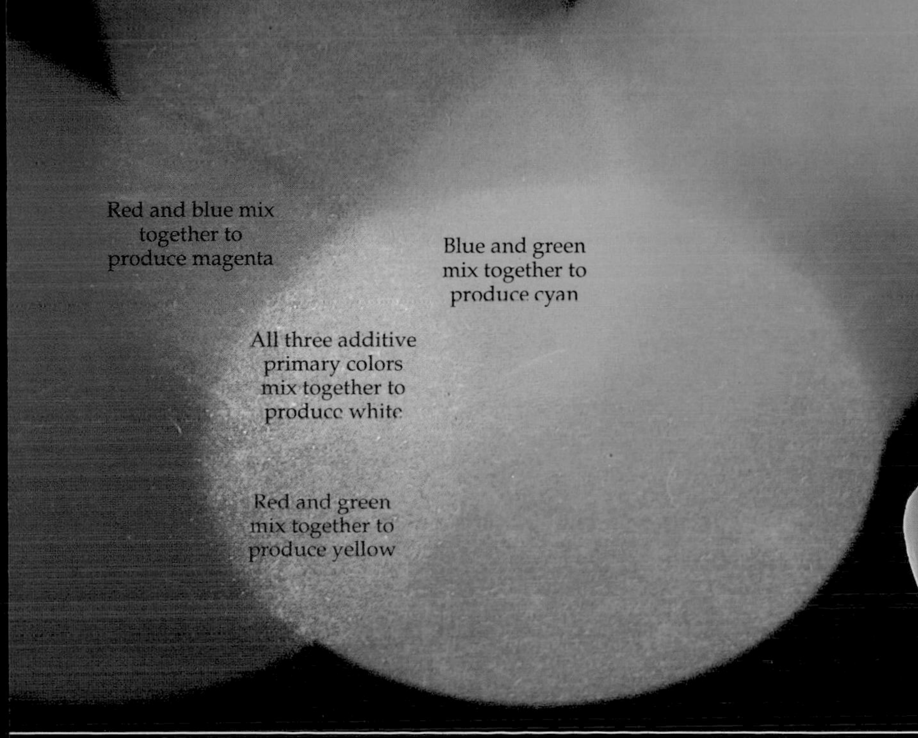

SEEING HIDDEN COLORS

A spectroscope is a device that disperses colors by bending them through different angles. Spectroscopes are used to show whether colors (reflected or created by an object) are pure or made by addition. The example below shows what would be seen when looking through a spectroscope at a red and a yellow pepper. The red pepper would give off red light only – red cannot be broken down into different colors. The yellow pepper would give off two hidden colors – green and red.

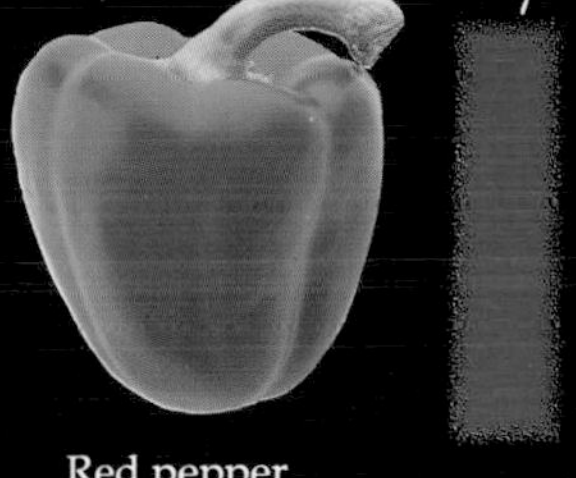

Red and blue mix together to produce magenta

Blue and green mix together to produce cyan

All three additive primary colors mix together to produce white

Red and green mix together to produce yellow

Only red light is reflected

Red and green are reflected and make yellow

Red pepper

Yellow pepper

Subtracting colors

ALL VISIBLE THINGS give off light, but they do it in two different ways. Some objects are light sources, meaning that they actually produce light. A flashlight, for example, produces light by using electrical energy to heat a filament. If a flashlight is shone at a wall, the wall gives off light as well. But the wall is not a light source. It simply reflects light that has already been made. Things that do not produce light themselves are colored by a process called "color subtraction." When white light falls on them, they absorb some of its colors and reflect or transmit others. This is why a leaf, for example, looks green. It absorbs almost all the colors in sunlight except one – green – and reflects this, so green is the color that is seen. For thousands of years, people have sought substances that are particularly good at subtracting colors. They are used in pigments, dyes, paints, and inks. All of these substances make our world a more colorful place – not by making color, but by taking it away.

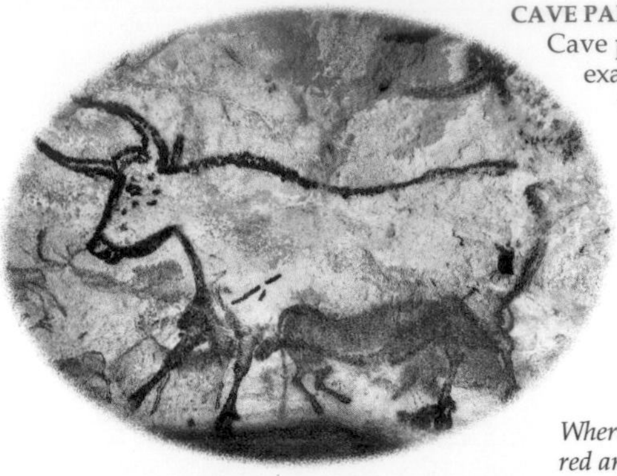

CAVE PAINTINGS
Cave paintings are the oldest surviving examples of human art. They were made with pigments that occur naturally in rocks, such as red ochre, and also with charcoal. Daylight makes most pigments fade over the years, but cave paintings are often deep inside the earth, so they have been well preserved. The painters would have worked by the flickering yellow light of burning torches.

Where the triangle and circle overlap, red and blue are removed, leaving green

Cyan

Where the triangle and square overlap, red and green are removed, leaving blue

Magenta

LEFTOVER COLORS
When the three primary colors of the spectrum are added together in pairs, they make three secondary colors. The main picture shows what happens when the secondary colors – cyan, yellow, and magenta – are then illuminated by white light. On their own, each of the colored shapes takes away or "subtracts" just one primary color from white light. The color that is seen is formed because the brain adds together the colors that are left. Where two secondary colors overlap, two colors are subtracted, leaving a primary light color – red, green, or blue. In the middle, where the three shapes overlap, all three primary colors are taken away from white light. This leaves no colors at all – or black. White cannot be made by color subtraction. This is why colored paints or inks cannot be mixed to produce white.

MAKING MAGENTA
The square takes away green from white light, to leave red and blue, which the brain adds together to give magenta.

Where the circle and square overlap, blue and green are removed, leaving red

MAKING BLACK
Where all three shapes overlap, red, green, and blue are removed, leaving no light.

FOOD DYES

Today, many artificial substances are used to give food a brighter color than it really has. In days gone by, many food dyes were made from plants or from animals. Cochineal, a brilliant scarlet dye, was made from tiny insects that feed on a type of cactus. These insects were painstakingly gathered by hand and then squashed to make the dye.

A bottle of cochineal – a natural food dye

SCATTERING LIGHT

When white light is shone through a jar of water containing just a few drops of milk, blue light is scattered by the tiny particles in the water. Red light is not scattered, and instead passes through. This effect is called Rayleigh scattering. It makes the liquid glow, and gives it a blue tinge. Smoke sometimes has a bluish color caused by Rayleigh scattering from tiny particles of ash.

MAKING CYAN

The triangle takes away red from white light, leaving green and blue, which the brain adds together to give cyan.

THE CHANGING COLORS OF SUNLIGHT

The color of sunlight changes as it passes through the atmosphere because air takes away some colors more than others. This is clearly seen as the sun sinks at dusk. To begin with, the sun's light looks yellow. As it gets nearer to the horizon, its light has to travel sideways through a longer and longer slice of air, and it begins to turn orange and then red. This happens because the air absorbs more and more of the sun's blue light, leaving the longer red wavelengths.

Yellow

MAN-MADE DYES

In 1856 a young English chemist named William Perkin stumbled across an important discovery that started a giant industry. He was trying to make a drug called quinine out of chemicals prepared from coal tar. In one experiment, he accidentally produced a brilliantly colored substance which later came to be known as "mauveine." Perkin realized that mauveine had great potential as a dye. He set up a company to produce it, and made a fortune in the process. Today, nearly all dyes are man-made (see also p. 238).

An original bottle of mauve dye

William Perkin (1838-1907)

Shawl colored with William Perkin's mauve dye

A sample-book showing a range of colors produced by synthetic dyes

MAKING YELLOW

The circle takes away blue from white light, leaving red and green. The brain adds these to make yellow.

Particles and waves

I<small>T IS EASY ENOUGH</small> to see the effects of light. But what is light made of, and how does it travel from one place to another? In the late 1600s Isaac Newton tried to answer these questions. He thought light could be made of particles or waves, and he did not want to rule either out. However, since the particle theory fitted most of the known phenomena and facts, it became popular with Newton's followers. The Dutch physicist Christian Huygens was not convinced by the particle theory. In 1690 he put forward a number of reasons for believing that light traveled in the form of waves. His evidence was strong, but over 100 years were to pass before an important experiment (p. 36) gave backing to the wave theory. In the early 1900s further discoveries were made (p. 44) about the nature of light. They showed that, in some ways, the followers of both Newton and Huygens were right.

The particles or waves of light bounce off the mirror, which then produces a reversed image of the candle

The flame produces particles or waves of light that radiate in all directions

MAKING SENSE OF LIGHT

Three of the most important characteristics of light are that it travels in straight lines, that it can be reflected, and that it can be bent when it passes from one medium to another. These two pages show how the two different ways of understanding light – the particle theory and the wave theory – explain each of these characteristics.

LIGHT AND WAVES

Christian Huygens (1629-1695) was a mathematician, physicist, and inventor who constructed the first pendulum clock and discovered the rings around the planet Saturn. In his book *Traité de la Lumière*, published in 1690, he rejected the particle theory of light. He decided that because light moves so quickly it must be made up of waves rather than particles. Huygens suggested that light waves were carried by the "ether," an invisible, weightless substance that existed throughout air and space. In "Huygens's Principle," he showed that each point on a wave could be thought of as producing its own wavelets, which add together to form a wave-front. This idea neatly explains how refraction (p. 14) works. Because waves can cross each other, his theory also explains why light rays do not crash into each other when they meet.

Christian Huygens

Huygens's wave model

Light wave spreads in all directions

Light rays are transmitted in straight lines

Wavelets add to form a "wave-front"

Each point on the wave is the source of a new "wavelet"

MAKING WAVES

Long after the days of Huygens and Newton, the inventor and physicist Charles Wheatstone (1802-1875) made this model to show how light waves work. The white beads represent the "ether," a substance that was thought to carry light waves. The model showed that ether carried light by vibrating at right angles to the light waves. Huygens had believed that ether vibrated in the same direction as light, squashing and stretching as it carried the light waves. It is now believed that ether does not exist.

Ether

Ether

Wheatstone wave machine

WAVES AND REFLECTION

According to the wave theory, a light source gives off light waves which spread out in all directions. If any of the waves strike a mirror, they are reflected according to the angles from which they arrive. Reflection turns each wave back to front – this is why the image seen is reversed. This diagram shows what happens. The shape of the waves depends on the size of the light source and how far the waves have traveled. The wave-front from a small nearby light will be strongly curved because it is close to the light source. The wave-front from a distant light is less curved.

The dark side of each vane absorbs more light and becomes warmer than white side

Light waves

Mirror

Waves are reflected and reversed by the mirror

PARTICLES AND REFLECTION

According to the particle theory, reflection is very straightforward. Light arrives at a mirror as a stream of tiny particles, and these bounce off the mirror's surface. The particles are very small, so many of them travel side by side in a light ray. They bounce at different points, so their order is reversed by reflection, producing a reversed image. As with the wave theory, this kind of reflection would happen only with a smooth surface. If the surface was rough the particles would bounce at many different angles, so the light would be scattered.

Light particles traveling toward the mirror from the foreground

Reflected, reversed particles travel away

Mirror

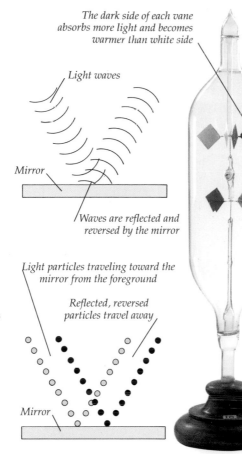

POWERED BY LIGHT

If light is made of particles, it should exert pressure when it hits a surface. Light does in fact do this, but the amount of pressure is tiny. How tiny can be seen with a radiometer, a device invented by William Crookes (1832-1919). In the radiometer light turns a set of finely balanced vanes. The glass bulb contains air at reduced pressure, and heated molecules of air bounce off the vanes and push them around. But if all the air is removed the vanes stop. Light pressure alone cannot push them around.

Air molecules collect heat energy from the dark side of vanes, bounce off the vanes, and push them around

PARTICLES AND SHADOWS

In his book *Opticks* of 1704, Isaac Newton wrote that "Light is never known to follow crooked Passages nor to bend into the Shadow." Newton explained this by saying that light particles always travel in straight lines. He thought that if an object stood in the path of the particles, it would cast a shadow because the particles could not spread out behind it. For everyday objects and their shadows, Newton was right. However, this idea did not agree with an important discovery made in 1665 by Francesco Grimaldi. Grimaldi found that on a very small scale, light could "bend into the shadow."

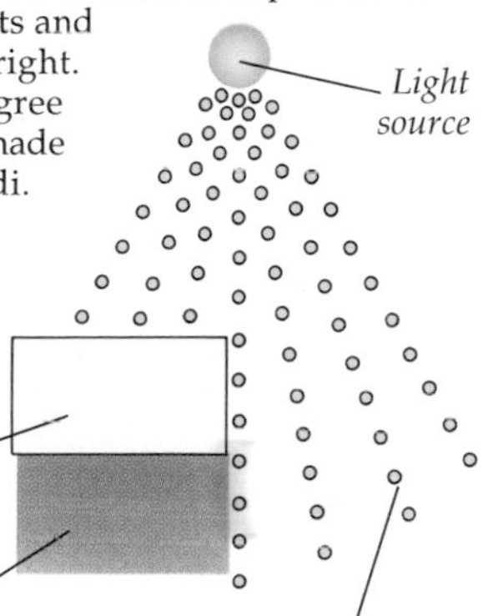

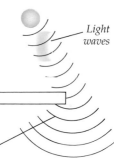

Light source

Object blocks some particles

On a large scale a shadow is cast in area where particles are blocked

Particles

WAVES AND SHADOWS

On a very small scale, shadows are not as simple as they seem. If light shines through a narrow slit it spreads out, and the light beam becomes wider than might be expected. This effect is very difficult to explain by the particle theory of light, but it is easy with the wave theory. Water waves and sound waves spread out after passing through small gaps. If light is also a wave, it should be able to do the same thing.

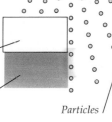

Light waves

Waves spreading out around a very small object

A shadow is formed by everyday objects when the waves or particles of light are blocked

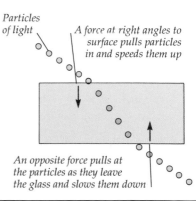

Light waves or particles are refracted by the lens, producing a magnified image

WAVES AND REFRACTION

What happens when a beam of light hits a glass block at an angle? According to the wave theory, part of each advancing wave should meet the glass before the rest. This part will start to move through the glass, but it will travel more slowly than the part still in air. Because the same wave is traveling at two different speeds, the wave-front will bend into the glass. This fits the facts of refraction.

Rest of wave still in air

Edge of wave meets glass and travels more slowly

Wave-front bends on entering and leaving the glass

PARTICLES AND REFRACTION

Newton had difficulty explaining why particles of light should change course when they pass from air into glass. He thought that a special force might speed the particles as they entered the glass, and slow them down as they left it. He explained how refraction could disperse colors by suggesting that the rays of each color move in "fits." Each color had "fits" of a different length – an idea very much like wavelengths.

Particles of light

A force at right angles to surface pulls particles in and speeds them up

An opposite force pulls at the particles as they leave the glass and slows them down

Diffraction and interference

IN 1801 AN ENGLISH PHYSICIST named Thomas Young described an experiment that led to a change in the understanding of light. Young had studied the eye and the human voice, and this made him think of similarities between light and sound. Many people believed that sound traveled in waves, and it seemed very likely to Young that light did as well. Like the Italian scientist Francesco Grimaldi, Young noticed that light rays spread out, or were "diffracted," when they passed through a very small slit. Young went on to see what happened when sunlight passed through two slits side by side, and then fell on a screen. He found that if the slits were large and far apart he saw two overlapping patches of light. But if the slits were very narrow and close together, the light produced bands of color, called "interference fringes." Young realized that these colored bands could be produced only by waves.

MAKING WAVES
Interference happens not only with light waves, but with sound and water waves, too. If the surface of a still pool of water is tapped with a thumb and forefinger, two sets of waves will be produced. Like light waves, they will spread out in all directions. Where two waves meet and are in step, they will interfere "constructively" to make a bigger wave. Where two waves meet and are out of step, they will interfere "destructively," or cancel each other out.

THOMAS YOUNG
Together with Augustin Fresnel, Thomas Young (1773-1829) put together important evidence showing that light travels in waves. He concluded that different colors are made of waves of different lengths. Young carried out his experiments with great care, but his conclusions were not immediately accepted. During the 18th century it was believed that light was made of particles, and people were slow to change their views.

MAKING LIGHT DIFFRACT (left)
A diffraction grating, like the one at the upper left of this picture, is a small glass slide engraved with many narrow slits, through which light is made to pass. The spreading light waves interfere with each other to produce streaks of color. In a typical diffraction grating, there are about 7,500 per inch (about 3,000 lines per cm), carefully positioned so that they are all exactly the same distance apart.

HOW INTERFERENCE WORKS
In Thomas Young's experiment, light shines through one narrow slit cut into a screen, which makes the light spread out, or "diffract." It then reaches a screen with two more narrow slits, which are very close together. This creates two sources of light, which diffract once more. As the light waves from each slit spread out, they meet each other. Sometimes the waves will be exactly in step, and sometimes they will be slightly or completely out of step. If the waves are in step they will add together – this is called constructive interference. If the waves are out of step they will cancel each other out – this is known as destructive interference. The effect of the two kinds of interference can be seen because they make bright or dark "fringes" where the light hits the screen. Interference is produced by anything that splits light into waves that can be added together or cancelled out. Diffraction gratings, bubbles, compact discs, and even butterfly wings all create interference patterns.

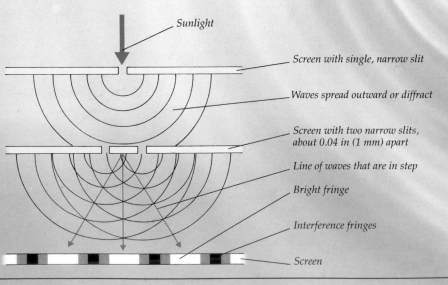

Sunlight

Screen with single, narrow slit

Waves spread outward or diffract

Screen with two narrow slits, about 0.04 in (1 mm) apart

Line of waves that are in step

Bright fringe

Interference fringes

Screen

The thumb and forefinger act like two light sources, producing waves of the same length that radiate outward

Where two waves meet and are exactly out of step, they interfere destructively, and the water stays level

Where the waves meet and are exactly in step, they interfere constructively to make a higher peak or a deeper trough

BENDING AROUND CORNERS

In everyday circumstances light seems to travel in straight lines. But in 1665 Francesco Grimaldi noticed that light seemed to bend and spread out when it passed through a narrow slit. He called this bending "diffraction." Today, microscopes and camera lenses are powerful enough to show how light is diffracted by sharp edges. This photograph, taken through a special filter, shows how light bends around the sharp edges of a metal bolt, giving it a fuzzy outline.

BARTON'S BUTTONS

These metal buttons were made by John Barton in about 1830. Each one has a pattern of fine lines scratched on its surface. The lines work like a diffraction grating. They reflect bright sunlight so that neighboring waves interfere with each other.

Interference in action

INTERFERENCE IS SOMETHING that can be seen not only in optical experiments, but in many different objects – living and nonliving. It makes up some of the most brilliant colors and intricate patterns in the world. Interference colors are created in a different way from colors that are produced by pigments. In daylight, a pigmented surface – like a piece of blue paper – always looks the same, no matter how it is seen. But if you look at a film of oil floating on water, or at a peacock's tail feather, things are different. The colors you see will depend on the angle from which you look. If you move your head, the colors will change, and may disappear altogether. This happens because these "iridescent" colors are produced by the shape of separate surfaces that are a tiny distance apart. The surfaces reflect light in a special way, making the light rays interfere with one another.

IRIDESCENT OPAL
Opal is made up of microscopic silicate spheres stacked in regular layers. Each sphere reflects light, and the reflected light rays interfere to produce brilliant colors. Turning the opal changes the colors that are seen.

NEWTON'S RINGS
When a convex lens is placed on a flat glass plate, light is reflected by the plate and by the lower surface of the lens. The two groups of rays interfere with each other to produce "Newton's Rings." These are named after Isaac Newton (1642-1727), who first investigated the effect.

Interference creates colorful patterns

BRIGHT EYES
The "eyes" in these peacock feathers are colored by tiny rods of a substance called melanin. The rods are arranged in a way that produces interference when light falls on them.

INSIDE A SHELL
The beautiful silvery colors inside this abalone shell are brought about by very thin layers of nacre – a hard mineral. Each layer reflects light, and the reflected rays interfere with each other to create colors. The metallic colors of some beetles are produced in the same way, by thin layers of a substance called chitin (pronounced *kytin*).

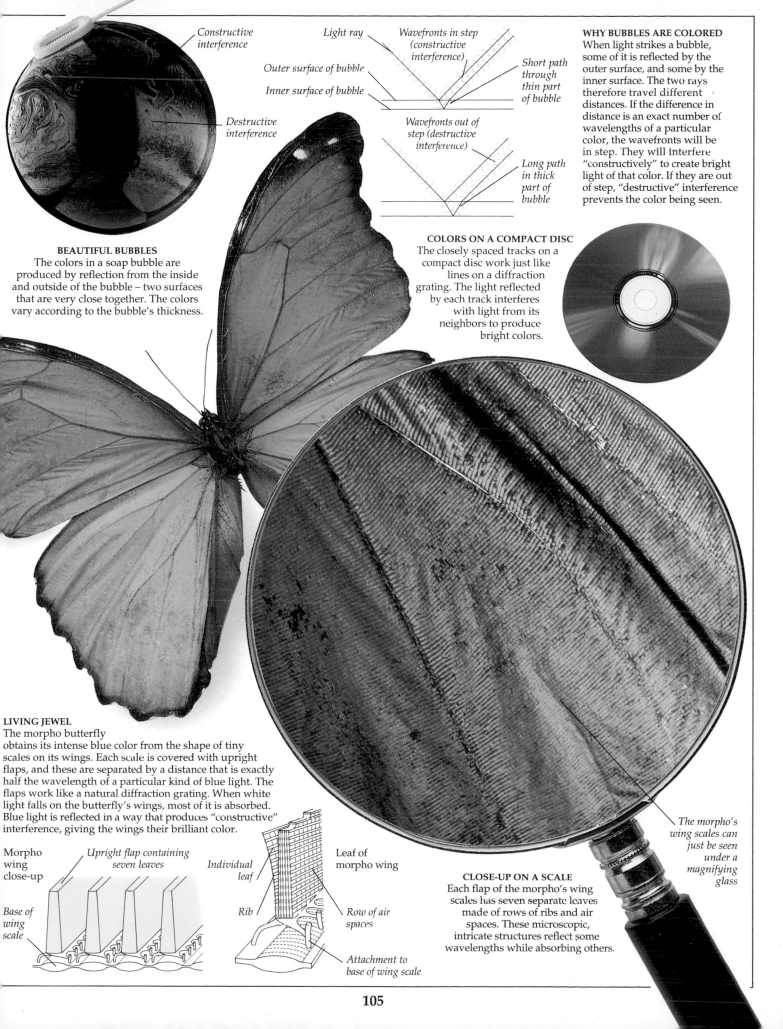

Constructive interference

Destructive interference

Light ray

Outer surface of bubble

Inner surface of bubble

Wavefronts in step (constructive interference)

Short path through thin part of bubble

Wavefronts out of step (destructive interference)

Long path in thick part of bubble

WHY BUBBLES ARE COLORED
When light strikes a bubble, some of it is reflected by the outer surface, and some by the inner surface. The two rays therefore travel different distances. If the difference in distance is an exact number of wavelengths of a particular color, the wavefronts will be in step. They will interfere "constructively" to create bright light of that color. If they are out of step, "destructive" interference prevents the color being seen.

BEAUTIFUL BUBBLES
The colors in a soap bubble are produced by reflection from the inside and outside of the bubble – two surfaces that are very close together. The colors vary according to the bubble's thickness.

COLORS ON A COMPACT DISC
The closely spaced tracks on a compact disc work just like lines on a diffraction grating. The light reflected by each track interferes with light from its neighbors to produce bright colors.

LIVING JEWEL
The morpho butterfly obtains its intense blue color from the shape of tiny scales on its wings. Each scale is covered with upright flaps, and these are separated by a distance that is exactly half the wavelength of a particular kind of blue light. The flaps work like a natural diffraction grating. When white light falls on the butterfly's wings, most of it is absorbed. Blue light is reflected in a way that produces "constructive" interference, giving the wings their brilliant color.

Morpho wing close-up

Upright flap containing seven leaves

Base of wing scale

Individual leaf

Rib

Leaf of morpho wing

Row of air spaces

Attachment to base of wing scale

CLOSE-UP ON A SCALE
Each flap of the morpho's wing scales has seven separate leaves made of rows of ribs and air spaces. These microscopic, intricate structures reflect some wavelengths while absorbing others.

The morpho's wing scales can just be seen under a magnifying glass

The electromagnetic spectrum

In 1799 and 1800 William Herschel set up dozens of different experiments to test the link between light and heat. In one he formed a spectrum with a prism and then screened out all but one of the colors. He let this light fall on a thermometer and recorded the temperature that it showed. Herschel found that violet light gave the lowest reading on the thermometer. Red gave a higher reading, but the highest reading of all was produced beyond the red end of the spectrum, where there was no light to be seen. He had discovered "infrared" radiation – a form of wave energy that can be felt, but not seen by human eyes. Herschel decided that the light and infrared rays were two quite different forms of energy. However, other scientists, including Thomas Young (p. 102), thought that they were similar. Today it is known that both light waves and infrared waves are part of a wide spectrum of wave energy – the "electromagnetic spectrum." Humans can see light because the eyes contain special nerve endings that are sensitive to a particular range of wavelengths. The rest of the electromagnetic spectrum is invisible to humans.

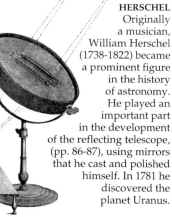

HEAT AND THE SPECTRUM
In this experiment Herschel tested the heating power of each color of the spectrum. He split light with a prism, and the spectrum fell onto a screen with a slit cut in it. Light of one color passed through the slit and fell on a thermometer. He also performed experiments to see if "invisible light" (infrared) could be refracted, and found that it could.

WILLIAM HERSCHEL
Originally a musician, William Herschel (1738-1822) became a prominent figure in the history of astronomy. He played an important part in the development of the reflecting telescope, (pp. 86-87), using mirrors that he cast and polished himself. In 1781 he discovered the planet Uranus.

BEYOND THE VISIBLE
William Herschel investigated the link between light and heat in order to solve a practical problem. He wanted to look at sunspots through his telescope, but he found that even with colored filters the sun's heat was too great for comfortable viewing. He thought that if he could find out exactly which colors were "more apt to occasion heat" he could do something to cut them out. His experiments helped him devise green lenses which blocked some of the heat.

THREE-COLOR VISION
Isaac Newton showed that sunlight is made of a spectrum of different colors. Each color merges gradually into its neighbors to give different "hues." Most people can see about five main colors in the spectrum, but the number of hues is almost limitless. So how do the eyes distinguish among them? In 1801 Thomas Young suggested that the eye has three types of color receptor, and that the mix of signals that they produce tells what kind of light is being seen. Young's idea of "trichromacy" was correct. The eyes have three types of nerve endings, or "cones," for colored light. Each type of cone is most sensitive to a different range of colors. If violet light is seen, only one type of cone produces a signal, which the brain interprets as "violet." With an equal mixture of red, green, and blue light, signals are produced by all types of cone. The brain interprets this as "white."

"Response curve" of cones most sensitive to blue

"Response curve" of cones most sensitive to green

"Response curve" of cones most sensitive to red

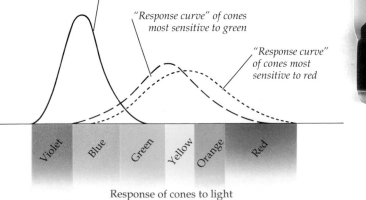

Response of cones to light
(measured by light absorption of each of the three types of cone)

Thermometer placed outside the visible spectrum is heated by invisible infrared light, which produces more heating than visible red light

Thermometer heated by visible red light

The visible spectrum

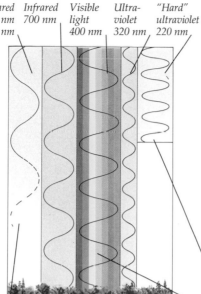

Far infrared
1,100 nm
2,300 nm

Infrared
700 nm

Visible
light
400 nm

Ultra-
violet
320 nm

"Hard"
ultraviolet
220 nm

A TEST FOR LIGHT

In 1614 the Italian chemist Angelo Sala (1576-1637) described how light broke down silver nitrate crystals, making them turn dark. Nearly 200 years later Wilhelm Ritter used this chemical change to search for "hidden" light at the blue end of the spectrum.

The visible spectrum

The far infrared waves are absorbed

Paper exposed to blue light

Paper exposed to violet light

Paper exposed to ultraviolet turns darkest

"Hard" ultraviolet waves are absorbed

Infrared, visible light, and ultraviolet reach the ground

THE DISCOVERY OF ULTRAVIOLET

In 1801 Wilhelm Ritter (1776-1810) investigated the light energy of different parts of the spectrum. To do this he used strips of paper soaked in silver nitrate solution. When light falls on silver nitrate there is a chemical reaction that produces tiny grains of silver. The grains look black, and so the silver nitrate turns dark. Carl Wilhelm Scheele (1742-1786) had found that light of different colors darkened the paper at different rates, so blue light had more effect than red. Following Herschel's technique a year before, Ritter decided to see what would happen if he tested beyond the blue end of the spectrum, where no light could be seen. To his surprise, he found that the reaction was even stronger. The invisible "light" that he discovered became known as ultraviolet.

LIGHT AND THE ATMOSPHERE *(left)*

Sunlight consists of an almost continuous spectrum of waves. Most of the energy is concentrated in wavelengths that are between 220 and 3,200 nanometers (or nm – a billionth of a meter). However, not all of these different waves reach the ground. As the far infrared waves travel through the atmosphere they are absorbed by carbon dioxide, water vapor, and ozone, a gas formed by oxygen atoms. The shorter, "hard," ultraviolet waves are also absorbed, this time by the ozone layer in the atmosphere. The filtering effect of the atmosphere narrows down the spectrum of waves, so that most of the waves reaching the ground have wavelengths between 320 and 2,000 nm. Visible light waves make up less than a third of this band, from 400–700 nm.

A DISAPPEARING SHIELD

This computerized satellite map shows a hole (the pink, purple, and black areas) in the earth's ozone layer, high in the atmosphere above Antarctica. The ozone layer is essential to all living things because it screens out short-wavelength ("hard") ultraviolet light, which can damage living cells. The hole in the Antarctic ozone layer was probably caused by man-made gases being released into the atmosphere.

Equipment to investigate the ultraviolet end of the spectrum

Water to dissolve crystals

Silver nitrate crystals are colorless until they are dissolved in water and exposed to light

Pipette

Paper soaked in silver nitrate solution will turn brown when light shines on it

Electromagnetic waves

AFTER WILLIAM HERSCHEL DISCOVERED the existence of infrared light beyond the red end of the visible spectrum, the Danish physicist Hans Christian Oersted (1777-1851) found that an electric current could make the needle of a compass change direction. In the same year the French scientist André-Marie Ampére (1775-1836) showed that two wires that were carrying electric currents could be made to attract or repel each other, just like magnets. More experiments followed thick and fast, and it became clear that electricity and magnetism were somehow linked. In 1865 the Scottish scientist James Clerk Maxwell used mathematics to explain the links between the two. He showed that electricity and magnetism are bound together so closely that they often act together as "electromagnetism." Maxwell realized that if an electric current was made to surge backward and forward, it would set up changing electromagnetic waves that would radiate outward at an immense speed. His calculations showed that these electromagnetic waves radiated at the speed of light. From this, Maxwell concluded that light itself was a form of electromagnetic wave.

CHANGING WAVES
Why do things glow when they are very hot? The answer is that they emit visible electromagnetic waves – or light. Even a very cold object, such as a block of ice, emits waves, but the waves are weak, and they are much too long for human eyes to detect. As an object becomes warmer, its atoms emit much more wave energy, and the waves it produces become shorter and shorter. If it is warmed enough, it will eventually start to glow. This happens because the waves it emits are now short enough for human eyes to see.

Heated atoms emit light at the red end of the visible spectrum

Cooler atoms give off longer infrared waves, which are invisible

1 BECOMING VISIBLE
A cold steel bar emits no visible light. It can be seen in daylight because it reflects light that falls on it. In the dark it is invisible. But if the bar is heated, it produces visible light. This bar is emitting light with wavelengths of about 700 nm – just within the red end of the visible spectrum.

TELEVISION
Television sound and pictures are carried on short-wavelength radio waves of less than 3.3 ft (1 m). The frequencies of the waves are modulated, to make them carry a signal.

Television
Typical wavelength: 1.65 ft (0.5 m)

Radio waves
Typical wavelength: 328 ft (100 m)

Radar
Typical wavelength: 0.03 ft (0.01 m)

A SPECTRUM OF WAVELENGTHS *(right)*
Electromagnetic radiation makes up a whole spectrum of waves of many lengths. Red light, for example, has a wavelength of about 650 nm (a nanometer is a billionth of a meter). Another way of describing red light is to say that it has a "frequency" of 450 million million cycles, this being the number of waves of red light that will pass any point in one second. Radio waves have much longer wavelengths. Long-wave radio uses waves of up to 6,562 feet (2,000 meters) long – three billion times longer than red light waves.

JAMES CLERK MAXWELL
Scotsman James Clerk Maxwell (1831-1879) (see also p. 46) was a gifted mathematician who made key discoveries in many different areas of physics. One of his first achievements was the "Kinetic Theory of Gases," a mathematical investigation showing how the temperature of a gas is linked to the overall movement of its atoms or molecules. Maxwell used the same mathematical skills to produce equations describing how electricity and magnetism are linked. He was also interested in mechanics and astronomy, and in 1861 he made the world's first color photograph.

RADIO WAVES *(left)*
Radio waves range from about 1 mm to several miles in length. Radars, microwave ovens, televisions, and radios work by using different bands of radio waves. Radio waves are also produced by many stars and galaxies and can be detected by special telescopes. These radiotelescopes in New Mexico work together to gather waves from very distant objects.

RADAR *(below)*
A radar scanner emits very short radio waves and detects echoes from objects in their path. Radar is short for "Radio Detection and Ranging."

Cold atoms emit no visible light

Cooler atoms produce red light

The hottest atoms emit orange light

Cooler areas on the surface absorb yellow light, so they look darker

The hottest atoms emit yellow light

The hottest atoms emit yellowish-white light

2 ORANGE HEAT

The bar is now hotter still, and it is emitting more light. At this temperature more of the light emitted has a shorter wavelength – about 630 nm – giving the bar an orange color. Farther away from the tip of the bar the color changes because the temperature gradually decreases.

3 YELLOW HEAT

The bar is now extremely hot. The most prominent color of light being emitted is yellow, with a wavelength of about 580 nm, though others are present. The hottest parts of the bar still emit orange and red light, but these colors are masked by the much more intense waves of yellow light.

4 WHITE HEAT

The heat is now so intense that the bar is radiating most colors of the visible spectrum, which add together to appear white.

X-RAYS (right)

These rays (or waves) carry more energy than visible light. They are able to penetrate the soft parts of our bodies, but they cannot pass through bone. X-rays can be detected by photographic film, so they are used to produce pictures of things that cannot normally be seen, like broken bones.

COSMIC RAYS

The highest-energy radiation that exists is in cosmic rays. They contain tiny particles of atomic nuclei, as well as some electrons and gamma rays. Cosmic radiation bombards the earth's atmosphere from remote regions of space.

MICROWAVES

Low-level microwave radiation permeates space. It is thought to have been released by the "Big Bang" that may have created the universe. In a microwave oven, microwaves rapidly change the alignment of water molecules, and this heats up the food.

*Microwaves
Typical wavelength: 0.003–0.328 ft
(.001–0.1 m)*

*Visible light
Typical wavelength: 0.000,001,5 ft
(0.000,000,5 m)*

*X-rays
Typical wavelength: 0.000,000,000,03 ft
(0.000,000,000,01 m)*

*Cosmic rays
Typical wavelength:
0.000,000,000,000,03 ft
(0.000,000,000,000,01 m)*

*Infrared waves
Typical wavelength: 0.000,164 ft
(0.000,05 m)*

*Ultraviolet waves
Typical wavelength: 0.000,000,3 ft
(0.000,000,1 m)*

*Gamma rays
Typical wavelength: 0.000,000,000,000,3 ft
(0.000,000,000,000,1 m)*

INFRARED WAVES (below)

Infrared waves are produced by things that are hot. In this satellite photograph of an erupting volcano, invisible infrared waves from molten lava have been processed by computer to make them a visible red color.

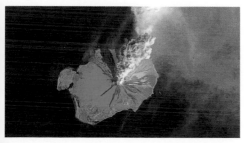

ULTRAVIOLET WAVES

Ultraviolet waves have lengths as short as 50 nm. They are produced by very hot objects, like the sun and other stars. Ultraviolet waves carry more energy than light waves, which is why they can penetrate and burn the skin. Some suntan lotions screen out the harmful ultraviolet light rays, and this prevents the skin from becoming damaged.

GAMMA RAYS (left)

Gamma rays (or waves), a form of radioactivity released by some atomic nuclei, have very short wavelengths. They carry a large amount of energy and can penetrate metals and concrete. They are very dangerous and can kill living cells, especially at the high levels released by nuclear reactions such as the explosion of a nuclear bomb.

Atoms and light

IN 1802 WILLIAM HYDE WOLLASTON made a surprising discovery about light from the sun. He found that the sun's spectrum was not a continuous band of light. Instead, it contained hundreds of narrow lines where particular wavelengths were missing. A German physicist named Joseph von Fraunhofer mapped over 500 of these, giving the main ones letters. In the late 1850s a physicist named Gustav Kirchoff found that all atoms can emit or absorb particular wavelengths of light, and that the gaps in the Sun's spectrum were caused by absorption. This was a major discovery, because it showed that there were strong links between atoms and light. As the 20th century began, an important new theory emerged that explained how atoms and light interact.

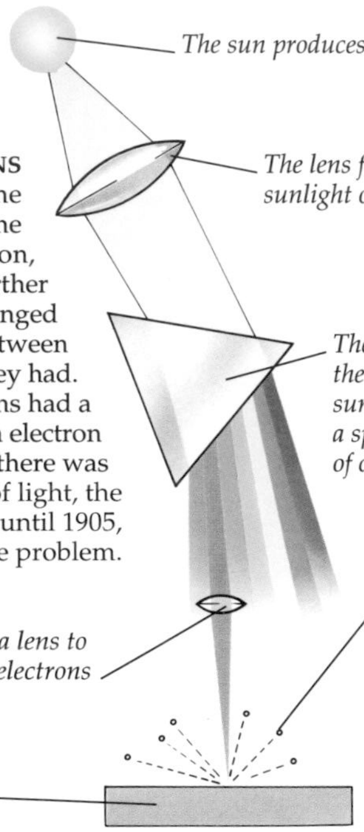

The sun produces light

The lens focuses the sunlight on to a prism

The prism then splits the sunlight into a spectrum of colors

EVIDENCE FROM ELECTRONS
It was known in the 19th century that light had an effect on some metals – it could dislodge electrons from the atoms (electrons are the tiny particles in atoms that form electric currents). This phenomenon, which became known as the photoelectric effect, was investigated further in 1902 by the German physicist Philipp Lenard. Using a prism arranged like the one shown here, he and other physicists looked at the links between the wavelength of light, the release of electrons, and the energy that they had. The results were strange. For a given wavelength of light, the electrons had a fixed amount of energy. Weak light produced fewer electrons, but each electron still had just as much energy as if the light had been bright. However, there was a link between wavelength and energy. The shorter the wavelength of light, the more energy the electrons had. These findings were not understood until 1905, when Albert Einstein used "quantum theory" to solve the problem.

Max Planck

A color is singled out with a lens to test its effect in dislodging electrons

The number and the energy of the electrons is measured

The colored light is focused on to a metal plate

FRAUNHOFER LINES
In 1814 Joseph von Fraunhofer (1787-1826) plotted the sun's spectrum, now called Fraunhofer lines.

Observer looks at spectrum through tube containing lenses

THE QUANTUM THEORY
During the late 19th century physicists thought that light and other forms of electromagnetic radiation were continuous streams of energy. However, by 1900 this idea had led to a number of theoretical problems. Max Planck (1858-1947) tackled them by suggesting that the energy in radiation was not continuous, but that it was divided into tiny packets, or "quanta." His quantum theory showed that in some circumstances light could be thought of as particles, as believed by the followers of Isaac Newton's particle theory.

EXAMINING A SPECTRUM
A spectrometer is a device used to investigate the light in a spectrum. This one was built in about 1905. The substance to be examined is placed in one tube, and white light shining through it is split by a diffraction grating (p. 36) on the central plinth. The observer looks at the spectrum through the other tube.

HOW ATOMS MAKE LIGHT
Why is light energy is produced in small packets, or "quanta"? The answer lies in the structure of atoms, the tiny particles that make up matter. An atom consists of a small and dense nucleus, surrounded by electrons – the same particles that produce electric currents. Electrons circle the nucleus at different distances. The farther they are from the nucleus, the more energy they have. If an electron moves from an outer orbit to one that is closer to the nucleus, it loses energy. This energy is released as a quantum of light, or photon. In most atoms, there are many electrons and many different energy levels. The wavelengths of light that each electron can produce depend on how much energy the electron loses in falling from one orbit to another. Together, these different wavelengths give an atom its characteristic "emission spectrum." By examining an emission spectrum, scientists can identify the kind of atom that produced it.

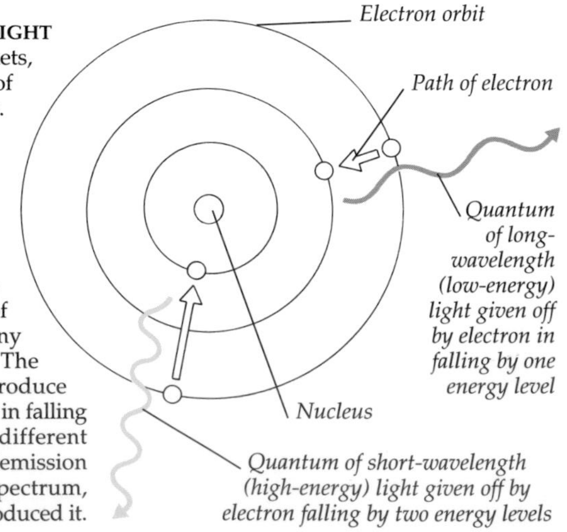

Electron orbit

Path of electron

Quantum of long-wavelength (low-energy) light given off by electron in falling by one energy level

Nucleus

Quantum of short-wavelength (high-energy) light given off by electron falling by two energy levels

LINES IN THE SPECTRUM
The strips above show the sun's spectrum in great detail. In it, hundreds of tiny lines called "Fraunhofer lines" can be seen. The sun's light is created by hot atoms on its surface. When this light travels through cooler atoms in the sun's outer atmosphere, some of its wavelengths are absorbed. Each kind of atom absorbs particular wavelengths, producing characteristic lines. Together they create an "absorption spectrum."

Fluorescence

Sometimes atoms absorb light of one wavelength, but almost immediately release the energy as light of another wavelength. This is called fluorescence. Fluorescence happens when an electron takes in energy and moves to a higher orbit, but then falls back to a lower orbit in a series of steps. Many substances fluoresce when ultraviolet light strikes them. We cannot see ultraviolet, but we can see the lower-energy light that fluorescence produces.

SOAP POWDER IN DAYLIGHT
In daylight soap powder looks bright and white. Some of this brightness is due to fluorescence.

WILLEMITE IN DAYLIGHT
Willemite is a mineral containing zinc and manganese. In daylight it looks brownish (the white is quartz).

SODALITE IN DAYLIGHT
This grayish mineral is a complex compound of sodium, aluminum, silicon, oxygen, and chlorine.

SOAP POWDER IN ULTRAVIOLET LIGHT
In ultraviolet light soap powder is intensely white. Fluorescence helps make clothes look clean.

WILLEMITE IN ULTRAVIOLET LIGHT
When willemite fluoresces, it emits a bright green light (the pink fluorescence is produced by quartz).

LIVING LIGHTS
These specks of light on the surface of the sea are created by luminescence in tiny plants and animals. They make light through a chemical reaction in which a protein combines with oxygen. The reaction produces light, but hardly any heat.

The diffraction grating splits the light from the substance to form a spectrum

SODALITE IN ULTRAVIOLET LIGHT
Sodalite absorbs ultraviolet light, and emits yellow or orange light.

Substance to be examined is placed in this tube and illuminated by a strong white light

SPECTRAL SAMPLES
Spectroscopy – the scientific study of spectra – began in the 1860s. These glass tubes were made in 1871 and contain solutions of different substances. They were used as a set of standards when examining spectra. Each of these substances absorbed particular wavelengths when light passed through it.

ULTRAVIOLET SPECTRUM
This photographic slide, made in about 1900, shows Fraunhofer lines of part of the "absorption spectra" of aluminum and hydrogen atoms. The atoms were illuminated with ultraviolet light, which was split into a spectrum to show which wavelengths were absorbed.

Letting light through

ABOUT 5,000 YEARS AGO, the Egyptians learned how to make glass. To begin with they shaped it into beads, but by Roman times glass was being "blown" to make cups and dishes as well. Glass became highly prized. Although it broke easily, it was almost transparent, and by comparison it made pottery look dull and uninteresting. Today, transparent objects – from plastic windows to glass bottles – are common, and they play an important part in day-to-day life. They let light through without scattering its rays. As a result, images can be seen through them clearly. Translucent objects also let light through, but scatter its rays. Because of this scattering, images behind a translucent object cannot be seen clearly. Opaque objects do not let any light through. They block light waves, though they may be transparent to other kinds of waves – X-rays, for example.

SEEING THE LIGHT
If a few drops of oil are added to a sheet of paper, the paper lets more light pass through.

Translucent comb

Translucent frame

Glasses
Transparent lenses

Translucent flower petals

Translucent leaf

Transparency

Transparent objects let light pass through without noticeably scattering its rays. As a result, a clear image can usually be seen from the other side. Transparent materials are common in nature. Pure water, some natural oils, and the crystals of many minerals are transparent. But apart from a vacuum, nothing is ever completely see-through. Some light energy is always absorbed by the material that it passes through. The thicker something is, the more energy it will absorb. This is why things look clear through a thin layer of glass, but dull through a thick block.

SEE-THROUGH FISH
This fish's body contains transparent oils that make it harder to see. This helps many small water animals to hide from their enemies.

Transparent molten wax

Metal oxides in the glass subtract colors from white light

Transparent quartz crystal

Transparent glass

Translucent bottle

Translucent bottle

Translucent bottle

Translucency

A translucent object lets some light through, but it scatters the rays so much that whatever is on the other side cannot be seen clearly. Many plastics, oils, fats, and waxes are translucent, as are thin layers of cells in plants and animals. Just like transparency, translucency depends on thickness. If a single sheet of paper is held up to a lamp, the fibers in the paper will scatter and absorb light, but some light will still pass through. If more and more sheets are gradually added to make a thicker layer, the light will eventually disappear. With some substances, translucency depends on temperature. Many fats and waxes scatter light less when they are liquid than when they are solid. This is why candlewax becomes see-through when it melts, and why butter becomes clear when it is warmed in a pan.

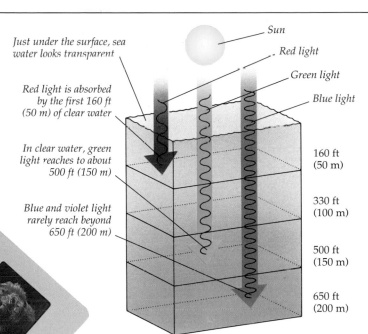

Just under the surface, sea water looks transparent

Sun

Red light

Green light

Blue light

Red light is absorbed by the first 160 ft (50 m) of clear water

In clear water, green light reaches to about 500 ft (150 m)

Blue and violet light rarely reach beyond 650 ft (200 m)

160 ft (50 m)

330 ft (100 m)

500 ft (150 m)

650 ft (200 m)

Different parts of a color slide allow different wavelengths to pass through

Color slides

Soap and beeswax let some light through, but the rays of light are scattered

LETTING COLORS THROUGH
Clear, coloured objects – such as tinted glass bottles or photographic slides – obtain their colors by subtracting some wavelengths from white light. Although shallow sea water sometimes looks transparent, sea water does absorb light. Red light is absorbed by the upper layers; blue and violet light penetrate farthest.

Blocking light

If a piece of aluminum foil is held up to a lamp, no light is seen, quite unlike the glow seen through a sheet of paper. This is because most metals are "opaque" – they do not let light pass through them. Some metals can let light through, but only if their atoms are formed into very thin layers. When you look at any opaque object, all the light you see is reflected by the object's surface. Shiny metals reflect nearly all the light that hits them, so they look bright. India ink reflects very little light, so it looks black.

This key reflects light but does not let it through

Opaque metal key

These painted scissors do not let light through but reflect red

Bottle of India ink

Most of the light that strikes the ink is absorbed

Translucent soap

Translucent beeswax

Opaque scissors

Opaque wood bark

Opaque pyrites

Polarized light

PRESENTING A PUZZLE
In his book about Iceland spar, Erasmus Bartholin (1625-1698) described how its crystals split light in two different ways. This phenomenon is called double refraction, or birefringence.

NORMALLY, AN OBJECT SEEN through something transparent appears as a single image – but not always. In 1669 Erasmus Bartholin described how crystals of a mineral called Iceland spar (calcite) produce a double image. He rotated a crystal, and found one image moved while the other stayed put. In 1808 Etienne Malus, a French physicist, looked through Iceland spar under reflected light and found that one of the images had disappeared. He decided that ordinary daylight is made of two forms of light, which the crystal bent in different ways. At a certain angle, only one form of light was reflected by the mirror, so under reflected light only one image could be seen. It is now known that the difference between these forms of light lies in their "polarity," or nature of their waves. Daylight is usually "unpolarized" – its waves move up and down at all angles to its direction of movement. Reflected light is partially "polarized" – its waves move mainly in one plane.

Gold chain

Crystal of Iceland spar

Polarizing filter

Light wave moving in one plane

Light waves moving in all planes

Light blocked by "crossed" polarizing filter

Double image of chain caused by birefringence

BIREFRINGENCE
This crystal of Iceland spar has been placed over a single gold chain, producing a double image. When light from the chain meets the crystal, it is refracted because it is passing from one medium to another. But the bending takes place in an unusual way. Waves that are moving on one particular plane are bent by a different amount than waves moving at right angles to them, so two sets of light rays are produced. The splitting of light is known as double refraction, or "birefringence," and the emerging light is polarized.

SCREENING OUT LIGHT
A polarizing filter lets through only light waves that move in one particular plane. If two polarizing filters are arranged at right angles or "crossed," no light can get through. You can see this for yourself with polarized sunglasses. Hold one pair in front of another, and then rotate one pair. The lenses will seem to turn black.

FRENCH CONNECTION
In the early 19th century the French statesman and scientist François Arago (1786-1853) followed the work of Etienne Malus with his own studies on the nature of polarized light. He investigated the polarity of light from different parts of the sky, and in 1812 he built one of the first polarizing filters, which he made from a stack of glass sheets.

HAND POLARISCOPE
Many substances that are normally colorless become brightly colored when viewed under polarized light. This 19th-century hand polariscope enabled people to look at transparent minerals under polarized light. Mineral specimens are mounted on a wheel so that each can be brought between two polarizing filters, in and below the eyepiece, made of Iceland spar. The filter nearest the eye (the "analyzer") can be turned to alter the intensity of the light that gets through.

Indicator label

Mineral specimen mounted on wheel

Eyepiece with polarizing filter

POLARIZED PICTURES
With the help of some transparent tape and two polarizing filters, pictures that have brilliant colors can be made. The pictures are built with up to 10 layers of tape. They are then placed between the filters, and the colors become visible.

1 NORMAL LIGHT
Under unpolarized light, the picture is transparent.

2 POLARIZED LIGHT
With filters in front and behind, the picture becomes colored. This happens because the different thicknesses of tape twist the polarized light waves by different amounts, according to their color.

Crowded stress lines show region under high stress

Widely spaced stress lines show region under low stress

3 ROTATING THE FILTER
If the front filter is turned, the colors change because the filter now cuts out different light waves.

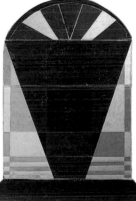

SEEING STRESS
This hook is made of a plastic that becomes slightly birefringent if it is stretched or bent. Under normal light, the birefringence is hardly noticeable. Under polarized light, conspicuous "stress patterns" become visible. Stress patterns are common in anything that is made of molded plastic or glass (they are easy to see in a car windshield if polarized sunglasses are worn). They are useful to engineers, because they enable areas of high stress to be seen.

4 BLOCKING LIGHT
Black areas on the picture show where the front filter has blocked all the light.

LIQUID CRYSTAL DISPLAY (LCD)
A liquid crystal display contains two "crossed" polarizing filters backed by a mirror. Normally, crossed polarizers block all light, so the display should look black. But between the filters is a layer of liquid crystals. As long as the power is switched off, the crystals twist light rays through 90°. The twisted rays can then pass through the rear filter. They are reflected by the mirror, so the display looks white. The numbers or letters on a display are made by "switching on" areas of liquid crystals. This changes them so that they no longer twist the light.

CRYSTALS OFF
When a liquid crystal display is "off," the liquid crystals twist the polarized light, allowing it to pass through the rear polarizer. The mirror reflects the light, which is then twisted once more as it passes through the crystals for a second time. The twisted light can now pass out through the front polarizer, and as a result, the display looks white.

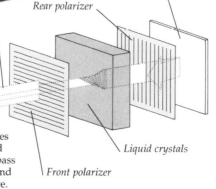

Mirror

Rear polarizer

Light

Liquid crystals

Front polarizer

CRYSTALS ON
Pressing a key sends an electric current to specific areas of the crystals. The crystals in these areas no longer twist the polarized light, so the light that passes through them is blocked by the rear polarizer. There is no light for the mirror to reflect, so the affected areas of the display now look black.

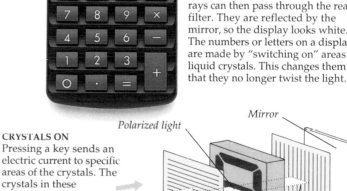

Polarized light

Mirror

Black number appears where light is not reflected back

Light blocked by rear polarizer

Light energy

EVERY DAY THE EARTH is bathed by a huge amount of energy from the sun. In the course of a year, a single square yard of ground in a sunny part of the world receives over 2,000 kilowatt hours of light energy. If all this energy could be collected and converted into electricity, it would be enough to keep a kettle boiling non-stop for nearly six weeks. In the natural world a small part of the energy in sunlight is collected by the leaves of plants and used to fuel their growth. Recently, scientists have begun to look at ways in which humans can make use of the energy in light. Solar energy never runs out. It is cheap and non-polluting. However, collecting solar energy and converting it into a useful form is not easy, because at each step a large amount of the energy is lost. Mirrors in solar power stations waste energy when reflecting light, and solar cells can use only certain wavelengths. However, despite these drawbacks it seems certain that in the future solar energy will play a growing part in providing power.

Some green light is reflected

Blue light is absorbed by the leaf

Red light is absorbed by the leaf

Leaf contains chlorophyll

Some green light passes through the leaf

Hydrogen atom

Carbon atom

Oxygen atom

Glucose molecule produced by photosynthesis

PLANTS AND OXYGEN
In 1771 chemist Joseph Priestley (1733-1804) found that animals took in oxygen, but plants seemed to emit it (p. 56). Eight years later Dutch doctor Jan Ingenhousz (1730-1799) investigated those findings and discovered that plants emit oxygen only when light shines on them. Ingenhousz's discovery was important because it showed that sunlight affects the chemical reactions that take place inside plants.

Jan Ingenhousz

PHOTOSYNTHESIS
When sunlight shines on a leaf, its energy is harnessed through a process called photosynthesis. This begins when chlorophyll, a chemical in the leaf's cells, traps the energy in sunlight. Chlorophyll passes this energy to other substances, and it is used to power a series of chemical reactions. During the day plants take in more carbon dioxide from the air than they give out. The energy from chlorophyll joins carbon dioxide with atoms of hydrogen to make a sugar called glucose. Glucose is an energy supply used for growth and a source of building materials for the walls of plant cells.

Solar cell panel used to power solar car

DRIVEN BY LIGHT
The Solar Flair is an experimental solar-powered car that can run at speeds of up to 40 mph (65 kph). Its streamlined body is made from a lightweight sandwich of aluminum honeycomb with a carbon-fiber composite material. It has nearly 900 solar cells arranged in panels on the top and rear of the car. The cells collect the energy in sunlight and convert it to electricity, which drives a special motor. In bright sunlight the cells can produce just over 1 kilowatt of power, or about 1.3 horsepower. (By comparison, the engine of a gasoline-driven car may produce over 100 horsepower.) Solar cars are still in their early days, and they may never be a practical proposition. However, many low-power devices, from telephones and calculators, work effectively on energy from the sun.

SOLAR CELLS
The cells that power the experimental solar car, Solar Flair, have no moving parts, so they need very little maintenance. Each one produces the same voltage as a flashlight battery. The cells are linked together in a line so that the small voltages add together to make a much bigger voltage.

When the light source is overhead, seedlings grow straight up

Cress seedlings

Motor

TURNED BY THE SUN
This small electric motor is driven by light energy falling on a solar cell. Solar cells work as a result of the photoelectric effect. Instead of pushing electrons out of a metal, light falling on a solar cell is used to loosen electrons within a "semiconductor," usually silicon. The light energy arrives at the cell in packets, or photons, and these dislodge electrons within the silicon to create the current. The voltage produced across the cell depends on the wavelength of light that it uses. Green light gives electrons the same energy as a 2-volt battery. However, most solar cells are designed to work with light of longer wavelengths. Although they produce a lower voltage, they waste less of the light energy.

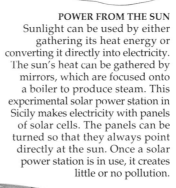

Solar cell

TURNING TO THE LIGHT
A plant cannot "see" sunlight, but it can grow toward it. If light shines on a plant from one side, that side of the plant's stem grows slowly, while the side away from the light grows more quickly. As a result, the stem bends. The cress seedlings here are growing toward the light. Together with some kinds of bacteria, plants are the only living things that can directly harness the energy of light. Animals obtain their energy by either eating plants or eating the animals that feed on plants.

When the source of light is to one side, the stems bend toward the light

POWER FROM THE SUN
Sunlight can be used by either gathering its heat energy or converting it directly into electricity. The sun's heat can be gathered by mirrors, which are focused onto a boiler to produce steam. This experimental solar power station in Sicily makes electricity with panels of solar cells. The panels can be turned so that they always point directly at the sun. Once a solar power station is in use, it creates little or no pollution.

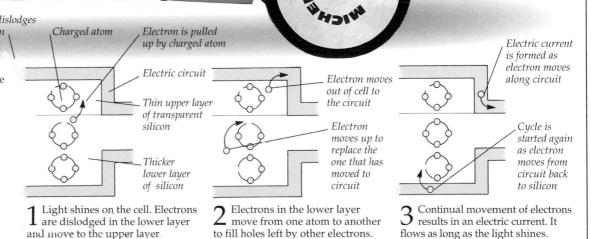

HOW SOLAR CELLS WORK
Solar cells contain two layers of silicon – the substance used to make computer microchips. Some atoms on the upper layer of silicon have an extra electron, while some in the lower layer are missing an electron. This causes electrons to move from the upper to the lower layer – creating an imbalance, or electric charge, in the atoms. So when light then strikes the cell, electrons in the lower layer are dislodged. These are then pulled into the upper layer by the electric charge, producing a current.

Light dislodges electron

Charged atom

Electron is pulled up by charged atom

Electric circuit

Thin upper layer of transparent silicon

Thicker lower layer of silicon

Electron moves out of cell to the circuit

Electron moves up to replace the one that has moved to circuit

Electric current is formed as electron moves along circuit

Cycle is started again as electron moves from circuit back to silicon

1 Light shines on the cell. Electrons are dislodged in the lower layer and move to the upper layer.

2 Electrons in the lower layer move from one atom to another to fill holes left by other electrons.

3 Continual movement of electrons results in an electric current. It flows as long as the light shines.

Electric light

ELECTRIC BIRTHDAY
This illustration from an early 20th-century advertisement shows an unusual use for electric lighting.

THE HISTORY OF practical electric lighting began in the early 1800s with the arc lamp. In this device, an electric current was made to jump across a small gap between two carbon rods. The light from arc lamps was much brighter than that from candles or gaslights, but arc lamps were difficult to install and were a fire hazard. In the mid 1870s the search began for ways to make a safe and reliable low-voltage electric light. Today, two men are credited with success in this venture. At practically the same time, Thomas Edison and Joseph Swan independently produced a new and different kind of lamp – the electric light bulb.

Lights for all uses

Modern electric lamps produce light in three different ways. A normal light bulb works by "incandescence" – it glows because an electric current heats up its filament. In a fluorescent lamp the electric current flows through a gas that is under low pressure. The gas gives off ultraviolet light, and this strikes a phosphor coating, making it fluoresce and produce visible light. A vapor lamp contains a gas under low pressure, but the gas glows with visible light when electricity passes through it. The color of the light depends on the type of gas.

SWAN'S LAMP
Joseph Swan demonstrated his lamp in Britain in February 1879. It had a carbon filament, which glowed when a current flowed through it. The glass "bulb" contained a partial vacuum. There was so little oxygen in the bulb that the filament could get very hot without catching fire.

Partial vacuum

Carbon filament made from a specially treated thread

Partial vacuum

Filament made of a single loop of carbon

Edison's lamp

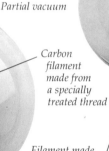

Joseph Wilson Swan
(1828-1914)

Swan's lamp

DAYLIGHT BULB
This filament bulb is designed to imitate natural daylight. Its light is actually made up of a broad mixture of colors, just like light from the sun. In this light, the colored walls around the bulb appear as they would in daylight.

THE GEISSLER TUBE
In the mid 1850s Johann Heinrich Wilhelm Geissler made tubes that contained gases at low pressure. It was known that passing electricity through them caused a colored glow. These tubes were the forerunners of today's streetlights and neon signs.

Electricity enters here

Partial vacuum

Light is produced between electrodes when electric current is switched on

Electrode   *Electrode*

Electricity passes through here

EDISON'S LAMP
This lamp made by Thomas Edison (1847-1931) was demonstrated in the United States in October 1879, and it went into commercial production in November 1880. It had reduced oxygen to keep the filament from burning. It quickly became popular. Some hotels had to remind guests they did not need matches to light the new lamps.

Art gallery lit with Edison lamps

MERCURY LAMP (left)
A mercury vapor lamp makes the left wall look blue, but the right turns a blue-gray. This is because the light contains no red, so the right wall cannot reflect it. The light does contain some yellow, so the bottom wall still reflects a bit of this color.

STANDARD LIGHT BULB (below)
An ordinary light bulb contains about 20 in (50 cm) of coiled tungsten filament surrounded by inert gases, such as argon, at low pressure. The filament emits a yellowish-white light. Only about 8 percent of the electrical energy is converted to light.

LOW-PRESSURE SODIUM LAMP (above)
This kind of lamp is also used for street lighting. It contains a small amount of sodium, which takes a few minutes to vaporize when the lamp is switched on. The colors around this lamp show that its light is an almost pure yellow.

HIGH-PRESSURE SODIUM LAMP (left)
These are used for street lighting in cities. They contain sodium and aluminum, which combine to make pinkish-blue light. This gives most objects a similar color as daylight. These lamps are quite efficient at converting electricity to light.

Total internal reflection

WHEN YOU LOOK INTO A MIRROR, you always see a reflection. This shows that the mirror reflects light rays arriving from all angles. But light can also be reflected in another way. In total internal reflection, light is reflected from some angles but not others. To understand this, think of a diver working underwater at night equipped with a powerful flashlight. The water's surface above is perfectly calm. If the diver points the flashlight straight up, the beam will shine out of the water and vertically into the air. If the flashlight is turned slightly to one side, the beam will no longer hit the surface at right angles. It will still shine into the air, but this time refraction will bend it so that the light makes a smaller angle to the water's surface. If the diver keeps slanting the beam down, it will meet the surface at a smaller and smaller angle. Refraction will bend it further and further. Eventually, the emerging light will be bent so far that it will be parallel to the water's surface. At this point the water's "critical angle" will be reached. If the flashlight is turned a little more, refraction stops altogether, and the water's surface becomes a mirror. Instead of letting the light out, it reflects it back down again. This is the principle behind fiber optics.

Internal reflection works around even gradual bends

Light ray

Prism focuses the light

The light rays are internally reflected if they hit the sides of the bar at a shallow angle

TRAPPING LIGHT
Here a beam of light is reflected by a bar of clear plastic. The reflection is "total" because little or no light escapes from the bar during each reflection. It is "internal" because the all the reflections take place inside the bar. This kind of reflection happens only under particular conditions. The light must be traveling inside a medium with a high refractive index, such as water, glass, or plastic. This must be surrounded by a medium with a lower refractive index, such as air. The light must also hit the boundary between the two at a shallow angle.

No light escapes when the beam is reflected

Tip of endoscope, which goes inside body

Depth scale shows how far endoscope has traveled into the body

Light source is attached here

Operator looks through eyepiece

SEEING INSIDE
An endoscope is a device used by doctors to look inside the body. It is made out of a bundle of fiber optics and control wires. One set of fibers conducts light from the light source to the tip of the endoscope, illuminating the surrounding organs. Another set of fibers conducts light back to the eyepiece, so that the operator can see an image. The control wires make the tip of the endoscope twist or turn, so it can be guided to different places in the body.

Dials for operating control wires that move the tip of the endoscope

The light rays travel through the end of the bar because they strike it at a steep angle

THE VIEW INSIDE
The view of an artery through an endoscope is made out of small points of light from the separate fibers. These build up an image in the same way that an image is formed by an insect's eye.

Beads reflect light back to its source

Eyepiece lens

Two prisms reflect light internally four times, during each reflection, the light changes direction by 90°

SEEING THE WAY

A reflecting cat's eye uses total internal reflection to bounce light back toward oncoming cars, showing the way ahead. Many road signs shine brightly in car headlights because they are covered with tiny transparent beads. The beads reflect light in the direction from which it comes.

Objective lens

PRISMS AS MIRRORS

Binoculars and cameras often use specially shaped prisms to reflect light. In binoculars, there are two pairs of prisms. Light is reflected four times as it passes from the objective lens to the eyepiece lens. The prisms turn the image so that it is the right way around, and also the right way up. Because the light goes backward and forward, binoculars can be made shorter than telescopes.

Needle

Single optical fiber

CARRYING A MESSAGE

When someone speaks through a telephone, the voice is converted into a form of energy that can be sent from one place to another. Before fiber optics, the form of energy was always electricity.

FIBER OPTICS

A fiber optic cable, or light pipe, is like a very long, thin version of the bar on the opposite page. When light shines through one end of the fiber, it bounces off the fiber's inside surface until it emerges at the other end – even if this is many miles distant. Fiber optics can carry signals in the form of pulses of light, just as wires can carry signals as pulses of electricity. The fibers are made from exceptionally pure glass, stretched until it is about about 0.02 in (0.5 mm) in diameter.

OLD AND NEW

Below are two telephone cables. The large, old-fashioned cable transmits signals in the form of electricity, and despite its size it can carry only a few dozen telephone calls at once. The tiny fiber optic cable transmits signals in the form of light, and it can carry over 1,000 calls at once.

Fiber optic cable

Reflected light emerges at the end of the cable

EARLY FIBER OPTICS

This experimental cable contains two optical fibers. Each one has a glass core that is surrounded by an overlay of resin. The resin has a lower refractive index than the glass. Optical fibers can reflect light of all wavelengths. Short-wavelength light can carry the most information, but longer wavelength light is less affected by Rayleigh scattering in the glass.

Copper cable carries signals

Protective metal casing

Insulation for cables

Laser light

THE LIGHT THAT WE SEE IS USUALLY a mixture of many different wavelengths, or colors. Because atoms normally give off light at random, the light waves that they produce are also out of step. These two factors mean that ordinary light is a mixture of many different types of waves. But laser light is different. Instead of containing many wavelengths, it contains just one. Not only this, but the waves are also "coherent," meaning that they are all exactly in step with one another. Laser light is made by feeding energy into a solid, liquid, or gas. As the substance takes in energy, its atoms start to release light of a particular wavelength. When light from one atom strikes its neighbors more light is released, and this chain reaction continues until many atoms are emitting light all at the same time. This light is reflected by special mirrors so that it surges backward and forward within the laser. Eventually the light becomes so intense that some of it passes through one of the mirrors and forms a laser beam.

THE FIRST LASER
The word laser stands for "Light Amplification by Stimulated Emission of Radiation." The first working laser was built in 1960 by Theodore Maiman, shown here pouring coolant into an early experimental model. It was built around a cylinder of synthetic ruby, surrounded by a spiral lamp. Maiman's laser was only a few inches long, but it worked very successfully. Since Maiman made his laser, many different uses have been found for its intense and organized light.

HELIUM-NEON LASER
This laser makes light by feeding an electric current through a tube containing helium and neon gases. The energy is passed to the helium atoms, which collide with the neon atoms – making them produce light. At the ends of the tube are two mirrors. One reflects light, but the other lets a small amount through so that the laser beam can emerge.

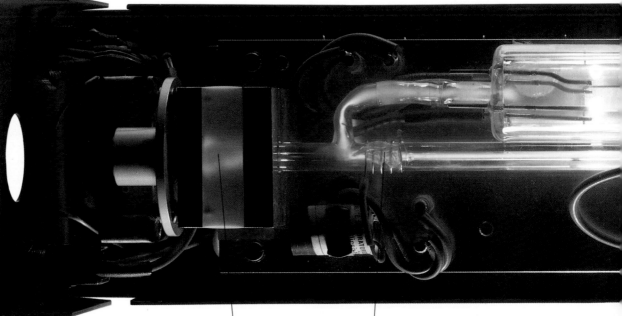

Power supply "excites" the light-producing substance

Laser light is reflected by the fully silvered mirror

Electrodes are the power supply producing a continuous electric discharge through the gas mixture

HOW LASER LIGHT WORKS
To make a laser beam, many atoms or molecules must be "excited" – given enough energy so that they reach high-energy states. They can then release light, which bounces back and forth in the light-producing substance. The intensity of the beam rises every time light travels from one end of the substance to another. The light escapes through a hole in one mirror, or through a mirror that lets through a small amount of light.

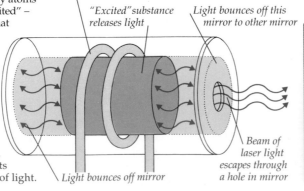

"Excited" substance releases light

Light bounces off this mirror to other mirror

Beam of laser light escapes through a hole in mirror

Light bounces off mirror

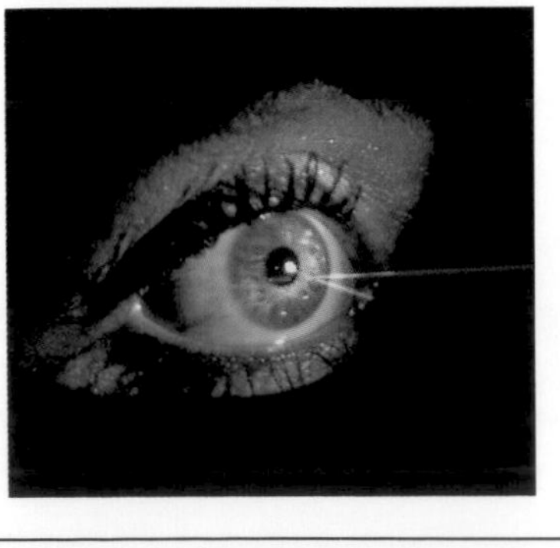

LIFESAVERS
If part of the eye's retina comes loose, the eye can no longer see clearly. A helium-neon laser beam can be shone through the pupil to weld the retina back in position. Laser beams are used by surgeons to cut or weld other parts of the body with great accuracy.

RUBY LASER
This ruby laser was made in the mid 1960s. It contains a long rod of synthetic ruby, which lies next to a lamp when the unit is closed and ready for use. The mirror like surface on the inside of the laser ensures that the ruby is bombarded with as much light as possible. The light produces a large amount of heat, so some lasers have a built-in water cooling system. Ruby lasers produce red light with a wavelength of about 695 nm.

Laser beam emerges through end of ruby rod

Rod of synthetic ruby

Laser light is produced by chromium atoms within the ruby

Reflecting surface

High-intensity lamp

Tube containing helium and neon at low pressure

DEADLY LIGHT
At one time deadly rays of light were no more than science fiction – in the 1958 film, *Colossus of New York*, a monster with the brain of a dead scientist emitted lethal light rays from his eyes. But with the invention of the laser, it really is possible to make a beam of light that can destroy objects at great distances. Unlike ordinary light, a laser beam does not spread out, so it can be aimed very precisely.

Most of the light is reflected by the semi-silvered mirror, but a small amount passes straight through and emerges as the laser beam

The narrow red laser beam consists of coherent light with a wavelength of about 694 nm

MADE TO MEASURE
Laser beams always follow a straight line, so they are often used in engineering projects, such as tunneling, to ensure the work is following the right course. Laser light can also be used to measure very small distances. This is done by using the interference that is produced when a laser beam is split and then reflected back by different surfaces. By then analyzing interference fringes, the distance between two objects can be calculated very accurately.

CUTTING WITH LIGHT
Long-wavelength lasers can be directed onto a surface to produce intense heat in a very small area. This heat can cut through materials of all kinds, from fabrics for clothing to steel plates used for building cars. Laser heat can also be used in spot welding, when two pieces of metal are glued together by making them melt. One advantage of a laser beam is that it does not become blunt like ordinary cutting tools, which must be sharpened or replaced.

Holograms

A PHOTOGRAPH RECORDS the intensity of light that falls on film. It is made by one set of light waves, and the image that the light waves form is flat, or two-dimensional. A hologram is different. It is taken in laser light, and instead of being made by one set of light waves it is made by two. One set of waves is reflected onto the film by the object, just as ordinary light waves are in a photograph. The other set of waves arrive at the film from a different direction without meeting the object at all. Where the two sets of waves meet each other, they produce interference fringes that are recorded in the film. When the hologram is viewed, these interference fringes produce a three-dimensional image.

THEORY AND PRACTICE
Dennis Gabor (1900-1979), shown here in a transmission hologram, outlined the principle of holography in 1948. He realized that a beam of light could be split to produce a three-dimensional image. But Gabor's holography needed a source of light waves that were "coherent," or in step. This did not appear until 1960 with the invention of the laser. In 1962 the first successful hologram was made by two Americans, Juris Upatnieks and Emmet Leith.

Transmission holograms

Transmission holograms are viewed in laser light. The diagram below shows how a transmission hologram is made by splitting laser light to form two separate beams. All of the equipment that is used (right) is mounted on a special heavy table. This prevents vibrations that could blur the interference fringes on the film.

Helium-neon laser fires a beam at the beam splitter

HELIUM-NEON LASER
This laser produces a narrow beam of red light that shines for several minutes to expose the holographic film.

Semi-silvered mirror splits laser beam in two

Knob used to adjust height of lens

Lens focuses beam on mirror

BEAM SPLITTER
The beam splitter divides the beam in two, keeping the two sets of light waves in step with each other. It is either a semi-silvered mirror or a glass prism.

LENS
Two identical lenses are used to make the narrow laser beams diverge, or spread out. The lenses must keep the two sets of light waves "in phase," or exactly in step with each other.

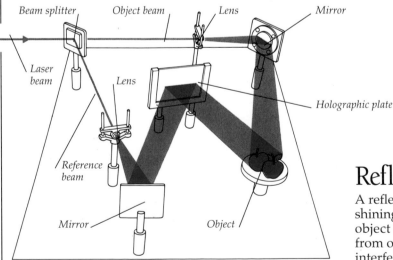

Beam splitter   *Object beam*   *Lens*   *Mirror*

Laser beam

Lens

Holographic plate

Reference beam

Mirror

Object

LIGHT PATH IN TRANSMISSION HOLOGRAPHY
The laser beam is split. The "object" beam passes through a lens and is reflected onto the object. Its light then shines onto the holographic plate, coated with photographic emulsion. The "reference" beam passes through a lens and is reflected onto the emulsion, where it meets light from the object beam and produces interference fringes.

Reflection holograms

A reflection hologram is made by shining a reference beam and an object beam onto a thick film from opposite sides. The beams interfere to produce tiny areas of light and dark throughout the film. When the hologram is viewed, this pattern reflects light in a way that produces a three-dimensional image.

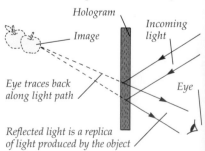

Viewing a reflection hologram

Hologram

Image

Incoming light

Eye traces back along light path

Eye

Reflected light is a replica of light produced by the object

MAKING A TRANSMISSION HOLOGRAM

A transmission hologram is made by two sets of laser waves that strike the same side of a special photographic emulsion. One set of waves is produced by the object beam, which here illuminates two apples. The apples reflect the waves, scattering them in the same way that they would scatter waves of ordinary daylight. The scattered waves spread outward from the apples until they reach the emulsion. At the same time, the waves from the reference beam also reach the emulsion. The two sets of waves then interfere with each other. Where two waves are in step, they produce a point of bright light. Where they are exactly out of step, they produce darkness. The emulsion records the pattern of light and darkness that interference creates.

Scattered waves of object beam

Regular waves of reference beam

Object

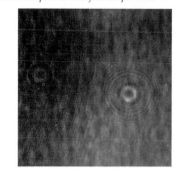

Glass plate covered with photographic emulsion captures interference patterns

Holographic mirror reflects light on to object or holographic plate

INTERFERENCE PATTERNS
The interference patterns in a transmission hologram are made of microscopic light and dark areas. They form an image only when the hologram is viewed in front of laser light of the correct wavelength.

Object to be shown in hologram

VIEWING A TRANSMISSION HOLOGRAM

Seen by daylight, a transmission hologram looks blank because the interference fringes on it are far too small to be seen. But if the hologram is illuminated by the reference beam, an image appears. This happens because the interference fringes in the film affect the laser light. They interfere with the laser beam in a way that "reconstructs" the original waves of light that were scattered by the apples. The reconstructed waves are exactly the same as those that would have been produced by the apples if the hologram was not there. The result is a three-dimensional image – one that changes according to the angle from which it is viewed.

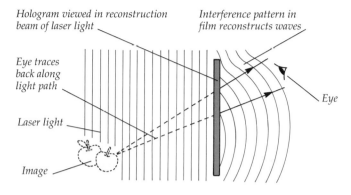

Hologram viewed in reconstruction beam of laser light

Interference pattern in film reconstructs waves

Eye traces back along light path

Laser light

Eye

Image

Glass plate covered with photographic emulsion

MIRROR
Two mirrors are used to bring the beams together so they interfere. The silvering on each mirror lies on the surface. This ensures that the beams are not refracted by traveling through the glass.

OBJECT
The object sits in a heavy plinth that helps prevent vibration. Most holograms need a long exposure time, so it is essential that the object keeps completely still.

HOLOGRAPHIC PLATE
The "film" in a transmission hologram is usually a glass plate coated with a special photographic emulsion. It has a fine grain used to record interference fringes that are far too small to be seen with the naked eye.

SECURITY HOLOGRAMS
Unlike transmission holograms, reflection holograms can be used in daylight. They are often used on credit cards to prevent forgery. They show color images, produced using laser light of the three primary colors. Each laser wavelength produces its own interference pattern, and the patterns add together to give a color image. These holograms are almost impossible to copy, so they are a valuable security device.

HEAD-UP DISPLAY
In a traditional aircraft cockpit the pilot can either look out of the windows or down at the controls. With a "heads-up display," the pilot can look at both at the same time. A three-dimensional transmission hologram is made, and reflected by the cockpit window. Here it is used in a fighter plane to show the target.

The speed of light

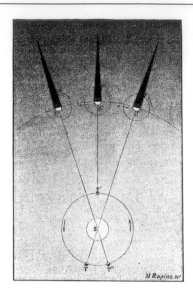

IN ANCIENT TIMES most people thought that the speed of light was infinite. Once the scientific study of light began, opinions slowly changed. Alhazen (p. 12) thought that light traveled very rapidly but still had a definite speed. The first estimate of the speed of light was made in 1675 by a Danish astronomer, Ole Roemer. Roemer had been watching the movement of Jupiter's moons, and he had noticed that the times they appeared and vanished seemed to vary throughout the year. He guessed that this was because the distance from the earth to Jupiter changed during a yearly cycle, and that so did the distance that the light had to travel. By some simple mathematics, Roemer estimated the speed of light to be about 137,000 miles (220,000 km) per second. The first land-based estimate was not made until 1849, by Armand Fizeau. Fizeau's figure, and the one calculated a year later by Léon Foucault, showed that Roemer's estimate was too low. Today, the speed of light in a vacuum is known to be almost exactly 186,000 miles (300,000 km) per second.

TIMING LIGHT ON LAND
Armand Fizeau (1819-1896) timed a beam of light as it flashed at a mirror about 5½ miles (9 km) away and was reflected back again. He timed it with a toothed wheel that turned very quickly. On its outward journey, the light passed through a gap between two of the wheel's teeth. If the wheel was turning fast enough, the light could pass through the neighboring gap on its return journey. By knowing the wheel's speed, Fizeau could calculate the speed of light.

Light passes through window with graduated scale

Glass plate reflects the returning beam into the microscope

Rotating toothed wheel is used to calculate the speed of the rotating mirror

Light enters through hole

Foucault's speed of light experiment

The shift of the light beam is measured by observing the image of the graduated scale through the microscope

The glass plate and microscope are mounted on a trolley so the distance the light travels can be adjusted

Stationary concave mirrors reflect the light in a zig-zag path

THE MOONS OF JUPITER
Jupiter is the biggest planet in the solar system, and it has at least 16 moons. As each of these moons travels around the giant planet, it moves in and out of "eclipse." This was first noted by Galileo, and it was used by Roemer to determine the speed of light. This photograph, taken in 1979 by the Voyager 1 spacecraft, shows two of the "Galilean" moons Io (in front of the planet) and Europa (to the right).

1 second

Speed of light in a vacuum 186,000 miles (300,000 km) per second; refractive index of air 1

Speed of light in water 140,000 miles (225,000 km) per second; refractive index of water 1.3

Speed of light in glass 124,000 miles (200,000 km) per second; refractive index of glass 1.5

Speed of light in diamond 77,500 miles (125,000 km) per second; refractive index of diamond 2.4

THE VARYING SPEED OF LIGHT
Armand Fizeau's method of calculating the speed of light relied on a very long light path to give an accurate result. For this reason it could be used only in air. In Foucault's method, shown below, the light path was much shorter. This allowed Foucault to test the speed of light in transparent substances other than air. He found that light's speed in water or glass was only about two-thirds of its speed in air. He also discovered that the speed of light was related to the substance's refractive index. The more the substance bent light, the slower the light traveled. This finding was exactly what the wave theory of light had predicted.

FOUCAULT'S SPINNING MIRROR *(below)*
Léon Foucault, who worked with Fizeau, devised a way of measuring the speed of light that used a spinning mirror. In his experiment a beam of light passed through a graduated scale and then struck the spinning mirror. The spinning mirror reflected the light to a series of stationary mirrors, which made the beam follow a zig-zag path. By the time the light had completed this journey and returned to the spinning mirror, the mirror had turned very slightly. It reflected the beam back toward its source, but along a slightly different path. Foucault's apparatus was arranged so that this tiny shift in the light path could be seen and measured. Foucault knew the distance that the light had travelled and the speed of the mirror. By combining these with the shift, he obtained a figure of about 185,000 miles (298,000 km) per second for light traveling in air.

A lens focuses the light on the spinning mirror

The mirror is turned at high speed by a compressed air turbine

LEON FOUCAULT
Léon Foucault (1819-1868) calculated the speed of light in air and water. He also invented the gyroscope and used the movement of a giant pendulum to demonstrate that the earth is rotating (p. 353).

(p. 353)

Stationary concave mirrors reflect the light in a zig-zag path

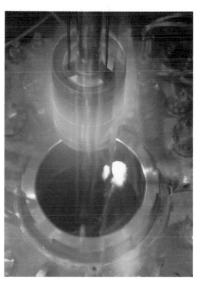

FASTER THAN LIGHT
Albert Einstein showed that nothing can move faster than light in a vacuum. But when light travels through a transparent substance it moves more slowly than it does in a vacuum. In these conditions, other things can sometimes overtake it. This photograph shows a rod of nuclear fuel in a pool of water. The fuel rod (center top) is surrounded by a blue glow called "Cherenkov radiation." The glow is caused by the slowing of high-energy particles, which travel through water faster than light.

Path of light in Foucault's experiment

DOUBLING BACK
In Foucault's experiment the light beam was shone through a graduated scale. It passed straight through a glass plate angled at 45° to the light beam. On the return journey the glass plate acted as a mirror and reflected the beam into a microscope. Here the image of the scale could be seen in the beam, and its sideways shift measured. Foucault's apparatus also included a toothed wheel, which was used for checking the speed of the mirror.

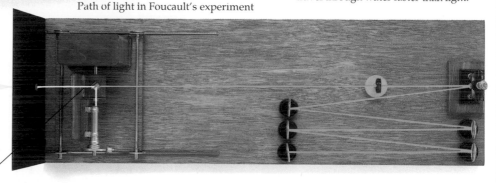

The total length of the light path is about 66 ft (20 m)

Light in space

DURING THE 19TH century most scientists thought "empty" space was not actually empty at all. Like Christian Huygens (p. 100), they believed it was filled with a substance called the "luminiferous ether." They thought light waves moved through the ether, as did the stars and planets. According to this theory the ether was invisible, frictionless, and absolutely still. In 1987 two American physicists, Albert Michelson and Edward Morley, tried to use interference to find out how fast the earth moved through the ether. But despite many attempts they were unable to detect any movement. In 1905 this perplexing result was explained by Albert Einstein in his Special Theory of Relativity. Einstein believed that all movement was relative. There could be no such thing as absolute movement, because there was nothing absolutely still to measure it against. His theory spelled the end for the ether, and today scientists believe that light can travel through nothingness itself.

LIGHT FROM ABOVE
In medieval times, people thought that the stars were fixed in the sky, and that the earth was the center of the universe. With the development of astronomy, it became clear that the stars were much farther away than was first thought. Today, measurement of starlight using spectroscopes shows that most galaxies (large groups of stars) are moving away from us at great speed.

Microscope used to view interference fringes on the semi-silvered mirror

Mirrors to reflect light beams

Adjustable mirror for altering length of light path

The Michelson–Morley experiment

The principle behind this experiment is simple. A beam of light is split in two, and the two beams are made to travel at right angles to each other by a set of mirrors. If the earth is moving through the ether, whichever beam is traveling back and forth across the flow of ether will have farther to go. This means that the waves in the two beams should become slightly out of step. When the two beams are brought together again, this should produce interference fringes. The faster the earth moves, the more out of step the waves should be. This is what the experiment was expected to show. Michelson and Morley designed the apparatus to ensure that the tiniest difference between the two sets of waves would produce a noticeable result.

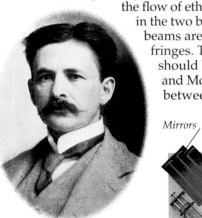

ALBERT MICHELSON
With Edward Morley (1838-1923), Albert Michelson (1852-1931) tried to use interference to investigate earth's movement in space.

A WEB OF LIGHT
In the Michelson–Morley experiment the light beams were shone back and forth on a slowly, steadily turning slab. The beam was first split in two by a semi-silvered mirror. The two beams were then reflected by mirrors and joined again. The light could then be examined through a microscope. As the slab turned, the observer could check to see if interference fringes were visible. None were ever seen.

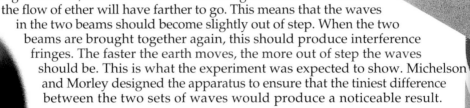
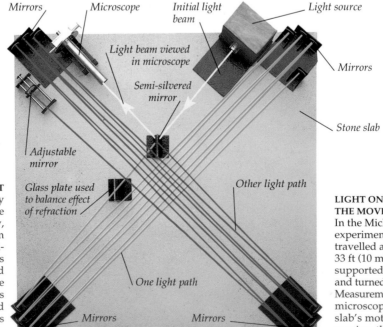

Mirrors   *Microscope*   *Initial light beam*   *Light source*

Light beam viewed in microscope

Mirrors

Semi-silvered mirror

Adjustable mirror

Stone slab

Glass plate used to balance effect of refraction

Other light path

One light path

Mirrors   *Mirrors*

LIGHT ON THE MOVE *(right)*
In the Michelson–Morley experiment the light beam travelled a distance of over 33 ft (10 m). The stone slab that supported the apparatus was 5 sq ft (1.5 sq m) and turned about once every 6 minutes. Measurements were taken by using the moving microscope. The pool of mercury made the slab's motion almost frictionless, so, once moving, the slab took hours to come to a halt.

SHIFTING LIGHT

In 1842 Christian Doppler (1803-1853) explained why a sound seems higher when its source is approaching than when it is moving away. He realized that the sound and light waves from an approaching source are "compressed," giving them a higher pitch or frequency. while sound waves from a receding object are "stretched," giving them a lower pitch. In 1848 Armand Fizeau predicted the change in the spectrum of stars traveling towards and away from the earth. Astronomers have since seen that the light from many stars is shifted towards the red end of the spectrum. This "red shift" shows that they are moving away from us.

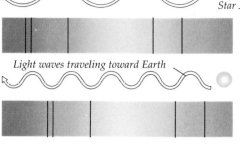

Star — *Direction of star's movement*

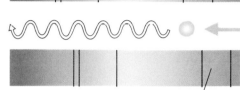

Light waves traveling toward Earth

Spectrum of star's light with spectral lines

RECEDING
Light from a star moving away from earth is shifted toward the red end of the spectrum. The position of the star's spectral lines indicates how fast it is receding.

STANDING STILL
This spectrum is formed by light from a star that is stationary relative to the earth. It shows no shift in either direction.

APPROACHING
Light from a star approaching earth is shifted towards the blue end of the spectrum. Again, the spectral lines indicate how fast the star is moving.

— *Light source*

— *Mirrors to reflect light beams*

— *Semi-silvered mirror*

— *Glass plate used to balance the effect of refraction in the other beam of light*

Mirrors to reflect light beam

— *Mirrors to reflect light beams*

Heavy block of stone over 5 ft (1.5 m) square and 14 in (35 cm) thick

LIGHT AND GRAVITY

According to Einstein's General Theory of Relativity (see below), light can be bent not only by refraction, but also by the force of gravity. If this is true, a massive object such as the sun should bend light rays that pass near it. In 1919 this was tested by simultaneous observations of a solar eclipse in two different parts of the world. The stars around the sun seemed to have shifted position, much as Einstein predicted. Today astronomers are searching the skies for whole galaxies that might act as "gravitational lenses." Because galaxies are vastly more massive than the sun, they should bend light rays farther.

Light rays traveling to earth   *Virtual image of star*

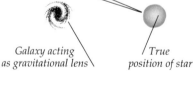

Observer sees virtual image of hidden star   *Galaxy acting as gravitational lens*   *True position of star*

A PUZZLE ANSWERED

Albert Einstein (1879-1955) is remembered for two of the most important theories in modern physics – the Special Theory of Relativity of 1905, and the General Theory of Relativity of 1915. The first theory investigated steady movement at very high speeds; the second examined acceleration and its links with gravity. These theories revolutionized physics because they challenged beliefs held by scientists such as Newton. Before Einstein published his ideas, physicists thought of motion or time as being "absolute" – existing independently of anything else. Einstein stated that both are "relative," meaning they can be measured only in relation to an object – for example, to the earth as it moves through space. Einstein's thinking affected all physics but had particular importance in the study of light. It explained why the Michelson–Morley experiment produced no results. It also showed that nothing can move faster than light in a vacuum, and that the speed of light in a vacuum is always the same.

Wooden float rotates in a trough filled with mercury, which prevents vibrations from reaching the stone block

Ring-shaped wooden float supporting stone block

Solid brick base

Open and shut mold for making apothecaries' vials (19th century)

Metals produced by electrolysis (mid 19th century)

Crookes's thallium compounds and notebook (1860s)

Measuring cylinder (19th century)

Model of adenovirus (20th century)

Ammonium dichromate crystals

Bunsen burner (19th century)

Graphite

Roman coins
(2nd century)

Boxes of chemicals
(19th century)

MATTER

Tyndall's boiling
point apparatus
(1880s)

Tongs and calcium
oxide powder

Heating limestone
(calcium carbonate)

What is matter?

Everything found everywhere in the universe – from the farthest star to the smallest speck of dust – is made of matter in an incredible variety of forms. About 200 years ago heat was regarded by many scientists as being a special sort of matter. But now it is known that heat is simply the motion of tiny particles of matter (p. 164). Sound, too, is a certain type of movement of matter. Forms of energy such as radiation (for example, light, radio waves, and X-rays) are generally regarded as not being matter, though they are very closely linked to it. All the different kinds of matter have one thing in common – mass. This is the amount of material in any object, and shows itself as resistance to being moved. A truck, for example, has more mass and is much harder to move than a toy car. Every piece of matter in the universe attracts every other piece of matter. The amount of matter is important – a large piece attracts other matter more strongly than a small piece.

A CONTAINED UNIVERSE
This terrarium is a microcosm of the living world. It contains the three states of matter - solids, liquids, and gases, as well as interesting substances found in the world of matter.

THE LIVING WORLD
All living matter can organize itself into intricate forms and behave in complicated ways. It was once thought that matter in living things was controlled by a "vital principle," a sort of ghostly force. But now scientists think that living and nonliving matter obey the same laws.

Plants grow upward to reach the light

MIXING AND SEPARATING MATTER
Gravel, sand, and water can be made into a mixture, and can easily be separated afterwards. Each of these materials is made of other substances that are more strongly combined and very hard to separate. Water, for example, is a combination of the gases hydrogen and oxygen. Such a close combination is called a chemical compound.

A mixture of gravel, sand, and water

METALLIC MATTER
Metals are found in rocks called ores. Pure metals are rare, and usually they have to be separated from their ores. Once separated, they are often combined with other materials to form alloys – mixtures of metals and other substances.

Lead is a metal which looks solid, but flows extremely slowly over decades

SOLUTIONS AND COLLOIDS

Substances can often dissolve in a liquid or solid. They form solutions – they are mixed very thoroughly with the liquid or solid, breaking up into groups of a few atoms, or even into single atoms (these are the smallest normally existing particles of matter). A colloid consists of larger particles of matter that are suspended in a solid, liquid, or gas.

Glass is transparent matter

THE WORLD OF GASES

When the particles of a substance become separated from each other, the substance becomes a gas. It has no shape of its own, but expands to fill any space available. Air (largely a mixture of nitrogen and oxygen) was the first gas to be recognized. It was many centuries before scientists realized that there are other gases as well as air. This was because gases tend to look similar – they are mostly colorless and transparent.

Condensation is caused by molecules of water vapor cooling and turning into a liquid

This butterfly is made of some of the millions of varieties of living matter on earth

LIQUID MATTER

Liquids, like gases, consist of matter that can flow, but unlike gases, they settle at the bottom of any container. Nearly all substances are liquids at certain temperatures. The most important liquid for living creatures is water. Most of the human body is made up of water. It forms the bulk of human blood, which transports dissolved foodstuffs and waste products around the body.

Water contains dissolved oxygen and carbon dioxide gases from the air

SOLID SHAPES

The metal and glass of this terrarium could not act as a container for plant and animal specimens if they did not keep a constant shape. Matter that keeps a definite shape is called solid. However, most solids will lose their shape if they are heated sufficiently, turning into a liquid or a gas.

Solids such as rock keep a definite shape

Ideas of the Greeks

ANCIENT GREEK PHILOSOPHERS vigorously debated the nature of matter and concluded that behind its apparent complexity the world was really very simple. Thales (about 600 BC) suggested that all matter was made of water. Empedocles (5th century BC) believed that all matter consisted of four basic substances, or elements – earth, water, air, and fire – mixed in various proportions. In the next century Aristotle thought there might be a fifth element – the ether. Leucippus (5th century BC) had another theory that there was just one kind of matter. He thought that if matter was repeatedly cut up, the end result would be an uncuttable piece of matter. His follower Democritus (about 400 BC) called these indivisible pieces of matter "atoms," meaning "uncuttable." But Aristotle, who did not believe in atoms, was the most influential philosopher for the next 2,000 years, and his ideas about elements prevailed.

THE FOUR ELEMENTS IN A LOG
Empedocles's idea of the four elements was linked to certain properties. Earth was dry and cold, water was wet and cold, fire was hot and dry, and air was hot and wet. In the burning log below, all four elements can be seen. Empedocles thought that when one substance changes into another – such as when a burning log gives off smoke, emits sap, and produces ash – the elements that make up the log are separating or recombining under the influence of two forces. These forces were love (the combining force), and hate or discord (the separating force).

Empedocles

Design on the coin has been smoothed away

WEARING SMOOTH
Ancient philosophers thought that when objects such as coins and statues wore smooth with the passing of time they were losing tiny, invisible particles of matter.

MODEL OF WATER
Plato (4th century BC) thought that water was made up of icosahedrons, a solid shape with 20 triangular faces.

LIQUID FROM A LOG
Empedocles believed that all liquids, even thick ones like the sap that oozes from a burning log, were mainly water. His theory also held that small amounts of other elements would always be mixed with the main element.

Sap is made from the element water

Ash and cinders are mainly the element earth

MODEL OF EARTH
Atoms of earth were thought by Plato to be cubes, which can stack tightly together to give strength and solidity.

ELEMENTAL ATOMS
Democritus developed the theory of atoms and combined it with the theory of elements. Like Plato, he thought there were only four shapes of atom, one for each element. He argued against the religious beliefs of his day, claiming that atoms moved randomly, and that there were no gods controlling the universe.

ASHES TO ASHES
The theory of the elements suggested that ash and cinders were mainly made of the element earth, with a little of the element fire. At the end of the burning process, there was not enough fire left for more ash to be produced, but some fire remained for a while in the form of heat. The Greeks thought that the elements earth and water had a natural tendency to fall.

THE FIVE ELEMENTS
The human figure in this engraving is standing on two globes, representing earth and water, and is holding air and fire in his hands. The sun, moon, and stars are made of the ether, the fifth element.

MODEL OF AIR
Plato's model of an air atom was an octahedron, a solid figure with eight faces.

Smoke is mostly air, with some earth in the form of soot mixed in

NO SMOKE WITHOUT FIRE
When a piece of matter is burned, the element air inside was thought to be released in the form of smoke. The Greeks thought that air, like fire, had a natural tendency to rise.

MODEL OF FIRE
According to Plato, the atom of fire was a solid shape with four sides called a tetrahedron.

PENETRATING FLAMES
The element fire could be seen most clearly in flames and sparks, but the Greeks thought that some fire was present in everything. Plato's model of the fire atom is sharp and pointed. This is because heat seemed to be able to penetrate virtually every piece of matter.

Flames and sparks are the element fire

Investigating matter

IDEAS ABOUT MATTER AND HOW IT BEHAVED changed little for hundreds of years. But in Europe during the 16th and 17th centuries "natural philosophers" looked again at the ancient theories about matter. They tested them, together with newer ideas about how matter behaved, by experiments and investigations, and used the newly invented microscope and telescope to look closely at matter. Measurements became more precise. News of discoveries was spread by the printing press. The scientific revolution had begun.

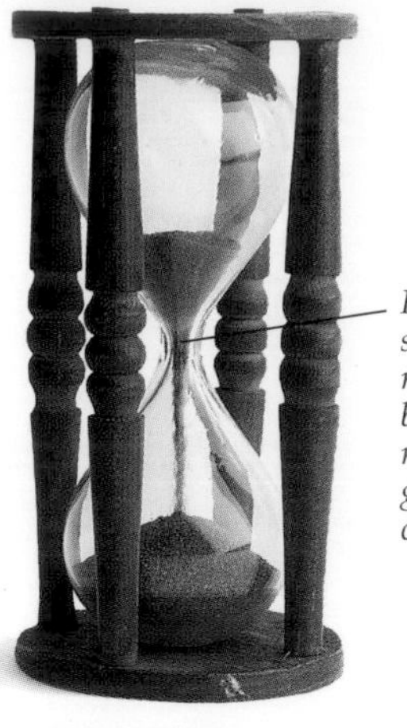

SANDS OF TIME
The sandglass was a simple timing device, which allowed scientists to work out how fast objects fell, or how long it took for chemicals to react. More accurate measurements of time were not possible until after the first pendulum clock was made in 1657.

Flow of sand is regulated by the narrow glass channel

LABORING IN THE LAB
This 17th-century laboratory illustrates just some of the processes used by "natural philosophers" to find out about matter.

Eyepiece

HEATING AND COOLING MATTER
Very early experiments showed the effects of heating or cooling of matter. Philo of Byzantium constructed his lead thermoscope (Greek for "observing heat") about 250 BC. When the globe on the right is warmed, the air inside expands and pushes its way up the tube, which is immersed in the water on the left. If the heat is strong enough, bubbles of air escape. When the globe is cooled, the air contracts and water is drawn back up the tube.

Reconstruction of Philo's thermoscope

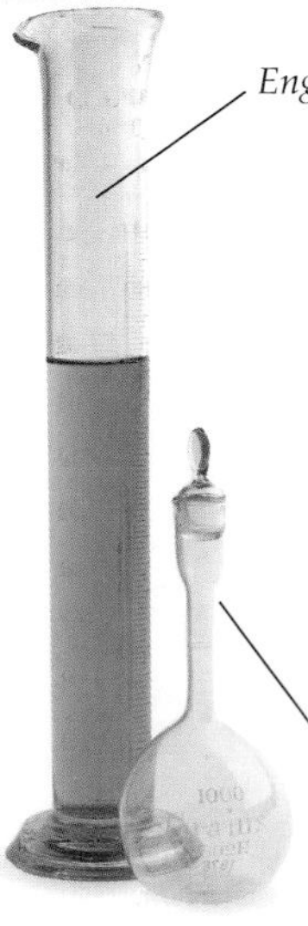

Tiny bubbles of air

Lead globe is full of air

Glass globe contains water

Engraved scale

MARKINGS FOR MEASURING
Scientific investigations often involved measuring the exact amount of a liquid. This tall measuring cylinder has a scale of accurate markings for this purpose, while the specific gravity bottle has just one very accurate marking. When the liquid inside is weighed, its density can be calculated.

Object to be viewed is placed on the glass

Small lens focuses light

Tilting mirror

Single accurate marking

SMALL WONDER
Microscopes began to open up the world of the very small from the mid-1500s onward. In the mid-1600s Anton van Leeuwenhoek found that a single drop of pond water could contain 8 million "animalcules" – tiny but intricately constructed creatures and plants. The more elaborate microscope shown here was made by Edmund Culpeper of London, in about 1728. It used a tilting mirror, visible at the bottom, to reflect light onto a specimen mounted above it on glass.

Enlarged view of a deathwatch beetle

DEGREES OF ACCURACY

As scientists looked closer at matter, they needed ever more accurate ways of measuring what they saw. This thermometer, a device for measuring changes in temperature, was made in Florence, Italy, in the 18th century. The bulb at the bottom contained alcohol, which expanded when it became warmer and moved along the coiled tube. The tube is marked with dots at equal intervals.

Dots are regularly spaced

Bulb of alcohol

NOVA
ATLANTIS
PER
FRANCISCUM BACONUM,
Baronem de Verulamio,
Vice-Comitem S. Albani.

ET FLORES FRUCTUS

VLTRAIECTI.

Apud Ioannem à VVuesberge,
Anno cIↃ IↃ c XLIII.

SCIENTIFIC IMPROVEMENTS

Francis Bacon (1561-1626), the English philosopher, hoped that the new science could increase human well-being. *The New Atlantis* was his 1626 account of an imaginary society, or "utopia," where the government organized teams of scientists to conduct research and use the results to improve industry.

Ivory arm

Brass ring

Pointer indicates equilibrium

Cord fulcrums

Alchemy

Before the scientific revolution of the 17th century, the closest approach to a systematic study of matter was alchemy – the "science" of changing one substance into another. This was studied in Egypt, China, and India at least as early as the 2nd century BC, and from the Middle East it eventually reached Europe. Alchemists learned much from the practical skills of dyers and metalworkers, and borrowed various ideas from astrologers. They tried, without success, to change "base" metals, such as lead, into precious ones, such as silver or gold. This series of operations was described as "killing" the metal and then "reviving" it. Alchemists also attempted to make the elixir of life, a potion that would give them the secret of everlasting life.

QUEST FOR GOLD

Alchemists used all kinds of scientific instruments and chemical processes in their mystical quest for gold. The laboratory above was imagined by a 19th-century painter.

Spoutlike alembic sits on the cucurbit

Alembic and cucurbit

PURE MATTER

Cucurbits and alembics were used by many alchemists to purify liquids. As the cucurbit was heated, vapor from the liquid inside rose to the top, then cooled and condensed. The pure liquid dripped from the alembic and was then collected.

"Fool's gold" – a compound made up of iron and sulfur

HANGING IN THE BALANCE

Scales are one of the most basic of measuring instruments. The weight at the right of these Chinese scales is moved along the longer arm until it balances the object in the pan. This particular method is quick, convenient, and fairly accurate. It was not until the 17th century that chemists realized that accurately weighing the substances involved in a chemical reaction is crucial to understanding what is going on.

Compound counterbalance

Greek lead weight

Solid matter

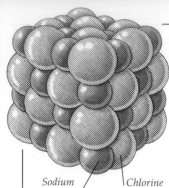

Sodium atom | Chlorine atom

HELD IN PLACE
As in most solids, the atoms (pp. 34-35) in this model of salt hold each other firmly in place, and form a regular pattern.

EVER SINCE PEOPLE began to observe the world carefully, they have classified matter into three main states - solids, liquids, and gases. A piece of solid matter has a fairly definite shape, unlike a liquid or a gas. Changing the shape of a solid always requires a certain amount of force, which can be either large or small. Squeezing or stretching a solid can change its volume (the amount of space it takes up) but generally not by very much. When they are heated, most solids will turn to liquid, then to gas as they reach higher temperatures. However, some solids such as limestone decompose when they are heated. Crystals and metals are two of the most important kinds of solid.

Screw

Gimbal ring keeps the compass level even when the ship is rolling

SOLID STRENGTH
Brass, which is a combination of metals, or an alloy, is made of copper and zinc. It is used for the compass's gimbal ring, mounting ring, and pivot. Brass is strong, so the gimbal ring's mountings will not quickly wear out. Like many metals, brass is not magnetic, and will not interfere with the working of the compass needle.

Mounting ring fixes the compass in its case and holds it under the glass

SOLID PROPERTIES
Like most artificial objects, this 19th-century mariner's compass contains several kinds of solids. The compass has been taken apart on these two pages to reveal four solids – metal, cardboard, wood, and glass. All the solids in the compass have been chosen for their special and varied properties.

Mariner's compass in its protective wooden box

Magnet

Pins are attracted to the ends of the magnet

MAKING MAGNETS
The ancient Chinese are thought to be the first magnet makers. They discovered that iron can be magnetized by making it red-hot and then letting it cool while aligned in a north-south direction.

Hole which rests on pointed pivot

FINDING THE WAY
Beneath the compass card is a magnet, made either of iron or a rock called a lodestone. Magnets attract or repel each other, and also respond to the earth's magnetic poles. They tend to swing into a north-south line if they are free to move. The compass showed the mariner the angle between the direction of the ship and the north-south direction of the magnet.

SIZE AND STRENGTH

Galileo Galilei (1564-1642) studied materials' strength and showed that there is a limit to land animals' size. If the largest dinosaur had doubled in size, its bones would have become larger and stronger. However, the increase in the dinosaur's weight would have been even greater, making its bones snap.

AT FULL STRETCH

Many solids are elastic – after being stretched or squeezed, they return to their original shape. A rubber band, for example, can be stretched to more than double its length and then return to its original length. But if a material is distorted too much its shape may be permanently altered.

Pointed pivot supports the compass

Brass knobs sit in holes in the gimbal ring

Glass flows over hundreds of years

QUALITIES OF WOOD

The protective container of the compass needs to be strong, and to be rigid (keep its shape). Wood has many different qualities – the wood used for this container is fairly hard and long-lasting. Yet it is also soft and light enough to be easily worked with metal tools, and can be carved to form a smooth bowl shape.

SEEING THROUGH THINGS

The top of the compass needs to be transparent and strong. It is made of glass - halfway between a solid and a liquid. Glass may seem rigid, but over hundreds of years it gradually flows and becomes distorted. Most solids block light completely, but the clearest kinds of glass absorb little of the light passing through them.

DIFFERENT VIEWS

Transparent (see-through) materials can give a clear and undistorted view, as in the glass front of a watch. Or they can be deliberately shaped to help give an even clearer view, as in eyeglasses.

Diamond
10

Considerable difference in hardness between diamond and the other minerals on the scale

FROM SOFT TO HARD

Scientists classify solid materials by their hardness, on a scale from one to ten named after Friedrich Mohs (1773-1839). These solids are all minerals (so-called because they are usually mined). Talc is the softest at one, and diamond the hardest at ten. Any solid on the scale will scratch a softer one, and will itself be scratched by a harder one.

Compass direction points

PAPER POINTERS

The compass points are printed on paper or cardboard. Paper is made by pulping up wood and treating it to make it soft and flexible. It consists of countless fibers, and absorbs ink well because the ink lies in the spaces between the fibers.

Corundum

Topaz

Quartz

Feldspar

Apatite

Fluorite

Calcite

Gypsum

Talc

1 2 3 4 5 6 7 8 9

The world of crystals

CRYSTALS HAVE BEEN VIEWED with awe since ancient times. They are often very beautiful, and their shapes can differ widely, yet all crystal forms are of just six basic kinds. The orderly shape of each crystal is created by the arrangement of the atoms (p. 160) inside. With the help of powerful microscopes, many objects and materials that seem irregularly shaped to the naked eye, such as stalactites and most metals, can be seen to be masses of tiny uniform crystals. Many crystals are valuable in industry, and some, such as quartz (used in watches) and silicon (used in computers), can be made in the laboratory.

SIX SHAPES
Abbé René Haüy (1743-1822) was one of the first to show that crystal shapes fall into six geometrical groups. He suggested how they could be built up by stacking identical units in regular patterns.

SCULPTED WATER
Stalactites are mainly limestone, created by centuries of dripping water. The atoms in the limestone have arranged themselves in regular crystalline patterns.

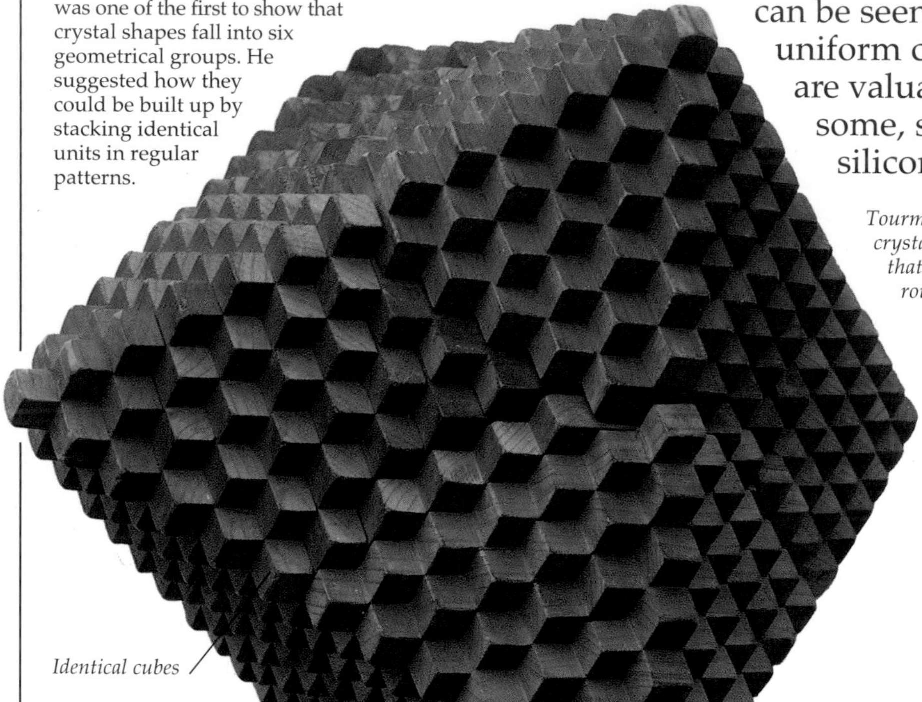

Tourmaline forms fine, long crystals with a cross-section that is triangular with rounded corners

Identical cubes

CRYSTAL CUBES
Wooden models like this octahedron (eight-faced solid) were used by Abbé Haüy to explain how crystal forms arise. The cube-shaped units of this crystal model are arranged in square layers, each larger than the previous one by an extra "border" of cubes.

HIGH-RISE CRYSTALS
Tourmaline crystals up to 10 ft (3 m) long have been found. They can occur in a wide variety of colors and are prized as gems. If warmed, one end of a tourmaline crystal becomes positively charged, and the other end becomes negatively charged.

THE EMERALD CITY
Crystals are often used as symbols of perfection and power. The magical Emerald City appears in the 1939 film *The Wizard of Oz.*

Outer part of the bismuth cooled fast and formed only microscopic crystals

Yellow sulfur crystals

Needle-shaped crystals formed where alloy solidified slowly

Crystals formed where the metal solidified slowly

BOXLIKE BISMUTH
Inside this piece of bismuth are intricate "nests" of crystal boxes, formed as the metal slowly solidified.

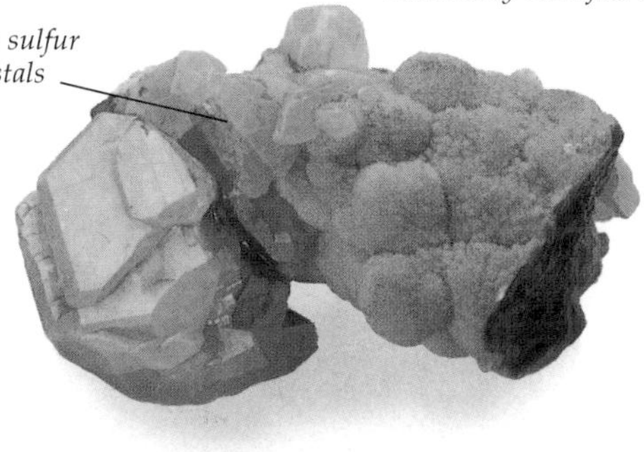

MELLOW YELLOW
At low temperatures, fairly flat sulfur crystals form. At high temperatures they are needle-shaped.

METAL MIXTURE
The thin, pointed crystals shown here are alloys of copper and aluminum.

Outer part of alloy cooled fast and formed few crystals

Aragonite often forms twin crystals

AMAZING ARAGONITE
Crystals of aragonite can be found in limestone caves and hot springs. They take many forms, such as fibers, columns, or needles. Their color is usually white, yellow, green, or blue.

MAKING CRYSTALS CLEAR
William Hyde Wollaston (1766-1828) made important contributions to crystallography (the scientific study of crystals). He recognized that a cubic crystal, for example, did not have to be built from cubes. Instead, it could be assembled from atoms of other shapes, as in his wooden models shown on this page. Scientists now know that atoms can take very complicated shapes when they join together.

Azurite crystals are "knobbly"

BLUE IS THE COLOR
The mineral azurite is blue, as its name implies. In the past azurite was crushed and used as a pigment. It contains copper and is found with deposits of copper ore. When azurite is made into a gem, it can be faceted – cut to display polished flat faces.

EGG-SHAPED ATOMS
In this model made by Wollaston, the atoms in the crystal are imagined to be egg-shaped. Each has six neighbors at the sides, forming a strong horizontal layer.

LOOSE LAYERS
If atoms in crystals are spheres, Wollaston realized that they would have neighbors on all sides. They would not form such strong layers as the atoms of the other shapes shown here.

FLAT ATOMS
Wollaston thought that if crystal atoms are flat, they would link most strongly where their flat faces were in contact. They might form columns or fibers.

LINING UP LIQUID CRYSTALS
Some crystals are liquid. The particles in a liquid can be temporarily lined up in regular arrays when an electric or magnetic field is applied. The liquid crystals shown here were revealed under an electron microscope. The liquid affects light differently when the crystals form, and can change from being transparent to being opaque, or colored. In digital clocks and watches, calculators, or laptop computers, electricity is used to alter segments of the display from clear to dark, to generate the changing numbers or letters.

Metals and alloys

The three metals most widely used are iron, steel, and aluminum. Iron and aluminum are both metallic elements, but steel is a mixture of iron and carbon. Such a combination, either of metals, or of metals and non-metals, is called an alloy. Combining a metal with other substances (either metallic or non-metallic) usually makes it stronger. Most metals are found in ore (rock), combined with other elements such as oxygen and sulfur. Heating the ore separates and purifies the metal. When metals are pure they are shiny, can be beaten into shape, and drawn out into wires. They are not brittle, but are often rather soft. Metals are good conductors (carriers) of electric current and heat.

Surface pitted by heating during fall

Rust formed by iron combining with oxygen from the air after the fall

GOLDEN CHARACTER
Gold is a precious metal. It is rare and does not tarnish. It can be beaten into sheets of gold leaf, which are used to decorate letters in illuminated manuscripts like the one above.

HEAVENLY METAL
A very pure iron comes from certain meteorites. They are bodies that have fallen to Earth from outer space and have been partly burned away by the friction of entering the Earth's atmosphere.

CUTTING EDGE
The use of bronze dates from about 5000 BC in the Middle East, and 2000 BC in Europe. Bronze is an alloy of copper and tin. It is very hard, and was used for the blades of axes, daggers, swords, and razors.

Blade of hammered bronze

Ancient Egyptian razor

Bronze handle

Mercury expands along thin tube when heated

THIS CARD **MUST** BE SENT UNDER COVER ONLY.
MAILABLE AS FOURTH CLASS MATTER UNDER RULING OF THE POSTMASTER-GENERAL.

1964-4

POST CARD

THE SPACE BELOW IS FOR THE ADDRESS ONLY.

PLACE STAMP UPON ENVELOPE

HARD WORDS
Aluminum makes up one-twelfth of the rock near the Earth's surface. It was discovered in 1809, but only came into widespread use after 1886. It is a very light metal, and was first used in jewelery and novelties, like this picture postcard. Aircraft parts are often made of aluminum alloys.

Bulb contains mercury

LIQUID METAL
The metal mercury, sometimes known as quicksilver, is a liquid at normal temperatures. It expands by a relatively large amount when warmed, and has long been used in instruments to measure temperature, such as this 18th-century thermometer.

Henry Bessemer

Molten pig-iron poured in

Converter

Air blown through inlets and carbon burned off

Purified iron poured into ladle

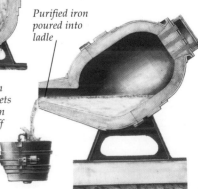

MAN OF STEEL
Henry Bessemer (1813-1898) greatly speeded up the steel-making process in the mid-19th century with his famous converter. Air was blown through molten pig iron (iron ore that had been heated in a furnace with coal or wood). This burned off the carbon from the coal or wood in a fountain of sparks. The purified iron, still molten, was tipped out of the coverter, and measured amounts of carbon and metals, such as nickel, manganese, or chromium, were added. These other substances turned the molten iron into steel, an alloy that is renowned for its strength (see also p. 226).

BELL OF BRONZE

Metals such as bronze are ideal for bells because they vibrate for a long time after being struck. From about 1000 BC bronze has been cast (poured in a molten state into a mold). Once cast, large bells must cool very slowly to prevent cracking. The Liberty Bell, which hangs in Philadelphia, Pennsylvania, weighs about 2,079 lb (943 kg), and is about 3 ft (1 meter) high. It was made in London and delivered in 1752, but it cracked and had to be recast twice before it was hung. It cracked again in 1835 and in 1846. Since then it has never been rung.

PURE QUALITY

Goldsmiths formerly judged gold's purity by scraping it on a type of dark rock called touchstone. Its streak was then compared with the streaks made by the gold samples on two "stars." The best match came from gold of the same purity.

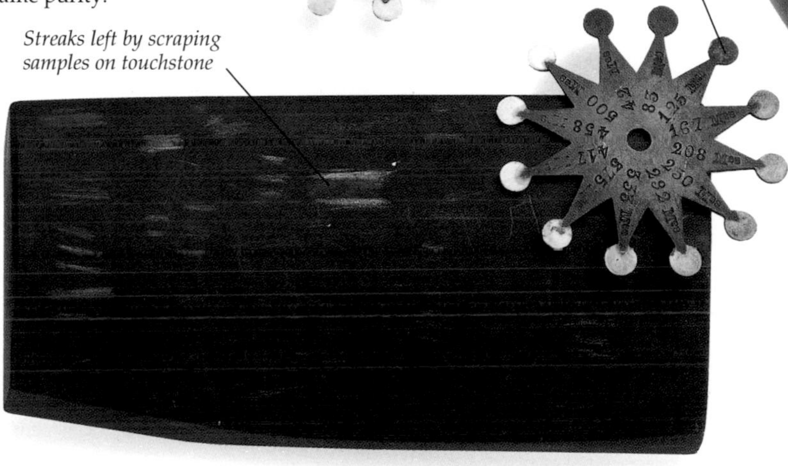

Sample has 875 parts of gold per thousand

Sample has 125 parts of gold per thousand

Streaks left by scraping samples on touchstone

Steel spring

Steel wheels

MULTIPURPOSE METALS

Various metals, each with its own particular job to do, are used in this old clock. The springs, chain, and cogwheels inside, which receive the most wear, are made of steel. The case is made of brass, an alloy of copper and zinc that is not so strong as steel. To make it look attractive, the brass has been gilded (coated with gold).

Cross-section of transatlantic cable

Rubberlike gutta-percha prevents electricity from leaking

Twisted steel cables

Copper strands

DEEP COMMUNICATION

A telegraph cable 2,325 miles (3,740 km) long was first laid across the seabed of the Atlantic Ocean in 1850, linking Britain with the US. The outer part of a typical cable was a strong sheath of twisted steel cables. It would resist rusting even in seawater (a solution known to rust metals quickly).

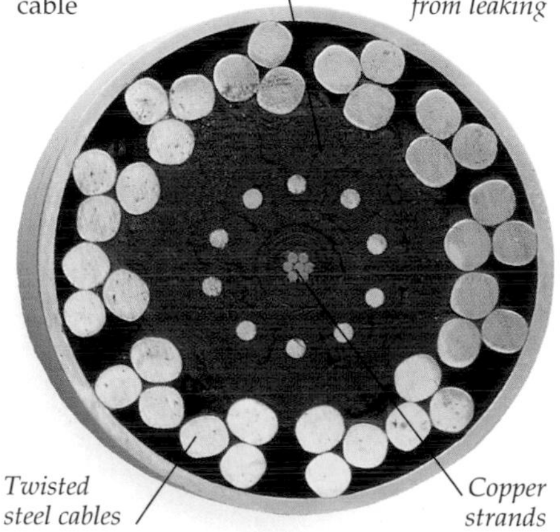

Twisted steel cables

OCEAN CURRENT

A seven-stranded copper wire lies at the heart of the undersea cable. Copper was chosen for the wire because of its very useful properties. It is an excellent carrier of electric current and is easily drawn out into wires.

Properties of liquids

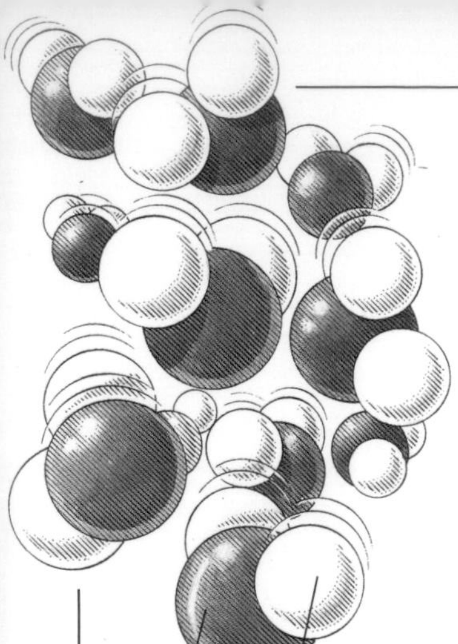

ACCORDING TO THE GREEKS who believed in the four elements, all liquids contain a large proportion of water. However, those who believed in atoms thought that the atoms in a liquid could slide around each other, making the liquid flow to take the shape of its container. This is also the modern view. Liquid particles attract each other and keep close together, so they cannot be easily squeezed into a smaller volume or stretched out into a larger one. When a liquid is heated, however, the spacing between the particles generally increases in size, so the liquid expands. When a liquid is cooled, the reverse effect occurs, and the liquid contracts. It is possible for liquids to dissolve some solid substances. For example, salt placed in water seems to disappear very slowly. In fact the salt breaks up into individual atoms of sodium and chlorine. The ions spread out through the water, forming a mixture called a solution of salt in water. Liquids can also dissolve gases and other liquids.

SLIPPING AND SLIDING
The smallest unit of water consists of one atom of oxygen joined to two hydrogen atoms. These clusters of three atoms slide around each other in liquid water.

Hydrogen atom

Oxygen atom

PRESSING MATTER
Most liquids, particularly water and oil, act as good transmitters of pressure. In 1795 Joseph Bramah (1749-1814) patented his hydraulic press, in which compressed fluid multiplied the force that could be exerted by a human operator.

SLOW FLOW
Some liquids flow easily, but honey flows very slowly, and is described as being "viscous." Liquids such as tar and pitch (a substance used to seal roofs) are even more viscous.

Slow-moving liquid

Droplets are forced into shape by surface tension

Meniscus

Level surface

Gas in a liquid is pressed into spherical or almost spherical bubble shapes by the surrounding liquid

Liquid spreads out in a thin film

CURVED EDGE
The surface of an undisturbed liquid is horizontal, except at the very edge, where it forms a curve called a meniscus. The meniscus can be sloped up as it is here, or sloped down.

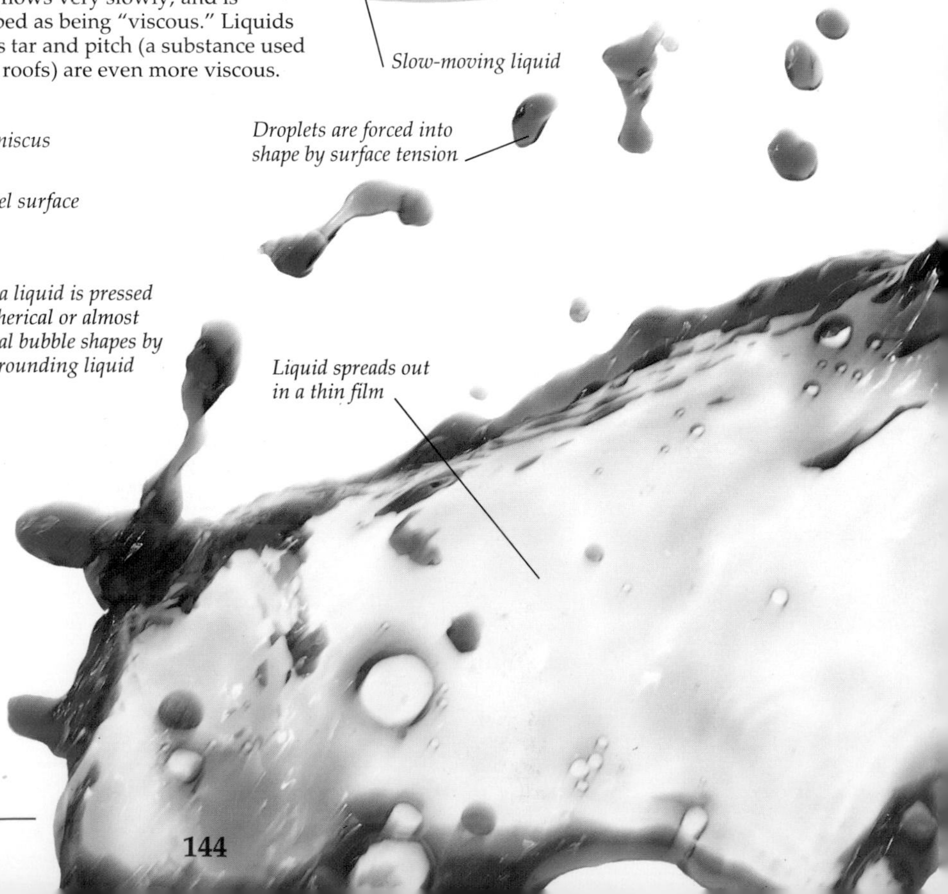

UPLIFTING MATERIAL

Because a liquid can flow, an object can be pushed down into it, forcing some of the liquid aside. But the displaced liquid tries to flow back, pushing the object upward. The object then seems lighter than the liquid, and floats, like this boat.

Narrow neck of vessel causes liquid to speed up as it flows through

WORN DOWN BY WATER

Given sufficient time, flowing liquids wear away solid surfaces, even rocks. The abrasive effect is increased when the liquid carries solid particles of rock and mud. Some rocks, such as clays and sandstones, have a low resistance to erosion. This canyon in the Arizona desert has been worn away by 10,000 years of flash floods.

Fast-moving liquid

Liquid takes the shape of its container

THE STRENGTH OF MOVING LIQUIDS

A stream of liquid can deliver a powerful force – a tsunami, or "tidal wave," can sweep away towns. Slower-moving liquid has time to break up and flow round obstacles, and does them less damage. Where a liquid has escaped from a container, surface tension (the inward pull at the surface) tries to pull it into shape. But because it is a relatively weak force, surface tension can pull only small amounts into drops – larger quantities of liquid are chaotic and formless.

WATER POWER

Streams and rivers have been used to turn waterwheels since ancient times. In 18th-century Britain water-powered looms featured heavily in the Industrial Revolution. Today, water from lakes, reservoirs, or the sea is used to turn electricity-generating turbines worldwide.

Level surface

BRIMMING OVER

The tiny particles that make up a liquid are held together by their attraction to each other. Surface tension makes the surface of a liquid behave like the tight elastic skin of a balloon. The wine in this glass is above the brim, but surface tension stops it from overflowing.

WALKING ON WATER

Surface tension lets this insect's feet walk instead of swim; its feet make dents in the water but don't go through.

Gases and their properties

Ancient philosophers were puzzled by the exact nature of gases. They realized air was not empty space. Some guessed the smell of a perfume was due to the spreading of tiny particles, and that frost was formed by the condensation of invisible water vapor. Many observed that the wind bent trees and vigorous bubbling made water froth. These early philosophers believed that there was a single element of air, which had "levity," a tendency to rise. In the 17th century Evangelista Torricelli (1608-1647) showed that air, like solids and liquids, can be weighed. In the next century, chemists showed that air is a mixture of gases, and identified the gases given off in chemical reactions. These newly discovered gases were soon put to use; for instance, gas obtained from coal produced light and heat.

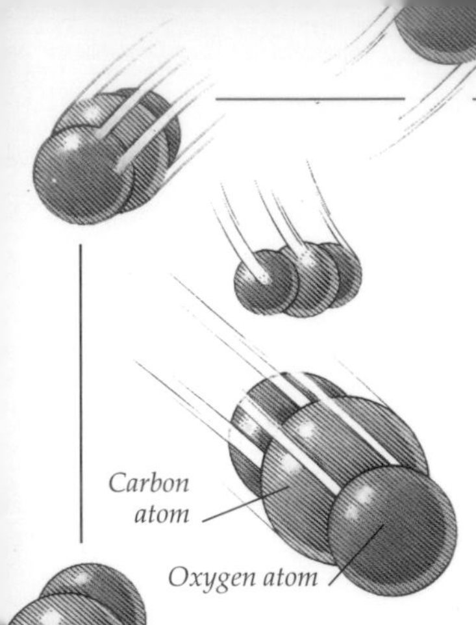

Carbon atom

Oxygen atom

IT'S A GAS
Gases, like the carbon dioxide shown here, consist of molecules that are separated from each other, and which are constantly moving. Gas molecules are usually complex, made up of atoms (pp. 34-35) that are closely bound together.

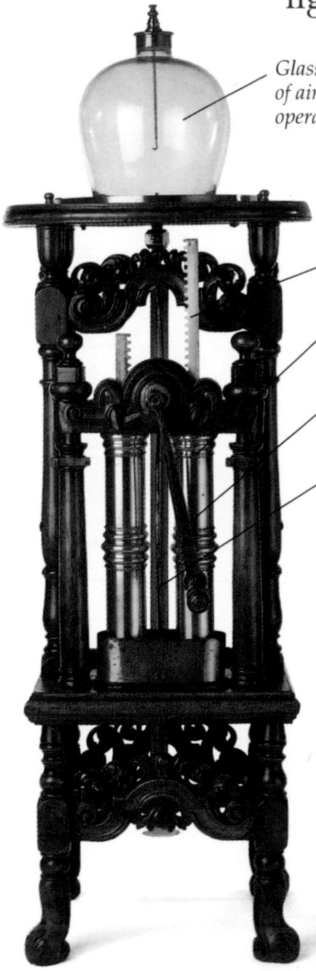

Glass dome is emptied of air when the pump operates

Piston

Cylinder

Handle

Tube connecting cylinders to glass dome

AIRLESS EXPERIMENTS
The airpump shown here was built by Francis Hauksbee (1666-1713). The lever was worked to operate twin pistons, which removed air from the glass dome. Experiments could then be performed under the dome in an airless environment. The first airpump was made in the 1650s by Otto von Guericke (1602-1686), to demonstrate the strength of air pressure.

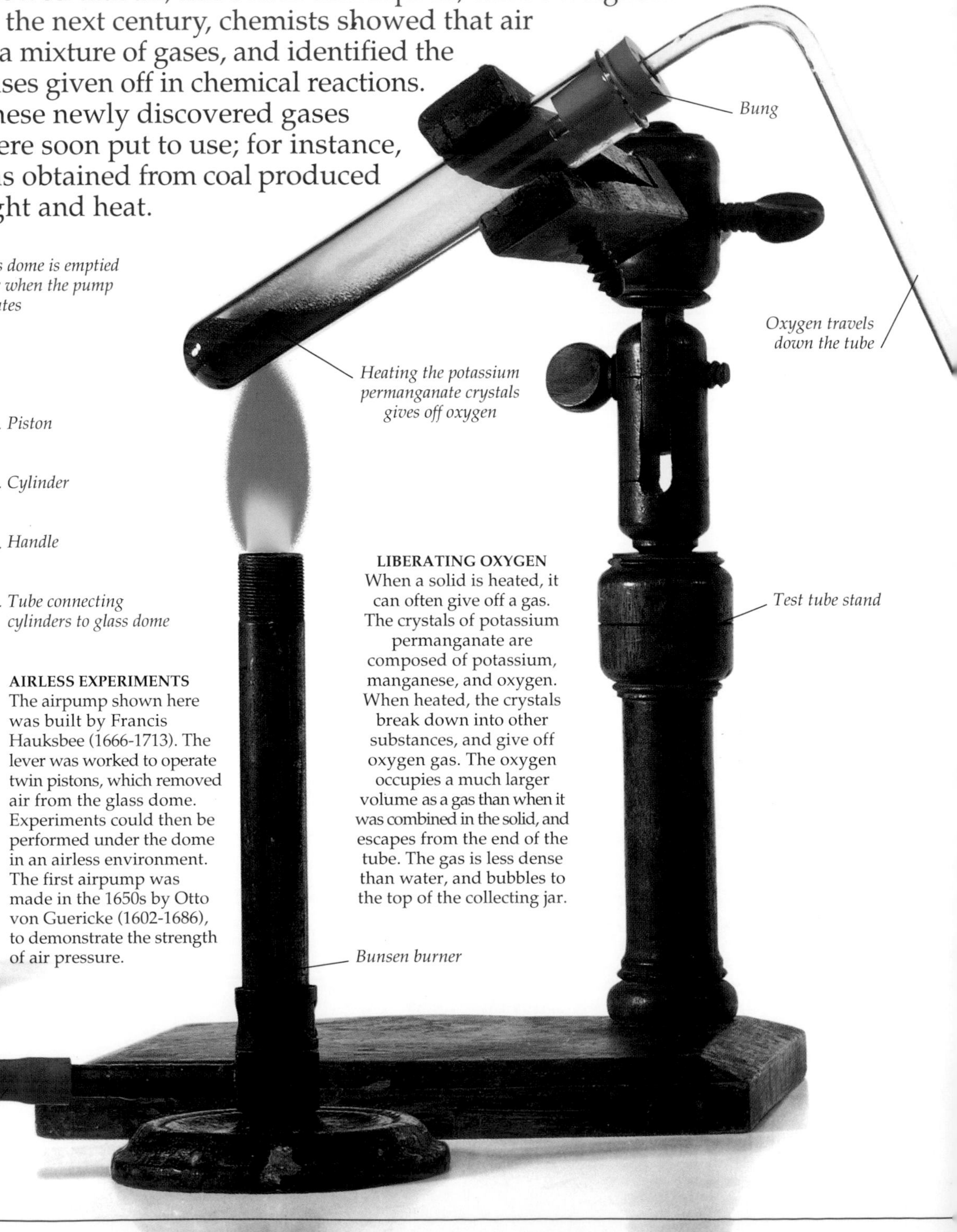

Bung

Oxygen travels down the tube

Heating the potassium permanganate crystals gives off oxygen

Test tube stand

LIBERATING OXYGEN
When a solid is heated, it can often give off a gas. The crystals of potassium permanganate are composed of potassium, manganese, and oxygen. When heated, the crystals break down into other substances, and give off oxygen gas. The oxygen occupies a much larger volume as a gas than when it was combined in the solid, and escapes from the end of the tube. The gas is less dense than water, and bubbles to the top of the collecting jar.

Bunsen burner

Gas supply

PRESSING FORCE
A barometer measures changes in atmospheric pressure. The early barometer made by Evangelista Torricelli had a mercury-filled upright glass tube. The tube's open end dipped in a bowl of mercury. Atmospheric pressure forced the mercury down in the bowl, and balanced the weight of the mercury in the tube.

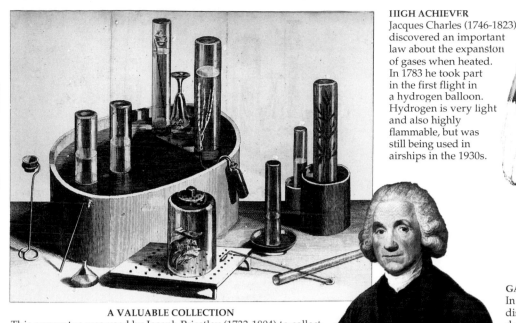

A VALUABLE COLLECTION
This apparatus was used by Joseph Priestley (1733-1804) to collect gases. The gases would bubble up through the water and be collected for experimentation in the glass jars (see also p. 147).

HIGH ACHIEVER
Jacques Charles (1746-1823) discovered an important law about the expansion of gases when heated. In 1783 he took part in the first flight in a hydrogen balloon. Hydrogen is very light and also highly flammable, but was still being used in airships in the 1930s.

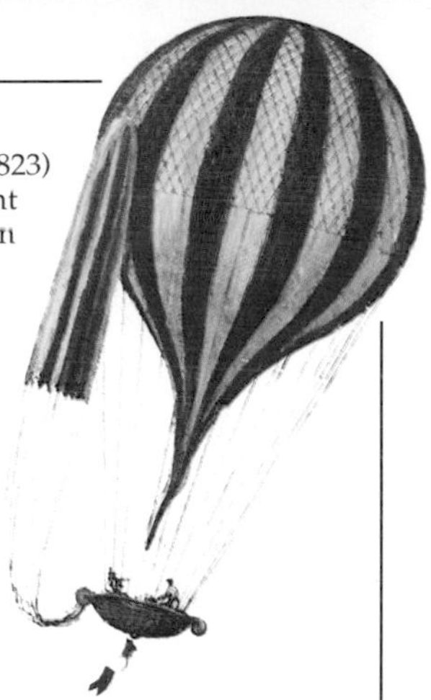

GAS WORKER
In 1775 Joseph Priestley discovered oxygen during his work with mercuric oxide. He found that oxygen supported breathing and burning, but did not recognize its exact nature. Using carbon dioxide from a local brewer to make water fizzy, he invented soda water.

Gas jar

Gas pressure pushes water out of the gas jar into the trough

Oxygen bubbles become larger as they reach the surface

"Beehive" stand for jar

ENERGY FROM SUNLIGHT
Photosynthesis is the process by which green plants take energy from sunlight, and produce food molecules from carbon dioxide and water. Parts of this process can be seen here, when sunlight shines on freshly cut leaves immersed in water. The oxygen from the carbon dioxide molecules is released, and is given off into the water in the form of small bubbles. They rise to the surface and push water out from the jar.

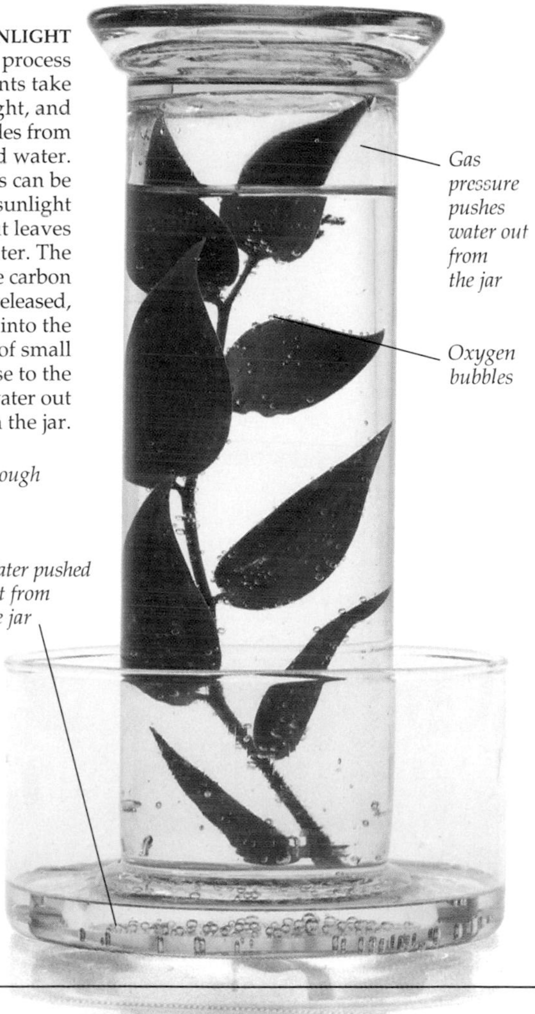

Trough

Gas pressure pushes water out from the jar

Oxygen bubbles

Water pushed out from the jar

Water

Changes of state

M ATTER CAN BE ALTERED in various ways. Heating a solid to a temperature called its melting point will make it change state – it will turn into a liquid. Heating a liquid to a temperature called its boiling point has a similar effect – the liquid will change state and turn into a gas. It is possible to affect both the melting and the boiling point of matter. For example, if an impurity such as salt is added to ice, the melting point of the ice is lowered. The mixture of salt and ice will melt, while pure ice at the same temperature will remain frozen. If salt is added to water, it raises the boiling point, and the water boils at a higher temperature. Pressure can also affect the state of matter. Where air pressure is low, the boiling point of water is lowered. An increase in pressure will lower the melting point of a solid.

YIELDING TO PRESSURE
Where a wire presses on ice, the melting point is lowered, and the ice melts. The wire cuts through the ice, which freezes again as the wire passes.

FROM SOLID TO GAS
In the following sequence, heating a solid – ice – to its melting point makes it change state to a liquid. Heating the liquid – water – to its boiling point makes it change state to a gas.

DROPPING LEAD
Bullets and lead shot used to be made by letting drops of molten lead fall from the top of a "shot tower." While still liquid, the lead droplets formed spheres, and then "froze" in this shape.

A WEALTH OF SUBJECTS
Scientist John Tyndall (1820-1893) was very interested in how heat causes changes of state. He also studied many other subjects, including the origins of life, and why the sky is blue.

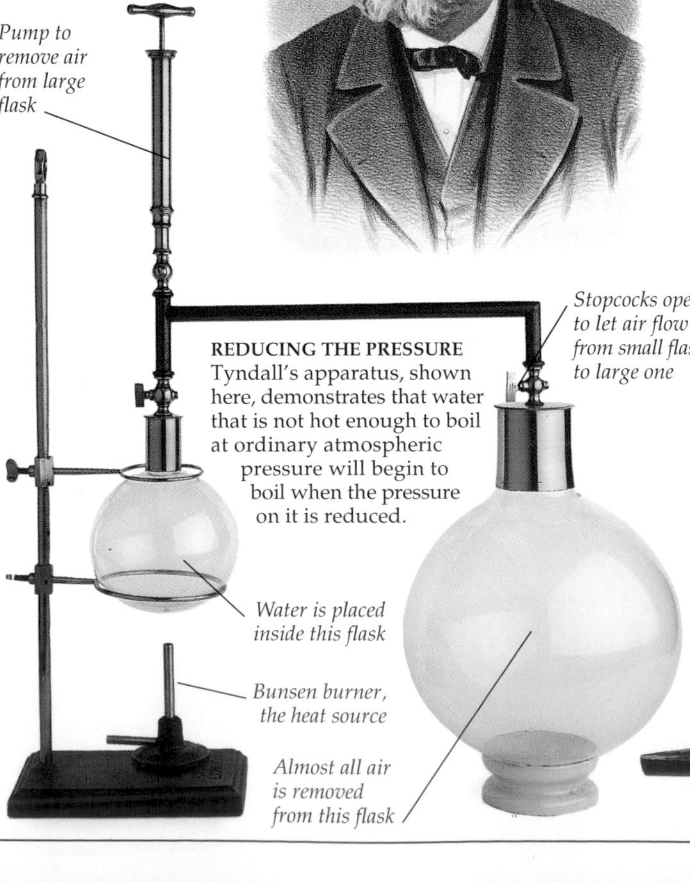

1 SOLID STATE
Like most other substances, water can exist as a solid, liquid, or gas. The solid state is ice, and it forms when liquid water is cooled sufficiently. Ice may look different from water, but chemically it is exactly the same.

Pump to remove air from large flask

REDUCING THE PRESSURE
Tyndall's apparatus, shown here, demonstrates that water that is not hot enough to boil at ordinary atmospheric pressure will begin to boil when the pressure on it is reduced.

Stopcocks open to let air flow from small flask to large one

Each piece of ice has a definite shape

Water is placed inside this flask

Bunsen burner, the heat source

Almost all air is removed from this flask

Safety valve

Pressure gauge

PRESSURE AT WORK
This is a cast-aluminum pressure cooker from about 1930. The very high pressure in a pressure cooker allows water to be heated above its normal boiling point, and the food inside is quickly cooked.

Holes formed by bubbles of gas

STONE FROM A VOLCANO
Pumice stone is molten lava which has cooled very quickly. It is honeycombed with holes, which are "frozen-in" bubbles of gas.

MOLTEN MOUNTAIN
When a volcano erupts, it can violently expel thousands of tons of lava – red-hot molten rock from the Earth's core. As the lava cools it changes state and solidifies.

HIDDEN HEAT
Joseph Black (1728-1798) measured the heat needed to turn a solid into a liquid, or a liquid into a gas. He called this heat "latent," or hidden (p. 27).

2 LIQUID STATE
When ice is warmed, it can turn into liquid water. This change happens at a definite temperature, which is normally 32° F (0° C). Under normal pressure water stays liquid up to 212° F (100° C).

3 GAS STATE
When water is heated sufficiently, it starts to turn into steam – a colorless, invisible gas. It can be "seen" only as bubbles in water. What is usually called steam is really a fine mist of water droplets.

Gas turns into liquid water where it touches a cooler surface

A liquid's surface is horizontal

Steam is invisible

Bubbles of steam form in the liquid

A liquid takes the shape of its container

Colloids and glasses

SOME MATTER IS DIFFICULT to classify. For example, lead, a metal, flows like a liquid over centuries. Glass, a seemingly solid substance, is actually a supercool liquid, and flows over decades. The atoms in such substances are not locked into a regular pattern. Instead they form a disorderly pattern, and the atoms move around, allowing the substance to flow. In a form of matter called a colloid, one substance is dispersed through another. The dispersed particles are much larger than atoms, but too small to be seen by the naked eye. Colloids include colored glass (solid particles dispersed in a solid), clay (solid in liquid), smoke (solid in gas), milk (liquid in liquid), mist (liquid in gas), and foam (gas in liquid).

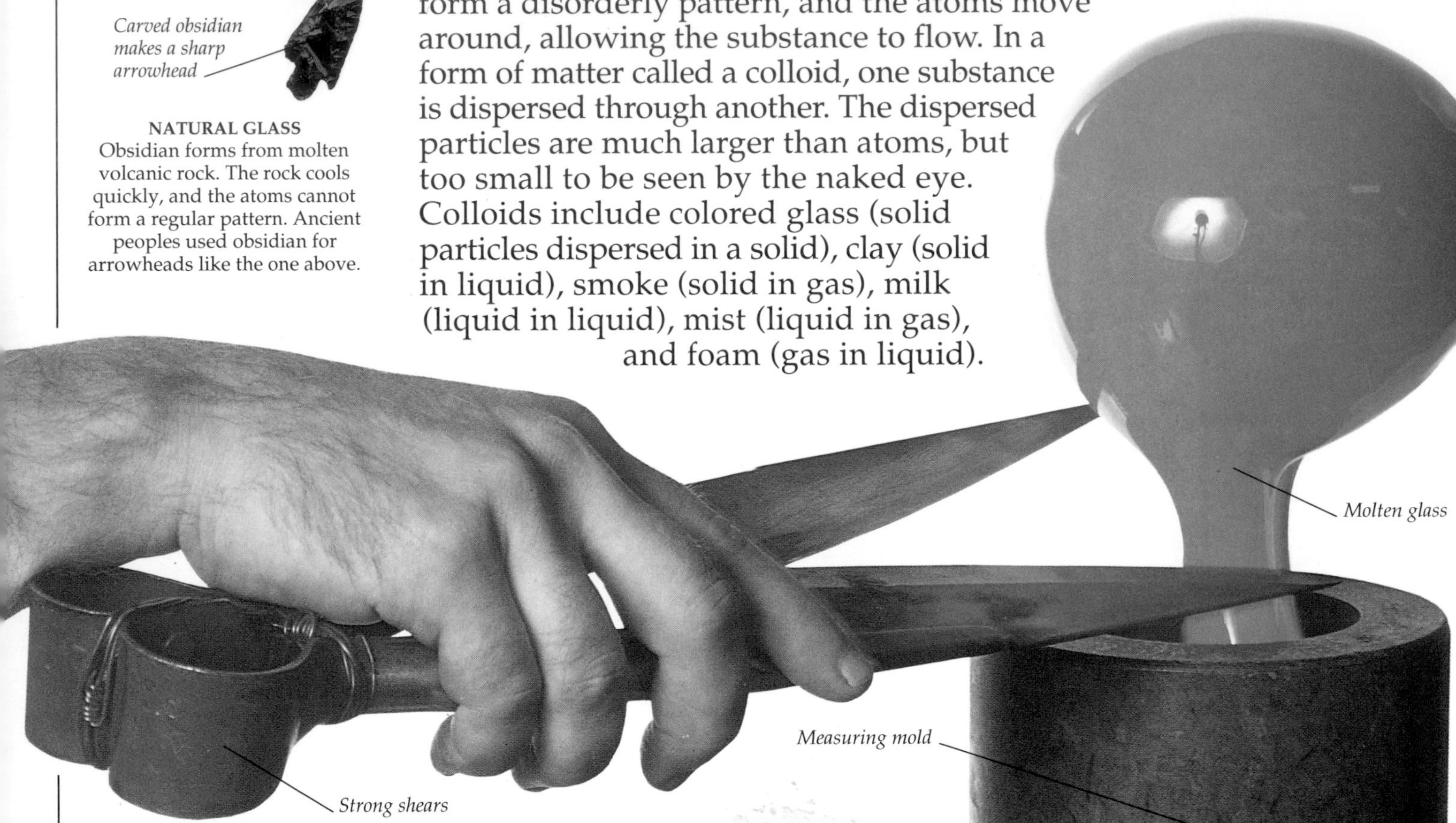

NATURAL GLASS
Obsidian forms from molten volcanic rock. The rock cools quickly, and the atoms cannot form a regular pattern. Ancient peoples used obsidian for arrowheads like the one above.

Carved obsidian makes a sharp arrowhead

Molten glass

Measuring mold

Strong shears

GLASSBLOWING
Glass is made by melting sand mixed with other ingredients, and then cooling the liquid rapidly. It was first made around 4000 BC in the Middle East. Glass was blown to fit tightly inside a mold from the 1st century AD. Most glassblowing is now done mechanically, but a traditional method is shown in the following sequence. It is now practiced only for specialized objects.

Soda ash (sodium carbonate)

Sand (silica)

Limestone (calcium carbonate)

1 A GLASS RECIPE
The main ingredient in the recipe for glass, called the batch, is sand. The next main ingredient is usually soda ash (sodium carbonate), which makes a glass that is fairly easy to melt. Limestone may be used to produce a water-resistant glass.

Iron oxide gives a green color

Barium carbonate gives a brown color

2 CUTTING GLASS
A large quantity of the molten glass is gathered on the end of an iron rod by the glassmaker. It is allowed to fall into a measuring mold, and the correct quantity is cut off, using a pair of shears. There are several other traditional glassmaking techniques. Flat glass for windows can be produced by spinning a hot molten blob of glass on the end of a rod. It is spread into a large disc, from which flat pieces can be cut. Glass with a decorated surface can be made by pressing molten glass into a mold.

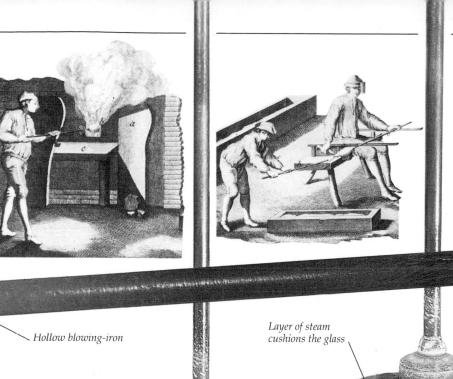

Hollow blowing-iron

Layer of steam cushions the glass

Shaping mold

Parison

Flat plate

Final product shows no signs of the joint between the two halves of the mold

3 **MAKING THE PARISON**
The correct quantity of molten glass is picked up from the measuring mold on a hollow blowing-iron and is reheated in a furnace. The glassmaker blows a little air through the blowing-iron and taps the glass on a flat plate a few times to shape it. The glass is now approximately the size and shape of the finished product – in this case a bottle – and is called a parison. Behind the parison is the open shaping mold, which is bottle-shaped. The parison is now ready to be placed inside.

4 **BLOWING, MOLDING, AND SPINNING**
When the mold has been tightly closed, the glass is gently blown again. The glass expands and takes the shape of the inside of the mold. As well as blowing, the glassblower also spins the blowing-iron rapidly. This ensures that the final object does not show any signs of the joint between the two halves of the mold, or any other defects. The glass never comes in direct contact with the material of the mold. This is because the inside of the mold is wet and a layer of steam forms, cushioning the glass.

5 **ONE BROWN BOTTLE**
The shaping mold is opened to reveal the final product – a reproduction of a 17th-century bottle. This specialized object has to be broken away from the blowing-iron. The jagged mouth of the bottle has to be finished off by reheating it in a furnace and using shaping tools. Since the glass has cooled slightly, the rich brown color provided by the special ingredients in the batch is revealed. In the very early days of glass, it was always colored. The first clear glass was made in the 1st century BC.

Mixtures and compounds

WHEN SALT AND SAND ARE MIXED TOGETHER, the individual grains of both substances can still be seen. This loose combination of substances is called a mixture. The mixture of salt and sand is easy to separate – if it is given a gentle shake, the heavier grains of sand settle to the bottom. Mixing instant coffee and hot water produces a closer combination, called a solution. Yet this is still fairly easy to separate. If the solution is gently heated, pure water is given off in the form of water vapor, while solid coffee is left behind. The closest combinations of substances are chemical. When carbon (in the form of charcoal) burns, oxygen from the air combines with it to form the gases carbon dioxide and carbon monoxide. These gases are difficult to break down, and are called compounds.

WHEAT FROM CHAFF
Traditionally, wheat was threshed to loosen the edible grains from the chaff (the husks). The grains and chaff formed a mixture that could be separated by "winnowing." Grains were thrown into the air and the breeze blew away the lighter chaff, while the grain fell back.

GOLD IN THE PAN
Gold prospectors have "panned" for gold since the 19th century. They swill gravel from a streambed around a pan with a little water. Any gold nuggets present separate from the stones because of their high density.

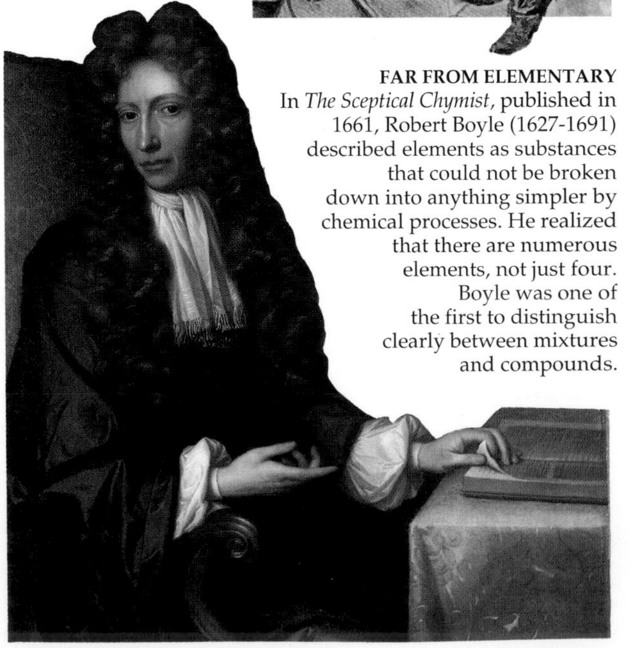

FAR FROM ELEMENTARY
In *The Sceptical Chymist*, published in 1661, Robert Boyle (1627-1691) described elements as substances that could not be broken down into anything simpler by chemical processes. He realized that there are numerous elements, not just four. Boyle was one of the first to distinguish clearly between mixtures and compounds.

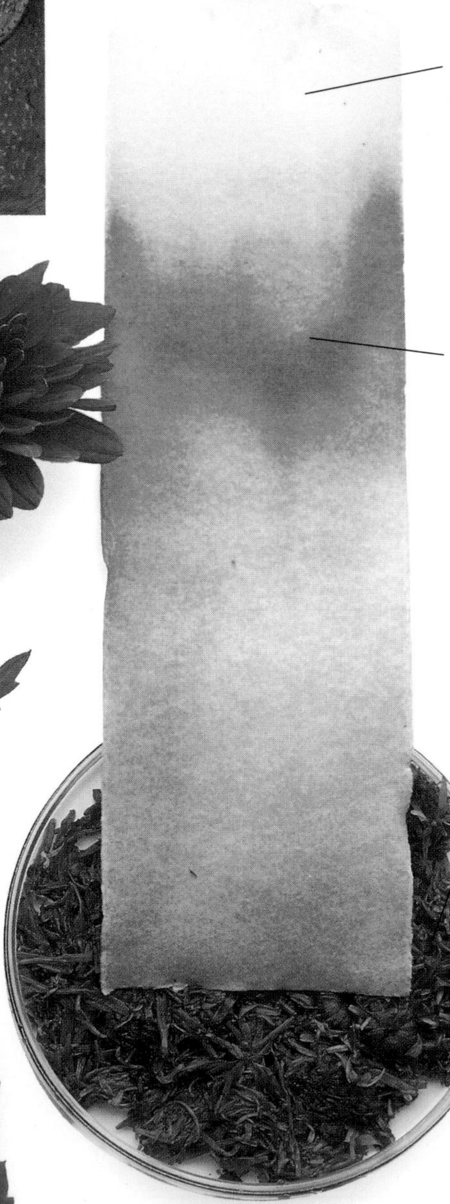

COLORFUL REPORT
Mixtures of liquids or gases can be separated by chromatography. The blotting paper shown here has been dipped into an extract of flower petals. Some of the liquid is drawn up into the paper, but the components flow at different rates, and separate out into bands of colors.

Blotting paper

Fastest moving component

Mashed petals and mineral alcohol

ANALYZING COMPOUNDS

This condenser was invented by the German chemist Justus von Liebig (1803-1873) around 1830, for analyzing carbon-containing compounds. The compound was heated into a gas, and passed over copper oxide in the glass tube. Oxygen from the copper oxide combined with carbon and hydrogen in the gas, and formed carbon dioxide gas and water vapor. The potassium hydroxide in the glass spheres absorbed the carbon dioxide. The amount of carbon in the original compound could be calculated by the increase in weight in the spheres.

REFLECTIVE THINKER

Justus von Liebig made many advances in the chemistry of "organic" substances. This originally meant substances made in living organisms, but now refers to most carbon-containing substances (p. 166). His scientific feats included devising standard procedures for the chemical analysis of organic compounds, inventing a method of making mirrors by depositing a film of silver on glass, pioneering artificial fertilizers, and founding the first modern teaching laboratory in chemistry.

Charcoal is used as the heat source

RUSTING AWAY

The compound rust is a red solid. It forms when iron, a grayish solid, combines with the gases oxygen and hydrogen. When iron is exposed to air, rust forms spontaneously, but the reaction is not easily reversed – the compound can only be broken down again by chemical means.

Sample experiences a strong force

Glass tube contains copper oxide

SALT OF THE EARTH

In the 19th century salt was shown to be a compound of two previously unknown substances – sodium, a silvery metal, and chlorine, a poisonous gas.

Potassium hydroxide in the glass spheres absorbs the carbon dioxide

IN A WHIRL

Mixtures of liquids, or suspensions of solids in liquids naturally separate out over a period of time. This process can be speeded up by whirling the sample round in a centrifuge.

Handle is connected to the shaft by gears so the speed of rotation is increased

Measuring device

Metal holders for the test tubes

Calcium chloride in this tube absorbs water, allowing the amount of hydrogen in the compound to be calculated

Test tube

Hand centrifuge in action

Hand centrifuge is operated by turning the handle

Components of the hand centrifuge

SALT OF THE SEA

These salt pans in India are shallow pits that are flooded with seawater (a mixture of salt and water). The water evaporates in the hot sunshine, but only pure water comes off as a vapor. The salt is left behind as a white solid.

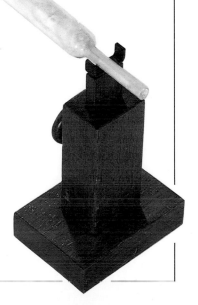

Conservation of matter

MATTER COMBINES, separates, and alters in countless ways. During these changes, matter often seems to appear and disappear. Hard deposits of scale build up in a kettle. Water standing in a pot dries up. Plants grow, and their increase in weight is much greater than the weight of the water and food that they absorb. In all everyday circumstances matter is conserved – it is never destroyed or created. The scale found in the kettle built up from dissolved matter that was present in the water all the time. The water in the pot turned into unseen gases that mingled with the air. The increased bulk of the plants came from the invisible carbon dioxide gas in the air. Only in nuclear explosions, or in the sun and stars, or in other extreme situations, can matter be created or destroyed.

GREAT SURVIVOR
The original matter in a long-dead organism is dispersed and survives. A fossil is the last visible trace of an organism.

THE BALANCE OF LIFE
Lavoisier weighed people and animals over long periods of time to discover what happened to their air, food, and drink. He calculated the quantities of gases involved by examining the measured quantities of solids and liquids that they had consumed.

WEIGHTY MATTER
In the late 18th century the balance became the chemist's most important measuring instrument. Accurate weighing was the key to keeping track of all the matter involved in a reaction. It led to the abandonment of the phlogiston theory (pp. 30-31) – that when a material burns, a substance called phlogiston is always released.

Glass dome traps gases

Fresh pear

WEIGHING THE EVIDENCE
Lavoisier's theory of the conservation of matter can be effectively demonstrated by comparing the weight of substances before and after an experiment. Here, a pear is placed under an airtight container and weighed. The pear is left for a few days and then weighed again. The two weights can be compared to discover whether the process of decay has involved any overall weight change.

A COUPLE OF CHEMISTS
Antoine Lavoisier (1743-1794) stated the principle of conservation of matter in 1789. This was not a new idea – matter had been assumed to be everlasting by many previous thinkers. Lavoisier, however, was the first to demonstrate this principle actively. His wide-ranging investigations were renowned for their rigor – he carried out experiments that were conducted in sealed vessels, and made accurate records of the many substances involved in chemical reactions. This work was extremely careful and laborious, but he was aided by another talented chemist and devoted coworker, his wife, Marie-Anne.

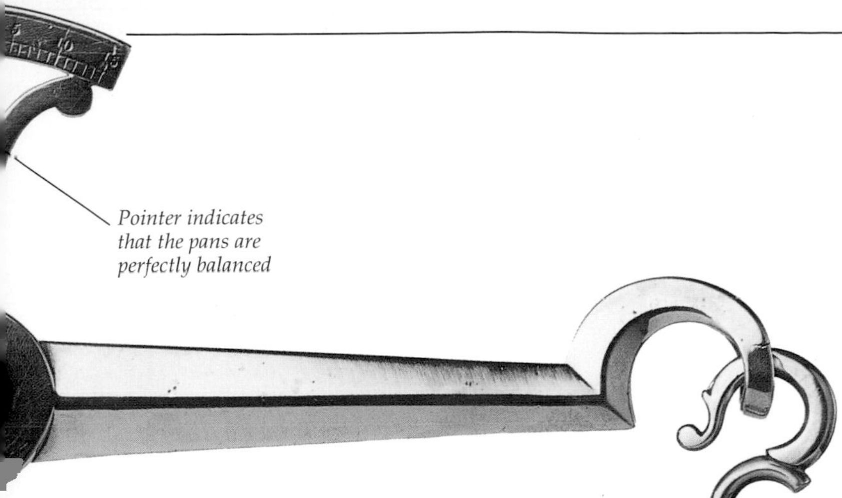

Pointer indicates that the pans are perfectly balanced

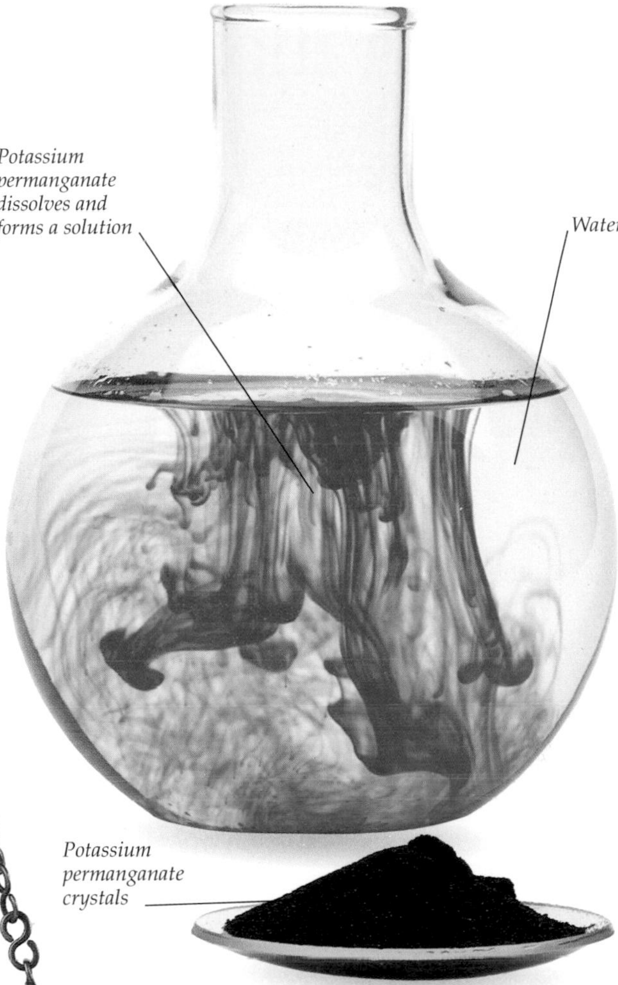

Potassium permanganate dissolves and forms a solution

Water

Potassium permanganate crystals

NATURAL EROSION

The land is constantly worn away by wind, rain, and waves, yet this is balanced by the natural building up of new land forms elsewhere. No matter is lost or gained overall.

AN OBVIOUS SOLUTION

Solids left in water often dissolve. If the solids are colorless, such as salt, it is easy to believe they have disappeared completely. In fact they have just thoroughly mixed, and broken into minute particles, which have spread through the liquid. When the solid is colored, like this potassium permanganate, it is easier to believe that it still exists in the liquid. Weighing the solution confirms that it weighs the same as the original liquid and solid.

OUT WITH A BANG

When fireworks go off, gunpowder burns, as well as other chemicals, plus the cardboard and paper of the firework packaging. The burning products form gases and a small quantity of solids. Though widely scattered, the combined products weigh the same as the original.

Glass dome contains air and gases produced by rotting pear

Condensation

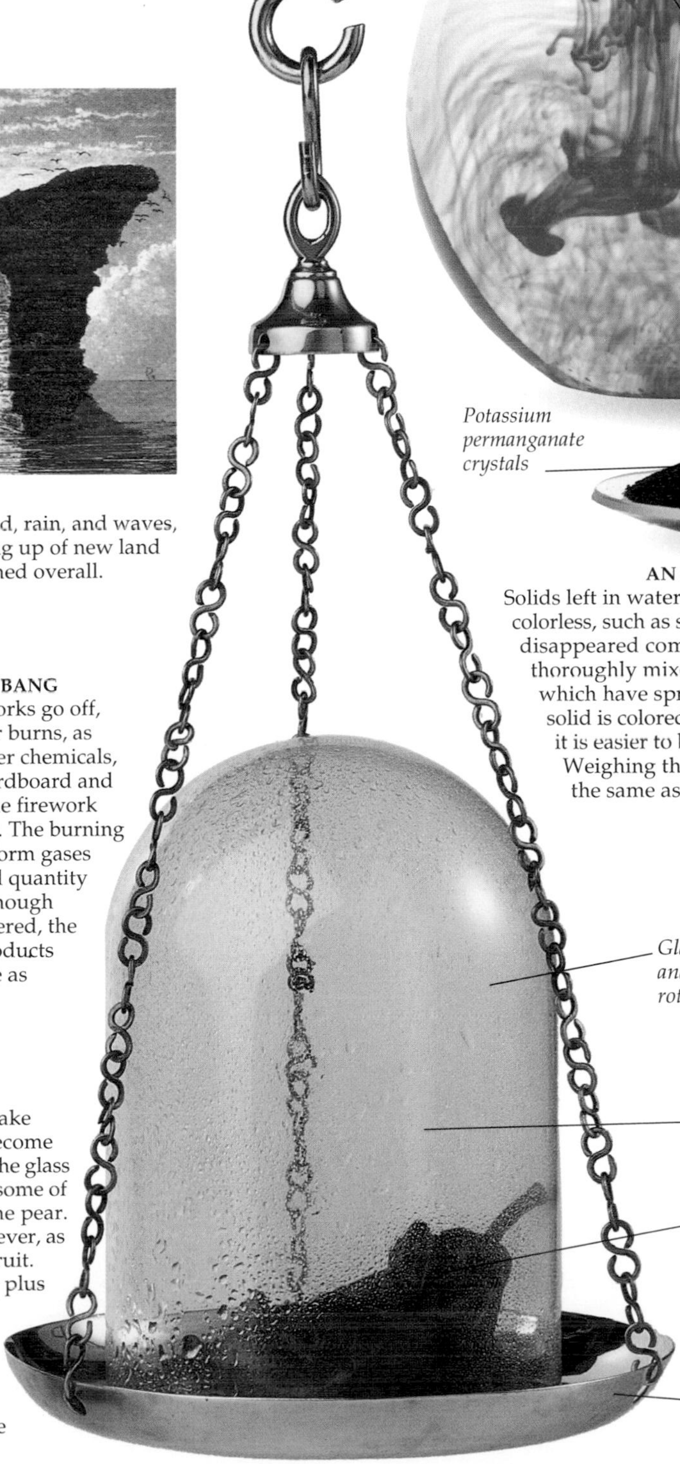

ROTTEN RESULT

After a few days, rotting begins to take place, and some parts of the pear become brown and mushy. In the air under the glass dome there is now less oxygen, for some of it combines with the substances in the pear. There is more carbon dioxide, however, as well as other gases released by the fruit. Overall, the weight of the container plus its contents does not alter in the slightest degree. Early chemists did not realize that if the glass dome is lifted before weighing, air is likely to enter or escape, and therefore affect the weight of the container and its contents.

Rotting pear

Scale pan

Burning matter

ONE OF THE FIRST great achievements of 18th-century science was the explanation of burning (also known as combustion). Georg Stahl (1660-1734) put forward the theory that an element, phlogiston, was given out in burning. His theory was wrong – it would mean that all substances would lose weight when they burn. Several chemists had already observed that some substances such as metals increase in weight during burning, and the theory of phlogiston was firmly denied by Antoine Lavoisier (p.154). He argued that air contains a gas that combines with a substance when it burns, and he named the gas oxygen. Sometimes substances can "burn" in gases other than oxygen. Some, such as ammonium dichromate, can change by themselves into other substances, producing flame, heat, and light.

FROM CRYSTALS TO ASH
In the following sequence, orange ammonium dichromate crystals produce flame, heat, and light, and turn into gray-green ash.

Low flames

Orange crystals of ammonium dichromate

Ash quickly forms

1 READY TO REACT
Ammonium dichromate is a substance used in indoor fireworks. It consists of nitrogen, hydrogen, chromium, and oxygen.

2 VITAL SPARK
When lit by a flame, the substance's atoms form simpler substances, and produce heat and light.

Brass pivot

Burning-lens is angled to catch sunlight

Wooden stand

Melting ice in flask

THE HEAT OF THE MOMENT
Antoine Lavoisier was particularly interested in chemical reactions that required great heat. One problem in his scientific work was to obtain heat that was both intense and "clean," for often the reacting substances were contaminated by smoke and soot from the heat source (usually a flame). His solution was this giant mobile burning-glass, or convex lens, with which he enthralled the French populace in 1774.

FOCUS OF ACTIVITY
Heat brings about many changes in matter. It can cause different substances to react together, or it can make a reaction go faster. Here the heat is produced as sunlight is focused by a large convex lens to fall on to a flask containing ice. This causes the ice to melt – a physical rather than a chemical change. If sunlight is focused on to paper, the paper can smolder, and even burst into flame. This is a chemical change, and is an example of combustion.

Higher, stronger flames

3 BREAKDOWN
The substance is rapidly converted into chromium oxide, a compound of chromium and oxygen, and into nitrogen and water vapor, both invisible gases.

4 ASHEN ENDING
The orange crystals of ammonium dichromate have broken down, leaving a large pile of chromium oxide. The nitrogen and water vapor have escaped into the air.

Gray-green ash of chromium oxide

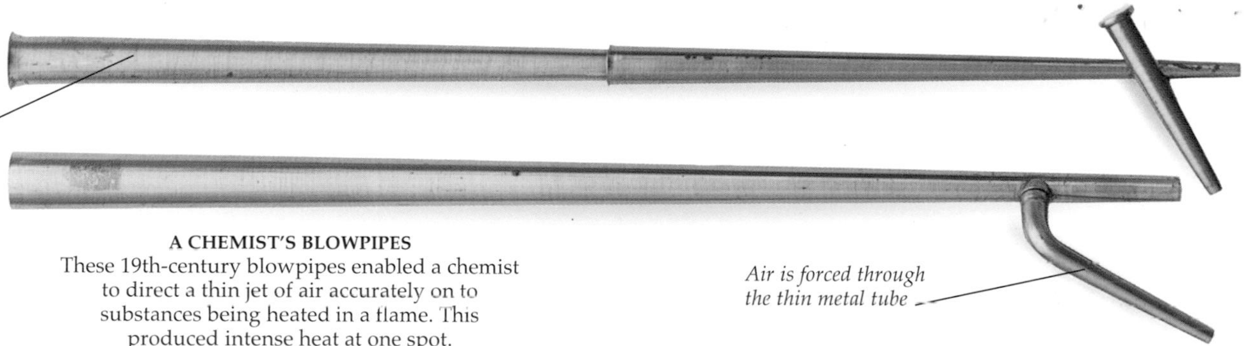

Air is blown through the mouthpiece

A CHEMIST'S BLOWPIPES
These 19th-century blowpipes enabled a chemist to direct a thin jet of air accurately on to substances being heated in a flame. This produced intense heat at one spot.

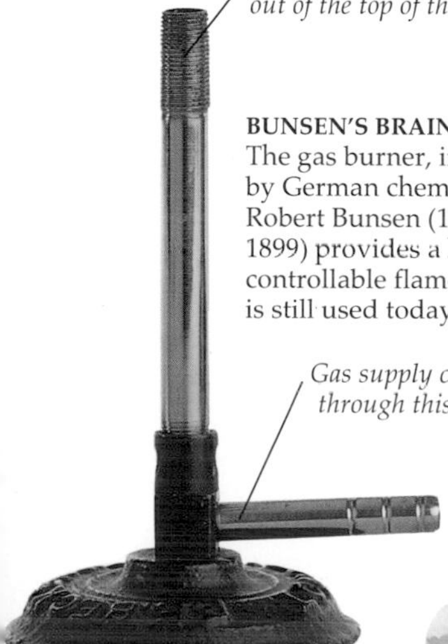

Air is forced through the thin metal tube

Controllable flame comes out of the top of the burner

Large surface area increases the amount of heat that can be delivered

BUNSEN'S BRAINCHILD
The gas burner, invented by German chemist Robert Bunsen (1811-1899) provides a hot, controllable flame, and is still used today.

Gas supply comes through this pipe

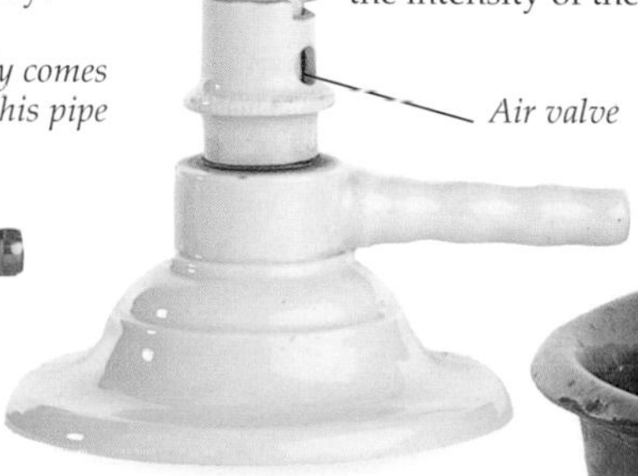

VERSATILE VALVE
The secret of the Bunsen burner lies in the adjustable air valve at the base of the tube, which can be opened in varying degrees to alter the intensity of the flame.

Air valve

A BETTER BURN
This elaborate version of the laboratory gas burner was made in 1874. It increased the amount of heat that could be delivered.

Enamelled iron

Bunsen burner from 1889

Bunsen burner made from flame resistant porcelain

Charting the elements

ELEMENTS ARE PURE SUBSTANCES – they do not contain anything else, and cannot be broken down into simpler substances. Many of the elements were discovered during the 18th and 19th centuries, particularly by using processes such as electrolysis and spectroscopy. In electrolysis, an electric current is passed through compounds to break them down. In spectroscopy, the light given out by hot substances is analyzed with a spectroscope to show an element's characteristic pattern of colors. Dimitri Mendeleyev (1834-1907) brought order to the elements with his "periodic table," based on patterns in properties of elements such as their reactivity.

FLAME TEST
Here common salt (sodium chloride) burns yellow in a flame, revealing the presence of the element sodium.

A BATTERY OF DISCOVERIES
After learning of Alessandro Volta's invention of the electric battery in 1800, Humphry Davy (1778-1829) built his own. It was large, and had 250 metal plates. He used it for electrolysis, and prepared pure samples of new metals (p. 232).

SPLITTING UP SALT
Humphry Davy discovered sodium by electrolyzing molten salt in this apparatus. Davy used electrolysis to obtain other metals with similar properties to sodium, such as barium, potassium, magnesium, calcium, and strontium. He then used potassium to extract another new element, boron.

BURNING QUESTION
This box of flame test equipment dates from the 19th century. It includes a blowpipe, tweezers, and different chemicals for testing. In a flame test, tiny quantities of a substance are held on a wire, which is put in to a flame. The color of the flame often indicates the substance's identity. For example, a flame is turned violet by potassium, and blue-green by copper. Flame tests require the hot flame of the Bunsen burner.

Terminal linked to battery

ELECTRICAL BREAKDOWN

Common salt consists of sodium and chloride ions – positively charged sodium atoms, and negatively charged chlorine atoms. When salt is melted, the ions move around each other. If metal plates connected to a battery are placed in the molten salt, the positive plate attracts the chloride ions, and the negative plate attracts the sodium ions.

Sodium deposited

Negatively charged chloride ion

Chlorine released

Positively charged sodium ion

Negative terminal linked to battery

Positive terminal linked to battery

Liquid compound was placed in glass dish to be electrolyzed

GETTING THE GREEN LIGHT
In 1861 William Crookes discovered a new element, thallium, by spectroscopy. His many samples of thallium compounds are shown here, with one of his notebooks detailing the discovery. He could detect minute quantities of the new element because it emits a brilliant green light when in a hot flame.

The periodic table

The properties of the elements can be described and understood in terms of the periodic table. It shows more than 100 elements, arranged vertically into columns (called groups) and horizontally into rows (called periods). Properties change systematically going down each group and along each period, but elements in each group have generally similar properties. For example, group VIII contains the very unreactive "noble" gases such as argon (Ar), while group I contains very reactive metals such as sodium (Na).

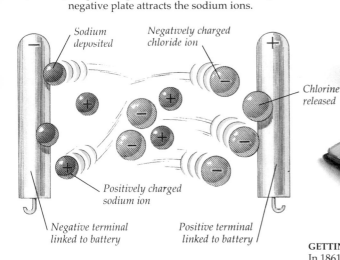

PATTERN FINDER
Dmitri Mendeleyev's periodic table suggested corrections to previously accepted chemical data, and successfully predicted the existence of new elements. The Russian periodic table shown here is based on Mendeleyev's original of 1869.

The building blocks

AS SCIENTISTS DISCOVERED more elements, they pondered over the ultimate nature of matter. The ancient idea of atoms (p. 134) received a boost from English chemist John Dalton (1766-1844) in 1808. He proposed that each element has its own unique atom, and that each compound is formed by a certain combination of atoms. He showed that the weights of atoms relative to each other could be found by weighing the elements that combined in particular compounds. The comparative weight of an atom could be found, but not the actual weight – a given atom could only be said to be so many times heavier than, for example, one of hydrogen, the lightest atom.

CLOSING IN ON ATOMS
Atoms make up the world in much the same way that the letters of the alphabet make up a book. Scientists need a close-up view to study atoms, just as readers have to peer closely at a page to study individual letters.

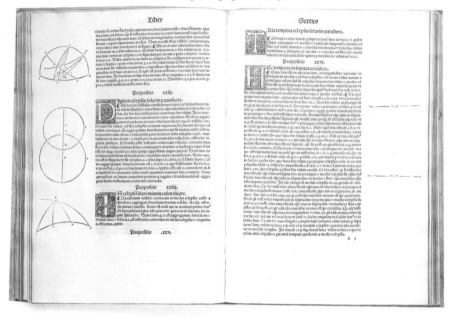

1 THE BOOK OF THE WORLD
A glance at any book shows that it is made up of many things, such as pictures, text of large and small print, and different chapters. Similarly, a glance at the "book of the world" shows that it is a kaleidoscopic array of many sorts of chemical substances. But such a glance does not reveal whether or not the world is made of atoms.

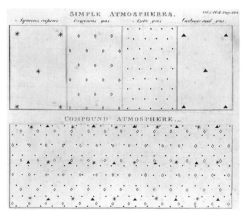

ATMOSPHERIC ATOMS
John Dalton drew these diagrams in 1802. He was an enthusiastic meteorologist and knew that air consists of oxygen, water vapor, carbon dioxide, and nitrogen (top diagram). He developed his atomic theory while explaining why these gases remain mixed, rather than forming separate layers.

2 A PAGE AT A TIME
If a reader concentrates on one page of the "book of the world" and temporarily ignores the rest of the pages, this still gives a sample of the world that is very large compared with the atom. Similarly, when studying matter scientifically a small part must be isolated, for example, by examining a substance in a flask in a laboratory. To obtain a more detailed view of matter, scientists need to use instruments.

ELASTIC FLUIDS
Dalton assumed that gases are made of atoms which are far apart and can move independently. This is why gases can be compressed and expanded. He called gases "elastic fluids," and pictured their atoms like these circles.

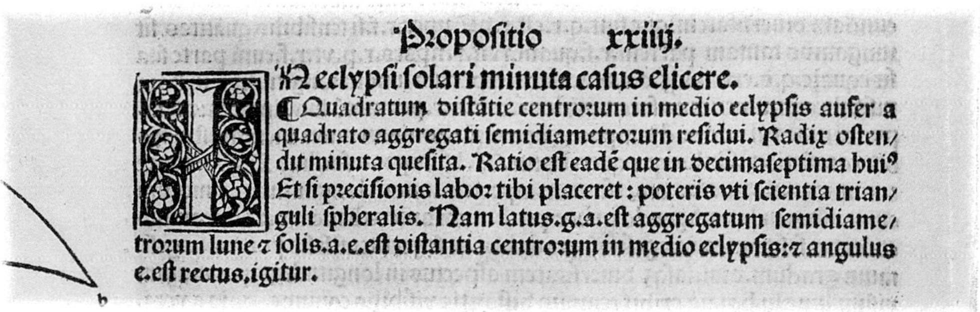

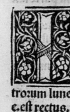

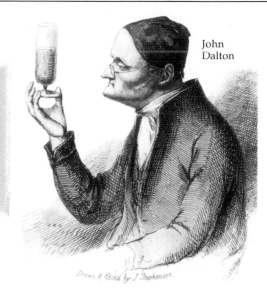

Propoſitio xxiiij.
In eclypſi ſolari minuta caſus elicere.
Quadratum diſtātie centrorum in medio eclypſis aufer a quadrato aggregati ſemidiametrorum reſidui. Radix oſten/dit minuta queſita. Ratio eſt eadē que in decimaſeptima hui⁹ Et ſi preciſionis labor tibi placeret: poteris vti ſcientia trian/guli ſpheralis. Nam latus.g.a.eſt aggregatum ſemidiame/trorum lune & ſolis.a.e.eſt diſtantia centrorum in medio eclypſis: & angulus e.eſt rectus.igitur.

3 ENDLESS VARIETY
In close-up, one piece of text consists of many different words. Similarly, with the aid of chemical analysis and instruments, matter can be seen to be made up of an enormous number of different substances.

quadrato aggregati ſemidiametrorum reſidui. Radix oſten/
dit minuta queſita. Ratio eſt eadē que in decimaſeptima hui⁹
Et ſi preciſionis labor tibi placeret: poteris vti ſcientia trian/
guli ſpheralis. Nam latus.g.a.eſt aggregatum ſemidiame/

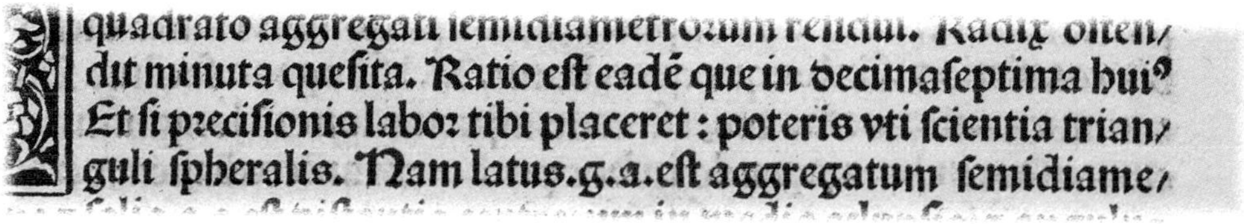

4 NARROW VIEW
A microscope can give a detailed view of a small sample of matter, but this sample may be composed of a variety of substances. It is similar to a sentence, which is made up of many different words.

Ratio

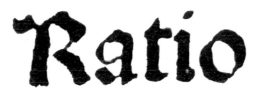

5 WORDS OF SUBSTANCE
"Words" in the "book of the world" are groups of atoms, or molecules. Here, the 26 letters of the Roman alphabet make up words. About 90 different kinds of atom make up molecules.

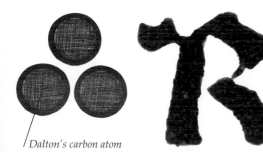

Dalton's carbon atom

6 SINGULAR CHARACTERS
The letters on the printed page correspond to atoms. Just as letters group into words, so atoms form molecules. There is no limit to the words that can be formed from the alphabet, and any number of compounds can be formed from atoms. Not all possible combinations of letters are permitted, and neither are all combinations of atoms.

Drawn & Etched by J. Stephenson

John Dalton

DALTON'S ATOMS AND ELEMENTS
In 1808 John Dalton published his atomic theory. It suggested that all matter is made up of indivisible atoms; each element is composed of atoms of characteristic weight; and compounds are formed when atoms of various elements combine in definite proportions. Below are Dalton's symbols for the atoms of the 36 elements that he believed to exist (over 100 elements have now been found). Some of Dalton's elements shown here, for example lime and soda, are actually compounds, not elements. Dalton also calculated the weight of each element's atom, by comparing it to hydrogen (see also p. 202).

ELEMENTS

Element	W	Element	W
Hydrogen	1	Strontian	46
Azote	5	Barytes	68
Carbon	54	Iron	50
Oxygen	7	Zinc	56
Phosphorus	9	Copper	56
Sulphur	13	Lead	90
Magnesia	20	Silver	190
Lime	24	Gold	190
Soda	28	Platina	190
Potash	42	Mercury	167

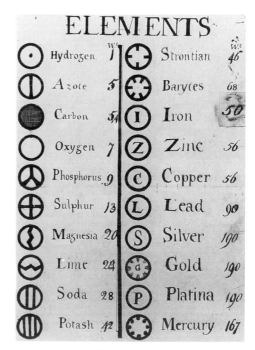

Dalton's elements

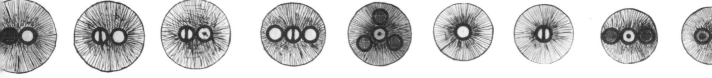

Molecules

ATOMS CAN EXIST SINGLY in some gases, but in many substances they form groups called "molecules." For example, the molecule of water consists of an oxygen atom (O) joined to two hydrogen atoms (H). Its chemical formula is H_2O. Some molecules can be much bigger than this, containing thousands of atoms. In the mid-19th century it was realized that chemical bonds could explain the ways in which atoms link together to form molecules. A bond is like a hook that can link to a similar hook on another atom. For example, an atom of the gas nitrogen has three hooks, while a hydrogen atom has one. Each bond on the nitrogen atom can link to the bond on one hydrogen atom, which produces the molecule NH_3, the gas given off by smelling salts.

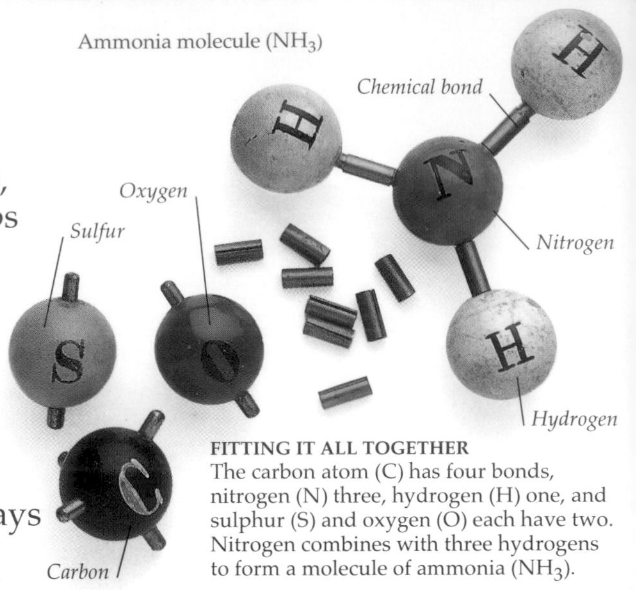

19th-century molecular model of monochloromethane, a type of solvent

Ammonia molecule (NH_3)

Chemical bond

Oxygen

Sulfur

Nitrogen

Hydrogen

Carbon

FITTING IT ALL TOGETHER
The carbon atom (C) has four bonds, nitrogen (N) three, hydrogen (H) one, and sulphur (S) and oxygen (O) each have two. Nitrogen combines with three hydrogens to form a molecule of ammonia (NH_3).

Calcium carbonate molecule ($CaCO_3$)

Oxygen

Carbon

Calcium

1 THE RAW MATERIAL
Limestone is a whitish rock with the chemical name of calcium carbonate. As this name suggests, the molecule of limestone contains atoms of calcium and carbon, but it also contains oxygen. Each atom of carbon is tightly joined to three of oxygen, and this group is more loosely linked to one atom of calcium.

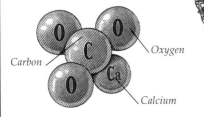

Limestone (calcium carbonate)

Limestone breaks up when heated

Bunsen burner

Pestle

Mortar

Calcium hydroxide paste

FORCEFUL SUGGESTION
Jöns Jakob Berzelius (1779-1848) was one of the first people to suggest that atoms are held together in molecules by electrical forces.

ITALIAN IDEAS
Amedeo Avogadro (1776-1856) suggested that in equal volumes of any two gases there are always the same number of molecules, if the gases are at the same temperature and pressure. For about 50 years his idea was largely ignored, until another Italian chemist, Stanislao Cannizzaro (1826-1910), publicized it. The idea was then quickly accepted, and it helped to clarify many chemical reactions.

Water

Pipette

Crumbly powder (calcium oxide)

Hydrogen

Calcium

Oxygen

Calcium hydroxide molecule (Ca(OH)$_2$)

Oxygen

Calcium carbonate molecule (CaCO$_3$)

Carbon

Calcium

3 ADDING WATER
When water is added to calcium oxide powder there is a strong reaction, and the powder swells up and gives out heat. The molecules of the calcium oxide and of the water, H$_2$O, rearrange themselves to form molecules of calcium hydroxide, a soft and pasty substance. As its name suggests, this molecule contains calcium, hydrogen, and oxygen. Its formula is Ca(OH)$_2$, showing that two oxygen-hydrogen pairs (OH) are joined to a calcium atom.

4 BACK TO CALCIUM CARBONATE
The calcium hydroxide dries and hardens. Water molecules (H$_2$O) are given off into the air, while carbon dioxide molecules (CO$_2$) from the air are absorbed. The calcium hydroxide (Ca(OH)$_2$) turns into calcium carbonate (CaCO$_3$), chemically identical to the raw material. The reconstituted calcium carbonate looks different from the original limestone because it was not formed under high pressure within the Earth.

Carbon dioxide molecule (CO$_2$)

Carbon

Oxygen

Calcium

Calcium oxide molecule (CaO)

2 HEATING THE LIMESTONE
When limestone is heated, it turns into a soft, crumbly powder called calcium oxide. This happens because each molecule of the original calcium carbonate breaks into two smaller molecules. One of these molecules consists of the calcium atom (Ca) joined to a single oxygen atom (O), making CaO. The other molecule consists of the carbon atom joined to the other two oxygen atoms, making CO$_2$. This is carbon dioxide gas, which escapes into the atmosphere.

Tongs

Reconstituted calcium carbonate

Molecules in motion

Highly magnified pollen grains – the key to molecular movement

U P UNTIL THE MID-18TH CENTURY, there was a widely accepted theory that heat was a "fluid" called caloric. However, in 1799 Count Benjamin Rumford (1753-1814) observed that limitless quantities of heat could be generated in the boring of cannon barrels. He suggested that the drilling work was increasing the motions of the atoms that made up the metal. This idea gained support when James Joule (1818-1889) did experiments to measure exactly how much work was needed to generate a definite amount of heat. When heat is applied to matter, the motion of the molecules is increased, and the temperature rises. Gradually it was realised that the differences between the three states of matter – solids, liquids, and gases – are caused by the motion of molecules. The molecules in a solid are fixed, but can vibrate. The molecules in a liquid move around, but still remain in contact with each other. In a gas the molecules fly around freely, and move in straight lines until they collide with each other or with other objects.

DANCE OF THE POLLEN
In 1827, Scotsman Robert Brown (1773-1858) observed pollen grains under a microscope. The grains were suspended in a liquid, and were in constant motion. He thought the motion originated in the pollen particles. But Albert Einstein in 1905, and Jean Perrin (1870-1942) in 1909, explained that the grains were being buffeted by the movement of the molecules in the liquid.

Pointer moves around the dial to show expansion of the rod

MEASURING HEAT EXPANSION
When a solid is heated, the vibration of its molecules increases. Each molecule then needs more space to vibrate, and the solid expands. This device, a pyrometer (meaning "heat-measurer") from the mid-19th century, showed how a metal rod increased in length as it was heated by a gas flame placed beneath it, and then shrank again as it cooled.

Lever turns when rod changes length

Alcohol burner for heating the rod

Free end of rod moves as it expands

Metal rod to be heated

Clamp at fixed end of rod

Support for free end of rod

Weight keeps lever mechanism in close contact with the end of the rod

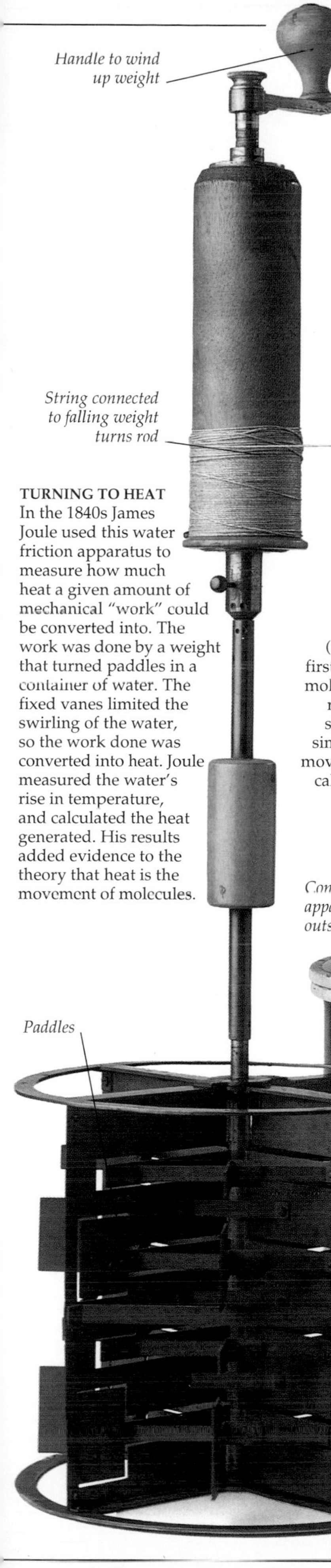

TURNING TO HEAT

In the 1840s James Joule used this water friction apparatus to measure how much heat a given amount of mechanical "work" could be converted into. The work was done by a weight that turned paddles in a container of water. The fixed vanes limited the swirling of the water, so the work done was converted into heat. Joule measured the water's rise in temperature, and calculated the heat generated. His results added evidence to the theory that heat is the movement of molecules.

Handle to wind up weight

String connected to falling weight turns rod

Paddles

TAKING TEMPERATURES

James Joule (p. 30, p. 270) measured the "rate of exchange" between heat, mechanical work, and electrical energy.

RACING AHEAD

Ludwig Boltzmann (1844-1906) was one of the first scientists to assume that molecules in gases move at a range of speeds (previous scientists had assumed for simplicity that all molecules moved at the same speed). He calculated that gas molecules can rotate and vibrate, as well as move through space.

Water inlet

Container insulates apparatus from outside heat

Water outlet

Fixed vanes resist movement of water

Glass separating plate

Bromine is brown

UPWARDLY MOBILE

Gases expand to fill available space. Here, the gas bromine, which is heavier than air, is confined in the lower jar. But when the separating plate is removed, the bromine molecules diffuse into the upper jar.

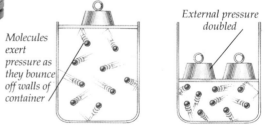

Molecules exert pressure as they bounce off walls of container

External pressure doubled

BOYLE'S LAW

Robert Boyle (p. 152) saw that when a gas is pushed into a smaller volume, it exerts greater pressure. This is because the molecules hit the container wall more frequently.

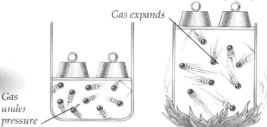

Gas expands

Gas under pressure

CHARLES'S LAW

Jaques Charles (p. 147) saw that when a gas is heated, it exerts greater pressure, and will expand if it can. The molecules move faster and collide more violently with the container walls.

Carbon rings and chains

CLOSING THE CIRCLE
The structure of the benzene molecule, a form of carbon, resembles a snake swallowing its own tail.

CARBON IS UNIQUE in the number and complexity of compounds it can form. More than 7 million carbon-containing compounds are now known, compared with about 100,000 compounds made from all the other elements. Carbon is essential to the chemistry of all living things. The carbon atom can easily link up with other carbon atoms and with most other types of atom, using its four chemical "hooks," or valency bonds. Its molecules can have a "backbone" of a long chain of carbon atoms, either straight or branched. The carbon atoms can also form rings, which can be linked to other rings or carbon chains, to form intricate structures, sometimes consisting of thousands of atoms.

PREHISTORIC PRESSURE
Coal is the fossilized remains of trees and other plants that were buried in swamps. Over about 345 million years, they have been turned into a soft black rock by intense, sustained pressure from layers of other rocks. Coal consists mostly of carbon, with some hydrogen, oxygen, nitrogen, and sulfur. The carbon takes oxygen from the air and burns vigorously, so coal is a useful source of fuel.

Benzene

SMUDGY CARBON
Charcoal, a form of carbon, is obtained when substances such as wood, bone, or sugar are heated strongly with no air present. Charcoal is soft and easy to smudge, and is an excellent drawing material.

Graphite

PLUMBING THE DEPTHS
Graphite, also known as plumbago, is a form of carbon found as a soft mineral. It can easily be made to split and flake. Graphite is the main component of pencil "leads," and is widely used as a lubricant.

LORD OF THE RINGS
Friedrich Kekulé (1829-1896) tried for a long time to calculate how a benzene molecule's six carbon atoms link to the six hydrogen atoms. He found the solution while dozing. He dreamed of a row of carbon and hydrogen atoms closing in a ring, like a snake swallowing its tail.

Carbon atoms are arranged in an intricate lattice

Diamond molecule

Single bond

Benzene molecule

Carbon atoms form a ring

Hydrogen atom

Diamonds

Single bond   *Double bond*

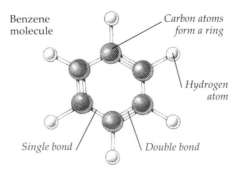

BAFFLING BENZENE
When coal is strongly heated, a colorless liquid – benzene – is obtained. The benzene structure is the basis of a huge number of important carbon compounds. Its molecular structure had baffled chemists until Kekulé thought of it as a ring of carbon atoms linked to hydrogen atoms.

DIAMONDS ARE FOR EVER
The hardest natural material is diamond. It is a valuable gemstone, but is also used as the cutting tip in drills, or for grinding material. It consists of virtually pure carbon. Its atoms are arranged in a very strong three-dimensional lattice (a repeated pattern within a crystal). Each atom is joined to four neighbors by single chemical bonds. Diamonds form where carbon has been subjected to huge geological pressures and temperatures.

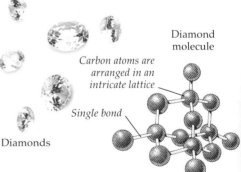

FAT FACTS
Butter is a mixture of fats – carbon-containing substances that are important in living things for storing energy. Similar substances that are liquid at room temperature are called oils.

Butter is an edible fat

Jet brooch

CLEANSING WITH CARBON
Soap is made from substances with long chains of carbon atoms, usually 15 or 17. One end of each soap molecule attaches to water and the other end attaches to oil. This enables soap to break up oil and grease into small drops in water.

BLACK BEAUTY
Jet is a form of coal called lignite, and is largely made up of carbon. It has a deep velvety black color, and is easy to carve and polish. Jet has been used for jewelery since early times.

Gasoline

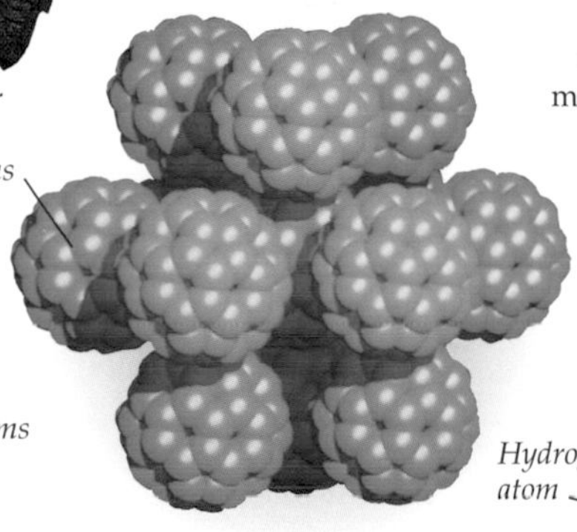

Each cluster contains 60 carbon atoms

Octane molecule

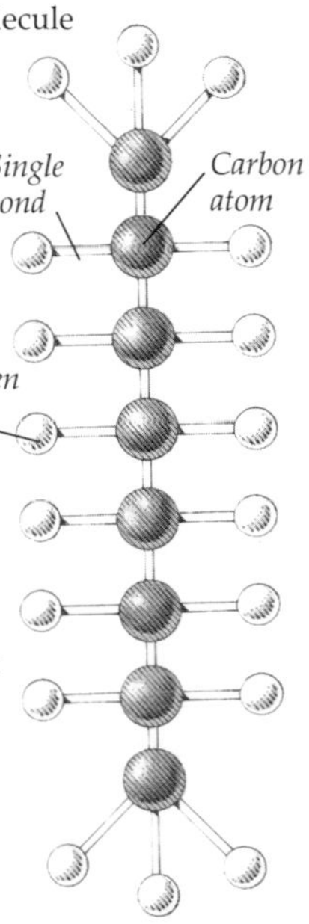

Graphite molecule

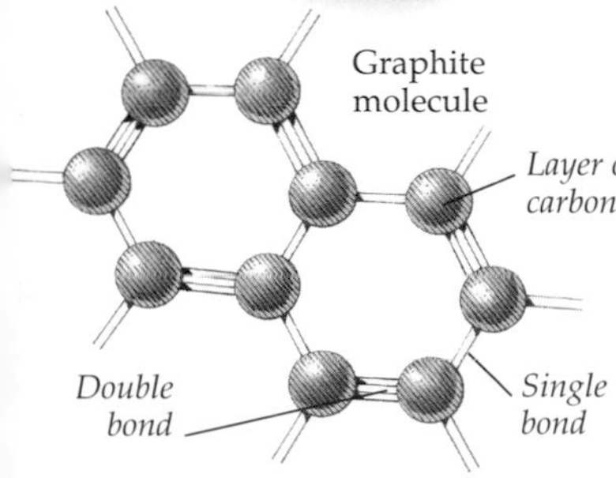

Layer of carbon atoms

Single bond

Carbon atom

Hydrogen atom

Double bond

Single bond

ATOMS IN LAYERS
Graphite and diamond are the two crystalline forms of carbon. Unlike diamond, the carbon atoms in graphite are joined in flat layers. Each layer is only weakly joined to the next, and so the layered atoms can easily slip over each other.

GLOBULAR CARBON
One of the strangest forms of carbon to be discovered consists of globular clusters of carbon atoms. The computer graphics color representation shown here is the simplest form, with each globe containing 60 atoms. It is named buckminsterfullerene, after Buckminster Fuller (1895-1983), an inventor who developed the similarly shaped geodesic dome. Though only recently discovered, buckminsterfullerene (also known as buckyballs) is fairly common, and can be found in soot particles.

LIQUID POWER
Most gasoline molecules are chains, containing between five and ten carbon atoms. The gasoline molecule octane (left) contains eight carbons. Gasoline is derived from petroleum oil, a mixture of liquids, solids, and gases that are the fossilized remains of microscopic life.

Living matter

Original templates from Watson and Crick's DNA model

ANIMALS AND PLANTS ARE AMAZINGLY complex forms of living matter. They can grow, reproduce, move, and respond to their environments. Until the late 19th century, many scientists thought a "vital principle" must control the behavior of living matter. Such beliefs changed when scientists began to be able to synthesize a range of "organic" substances (substances previously found only in living things), and started to explain the chemistry of the processes within living creatures. It was once thought that flies and other small creatures could develop spontaneously from rotting matter, but Louis Pasteur (1822-1895) showed that new life can only arise from existing organisms. Life has never yet been made in a scientific laboratory from nonliving matter. This leaves the problem of how life developed on earth from a "soup" of nonliving molecules.

FLIES IN THE SOUP
In the 1860s, when Louis Pasteur boiled a flask of broth and left it, he learned that new life arises only from living matter. Dust from the air fell in the broth, and microorganisms grew. But when only dust-free air reached the broth, nothing grew.

ANALYSING THE ORGANIC
In the 19th century many "organic" substances were closely examined. This apparatus (left) was used in the 1880s to measure the nitrogen in urea.

Saturated solution of common salt was placed in glass cup

Measuring tube was filled with distilled water

Central tube

Sodium hypobromite solution was placed in here

UNDERSTANDING UREA
A landmark in understanding life was the synthesis of urea, a nitrogen-containing chemical found in animal waste. Friedrich Wöhler (1800-1882) made urea in 1828 from ammonia and cyanic acid.

When the tap was opened, the solutions mixed, and nitrogen was produced and collected in the measuring tube

Sample of urea containing unknown concentration of nitrogen was placed in here

CO_2

Animals take in carbon from green plants, and animal wastes and remains contain carbon

Green plants absorb and give out CO_2

Rocks absorb and give out CO_2

NEVERENDING CYCLE
Carbon is the basis for all living matter, circulating between air, oceans, rocks, and living things. Carbon dioxide gas (CO_2) is absorbed from the air by green plants. Plant-eaters use the plant's carbon for tissue-building. Carbon is returned to the environment in animals' waste products, and when dead animals decay. Rocks and water also absorb and give off CO_2 and complete the cycle.

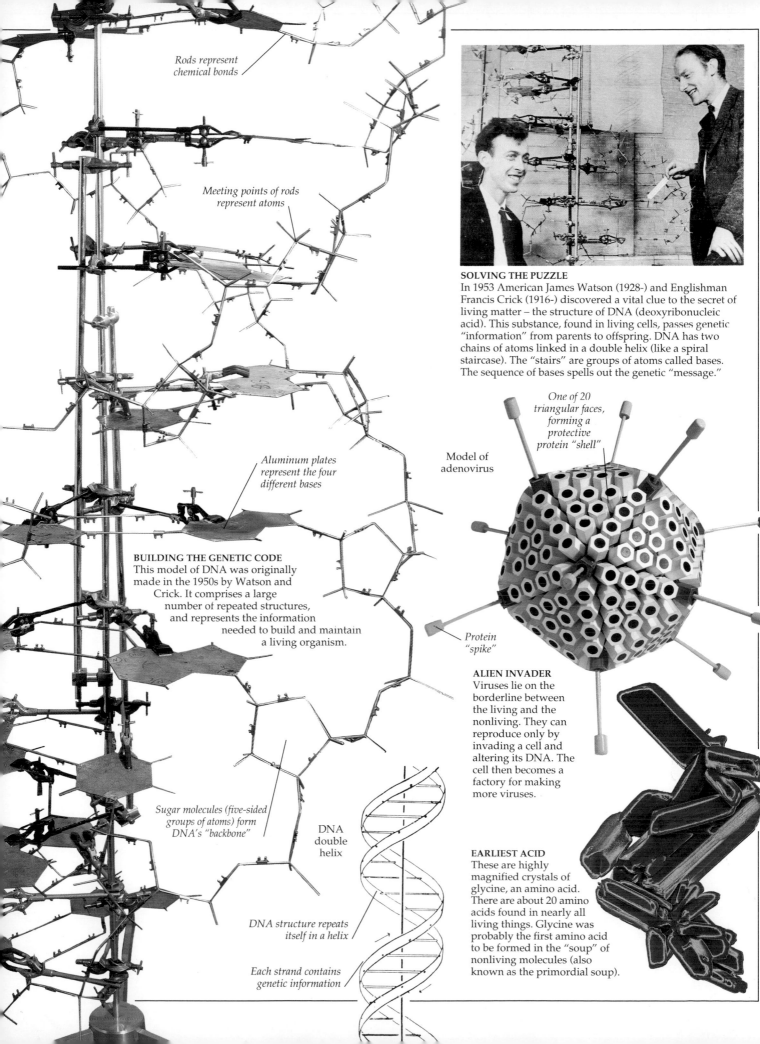

*Rods represent
chemical bonds*

*Meeting points of rods
represent atoms*

*Aluminum plates
represent the four
different bases*

BUILDING THE GENETIC CODE
This model of DNA was originally
made in the 1950s by Watson and
Crick. It comprises a large
number of repeated structures,
and represents the information
needed to build and maintain
a living organism.

*Sugar molecules (five-sided
groups of atoms) form
DNA's "backbone"*

DNA
double
helix

*DNA structure repeats
itself in a helix*

*Each strand contains
genetic information*

SOLVING THE PUZZLE
In 1953 American James Watson (1928-) and Englishman
Francis Crick (1916-) discovered a vital clue to the secret of
living matter – the structure of DNA (deoxyribonucleic
acid). This substance, found in living cells, passes genetic
"information" from parents to offspring. DNA has two
chains of atoms linked in a double helix (like a spiral
staircase). The "stairs" are groups of atoms called bases.
The sequence of bases spells out the genetic "message."

*One of 20
triangular faces,
forming a
protective
protein "shell"*

Model of
adenovirus

*Protein
"spike"*

ALIEN INVADER
Viruses lie on the
borderline between
the living and the
nonliving. They can
reproduce only by
invading a cell and
altering its DNA. The
cell then becomes a
factory for making
more viruses.

EARLIEST ACID
These are highly
magnified crystals of
glycine, an amino acid.
There are about 20 amino
acids found in nearly all
living things. Glycine was
probably the first amino acid
to be formed in the "soup" of
nonliving molecules (also
known as the primordial soup).

Designing molecules

Artificial teeth and dental plate from the 1870s

IN THE MID-19TH CENTURY chemists began to use their new knowledge of organic molecules to make new materials with valuable properties. Parkesine, an imitation ivory, was made in 1862 by Alexander Parkes (1813-1890). In 1884 Hilaire de Chardonnet (1839-1924) made rayon, the first artificial fiber, by imitating the chemical structure of silk. Rubber was toughened and made more useful by the vulcanizing process (heat treatment with sulfur), invented in 1839. The age of plastics was ushered in by Leo Baekeland (1863-1944), who invented Bakelite in 1909. Plastics are polymers – large molecules with possibly thousands of identical groups of atoms chained together. Plastics can be molded by heat and pressure, but then become fixed in shape. They are unreactive, and do not disturb the body's chemistry when used as a replacement hipjoint, for example. Plastics pose a waste disposal problem, however, for most are not biodegradable. In addition to plastics, modern chemists have designed many useful products, such as drugs, detergents, and alloys.

Matte bakelite

BAEKELAND'S BAKELITE
The first entirely synthetic plastic, bakelite was used in early telephones and other electrical devices. It was developed in the United States in 1909.

EBONITE ARTIFACT
This saxophone mouthpiece is made of ebonite, a type of vulcanized rubber. It is also known as vulcanite.

Ebonite resembles ebony

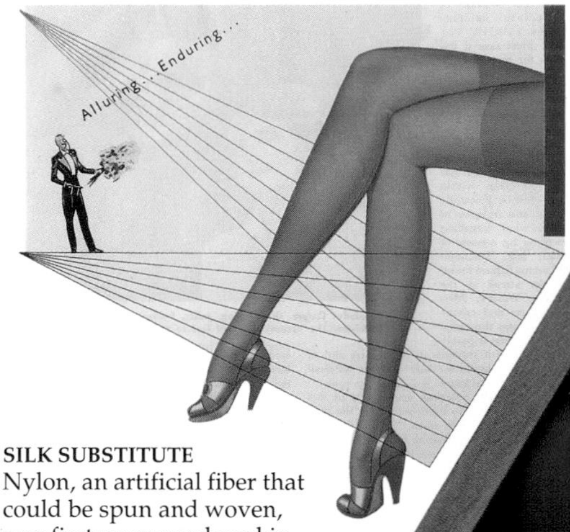

Alluring... Enduring...

Bakelite hairdryer

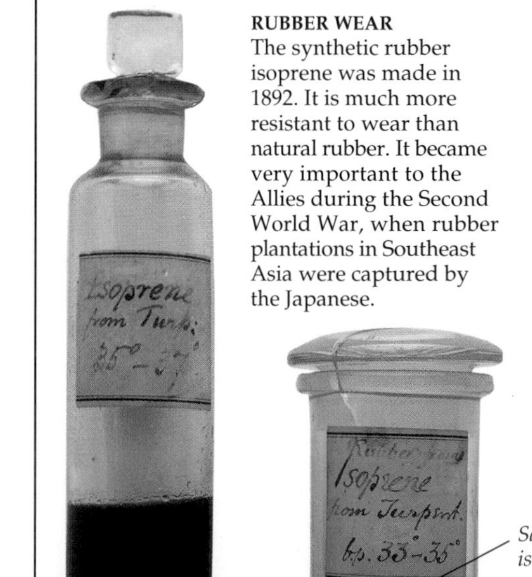

RUBBER WEAR
The synthetic rubber isoprene was made in 1892. It is much more resistant to wear than natural rubber. It became very important to the Allies during the Second World War, when rubber plantations in Southeast Asia were captured by the Japanese.

SILK SUBSTITUTE
Nylon, an artificial fiber that could be spun and woven, was first mass-produced in the 1940s. It was mainly used in stockings and underwear.

FLEXIBLE HARDNESS
These billiard balls are made of celluloid, a hard plastic. It is also flexible, and was used as a base for photographic film, and in shirt collars.

Samples of isoprene

A BALATA BALL
Balata, a hard, rubberlike substance, is used for the outer casing of golf balls. Natural balata is now extremely rare, and has had to be replaced by synthetic plastics.

Outer casing of a golf ball is made of balata

IN THE FRAME
A tough high-density form of polyethylene is used for spectacle frames. Polyethylene is most familiar as packaging.

MARBLED FOUNTAIN
Plastic cases made fountainpens cheaper. Their "marbled" appearance was created by mixing different colored plastics.

PLASTIC PLATTER
This plastic plate is a thermoset – it has been hardened by heating during its manufacture, and is consequently heat-resistant.

HOT STUFF
Bakelite is a good thermal and electrical insulator, and was used in items such as this 1930s hairdryer.

Slightly marbled bakelite

PLASTIC PERSONALITY
The plastic Michelin Man advertises Michelin car tires, which are made of vulcanized rubber.

SCREEN TEST
Chemists now work with molecules on computer screens. This is a molecule of enkephalin, a natural substance in the brain that affects the perception of pain. The atoms in the molecule are color-coded, positioned, and in their correct proportions. Their positions can be modified, or new groups can be added. The computer has stored information about the forces between the atoms, so chemically impossible groupings are not permitted. The proposed molecule can be rigorously tested on screen, and precious laboratory research time can be saved.

Radioactivity

IN 1880 THE ATOM WAS STILL THOUGHT TO BE impenetrable and unchanging. However, by 1900 this picture was seen to be incorrect. An important new discovery was radioactivity. This is the emission of invisible radiations by certain kinds of atoms, happening spontaneously and unaffected by chemical reactions, temperature, or physical factors. The radiations are alpha, beta, or gamma (α, β, or γ). Ernest Rutherford (1871-1937) did most to clarify radioactivity. He found that α-particles were helium atoms, without electrons and β-particles were fast electrons. When α- or β-particles were shot out from the atom, a different sort of atom was left. Such changes could cause γ-radiation, a type of electromagnetic radiation, to be emitted. Transmutation, long dreamed of by the alchemists as they tried to change one element into another, really was possible. It is now known that radiations in large doses, or in small exposures over long periods, can cause sickness and death. Nevertheless, radioactivity has many important uses. For example, metal objects can be "X-rayed" with γ-rays, medicines moving around the body can be tagged with radioactive "tracers," and archaeological finds can be dated by measuring their radioactivity.

BECQUEREL'S RAYS
While studying Xrays (radiation that could penetrate certain materials) Antoine Becquerel (1852-1908) stumbled on a new kind of invisible, penetrating radiation. In 1896 he found that crystals of a uranium compound could "fog" photographic film, even when the film was wrapped in black paper.

Cartoon of the Curies

A CURIOUS COUPLE
Marie Curie (1867-1934), assisted by her husband Pierre (1859-1906), found that the uranium ore pitchblende was considerably more radioactive than pure uranium. They realized that pitchblende must contain additional, more highly radioactive substances. In 1902, after four years of laborious effort, they isolated tiny quantities of two new elements, polonium and radium. Like other early scientists working with radioactivity, the Curies knew little of its dangers, and Marie Curie died of leukemia. The high radiation levels with which she worked are evident from her glass flask – exposure to radiation turned it from clear to blue.

Marie Curie's glass flask

URANIUM ORE
Pitchblende is a brownish-black rock consisting mainly of uranium chemically combined with oxygen. It forms crystals called uraninite. Once considered useless, pitchblende is now the main source of uranium and radium.

FLASH GADGET
William Crookes invented the spinthariscope, for detecting α-particles. The α-particles struck a screen coated with zinc sulfide, creating a tiny flash seen through the eyepiece.

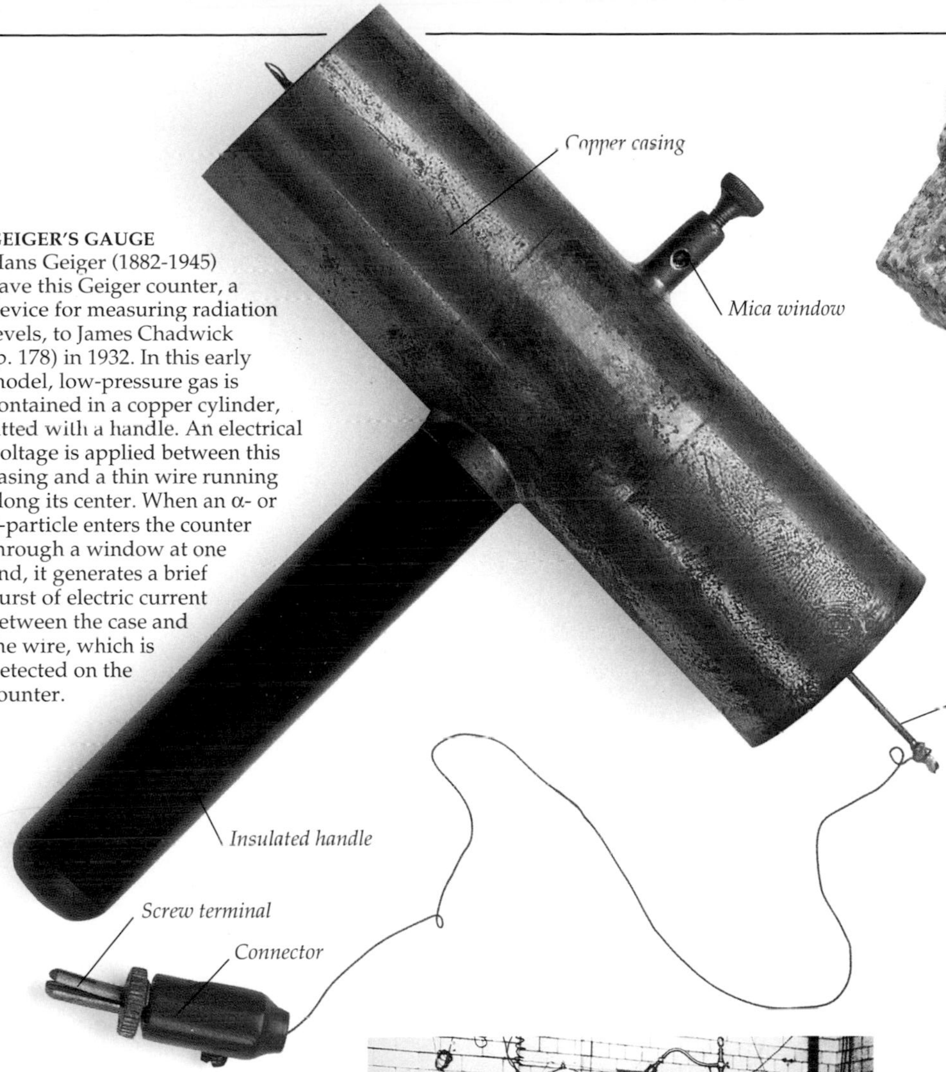

GEIGER'S GAUGE

Hans Geiger (1882-1945) gave this Geiger counter, a device for measuring radiation levels, to James Chadwick (p. 178) in 1932. In this early model, low-pressure gas is contained in a copper cylinder, fitted with a handle. An electrical voltage is applied between this casing and a thin wire running along its center. When an α- or β-particle enters the counter through a window at one end, it generates a brief burst of electric current between the case and the wire, which is detected on the counter.

Copper casing

Mica window

Thin wire runs the length of the counter

Insulated handle

Screw terminal

Connector

RADIATION OF THE ROCKS

A low level of "background" radioactivity is present in everything, even in our bodies. Levels are higher in regions of granite rock, for granite contains uranium. Granite emits radon gas, which can accumulate in homes and threaten health.

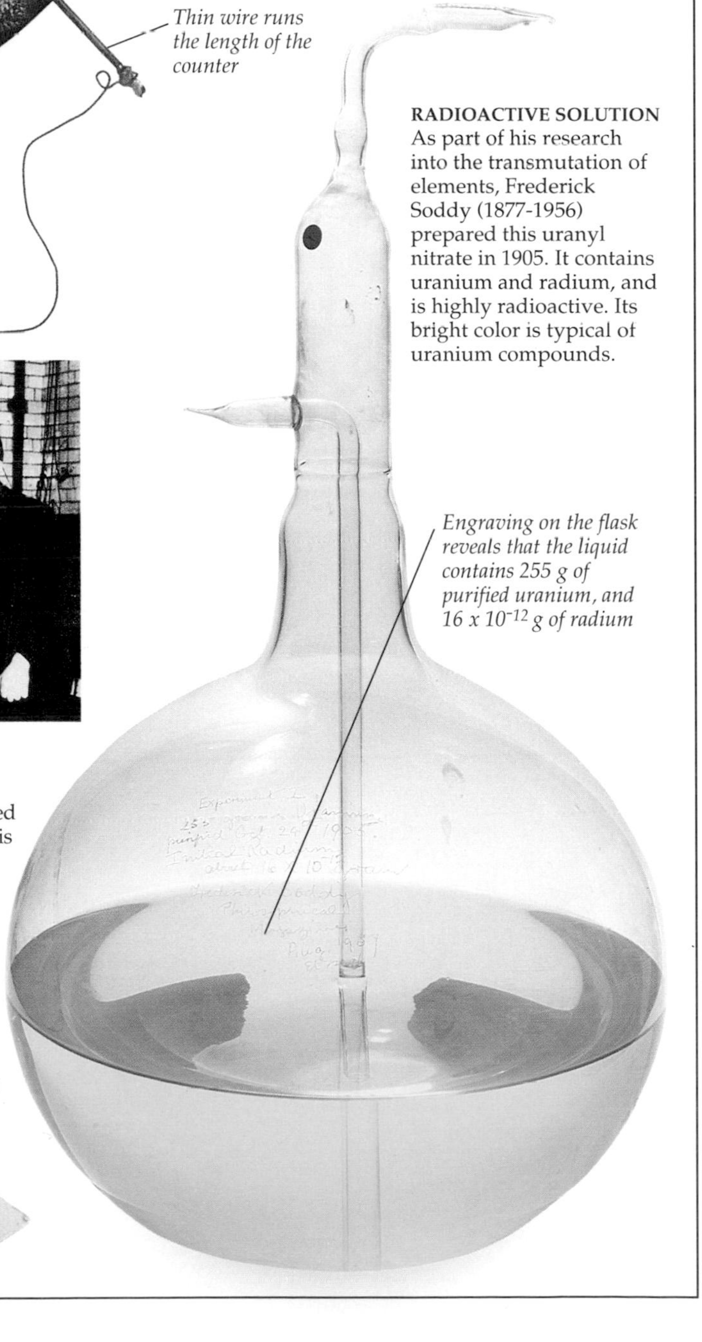

RADIOACTIVE SOLUTION

As part of his research into the transmutation of elements, Frederick Soddy (1877-1956) prepared this uranyl nitrate in 1905. It contains uranium and radium, and is highly radioactive. Its bright color is typical of uranium compounds.

PHYSICISTS AT WORK

Ernest Rutherford (right) and Hans Geiger in their laboratory at Manchester University in England, about 1908, with apparatus for detecting α-particles. Geiger and Rutherford realized that α-particles were helium atoms without electrons.

Part of image on shroud

CARBON DATING THE TURIN SHROUD

The body of the crucified Christ was reputedly wrapped in a shroud, and was said to have created a life-size image still visible on the cloth. Analysis of a radioactive form of carbon taken from tiny samples of the shroud, now kept at Turin, showed that in fact the cloth was from medieval times.

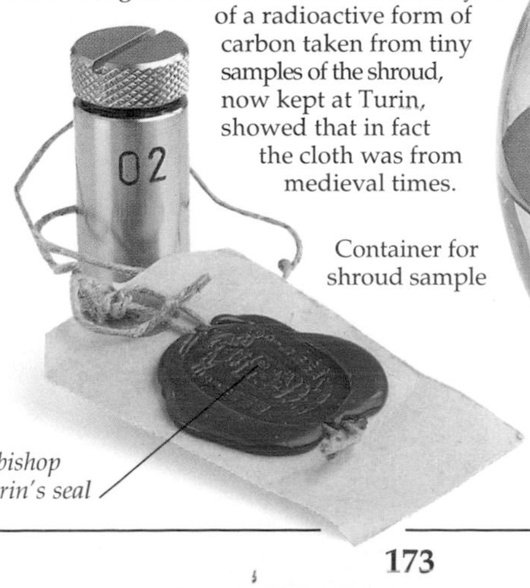

Container for shroud sample

Engraving on the flask reveals that the liquid contains 255 g of purified uranium, and 16×10^{-12} g of radium

Archbishop of Turin's seal

Inside the atom

THE FIRST CLUE TO THE STRUCTURE of the atom came from experiments by English physicist J. J. Thomson (1856-1940) in 1897. He discovered particles that were smaller than atoms in cathode rays. These rays were seen passing between high voltage terminals in a glass tube filled with low pressure gas. The particles, called corpuscles by Thomson and later known as electrons, had a negative electric charge and were about 2,000 times lighter than a hydrogen atom. They were exactly the same whatever gas was used in the tube, and whatever metal the terminals were made of. This strongly suggested that electrons were present in all matter. Atoms must also contain positive electric charge to balance the negative charge of electrons. Ernest Rutherford probed atoms with particles produced in his radioactivity experiments, and found that the positive charge was concentrated in a tiny nucleus. He reached the conclusion that the atom resembled a miniature solar system, where the "planets" were the electrons and the "sun" was the nucleus.

MYSTERY RAYS
William Crookes (1832-1919) devised a glass tube that could contain a vacuum. It was used for the study of cathode rays (electrons emitted by a cathode – a negative terminal – when heated). He placed small obstacles in the rays, which cast "shadows," showing that their direction of travel was from the cathode to the positive terminal (the anode). They could make a small wheel turn in the tube, and Crookes concluded that the rays consisted of charged particles. The tube later became known as the Crookes tube.

High voltage between the metal plates creates an electric field, which bends the paths of charged particles

Paper scale for measuring deflection of electron beam

Low-pressure gas

Particles make glowing spot on glass

ATOM ATTACK
In 1911 Ernest Rutherford studied the effects of bombarding pieces of gold or platinum foil with alpha (α) particles – positively charged particles given out by radioactive materials. Most α-particles passed through the foil, but about one in 8,000 was deflected by more than 90°. Rutherford explained that this was due to the nucleus – a dense centre of positive charge within the atom.

Positively charged nucleus

α–particle deflected by more than 90°

α–particle scarcely deviated

α–particle track strongly bent

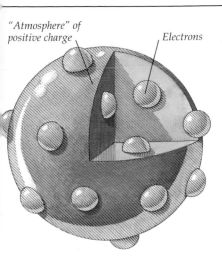

"Atmosphere" of positive charge

Electrons

THOMSON'S DISCOVERIES

J. J. Thomson intended to be an engineer, but instead became a brilliant physicist. He studied cathode rays with great success because he managed to achieve very low gas pressures in his modified Crookes tube. Thomson's discovery of the electron – the fundamental unit of electric current, present in all matter – revolutionized the theories of electricity and atoms. He also confirmed the existence of isotopes (pp. 178-179) - elements that each have several types of atom, chemically identical, but differing in weight (p. 301).

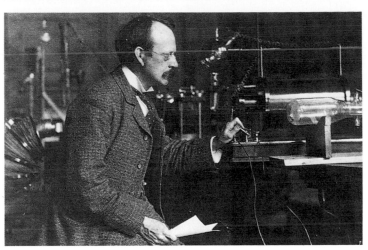

THE PLUM PUDDING ATOM

In his plum pudding theory, J. J. Thomson suggested that every atom consists of a number of electrons, and an amount of positive charge to balance their negative charges. He thought the positive charge formed an "atmosphere" through which the electrons moved, like plums in a plum pudding.

Electrons pass through slits in anodes (positive terminal)

Heated cathode (negative terminal) produces electrons

WEIGHING THE ELECTRON

This is Thomson's original apparatus for studying cathode rays. It contained low pressure gas, through which cathode rays passed. The paths of the rays were bent by an electric field and Thomson measured the amount of bending. The electric field was switched off, a magnetic field was switched on, and again the bending was measured. Thomson calculated that if the particles had the same charge as the hydrogen ion (an "incomplete" atom) found in electrolysis they must be about 2,000 times lighter.

Coils for magnetic field, which bends the charged particles

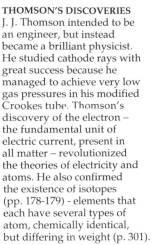

RUTHERFORD'S DISCOVERIES

During his experiments with radioactivity, Ernest Rutherford discovered the transmutation of one element into another. He also studied the half-life of an element – the time taken for half of a sample of a radioactive element to decay, or change into another element. He published his discoveries in 1904 in his book *Radioactivity*.

THE NUCLEAR ATOM

After Rutherford's explanation of the scattering of α–particles, the structure of the atom became clearer. Negatively charged electrons were thought to move around a positively charged, dense nucleus, much like planets moving around the sun. However, there were problems with this "solar-system" model. According to the laws of physics at that time, such an atom should have collapsed instantly in a burst of electromagnetic radiation. (It is now known that the atom does not collapse because electrons are only "allowed" certain energies.)

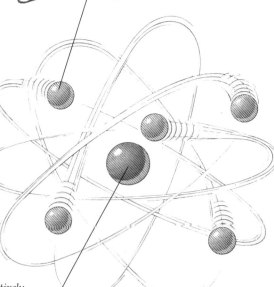

Negatively charged electron

Positively charged nucleus

Electrons, shells, and bonds

IN THE EARLY 1900s the structure of the atom became clearer, but the laws of physics at the time could not explain why electrons did not quickly spiral in toward the nucleus. Niels Bohr (1885-1962), a student of Rutherford, helped to solve the mystery by suggesting that electrons were only "allowed" certain energies. He found that electrons with the lowest allowed energy orbit closest to the nucleus, and electrons with the highest allowed energy orbit furthest away. It was soon discovered that there is a limit to the number of electrons with each energy. Electrons in an atom behave as if they are stacked, lowest energies first, in "shells" around the nucleus. It is the electrons in an atom's outermost shell that decide an atom's chemical properties. Atoms with outer shells "filled" with electrons are less reactive than those with only one electron in their outer shell. The outermost electrons join, or bond, with other atoms to form molecules. This new picture of the atom explained the reactions of atoms in processes such as electrolysis.

THE EXPENSE OF EROS
In 1884 this aluminum statue of the Greek god Eros was highly expensive, but now aluminum can be cheaply produced by electrolysis.

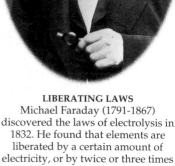

LIBERATING LAWS
Michael Faraday (1791-1867) discovered the laws of electrolysis in 1832. He found that elements are liberated by a certain amount of electricity, or by twice or three times this amount. This depends on the number of outer electrons (see also p. 28, p. 176).

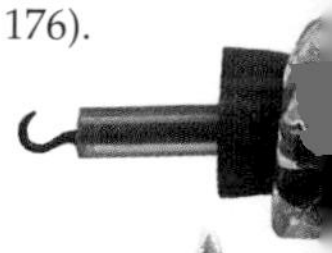

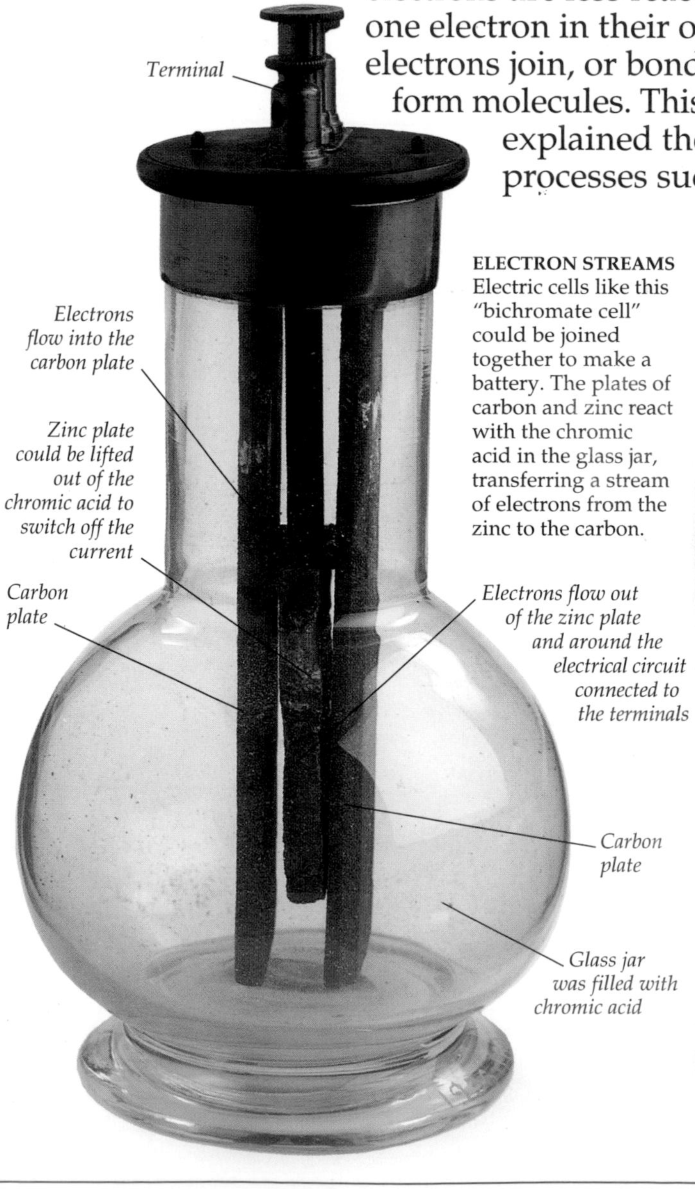

Terminal

Electrons flow into the carbon plate

Zinc plate could be lifted out of the chromic acid to switch off the current

Carbon plate

Electrons flow out of the zinc plate and around the electrical circuit connected to the terminals

Carbon plate

Glass jar was filled with chromic acid

ELECTRON STREAMS
Electric cells like this "bichromate cell" could be joined together to make a battery. The plates of carbon and zinc react with the chromic acid in the glass jar, transferring a stream of electrons from the zinc to the carbon.

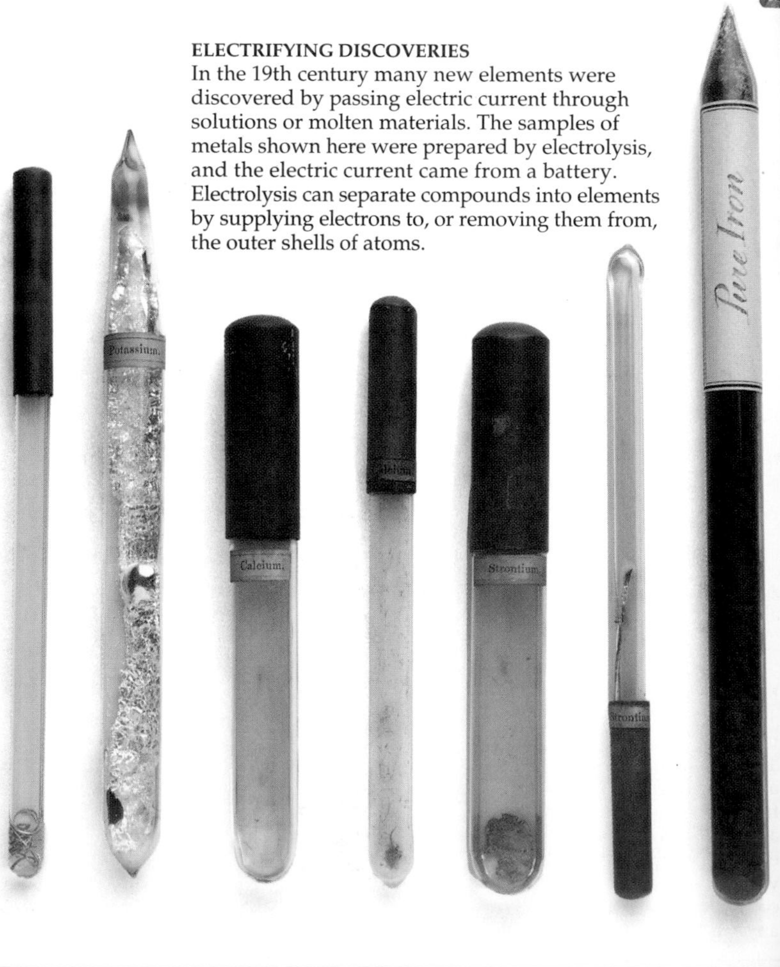

ELECTRIFYING DISCOVERIES
In the 19th century many new elements were discovered by passing electric current through solutions or molten materials. The samples of metals shown here were prepared by electrolysis, and the electric current came from a battery. Electrolysis can separate compounds into elements by supplying electrons to, or removing them from, the outer shells of atoms.

BREAKING DOWN WATER

This equipment was used by Michael Faraday (left) to study the decomposition of water by electricity. Hydrogen came off at one electrode and oxygen at the other. The amounts of these gases were measured, as was the amount of electricity required to release them from water. Faraday worked out the laws of electrolysis in this way. In his honour, the basic amount of electricity used in electrolysis is called the Faraday constant.

Tube for collecting oxygen or hydrogen

Terminals were connected to a battery

Glass globe was filled with water and a little acid

Platinum electrode

LIGHT ON THE MATTER

Niels Bohr explained the connection between matter and light in 1913. He suggested that when electrons move from one energy level to another, they give out or absorb "packets" of radiation in the form of light. These packets are called photons, or quanta. The shorter the radiation's wavelength, the higher the photon's energy.

Eight electrons in second level or "shell"

Lone electron

Two electrons in first level or "shell"

Nucleus

BOHR'S ATOM

In Bohr's theory of the atom, electrons that are farther out from the nucleus have higher energy, and an electron can jump to a higher level by absorbing energy. This can happen at high temperatures, or when photons with enough energy hit the atom. If there is a gap in a lower level, an electron can fall down to that level, giving out energy in the form of radiation.

IONIC BONDS

Sodium and chlorine ions are held together by their opposing electric charges. The sodium atom "wants" to lose its outer electron because the atom is unstable, and the incomplete atom (ion) is left with a positive electric charge. A chlorine atom "wants" to gain an electron to fill its outer shell, and gains an extra negative charge.

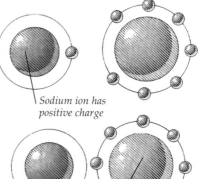

Sodium ion has positive charge

Chlorine ion has negative charge

Sodium chloride – common salt

Mask to avoid poisoning from chlorine gas

COVALENT BONDS

Atoms can share electrons in their outer shells to produce filled shells, forming a "covalent" bond. Chlorine atoms, with seven electrons in the outer shell, can pair off, each pair sharing two electrons. Each atom effectively has eight electrons in the outer shell. Like many other gases, chlorine normally exists in the form of two-atom molecules. The bond is easily broken, making chlorine reactive and dangerous.

Chlorine atoms can pair off and share two electrons

"Pool" of shared electrons

Aluminum aircraft

METALLIC BONDS

The atoms of metals share their outer electrons. They are contributed to a "pool," and wander freely from atom to atom. The electrons' ease of movement is why metals are good conductors of heat and electricity.

CLOUDS OF MYSTERY

Bohr's sharply defined electron orbits have been superseded by fuzzy electron "clouds" (right), which can be seen with an electron microscope. It is now known that electrons behave as waves, as well as like particles. An electron is most likely to be found where the electron "cloud" is dense. But there is always a definite, if small, chance of finding it closer to, or farther from, the nucleus.

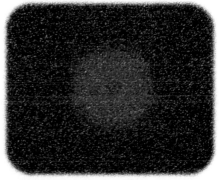

Architecture of the nucleus

By THE EARLY 20TH CENTURY, it was known that the atom had a positively charged nucleus. Ernest Rutherford suggested that the nucleus contained positively charged particles called "protons" (Greek for "first things"). He demonstrated their existence in 1919 by knocking them out of nitrogen nuclei using alpha (α) particles. James Chadwick (1891-1974) discovered another particle in the nucleus in 1932 – the neutron, an uncharged particle of about the same mass as the proton. All nuclei comprise protons and neutrons. The number of protons determines the number of electrons circling the nucleus, and therefore the chemical properties of the atom. All elements have different isotopes – atoms with the same number of protons but different numbers of neutrons.

PARTICLE DISCOVERER
James Chadwick, a student of Rutherford, discovered neutrons by exposing the metal beryllium to α-particles. He observed a new kind of particle ejected from its nucleus, the neutron. Later he studied deuterium (also known as "heavy hydrogen"). This isotope of hydrogen was discovered in 1932 and is used in nuclear reactors.

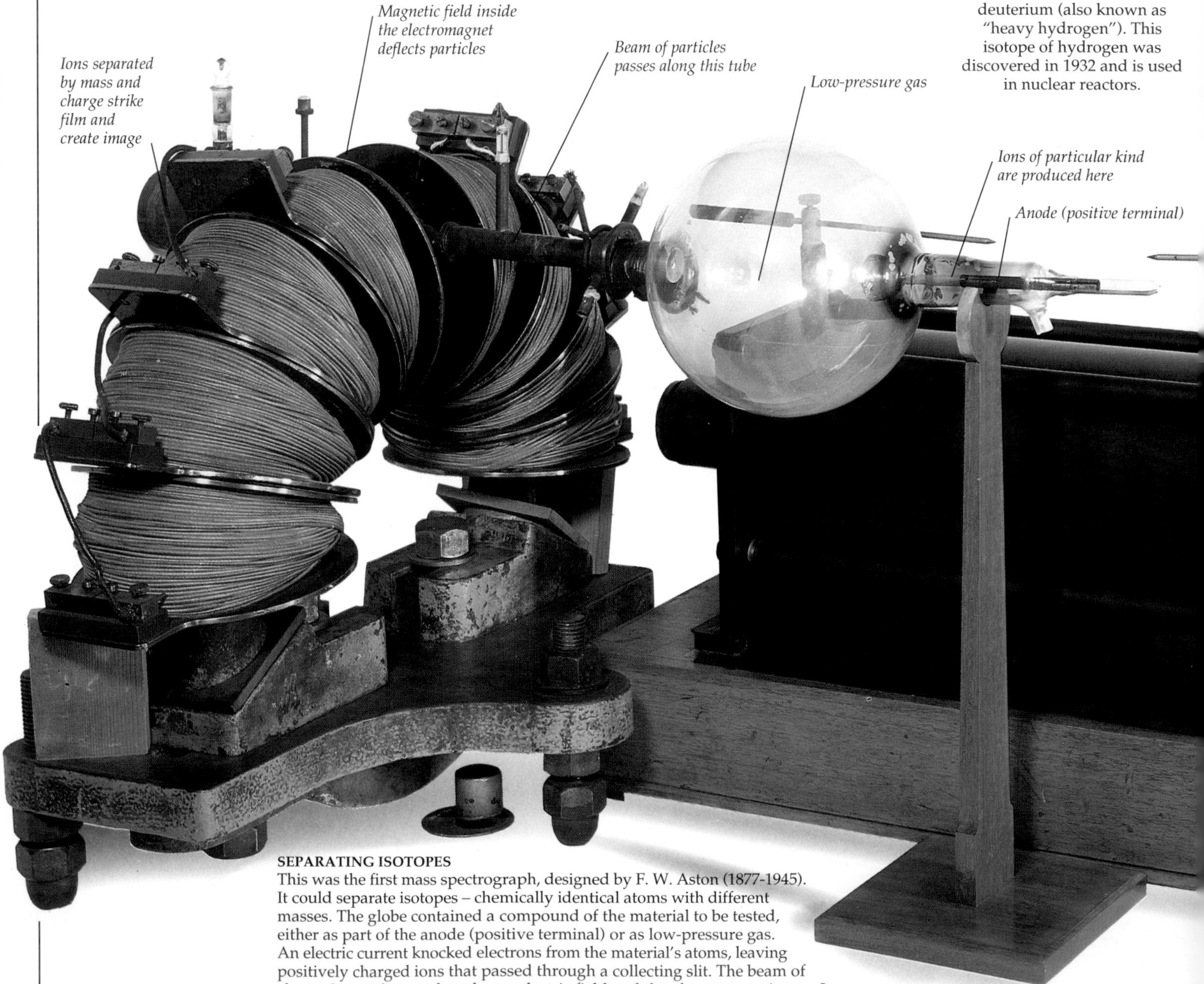

Ions separated by mass and charge strike film and create image

Magnetic field inside the electromagnet deflects particles

Beam of particles passes along this tube

Low-pressure gas

Ions of particular kind are produced here

Anode (positive terminal)

SEPARATING ISOTOPES
This was the first mass spectrograph, designed by F. W. Aston (1877-1945). It could separate isotopes – chemically identical atoms with different masses. The globe contained a compound of the material to be tested, either as part of the anode (positive terminal) or as low-pressure gas. An electric current knocked electrons from the material's atoms, leaving positively charged ions that passed through a collecting slit. The beam of charged particles was bent by an electric field and then by a magnetic one. It was spread into separate bands on a photographic film, according to the ions' charge and mass.

Electrons, protons, and neutrons

Rutherford believed the nucleus was made up of protons and a smaller number of electrons. He thought that each electron was closely paired with a proton to make a "doublet" that was neutral (had zero electric charge). In 1932 James Chadwick produced a type of radiation that did not bend in an electric field, but was far more penetrating than gamma rays. This radiation consisted of uncharged particles, known as "neutrons," that were about as massive as hydrogen atoms. Chadwick realized that these neutrons might be particles themselves, and not a proton and electron combined. This view is now accepted. However, a free neutron has a 50 percent chance of "decaying" into a proton and electron in 15 minutes. If a proton and electron collide they will produce a neutron.

NEUTRON DETECTOR
Inside this intriguing apparatus built by Chadwick, α-particles from a radioactive source struck a beryllium target. The neutrons given off could be detected only when they knocked protons from a piece of paraffin wax. The protons were detected with a Geiger counter (p. 173).

Tube was fixed to an air pump to take air out of the chamber

Chamber contained a radioactive source

A SCIENTIST'S TOOLS
This cigarette carton was Chadwick's "toolbox." He used the pieces of paraffin wax to observe neutrons. The silver and aluminum foils, of different thicknesses, were used as barriers to determine the penetrating power of the radiation.

Power supply

One of six orbiting electrons – negative charge

CARBON-12
The chemical properties of carbon are determined by its six negatively charged electrons. These six electrons balance the six positively charged protons of the nucleus. In a carbon-12 atom, the nucleus also has six neutrons, of about the same mass as the protons, giving the atom a "mass number" of 12.

One of six protons – positive charge

One of six neutrons – zero charge

One of six orbiting electrons – negative charge

CARBON-14
The isotope carbon-14 is chemically identical to ordinary carbon. It has six protons and six electrons. But carbon-14 has two extra neutrons, giving it a mass number of 14. This isotope is radioactive, 50 percent of it decaying every 5,730 years. Environmental levels are roughly constant, since new carbon-14 atoms are constantly being formed by cosmic rays smashing into ordinary carbon atoms.

One of six protons – positive charge

One of eight neutrons – zero charge

Splitting the atom

AFTER THE DISCOVERY of the nucleus in 1911, it was found that bombarding certain atoms with particles from radioactive materials could disintegrate their nuclei, releasing energy. The heaviest nuclei, those of uranium, can be split by neutrons in this way. Otto Hahn (1879-1968) and Lise Meitner (1878-1968) discovered that the uranium nucleus splits in half, or "fissions," and also gives out further neutrons. These neutrons can go on to cause further fissions. In 1942 a team led by Enrico Fermi (1901-1954) achieved this "chain reaction" in the world's first nuclear reactor. Three years later the chain reaction was used in the nuclear bombs that destroyed the Japanese cities of Hiroshima and Nagasaki.

Neutrons produced by fission

Typical products of fission are barium and krypton

Nucleus fissions into two smaller nuclei

CHAIN REACTION
The source of energy in a nuclear reactor or a nuclear explosion is a chain reaction. A nucleus of uranium or plutonium splits (fissions), giving out neutrons that split further nuclei. Immense heat is created by the energy of the splitting fragments and by radiation. In a reactor this heat is used in a controlled way to generate electricity. In an explosion it is released violently.

Neutron about to hit uranium nucleus

1 WANDERING NEUTRONS
Neutrons can be released by bombarding atoms with radiation. Neutrons are also occasionally given out by decaying uranium nuclei, but these neutrons rarely react with uranium nuclei to build a chain reaction. Many nuclear reactors use uranium-235, a very reactive but uncommon isotope.

2 NUCLEAR SPLIT
When a neutron hits another uranium nucleus, the nucleus fissions into two smaller nuclei of approximately half the size. Several neutrons are also given out, together with high-energy radiation. The neutrons can go on to cause further fissions in a chain reaction. Neutrons can be slowed down by graphite or heavy water mixed with the uranium.

Uranium nucleus (U-235)

Unstable uranium
The main isotope of uranium is uranium-238 (symbol U-238). It has 238 particles in its nucleus – 92 protons and 146 neutrons. The neutrons prevent the protons from blowing the nucleus apart because of their mutual repulsion. Even so, an unstable U-238 nucleus breaks down from time to time, giving out an alpha (α) particle and turning into a thorium nucleus. The thorium nucleus in turn breaks down, and so do its products, in a chain of decays that ends when a lead nucleus is formed. Other uranium isotopes go through a similar chain of radioactive decays, ending in a different isotope of lead. This is why uranium-bearing rocks can be detected by their radioactivity. Uranium can also break down by fission, and this process can build up into a chain reaction. For a chain reaction to occur, there must be special conditions, and a sufficient quantity of relatively pure uranium must be used.

FAMILY FISSION
In 1917 Lise Meitner and Otto Hahn discovered a new element, protactinium, found in uranium ores. In 1939 Meitner and her nephew Otto Frisch (1904-1979) announced the fission of uranium.

PUZZLING PRODUCT
Otto Hahn studied the disintegration of uranium nuclei by neutrons. Among the by-products of this disintegration were barium nuclei, which are about half the weight of uranium nuclei.

HEAVY WATER
Neutrons in a nuclear reactor's chain reaction can be controlled by a moderator such as heavy water. It is 11 percent heavier than an equal volume of ordinary water.

NORSK HYD
KVÆLSTOF

DEUTERI
Gr
d

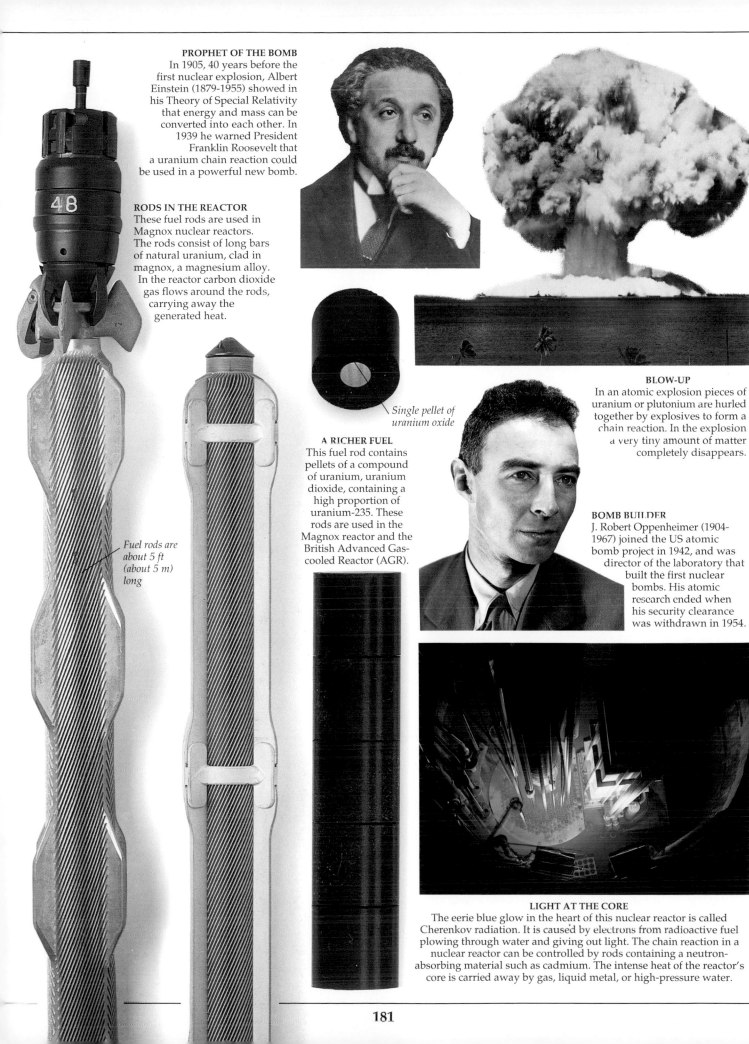

PROPHET OF THE BOMB
In 1905, 40 years before the first nuclear explosion, Albert Einstein (1879-1955) showed in his Theory of Special Relativity that energy and mass can be converted into each other. In 1939 he warned President Franklin Roosevelt that a uranium chain reaction could be used in a powerful new bomb.

RODS IN THE REACTOR
These fuel rods are used in Magnox nuclear reactors. The rods consist of long bars of natural uranium, clad in magnox, a magnesium alloy. In the reactor carbon dioxide gas flows around the rods, carrying away the generated heat.

Fuel rods are about 5 ft (about 5 m) long

Single pellet of uranium oxide

A RICHER FUEL
This fuel rod contains pellets of a compound of uranium, uranium dioxide, containing a high proportion of uranium-235. These rods are used in the Magnox reactor and the British Advanced Gas-cooled Reactor (AGR).

BLOW-UP
In an atomic explosion pieces of uranium or plutonium are hurled together by explosives to form a chain reaction. In the explosion a very tiny amount of matter completely disappears.

BOMB BUILDER
J. Robert Oppenheimer (1904-1967) joined the US atomic bomb project in 1942, and was director of the laboratory that built the first nuclear bombs. His atomic research ended when his security clearance was withdrawn in 1954.

LIGHT AT THE CORE
The eerie blue glow in the heart of this nuclear reactor is called Cherenkov radiation. It is caused by electrons from radioactive fuel plowing through water and giving out light. The chain reaction in a nuclear reactor can be controlled by rods containing a neutron-absorbing material such as cadmium. The intense heat of the reactor's core is carried away by gas, liquid metal, or high-pressure water.

Hot matter

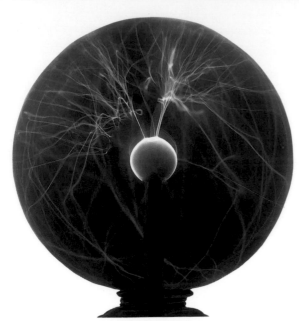

ATOMS ARE LAID BARE as they are subjected to high temperatures. The spectroscope reveals their secrets by analyzing the light they give out. In a spectroscope the light falls on a diffraction grating – a flat surface with thousands of lines – or a prism. Light passes through or is reflected, and is broken up into different colors. Sunlight consists of the whole color spectrum and beyond. Gases at the sun's surface produce sunlight, at temperatures of about 10,000° F (about 5,500° C). Here, the atoms' outer electrons are knocked to higher orbits and give out light as they fall back. Inside the sun and other high-temperature stars, inner electrons are knocked to higher orbits. As they fall back, they give out ultraviolet and X-rays. At the centers of the sun and stars, at temperatures of about 27 million° F (around 15 million° C), nuclei are stripped bare and welded together, producing heavier nuclei.

INSIDE THE PLASMA BALL
A powerful voltage at the center of this glass globe tears electrons from the atoms of the low-pressure gases inside. Avalanches of electrons build up, forming bright squiggly lines of hot gas. The mixture of electrons and charged atoms in these lines is called a plasma.

A LIGHT SIGNATURE
The spectrometer "reads the signature" of materials by analyzing their light. The light first passes through a narrow slit into a small telescope, which focuses the light into a narrow parallel beam. The beam passes through a glass prism, and is spread out, with each wavelength (color) of light going in a slightly different direction. Through a viewing telescope a rainbow-colored "spectrum" can be seen. This may appear as a host of bright lines, or a continuous band of color, crossed by dark lines, where wavelengths have been absorbed.

Photographic plate

Camera

Plateholder

THE VANISHING SUN
The sun is kept at a high temperature by the flood of energy from the nuclear reactions at its heart. Every second, four million tons of the sun's matter vanish, converted into energy that escapes from the surface as radiation.

ABSORBING EXPERIMENT
This 19th-century spectroscopic experiment shows light from a gas flame passing through a liquid containing dissolved materials. The spectrum that is produced reveals the identity of the dissolved materials in the liquid.

HARNESSING FUSION

At temperatures of millions of degrees, electrons are completely stripped from atoms. Light nuclei such as hydrogen can collide, despite the mutual repulsion of their positive electric charges. The fusion of hydrogen nuclei to form helium nuclei powers the sun, a hydrogen bomb, and the prospective fusion reactors of the future.

Neutron

Tritium nucleus

Deuterium nucleus

Electron

Proton

Building nuclei by fusion

Merging (fusing) light nuclei yields an immense amount of energy. Hydrogen has the very lightest nucleus, containing just one proton. Hydrogen nuclei can be fused to form one nucleus of helium (two of the protons are turned into neutrons, forming a helium nucleus with two protons and two neutrons). Energy is given out at the same time. This fusion process takes place in the sun and stars in a series of stages, with other nuclei forming briefly, then changing into other nuclei. On earth, hydrogen isotopes such as deuterium and tritium are used for fusion. The supply of deuterium, also known as heavy hydrogen, is limitless, because it is found in the ocean.

1 PATHWAYS TO POWER
There are several ways in which helium nuclei can form from hydrogen nuclei. One process involves two isotopes of hydrogen – deuterium and tritium. The deuterium nucleus has one proton and one neutron. Tritium has one proton and two neutrons. When a gas of these isotopes is heated to millions of degrees, a plasma is formed, and the nuclei can occasionally collide.

Unstable helium-5 nucleus

2 FORMING HELIUM-5
A deuterium nucleus and tritium nucleus collide and briefly form a nucleus of helium-5. At the same time other short-lived nuclei are also formed.

Neutron shed by helium-5

Stable helium-4

Telescope focuses light from source

Triangular prism bends violet light most strongly and red light least

STAR MAN
In 1939 Hans Bethe (1906-) was the first scientist to explain how the sun and stars are powered mainly by the fusion of hydrogen into helium. He was also a member of the team that worked on the atomic bomb project.

3 KEEPING THE HEAT IN
The helium-5 nucleus sheds a neutron, and gives out radiation. A stable helium-4 nucleus remains. The energy of the neutron and the radiation is absorbed by plasma, or by surrounding matter, and is turned into heat. The plasma must not be cooled by contact with other matter, and is confined within magnetic fields. To work efficiently, this confinement must be sustained long enough for the reaction to give out more energy than has to be put in.

A TOUR OF THE TORUS
The plasma in a fusion reactor circulates in a doughnut-shaped ring, or torus, and is kept at very low pressure. This is the interior of JET, the Joint European Torus, a research fusion reactor operated by 14 countries. Electric current in coils wrapped around the Torus creates a powerful magnetic field that traps the plasma. Bursts of power from the field also heat the plasma. Inside the Torus temperatures can reach as high as 550 million° F (about 300 million° C).

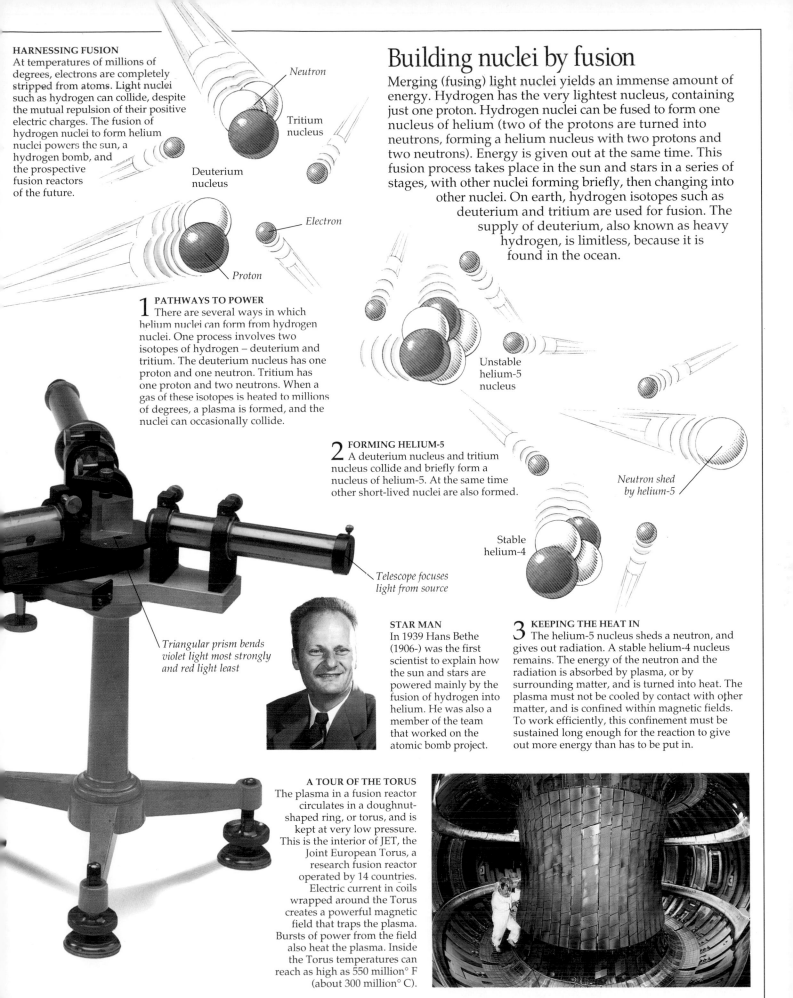

Subatomic particles

IN THE EARLY 1930s the atom was thought to be made of three kinds of particle – the proton, neutron, and electron. But soon more particles were found. The existence of the neutrino – a ghostlike particle that "carries away" energy when a neutron decays – was suspected. Then the muon, much like a heavy electron, and the pion, which binds protons and neutrons together in the nucleus, were both discovered in cosmic rays. Accelerators were built to smash particles into nuclei at high speed, creating new particles. Today hundreds of particles are known. They seem to fall into two main classes, hadrons and leptons. Hadrons include the proton and neutron, and are made of pairs or triplets of quarks, which are never seen singly. Leptons, the other class, include electrons and neutrinos.

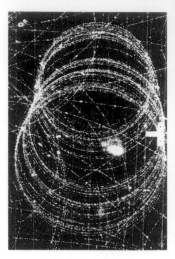

MAKING TRACKS
Trails of water droplets in a cloud chamber mark the paths of electrons and positrons (similar to an electron but with a positive charge). Because of their opposite electric charges, they curve in different directions in the chamber's magnetic field. An electron produced near the bottom of the picture circles 36 times before losing its energy.

Chamber contains water vapor

AMAZING REVELATIONS
The cloud chamber, invented by Charles Wilson (1869-1959) in 1911, was the first detector to reveal subatomic particles in flight. Particles from a radioactive source pass through a glass chamber, which contains air and water vapor. In the glass chamber, particles knock electrons out of the atoms in the air, leaving positively charged ions (incomplete atoms). The pressure in the chamber is suddenly reduced, and water vapor condenses on the ions, forming trails of small drops.

The piston at the bottom of the chamber moves to form water vapor, which condenses on the tracks of particles as they pass through

To lower the piston the flask is emptied of air – the connection between the flask and the space below the piston is opened and the piston is suddenly sucked downward

Glass negatives of cloud chamber photographs

PARTICLE PICTURES
Photographic plates of cloud chamber tracks often show particles being created and destroyed. Measuring the tracks can reveal the particles' electric charge, mass, and speed.

IN A WHIRL

The cyclotron, invented by Ernest Lawrence (1901-1958) in 1930, accelerated particles and smashed them into atomic nuclei to form new particles. The vacuum tank of the cyclotron shown here housed a metal "dee" (a D-shaped box). Charged particles entered the dee at the center of the apparatus, and a magnetic field moved them in a small circle, half in and half out of the dee. A rapidly varying electric voltage was applied to the dee, giving a "kick" to a particle whenever it left or reentered the dee. The particle spiraled outward, traveling faster and faster, until it left the cyclotron.

Vacuum tank is sealed and the air is removed

"Dee"

The vacuum tank of the cyclotron

Source of protons

JESTER OF PHYSICS

Richard Feynman (1918-1988) shared a Nobel Prize in 1965 for his work on the forces between particles and electromagnetic radiation. He was considered a brilliant teacher and was famous for his practical jokes.

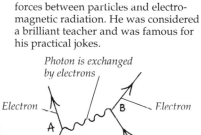

Photon is exchanged by electrons

Electron

A

B

Electron

FEYNMAN DIAGRAM

This strange squiggle is a Feynman diagram. It illustrates that electromagnetic force between electrons occurs when they exchange a photon (the "carrier" of the electromagnetic force).

Bubble chamber contained liquid hydrogen

PARTICLE FROTH

This bubble chamber, made in 1956, contained liquid hydrogen at low temperature and high pressure. The pressure was suddenly released, and particles passed through the chamber. The liquid boiled on the trails of charged atoms left by the particles. The trails were photographed, and the chamber was quickly repressurized.

MAGIC CIRCLE

The underground Tevatron at the Fermi National Accelerator Laboratory in Illinois has two accelerators, one above the other. The upper one feeds particles to the more powerful lower one.

BEAUTY IN DECAY

In this computer graphic representation bubble-chamber image, a high-speed proton (yellow, bottom) collides with a proton in a hydrogen atom and disappears, creating a shower of particles. An uncharged particle called a lambda leaves no track, but reveals itself by "decaying" into a proton and a pion (yellow and purple, center).

"Porthole" for viewing tracks

When in use, the bubble chamber sat in this lower chamber and was kept at a low temperature

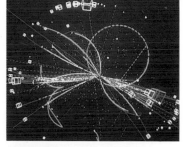

RECONSTRUCTING THE EVENT

Computers are now used to reconstruct subatomic events. This is a computer simulation of the decay of the Z^0 particle, one of the carriers of the weak nuclear force.

The four forces

ALL MATTER IS SUBJECT TO four forces – gravity, electromagnetism, and the weak and strong nuclear forces. Gravity holds people on the earth and the planets in orbit around the sun. Electrons are held in atoms by electromagnetism, a force that is enormously stronger than gravity. The weak nuclear force, a hundred billion times weaker than electromagnetism, is involved in radioactivity and nuclear fusion. The strong nuclear force, a hundred times stronger than electromagnetism, affects particles called quarks. Protons, neutrons, and other particles are made up of pairs or triplets of quarks. Electromagnetism is "carried" by particles called photons, the weak nuclear force by W and Z particles, and the strong nuclear force by particles called gluons. Gravity is probably carried by particles, too – these have been dubbed gravitons. Electricity and magnetism are "unified" because electricity in motion produces magnetic fields, and changing magnetic fields produces electrical voltages. Electromagnetism is in turn unified with the weak nuclear force, because at extremely high energies and temperatures they merge into one "electro-weak" force. The evidence for this comes from ideas about the first moments of the Big Bang (p. 188) and from experiments in particle accelerators. Physicists are now working to develop a theory in which all four forces would be aspects of one superforce.

NOT-SO-WEAK FORCE
The sun is powered by the weak nuclear force, which is responsible for the conversion of hydrogen into helium at the sun's core.
Under the less extreme conditions on earth, the weak nuclear force is involved in radioactivity. This force does not extend beyond the atomic nucleus and could not be detected until scientists had learned how to probe inside the atom. The particles that carry the weak force, the W^+, W^-, and Z^0, were discovered in 1983 among the debris formed when subatomic particles collided in a giant accelerator.

Sun

Earth

Moon

An orrery, a mechanical model of planetary motions

PULLING POWER
Gravity is the force in control of the entire solar system – it holds planets, asteroids, comets, and smaller bodies in orbit. The farthest known planet, Pluto, is firmly held by gravity even when it is about 4 billion miles (over 7 billion kilometers) away from the sun. Gravity extends far beyond this, however – clusters of galaxies millions of light-years across are held together by their own gravity. Yet it is by far the weakest of the four forces. It dominates the universe because it is long-range, whereas the far stronger nuclear forces do not extend beyond the nucleus. Gravity is cumulative – it always attracts, never repels, so when matter accumulates into planet-sized or star-sized objects, a large gravitational force is developed. Electromagnetic forces are also long-range, but unlike gravity can both attract and repel, and generally cancel themselves out.

EVERYDAY INTERACTIONS

Many forces can be easily seen, such as the way materials hold together and the friction between objects. These are both examples of the electromagnetic force. Gravity is the other force that is most obvious in human life. The electromagnetic force and gravity are shown in the following sequence.

1 GETTING THINGS GOING

A ball falls to the floor because the earth's gravity pulls it, but the ball also pulls the earth with exactly the same force. However, since the earth has so much more mass, it does not move visibly, while the ball moves faster and faster. It is described as gaining energy of movement, or kinetic energy. Energy can be defined as making things happen – for example to break things, to make them hotter, and to set them in motion.

QUARK-FINDER

The strongest force of all, the strong nuclear force, is felt only by quarks. It binds them tightly together, and they have never yet been observed singly. During the 1980s evidence about the strong force carrying quarks, and the weak force, came from experiments in this giant accelerator, called the Super Proton Synchrotron.

EXCHANGING MESSAGES

When two particles are interacting through one of the four fundamental forces, they constantly exchange messenger particles. The messenger particles influence the other particles' movements the way a tennis ball influences the tennis players' movements. The force can be a repulsion or an attraction.

3 GREAT POTENTIAL

The potential energy that was momentarily stored in the ball is converted into kinetic energy, and the ball shoots upward. As the ball rises, it loses kinetic energy. If it should fall back to the ground later it will regain its speed. It is therefore described as converting kinetic into potential energy as it rises. In this case the potential energy is associated with height above the ground.

Gravity pulls the ball to the floor, but the ball pulls the earth with exactly the same force

Potential energy is converted into kinetic energy and the ball bounces up

2 DOWN WITH A BUMP

When the ball hits the floor, the force of gravity is opposed by electromagnetism. The electrons in the outer layers of atoms in the ball and the floor repel each other. The upward push of electromagnetism overcomes the downward pull of gravity. The motion is abruptly stopped, but the ball's kinetic energy is converted into other forms. Some is dispersed through the material of the ball and floor as heat. Some is stored as potential energy (energy waiting to be released) in the ball. The electromagnetic forces between the atoms are distorted by the impact, and try to restore the ball to its normal shape. When they succeed the ball regains its kinetic energy.

CONSTANT QUANTITY

In any isolated system the total quantity of mass and energy is conserved. In a steam engine, for example, chemical energy of the fuel is converted into heat energy of the fire and of the steam. This heat energy is in turn converted into kinetic energy of the wheels driven by the engine. The total amount of mass and energy is always conserved whichever of the four fundamental forces are involved.

The birth and death of matter

THE TOTAL AMOUNT of mass and energy in the universe never changes. According to a widely held theory, billions of years ago the universe contained matter and energy of extraordinarily high density and temperature, which exploded in the Big Bang. As the gas expanded and cooled, quarks formed protons and neutrons, and some of these built helium nuclei. Eventually complete hydrogen and helium atoms formed. The gas condensed into galaxy-sized clouds which broke up into stars. In the far future, the universe could collapse, be rejuvenated in a new Big Bang, and re-expand, but it is more likely that it will always expand. After the last star has faded, even protons may decay into much lighter particles, and the universe may end as a sea of electrons, neutrinos, and forms of radiation.

VIOLENT UNIVERSE
Early astronomers thought that the stars were tranquil and unchanging. It is now known, however, that they are born, lead violent lives, and die.

PUTTING THE CLOCK BACK
Time does not necessarily go forward, or even at the same speed. If the universe were to collapse, it is possible that time could go backward. Time slows down for high-speed objects – a person in orbit for a year ages less (by a hundredth of a second) than people on earth. Even time travel may be possible. In theory, two regions of the universe can be connected by a "wormhole," passing though other dimensions. An object entering one end of a wormhole could reappear from the other end, at an earlier time.

Time could go backward in the extreme conditions found in the cosmos

SCATTERED SEED
The Crab Nebula is a mass of gas from a supernova – the explosion of a giant star, seen by Chinese astronomers in 1054. The gas is rich in elements made in the star's core. These will be scattered through space and some will be incorporated into new planets as they are born. All the elements in our bodies were made in some ancient supernova.

THE GRAVITY OF DARK MATTER

Galaxies are huge collections of stars, gas, and dust. Light, travelling at about 200,000 miles (300,000 km) per second, can take as long as 100,000 years to cross a galaxy. Galaxies are grouped into clusters, which hurtle apart. There may be undetected dark matter in the vast spaces between galaxies. The gravity of dark matter may be sufficient to slow the galaxies' expansion and turn it into a collapse.

A BRIEF HISTORY OF BLACK HOLES

Stephen Hawking (1942-) (p. 367) is renowned for his work on explaining the birth of the universe and also for his theories about black holes. When matter becomes extremely dense, as in the core of an exploded star, its gravity becomes so powerful that both matter and radiation, including light, are trapped inside. The result is a black hole. Hawking showed that a black hole gives off radiation very slowly. His most popular work is the 1988 book *A Brief History of Time*.

AN INTELLIGENT UNIVERSE?

Fred Hoyle (1915-) is associated with the Steady State theory, which holds there was no Big Bang, and matter is always being created throughout space. He claims that some physical laws have been designed by a superior intelligence specifically to produce conditions that make the development of carbon-based life possible.

BACK TO THE BEGINNING

So far, the strongest evidence available to scientists for the Big Bang theory is cosmic background radiation. This is microwave radiation that can be detected by large radio telescopes like the one shown here. The radiation always comes with the same strength from all directions in the sky, and is believed by some to have traveled through space since the universe was 100,000 years old. Until this time the universe is thought to have been made of hot expanding plasma. The plasma then cooled sufficiently to allow electrons and nuclei to join up and form the first complete atoms.

189

Model of the molecular structure of tartaric acid (1914)

Silica gel is used in a desiccator to remove moisture

A precipitation reaction where potassium iodide is added to lead nitrate

Kipps apparatus for the preparation of hydrogen sulfide

Early 20th-century view of what an atom looks like

Saffron, and turmeric, used to color foods and fabrics since ancient times

Precipitates of substances with hydrogen sulfide

The acid in a bee sting can be soothed by alkaline ointment

Bromine: one of the nonmetal elements

CHEMISTRY

The molecules in citrus fruits contribute to their odor

Potassium permangenate dissolving in water

Egyptian mummified cat

Two metal salts derived from the element copper

What is chemistry?

CHEMISTRY IS THE SCIENCE OF CHANGE. It looks at all the different kinds of substances and how they interact with each other. It is going on all around us all the time, as well as in the scientific laboratory and in the chemical industry. People in widely differing walks of life use chemistry everyday – the doctor and the chef, the farmer and the builder. Chemisrty comes to the aid of the manufacturer of food, and also to the brewer and wine maker. The technician in the hospital laboratory uses chemistry to check for infections in blood samples (p. 229). The forensic scientist uses chemistry to solve crimes. In agriculture, chemistry is used to increase the yield of crops and to control many pests. Chemicals keep the water supply safe and swimming pools clean. One of the largest industries in the world is the petrochemical industry – this industry is mainly associated with gasoline and the chemicals that come from crude oil (p. 248). Drugs, synthetic dyes, plastics, and fabrics are produced by chemical means from nature's raw materials.

PLASTER CAST
Gypsum is a form of calcium sulfate that contains some water in its structure. Heating it removes 75 percent of the water, producing powdered plaster of Paris, used here to correct a deformity of the spine.

ACID RAIN FOREST
These spruce trees in Poland have been badly damaged by acid rain. This is caused by gases such as sulfur dioxide, which are emitted from factories. When these gases react with moisture in the atmosphere, they form dilute acids. The prevailing wind can carry this pollution some distance before releasing it in rainfall that damages vegetation and lakes.

CHEMISTRY IN ACTION
The popular view of chemistry is one with test tubes, strange smells, and evil-looking mixtures in the laboratory. Chemists study the chemical reactions that occur when substances are mixed together to form new substances. Here nitric acid is added to copper metal. The brown gas (the pollutant nitrogen dioxide) is produced so quickly that it makes the liquid fizz up and spill. To describe chemical reactions, chemists have developed a language, using internationally recognized symbols and equations. This reaction can be written as:

$$Cu + 4HNO_3 \rightarrow Cu(NO_3)_2 + 2NO_2 + 2H_2O$$

Nitrogen dioxide gas (NO_2) is a pollutant produced in car engine exhaust fumes

Blue copper nitrate ($Cu(NO_3)_2$) is formed in the solution

Water (H_2O) is also produced in the reaction

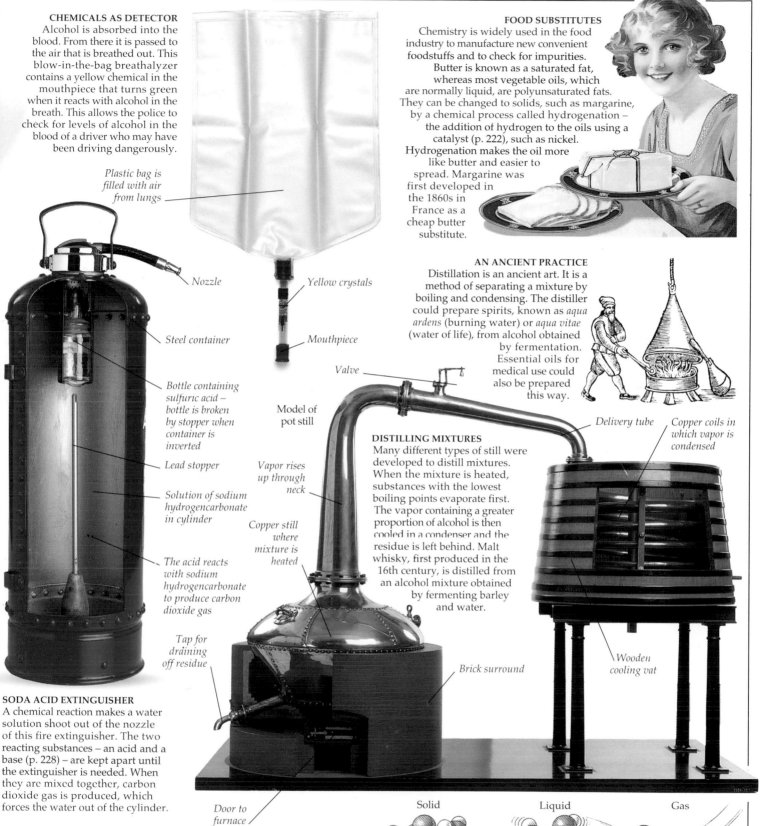

CHEMICALS AS DETECTOR
Alcohol is absorbed into the blood. From there it is passed to the air that is breathed out. This blow-in-the-bag breathalyzer contains a yellow chemical in the mouthpiece that turns green when it reacts with alcohol in the breath. This allows the police to check for levels of alcohol in the blood of a driver who may have been driving dangerously.

Plastic bag is filled with air from lungs

Nozzle

Yellow crystals

Steel container

Mouthpiece

Bottle containing sulfuric acid – bottle is broken by stopper when container is inverted

Model of pot still

Lead stopper

Solution of sodium hydrogencarbonate in cylinder

Vapor rises up through neck

The acid reacts with sodium hydrogencarbonate to produce carbon dioxide gas

Copper still where mixture is heated

Tap for draining off residue

Valve

FOOD SUBSTITUTES
Chemistry is widely used in the food industry to manufacture new convenient foodstuffs and to check for impurities. Butter is known as a saturated fat, whereas most vegetable oils, which are normally liquid, are polyunsaturated fats. They can be changed to solids, such as margarine, by a chemical process called hydrogenation – the addition of hydrogen to the oils using a catalyst (p. 222), such as nickel. Hydrogenation makes the oil more like butter and easier to spread. Margarine was first developed in the 1860s in France as a cheap butter substitute.

AN ANCIENT PRACTICE
Distillation is an ancient art. It is a method of separating a mixture by boiling and condensing. The distiller could prepare spirits, known as *aqua ardens* (burning water) or *aqua vitae* (water of life), from alcohol obtained by fermentation. Essential oils for medical use could also be prepared this way.

Delivery tube

Copper coils in which vapor is condensed

DISTILLING MIXTURES
Many different types of still were developed to distill mixtures. When the mixture is heated, substances with the lowest boiling points evaporate first. The vapor containing a greater proportion of alcohol is then cooled in a condenser and the residue is left behind. Malt whisky, first produced in the 16th century, is distilled from an alcohol mixture obtained by fermenting barley and water.

Brick surround

Wooden cooling vat

SODA ACID EXTINGUISHER
A chemical reaction makes a water solution shoot out of the nozzle of this fire extinguisher. The two reacting substances – an acid and a base (p. 228) – are kept apart until the extinguisher is needed. When they are mixed together, carbon dioxide gas is produced, which forces the water out of the cylinder.

Door to furnace

Solid

Liquid

Gas

PHYSICAL OR CHEMICAL?
Not all changes are chemical. When ice melts to form water, or water boils to form steam, no chemical reaction takes place, but the physical state changes. The behavior of the individual units (molecules) of the water is different in each case. The attractions between the molecules form a rigid structure in a solid. As the molecules slide over each other, the structure is less rigid in the liquid. Heating causes the molecules to dart around and bump into each other in a gas.

Molecules form a rigid structure

Molecules slide over each other

Molecules are widely spaced

Chemistry in nature

CHEMICAL CHANGE HAS ALWAYS BEEN part of the Universe, even before human beings evolved. Indeed, scientists believe that life began on Earth as a result of complex chemicals reproducing themselves over billions of years. Chemistry is a physical science; it lies between the biological sciences, helping to explain many of life's processes, and the laws of physics, which include matter and energy. Chemical processes are constantly occurring within us – when our bodies move, a series of chemical reactions takes place to give the muscles the energy that is taken in from food. Many species of the animal world make use of chemistry to defend themselves, to kill their prey, and to build fragile structures that have incredible strength. Modern methods of chemical analysis have led to a greater understanding of the chemistry of nature, so that it is possible to identify those chemical compounds (pp. 20-21) that produce the color, taste, and smell of a flower or a fruit.

STRONGER THAN STEEL
This garden spider makes its web from fine, silk threads of protein. Amazingly, this thread of protein is stronger than a thread of similar thickness made of steel. The spider can even vary the thread – firm, dry threads for the spokes, and sticky threads to capture prey.

Red chilis

BURNING SENSATIONS
The burning sensation experienced when eating chilis is caused by the organic compound capsaicin. This aids digestion by triggering the production of saliva. It also helps remove waste products from the system. Capsaicin is also found in the spice paprika.

POISONOUS CHEMICALS
This snake injects venom into its prey through fangs, or hollow teeth. Produced in special glands situated behind the mouth, the venom is a protein that attacks the blood circulation of the victim, causing swelling and bleeding. Snake venom is not poisonous when swallowed, because the digestive system can break down proteins.

Fer-de-lance snake

CHEMICAL SMELLS
The taste and smell of fruits are the result of mixtures of a large number of organic compounds. The smell of freshly picked raspberries is produced partly by a ketone (a kind of organic compound) called ionone. The same ketone is found in freshly mown hay. This explains why the smells are similar. Ionone is used to give foods such as artificially flavored raspberry yogurt a raspberry-like smell. The essential oil derived from violets also contains ionone. It is now made synthetically for use in flavorings.

Raspberries

Mowing hay

Nettle leaves also give a sting

Barbs contain formic acid

PAINFUL CHEMICALS
Tiny barbs on the stem and leaves of a stinging nettle can give painful stings when they brush against skin. One of the compounds responsible is formic acid, the smallest and most acidic organic acid The sting of nettles, like bees, can be eased with the application of an alkali to the skin. Formic acid is also found in stinging ants – *formica* is Latin for ant. The ants inject venom containing formic acid.

Stinging nettle

UNDERGROUND LIMESTONE DEPOSITS

Limestone rocks consist mainly of calcium carbonate derived from the shells and skeletons of species such as shellfish. As rainwater percolates through rocks, it dissolves small amounts of the calcium carbonate. Where underground caverns have been formed, the water drips through the roof, and some evaporates, depositing solid carbonate on the roof. Over thousands of years, the deposit grows into a stalactite, like these in caverns in Florida.

DIGESTIVE PROCESS

Escherichia coli (or *E. coli* for short) are bacteria that inhabit our intestines. They are able to break down some of the foods we eat, such as green vegetables and beans, into different nutrients. In the chemical process, gases are released, which is the reason for flatulence after a meal of legumes. *E. coli* also make vitamin K, which is needed to make blood clot. They cause disease only if they get into the bloodstream; in the intestine, they are harmless.

Melanin changes in the skin mimic the colors of the branch

CHEMICAL CAMOUFLAGE

The chameleon, like the octopus, squid, and cuttlefish, can alter the color of its skin to disguise itself from prey. The compound chiefly responsible is melanin, which also helps the human skin tan in the sun. The chameleon's melanin-producing cells can be activated by fear or anger; they disperse melanin granules to produce colors ranging from yellow to brown and black, masking the chameleon's normal coloring. When the melanin comes together again, the color returns to the original green. Some chameleons are able to change their skin color to blue and bright red.

Peel contains essential oils

Carotene provides the orange color

Citric acid from lemons is used to flavor lemonade

ORANGES AND LEMONS

The odor of a lemon is caused partly by limonene, an essential oil in the peel. This group of organic compounds provides the smell and color of many plants. The structure of limonene has a mirror image; this is found in orange peel. All citrus fruits contain citric acid, which gives them their tart flavor; lemons have a greater concentration of citric acid than is found in oranges.

Flavor of an orange comes from hundreds of compounds

Chemistry in ancient worlds

EARLY PEOPLE FIRST PRACTICED CHEMISTRY after they learned to use fire. Once fire could be controlled, people began cooking their food and baking clay to produce pottery vessels. Natural curiosity about materials led to experimentation, and ores were smelted to obtain metals. As communities were established, people discovered that particular substances could be used for special purposes. Yeasts were used to prepare beer and wine, and foods were preserved by salting or smoking. Extracts from plants were used to dye clothes, barks provided materials to tan leather, and cosmetics were made from pigments and dyes. Glass, first used as a glaze for beads or pottery, was being blown into shapes by 100 BC. The ancient Egyptians mummified their dead using chemical preparations. The Chinese have a long history of chemical crafts. Lacquer, perhaps the most ancient industrial plastic, was in use in China in an organized industry by 1300 BC. Paper manufacturing and gunpowder were Chinese developments.

FACE PAINTING
People have always used color to decorate themselves and their possessions. This Native American Indian used his warlike face colorings to frighten the enemy and show his status.

Indigo dye, extracted from the leaves of *Indigofera* plant

Saffron from the crocus flower

Red lead decoration

Turmeric

DYES AND DYESTUFFS
Organic dyes such as madder, woad, and indigo attach themselves chemically to textiles. Sometimes the material is treated with a chemical to "fix" the color – this is known as a mordant. Alum (p. 198) was an early mordant. Another method of coloring is to use pigments. Many of these are obtained from minerals that are ground into fine powders for use in cosmetics, paints, and inks.

GREEK PERFUME
Clay is a substance that can be easily molded. When dried and baked, water is lost and chemical changes occur, producing pottery. This perfume bottle has been decorated using pigments such as red lead, which is a lead oxide. The perfume was made from oils which were extracted from flowers and spices by gentle heating in oils, such as olive oil.

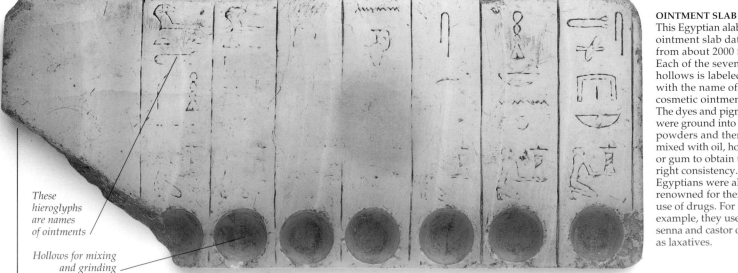

OINTMENT SLAB
This Egyptian alabaster ointment slab dates from about 2000 BC. Each of the seven hollows is labeled with the name of a cosmetic ointment. The dyes and pigments were ground into fine powders and then mixed with oil, honey, or gum to obtain the right consistency. The Egyptians were also renowned for their use of drugs. For example, they used senna and castor oil as laxatives.

These hieroglyphs are names of ointments

Hollows for mixing and grinding

MUMMIFIED CAT
A belief in life after death led the ancient Egyptians to preserve the bodies of their dead. Animals which represented gods were often mummified. This mummy dates from about 1000 BC. First the body was covered with dry natron, a naturally occurring chemical that is chiefly washing soda. This absorbed water from the body, preserving it. After 40 days the body was cleaned, anointed with aromatic resins, and wrapped in linen strips.

Features are painted in kohl, a black pigment derived from antimony

Linen strips woven from flax

Dyed strips

Cutting edge

Surface beaten during working

Barb

Shaft

MAKING GLASS
Glass was probably first made in Egypt around 3000 BC by fusing together sand, soda to lower the melting point, and lime as a stabilizer. The addition of certain metal oxides to the mixture gave colored glass. For example, blue glass could be obtained by adding copper oxide. By Roman times many household vessels were made of glass. This glass bottle was found in a Roman grave. The pearly patina is due to the glass crystallizing with age. The materials for making glass today are little changed since ancient times.

LEATHERMAKING
Hides of animals were valuable materials to early people, but when dried out, raw skin becomes hard. Tanning is a process which combines the skin with substances that preserve it as leather so that it remains flexible when dried. After cleaning and soaking, the leather is treated with extracts of bark, wood, and leaves containing a mixture of special acids called tannins. These react with the protein that makes up skin. After drying, the skins were used for all kinds of purposes – water carriers, harnesses, and shoes, for example.

SUDANESE IRON SPEAR
This barbed spear from the Sudan in Africa dates from the 1930s but was produced by the same methods as spears made 2,000 years before. Iron was harder to extract from its ores than copper or tin because its melting point was too high for early furnaces. The material had to be heated red-hot and worked over and over again to get rid of impurities. Carbon, in the form of charcoal, was added to the ore to improve the properties of the metal, making it easier to sharpen, with a good cutting edge.

Patina

Roman glass bottle

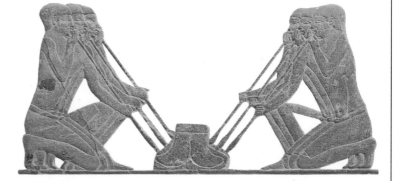

EGYPTIAN METALWORKERS
The metalworkers in this Egyptian relief are using blowpipes to make the fire hot enough to melt metal. Gold and silver were used extensively for jewelry. However, bronze – an alloy of copper and tin – was preferred for other articles because it was easier to make and work.

The first chemists

STAR OF ANTIMONY
When antimony is cooled from the molten state, it forms a starry pattern. Its minerals were considered suitable raw material by the alchemists for transmutation of metals (turning them to gold).

IN ANCIENT GREECE, philosophers began to put forward theories about matter. These theories, mixed with religious ideas and knowledge gained from the chemical crafts of ancient peoples, gave rise to alchemy. The alchemists combined mystical ideas of achieving perfection with practical experiments. A belief that one substance could be changed to another led them to seek to change so-called base metals, such as lead, into gold, which was believed to be the most perfect metal. Distillation, a technique introduced by these early alchemists, was used to prepare essential oils and perfumes. Later alchemists learned to prepare mineral acids that were much stronger than the acids previously known to them, such as fruit juices. Out of this work, new medical theories developed. The idea arose that disease represented an imbalance of the body's chemical system and should be treated with chemicals to restore the balance. Mining became an important activity; new metals were identified and methods of recognizing them became vital. Techniques of assaying metals – judging their worth – were also developed.

THE IMPORTANCE OF METALLURGY
As mining became economically important, works such as *De Re Metallica* appeared. Written by Georg Bauer (1494-1555), a German physician who used the pen name Agricola, it covered the techniques of mining, smelting to convert the ore to the metal, and assaying, or testing to see what metals were present.

TESTING THE METAL
Assayers worked in the first industrial laboratories in the mining areas of Central Europe, testing minerals for their metal content. They became familiar with a number of chemical reactions, even if they did not understand the chemistry behind them. They had access to a number of chemicals, such as saltpeter (potassium nitrate), alum (potassium aluminium sulfate), and green vitriol (ferrous sulfate). Distilling these together produced *aqua fortis*, or nitric acid, which could be used to separate silver (which dissolved in it) from gold (which did not). *Aqua regia* (concentrated nitric and hydrochloric acids) was used to dissolve gold, leaving silver.

THE ASSAYER'S LABORATORY
A common way of testing the purity of precious metals was by cupellation. The new, smaller furnaces meant that it was possible to maintain a uniform heat for long periods of time. The metal samples, with some lead to help them melt, were placed in a porous cupel, or crucible, and heated in the furnace. Lead and all metals except gold and silver would be converted to the metal oxides. These were absorbed by the cupel, which was made of bone ash, leaving a button of the pure gold or silver for testing with acid and weighing.

Round-bottomed flask

Aqua regia

Flat-bottomed flask

Aqua fortis

Saltpeter

Alum

Gold button

DISTILLATION APPARATUS

Distillation, or heating liquids to separate them, was an important part of alchemy and many pieces of apparatus were associated with it. The first "still" is thought to have been developed from observations that a pot lid collected condensation. Subsequent apparatus included the retort, which evolved from the alembic (see below). They could be made of glass, metal, or earthenware. The glass was green or brown because of iron impurities in the sand (p. 231).

Glass retort

Early distillation apparatus

Substance for distillation placed in here

Green color from iron impurities in early glassmaking

Long spout helps vapors to condense

Iranian alembic

Alembic head

Condensed vapors collects in rim

Cucurbit

Condensed vapor trickles down the long neck

ESSENTIAL OILS FOR MEDICINE

In the Middle Ages essential oils, such as oil of roses, were obtained by heating extracts of plants in a retort. The oils were vaporized and cooled during their passage down the long neck of the retort to condense in a flask which was often cooled by immersing it in water. The furnaces were usually fueled by charcoal.

خشتخاش قمب ٣٠. Papaver *142.*

حرف الزاقمط XXV. Litera
Adſdſal 149.

AVICENNA'S LEGACY

The word alchemy comes from the Arabic *al kimia*, meaning Egyptian art. The tradition of alchemy spread from Alexandria in Egypt and its language was Arabic. This glossary, with a Latin translation, was compiled by Avicenna (980-1037), a Persian philosopher. It features words such as *alkali* and *alembic*, still part of the language of chemistry today.

THE ALEMBIC

The alembic is an apparatus used in distillation. It comprises the head and the cucurbit (gourd-shaped base) and is believed to have been invented by Maria the Jewess, after whom the bain-marie (water bath), an early source of gentle heat, is named.

STUDYING CHEMISTRY

In the Middle Ages people began to teach the ideas of the alchemists. A new science known as iatrochemistry developed, based on the alchemists' belief that the human body was a chemical system that could be cured with chemicals. Andreas Libavius (1560-1616) published one of the first chemical textbooks, *Alchymia*, in 1597. He documented contemporary findings on pharmacy and metallurgy.

Door for stoking charcoal fire

Furnace

Engraving from *Alchymia*

Cupel made from bone ash

Long-handled metal tongs

CHEMICAL TOOLS

A bone ash cupel, or crucible, and long metal tongs were used to remove metals from a furnace and to pour them into molds. Other tools used by alchemists and assayers are still seen today in laboratories – mortars and pestles (p. 210), flasks, beakers, funnels, and filters.

Alchemical symbols for metals

SYMBOLS FOR SECRECY

Alchemy was closely linked with astrology, and the seven metals known to alchemists shared the symbols of the seven known heavenly bodies. The use of symbols for chemicals arose because of the alchemists' desire to keep their discoveries secret.

Investigating mixtures

EVERYTHING AROUND US IS MADE UP OF CHEMICALS, including ourselves. Some things are made up of a single chemical, or substance. For example, pure water is a substance made up of only one kind of molecule. Orange juice, however, contains different kinds of molecules and is a mixture of substances. Vinegar is a solution with water acting as a solvent in which the other substances are dissolved. These substances can be separated physically from one another. Most foods are mixtures. Salad dressing is a mixture, called an emulsion, containing oil and vinegar. They do not mix properly, but separate out into the lighter oily layer and the heavier water layer containing the vinegar. Other kinds of mixtures may be solids, like coins, or gases, like the air around us. Toothpaste is a mixture called a suspension, in which fine particles are suspended in a liquid, and they do not dissolve. It is often necessary for chemists to separate out the different chemicals to find out what they are.

SEPARATING LIQUIDS
This separatory, possibly from the 17th century, was used to separate two immiscible liquids (liquids that do not mix) from each other. The heavier liquid is poured off from the bottom, leaving the lighter one behind.

Filter paper

Solid sulfur particles do not pass through filter paper

Filter funnel

Conical flask

MAKING AND SEPARATING MIXTURES
It is possible to extract chemicals from mixtures in several different ways. Filtering and evaporation are two methods demonstrated here. Copper sulfate is a blue salt that dissolves in water – it is soluble. Sulfur is a solid element that does not dissolve in water – it is insoluble.

Beaker

Suspension of sulfur

$CuSO_4$

S

Blue solution of copper sulfate in water

Copper sulfate

Sulfur

Solution of copper sulfate

1 MIXING SUBSTANCES TOGETHER
When copper sulfate and sulfur are added to water, the copper sulfate dissolves, but the sulfur does not. Water is not a solvent for sulfur.

2 SEPARATING THE SULFUR
If the mixture is filtered, the yellow sulfur is easily separated and remains in the filter paper. The water and copper sulfate are not separated. They remain together in a solution. The yellow sulfur can be washed with water to remove any traces of copper sulfate. This technique of filtration is used to extract pure chemicals.

3 HEATING THE SOLUTION
The water can be removed by evaporation to leave blue copper sulfate crystals.

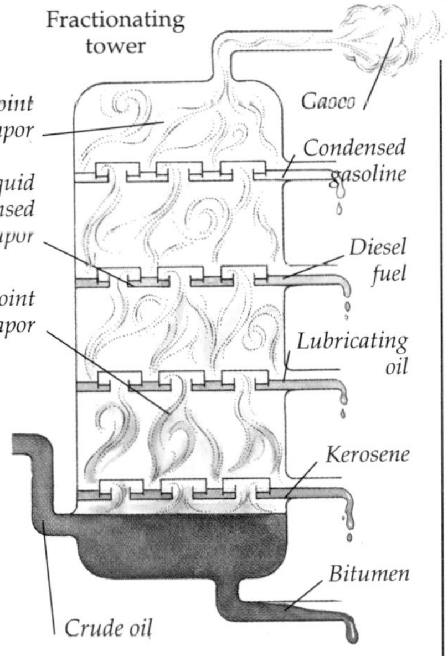

Water lost to atmosphere

Crystals of copper sulfate recovered from solution

Evaporating dish

Wire gauze spreads heat evenly

Bunsen burner

Tripod

CHROMATOGRAPHY
Black ink is a mixture of several different dyes. These can be separated by a technique called chromatography. As the ink and solvent (here water was used) travels up a piece of inked blotting paper, any substances dissolved in it will move up at a rate depending on the size, shape, and chemical characteristics of their molecules.

Different dyes move at different speeds

Blotting paper

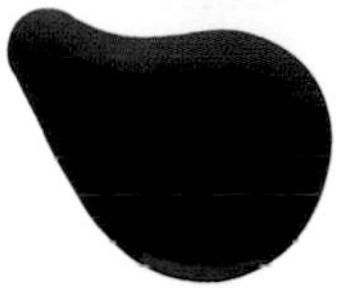

Black ink

Fractionating tower

Low boiling point vapor

Tray holds liquid from condensed vapor

High boiling point vapor

Gases

Condensed gasoline

Diesel fuel

Lubricating oil

Kerosene

Bitumen

Crude oil

FRACTIONAL DISTILLATION
Crude oil is the basis of the modern petrochemical industry (p. 248). It contains many different chemical compounds which can be separated into groups using fractional distillation. The crude oil is heated and pumped into the fractionating tower. The vapors cool as they rise. The products from the oil condense when they reach the temperature just below their boiling points and collect on trays. They are drawn off through pipes.

Red wine

THE COMPLETE FOOD
Although milk looks like a uniform liquid, viewed through a microscope it is a mixture of watery liquid with oily drops suspended in it. This mixture is known as a colloid, in which very small particles are dispersed through the liquid but they do not dissolve. The particles are smaller than those in toothpaste, which is a suspension.

ORGANIC MIXTURES
Wine is a complex mixture of organic chemicals (chemicals that are derived from living things), but the differences in it are not clearly seen, even under a microscope: it is homogeneous. Wood is an example of a heterogeneous mixture. It is clear from looking at it that it is not uniform.

Bronze coin

Nickel alloy coin

CURRENCY MIXTURES
Gold, silver, and copper have been used as coinage metals since antiquity, sometimes in mixtures called alloys. Copper, tin, and zinc alloys are used to make bronze coins.

201

Atoms and molecules

THE IDEA THAT MATTER IS MADE OF tiny indivisible particles was first suggested by the Greek philosopher Democritus (c. 460-370 BC). He called these particles atoms. In the late 18th century a modern theory about atoms originated. By then new gases, metals, and other substances had been discovered. Many chemical reactions were studied and the weights of substances involved were measured carefully. John Dalton's atomic theory arose from these observations. He believed that the atoms of an element were all identical and differed from those of a different element. Two or more of these atoms could join together in chemical combination producing "molecules" of substances called compounds. The molecules in a compound were all identical. The Italian thinker Amadeo Avogadro (1776-1856) asserted that the same volume of any gas would contain the same number of molecules. Although this idea was not immediately accepted, it eventually helped chemists calculate atomic and molecular weights. These weights are related to the weight of hydrogen, which is counted as one (p. 208).

THE NATURE OF MATTER
Englishman John Dalton (p. 161) (1766-1844) was the self-taught son of a Quaker weaver. He was the main advocate of the existence of atoms and his ideas dramatically influenced the study of chemistry. He was interested in everything around him, especially the weather, and began to investigate the marshes near his home in the north of England. He used his experimental findings on gases and those of Antoine Lavoisier (1743-1794) in France. Dalton also devised his own set of symbols for the elements.

Dalton's wooden balls

THE FIRST ATOMIC MODELS
Dalton used these balls, the first models of atoms, to demonstrate his ideas. He stated that matter is made up of small indivisible particles, or solid atoms. With the discovery that atoms were surrounded by negatively charged particles called electrons, Dalton's concept of solid atoms began to be less satisfactory.

ATOMS MOVING
Atoms are so small they cannot be seen by the naked eye, but their existence can explain many everyday observations. Look at the way the purple color of the potassium permanganate spreads when its crystals dissolve in water. This is because atoms are constantly moving, so as they come away from the crystals, they move through the water until they are evenly distributed.

ONE VIEW OF AN ATOM
The early years of the 20th century saw the development of ideas about the structure of the atom, with its central nucleus and orbiting electrons. Alongside these developments came an understanding of how atoms bond together to form molecules. Niels Bohr (1885-1962), a Danish physicist, constructed models with fixed orbits; the central nucleus, consisting of protons (positive particles) and neutrons (uncharged particles), had electrons orbiting around it in groups or "shells." This proved to be a convenient and useful model of an atom, but it is not the only view – electrons also behave as if they are waves of energy (like light) and are sometimes best imagined as being spread around the nucleus in a sort of cloud. This Bohr model represents a sodium atom with its nucleus at the center. There are ten electrons in the two inner shells – known as the inner electron orbits – and in the outer electron orbit there is one electron in an incomplete shell. The number of protons in an atom is equal to the atomic number.

Sodium atom model

Inner electron orbit

Nucleus containing protons and neutrons

Outer electron orbit

Potassium permanganate crystals added to water

Molecules and measures

Atoms and molecules are tiny, and the number in even a small amount of a substance is huge. To help calculate how many there are, Avogadro's number (6.02×10^{23}) is used as a constant. The amount of a substance containing this number of molecules is called a "mole." Using this measure, the chemical formula (p.192) can be worked out. Each chemical sample shown here has the same number (Avogadro's) of molecules in it. The weight of each is determined by calculating, in grams, the molecular weight – the atomic weights of all the atoms in the molecule added together.

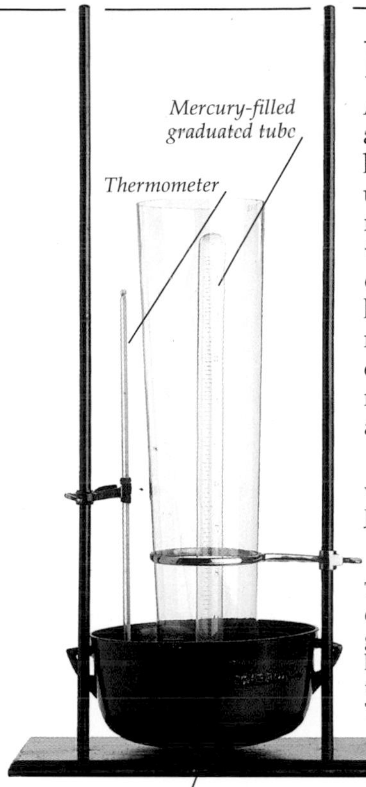

Mercury-filled graduated tube

Thermometer

Iron trough filled with mercury

VAPOUR DENSITY APPARATUS
Joseph Gay Lussac (1778-1850) developed this apparatus to measure the weight of the vapor of a compound.
The compound was sealed in a glass tube which was heated until it burst and the sample had vaporized. The vapor density was then calculated from the volume of mercury displaced from the tube. From this, the molecular weight and chemical formula

NaCl

SODIUM CHLORIDE
The atomic weights are sodium 23, chloride 35.5, making the mole weight 58.5 g.

Zn

ZINC
The atomic weight of zinc is 65, making the mole weight 65 g.

$CuSO_45H_2O$

HYDRATED COPPER SULFATE
The atomic weights are copper 63.5, sulfur 32, oxygen 16 (x 4), water 18 (x 5), making the mole weight 249.5 g.

ACETIC ACID
The atomic weights are carbon 12 (x 2), oxygen 16 (x 2), hydrogen 1 (x 4), making the mole weight 60 g. (Indicator has been added to show it is acidic.)

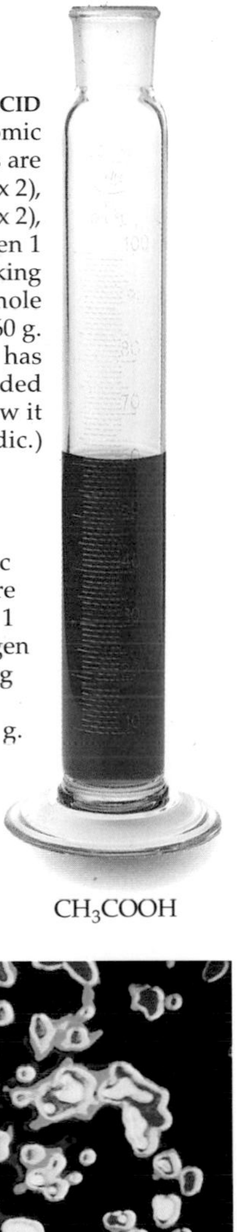

WATER
The atomic weights are hydrogen 1 (x 2), oxygen 16, making the mole weight 18 g.

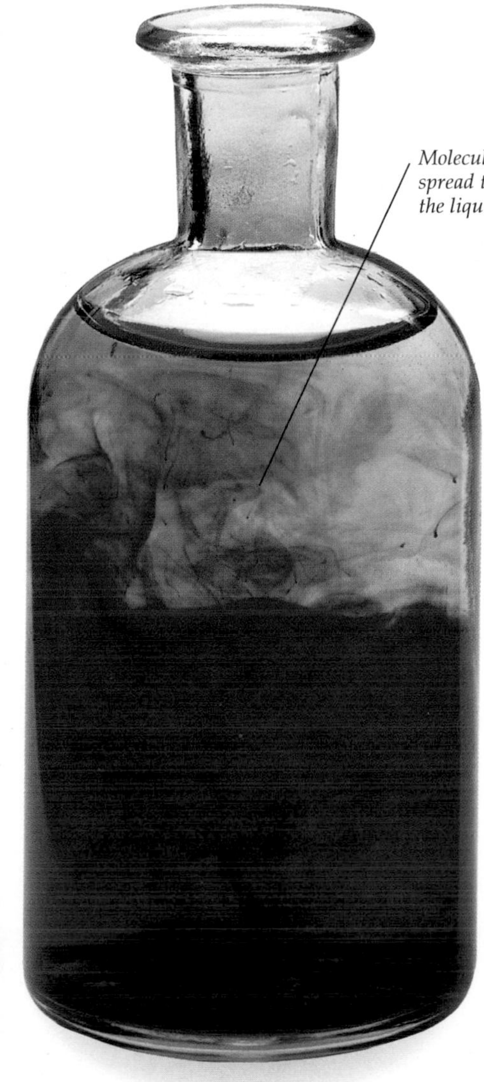

Molecules begin to spread through the liquid

Crystals have dissolved, forming a uniform solution

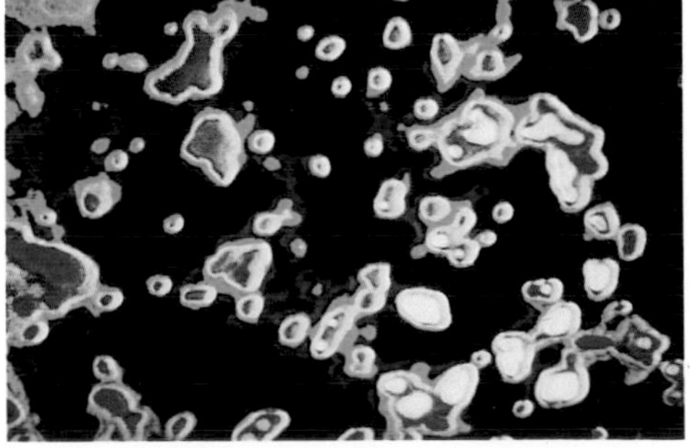

H_2O

CH_3COOH

LOOKING AT ACTUAL ATOMS
These uranium atoms cannot be seen with an ordinary microscope – they are too small. An electron microscope uses electron beams instead of light because electrons have shorter wavelengths, allowing smaller objects to be seen. The microscope used here is known as a scanning tunneling microscope.

The elements

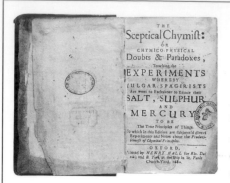

AN ELEMENT IS A SUBSTANCE that contains only one kind of atom. Gold contains only gold atoms and hydrogen contains only hydrogen atoms. Water, on the other hand, contains both hydrogen and oxygen atoms and is therefore a compound. Antoine Lavoisier (1743-1794) (p. 154) treated elements as substances that could not be broken down into other substances. He produced a list of elements in 1789. Almost all these are found in modern lists, although he also included heat and light. The number of known elements increased during the 18th century as mineralogists analyzed ores and found new metals. New instruments, such as the spectroscope, helped chemists recognize more elements in the 19th century.

Green vegetables are a source of sodium, calcium, and iron

Watercress

Apricots

BAUXITE MINE
The claylike mineral bauxite is aluminum oxide from which the element aluminum can be extracted. Here it is being mined in Jamaica. Bauxite is the chief source of aluminum metal. Aluminum is used in aircraft parts and engines because it is lightweight, tough, and does not corrode.

Dried fruits are rich in magnesium, calcium, and iron

Berry fruit is a source of folic acid, which helps the absorption of iron

Strawberry

Egg yolk

Seaweed

Sardine

Nuts and seeds

ELEMENTS FROM SPACE
Hydrogen is the simplest element. Over 90 percent of the Universe is made up of hydrogen created at the time of the Big Bang – the explosion that produced the Universe. All other heavier elements have been formed from hydrogen by nuclear reactions. This rock is from a meteorite that collided with the Earth about 20,000 years ago. The elements in it, such as iron and nickel, are identical to those found on Earth or on the Moon, though in different amounts.

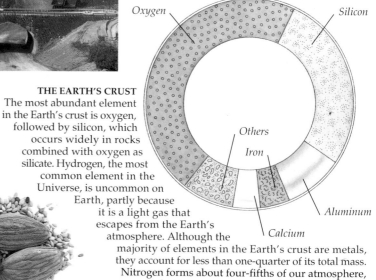

Oxygen

Silicon

Others

Iron

Calcium

Aluminum

THE EARTH'S CRUST
The most abundant element in the Earth's crust is oxygen, followed by silicon, which occurs widely in rocks combined with oxygen as silicate. Hydrogen, the most common element in the Universe, is uncommon on Earth, partly because it is a light gas that escapes from the Earth's atmosphere. Although the majority of elements in the Earth's crust are metals, they account for less than one-quarter of its total mass. Nitrogen forms about four-fifths of our atmosphere, but is so unreactive that it forms only a tiny percentage of the Earth's crust.

TRACE ELEMENTS
Humans need a balanced diet to stay healthy. Tiny amounts of many elements are vital to the chemical processes that go on within us. To prevent deficiencies, staple foods such as bread and margarine often have supplements added to them. Foods from the sea, such as seaweed and oily fish, are rich sources of calcium and iodine. Nuts and seeds are also rich in calcium, which ensures healthy bones and teeth. Egg yolk is a good source of sulfur, sodium, and zinc.

CROOKES'S SPECTROSCOPE

Crookes viewed the green line that he identified as characteristic of thallium through a spectroscope. During the 19th century new elements were discovered in a variety of ways. Robert Bunsen (1811-1899) first used a spectroscope to identify the metals cesium and rubidium by looking at their spectra in 1859. The spectroscope became a powerful tool for identifying new chemical elements. It has a prism inside it which splits a light beam into its different colors or wavelengths (its spectrum). If solutions of metals are put in a flame they produce characteristic colors that show as lines on a spectrum. Gases can be put in a discharge tube for observation.

Contains mirror to reflect micrometer scale

Micrometer to measure wavelength

Eyepiece

Pivot

Barrel contains prism

Slit to let in light

Green line characteristic of thallium

The spectrum of thallium

A CHANCE DISCOVERY

Sir William Crookes (1832-1919) was interested in applied chemistry, such as dyeing, and he practiced as an expert chemical analyst. His influence spanned 60 years of chemical research. He was quick to adopt the new technique of chemical spectroscopy, to look for previously unknown elements. In 1861 Crookes was examining deposits left over from the production of sulfuric acid when he saw a new green line in the spectrum and realized that there was another element present. He called it thallium, from the Greek *thallos*, meaning a budding or green twig. More elements have since been discovered, and we now know that 92 different elements are present in the Earth's crust. Many people have contributed to their identification and isolation (see also p. 174).

A NEW, GREEN SHOOT

Thallium compounds will give a green flame when burned. Looked at through a prism (contained in a spectroscope), the flame gives a spectrum with a characteristic green line. It was this green line that Crookes saw and was puzzled about because he had expected to identify one of two other elements – selenium or tellurium – which give blue and yellow lines, respectively.

Phosphorescent screen of zinc sulfide

Microscope slide

Trace of radium

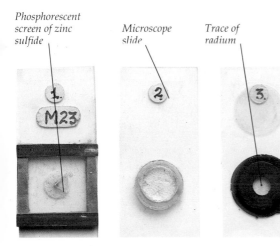

Three of Crookes's spinthariscopes

INVESTIGATING THALLIUM

Thallium is a blue-white, malleable metal similar to tin, but softer. It is sensitive to moisture in the air and crumbles after exposure. Like other metals, it forms many salts (p. 170). These thallium salts were prepared by Crookes soon after he discovered thallium and was studying the chemical properties of the element. The thallium salts are sealed in glass containers for display purposes. Thallium has few commercial applications, although it was used as a rat poison because it mimics the action of sodium, which is an element vital for living processes.

Thallium salt in display bottle

OBSERVING RADIUM

Crookes designed the spinthariscope (from the Greek *spintharis*, a spark) to measure the radioactivity of radium. They consist of phosphorescent screens of zinc sulfide behind which are placed tiny traces of radium, supplied to Crookes by Marie Curie, the Polish chemist who isolated radium. The radium emits alpha-particles that cause visible flashes of light when they fall on the screen placed in front of it. These are observed through a microscope. Radium is a radioactive element that occurs naturally. Since 1940, 17 more elements have been added to the 92 already known. They are all radioactive and usually short lived, breaking down into smaller atoms and emitting radioactivity. They do not occur naturally so must be prepared by scientists in nuclear reactors. With some elements only a few atoms have ever been prepared.

Investigating compounds

WHEN ELEMENTS COMBINE, THEY FORM COMPOUNDS. Compounds contain more than one type of atom, bound together to form molecules. A pure compound contains a single kind of molecule. Modern atomic theory helps explain how atoms are held together (bonded) to form molecules. Chemical bonds are formed using the electrons in the outer shell of the atom. The atoms either gain, share, or lose their electrons in the process. If one atom gives electrons to another, each then has an electric charge and is attracted to the other like opposite poles of a magnet, forming an *ionic* bond. Metals tend to form ionic bonds. Nonmetals tend to form *covalent* bonds with each other. Instead of handing over electrons to another atom, they prefer to share electrons. Elements that do not give up their electrons, such as the noble gases (p. 218), do not usually react with other elements. They are said to be unreactive, and they do not form compounds easily.

H_2O

Simple formula of water $\quad H_2O$

Structural formula of water

H — H
O

Ball-and-stick model of water

DOROTHY HODGKIN
The complex vitamin B_{12} molecule contains a total of 181 atoms, compared to water which has three. In 1948 the vitamin was isolated as a red crystalline material; Dorothy Hodgkin (b. 1910) examined it using X-ray crystallography. Together with Alexander Todd (b. 1907), who studied its chemical reactions, they worked out the chemical formula and structure in 1955.

COVALENT BONDS
Covalent compounds may be solids, liquids, or gases at normal temperatures. Water, the commonest and most important compound on Earth, is made up of molecules of two atoms of hydrogen bound to one of oxygen (H_2O). Each hydrogen atom shares its single electron with one from the oxygen, forming covalent bonds.

Space-filling model of water

Cl

Na

IONIC BONDS
An ion is an atom, or group of atoms with an electric charge. Sodium (Na), a metal, and chlorine (Cl), a nonmetal, react to form an ionic compound – common salt, or sodium chloride (NaCl). The sodium atom gives the single electron in its outer shell to the chlorine atom, completing the chlorine atom's own outer shell. In the crystalline solid of salt, the sodium and chloride ions are arranged alternately in a lattice with ions held together by the electrostatic force of attraction.

Positive and negative ions are attracted to one another

MAKING A COMPOUND
In this experiment, iron filings (Fe) are mixed with powdered sulfur (S). Although they are thoroughly mixed, no chemical reaction takes place between them. When heat is applied (step 2), sulfur combines with the iron to form a metal salt – iron, or ferrous sulfide. Metals often form salts with nonmetals.

Magnet attracts iron filings

1 MIXING ELEMENTS
The sulfur and iron filings are easily separated using an ordinary magnet that attracts the iron filings, but not the sulfur.

Yellow sulfur powder stays behind

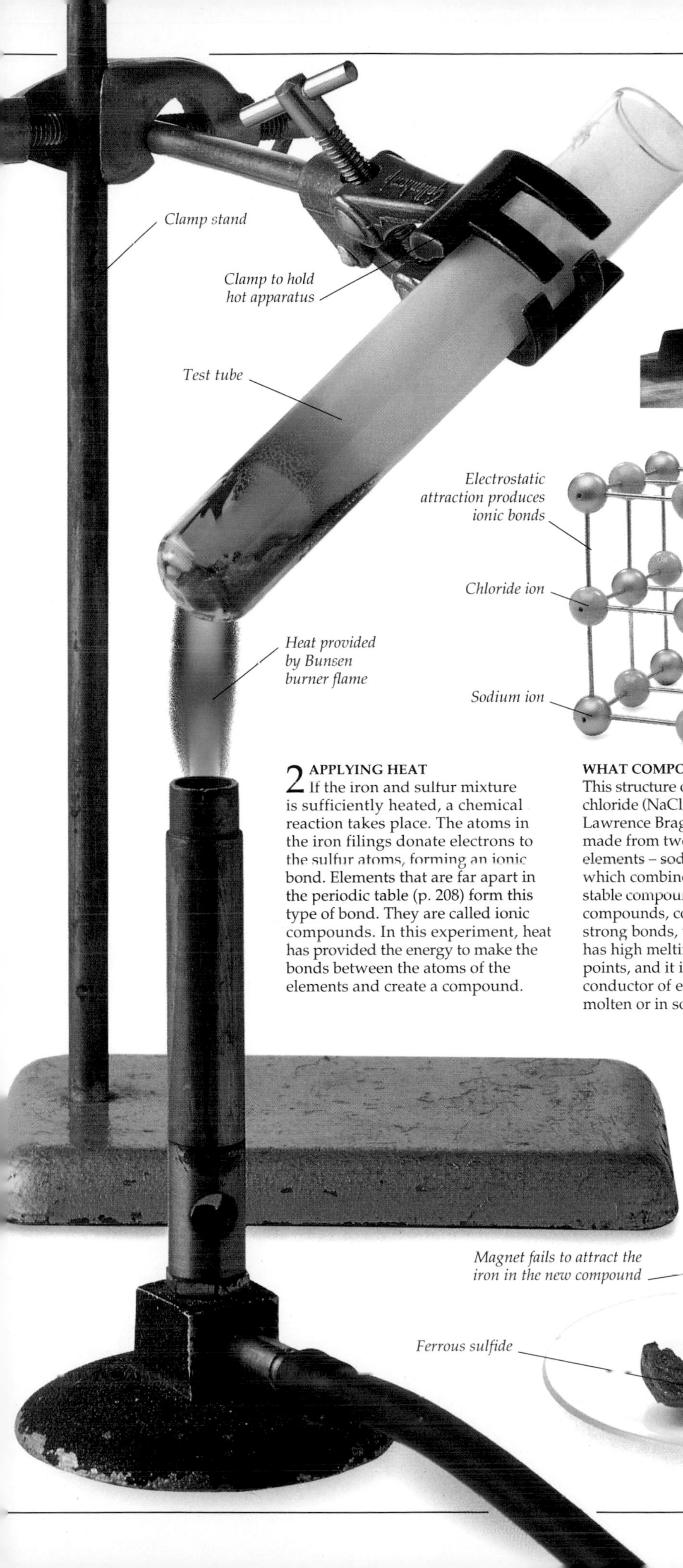

Clamp stand

Clamp to hold
hot apparatus

Test tube

Heat provided
by Bunsen
burner flame

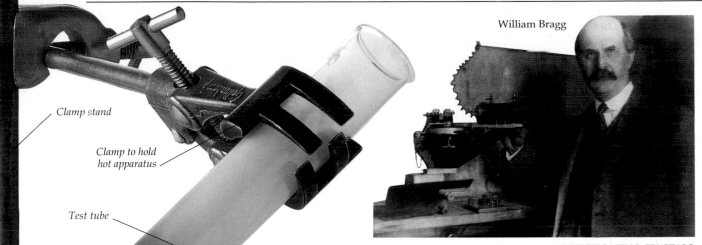

William Bragg

Electrostatic
attraction produces
ionic bonds

Chloride ion

Sodium ion

INVESTIGATING CRYSTALS
William Bragg (1862-1942)
developed the X-ray
spectrometer. Lawrence Bragg
(1890-1971), his son, used it to
work out the arrangement of
atoms in crystalline structures
by measuring the way X-rays
are diffracted (bent) on
passing through them. Salts
form crystalline structures; some
compounds like vitamin B_{12} can
form crystals with an extremely
complex structure.

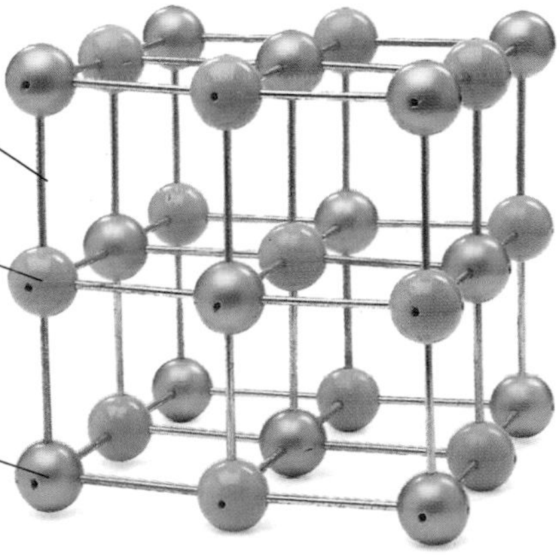

2 APPLYING HEAT
If the iron and sulfur mixture
is sufficiently heated, a chemical
reaction takes place. The atoms in
the iron filings donate electrons to
the sulfur atoms, forming an ionic
bond. Elements that are far apart in
the periodic table (p. 208) form this
type of bond. They are called ionic
compounds. In this experiment, heat
has provided the energy to make the
bonds between the atoms of the
elements and create a compound.

WHAT COMPOUNDS LOOK LIKE
This structure of common salt, or sodium
chloride (NaCl), was determined by
Lawrence Bragg. Sodium chloride is
made from two extremely reactive
elements – sodium and chlorine –
which combine to form a remarkably
stable compound. Like all ionic
compounds, common salt has
strong bonds, which means it
has high melting and boiling
points, and it is a good
conductor of electricity when
molten or in solution.

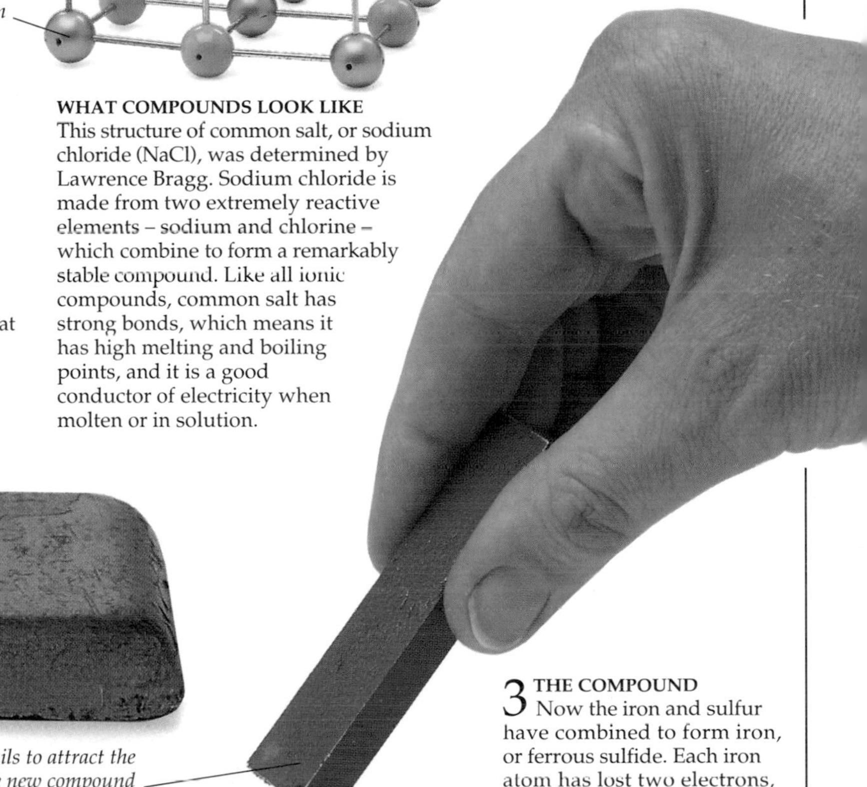

Magnet fails to attract the
iron in the new compound

Ferrous sulfide

3 THE COMPOUND
Now the iron and sulfur
have combined to form iron,
or ferrous sulfide. Each iron
atom has lost two electrons,
while the sulfur atoms have
each gained two. The sulfur
no longer looks yellow, and
the magnet cannot pull
out the iron because it is
now chemically bound
to the sulfur. The
chemical equation can be
written as Fe + S → FeS.

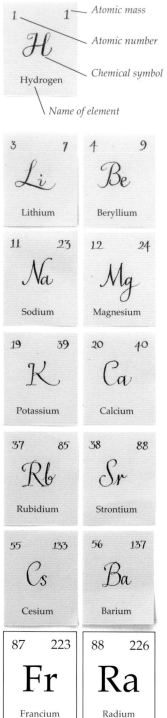

1 / 1
H
Hydrogen

- 1 — Atomic mass
- 1 — Atomic number
- H — Chemical symbol
- Hydrogen — Name of element

3	7	4	9
Li		Be	
Lithium		Beryllium	

11	23	12	24
Na		Mg	
Sodium		Magnesium	

The periodic table

AS NEW ELEMENTS WERE DISCOVERED, their atomic masses were determined, and the way each reacted with other substances was studied. Chemists began to notice families of elements that showed similar behavior. As early as 1829 Johann Döbereiner (1780-1849) had introduced the idea of triads of elements (groups of three): thus lithium, sodium, and potassium, all similar metals, formed one group, and they tended to behave in the same way. The Russian chemist Dmitri Mendeleyev (1834-1907) observed that elements listed in order of atomic mass showed regularly (or periodically) repeating properties. He announced his Periodic Law in 1869 and published a list of known elements in a tabular form. He had the courage to leave gaps where the Periodic Law did not seem to fit, predicting that new elements would be discovered to fill them.

| 19 / 39 K Potassium | 20 / 40 Ca Calcium | 21 / 44 Sc Scandium | 22 / 48 Ti Titanium | 23 / 51 V Vanadium | 24 / 52 Cr Chromium | 25 / 55 Mn Manganese | 26 / 56 Fe Iron | 27 / 59 Co Cobalt |

| 37 / 85 Rb Rubidium | 38 / 88 Sr Strontium | 39 / 89 Y Yttrium | 40 / 91 Zr Zirconium | 41 / 93 Nb Niobium | 42 / 96 Mo Molybdenum | 43 / 99 Tc Technetium | 44 / 101 Ru Ruthenium | 45 / 103 Rh Rhodium |

| 55 / 133 Cs Cesium | 56 / 137 Ba Barium | 57 / 139 La Lanthanum | 72 / 178 Hf Hafnium | 73 / 181 Ta Tantalum | 74 / 184 W Tungsten | 75 / 186 Re Rhenium | 76 / 190 Os Osmium | 77 / 192 Ir Iridium |

| 87 / 223 Fr Francium | 88 / 226 Ra Radium | 89 / 227 Ac Actinium | 104 (261) Unq Unnilquadium | 105 (262) Unp Unnilpentium | 106 (263) Unh Unnilhexium | 107 (262) Uns Unnilseptium | 108 (265) Uno Unniloctium | 109 (266) Une Unnilennium |

Elements in the transition series make up the center rows of the table

READING THE TABLE
The elements Mendeleyev knew about in his table published in 1871 are shown here as cards. The atoms are arranged in order of increasing "atomic number." This number represents the number of protons (positively charged particles) there are in the nucleus of the atom. This is the same as the number of electrons (negatively charged) surrounding the free atom. Atomic masses are determined by comparing the masses to that of a carbon atom, whose atomic mass is counted as 12.

Lanthanides

| 58 / 140 Ce Cerium | 59 / 141 Pr Praseodymium | 60 / 144 Nd Neodymium | 61 / 147 Pm Promethium | 62 / 150 Sm Samarium | 63 / 152 Eu Europium | 64 / 157 Gd Gadolinium |

Actinides

| 90 / 232 Th Thorium | 91 / 231 Pa Protactinium | 92 / 238 U Uranium | 93 / 237 Np Neptunium | 94 / 242 Pu Plutonium | 95 / 243 Am Americium | 96 / 247 Cm Curium |

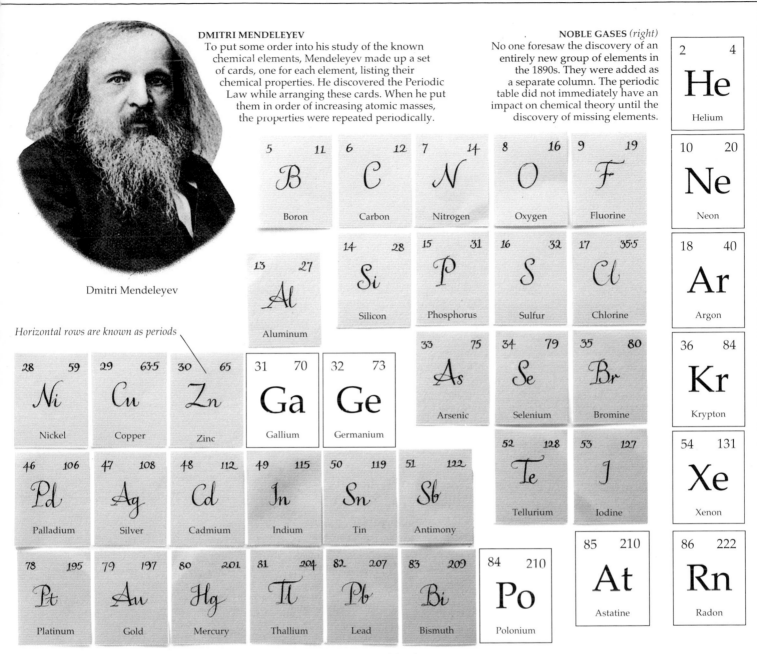

DMITRI MENDELEYEV
To put some order into his study of the known chemical elements, Mendeleyev made up a set of cards, one for each element, listing their chemical properties. He discovered the Periodic Law while arranging these cards. When he put them in order of increasing atomic masses, the properties were repeated periodically.

NOBLE GASES (right)
No one foresaw the discovery of an entirely new group of elements in the 1890s. They were added as a separate column. The periodic table did not immediately have an impact on chemical theory until the discovery of missing elements.

Dmitri Mendeleyev

Horizontal rows are known as periods

MODERN NUCLEAR ELEMENTS (left)
To avoid disputes over the names of new elements, they have been given systematic names based on their atomic numbers. Therefore, element 104 became unnilquadium from un-nil-quad, or one-zero-four, and so on.

FITTING IN NEW ELEMENTS (above)
The crowning achievement of Mendeleyev's periodic table lay in his prophecy of new elements. Gallium, germanium, and scandium were unknown in 1871, but Mendeleyev left spaces for them and even predicted what the atomic masses and other chemical properties would be. The first of these to be discovered, in 1875, was gallium. All the characteristics fitted those he had predicted for the element Mendeleyev called eka-aluminum – because it came below aluminum in his table.

INNER TRANSITION SERIES (left)
These two rows are known as the lanthanides and actinides after the first members of their groups – lanthanum (atomic number 57) and actinium (atomic number 89). They are traditionally separated out from the rest of the table to give it a coherent shape. The lanthanides are often found together in minerals. They are sometimes called the rare earth elements, although they are not particularly scarce. The actinides are all radioactive. Only the first three are found in nature; the rest have to be made artificially.

Looking at metals

MOST ELEMENTS ARE METALS. Metals are often described as strong, heavy, shiny, and difficult to melt. They are good conductors of heat and electricity and may clang when hit. Many metals are malleable: they can be hammered into shape. Some are ductile: they can be drawn out into thin wires. There are exceptions – mercury is a metal, but is a liquid at room temperature. Metals also have distinctive chemical properties. They react with acids to form salts and with oxygen in the air to form basic oxides. Although there are many similarities between metals, there are also differences which determine how appropriate a metal is for a particular use. Some metals are light, such as aluminum, making it ideal as components in the aeronautics industry. Some are resistant to corrosion, such as chromium, which is used for bathroom fittings.

AN ALLOY
The mortar and pestle are essential tools of the chemist and pharmacist. They were often cast by bell founders so they were made from the same metal as bells – an alloy of chiefly tin and copper. An alloy is a mixture of metals. Alloys are often preferred to pure metals because they can be mixed to give properties such as rigidity or a low melting point.

LIQUID METAL
This late 18th-century thermometer uses mercury to indicate the temperature. Heat makes the mercury expand. For centuries, it was thought that mercury could exist only as a liquid, but during a cold winter in Russia in 1759 it was observed that mercury froze at about −36.4° F (−38° C).

MINING AND CHEMISTRY
Prospectors looked for mineral deposits and helped identify many new metals. Blowpipes were an important tool in their work. A portable "laboratory" was first described by Karl Friedrich Plattner (1800-1858) in his treatise on blowpipe analysis. This 19th-century set contains mineralogical tools for use in the field. Using the blowpipe for heat, metal samples were fused with lead in a tiny cupel (p. 198) and tested for their reactions with standard chemical reagents.

Bottles containing reagents

Tray holding prospecting tools

Magnifying glass

Wooden case

Bottle containing reagent

Indicator papers

Lead strips

Mortar and pestle

Cupel

Wick

Alcohol burner

SANDSTONE ROCK
This sample of sandstone rock contains a copper ore, which is mainly greenish copper carbonate. Sandstone is a sedimentary rock, which is chiefly silica; the layers of silica in the form of sand have been built up over millions of years. Other substances are mixed in with it as it forms. Analysts find out how much metal is in the rock to determine whether mining will be economically feasible.

Mouthpiece

Blowpipe

ISOLATING THE REACTIVE METALS

Sir Humphry Davy (1778-1829) became a professor at tEngland's Royal Institution in 1801, a year after it was founded. His lectures on scientific topics were very successful, and fashionable society flocked there to listen to him. After the discovery of the voltaic pile (p. 232), Davy built himself a huge battery of voltaic cells and used the electricity they produced to isolate first potassium, then sodium metals from their hydroxides. The following year he isolated magnesium, calcium, strontium, and barium. These metals must be extracted from their molten ores by means of electricity because they are highly reactive. Less reactive metals, for example copper, can be extracted from ores by roasting at high temperatures.

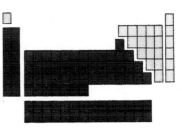

METALS ON THE PERIODIC TABLE

Vertical groups of elements have similar properties. The alkali metals on the left of the table all react with water to form an alkali. The transition metals, which occur from the fourth horizontal row downward, are notable for the variety of colored salts they form.

STRONTIUM

This metallic element is named after the Scottish town Strontian, where ores containing strontium were first found. A soft, silvery metal, it reacts with water and burns in air. Its red flame is used in fireworks. These sample bottles were specially made to fit a display board.

GALLIUM

This metal is soft, silvery, and white, similar to aluminium. Its existence was predicted by Mendeleyev (p. 209). With a low melting point of about 86° F (30° C), it will melt if held in a warm hand. It is extracted by electrolysis as a by-product of bauxite mining (pp. 18-19) and is used in the electronics industry.

How metals react

If an element easily gains or loses the electrons used for bonding, it is said to be reactive. All metals can be put in order of their reactivity with water and with air. This is known as the reactivity series, and the order also indicates the ease with which metals can be extracted from their ores. Gold, the least reactive metal, comes at the bottom: it does not react with water, dilute acids, or air, and it is found as the element in nature.

REACTIVITY OF DIFFERENT METALS

Potassium and tin behave differently when put into contact with water. Potassium metal (right) reacts vigorously, and so much heat is generated that the hydrogen gas produced catches fire and burns with a lilac flame. Tin (above), which is lower down the reactivity series, reacts hardly at all with water. If dilute acid is used, potassium reacts even more vigorously, and tin reacts very slowly to produce hydrogen.

Discovering nonmetals

MOST ELEMENTS ARE METALS. Those that are not are called nonmetals. Half of these are gases such as oxygen, nitrogen, and chlorine. Bromine is a liquid at room temperature, and the rest are solids. The physical characteristics of nonmetals are usually the opposite of those of metals. When solid, they are brittle and cannot be beaten into shape (not malleable) or drawn into wires (nonductile). The elements themselves have a different chemical structure from that of metals. They are not good conductors of electricity or heat. The chemical reactions of nonmetals also differ from those of metals. They do not react with dilute acids and, when they burn in air or oxygen, they form oxides, which produce acids with water. Some of the solids show behavior between that of a metal and a nonmetal: these are called semimetals or semiconductors. One complete group of nonmetals was unknown until the 1890s. These are the noble gases (p. 218).

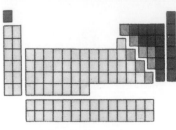

ON THE PERIODIC TABLE
The nonmetals are to the upper right of the table. The so-called semimetal elements (light pink) show both nonmetal and metal behavior. Some, like silicon, are semiconductors. Hydrogen is also a nonmetal.

Oxidizing agent reacts with the phosphorus

Phosphorus

LIGHT BEARER
Discovered in 1669, white phosphorus glows in the dark and was used in matches because it ignites easily. Because it was highly toxic, it was replaced by red phosphorus in 1845. In these safety matches, the phosphorus is included on the box; the match head contains an oxidizer, which ignites when struck against the phosphorus.

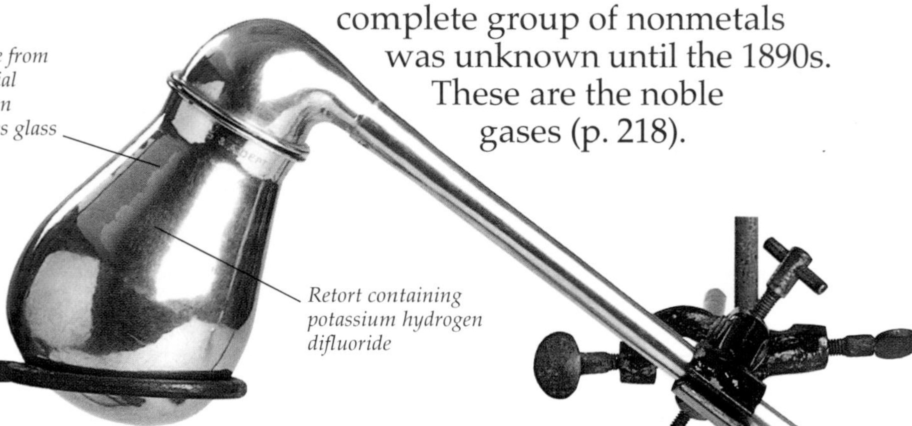

Apparatus made from platinum material because hydrogen fluoride dissolves glass

Clamp stand with retort ring

Retort containing potassium hydrogen difluoride

DISCOVERING FLUORINE
Although salts of fluorine – fluorides – had been used for centuries, fluorine gas, the most reactive element of all, was not isolated until 1886. No compounds will easily give up their fluorine. Therefore, like the more reactive metals, the only way to isolate it is by electrolysis (p. 232), using this equipment. The gas was obtained from a solution of potassium hydrogen difluoride (KHF_2) in liquid hydrogen fluoride (HF). The hydrogen fluoride used must be anhydrous (completely free from water); otherwise oxygen will be obtained.

MOISSAN IN HIS LABORATORY
Henri Moissan (1852-1907) is shown here in his laboratory in Paris. Moissan finally succeeded in obtaining fluorine – a yellowish gas. In his experiments, he made sure the gases from the electrodes did not come into contact, he used a mixture of chemicals, and he constructed the apparatus from platinum because hydrogen fluoride attacks glass vessels. Like fellow scientists who tried to isolate this dangerous chemical, Moissan suffered from the poisonous effects of hydrogen fluoride and fluorine gases.

Delivery tube

STRONGER, HEALTHIER TEETH
Tiny amounts of fluoride protect teeth from attack by acids in food. This can be achieved by adding fluoride to water supplies. Modern toothpastes now have fluoride added to them. This fluoridation has reduced serious tooth decay.

Bunsen burner provides heat

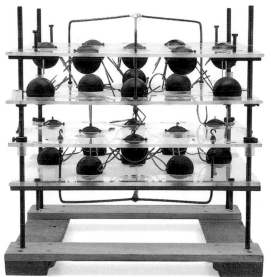

DIAMOND AND GRAPHITE

Many nonmetal elements exist in more than one form (allotrope) – carbon is no exception (p. 294). Diamond, the hardest substance, is colorless, while graphite is soft and black. Both contain only carbon atoms. Kathleen Lonsdale (1903-1971) used this model to illustrate the different arrangement of carbon atoms in the two allotropes. Graphite has widely spaced flat layers of carbon atoms. The layers slide easily over each other, making graphite a good lubricant. Electrons binding the layers together are not strongly attached to particular atoms, so they conduct electricity fairly well. In diamond, each carbon is bound to four others in a regular structure of very strong bonds. (Elastic bands represent the bonds in the models shown here.)

Arrangement of carbon atoms in graphite

Arrangement of carbon atoms in diamond

Gas mask (1917)

Thistle funnel for topping up methyl chloride

Face mask

TRAGIC USE OF CHLORINE

Toxic gases were used by both sides throughout World War I (1914-1918). Chlorine was first used at Ypres in Belgium in 1915. The heavy green gas rolled over the countryside and was inhaled by Allied troops, causing their lungs to fill with liquid, drowning them. Those who did not die were invalids for the rest of their lives. Masks were produced in great numbers during World War II (1939-1945); fortunately, chemical warfare played no part in the hostilities.

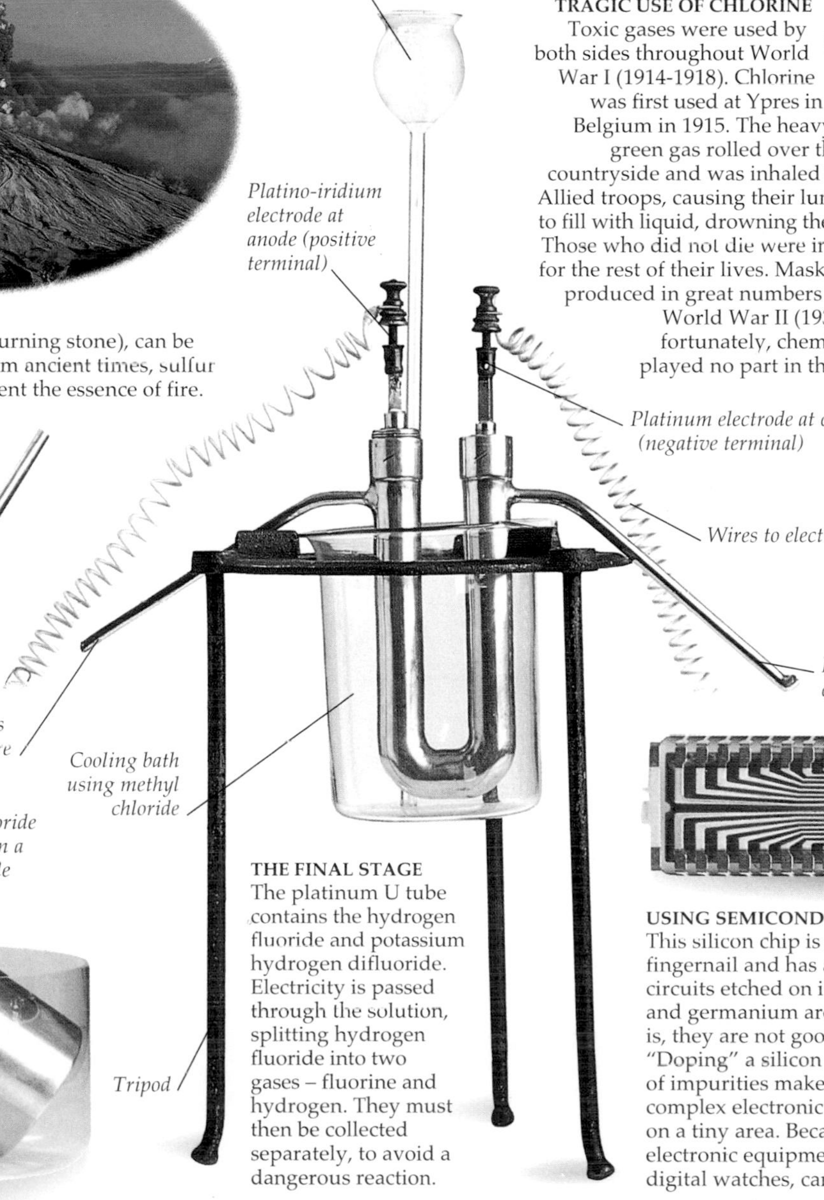

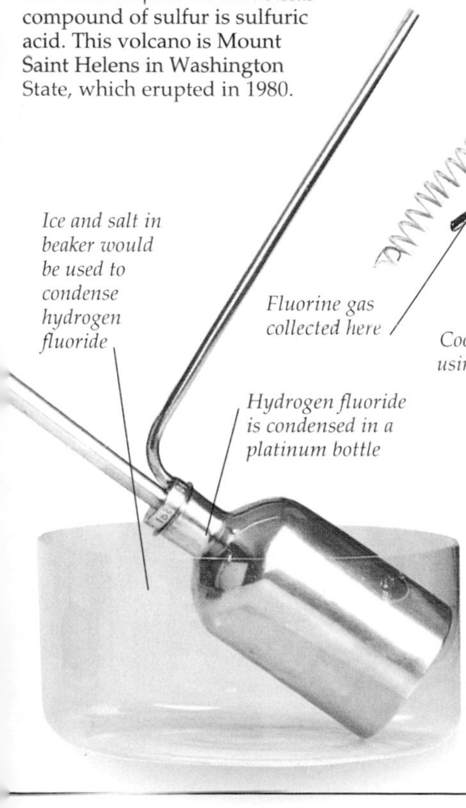

Flexible rubber tube

Platino-iridium electrode at anode (positive terminal)

Platinum electrode at cathode (negative terminal)

Wires to electricity supply

Bottle contains chemicals to neutralize the chlorine

ELEMENTS FROM VOLCANOES

Sulfur, or brimstone (which means burning stone), can be found on volcanic slopes. Known from ancient times, sulfur was believed by alchemists to represent the essence of fire. The most important industrial compound of sulfur is sulfuric acid. This volcano is Mount Saint Helens in Washington State, which erupted in 1980.

Hydrogen gas collected here

Ice and salt in beaker would be used to condense hydrogen fluoride

Fluorine gas collected here

Hydrogen fluoride is condensed in a platinum bottle

Cooling bath using methyl chloride

THE FINAL STAGE

The platinum U tube contains the hydrogen fluoride and potassium hydrogen difluoride. Electricity is passed through the solution, splitting hydrogen fluoride into two gases – fluorine and hydrogen. They must then be collected separately, to avoid a dangerous reaction.

Tripod

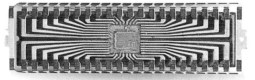

USING SEMICONDUCTORS

This silicon chip is smaller than a baby's fingernail and has a series of electrical circuits etched on its surface. Both silicon and germanium are semiconductors – that is, they are not good conductors of electricity. "Doping" a silicon chip with small amounts of impurities makes it conduct electricity, and complex electronic circuits can be designed on a tiny area. Because chips are so small, electronic equipment, such as computers and digital watches, can be of manageable size.

Looking at air

GASES FROM BURNING
J.B. van Helmont recognized that different gases could be produced chemically by burning substances. He realized that these gases were different from the air we breathe.

THE AIR AROUND US is made up of a mixture of gases. Oxygen and nitrogen are the two main ones. Most gases cannot be seen or felt. Indeed, until the 17th century people did not realize that there were different gases – there was just air, which was one of the original Greek elements. Johann van Helmont (1577-1644) tried making "airs" chemically. Because his glass apparatus often broke he used the word "gas" for them, which comes from the Greek word for chaos. Investigation of gases started in earnest in the 18th century. The major obstacle was how to handle gases. The pneumatic trough, a device for collecting gases under water or mercury, was introduced by Joseph Priestley and it is still used in laboratories today. The first gas to be studied in detail was carbon dioxide. Joseph Black made it in several different ways and, recognizing that it was not ordinary air, he called it "fixed air." By the end of the 18th century, many of the common gases had been prepared and studied in a science known as pneumatic chemistry.

HANDLING GASES
Pig's bladders were widely used in the 18th century to contain gases for use in experiments. They also held the gases that were to be weighed. Priestley used carbon dioxide contained in a bladder to prepare his artificial mineral water. John Nooth complained of the flavor imparted to the water by the bladder and introduced his glass apparatus.

Thistle funnel

Delivery tube

JOSEPH PRIESTLEY (1733-1804)
This medallion of the renowned English clergyman and scientist was made by the English potter Josiah Wedgwood, who also supplied Priestley with much of his chemical apparatus. Using his pneumatic trough, Priestley investigated many gases before his discovery of oxygen. He studied carbon dioxide, obtained as a by-product from the neighboring brewery, and invented a way of preparing carbonated water (p. 147).

JOSEPH BLACK (1728-1799)
A leading Scottish chemist, Black's careful experiments increased chemical knowledge enormously. His work finally proved that there were other gases besides those present in the atmospheric air. Black first prepared carbon dioxide while studying stomach acidity and how to cure it.

Hydrochloric acid

MAKING CARBON DIOXIDE
In this experiment, carbon dioxide (CO_2) is being prepared by one of the methods used by Joseph Black. Hydrochloric acid is added to magnesium carbonate ("magnesia alba" as Black called it). The resulting gas is collected using a pneumatic trough. Black realized that he could also produce this gas by heating a carbonate, or calcinating limestone. He called it "fixed air" because he recognized that it was not the same as the atmospheric air he breathed, although he did show that small amounts of the gas were present in the atmosphere.

Magnesium carbonate reacting with acid

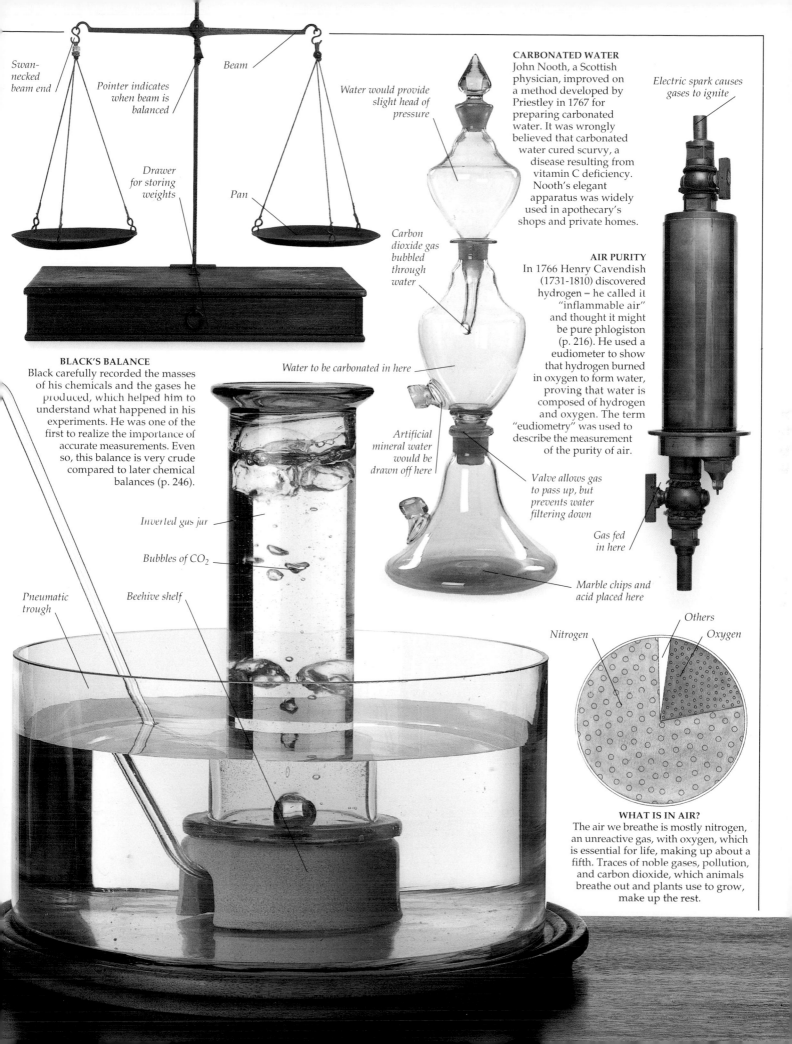

Swan-necked beam end

Beam

Pointer indicates when beam is balanced

Drawer for storing weights

Pan

CARBONATED WATER
John Nooth, a Scottish physician, improved on a method developed by Priestley in 1767 for preparing carbonated water. It was wrongly believed that carbonated water cured scurvy, a disease resulting from vitamin C deficiency. Nooth's elegant apparatus was widely used in apothecary's shops and private homes.

Water would provide slight head of pressure

Carbon dioxide gas bubbled through water

Electric spark causes gases to ignite

AIR PURITY
In 1766 Henry Cavendish (1731-1810) discovered hydrogen – he called it "inflammable air" and thought it might be pure phlogiston (p. 216). He used a eudiometer to show that hydrogen burned in oxygen to form water, proving that water is composed of hydrogen and oxygen. The term "eudiometry" was used to describe the measurement of the purity of air.

BLACK'S BALANCE
Black carefully recorded the masses of his chemicals and the gases he produced, which helped him to understand what happened in his experiments. He was one of the first to realize the importance of accurate measurements. Even so, this balance is very crude compared to later chemical balances (p. 246).

Water to be carbonated in here

Artificial mineral water would be drawn off here

Valve allows gas to pass up, but prevents water filtering down

Gas fed in here

Inverted gas jar

Bubbles of CO_2

Marble chips and acid placed here

Pneumatic trough

Beehive shelf

Nitrogen

Others

Oxygen

WHAT IS IN AIR?
The air we breathe is mostly nitrogen, an unreactive gas, with oxygen, which is essential for life, making up about a fifth. Traces of noble gases, pollution, and carbon dioxide, which animals breathe out and plants use to grow, make up the rest.

Burning reactions

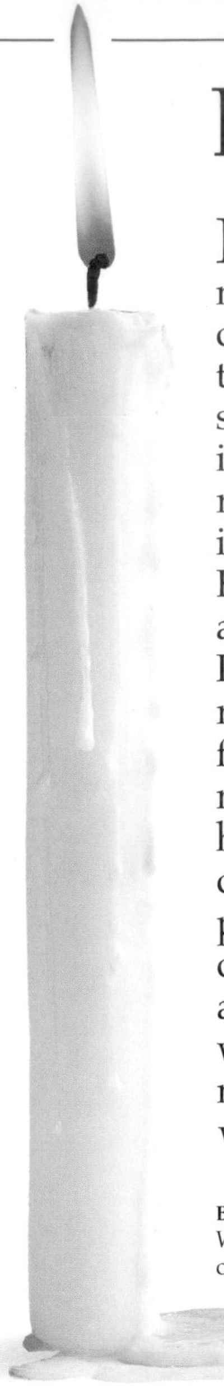

Fire PROVIDES HUMANITY WITH LIGHT and heat, the means to cook and to smelt metals. Burning, or combustion, was one of the first chemical reactions to be studied in detail. We now know that when substances burn in air they react with the oxygen in it, forming new compounds and sometimes leaving a residue of ash. Some compounds are gases which disappear into the air; some are solids which remain behind. Early theories assumed that burning wood to form ash was essentially the same as burning metals. In both cases it was believed that burning released part of the original material in the form of phlogiston (from the Greek *phlogistos*, meaning inflammable). This idea proved helpful to the understanding of the chemical processes involved. When products were weighed more carefully, it was realized that although the ash left behind when wood burned was lighter, metals actually increased in weight when burned.

PHLOGISTON THEORY
The German chemist Georg Ernst Stahl (1659-1734) believed that when substances burned they gave up a substance he called phlogiston. This theory proved helpful in explaining reactions, and it diverted many thinkers, but it was proved wrong by Antoine Lavoisier (see below).

Mercury would be heated in retort to form calx

BURNING A CANDLE
Wax is a mixture of compounds containing chiefly carbon and hydrogen. When the wick is lit, some wax is drawn up the wick and vaporizes. The vapor burns, using oxygen in the air. The yellow part of the flame is caused by carbon particles incandescing (glowing) at high temperatures. Unburned carbon forms soot.

Carrying handle

THE FATHER OF CHEMISTRY
After Englishman Joseph Priestley discovered oxygen in 1774, Frenchman Antoine Lavoisier (1743-1794), who gave the gas the name oxygen, started examining its properties and those of air. He proposed a totally new theory which explained both the formation of metal oxides and allowed for the reactions which occur when burning wood or candles. Lavoisier came from a wealthy family. Because of his involvement with tax collection, he was tried and guillotined during the French Revolution.

Opening for fuel

Fire clay furnace

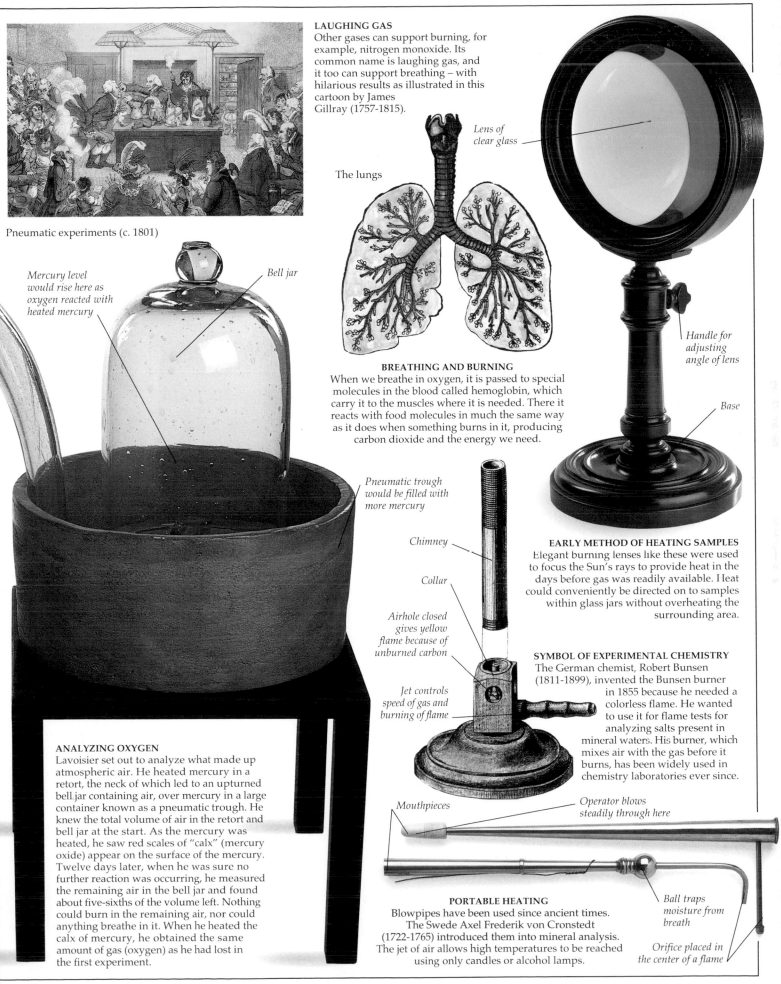

LAUGHING GAS
Other gases can support burning, for example, nitrogen monoxide. Its common name is laughing gas, and it too can support breathing – with hilarious results as illustrated in this cartoon by James Gillray (1757-1815).

Pneumatic experiments (c. 1801)

Lens of clear glass

The lungs

Mercury level would rise here as oxygen reacted with heated mercury

Bell jar

Handle for adjusting angle of lens

Base

BREATHING AND BURNING
When we breathe in oxygen, it is passed to special molecules in the blood called hemoglobin, which carry it to the muscles where it is needed. There it reacts with food molecules in much the same way as it does when something burns in it, producing carbon dioxide and the energy we need.

Pneumatic trough would be filled with more mercury

Chimney

Collar

Airhole closed gives yellow flame because of unburned carbon

Jet controls speed of gas and burning of flame

EARLY METHOD OF HEATING SAMPLES
Elegant burning lenses like these were used to focus the Sun's rays to provide heat in the days before gas was readily available. Heat could conveniently be directed on to samples within glass jars without overheating the surrounding area.

SYMBOL OF EXPERIMENTAL CHEMISTRY
The German chemist, Robert Bunsen (1811-1899), invented the Bunsen burner in 1855 because he needed a colorless flame. He wanted to use it for flame tests for analyzing salts present in mineral waters. His burner, which mixes air with the gas before it burns, has been widely used in chemistry laboratories ever since.

ANALYZING OXYGEN
Lavoisier set out to analyze what made up atmospheric air. He heated mercury in a retort, the neck of which led to an upturned bell jar containing air, over mercury in a large container known as a pneumatic trough. He knew the total volume of air in the retort and bell jar at the start. As the mercury was heated, he saw red scales of "calx" (mercury oxide) appear on the surface of the mercury. Twelve days later, when he was sure no further reaction was occurring, he measured the remaining air in the bell jar and found about five-sixths of the volume left. Nothing could burn in the remaining air, nor could anything breathe in it. When he heated the calx of mercury, he obtained the same amount of gas (oxygen) as he had lost in the first experiment.

Mouthpieces

Operator blows steadily through here

PORTABLE HEATING
Blowpipes have been used since ancient times. The Swede Axel Frederik von Cronstedt (1722-1765) introduced them into mineral analysis. The jet of air allows high temperatures to be reached using only candles or alcohol lamps.

Ball traps moisture from breath

Orifice placed in the center of a flame

The noble gases

IDENTIFYING HELIUM
During the 1868 eclipse of the Sun French astronomer Pierre Janssen (1824-1907) observed a bright yellow spectral line. This was thought to signify a new element, named helium from the Greek word *helios*, the Sun.

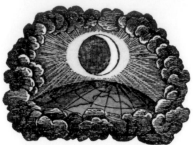

AT THE START OF THE 1890s, no one had any idea that there was a separate group of gases in the periodic table (p. 208), the noble gases. Noble gases are familiar to us from their use in neon signs and helium balloons. By 1900 this whole new group had been identified and isolated. While trying to determine an accurate atomic mass for nitrogen, British physicist Lord Rayleigh (1842-1919) discovered that nitrogen prepared from ammonia was noticeably lighter than nitrogen that came from the atmosphere. He and William Ramsay (1852-1916) both studied "atmospheric" nitrogen. By removing the nitrogen from it, they produced a tiny quantity of another gas. Since it did not react with anything they called it argon, from the Greek word for lazy. The discovery of helium followed a year later in 1895. Ramsay and his assistant Morris Travers (1872-1961) then started to search for additional elements in this new group. They attempted this by fractional distillation of large quantities of liquid air and argon. In 1898, their efforts were rewarded; they had prepared krypton, neon, and xenon.

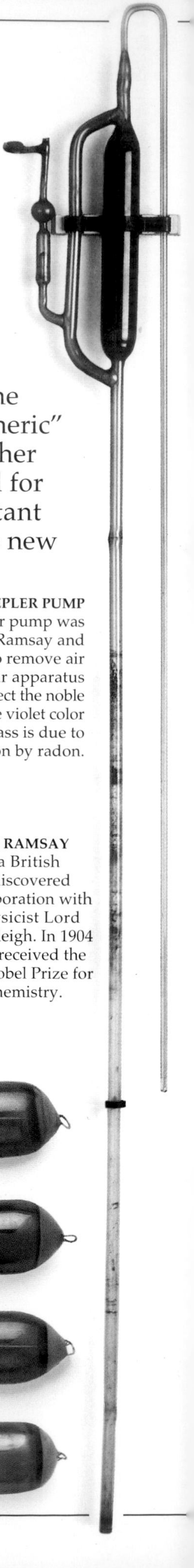

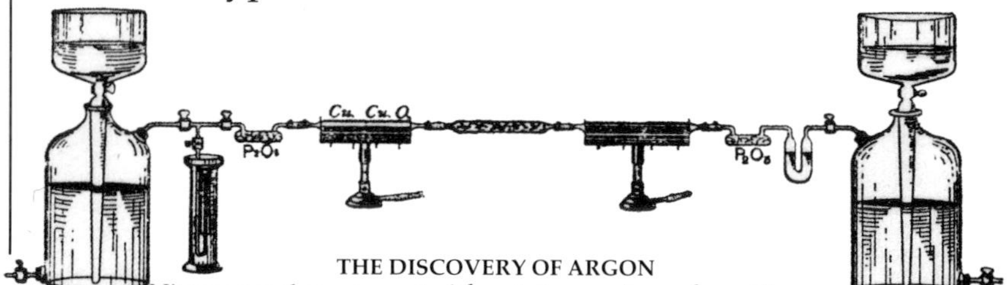

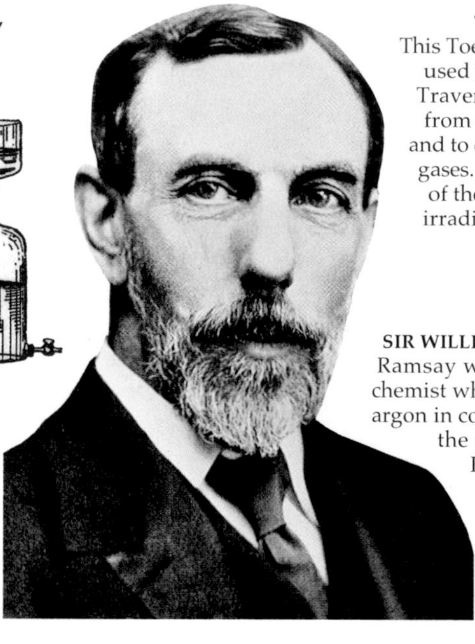

TOEPLER PUMP
This Toepler pump was used by Ramsay and Travers to remove air from their apparatus and to collect the noble gases. The violet color of the glass is due to irradiation by radon.

THE DISCOVERY OF ARGON
Nitrogen makes up most of the air in our atmosphere. Ramsay devised this apparatus to absorb all the known gases from atmospheric nitrogen. Air was first passed over heated copper to remove the oxygen, and the remaining gases were then passed through the apparatus which removed moisture, any remaining oxygen, pollutants, carbon dioxide, and nitrogen, leaving only one-eightieth of the volume of gas at the end. Ramsay examined this with a spectroscope and found new spectral lines that did not belong to any known gas. He and Rayleigh jointly announced the discovery of argon in 1894.

SIR WILLIAM RAMSAY
Ramsay was a British chemist who discovered argon in collaboration with the physicist Lord Rayleigh. In 1904 he received the Nobel Prize for chemistry.

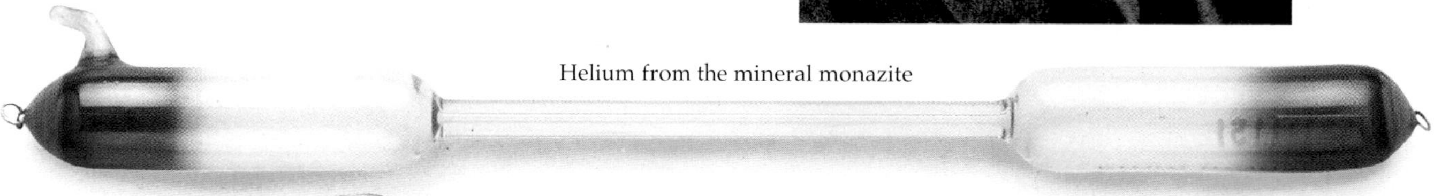

Helium from the mineral monazite

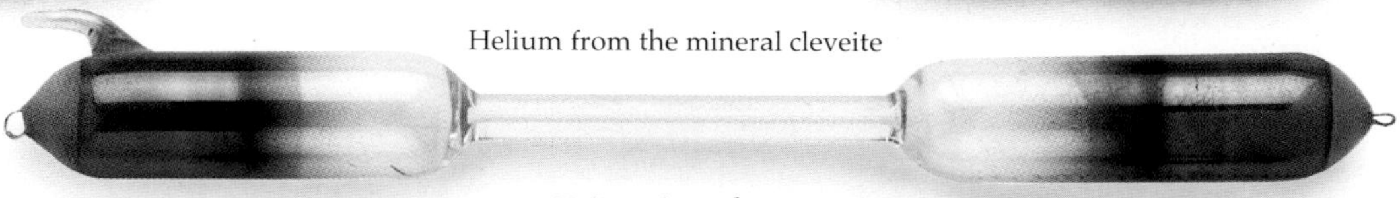

Helium from the mineral cleveite

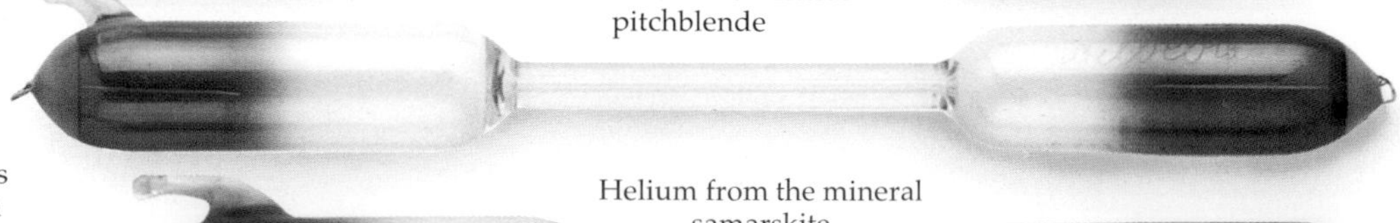

Helium from the mineral pitchblende

Helium from the mineral samarskite

HELIUM SAMPLES
Janssen's discovery of an element in the Sun set off a search for helium on Earth. Ramsay obtained it by boiling the mineral cleveite with dilute acid. Seeing a brilliant yellow line in its spectrum, he realized that it was identical to that observed in the Sun during the 1868 eclipse. He sent his samples shown here to Sir William Crookes and the astronomer Norman Lockyer (1836-1920). In 1895 they confirmed by spectroscopy that it was helium.

Argon gas

Tungsten
filament

Connection to
electric current

USING ARGON IN LIGHT BULBS
Since their discovery, the noble gases have found many
uses, not least because of their unreactivity. Argon is
often used in experiments to provide an inert atmosphere,
as here in this light bulb. It does not react with the
tungsten filament, even at high temperatures.

THE USES OF HELIUM
As it is much lighter than air,
helium is used to fill balloons
and airships. Because it does not
react (it is inert), it is safer than
hydrogen, which can explode in
air. The meteorological balloons
shown above were used to carry
equipment to investigate the
hole in the ozone layer above
the Arctic in 1990. Some balloons
reached an altitude of 18 miles
(28 km). Helium is also used
to make the voice of the cartoon
character Donald Duck. Sound
waves travel faster through the light
gas and so when the actor breathes
helium, his voice becomes high pitched.

Helium-filled
balloons

SOURCES OF RADON
Radon, the heaviest noble gas, was
first observed as the gas produced
by the radioactive element radium
when it decayed. Some granites
used for building houses
have been found to give off tiny
amounts of radon, which can
accumulate in confined areas.

Granite rock

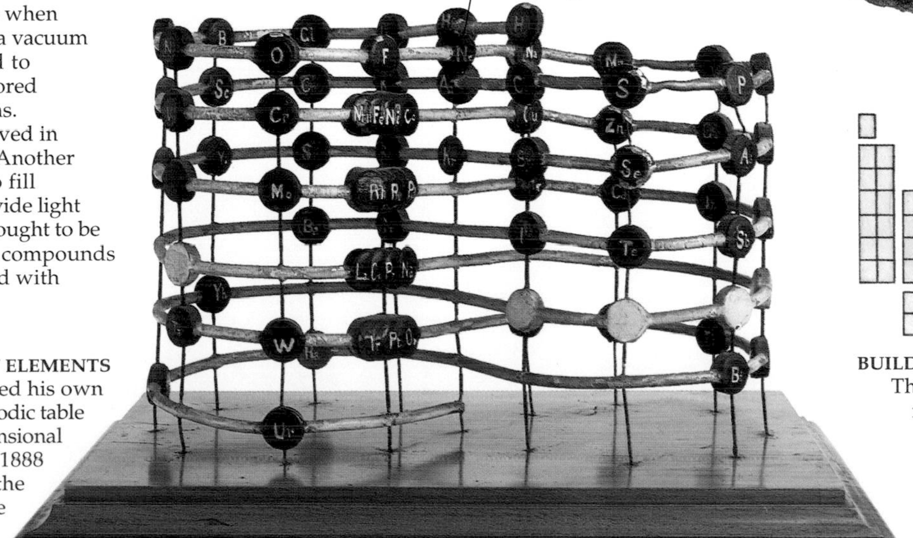

NEON SIGNS
Neon lets off a reddish light when
electricity is passed through a vacuum
tube containing it. It is used to
produce these brightly colored
advertising signs in Las Vegas.
A high light output is achieved in
relation to the power used. Another
noble gas, xenon, is used to fill
fluorescent tubes and to provide light
for lighthouses. Although thought to be
unreactive, since 1962 some compounds
of xenon have been prepared with
highly reactive fluorine.

The noble gases

ADDING NEW ELEMENTS
Sir William Crookes devised his own
way of representing the periodic table
in this elaborate, three-dimensional
spiral model made in 1888
before the discovery of the
noble gases. However, the
model easily fitted in the
new group of elements
at the center.

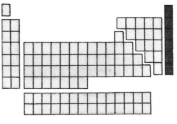

BUILDING UP THE PERIODIC TABLE
The noble gases are placed to the
right of Mendeleyev's periodic
table (p. 208) after the
halogen elements. Each gas
has a full outer shell of
electrons, which explains
their lack of reactivity and
the reason why they were
not discovered sooner.

Chemical reactions

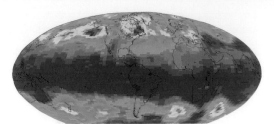

CHEMICAL REACTIONS CAN HAPPEN NATURALLY, without human intervention. Reactions happen in living things by making use of proteins called enzymes in complex catalytic reactions. Humans can also make chemical reactions happen to provide some of the products we use every day. When a chemical reaction takes place, atoms are rearranged, and new chemical substances are formed. The starting materials in a chemical reaction are called reactants that react to form products. In a chemical reaction there are changes of energy, often in the form of heat. If heat is given off, the reaction is said to be exothermic (potassium in water, p. 211); if heat is absorbed, this is an endothermic reaction (synthesis of fluorine, p. 212). Some chemical reactions are reversible; some are difficult, if not impossible to reverse. In a chemical reaction, a compound may be prepared or synthesized from its elements. For example, iron and sulfur form iron sulfide when they are heated together. A compound can also be broken down – for example, heating metal ores to obtain metals.

THE OZONE LAYER
Ozone is a reactive gas that contributes to pollution when it builds up in the atmosphere over cities. However, ozone in the stratosphere (red here shows maximum ozone concentration) does the useful task of absorbing damaging ultraviolet (UV) light from the Sun, screening it from the Earth. Some synthetic chemicals, especially chlorofluorocarbons (CFCs), react with ozone, creating holes in the ozone layer. These holes allow more UV light through, tending to cause an increase in skin cancer.

USING LIGHT FOR A REACTION
Plants make carbohydrates to build up stems, trunks, leaves, and roots in a process called photosynthesis. The plants take in water from the soil, and carbon dioxide from the atmosphere, and use light energy from the Sun to convert them to carbohydrates. They also produce oxygen as a by-product, which they release into the atmosphere through their leaves.

A DISPLACEMENT REACTION
When a coil of copper is dipped into a solution of a silver salt, the copper displaces the silver in the salt. Copper is able to do this because it is higher in the reactivity series of metals. Copper and silver nitrate are the reactants in this reaction, and copper nitrate and silver metal are the products. This is called a displacement reaction beacuse one metal has displaced another metal from a solution of one of its salts (pp. 230-231).

1 THE REACTANTS
The coils of copper are dipped into a flask of a silver salt in solution. In this reaction, the salt is the colorless silver nitrate.

Cork stopper

Copper coil

Glass flask

Silver nitrate dissolved in water

2 SILVER COATING
As soon as the copper coil and the salt solution come into contact, the silver is precipitated out of the solution – that is, it becomes an insoluble solid and can be seen as the metal clinging in crystals to the copper strip. The solution turns blue because copper ions displace silver ions in the solution, to produce copper nitrate. The equation can be written as $Cu + 2AgNO_3 \rightarrow Cu(NO_3)_2 + 2Ag$.

Silver crystals grow on the copper coil

Blue copper nitrate is formed in the solution

ROCKET FUEL

The Space Shuttle sits on a large fuel tank holding liquid hydrogen and liquid oxygen in separate containers. They are mixed in the correct proportion and react to provide power. The hydrogen burns in oxygen with a clean flame producing water, seen here as steam.

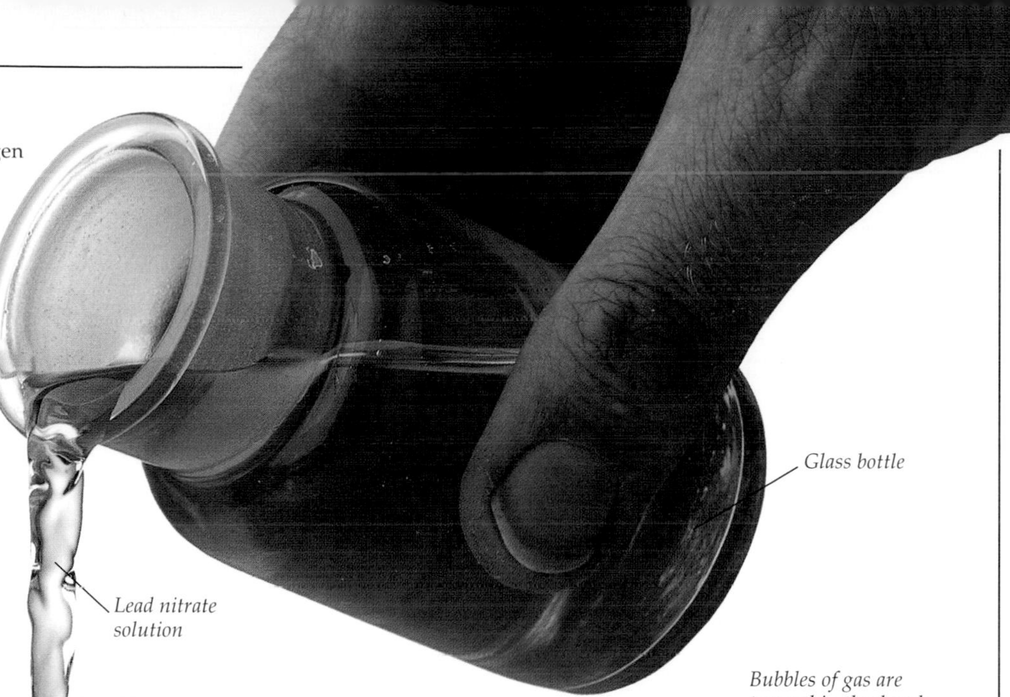

Glass bottle

Lead nitrate solution

Filter funnel

MAKING A PRECIPITATE

Both potassium iodide and lead nitrate are salts that are soluble in water, they form colorless solutions. However, lead iodide is insoluble, so when the two solutions are mixed, yellow lead iodide is precipitated out of the solution. The other product, potassium nitrate, is colorless and soluble and therefore remains in solution. This is called a precipitation reaction because an insoluble solid is produced during the reaction. This type of reaction is useful for making compounds that are insoluble – the solid precipitate can be filtered off and washed. It can also be used to recognize chemicals in unknown substances. The equation can be written as $2KI + Pb(NO_3)_2 \rightarrow 2KNO_3 + PbI_2$

Lead iodide forms a yellow precipitate

Flask contains potassium iodide in solution

CHEMISTRY IN THE KITCHEN

Like most chemical reactions involving living things, the process of making dough is controlled by enzymes which act as catalysts. These start to work as soon as the raising agent, yeast, is mixed with warm water and sugar. (Yeast is a living organism that needs air and moisture to grow; sugar provides food.) Bubbles of carbon dioxide are produced, and when the mixture is added to flour and water to make a dough, the dough rises. Heating kills the yeast and bakes the dough.

Bubbles of gas are trapped in the dough, causing it to expand

The ingredients are left to stand in a warm place

Yeast mixture becomes frothy as carbon dioxide is produced

MODERN ALCHEMY

Ernest Rutherford (1871-1937) was the first person to bombard atoms artificially to produce transmutated elements. The physicist from New Zealand described atoms as having a central nucleus with electrons revolving around it. He showed that radium atoms emitted "rays" and were transformed into radon atoms. Nuclear reactions like this can be regarded as transmutations – one element changing into another, the process alchemists sought in vain to achieve by chemical means.

What drives a reaction?

CHEMICAL REACTIONS SOMETIMES HAPPEN SPONTANEOUSLY; others need energy to make them happen. It is as if reactants have to jump over a barrier to become products. Heat may give them this energy. Light can provide energy, as in photosynthesis, and when pollutants react, they cause photochemical smogs over our cities. Mechanical energy is sometimes responsible for reactions. Dynamite is usually safe until it is detonated, often by a blast from a detonator which is itself highly sensitive to shock. Reactions can be induced by electrical energy; for the more reactive metals, such as sodium, this is the only practical means of extracting them from their compounds. Another way to make a reaction happen is to lower the barrier over which the reactants have to jump. A catalyst does just this by providing a different, easier, path for the reactants to take – it catalyzes the reaction. Often catalysts temporarily combine with a reactant, making it easier for another compound to react with it. In industry, catalysts make processes economically viable by speeding up reactions.

Lamp and cigar light up

Instantaneous light machine

DÖBEREINER'S LAMP
In 1823 Johann Döbereiner (1780-1849) observed that hydrogen gas caught fire in air if platinum metal was present. He exploited this catalytic reaction in his novelty light machine. When the tap is opened, sulfuric acid drips on to zinc, causing a reaction that produces hydrogen. The hydrogen emerges from the urn, where the platinum catalyst causes it to ignite, lighting a small oil lamp and the cigar.

CLEANING UP THE ENVIRONMENT
Car exhaust fumes are a source of pollution. Exhaust fumes contain poisonous gases, such as carbon monoxide, and gases that contribute to smog. Catalytic converters dramatically reduce the amounts of these gases emerging from car exhausts. They contain precious metals – the catalysts – which catalyze reactions that convert the gases to harmless ones. Catalysts are easily poisoned: lead is one such poison, so catalytic converters can be fitted only to cars using unleaded gasoline.

1 POISONOUS PRODUCTS
When petrol burns, the main products are carbon dioxide and steam. Also formed are nitrogen oxides (some nitrogen in the air reacts at the high temperatures of the engine), carbon monoxide from incompletely burned hydrocarbon, and fragments of unburned hydrocarbons. From the engine, these gases are passed straight into the catalytic converter.

Pollutant gas includes carbon monoxide, nitrogen oxides, and fragments of unburned hydrocarbons

Gases pass straight from engine into the converter

Glass negative
(1890s)

Black-and-white print

CHEMICALS USED FOR PHOTOGRAPHY
These 19th-century glass negatives were covered with a sticky solution of potassium iodide. Immediately before exposure, they are dipped in silver nitrate solution to form light-sensitive silver iodide. When light falls on the plate during exposure, the molecules of silver iodide are activated by the energy from the light. The plate is then developed by immersing it in a solution that converts the activated silver salt to metallic silver particles so fine they look black. Objects that reflect most light on to the plates show as dark areas in the negative, while those that do not reflect light are transparent.

MAKING A PRINT
Light is shone through the glass negative on to paper coated with another chemical – silver chloride. Where the negative is dark, no light reaches the paper and the silver salt is not activated, but where the negative is transparent, light activates the silver salt. When the paper is developed and fixed with more chemicals, the activated areas react to give dark silver where the negative was transparent, and light areas where the negative was dark.

ENZYMES AT WORK
Almost all reactions that take place in living things are directed by enzymes – biological catalysts. Amylase is an enzyme in saliva that starts to break down starch molecules from food into sugar units that provide our energy. It starts to work as soon as the food is in the mouth. Lysozyme is another enzyme, found in tears. It attacks the cell walls of bacteria, preventing them from infecting the eye.

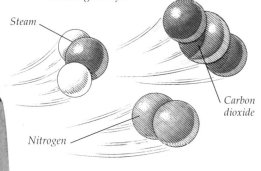

Steam

Carbon dioxide

Nitrogen

3 CLEAN AIR
By the time the gases reach the exhaust, the nitrogen oxides have been converted back to nitrogen by rhodium (one of the platinum metals); platinum has catalyzed the unburned hydrocarbons and the carbon monoxide to steam and carbon dioxide. With an efficiently running engine, the converter can remove up to 95 percent of pollutants.

Steel casing

Thin layer of platinum and rhodium catalysts coat ceramic honeycomb

2 HONEYCOMB STRUCTURE
The stainless steel casing of the catalytic converter houses a ceramic honeycomb structure. So fine is this honeycomb that it provides a surface area as large as about two football pitches on which the catalytic reactions take place. Although the metal catalysts are rare and expensive (platinum metals are used), only $\frac{1}{14}$ oz (2 g) are required to coat the honeycomb with a thin layer. This is enough to clean up exhaust gases for 50-100,000 miles (80-160,000 km).

USING FRICTION IN A REACTION
"Strike anywhere" matches contain the nontoxic red form of phosphorus with sulfur in the head. When the match is struck on a rough surface, the friction provides the energy that causes the phosphorus to ignite.

Friction causes phosphorus to ignite

Rates of reaction

SOME CHEMICAL REACTIONS TAKE PLACE ALMOST INSTANTLY – the reactions of explosives, for example. Others can proceed so slowly it may take years to see the results. Reactions will take place only when the reacting molecules come into contact with each other. Increasing the number of times molecules collide with each other will therefore increase the speed of a reaction. This can be done by increasing the amount of surface area so that more reactant is exposed. In a solution, the same effect is achieved by increasing the concentration – the number of molecules of compound in the solvent. Adding heat can speed up most reactions. This makes the molecules move around more quickly, so they collide more often. Catalysts are another way of speeding up a reaction. All these factors are taken into account in industrial processes, where time and economics play an important part. In theory, all reactions could proceed in either direction, but in practice many reactions are difficult to reverse. Those that proceed in either direction are said to be reversible and the amounts of reactants and products will reach equilibrium.

INSTANT REACTION
The spectacular displays provided by fireworks are initiated by the burning of gunpowder, a very fast reaction. Strongly exothermic, this reaction gives out the heat required to cause the metal atoms to emit characteristic colors.

REACTION TAKING YEARS
Although copper is fairly resistant to corrosion, it slowly reacts with moisture and carbon dioxide in the air to form the hydrated green carbonate. This green coating can often be seen on copper roofs. In industrial areas, basic copper sulfate is also formed due to sulfur dioxide in the air.

INCREASING THE SPEED
When hydrochloric acid is added to chips of marble (a naturally occurring form of calcium carbonate), bubbles of carbon dioxide gas are produced. The acid reacts when it comes into contact at the surface of the marble. If the marble is ground up into a fine powder, its surface area is increased enormously, and the reaction goes so fast that the bubbles cause the reactants to fizz up and overflow.

Glass beaker

Carbon dioxide gas gently bubbles to the surface

Chips of marble

Only the outer surface of the marble chips have reacted with acid

Gas bubbles up rapidly, causing spillage

Ground marble

LE CHATELIER'S PRINCIPLE

Henri Louis Le Chatelier (1850-1936) was a French professor of chemistry. He studied the gases that caused explosions in mines and the reactions that occur in a blast furnace. These studies led him to put forward the principle that bears his name. This principle explains that if conditions such as temperature or pressure are changed in a system containing reactants and products, then any chemical reaction occurring will tend to counteract the change and return the conditions to equilibrium.

Henri Le Chatelier

HELPING THE WAR EFFORT

Fritz Haber (1868-1934), a German chemist, succeeded in manufacturing ammonia from nitrogen and hydrogen gases using a catalyst of osmium. Saltpeter was used to prepare nitric acid, needed for the manufacture of explosives. During the World War I Germany's supplies of saltpeter from Chile were cut off. However, ammonia could be oxidized to nitric acid, so the new Haber process ensured the continuing supplies of explosives. Haber used Le Chatelier's principle to work out the best conditions of temperature and pressure. Only 10-20 percent of the nitrogen and hydrogen combine, so the gases are recycled.

Fritz Haber

Pipette

Drop of sodium hydroxide

REVERSIBLE REACTIONS

A reversible reaction can go in either direction. The products that are formed during the reaction are able to react with each other and re-form the reactant. This experiment demonstrates that the formation of dichromate ions from chromate ions is reversible.

Pipette

Drop of hydrochloric acid

1 A REACTANT

Potassium chromate dissolves in water to form a bright yellow solution containing potassium and chromate ions.

2 THE REACTION

Hydrochloric acid is added to the potassium chromate a drop at a time. The solution begins to turn bright orange, as the acid causes a chemical reaction to take place. The chromate ions in the solution are turned into orange dichromate ions, making another salt, potassium dichromate.

Sodium hydroxide neutralizes the acid

Potassium chromate dissolved in water

Adding acid turns the solution orange

3 REVERSING THE REACTION

Sodium hydroxide, which is a base, is added a drop at a time to remove the acid by neutralizing it. The solution is returning to the original bright yellow color as the chromate reforms. The equilibrium was disturbed by changing the amount of a reactant.

Oxidation and reduction

WHEN OXYGEN COMBINES WITH A REACTANT (p. 220), an oxidation reaction has taken place. Oxygen in the air frequently causes oxidation, either rapidly, by burning substances, or more slowly, in reactions such as rusting. The removal of oxygen from a reactant is called reduction. Extracting iron from its oxides (compounds containing iron and oxygen) in iron ore is a reduction reaction. If one reactant is oxidized while the other is reduced, it is called a redox (*red*uction-*ox*idation) reaction. The removal of hydrogen from a compound is also a type of oxidation: fluorine is obtained by oxidizing hydrogen fluoride. The addition of hydrogen is a reduction reaction. This happens during the hydrogenation of fats to make margarine. Oxidation is the cause of food deterioration: the cut surface of an apple quickly browns in air.

FLASH PHOTOGRAPHY
Magnesium metal was produced commercially from the 1860s as wire or ribbon. It readily burns in air, the metal being oxidized to magnesium oxide. The brightness of the white flame made it useful in photography to provide studio lighting.

Molten pig iron poured in here

Steel shell of converter

Lining made from silica firebricks to withstand heat

BESSEMER PROCESS
Most metals produced by reducing metal ores need further purification. Iron is produced by reducing iron ore (mostly oxides) with coke in a blast furnace. The resulting pig iron contains mainly carbon, silicon, and phosphorus. The conversion of this brittle metal to steel was revolutionized by the introduction of the Bessemer process by 1857. However, the iron ore from some localities contained large amounts of phosphorus that were not all removed in Bessemer's process. In 1878, the metallurgist Sidney Thomas suggested lining the converter with dolomite (a carbonate ore). This reacted with phosphorus to form phosphates, which were absorbed into the lining.

SIR HENRY BESSEMER (1813-1898)
A British engineer, Bessemer revolutionized the process of converting cast iron directly to steel by burning out the impurities in his steel converter. The shorter process and lower production costs made steel readily available in large quantities for the first time.

Converter pivoted to the horizontal to receive molten iron

1 LOADING THE FURNACE
The converter is filled with about 30 tons of molten pig iron together with fluxes such as limestone and fluorite to help extract the impurities in the form of molten slag. Initially, the process was carried out in a fixed converter. This more efficient moving converter, which could tilt to receive the metal, was introduced in 1860.

AMERICAN STEEL

The American engineer William Kelly (1811-1888) independently developed a similar process to Bessemer for making steel in the US. He realized that blowing air through molten pig iron raised the temperature sufficiently to burn out the impurities in the iron without using more fuel.

William Kelly

Converter vertical, to receive blast of air

Handle to rotate converter

Blast of air is injected through here

TAKING A REST

With strenuous exercise, lack of sufficient oxygen leads to lactic acid being produced in the muscles. As lactic acid builds up in the blood, it produces fatigue. Rest and oxygen allow it to be carried away and oxidized in the liver.

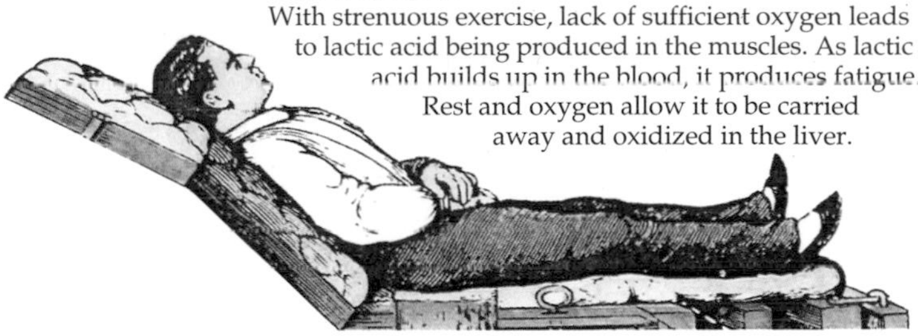

FOOD PRESERVATIVES

When margarine and other fats and oils turn rancid, it is due to oxidation reactions caused by oxygen in the air. If special antioxidant preservatives are used, the shelf life of the fats can be extended. Antioxidants have been used in cooking for thousands of years. Spices and herbs such as sage and rosemary contain compounds that prevent oxidation reactions taking place, and they also mask unpleasant smells.

Sage

Rosemary

2 MELTING THE IRON

The converter is tilted upright, and a blast of air is injected into the bottom. The oxygen in the air oxidizes some iron to an iron oxide in a reaction that gives off a lot of heat. In this way, the iron stays in a molten state. Impurities such as silicon then react with the oxide, reducing it back to iron and being oxidized themselves in a redox reaction. Carbon is burned off as the gas carbon dioxide. The molten slag containing the impurities is poured off when the converter is tilted again, leaving the purified metal.

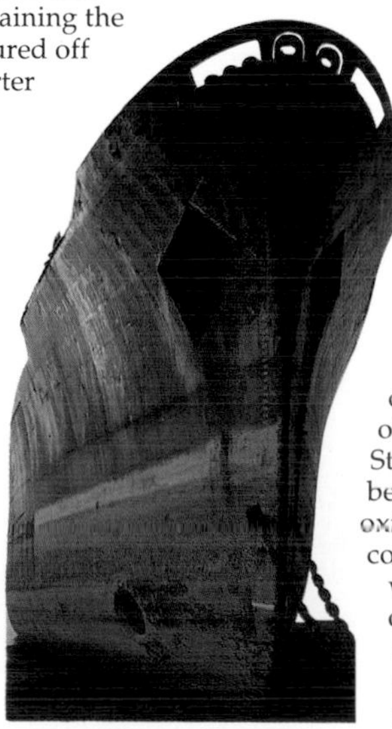

RUSTING SHIP

The oxidation of iron and steel is a major problem in industry. Both air and moisture must be present for the formation of rust – a hydrated iron oxide – in a complicated series of oxidation reactions. Structural iron can be protected from oxidation by being coated with paint, while in machinery, oil is used. Another method uses an electrochemical reaction.

Acids and bases

A BASIC REMEDY
A bee sting is acidic, so the pain can be relieved with bicarbonate of soda or ammonia, which are alkalis. Although the victim of a wasp sting feels the same pain, this sting is alkaline and can be relieved by treating with vinegar, which contains an acid.

IN NATURE, ACIDS CAN BE FOUND IN FRUITS: citric acid is responsible for the sharp taste of lemons. Vinegar contains acetic acid, and tannic acid from tree bark is used to tan leather. The stronger mineral acids have been prepared since the Middle Ages. One of these, *aqua fortis* (nitric acid), was used by assayers to separate gold from silver. Car batteries contain sulfuric acid, also strong and corrosive. A base is the opposite of an acid. Bases often feel slippery; bicarbonate of soda and soap are bases, and so is lyre, a substance that can burn skin. Bases that dissolve in water are called alkalis. In water, acids produce hydrogen ions, while alkalis produce hydroxide ions. When an acid and a base react together, the hydrogen and hydroxide ions combine and neutralize each other, forming water together with a salt. The strength of acids and bases can be measured on a pH scale.

WATER SPLITTING
Pure water is neither acidic nor basic: it is neutral. It can split (dissociate) into two ions: a positively charged hydrogen ion (H^+) and a negatively charged hydroxide ion (OH^-). In solutions of acids, there are more hydrogen ions than hydroxide ions. In solutions of alkalis, hydroxide ions outnumber the hydrogen ions.

Water molecule
H_2O

*Hydrogen ion
H^+*

Hydroxide ion OH^-

CHOOSING THE COLOR
The compounds responsible for color in plants are often sensitive to acids and alkalis. Blue hydrangeas grow only in acidic soils; in neutral or alkaline soils, they will revert to pink.

Pink hydrangea from alkaline soil

Hydrangea is blue in acidic soil

Color codes

S.P.L. Sørensen (1868-1939) introduced the pH scale to measure the concentration of hydrogen ions in solution. The more hydrogen ions, the stronger the acid. The amount of hydrogen ions in solution can affect the color of certain dyes found in nature. These dyes can be used as indicators to test for acids and alkalis. An indicator such as litmus (obtained from lichen) is red in acid. If a base is slowly added, the litmus will turn blue when the acid has been neutralized, at about 6-7 on the pH scale. Other indicators will change color at different pHs. A combination of indicators is used to make a universal indicator. Here universal indicator papers have been used with a range of pH from 2-11 (some papers measure 0-14). Starting with pink for strong acids below pH 2, it goes through various colors to green at the neutral pH 7 and to dark purple for strong alkalis at pH 11 and above.

STRONG ACIDS
Dilute hydrochloric acid, like other mineral acids such as sulfuric and nitric acids, has a pH of about 1.

SHARP TASTES
Vinegar contains acetic acid. This acid is also produced when wine is exposed to the air. It has a pH of about 4.

Hydrochloric acid

Vinegar

Chart for universal indicator papers

FORENSIC SCIENCE
Chemistry often comes to the aid of the forensic scientist when solving a crime. The pH of soil samples from a suspect's shoes or perhaps from the tread of a car tire can be measured to compare it with soil at the scene of the crime. Samples of the two soils are mixed thoroughly with distilled water (with a neutral pH), then filtered. Drops of universal indicator solution change the color according to acidity. This color is then compared with those on a chart, to find out the precise pH of the soils.

RECOGNIZING ACIDS
Svante Arrhenius (1859-1927), a Swedish scientist, won the 1903 Nobel Prize for his work on ionization. He introduced the idea of compounds dissociating, or splitting, into their constituent ions in solution. He explained how the strength of acids in aqueous (water) solution depended on its concentration of hydrogen ions.

Svante Arrhenius

Filter paper traps solid soil particles

Distilled water with soluble material from soil

Universal indicator solution

Soil sample mixed with distilled water

Universal indicator turns the solution orange – a mildly acidic soil

Dropper

DRINKING WATER
Tap water has a pH of 6. It changes with the area but is usually slightly acid because of dissolved materials. Pure water is neutral at pH 6-7.

CLEANING MATERIALS
Soaps are made by reacting organic acids with a strong base. Because the organic acid is weak, soaps are mildly basic with a pH of 8-9.

HOUSEHOLD CLEANER
Household cleaners range in strength depending on their purpose. Oven cleaners contain lye. This brand contains ammonia and is pH 10.

Tap water

Liquid soap

Household cleaner

Forming salts

Sᴀʟᴛꜱ ᴄᴀɴ ʙᴇ ᴘʀᴇᴘᴀʀᴇᴅ ʙʏ ᴍɪxɪɴɢ an acid with a base or a metal. If the acid is sulfuric acid, the salt is called a sulfate; hydrochloric acid forms salts called chlorides; nitric acid forms salts called nitrates. Salts are ionic compounds consisting of a positive ion, usually a metal, and a negative ion, which may be a nonmetal or a group of atoms bound together. The best known salt is probably sodium chloride – an essential part of our diet. Not all salts are harmless; thallium salts were used as a rat poison. If allowed to form slowly, salts become regularly shaped crystals. Some are soluble in water; some are not. Their solubility can be used to determine which metals are present in substances. Some salts take up water from the air; they are deliquescent. Some salt crystals gradually lose their attached water; they are efflorescent (washing soda). Sometimes salts come out of solution in inconvenient ways: kettles and central heating pipes become clogged up with calcium and magnesium salts in areas with hard water.

COMMON SALT
Sodium chloride is called common or table salt. Traces of another edible salt – magnesium carbonate – are added to help it flow.

Ruby

PRECIOUS IMPURITIES
Emerald is mainly the colorless mineral beryl. It owes its green color to the presence of tiny amounts of the green salt, chromium oxide. Rubies are chiefly made up of aluminum oxide in the form of corundum (a hard, natural mineral). Pure corundum is colorless, and ruby gets its red color from the same chromium salt because it is forced into the crystal structure of corundum, causing its spectrum to shift slightly.

Emerald

SALTS FROM COPPER
The metal copper, like other metals, forms a wide variety of salts. The copper salts shown here can be prepared in many different ways. Copper oxide (CuO) can be prepared by heating the metal with air. It is used as a pigment. Copper carbonate ($CuCO_3$) will yield carbon dioxide and copper oxide on heating. The green color on copper roofs is a form of copper carbonate. Copper chloride ($CuCl_2$) is soluble in water. It is used as a catalyst. Copper hydroxide ($Cu(OH)_2$) comes out of solution when alkali is added to soluble copper salts. Copper sulfate ($CuSO_4.5H_2O$) forms hydrated crystals (containing water molecules). It is used in agriculture as a fungicide. Copper nitrate ($Cu(NO_3)_2$) is very soluble and will even take up water from the air and dissolve itself.

Copper turnings

Cap traps waterborne solids

Ion-exchange resin removes positive and negative ions

Charcoal absorbs organic pollutants such as pesticides

Final filter for any remaining waterborne solids

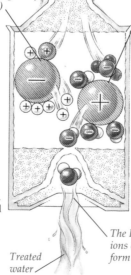

Positive metal ions are trapped and replaced with hydrogen ions (H^+)

Negative ions are trapped and replaced with hydroxide ions (OH^-)

Copper oxide

PURIFYING WATER
Tap water contains a number of impurities that impair the taste, cause the buildup of scale in kettles, and form a scum with soaps. Many impurities are salts that can be removed by a process called ion exchange. This uses a resin made up of small plastic beads with ions bonded to their surface. They replace positive metal ions, such as aluminum and calcium, with hydrogen ions, and they replace negative ions, such as nitrate, with hydroxide ions. Hydrogen and hydroxide ions make up water.

The H^+ and OH^- ions combine to form water (H_2O)

Treated water

Copper
nitrate

Copper sulfate

*Airtight
seal*

*Rock salt
prism*

Silica gel

KEEPING A PRISM DRY
The prism in this desiccator is made of rock
salt and is used for spectroscopy. It must
be kept absolutely dry; otherwise, it will
deteriorate. The atmosphere is kept dry using
silica gel, a hydrated form of silicon dioxide
that absorbs water very efficiently. It is
colored blue by another salt, cobalt chloride,
which turns pink in the presence of water.

Copper
hydroxide

*Sodium
carbonate*

Limestone

Sand

THE INGREDIENTS IN GLASS
Glass is made from several salts. The
main constituent is silicon dioxide in
the form of sand. Limestone (calcium
carbonate) and sodium carbonate are also
added to make the common soda glass
used for bottles. The greenish tinge of
old glass is due to iron impurities in the
sand. Other metal salts can be added
to the mix to make colored glass.

Copper chloride

Copper carbonate

231

Electricity and chemistry

CHEMICALS ARE USED TO PRODUCE ELECTRICITY; and electricity can produce chemicals. Alessandro Volta succeeded by 1800 in making electricity with the first battery, using different metals separated by salt solutions. Investigations of the effects of passing electricity from these batteries through solutions (electrolytes) began immediately. It was found that passing a current through water separated it into hydrogen and oxygen gases, the elements that make up water. Michael Faraday (1791-1867) showed that pure water does not conduct electricity well, but if salts are added, conductivity increases. This is because the electricity is carried by ions in the solution; water is a poor conductor, or electrolyte, because it is only slightly ionized. Salts, acids, and bases are good electrolytes. Electricity is also used to produce chemicals in electrolytic cells, and to purify substances.

Zinc disc

Copper disc

Cardboard disc soaked in brine

THE FIRST BATTERY
Alessandro Volta (1745-1827), an Italian scientist, noticed that two different metals in contact produced a "bitter taste" when they touched his tongue. Further experiments convinced him this was caused by an electric current. Volta found he could generate electricity by putting a layer of cardboard soaked in brine between discs of copper and zinc – a voltaic cell. When he made a "pile" of these cells, he increased the amount of electricity generated. This was the first battery – a collection of cells.

A voltaic pile

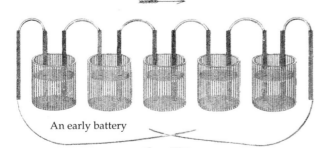
An early battery

PIONEER OF ELECTROLYSIS
Humphry Davy (1778-1829) started studying electrochemistry soon after the introduction of the voltaic cell. He succeeded in extracting sodium and potassium metals from their hydroxides, which had previously resisted all attempts to break them down to simpler substances. Davy also isolated other metals, such as strontium, by electrolysis (p. 158, p. 211).

Steel clip   Copper layer   Nickel layer   Gold finish

COATING METALS
Electroplating is used to give attractive and durable finishes to metals. The gold finish on this pen clip involves several stages. The steel clip is suspended from the cathode (the negative terminal) and then dipped into the electrolyte – copper cyanide. The cyanide cleans the steel, while the copper layer provides a better base for further electrolysis. A layer of nickel plating ensures a bright final product and improves resistance to corrosion. The gold plating is the final layer.

A FLOWING CURRENT
This early battery has zinc and copper electrodes dipping into cups of salt solution (the electrolyte). When the electrodes are connected, zinc dissolves, losing electrons, while hydrogen ions at the copper electrode gain electrons to form hydrogen gas. These reactions cause a current to flow.

SPLITTING SALT
The electrolysis of brine (concentrated sodium chloride) is a major industrial process. These huge cells are used to pass current through the brine. The chemical products are chlorine and hydrogen gases, and sodium hydroxide (lye).

ALUMINUM METAL STRIPS
Aluminum is an abundant metal that is difficult to extract from its ores because it is so strongly bonded. It is produced by electrolysis from molten bauxite, or aluminum oxide, and is high on the reactivity series. The process uses a lot of electricity.

PURIFYING COPPER
Copper is obtained mostly from copper pyrites, a copper ore containing iron and sulfur. The ore is crushed and added to frothy, oily water to remove stones. It is then dried and roasted to remove iron. Further heating with air converts the copper sulfide to copper which is poured into molds and purified by electrolysis. This experiment in a beaker shows the principles of that process of purification.

Negative electrode (cathode)

Positive electrode (anode)

Current-carrying wire

1 CONNECTING TO ELECTRICITY
The impure copper strip is connected to the positive electricity supply. It becomes the anode. The pure copper strip is connected to the negative electricity supply. It is the cathode. The beaker is filled with electrolyte – copper sulfate solution. Electricity is carried through the solution by ions.

Negative electrode (cathode)

HAMILTON CASTNER (1859-1899)
An American inventor, Castner started a company to extract aluminum metal from aluminum chloride using sodium just before a better process – electrolysis – emerged. He still made a fortune because, to obtain sodium, he had developed an electrolytic process for preparing pure sodium hydroxide from brine, using a flowing mercury cell.

Positive electrode (anode) of impure copper dissolves

2 PURIFIED METAL
When the electricity is turned on, a current flows through the electrolyte. At the anode, impure copper dissolves to form copper ions, and the anode gets thinner. Copper ions move to the cathode and are converted to the metal, so copper is deposited on the pure copper strip, making it thicker. The impurities from the anode form a sludge. This sludge is also valuable because it contains tiny amounts of silver and gold which can be extracted.

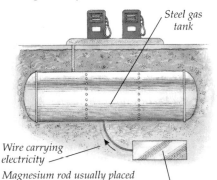

Steel gas tank

Wire carrying electricity

Magnesium rod usually placed near the surface for ease of replacement

RUST PREVENTION
Underground steel tanks can rust, and replacing them is costly. They are protected from corrosion using an electrochemical reaction. This is known as cathodic protection. A magnesium rod is connected to the steel using copper wire, a good conductor of electricity that will not corrode. Magnesium is more reactive than steel, and corrodes instead.

Copper sulfate solution (the electrolyte)

Pure copper deposited on cathode

Impurities from the copper anode

233

The chemistry of carbon

CARBON IS A REMARKABLE ELEMENT. It exists as the element in two very different forms: soft black graphite and sparkling diamond. It also forms a vast number of compounds. Organic chemistry was originally a term for the study of compounds found only in living things; now it is more widely seen as the chemistry of carbon compounds, except for a few simple compounds such as carbon dioxide and the carbonates, which nclude marble and limestone. For a long time, it was believed that such compounds had some hidden "vital force," and so the chemist could not make them without the aid of a plant or animal. This vital force theory received a blow in 1828 when Friedrich Wöhler (1800-1882) obtained urea, a known organic compound, by heating ammonia with cyanate, usually considered an inorganic compound of carbon. As he had prepared cyanate from animal horn, an organic material, a question mark remained about his findings.

THE ORGANIC CHEMIST
Marcellin Berthelot (1827-1907) prepared many organic compounds from inorganic compounds or elements. He demonstrated that plants and animals are not unique as the only sources of organic compounds. His work in this field finally disproved the vital force theory.

SYNTHESIZING APPARATUS
Berthelot systematically produced many organic compounds. Acetylene is a simple carbon compound (C_2H_2) – a colorless, inflammable gas. In 1866 Berthelot prepared acetylene from its elements hydrogen and carbon. He then passed it through this red-hot glass tube and prepared benzene (C_6H_6), another organic compound.

Glass tube in which acetylene was heated

Thistle funnel to trap gases

Unburned carbon forms soot particles

Berthelot's illustration of the synthesis of benzene

Burning candle wax

WHAT MAKES AN ORGANIC COMPOUND?
This experiment demonstrates that organic compounds (in this case, candle wax) contain carbon and hydrogen. The candle is lit, and the carbon dioxide and hydrogen gases produced from the burning wax are collected. Hydrogen is converted to water vapor, which is trapped by a solid drying agent. The presence of carbon is shown using calcium hydroxide in solution (limewater), the standard test for carbon dioxide.

Cover open to reveal tube

Eyepiece

Sugar solution placed in tube

TWO FORMS OF LACTIC ACID
In 1874 J.H. van't Hoff (1852-1911) realized that optical activity (see right) could be explained only if the four atoms attached to a carbon atom were arranged at the four corners of a pyramid around the central carbon atom. This model is one of two illustrating optical activity.

Pyramid shape

Carbon atom

Bond formed by carbon atom

Model of optically active lactic acid

Polarimeter

OPTICALLY ACTIVE SUGAR
A carbon atom's ability to bond to four other atoms (or groups of atoms) leads to an unusual property. If these four atoms or groups are all different, they can form two distinct molecules that are mirror images of each other. Although chemically identical, two such compounds behave differently when polarized light (where the light waves are in only one plane) is shone through them. They rotate the light in opposite directions and are said to be optically active. The polarimeter was introduced in 1840 to measure this optical activity. Sugars show this property; polarimeters were used routinely to analyze sugar syrups. After the 1860s, they became valuable tools for collectors of excise duty to determine the strength of sugar solutions for taxation purposes.

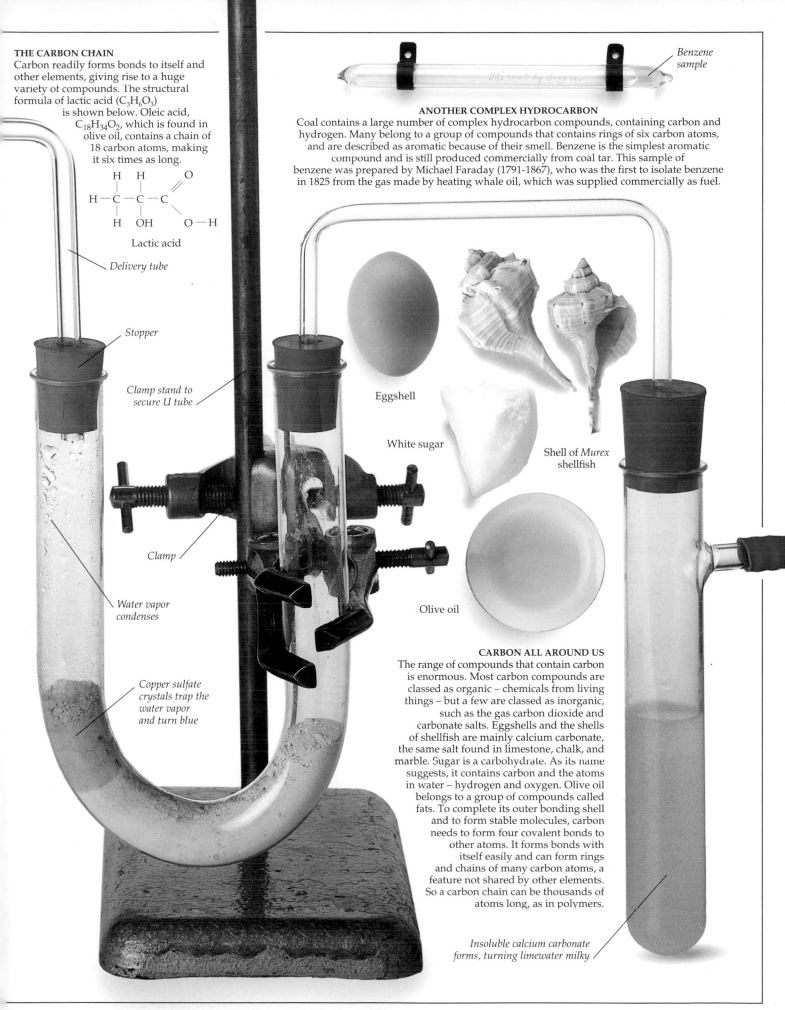

THE CARBON CHAIN

Carbon readily forms bonds to itself and other elements, giving rise to a huge variety of compounds. The structural formula of lactic acid ($C_3H_6O_3$) is shown below. Oleic acid, $C_{18}H_{34}O_2$, which is found in olive oil, contains a chain of 18 carbon atoms, making it six times as long.

Lactic acid

Delivery tube

Stopper

Clamp stand to secure U tube

Clamp

Water vapor condenses

Copper sulfate crystals trap the water vapor and turn blue

Benzene sample

ANOTHER COMPLEX HYDROCARBON

Coal contains a large number of complex hydrocarbon compounds, containing carbon and hydrogen. Many belong to a group of compounds that contains rings of six carbon atoms, and are described as aromatic because of their smell. Benzene is the simplest aromatic compound and is still produced commercially from coal tar. This sample of benzene was prepared by Michael Faraday (1791-1867), who was the first to isolate benzene in 1825 from the gas made by heating whale oil, which was supplied commercially as fuel.

Eggshell

White sugar

Shell of *Murex* shellfish

Olive oil

CARBON ALL AROUND US

The range of compounds that contain carbon is enormous. Most carbon compounds are classed as organic – chemicals from living things – but a few are classed as inorganic, such as the gas carbon dioxide and carbonate salts. Eggshells and the shells of shellfish are mainly calcium carbonate, the same salt found in limestone, chalk, and marble. Sugar is a carbohydrate. As its name suggests, it contains carbon and the atoms in water – hydrogen and oxygen. Olive oil belongs to a group of compounds called fats. To complete its outer bonding shell and to form stable molecules, carbon needs to form four covalent bonds to other atoms. It forms bonds with itself easily and can form rings and chains of many carbon atoms, a feature not shared by other elements. So a carbon chain can be thousands of atoms long, as in polymers.

Insoluble calcium carbonate forms, turning limewater milky

The chemistry of life

THE CHEMISTRY OF LIVING SYSTEMS is known as biochemistry. Living organisms and the cells that make them up are composed of water (about 70 percent) and carbon compounds, together with traces of metals and other elements. Plants and animals need carbon compounds to grow; when they die and decay, their carbon is recycled back to the earth. The lives of cells are programmed by DNA, which behaves rather like a computer program, storing information for specifying the proteins we need. Proteins build our structure (hair and skin); they act as enzymes which provide the catalysts in humans; as hormones they regulate growth and metabolism. Metabolism describes the chemical processes in living organisms that break down complex substances into simpler ones, gaining energy from them. This energy is then used by organisms to live, grow and reproduce.

Carbon dioxide emitted by burning fossil fuels

Carbon dioxide

Fungi give off carbon dioxide

Fungi

Carbon dioxide breathed out by animals

Fungi feed on carbon-rich decaying matter

Carbon taken in food by herbivores

Coal

Carbon present in fossil fuels

Carbon returns through decaying animal matter

Mouse

Hans Krebs

GENERATING ENERGY
The biochemist Sir Hans Krebs (1900-1981) arrived in England from Germany in 1933. He proposed a series of reactions to explain how glucose, a sugar, is broken down to yield carbon dioxide, water, and energy. The reactions occur in a cycle; after breaking down one molecule of sugar, the necessary compounds are ready to repeat the process.

THE CARBON CYCLE
Carbon is the key element in compounds produced by living things. It moves around our world in a cyclic process. Carbon dioxide in the atmosphere is combined with water to form carbohydrates in plants by a process called photosynthesis. These carbohydrates include cellulose, which is the main structural component of stems and leaves. Many animals eat plants, which give them the carbon they need. The plant-eating animals (herbivores) are eaten by other animals, passing carbon along the food chain. When they die, their carbon is recycled through decay. Decaying plant and animal matter provides food for fungi and bacteria, which produce carbon dioxide. Plants may also be buried and converted under pressure to coal and oil – fossil fuels. When these fossil fuels are burned, they return carbon to the atmosphere as carbon dioxide. Animals too return carbon to the atmosphere as they breathe out carbon dioxide.

Atmospheric carbon dioxide is regulated by plants

Plants use carbon dioxide to grow

Plants take in carbon dioxide through their leaves

Plant

Root system through which plants take in water

Decaying plants and animals may form fossil fuels

Soil

Decaying plants provide food for fungi

Water vapor in clouds absorbs heat and reflects it back to Earth

Increase in carbon dioxide means more heat trapped in the Earth's atmosphere

Heat from the Sun

Temperatures on Earth are rising

THE GREENHOUSE EFFECT

Heat from the Sun maintains a reasonable temperature on the Earth's surface, one in which organisms can live. Much of the heat that reaches the Earth is reflected back. Various compounds in the atmosphere prevent this heat loss – for instance water vapor in the form of clouds. Carbon dioxide also traps the heat. Since the amount of carbon dioxide in the atmosphere seems to be rising, it is feared that temperatures on Earth will start to warm up, possibly leading to flooding, as polar ice caps melt.

TRANSPORTING OXYGEN

The heart circulates blood around the body through a system of blood vessels. Blood carries oxygen and nutrients to tissues and removes carbon dioxide and waste products. Red blood cells contain hemoglobin, which reacts with oxygen in the lungs and carries it around the body, releasing it in the muscles where it is needed.

Red blood cell magnified 5,000 times

T pairs with A

Strands unzip down the center

Four units make up sequence

C pairs with G

GENETIC BLUEPRINT

All the information necessary to reproduce life is held in DNA – deoxyribonucleic acid – which is found in the nuclei of living cells. This substance is made up from four different chemical units (A, C, G, and T) strung together in long chains. Within the chain, the sequence of these four units provides the information, in code form, to make proteins which control living processes. The structure of DNA makes it easy to produce copies. It is arranged in a double helix structure, two complementary strands wound around each other. When a cell divides, these strands are "unzipped"; each strand can be copied to produce two identical strands. In this way, the genetic information in the DNA can be repeated each time a cell divides.

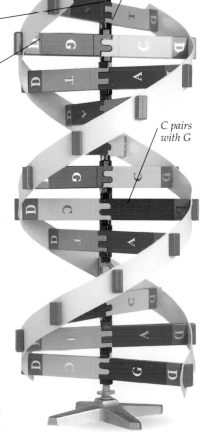

A teaching model of DNA

Organic synthesis

H EATING COAL IN THE ABSENCE OF AIR GIVES OFF A GAS and a thick tarry substance, to leave coke. Coal gas was produced in large quantities for gas lighting from about 1812. The coal tar residue collected in large amounts, to the embarrassment of the gas industry. During the 1840s, Charles Mansfield (1819-1855) succeeded in fractionally distilling the tar to produce aromatic compounds – so called because of their pleasant smells. The simplest aromatic compound is benzene, and the chemistry of it and the compounds derived from it is called aromatic chemistry. These compounds were initially used as industrial solvents. William Perkin synthesized a dye from one of them – aniline – and opened up a new industry. Other uses for coal tar chemicals rapidly followed. Today most organic chemicals are produced from petroleum and natural gas.

WORKING WITH RUBBER
Rubber from the latex of the rubber tree reacts badly to extremes of temperature. Charles Goodyear (1800-1860), an American inventor, simultaneously with Thomas Hancock in England, heated rubber with sulfur and found that this rubber remained flexible over a range of temperatures. He called this process "vulcanization," after the Roman god of fire, Vulcan.

SYNTHETIC DYES
William Henry Perkin (1838-1907) revolutionized the chemicals industry by making an artificial dye. He was trying to prepare the drug quinine from aniline, a compound derived from coal tar, but he obtained only a dark sticky mess. While cleaning this with alcohol, he found it dissolved to give a dark purple solution, from which he was able to crystallize the dye mauveine. Before this time, dyes had been prepared from vegetable materials such as indigo. The new synthetic dye was eagerly bought up by the textiles industry and called "mauve." Perkin went on to synthesize natural smells from chemicals, the beginning of the synthetic perfume industry.

Asphalt

Naphthalene

Anthracene

USING ASPHALT
The fractional distillation of coal tar produced a wide number of significant substances that were used to synthesize useful products in the 19th century. Asphalt is the residue from this process, and it is used for covering road surfaces.

THE FIRST "MAC"
Thomas Hancock (1786-1865), a rubber manufacturer, and Charles Macintosh (1766-1843), a Scottish chemist, used naphtha from fractional distillation of coal tar to dissolve rubber. This rubber solution was used to produce waterproof cloth for coats that became known as "mackintoshes." One component of naphtha, naphthalene, is used in mothballs. It is a valuable starting point for many synthetic dyestuffs and other materials, such as insect repellents.

RAINBOW COLORS
After the success of mauveine, bright synthetic dyes were sought after by textile manufacturers. Alizarin, the compound giving the natural dye madder its red color, was successfully synthesized from anthracene in the 1868.

Traditional road surface

Protection in the rain

Synthetic red dye

Synthetic dyes tend to be brighter than traditional vegetable dyes

Synthetic green dye

SOAPLESS DETERGENTS

Soap made from animal fats is a detergent or cleaning agent. It tends to form insoluble scum with hard water, so soapless detergents were developed to overcome this problem. Many of these are based on benzene, to which a long hydrocarbon chain, similar to those in soaps, is added. Unlike ordinary soaps, the calcium and magnesium salts of these are soluble, so scum does not form.

Creosote

Benzene

Soapless detergent

COMMON PRESERVATIVE

Creosote is a distillation product of coal tar. Its insecticide and disinfecting properties make it useful as a wood preservative.

HIGH EXPLOSIVE

The explosive TNT became widely used in World War I (1914-1918). Toluene obtained from coal tar is here being nitrated by pouring it into concentrated nitric and sulfuric acids to produce trinitrotoluene (TNT). When subjected to a mechanical shock, the atoms in this unstable molecule rearrange themselves to form carbon dioxide, steam, and nitrogen gases, causing a thousandfold increase in volume. This sudden expansion is what produces the destructive shock.

THE FIRST SYNTHETIC PLASTIC

Leo Baekeland (1863-1944) made a valuable plastic in 1907 by reacting phenol with another chemical, formaldehyde. He called this phenolic resin "Bakelite." The material was heat resistant, although it had the disadvantage of being dark in color. The new radio, and later the television, industry took advantage of the ease with which Bakelite could be molded, as well as its insulating properties.

Carbon disulfide

Aniline

Phenol

ARTIFICIAL SILK

Carbon disulfide is a poisonous liquid obtained by heating coke and sulfur in a furnace. It is used as an industrial solvent. In 1892, two British chemists, C.F. Cross and E.J. Bevan, dissolved cellulose in carbon disulfide and alkali, to obtain a viscous solution. Cellulose could be regenerated as fibers by pumping the "viscose" solution through a hole into acid. Originally marketed as artificial silk, these textiles became known as rayon.

Artificial silk fibers

THERAPEUTIC DRUGS

Drugs were derived from natural materials, such as willow bark, for centuries. Perkin was trying to synthesize the anti-malarial drug quinine from aniline when he discovered mauveine and launched the dye industry. By the end of the 19th-century, synthetic painkilling and anti-fever drugs had been made from organic compounds. They were overshadowed in 1899 when the German chemical company Bayer introduced aspirin, or acetylsalicylic acid, which is made from benzene in a complicated process.

Painkilling drugs

Bakelite television (1950s)

The first plastics

THE FIRST SYNTHETIC PLASTIC was made in the 1860s. Before that, natural materials such as ivory and amber were widely used. Many of these are polymers – from the Greek word *poly*, meaning many, and *mer*, meaning part. Polymers are composed of giant molecules, made up of large numbers of a small molecule strung together in long chains. This small molecule is called a monomer (*mono* means one). The search for synthetic materials started over a hundred years ago to replace materials like ivory, which were becoming scarce, and to make materials that could be molded or extruded as fibers. The first plastics were semi-synthetic polymers and worked by modifying cellulose, the natural polymer in cotton. Later, completely synthetic plastics, such as Bakelite, were made.

DECORATED BAG
Synthetic materials resembling ivory were widespread by 1900. They were used for all kinds of products, from knife handles, collars, and cuffs, to this evening handbag. These plastics could be molded when hot into shapes which became rigid after cooling.

THE FIRST PLASTIC
Alexander Parkes (1813-1890) introduced a moldable material made from cellulose nitrate. He dissolved cotton fibers in nitric acid, added a plasticizer such as camphor, and evaporated off the solvent. The material called Parkesine was used to make all kinds of domestic goods like this barrette. Parkes exhibited this first successful plastic in London in 1862.

Black inlay

Decorative diamante

Silk tassels

Molded decorative detail

Clasp

Braided leather strap

HAND MIRROR
This hand mirror is made from ivoride, an ivory substitute. Ivoride, like other plastics, could be easily molded to resemble intricately carved ivory. The early synthetic plastics were modeled to resemble the natural polymers.

CELLULOID EVENING BAG
By 1870, John Wesley Hyatt (1837-1920) was manufacturing celluloid, an ivory substitute, from cellulose nitrate. It was widely used for billiard balls and all kinds of decorative products, such as this evening bag made in 1900.

IMITATION EBONY
This matchbox, dating from 1890, is made of dark-brown ebonite. The plastic is made by vulcanizing rubber.

PLASTIC PEN
When sulfur-containing compounds are heated with rubber, the rubber absorbs them, forming crosslinks between the chains of molecules. Large amounts of sulfur lead to hard, chemically resistant materials, such as the vulcanite used to make this fountain pen.

LEO BAEKELAND (1863-1944)
Belgian-born Baekeland emigrated to the US, where he studied the reaction of phenol and formaldehyde. The dark, tarry mass obtained had previously been ignored by chemists who were interested only in pure crystalline products. In 1907, Baekeland succeeded in controlling a polymerization reaction to produce a synthetic plastic which he called "Bakelite."

Volume control / *Speakers* / *Tuning knob*

BAKELITE RADIO
Bakelite, or phenolic resin, was used for domestic items, such as clocks and electrical fittings. It is resistant to heat and has good insulating properties. The phenolic resins are always dark in color. They are easy to mold and are strengthened using fillers such as textiles.

PLASTIC FILM
Film made of cellulose nitrate was introduced for motion pictures in 1887 and for still pictures in the following year. Cellulose nitrate is notoriously inflammable, so modern film is made from the safer plastic, cellulose triacetate.

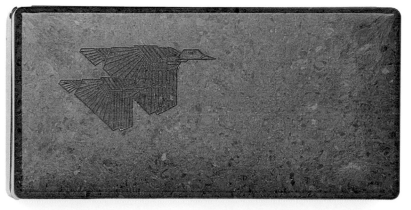

CIGARETTE BOX
In the 1920s the search for a light-colored plastic with similar properties to Bakelite, which was always black or reddish-brown, led to the ureaformaldehyde plastics. Using cellulose fillers and suitable coloring materials, both white and colored articles could be manufactured.

SYNTHETIC FIBERS (below)
Some plastics can be extruded to form fibers. Textiles used to be derived from natural fibers. Regenerated cellulose from a viscose solution was introduced in 1892. This plastic material could be pumped through fine holes into acid to produce an artificial thread for textiles. Large-scale production was possible with the introduction of a spinning box in 1900. The box collected the filaments without tangling them.

Silk samples from viscose

THE PLASTIC AGE
By the 1950s, many different plastics had been developed. They were used in industry and throughout the house, especially the kitchen. Strong polyvinyl chloride (PVC) is used as a floor covering. Melamine formaldehyde plastics, which have a good resistance to heat, water, and detergents, were introduced in the mid-1930s. They are laminated by sandwiching alternate layers of plastic and paper or cloth and pressing them to make formica for work surfaces. Other plastics, such as polystyrene, are used for buckets, bowls, and jars. Unfortunately most plastics are not biodegradable; they do not rot away, and they may emit poisonous fumes when burned.

Making synthetic materials

New plastics are being introduced all the time. The first of the thermoplastic materials was polyvinyl chloride (PVC). Observed in the 1870s, it was not successfully produced until the 1930s. Waterproof and weather resistant, it has a wide range of uses: rigid when thick, it makes up guttering, toys, and curtain rails; flexible when thin, it covers electric cables, makes baby pants, and upholstery. Polyacrylic plastics include perspex, a plastic of exceptionally high transparency. Its resistance to shattering makes it invaluable for aircraft canopies. Polythene, or polyethylene, was first discovered in 1933. Like many plastics, it was some time before successful commercial production was achieved in the late 1930s, when its valuable insulating properties were immediately pressed into service for wartime radar equipment. Rigid polyethylene was not produced until the introduction of a catalyst in the 1950s. In the US, the Du Pont company successfully launched nylon-66, which revolutionized the textiles industry. It was strong, stretchy, and nonabsorbent. Today, it is difficult to imagine a world without plastics. Many new processes and products depend upon them.

MAKING NYLON FIBERS
Wallace H. Carothers (1896-1937) joined Du Pont in 1928. He used two chemicals in solutions (an acid and a diamine) to prepare nylon-66. Where the two solutions met, the liquid could be pushed out (extruded) into threads that were stronger than natural fibers. The discovery gave a huge boost to the textile industry and led to a revolution in fabrics.

Nylon drawn out as a thread

MAKING NYLON
Two alternating monomers are used to make nylon-66: adipic acid and hexamethylene diamine. Each has reactive groups of atoms at both ends of a straight molecule – acid groups in the former, and amine in the latter. Each acid group combines with an amine to form long chains of alternating monomers. The diamine is dissolved in water forming the lower layer in the beaker, while the upper layer is a solution of the acid in hexane. Nylon is formed where the two reactants meet and can be pulled out of the beaker and wound around the rod.

Where layers meet, nylon is formed

Adipic acid dissolved in hexane

Hexamethylene diamine in water

FASHIONABLE STOCKINGS
Women's stockings made of the new nylon fiber were first marketed in 1940, and nylon soon caught on.

EARLY SAMPLE
This piece of nylon tubing was knitted in 1935 at Du Pont using a slightly different polyamide from the more usual nylon-66. The success of nylon for stockings lies in its strength and its elasticity, which makes it cling rather than wrinkle.

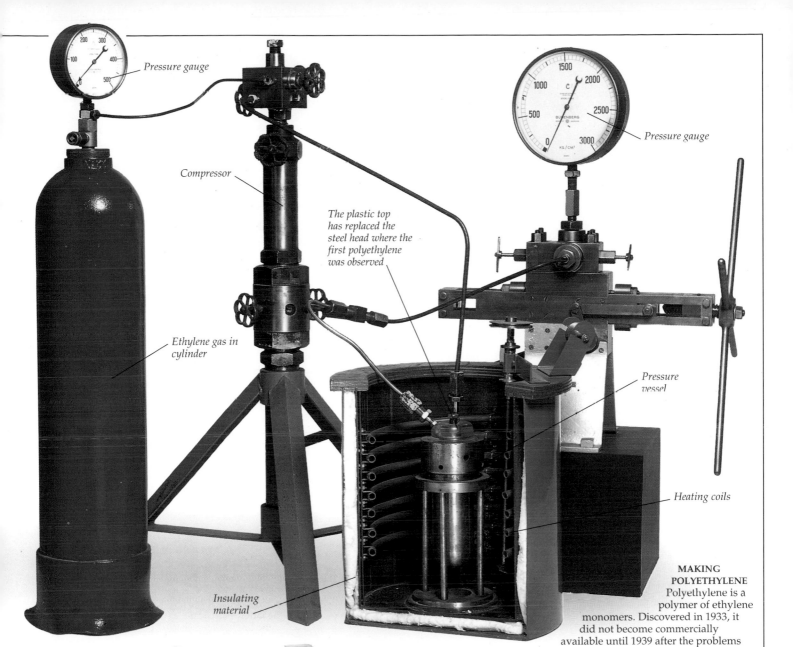

Pressure gauge

Compressor

The plastic top
has replaced the
steel head where the
first polyethylene
was observed

Ethylene gas in
cylinder

Pressure gauge

Pressure
vessel

Heating coils

Insulating
material

POLYETHYLENE ICON
This piece of polyethylene
is part of the first ton to be
manufactured commercially in
1938. Today millions of tons are
produced annually for plastic film
and molded items.

MAKING POLYETHYLENE
Polyethylene is a
polymer of ethylene
monomers. Discovered in 1933, it
did not become commercially
available until 1939 after the problems
of attaining high temperatures and pressures on a large scale were solved. This
pressure vessel was used to prepare the first polyethylene samples. While
examining the effects of very high pressures on ethylene gas, solid, white
particles were observed. Fortuitously, a hole in the equipment had allowed
oxygen from air to enter the chamber, which initiated (started) the reaction.
This low-density polyethylene is soft, flexible, and clear. In the 1950s a catalyst
was introduced, and rigid, high-density polyethylene was obtained.

Stainless steel shaft

Polyethylene joint

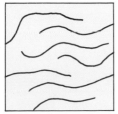

Thermoplastic molecules

Thermosetting molecules

MOLECULAR STRUCTURE OF PLASTIC
All plastics fall into one of
two categories depending
on how they act when
heated. Thermoplastic
materials (polyethylene)
soften each time they are
heated. Thermosetting
plastics will not soften
again once they have
been heated and cooled
down (Bakelite). On first
heating, these molecules
form cross linkages
which lead to a
permanent rigid
structure. They are used
to make components
such as electric plugs.

PLASTICS IN SURGERY
Plastics
increasingly find
applications in
replacement surgery,
because they do not
react with their
surroundings. Unlike
transplant material from
human donors, they do
not prompt the body to
reject them as foreign
material. This hip
replacement uses a special
ultra-high molecular
weight polyethylene.

RECYCLING PLASTICS
This plastic tubing is
being made from pellets
of polyethylene. Waste
polyethylene has been
softened with hot
water and ground up
to produce the pellets.
The plastic tubing is
blown out using hot
air, which shapes and
dries the tubing.
Recycled plastic is used
in the construction
industry, where
impurities in it are not
so important. Only
thermoplastics can be
recycled in this way.

The story of chemical analysis

FROM EARLY TIMES, assayers (p. 188) tried to analyze basic substances. Chemists often used the senses of smell and taste to detect what things were – sometimes with dreadful consequences. Sir Humphry Davy (p.158) breathed in all the gases he made – he died young. Johann Glauber (1604-1670) knew that silver forms precipitates with alkalis and carbonates, and he recognized the importance of color in identifying substances. By 1800, the ability of hydrogen sulfide gas to form insoluble salts with certain metals was understood. Karl Fresenius (1818-1897) developed this body of knowledge into a systematic analysis of metals. Other characteristics of substances were also important. When mineral oils began to replace traditional vegetable oils, analytical equipment was developed to measure their volatility.

THE LABORATORY
Karl Fresenius was professor of chemistry, physics, and technology at Wiesbaden from 1845. He established the Fresenius Laboratory in 1848 to teach analytical chemistry and to conduct chemical analyses.

Kipps gas generator

Glass tube allows acid to pass through chamber

Reactants produce gas in here

Iron sulfide

When gas supply is turned off, gas pressure forces acid back up tube to top chamber

Acid poured into here flows down into bottom chamber

Gas is siphoned off through here

Clip to open and close gas supply

Acid rises into central chamber when gas supply is turned on

KIPP'S APPARATUS
P.J. Kipp introduced his gas generator in 1862, to provide a convenient source of the gas hydrogen sulfide. Hydrochloric acid reacts with iron sulfide, to produce this extremely toxic gas. Hydrogen sulfide bubbling through solutions of metals salts will form insoluble metal sulfides for analysis.

Thermometer for water bath

Thermometer to measure oil

Burning jet moved past here

Cup to hold oil

Water bath

FLASHPOINT APPARATUS
The new mineral oils that came into use during the 19th century had unknown properties. This apparatus was developed to determine their flashpoint – the temperature at which oils give off vapor that easily ignites. A water bath heats the oil, and the vapor is tested regularly by moving a burning jet into a hole in the lid. When a slight explosion takes place, the flashpoint has been reached. Oils with low flashpoints can be dangerous, since they can explode or cause a fire.

Spirit lamp to heat water bath

TESTING METALS (below)
To analyze an unknown material, it is first dissolved in concentrated hydrochloric acid. Adding hydrogen sulfide causes some metals to form insoluble sulfides. The color of these precipitates gives an indication as to which metals are present, and further tests can be carried out. If the remaining solution becomes alkaline, other metals are made to precipitate.

Test tube rack

| Lead sulfide | Manganese sulfide | Copper sulfide | Cadmium sulfide | Iron sulfide |

Beam of light
produced in here

Prism separates
light into spectrum

Telescope to
view spectrum

Eyepiece

Light from
source enters here

Divided circle allows
wavelength to be measured

Magnifier to read scale

ANALYZING DYES
By 1876 it was known that the color of compounds such as dyes is affected by particular groupings of atoms. Additional groups of atoms are sometimes needed to bring out the color or vary the shade. The groups produce characteristic bands in a spectrum. When the dye indigo was made synthetically, it was checked spectroscopically with indigo from the *indigofera* plant to see that the samples were identical.

Indigo spectrum

ANALYSIS BY SPECTROSCOPE
Spectroscopy was first used to identify metals in 1859. This 19th-century spectroscope was based on the inventive German chemist Robert Bunsen's design. Spectroscopy rapidly caught on as a technique for chemical analysis and was expanded to use both infrared and ultraviolet radiation. As well as identifying elements, spectroscopy can be used to study a wide range of compounds. The characteristic spectra provide information about types of chemical bond and how atoms move within the molecule. The engraving on the left shows Robert Bunsen (1811-1899) looking at the spectrum of a flame through his spectroscope. In 1955 the Australian Alan Walsh devised the more sensitive technique of atomic absorption spectroscopy, which can detect minute traces of elements.

Robust
stand

Bunsen using
a spectroscope

JONS JAKOB BERZELIUS (1779-1848)
This famous Swedish chemist was a giant of chemical analysis. He was expert at blowpipe analysis and discovered several elements while carrying out analyses. He determined atomic weights for most elements known in the early 19th century. He also introduced modern symbols for elements, using the first one or two letters, such as H for hydrogen. He believed that these did not disfigure the printed page as much as pictorial symbols. He also analyzed many organic compounds and tried to understand their complex properties.

Screw for
adjusting
height of
equipment

Knob to adjust
level of wick

Chimney

Wick
would be
here

Reservoir
for alcohol

Shield for
circular wick

Strontium chloride   Barium chloride   Calcium chloride   Potassium chloride

FLAME TESTS FOR METALS
A flame test is one of the first tests used to analyze what a substance is. Johann Glauber noticed that colored flames indicate what metals are present as long ago as 1659. When a clean wire dipped in a solution of a metal salt is held in a flame – a Bunsen burner or an alcohol lamp flame – it makes it burn with a characteristic color. The color appears because the metal atoms take in energy from the flame. This energy is given out as light when the atom returns to its normal state. The colored flames can be analyzed using a spectroscope. Metals such as strontium and potassium are used to give fireworks their color.

BERZELIUS ALCOHOL LAMP
Some form of heat and flame is often necessary in chemical analysis. Charcoal furnaces were used from early times for heating. For small-scale work, the chemist had burning lenses and alcohol lamps. This type of alcohol lamp was used by Berzelius.

Base

Monitoring materials

CHEMICAL ANALYSIS IS USED in manufacturing operations to check raw materials and finished products; it can monitor food quality; and medicines are designed, tested, and manufactured with the benefit of chemical analysis. One vital part of analysis is weighing, and accurate balances have been developed since 1800. Some methods of analysis depend on volume measurement – the early studies of gases used a eudiometer (p. 215). For liquids, specialized apparatus such as pipettes and burettes are used. Food analysis assumed great importance during the 19th century; as governments took more responsibility for public health, so chemists were called on to check that foodstuffs were what they were said to be.

ANALYZING COLOR
Mikhail Tswett (1872-1919) studied plant pigments and developed chromatography (p. 201) while trying to extract and separate the pigments.

Eyepiece

Screw opens instrument to insert sample

Thermometer

Water jacket to control temperature

FOOD ADULTERATION
The first margarine, invented as a butter substitute in 1869, was made from a mixture of beef products. Both this and butter were sometimes adulterated by having cheaper vegetable fats added. This could be detected using a butter refractometer. Refractometers were introduced by Ernst Abbe, an optical instrument maker, in 1869. These instruments measure the refractive index of substances – how much light is bent when it passes from air into the substance.

Sample between two prisms in here

Tube connects water jacket around each prism

WEIGHING PRODUCTS
The balance was the major tool of practical analysis. Joseph Black was the first to use a balance to study chemical reactions by weighing reactants and products. His balance was fairly crude. This chemical balance, made in 1876, was one of the first to incorporate a short beam, using light aluminum to reduce the weight of the beam.

Rider carries small weights for final adjustments

Pans are suspended on knife edges

Knob opens side door

Mirror to reflect light through instrument

Pan

Knob lifts pans

ANALYZING ORGANIC COMPOUNDS
Joseph Gay-Lussac (1778-1850) and Louis Thenard (1777-1857) introduced this apparatus in 1811 to measure the amounts of carbon and hydrogen in organic compounds, such as sugars and starches, by burning them to form carbon dioxide and water. They used an oxidizing agent to make sure the compound burned completely. The carbon dioxide was absorbed and the water vapor was collected and measured. They confirmed that sugars and starches contained hydrogen and oxygen in the same proportions as in water, leading to the name "carbohydrates."

F. Sartorius,

Balance made by F. Sartorius

ANALYZING LIQUIDS

The hydrometer has been used since the 17th century to measure the amount of alcohol in liquor. An essential tool of the brewer, it measures the specific gravity of a liquid – its weight compared with that of the same volume of water. This type of hydrometer, designed by Bartholomew Sikes, was used from 1816 to levy excise duty on alcoholic liquids. The "proof" strength is found by looking up tables which take account of the temperature of the liquid.

Analyzing the quality of liquor

Circular weight slots on to the stem

Stem

Eyepiece views both samples at the same time

VOLUMETRIC ANALYSIS

This burette was used in the 19th century to measure the amount of a solution needed to complete a chemical reaction. The flow of liquid is controlled by placing a thumb on the side arm. By lifting the thumb slightly, the liquid can be poured slowly into a flask containing the second solution. The liquid is added until the reaction is complete: in acid-base experiments (p. 228) this may be shown using an indicator that changes color.

Side arm

Hydrometer is suspended in the liquid and the reading on the stem is noted

Glass rod

Beckmann thermometer

Glass rod

Standard solution

Aluminum short beam

Sample introduced through here

Stirrer

Cooling jacket

Sample solution

White background

KLETT COLORIMETER

The colorimeter was developed during the 19th century to quantify observations based on the depth of color in solution. Industries such as brewing, tanning, dyeing, and printing used colorimetry to check product quality in the early 20th century.

Pan stop for pans to rest on when not in use

Leveling screw

TEMPERATURE CHANGE

Measurement of the physical properties of compounds uses apparatus like this. Ernst Beckmann (1853-1923) developed this thermometer to measure the lowering of the melting point for a known weight of a dissolved substance. The thermometer can measure extremely small temperature changes. The scale has gradations of $\frac{1}{100}$ ° C.

MEDICAL ANALYSIS

The presence of particular compounds in medical samples is vital to medical diagnosis. A variety of ways of analyzing samples – some chemical – can be used. The computer age has changed the look of the chemistry laboratory from a room filled with glass, wooden, and brass apparatus to one that includes blinking screens and high-technological equipment.

The chemical industry

Up to the mid-18th century, chemical industries were mainly crafts with their roots in ancient times. These included the manufacture of glass, ceramics, soaps, and dyestuffs. In modern times, the most important industrial chemical is sulfuric acid. It is essential for all kinds of industries, from dyestuffs and fertilizers to metallurgy and plastics. Industries such as soap and glass manufacture depend on alkalis, such as potassium and sodium carbonate. Potassium carbonate is obtained from vegetable sources. Nicholas Leblanc (1742-1806) devised a process to produce sodium carbonate from common salt. This process was replaced by the Solvay process, developed in Belgium in 1865. Setting up plants and equipment to make large quantities often causes problems, so for reasons of economy, processes are usually continuous – a supply of reactants are fed in and products are removed continuously, unlike the "batch" process in the laboratory.

Ammonia recovery tower

Ammonium chloride travels up here for recycling

Ammonia is recovered using slaked lime from the kiln

The slaker where lime is slaked with water

CHEMICALS FOR WASHING
Many industries were associated with textiles and clothing. Soaps made by boiling animal fats with alkali have been known since the 12th century. Michel Eugene Chevreul (1786-1889) studied the composition of animal fats. His research led to practical improvements in both the soap and candle-making industries. In major textile-producing areas bleaching was an important industry. In large bleaching fields, textiles were bleached by the combined action of sunlight and lactic acid in buttermilk. Chlorine solutions were used after the late 18th century, but these were unpleasant to produce.

ALFRED NOBEL (1833-1896)
Black gunpowder, invented in China, was the standard military explosive until the 19th century. Nobel was a Swedish inventor who introduced a commercial process for nitrating glycerol and produced nitroglycerine in the relatively safe form of dynamite in 1866. Blasting gelatin was introduced in 1875. Both these explosives were extremely profitable during that era of great industrial expansion, and on his death Nobel left his estate as an endowment for the annual Nobel Prizes.

Filter separates out sodium hydrogencarbonate

SODIUM CARBONATE FROM THE SOLVAY PROCESS
The reaction of ammonia, carbon dioxide, and brine (concentrated salt solution) to produce sodium carbonate (soda ash) was studied in 1811, but it was not until 1865 that Ernest Solvay (1838-1922) succeeded in developing a commercial process. In a carbonating tower, brine containing ammonia is saturated with carbon dioxide gas. The resulting sodium hydrogencarbonate is filtered off and heated to give off sodium carbonate and some carbon dioxide, which is recycled. Additional carbon dioxide is obtained by heating limestone (calcium carbonate) in a kiln. Lime, the other product obtained from the kiln, is "slaked" with water and used to regenerate the ammonia, which is the most expensive reactant. The efficient recovery of ammonia is crucial to the commercial success of the process.

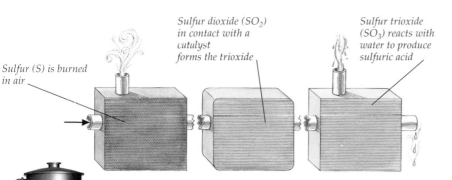

Sulfur (S) is burned in air

Sulfur dioxide (SO₂) in contact with a catalyst forms the trioxide

Sulfur trioxide (SO₃) reacts with water to produce sulfuric acid

THE CONTACT PROCESS

Sulfuric acid was first produced by the alchemists. Today it is made directly from sulfur. Sulfur is first burned in air to produce sulfur dioxide. In the second stage, sulfur dioxide is oxidized to the trioxide. This is a slow reaction and a catalyst (vanadium pentoxide) is used to speed it up. Heating also speeds up the reaction. Finally, sulfuric acid is formed by reacting the trioxide with water. Sulfur trioxide is so reactive that the most convenient way to do this is to absorb it in sulfuric acid which can then be diluted to the required strength.

Limestone to make carbon dioxide

Brine and ammonia travel along here

Cooler

Lime kiln

Carbonating tower where carbon dioxide and brine are added to ammonia

Sodium hydrogen–carbonate is heated here to give sodium carbonate

CHEMISTRY OF AGRICULTURE

Justus von Liebig (1803-1873) set up his teaching laboratory in Germany in 1839. Liebig emphasized the importance of inorganic elements such as phosphorus and potassium in stimulating the growth of plants. His enthusiasm for soil chemistry helped initiate the fertilizer industry, which has revolutionized agriculture.

CHEMICALS FOR GROWTH

Plants require nitrogen to build proteins. Increasing the nitrogen content of the soil improves crop yields. Modern-day fertilizers, sometimes sprayed on to crops from the air, contain nitrogen compounds produced largely from ammonia manufactured by the Haber process.

CHEMICALS FROM OIL

The chief product of the giant petroleum industry is fuel. About 10 percent of the petroleum processed provides raw material for much of the modern organic chemical industry, especially plastics and synthetic rubber, largely replacing the 19th-century source of coal tar. Although the chemical industry is fundamental to modern life, it does have its drawbacks. Waste materials from the huge chemical plants have been allowed to pollute the oceans and the atmosphere. However, strict controls are gradually being introduced in an effort to control this pollution.

Porcelain insulator for telegraph wires (20th century)

Wimshurst machine (1882) for making electric charge

Demonstration model showing shadow of Maltese cross produced by cathode rays

Lid and chain from a late 19th-century Leyden jar

Domestic electric heater (1913)

Receiver used by Marconi in 1901 to detect first transatlantic radio transmissions

Early British vacuum tube (1905)

Gold leaf electroscope for detecting charge (1895)

Electric doorbell (early 20th century)

Voltaic pile (1800)

Voltameter used in the electrolysis of water (1807)

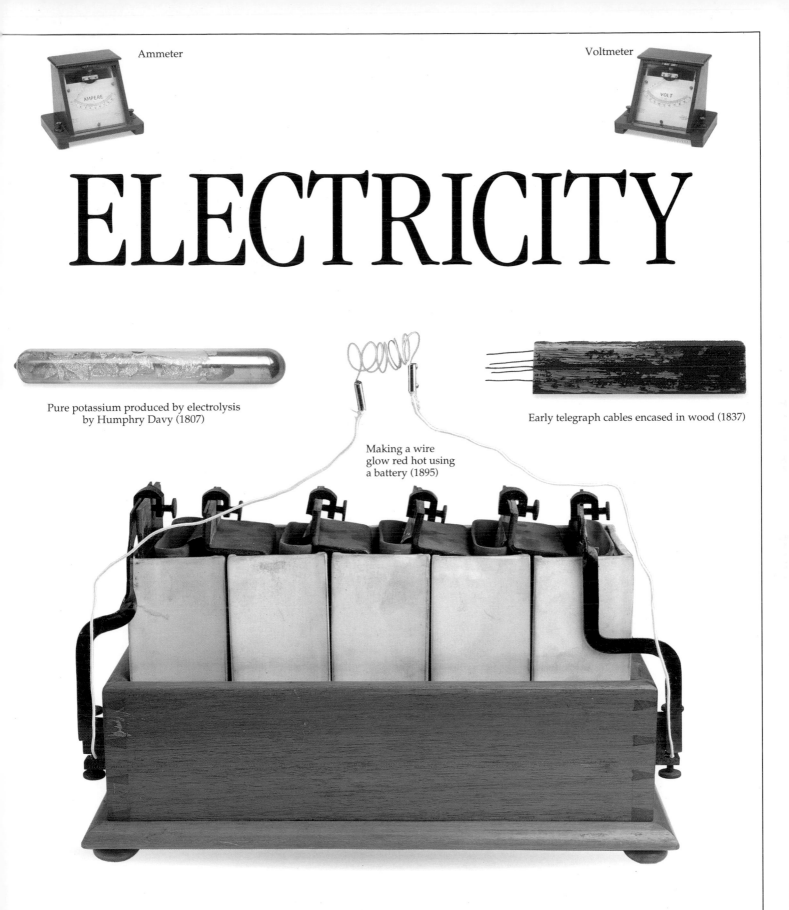

Ammeter

Voltmeter

ELECTRICITY

Pure potassium produced by electrolysis
by Humphry Davy (1807)

Early telegraph cables encased in wood (1837)

Making a wire
glow red hot using
a battery (1895)

A mysterious force

Since the beginning of the universe, there was electricity. Even when there was no life on our planet, more than 4 billion years ago, great bolts of lightning lit up the skies. Lightning is one of nature's most dramatic demonstrations of the energy form we call electricity. As life evolved, electricity became a vital part of the living world. It forms the basis of a nerve signal. Eyes receive light rays and turn them into tiny electric signals that pass along nerves into the brain and the rest of the body. Our whole awareness and ability to think and move depends on tiny electrical signals whizzing around the nerve pathways inside the brain. In the past two centuries, scientists have gradually begun to unravel the mysteries of electricity. Their advances were often linked to progress in other areas of science. Following this scientific research came exploitation. Inventors turned electrical energy into our servant.

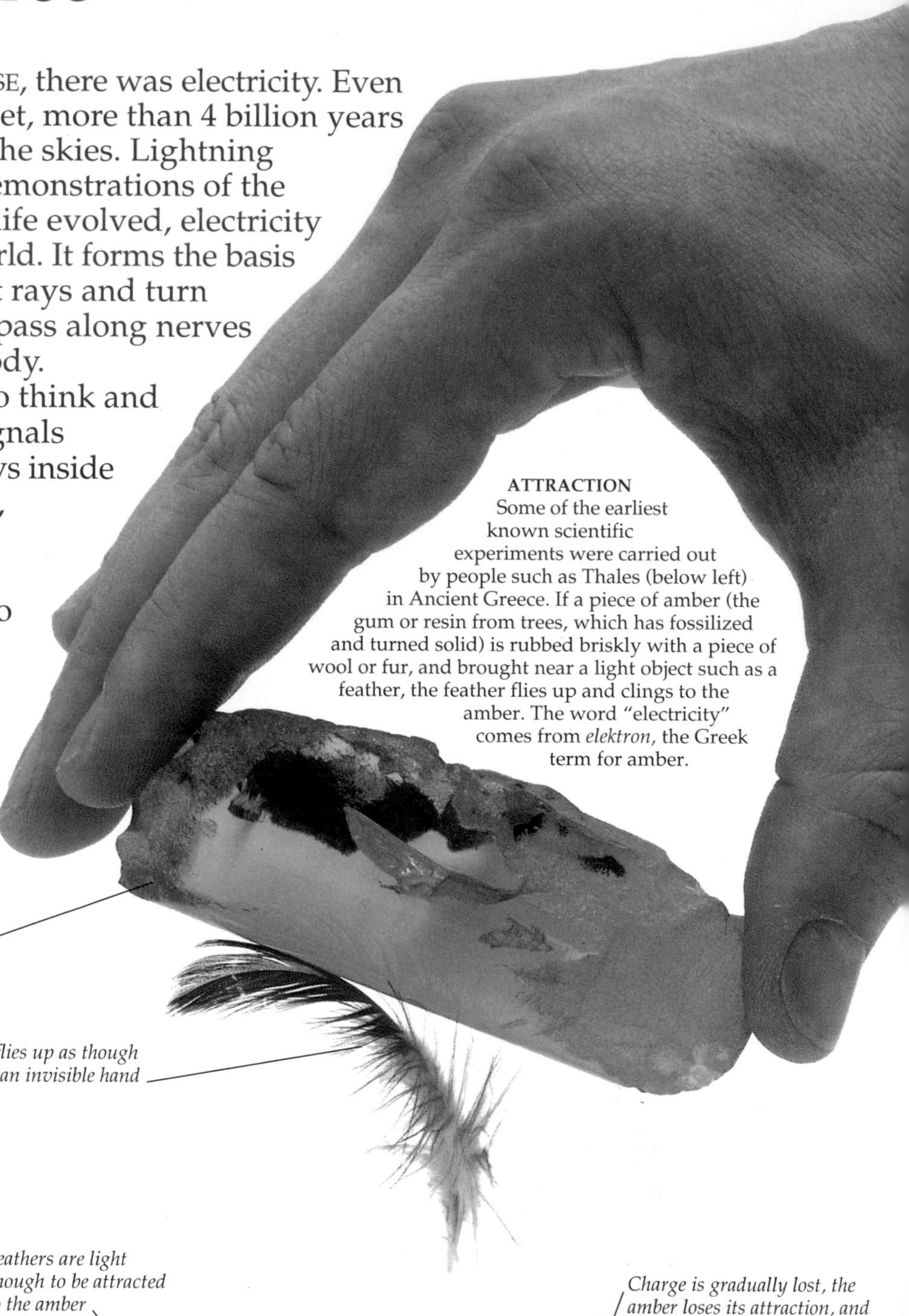

ATTRACTION
Some of the earliest known scientific experiments were carried out by people such as Thales (below left) in Ancient Greece. If a piece of amber (the gum or resin from trees, which has fossilized and turned solid) is rubbed briskly with a piece of wool or fur, and brought near a light object such as a feather, the feather flies up and clings to the amber. The word "electricity" comes from *elektron*, the Greek term for amber.

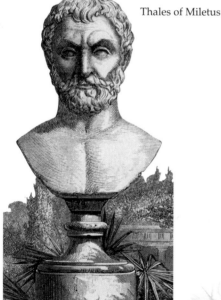

Thales of Miletus

Amber

Feather flies up as though lifted by an invisible hand

Feathers are light enough to be attracted to the amber

Charge is gradually lost, the amber loses its attraction, and the feathers float down

THE VIEWS OF THE ANCIENTS
The Ancient Greeks were among the first thinkers in the European scientific tradition. One of the earliest Greek scientists was Thales of Miletus (*c.* 625-547 BC), a skillful mathematician. None of Thales' own writings survives, but reports of his work show that he probably carried out simple experiments into the effects of what we now call electricity and magnetism.

ELECTRICITY IN THE AIR

The lightning bolt is an awesome example of electricity in action. The explanations of what electricity is, where it comes from, and how it works, are central to our understanding of matter and the fundamental forces of nature. Lightning is the result of the discharge of an electric charge in a cloud. The energy of the discharge is so great that it produces an intense trail of light, heat, and sound – thunder. It can destroy buildings, kill humans, and consume trees in a sheet of flame. Observations of lightning led scientists and thinkers such as Benjamin Franklin (p. 25, p. 254) to investigate and begin to unravel the mysteries of electric charge.

PLAYING TRICKS

In times gone by, teachers showed the attraction of magnetic and electrically charged objects, even though they did not understand their nature. Magicians still use the attracting powers of magnetism and "static" electricity (or electric charge) in their acts.

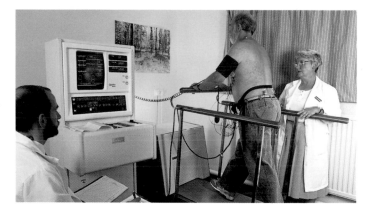

ELECTRICITY IN THE BODY

Human life depends on electricity. About every second, tiny electric signals spread through the heart muscle, triggering and coordinating a heartbeat. These signals send "echoes" through the body tissues to the skin. Here they can be detected by metal sensors and displayed as a wavy line called the electrocardiogram.

ELECTRICITY IN ANIMALS

In the animal world, a busy muscle produces small pulses of electricity. Creatures have capitalized on this for hunting and killing. The electric ray has modified muscle blocks on either side of its head. These jellylike "living batteries" send shock waves through the water to stun or kill a nearby victim. A typical shark has 1,000 electricity-sensing pits on its skin, mainly around its head. They pick up tiny electric pulses from the active muscles of fish. In complete darkness a shark can home in on its meal with unerring accuracy, using its electrical-navigation sensors.

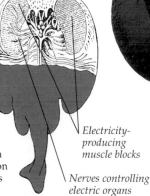

Electricity-producing muscle blocks

Nerves controlling electric organs

Atlantic torpedo or electric ray

Shark

Ideas about electricity

IN THE EARLY DAYS of experiments with electricity, scientists had no batteries to make electricity. Instead, they made it themseleves by rubbing certain materials together. Around 1600 William Gilbert suggested there were two kinds of electricity, based on the material used to do the rubbing, though he did not know why this was so. Glass rubbed with silk made vitreous electricity, and amber rubber with fur made resinous electricity. His experiments showed that objects containing the same kind of electricity repelled each other, while those containing different kinds attracted each other.

Benjamin Franklin also believed that there were two kinds of electricity. He proposed that electric charge was like "fluid" spreading itself through an object. It could jump to another object, making a spark.

Versorium

Thin, finely balanced pointer of light wood

Upright rod

GILBERT'S VERSORIUM
William Gilbert (1544-1603) was a doctor to Queen Elizabeth I of England. In 1600 he wrote about the mysterious forces of magnetism and electricity in his book *De Magnete* (*On the Magnet*). Gilbert was the first person to use the word "electric," and he invented possibly the earliest electrical instrument, the versorium. Objects like paper and straw, which had an electric charge when rubbed, made the pointer of the versorium swing toward them. He called these attracting substances "electrics." Those that did not attract the pointer were "nonelectrics."

Tip bent by intense heat

Lightning rod

Charge-collecting metal combs

Charge conducted down chains to jars

Leyden jar

Outer metal coating of Leyden jar

Brush touches across disc as part of charge buildup

DIRECT HIT
A lightning bolt is a giant spark of electric charge jumping from a thunder-cloud to the ground. If lightning hits anything, it burns it. A rod directs charge through a copper strip to the earth, leaving the building safe.

A RISKY EXPERIMENT
The lightning experiments of Benjamin Franklin (1706-1790) were copied by other investigators. The scientist Georg Richmann at St. Petersburg, Russia, was killed by the electric charge of lightning when he held a wire-tipped pole up high in a storm. The sparks from lightning were in fact similar to those obtained in laboratories (see also p. 25).

BENJAMIN FRANKLIN
To "collect" electricity from lightning, Franklin flew a kite in a thunderstorm. Sparks jumped when the lightning flowed along a kite string to which a key had been tied.

Discharging spheres

Wimshurst machine

As the charge builds up, a spark leaps across the small gap

Conductor arms

PRODUCING ELECTRIC CHARGE

For many years, the Wimhurst machine was used to produce electric charge. The machine works by induction. Turning the crank handle starts a process involving the metal sectors which are stuck on the outside of two glass discs – one wheel rotates in the opposite direction to the other – and metal combs that point to the discs, but do not actually touch them. This process multiplies small stray electric charges many times. The charge produced is stored in Leyden jars. When enough charge has built up, it jumps between the two discharging spheres, producing a bright spark. The device was developed by James Wimshurst (1832-1903). Wimshurst machines were used to demonstrate making static electricity – as the charge is sometimes called – until at least the 1960s. The largest machine had discs that were 7 feet (2.12 m) in diameter.

James Wimshurst

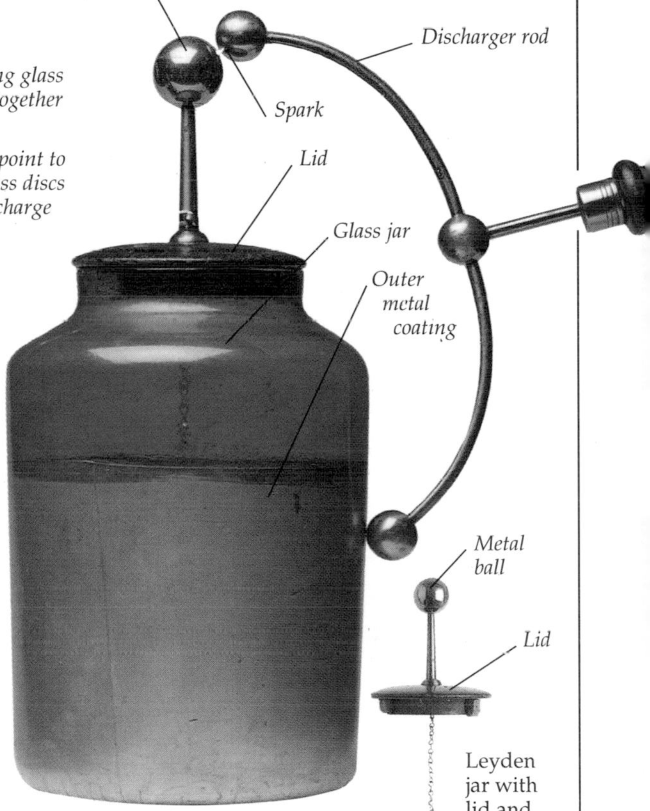

Leyden jar being discharged

Metal sectors stuck to outside of both discs

Two contra-rotating glass discs placed close together

Metal combs point to sectors on glass discs and collect charge

Metal ball

Spark

Discharger rod

Lid

Glass jar

Outer metal coating

Pulley

Crossed drive belt

Drive belt

Metal ball

Lid

Leyden jar with lid and chain

STORING CHARGE

The Leyden jar was an early device scientists used for storing the electric charge they were making. It is named after the place where it was developed in 1746, the University of Leyden in the Netherlands. The electric charge flows down the metal chain to metal coating inside the jar. It cannot leak away through the glass jar, so it builds up. If the discharger rod is held near the jar (above), the charge leaps from the ball on top, through the discharger to the outer metal coating on the jar – causing a spark. The Leyden jar was an early type of capacitor or condenser.

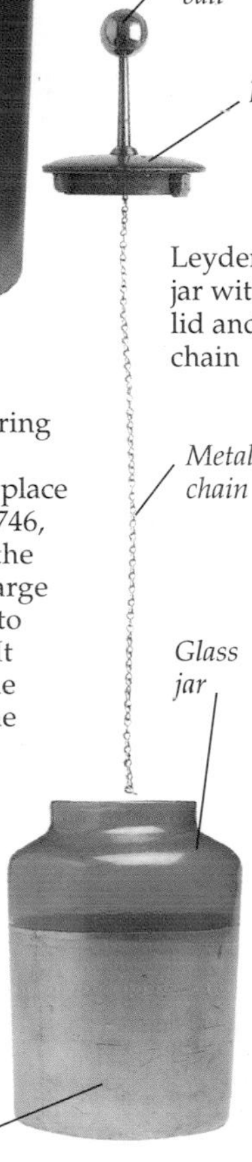

Metal chain

Glass jar

Leyden jar

Hand-turned crank handle

Drive pulley

Outer metal coating

The quest for knowledge

DURING THE 18TH CENTURY many scientists experimented with electric charge in their laboratories. As yet, there were no practical uses for electricity; what interested scientists was the quest for knowledge. They observed how electric charge could be seen as sparks, and how it behaved differently with different substances. Since electricity was invisible, instruments were needed to detect and measure it. Initially, progress was haphazard. There was no way to make a sustained flow of electric charge – that came later from the battery. Startling new discoveries were made that are now taken for granted. For instance, in the 1720s the English scientist Stephen Gray (1666-1736) proposed that any object which touches an "electrified (charged) body will itself become electrified." Charge transferring from one substance to another one that touches it is a process called electrical conduction.

JOSEPH PRIESTLEY
Before achieving fame as a chemist and the discoverer of oxygen, Priestley (1733-1804) was interested in electricity. In 1767 he published the earliest history of electrical science – *The History and Present State of Electricity*. This was his personal assessment of contemporary studies.

Electrostatic machine

Friction from leather pressing on glass produces electric charge

Electric charge can jump from the metal ball as a spark

Electric charge collected by comb-shaped metal collector

Electric charge can be stored in the Leyden jar

Hand-turned crank causes glass cylinder to revolve

GENERATING ELECTRIC CHARGE
Electrostatic generators, first developed by English experimenter Francis Hauksbee (1666-1713) in 1710, generated larger and larger amounts of electric charge. They were used by scientists in experiments about the nature of electricity, and also in public to produce bigger sparks for amazed audiences. This machine was one of those made by the successful scientific instrument maker George Adams (1750-1795).

Horse and rider electrostatic toy

Charge sprays off the end of the point

Vanes spin

Connection to source of charge

MOVING TOYS
Electric charge was used to work this country scene from the mid-19th century. The metal point was connected to a source of charge; the charge "sprayed" off the end of the point and jumped to the vanes, moving them and the model around.

Rider and horse go round

DEMONSTRATION HOUSE
Model wooden houses such as the one in this engraving were used to demonstrate how a lightning rod works. The walls and roof were made to fall apart easily. Hidden inside was a container of gunpowder. Electric charge from an electrostatic generator, representing lightning, would normally be guided down into the ground by a metal lightning rod. If this was disconnected in the model, the charge created a spark which set off the gunpowder, blowing off the roof so the walls fell flat.

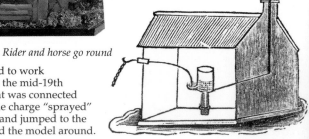

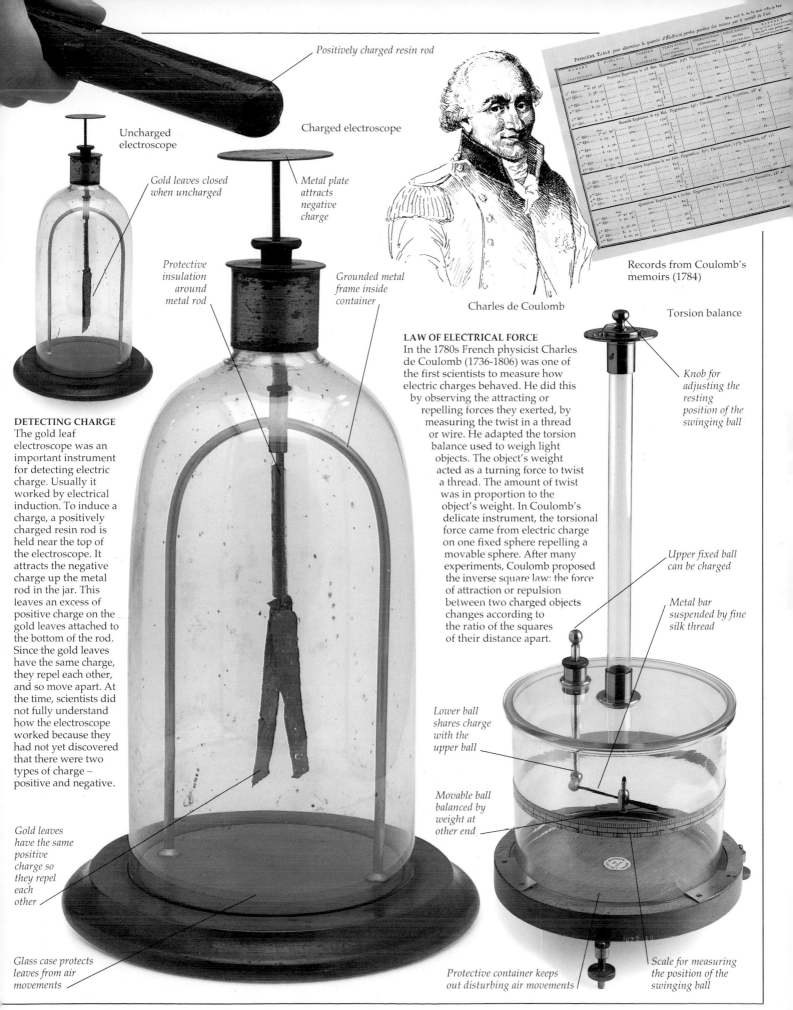

Positively charged resin rod

Uncharged
electroscope

Charged electroscope

Gold leaves closed
when uncharged

Metal plate
attracts
negative
charge

Charles de Coulomb

Records from Coulomb's
memoirs (1784)

Protective
insulation
around
metal rod

Grounded metal
frame inside
container

Torsion balance

LAW OF ELECTRICAL FORCE
In the 1780s French physicist Charles
de Coulomb (1736-1806) was one of
the first scientists to measure how
electric charges behaved. He did this
by observing the attracting or
repelling forces they exerted, by
measuring the twist in a thread
or wire. He adapted the torsion
balance used to weigh light
objects. The object's weight
acted as a turning force to twist
a thread. The amount of twist
was in proportion to the
object's weight. In Coulomb's
delicate instrument, the torsional
force came from electric charge
on one fixed sphere repelling a
movable sphere. After many
experiments, Coulomb proposed
the inverse square law: the force
of attraction or repulsion
between two charged objects
changes according to
the ratio of the squares
of their distance apart.

Knob for
adjusting the
resting
position of the
swinging ball

DETECTING CHARGE
The gold leaf
electroscope was an
important instrument
for detecting electric
charge. Usually it
worked by electrical
induction. To induce a
charge, a positively
charged resin rod is
held near the top of
the electroscope. It
attracts the negative
charge up the metal
rod in the jar. This
leaves an excess of
positive charge on the
gold leaves attached to
the bottom of the rod.
Since the gold leaves
have the same charge,
they repel each other,
and so move apart. At
the time, scientists did
not fully understand
how the electroscope
worked because they
had not yet discovered
that there were two
types of charge –
positive and negative.

Upper fixed ball
can be charged

Metal bar
suspended by fine
silk thread

Lower ball
shares charge
with the
upper ball

Movable ball
balanced by
weight at
other end

Gold leaves
have the same
positive
charge so
they repel
each
other

Glass case protects
leaves from air
movements

Protective container keeps
out disturbing air movements

Scale for measuring
the position of the
swinging ball

Collecting electric charge

TODAY, CHARGE-PRODUCING ELECTROSTATIC GENERATORS are an unfamiliar sight, confined to museums and research laboratories. These machines were designed to produce large charges and extremely high voltages. Charge-storing devices are vital components found inside many electrical devices, from washing machines to personal stereos. There are many different types of condenser (opposite), yet they all use the same principle as the Leyden jar (p. 255), the first electrical storage container. Condensers, sometimes called capacitors, are the only electric devices, other than batteries, that can store electrical energy. They are also used to separate alternating current (AC) from direct current (DC).

THE SPARK OF LIFE

The electrostatic generator's giant sparks made impressive special effects at the movies. Their similarity to lightning bolts fitted neatly into the plot of Mary Shelley's horror story *Frankenstein*. Doctor Frankenstein's monster, made from sewn-together bits of dead bodies, is jolted into life by the shock from a lightning bolt.

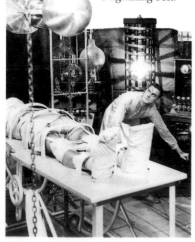

VAN DE GRAAFF GENERATOR

American scientist Robert Van de Graaff (1901-1967) developed a machine in the early 1930s for collecting and storing huge amounts of electric charge. He is shown here with one of his smaller electrostatic generators. The charge in the machine, which is named after him, builds up on a metal sphere, and reaches an incredible 10 million volts. The machine is mostly used as a research tool for studying the particles that make up atoms. The vast energy represented by its accumulated charge is transferred to the atoms' particles by accelerating the particles to enormous speed, so that scientists can study their interactions as they smash together.

Robert Van de Graaff

SPEEDING PARTICLES

The Cockcroft-Walton generator at Brookhaven Laboratory on Long Island, New York, generates electrical energy in the form of ultra-high voltages. The energy speeds up bits of atoms so fast that they travel a distance equivalent to the moon and back in four seconds.

ACCUMULATING CHARGE

In the Van de Graaff generator (below), the source of positive electric charge is a comb-shaped charge-sprayer connected to the electricity supply. The charge is carried on a moving belt to a charge collector above. This transfers it to the exterior of the large metal sphere. The sphere is mounted on a column that prevents the charge from leaking away. In atomic research there are no sparks; the fast-moving sub-atomic particles carry the charge away. In public demonstrations such as this model at the Boston Museum in Massachusetts (right), the accumulated charge leaps across to another piece of metal nearby, with a giant spark like a mini-lightning bolt.

How the Van de Graaff works

Charge collector

Sphere

Tube in which sub-atomic particles can be accelerated

Moving belt

Charge spraying comb

Electricity supply

Condensers

There are many different types of condenser that store electric charge. Two sheets of metal, or a similar electrical conductor, are separated by an insulating material such as paper or air. Capacitance is measured in units called farads, after Michael Faraday. One farad is a huge amount of charge, and most modern condensers are fingertip-sized items rated at microfarads (millionths of a farad) or less.

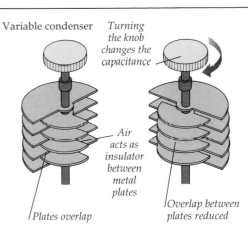

Variable condenser

Turning the knob changes the capacitance

Air acts as insulator between metal plates

Plates overlap

Overlap between plates reduced

CONDENSERS AT WORK

In electric devices, a condenser is used to store charge and release it at a certain moment, or to resist the continuous flow of charge through it. Bigger conducting plates, and a narrower gap between them, increase the amount of charge stored. The tuning knob on this 1950s radio operates a variable condenser, altering the overlap between its stack of metal plates. This changes the capacitance and causes the radio to respond to signals of a different frequency, that is, to pick up a different radio station.

Tuning knob

Metal plates of variable condenser

Using charges

THE DUST RESTING on a television screen is an example of electrostatic attraction. The glass surface of the screen becomes electrically charged while the television is on. It then attracts and holds any floating specks which happen to come near. This phenomenon of electrostatic forces, where there is attraction by unlike charges, and repulsion by like ones, is put to work in a variety of modern machines and processes. For instance, in the body-painting shop of a car manufacturer, tiny droplets of spray paint are all given the same electric charge. They repel each other and are attracted towards the car's body, and so settle on it as a more even coating. This is exactly the same principle as the charge that amber, when rubbed, produces to pick up feathers.

THE CARLSON COPIER
In 1938 American lawyer Chester Carlson (1906-1968) devised a process known as electrophotography. He wanted a machine that could duplicate patent application forms – not only the words, but also complicated drawings. He invented an electrostatic printer, or xerography machine, (from the Greek words *xeros* meaning "dry," and *graphos* for "writing.") The first xerographic print (above) was made by Carlson in 1938, but the first commercial copies were not produced until the 1950s.

Carlson's first print

Carlson with his early copier

Early copier (1960)

Charging chamber with top removed

Outer casing

Selenium-coated plate

Charging wires

Plate-charging button

Edge of selenium-coated plate

Developing tray with toner inside

Special toner tray (used for copying half-tone pictures)

TONE TRAY

"DRY WRITING"
The early copier uses the attraction of unlike electric charges. At its heart is a special metal plate coated with a substance called selenium. A pattern of positive charges on the plate representing the black areas to be copied, attracts negatively charged particles of a fine black powder – the toner. (The toner becomes negatively charged by contact with tiny glass beads in the developing tray.) The toner pattern is transferred to a blank sheet of paper and heat-sealed in place. In a modern copier, the selenium-coated plate is on a rotating drum. Otherwise the process is much the same as this 1960s machine, but now it happens automatically.

Making a
photocopy

*Light must be
kept out until the
developing stage
is complete*

*Plate is
locked in
developing
tray*

*Plate in charging
chamber is
positively charged*

1 CHARGING AND EXPOSING THE PLATE

The selenium-coated plate is put in the charging chamber and, as the electrified wires pass over, it receives an even coating of positive charges. The protective shield is replaced and the plate removed to a camera, where it is exposed to the document to be copied. An image of the document is shone on to it by a camera lens. Where light hits the plate, from the white areas of the original document, the selenium becomes a conductor, and the charge flows away. Where no light reaches, the charge remains.

2 DEVELOPING THE PLATE

The plate now has an exact mirror copy of the original document on its surface, in the form of a pattern of positive electrostatic charge. With the protective shield in place the plate is locked to the developing tray. The shield is removed, and the plate swung backward and forward. As this happens the toner in the developing tray cascades over the plate. Its tiny negatively charged grains are attracted to the positively charged areas of the plate, where they stick.

*Selenium-coated plate
with toner adhering to it*

3 THE DEVELOPED IMAGE

The plate is removed from the developer tray. This reveals the selenium-coated plate with the fine powder adhering to it, as an exact but mirror-image replica of the original document. The plate is returned to the charging chamber.

*The plate and paper
are slid into the
charging
chamber*

4 POWDER TO PAPER

The next stage also depends on electrostatic attraction. A sheet of blank paper is placed over the plate and its powder image. The plate and paper are pushed back into the charging chamber and withdrawn again while the transfer switch is depressed. The paper becomes positively charged so that it attracts the toner powder away from the plate.

*The paper now
holds a duplicate
of the original*

5 REMOVING THE COPY

The paper is carefully lifted from the plate, bringing with it the pattern of toner, which is now stuck to it by electrostatic attraction. The copied parts have been reversed again, so that they are an exact duplicate of the original.

*The paper is baked
in the fuser*

6 HEAT-SEALING THE COPY

Finally, the plain paper with its powder pattern is placed on the fuser tray and pushed into an oven-like chamber for a few seconds. The powder bakes and melts into the fibers of the paper, permanently sealing the image. The entire process takes about three minutes – much longer than the couple of seconds in a modern photocopier.

DUST-EATING AIR FILTER

The electrostatic air filter on this 1930s cigarette card, showing a man demonstrating the filter with cigarette smoke, uses a fan to draw in a stream of dusty, impure air. A prefilter traps the bigger floating particles. The remaining small ones pass through the first electrified grid of a device called the electrostatic precipitator. This grid gives each particle a negative charge. The particles are repelled from the negative wires onto the precipitator's second, positively charged grid. They are attracted to it, and stick to its mesh. A filter then absorbs any odors and cleaned air blows out the other end.

How an electrostatic precipitator works

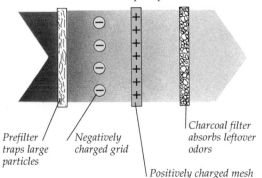

*Prefilter
traps large
particles*

*Negatively
charged grid*

*Charcoal filter
absorbs leftover
odors*

Positively charged mesh

A flow of charge

In 1780, while Italian anatomist Luigi Galvani (1737-1798) was dissecting and studying a frog, he noticed that when his sharp scalpel touched the nerves in the frog's leg, the leg twitched. Galvani suspected that there was electricity in the frog's muscles, and experimented to explain what he had seen. Soon another Italian, Alessandro Volta (1745-1827), heard of the incident. Volta disagreed with Galvani's ideas. He had already developed a device for producing small amounts of electric charge – the electrophorus. In 1800 he announced that he had found a new source of electricity, one which produced electricity continuously (unlike the Leyden jar, which discharged instantly). It became known as the voltaic pile. Galvani thought electricity came from animals' bodies when touched by two metals, calling it "animal electricity." Volta thought it came from contact between metals only; he called it "metallic electricity." Galvani and Volta disagreed strongly, and they and their supporters argued for years. We now know that neither was totally correct.

Galvani's laboratory

THE VOLTAIC PILE
This device used two different metals, separated by moist chemicals, to produce a flow of electric charge. The original voltaic pile used three types of disc: zinc, pasteboard or leather, and copper. The pasteboard was soaked in a solution of salt or weak acid such as vinegar. In an electrochemical reaction, the copper loses electrons to the solution and the zinc gains electrons from the solution. At the same time, zinc dissolves and hydrogen gas is produced at the surface of the copper. When the charge flows away along wires, the chemicals separate out more charge. And so electric charge continues to flow. Volta had invented the earliest electric cell. He piled up many of these cells or three-disc units to strengthen the effect. In this way he produced the first battery, which is a collection of cells (pp. 264-265).

Voltaic pile

Glass supporting rod

Copper disc

Zinc disc

Pasteboard disc

Wooden base

LUIGI GALVANI
Galvani studied the effects of electric charge from Leyden jars and electrostatic machines on animals. In a number of ways Galvani brought animal tissue into contact with two metals in his laboratory (above). He noticed convulsions in the limbs of the dead animals. Chemicals in the nerves and muscles, when placed between the metals, had caused an electrochemical reaction, making an electric cell.

Luigi Galvani

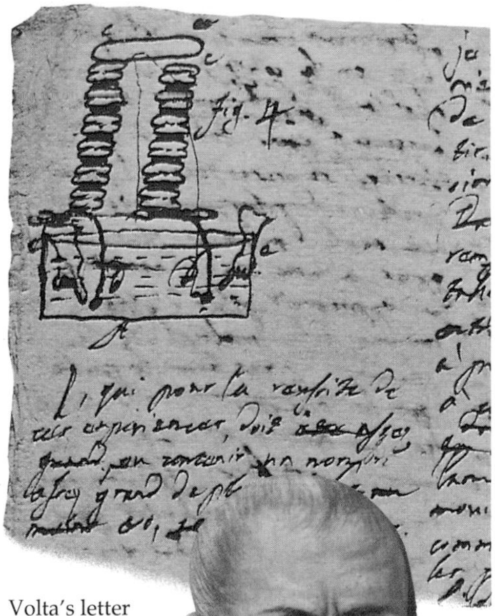

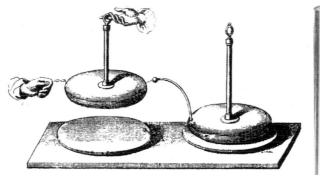

Volta's letter
to the Royal
Society (1800)

Alessandro
Volta

THE ELECTROPHORUS
Volta invented the electrophorus in 1775. It consisted of a metal plate, which could be charged, placed on an insulated base. With a handle, which was also made from an insulating material, the electrophorous could be used as a portable carrier of electric charge, to transfer charge to another apparatus, or further charge a Leyden jar. The process of charging and discharging the electrophorus could be repeated many times.

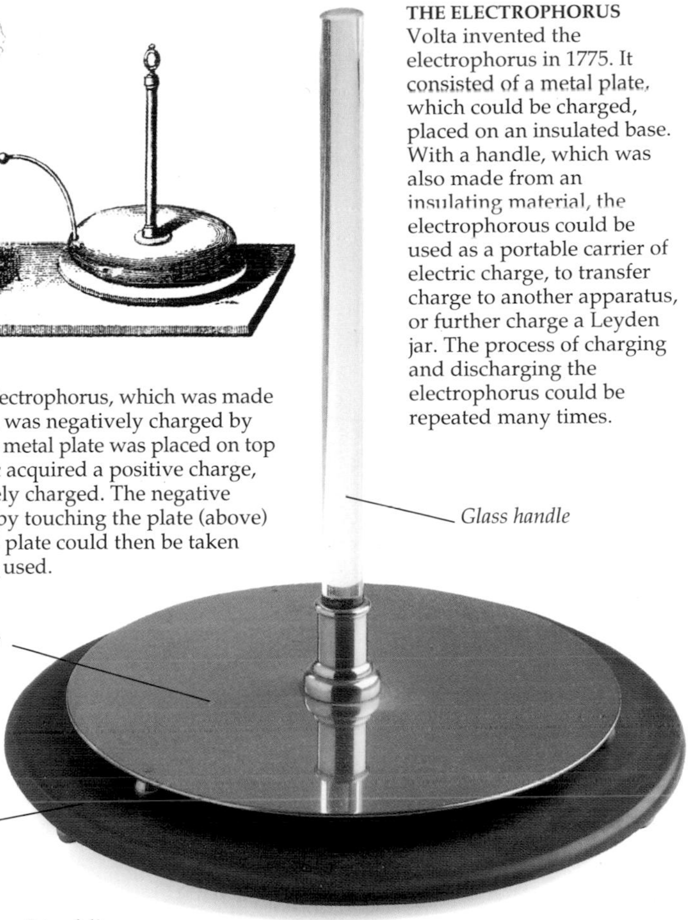

STORING CHARGE
The insulated base of the electrophorus, which was made from a resinous substance, was negatively charged by rubbing it so that when the metal plate was placed on top of it, the bottom of the disc acquired a positive charge, while the top was negatively charged. The negative charge was drained away by touching the plate (above) and the positively charged plate could then be taken away, and the charge on it used.

Glass handle

Brass disc carries the charge

Ebonite base which can be charged

ALESSANDRO VOLTA
On 20 March 1800 Volta sketched a U-shaped voltaic pile in a letter to Sir Joseph Banks, president of the Royal Society of London. The pile was the first practical battery. The modern unit of electric potential, which is the strength or "electric push" of the flowing charge, is the volt, named in honor of Volta. his apparatus produced just over one volt for every set of discs. The electric ray can send a 100-volt shock through the water. A modern house circuit carries 110 or 220 volts and high-voltage power lines carry up to half a million volts or more.

Sets of discs

Insulated wire

Wire inserted under disc

Components of a voltaic cell

Zinc disc

Salt-soaked pasteboard disc

Copper disc

Copper disc

Zinc disc

WIRING UP THE BATTERY
To connect up the voltaic pile to a piece of equipment, two insulated copper wires were attached to sets of discs. With 24 sets of discs this battery produced about 24 volts, which Volta detected with the tip of his tongue on the connecting wires.

Electricity from chemicals

RESEARCHERS FOUND THAT THE SIMPLEST electricity-making unit, or electric cell, was two plates of different metals in a jar filled with liquid. The metal plates are called electrodes. They are conductors through which electricity can enter or leave. The positive electrode is called the anode and the negative electrode is called the cathode. The liquid, which must be able to conduct electricity, is called the electrolyte. Several cells joined together form a battery. There have been many types and sizes of cells and batteries. Some of them used strong acids or other noxious chemicals as the electrolyte. The first batteries supplied electricity for research, in the laboratory. Large numbers of batteries were used for electric telegraphs. An important advance was the "dry" cell, a development of the Leclanché cell (below), which uses a jellylike paste instead of liquid. More recent advances include alkaline and other long-life cells.

Terminal

Leclanché cell

Carbon rod

Zinc cathode

Glass jar

Zinc rod

Electrolyte in jar – ammonium chloride solution

Corrosion-resistant glass container

Central part of Leclanché cell

Terminal

Carbon rod

Manganese dioxide and carbon granules

THE CELL AT WORK
A basic electrical cell has copper and zinc plates immersed in sulfuric acid. When the plates are connected by a conducting wire, chemical reactions occur. Hydrogen gas is given off at the copper plate, which loses electrons to the solution, becoming positively charged. Zinc dissolves from the zinc plate, leaving behind electrons which make the plate negative. The electrons move through the wire from the zinc plate towards the copper. This constitutes the electric current which continues until the zinc is eaten away or the acid used up.

LECLANCHE CELL
During the 1860s French chemist Georges Leclanché (1838-1882) devised a cell in which one electrode was a zinc rod, and the other was a carbon rod inside a pot of manganese dioxide and carbon granules. Between was a solution of ammonium chloride. The cell produced about 1.5 volts. It did not contain dangerous acid, and it soon became a popular and relatively portable electricity-maker, and the forerunner of the flashlight battery.

MASSIVE BATTERY
Humphry Davy (1778-1829) was professor at London's Royal Institution. In 1807 he used a roomful of batteries, some 2,000 cells in all, to make enough electricity to produce pure potassium metal by the process of electrolysis.

HIGH-TENSION BATTERY
This 1920s lead-acid storage battery was used to provide electricity for a domestic radio set. "High tension" means that the electricity had a high pressure, that is, a large voltage. Each glass jar contained two lead plates and the electrolyte – dilute sulfuric acid. The battery was recharged at the local garage, where batteries used in the new and popular automobiles were maintained, by being connected to an electricity supply to reverse the chemical reaction. It was then topped up with water to compensate for any water loss through evaporation.

Copper anode

Wire carries electric current

Wooden case

High-tension battery without lid

Glass containers – each one a single cell

Sulfuric acid

Connecting bars

Swinging bar lifts electrodes up when battery not in use

PORTABLE LIGHT TO READ BY
A safe, portable battery, combined with the electric light bulb, supplied light wherever it was needed. This late 19th-century train traveler reads with the battery in the bag by his side.

Hydrogen gas

1940s car battery

Sealed top-up hole

Terminal

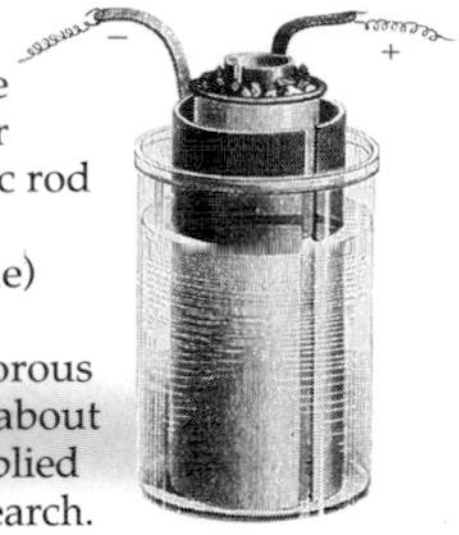

THE CAR BATTERY
These rechargeable lead-acid batteries are known as storage batteries. Each cell consists of two lead plates, or electrodes, separated by sulfuric acid. As the battery is charged, lead oxide forms on one of the plates, storing the incoming electrical energy in chemical form.

DANIELL CELL
English professor John Daniell (1790-1845) developed a simple cell in 1836 that provided current for a longer period. His cell (right) had a copper cylinder as the positive electrode (anode) in copper sulfate, and a zinc rod as the negative electrode (cathode) in sulfuric acid, separated by a porous pot. It produced about one volt and supplied electricity for research.

Sulfuric acid fills void

Cell divider

Lead oxide plate

Lead metal plate

Circuits and conductors

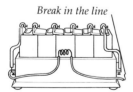

HENRY CAVENDISH
Forgetful and reclusive, Cavendish (1731-1810) was a great experimenter. His electrical research was wide ranging, and like other scientists of the time he assessed the intensity of electricity by how severely he was shocked by it. One of Cavendish's theories was the idea of electric potential or voltage to explain how the "push" of the electricity was produced.

As SCIENTISTS EXPERIMENTED with batteries, they discovered that some substances let electric charge pass through them without difficulty, while others would not. The former were called conductors, and the latter insulators. But why do some substances conduct? It is because all matter is made of atoms. An atom, in turn, is made of particles called electrons orbiting around a central nucleus. Each electron has a negative charge, and the nucleus has balancing positive charges. An electric current occurs when the electrons move. Certain substances, especially metals, have electrons that are not tightly held to their nuclei. These "free electrons" are more mobile, and they can be set in one-way motion easily, to produce an electric current.

INSIDE A CONDUCTOR
Metals are good conductors. In a good conductor, each atom has one or more free electrons. The nucleus cannot hold on to them strongly, and they can move within the conductors. Normally this happens at random, and there is no overall one-way flow of electrons. But if there is a difference in voltage between one end of the conductor and the other, the negative electrons are attracted to the positive end and so the current flows.

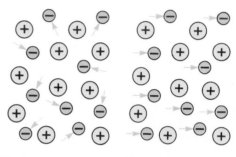

Electrons move at random

Flow of electrons producing current

MAKING A CIRCUIT
A cell or battery on its own does not produce an electric current. Electrons flow only if they have somewhere to go, and if a voltage pushes them. When conductors link one terminal of a battery to the other, a current flows. This series of conductors is a circuit. In an open or broken circuit, there is a break along the line, and the current stops. In a closed or complete circuit (right), the electrons flow from the negative side of the battery to the positive side. They can then do work, such as producing light.

Open circuit

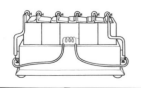

Break in the line

Closed circuit

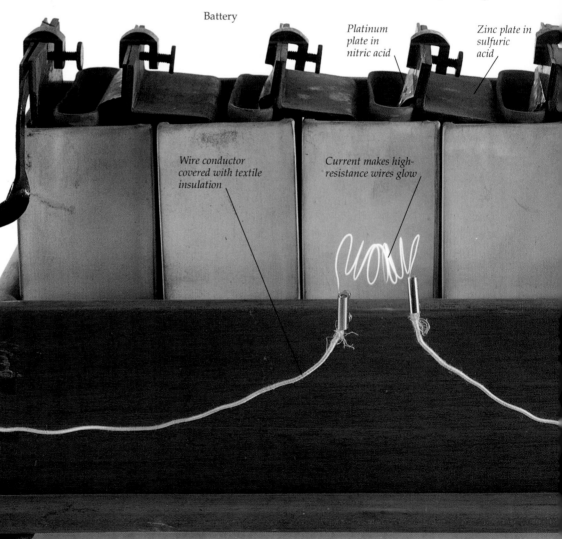

Battery

Platinum plate in nitric acid

Zinc plate in sulfuric acid

Wire conductor covered with textile insulation

Current makes high-resistance wires glow

Carrying current

Early experiments on conductors and insulators showed that most metals were good at carrying current. Soon wires of iron or, even better, copper and silver were being used in electrical research. Some forms of carbon, such as graphite (the "lead" in a pencil) and charcoal were also conductors. So was any watery substance, from solutions of acids and salts, to parts of vegetables and animals. Insulators tended to be woody, fibrous, or made of minerals. An early list of insulators included leather, parchment, ashes, chalk, hair, porcelain, feathers, precious stones, dried vegetables, resin, and amber.

A good conductor

A poor conductor

Charcoal conducts the charge away rapidly

Wool conducts the charge away very slowly

TESTING CONDUCTORS

An electroscope can show whether a substance was a conductor or an insulator. It was charged from a Leyden jar or electrostatic generator so that its two gold leaves repelled each other and moved apart. Then the test substance was held in the hand, against the metal cap. If the substance was a good conductor, it conducted the charge away from the electroscope, to the body and then into the ground. The leaves would lose their charge and flop back down. The speed with which they came to rest together showed how fast their charge was being conducted away, and so indicated the efficiency of the conductor.

Gold leaves lose their charge and close together

Porous pot

Gold leaves keep their charge and repel each other

INSULATING PLUGS

For safety's sake, the outside of a plug must be well insulated from the conducting metal prongs inside. Bodies of early plugs were made of wood and porcelain. Bakelite, a synthetic resin and a good insulator, came into use in the 1910s.

Bakelite body (1930)

Wooden body (1915)

Porcelain body (1920)

WEATHERPROOF INSULATION

High-voltage power lines must be well insulated or the electricity may force its way through a poor insulator or spark across a gap. Porous materials like wood are not used because they can absorb moisture. Nonporous substances such as ceramics and glass are shaped to keep rain, dew, and other moisture from creating a circuit into the ground.

Early porcelain insulator on a telegraph pole

Ceramic insulator (1956)

Toughened glass suspension insulator (1956)

Aluminum power line

Resisting electricity

IN A SERIES OF EXPERIMENTS around 1825, the German scientist Georg Ohm (1787-1854) demonstrated that there were no perfect electrical conductors. Each type of substance, even the best metals, put up some resistance to the current. Ohm showed that a long wire had more resistance than a short one of the same metal, and thin wires had more resistance than fat ones. Also, in a circuit, the greater the resistance, the more potential difference (volts) was needed to push the current through the wire. The relationships between potential difference, current, and resistance became known as Ohm's law.

ADJUSTABLE RESISTANCE

Scientists needing to vary the current in a circuit developed adjustable resistors, or rheostats. (Their uses today include dimmer switches.) One simple design used special resistance wire, made from a combination of metals, such as nickel and copper. This put up some resistance to the current, but not too much. A long piece of the resistance wire was wound as a coil on an insulating tube. This was more convenient than having it stretched out straight. The wire touched a contact that slid along the top. Electricity from a battery came in through one terminal, then into the resistance coil. As the contact slid one way, the electricity went through more resistance wire, so the rheostat's resistance rose. As the contact moved the other way, its resistance fell.

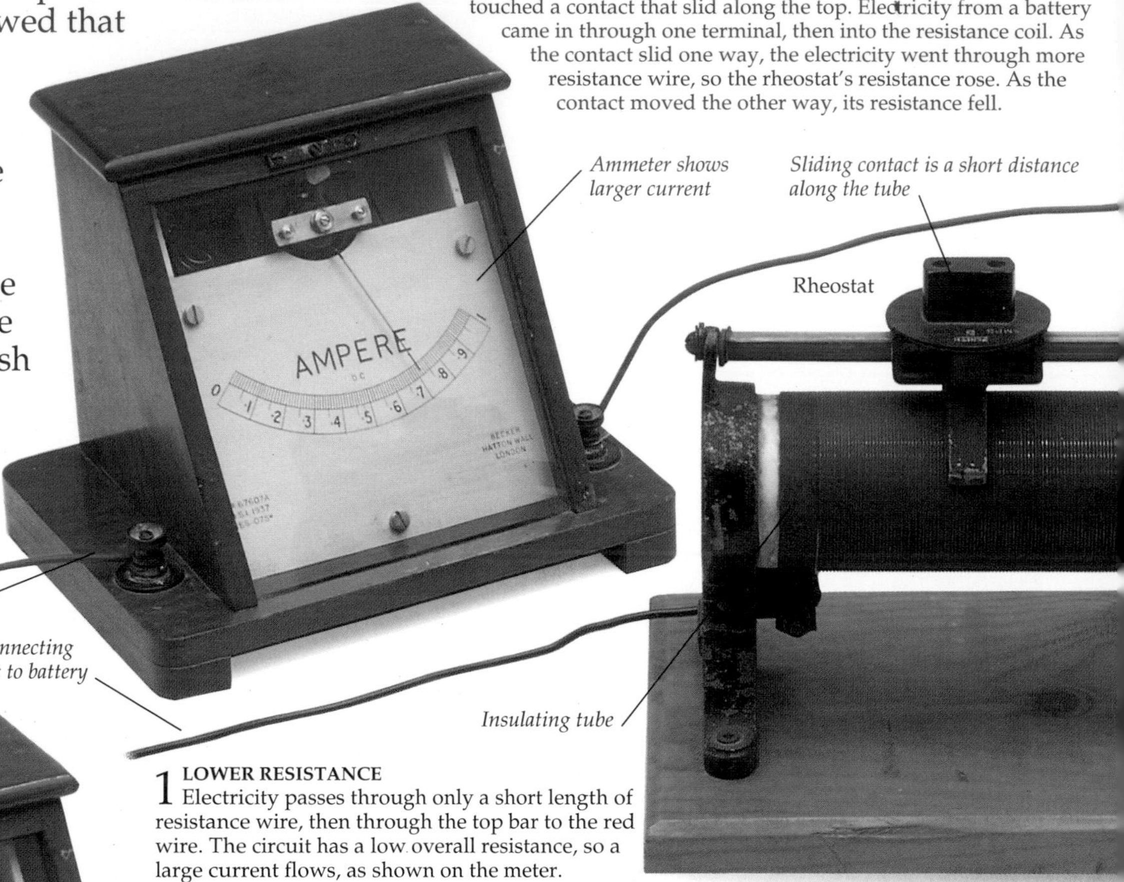

Ammeter shows larger current

Sliding contact is a short distance along the tube

Rheostat

Wire to battery

Wire connecting rheostat to battery

Ammeter

Insulating tube

1 LOWER RESISTANCE

Electricity passes through only a short length of resistance wire, then through the top bar to the red wire. The circuit has a low overall resistance, so a large current flows, as shown on the meter.

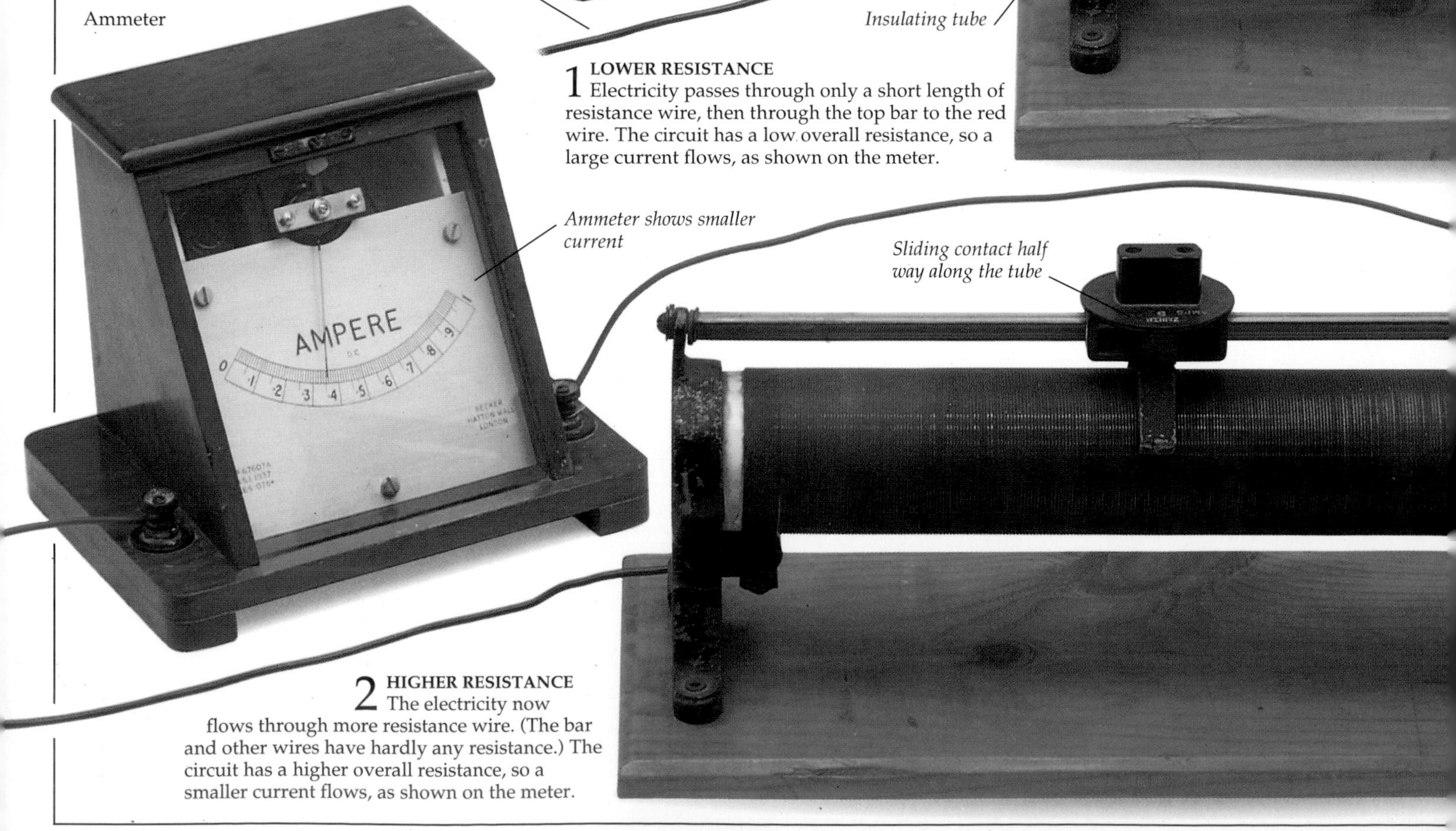

Ammeter shows smaller current

Sliding contact half way along the tube

2 HIGHER RESISTANCE

The electricity now flows through more resistance wire. (The bar and other wires have hardly any resistance.) The circuit has a higher overall resistance, so a smaller current flows, as shown on the meter.

Georg Ohm

Ohm's practical experiments showed the mathematical links between resistance, potential difference, and current. Ohm's law of 1826 states that provided the temperature does not change, the current flowing through certain conductors is proportional to the potential difference (voltage) across it. This is written as I (current) = V (voltage) divided by R (resistance) and is now a cornerstone of electric circuit design.

Coiled resistance wire

Metal bar

OHM'S APPARATUS
To test his theory, Ohm used a thermocouple (below), which produced a small voltage when there was a temperature difference between the junctions of two metals. To measure the current through the wire under test, he used a torsion balance similar to the one used by Coulomb (p. 257). In this reconstruction of his apparatus, he measured the deflection of the magnetized needle.

Torsion head twists to bring magnetic needle back to zero

Suspension wire

Magnetized needle turned by current in copper bar

Cold junction of thermocouple

Hot junction of thermocouple

Magnifying glass to detect swing of the needle

Copper bar

Bismuth bar

Cups of mercury into which ends of resistor are dipped

Container for ice

Boiler producing steam

THE SEARCH FOR BETTER CONDUCTORS
With a knowledge of resistance, engineers could improve the design of long-distance electrical and communication cables. Better conductors surrounded by better insulators would carry higher currents farther, without expensive loss of electricity. Copper was the preferred conductor. After silver, it has the lowest resistance; it does not rust or corrode like iron or steel; and it is easily drawn out into a wire.

Power cable (20th century)

STANDARD RESISTOR
After Ohm's work revealed the importance of resistance, standard resistors like this were made. It was connected up in an electric circuit and measurements were made to calculate the resistance using Ohm's law. In 1861 the British Association Standards Committee was set up to determine the most convenient unit for resistance. It was adopted in 1865. Later, it was named "ohm" with the symbol Ω.

Brass casing for resistance wire

Copper connecting leads

Wooden storage box

Copper cores

Flexible lead sheath

Paper insulation

Telegraph cable (1837)

Resin

Wood

Copper cores

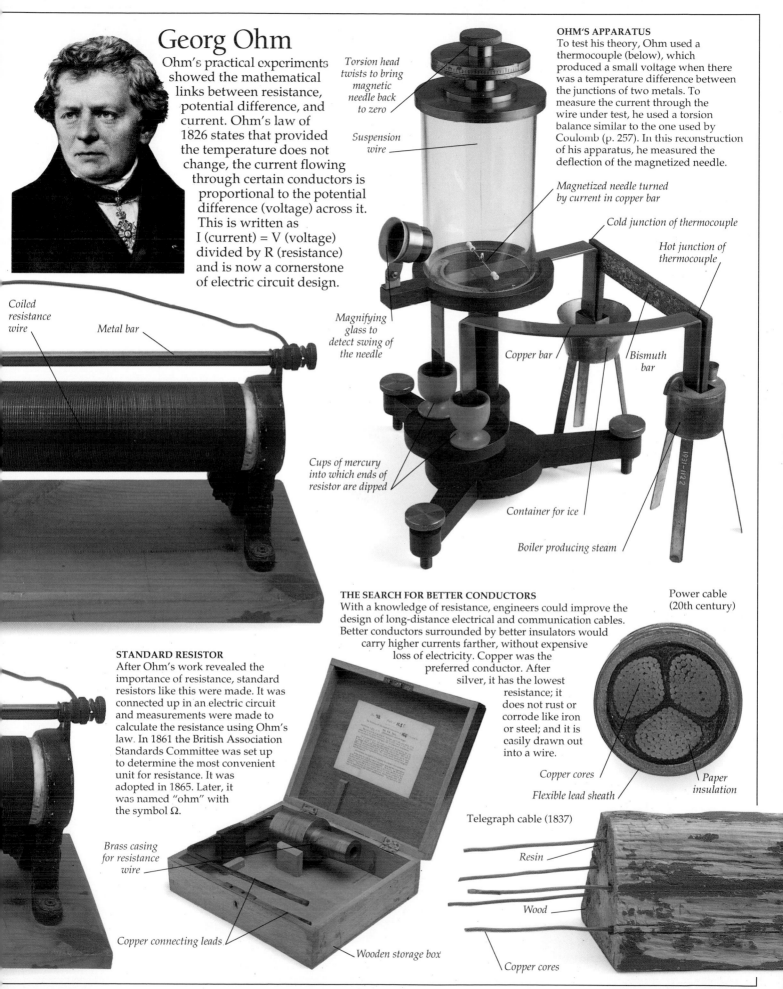

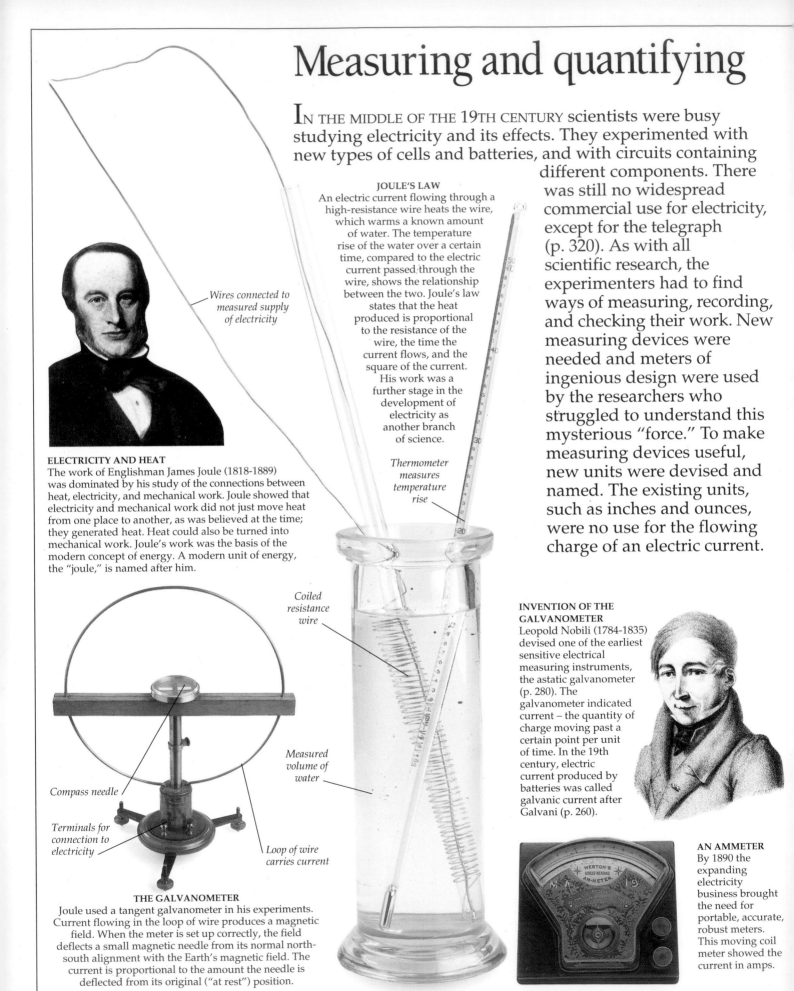

Measuring and quantifying

IN THE MIDDLE OF THE 19TH CENTURY scientists were busy studying electricity and its effects. They experimented with new types of cells and batteries, and with circuits containing different components. There was still no widespread commercial use for electricity, except for the telegraph (p. 320). As with all scientific research, the experimenters had to find ways of measuring, recording, and checking their work. New measuring devices were needed and meters of ingenious design were used by the researchers who struggled to understand this mysterious "force." To make measuring devices useful, new units were devised and named. The existing units, such as inches and ounces, were no use for the flowing charge of an electric current.

JOULE'S LAW
An electric current flowing through a high-resistance wire heats the wire, which warms a known amount of water. The temperature rise of the water over a certain time, compared to the electric current passed through the wire, shows the relationship between the two. Joule's law states that the heat produced is proportional to the resistance of the wire, the time the current flows, and the square of the current. His work was a further stage in the development of electricity as another branch of science.

Wires connected to measured supply of electricity

Thermometer measures temperature rise

ELECTRICITY AND HEAT
The work of Englishman James Joule (1818-1889) was dominated by his study of the connections between heat, electricity, and mechanical work. Joule showed that electricity and mechanical work did not just move heat from one place to another, as was believed at the time; they generated heat. Heat could also be turned into mechanical work. Joule's work was the basis of the modern concept of energy. A modern unit of energy, the "joule," is named after him.

Coiled resistance wire

Measured volume of water

Compass needle

Terminals for connection to electricity

Loop of wire carries current

THE GALVANOMETER
Joule used a tangent galvanometer in his experiments. Current flowing in the loop of wire produces a magnetic field. When the meter is set up correctly, the field deflects a small magnetic needle from its normal north-south alignment with the Earth's magnetic field. The current is proportional to the amount the needle is deflected from its original ("at rest") position.

INVENTION OF THE GALVANOMETER
Leopold Nobili (1784-1835) devised one of the earliest sensitive electrical measuring instruments, the astatic galvanometer (p. 280). The galvanometer indicated current – the quantity of charge moving past a certain point per unit of time. In the 19th century, electric current produced by batteries was called galvanic current after Galvani (p. 260).

AN AMMETER
By 1890 the expanding electricity business brought the need for portable, accurate, robust meters. This moving coil meter showed the current in amps.

Flowing currents

Electricity has been likened to a fluid flowing unseen from place to place. Some of the words used to describe electricity, such as "current" and "flow," relate to these notions. The comparison between electricity passing along wires and water flowing through pipes is not an exact parallel, but it can help to explain some of electricity's stranger properties by making them more physical and familiar.

WATER ANALOGY
The rate of water flow (the volume passing a certain point in a given time) is similar to the current in an electric circuit, measured in amps. The pressure, or pushing force, of the water can be thought of as the potential difference in an electric circuit, measured in volts. A narrower pipe resists water flow, as thin wire in a circuit resists the flow of electricity.

Flow meter shows two units of flow in this part of the circuit, where the water flow is slowed down because it had to turn the propeller

THE PROPELLER
The propeller turns when the water flows by it. It resists the flow of water and this results in a slower flow, and a reduction in the number of units shown on the meter.

Propeller

Flow meter shows one unit of flow in this part of the circuit, where there is resistance to flow set up by the long, thin pipe

RESISTANCE TO FLOW
Certain factors set up a resistance to flow. The propeller and the coils of tubing do this in the circuit shown here. The flow meters show less flow or current in their branches of the circuit, but the flows add up to the total flow from the pump. In electricity, resistance to the current could be provided by an electric motor or a conducting wire.

METERS
Meters show the units of flow in the pipes, and they register how these units are shared between the parallel pipes in the circuit. In electricity these would be ammeters, measuring the current in amps.

POWER SOURCE
The pump represents the battery or other electricity source which provides the "pushing power," or pressure, to force the water through the pipes. In electricity this is measured by the voltage.

A resistance coil is made up of a long length of thin piping wound into a coil to make it more manageable in the circuit

Flow meter shows three units of flow as the water is pushed around the circuit by the pump

Pump provides the pushing power

Water flows in a counter-clockwise direction

THE INTERNATIONAL VISUAL LANGUAGE OF ELECTRICITY

It would be time consuming if all the information about electricity was written out in full. Symbols are used as an international visual language that is understood by electrical engineers, circuit designers, and teachers.

A = ampere/amp	**J** = joule
AC = alternating current	**KWH** = kilowatt-hour
C = coulomb	**p.d.** = potential difference
DC = direct current	**V** = volt
emf = electromotive force	**W** = watt
F = farad	**Ω** = ohm
H = henry	

AC supply	relay
ammeter	resistor
battery	switch
cell	transformer
fuse	voltmeter

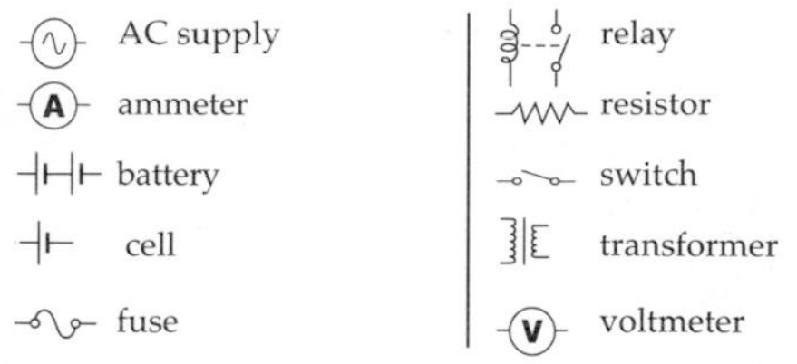

Magnetism from electricity

WITH THE DEVELOPMENT OF VOLTA'S BATTERY IN 1800, scientists had a source of steadily flowing electric current. This opened up new fields of research. Twenty years later an observation by Hans Christian Oersted (1777-1851) from Copenhagen began to link the two great scientific mysteries of the age: electricity and magnetism. Oersted noticed that a metal wire carrying a current affected a magnetic compass needle that was brought near to it. This revelation, which contradicted the orthodox philosophy of the time, was published in scientific journals. French scientific thinker André-Marie Ampère (1775-1836) heard about Oersted's work from a fellow scientist. He doubted it at first, so he repeated the tests, but had similar results. Ampère therefore set to work to describe the effect more fully and to explain the connection between electricity and magnetism. In repeating the experiments, he provided a theoretical and mathematical description of the practical results of Oersted's work. From this flowed discoveries such as the electromagnet and the telegraph receiver.

Overſigt
over
det Kongelige Danſke Videnſkabernes Selſkabs
Forhandlinger
fra Mai 1820 til Mai 1821.

Af
Profeſſor H. C. Ørsted,
Ridder af Dannebrogen, Selſkabets Secretair.

I ſidſte Forſamlingsaar har Selſkabet optaget:
Til indenlandſke Medlemmer:
Herr Profeſſor og Ridder Rahbek, for den hiſtoriſke Claſſe.
Herr Juſtitsraad og Profeſſor Werlauff, for ſamme Claſſe.
Herr Profeſſor Reinhardt, for den phyſiſke Claſſe.
Til udenlandſke Medlemmer:
Herr Profeſſor Henrik Steffens, for den philoſophiſke Claſſe.
Sir Humphry Davy, Præſident for det Kongelige Videnſkabernes Selſkab i London, for den phyſiſke Claſſe.
Herr Kammerherre v. Buch i Berlin, for den ſamme Claſſe.
Herr Hofraad, Profeſſor og Ridder Gauss i Göttingen, for den mathematiſke Claſſe.
A

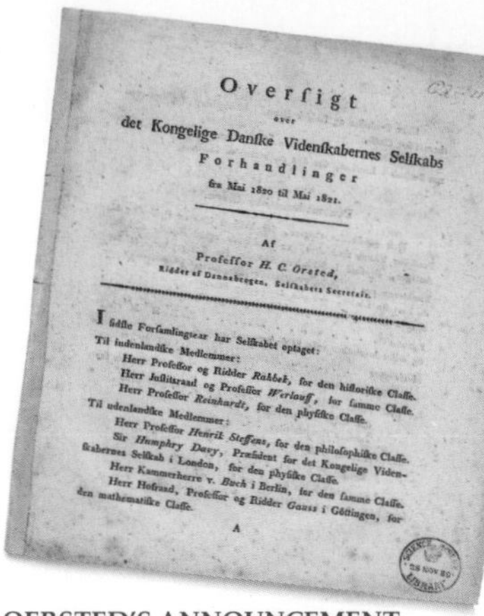

OERSTED'S ANNOUNCEMENT
Oersted published his discovery of the interaction between electricity and magnetism on July 21, 1820. The pamphlet was written in Latin but was translated into various languages including his own, Danish. Michael Faraday (pp. 34-35) would probably have heard about the discovery in this way.

Current off

With no current in the wire, the filings lie haphazardly

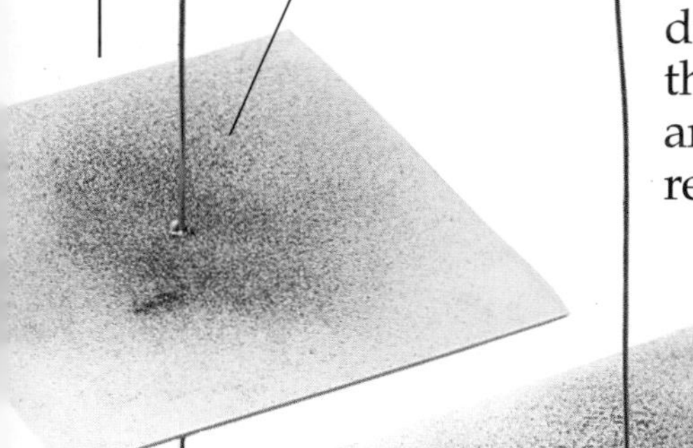

Current on

Filings line up indicating circular magnetic field

Wooden clamp
Current-carrying wire
Dilute acid between plates
Battery
Battery terminal

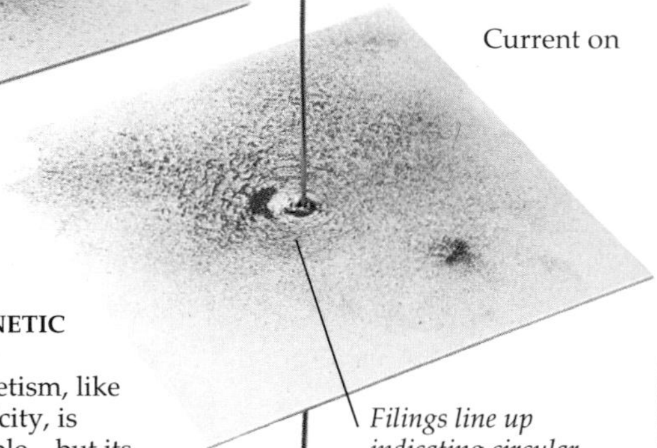

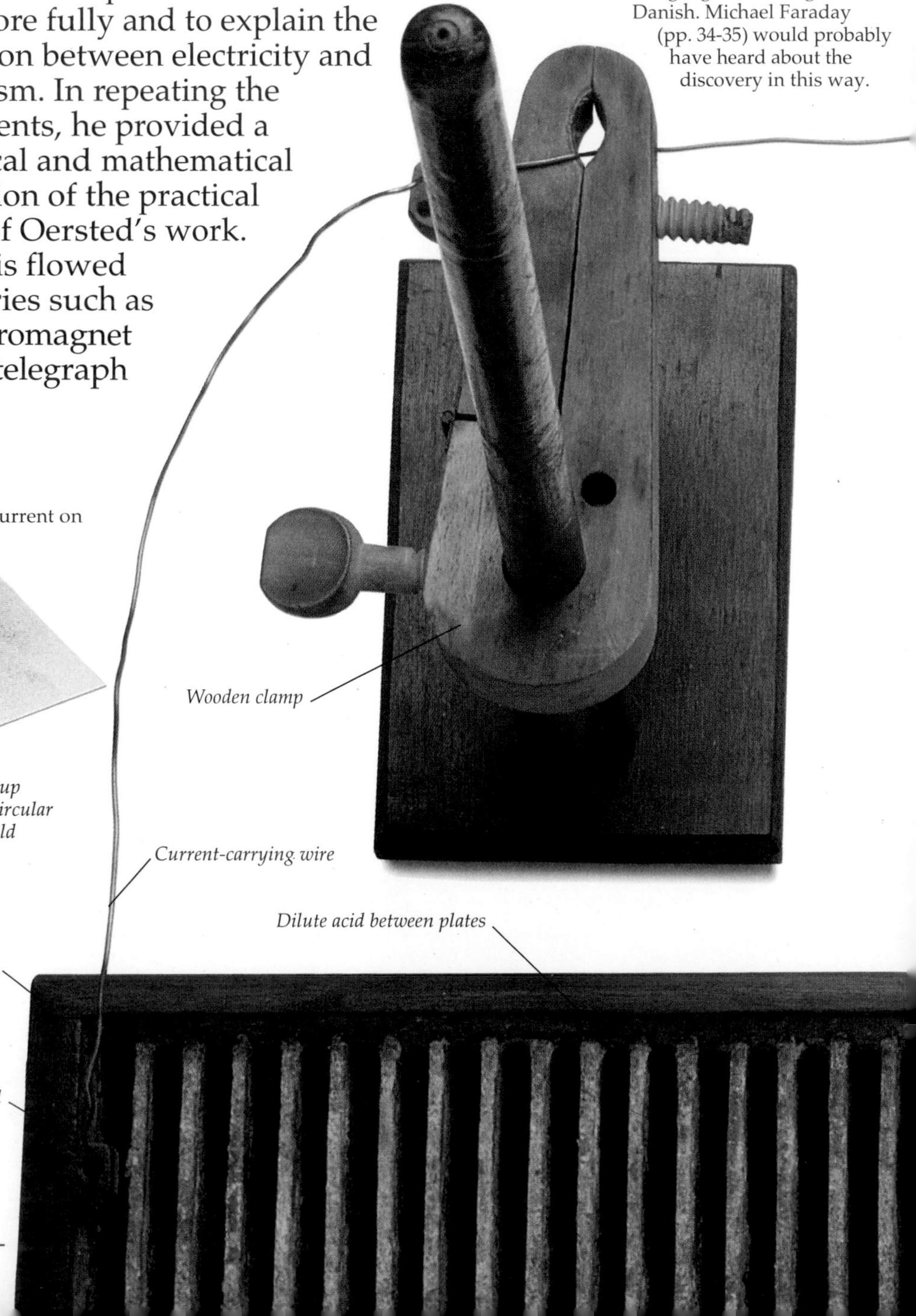

THE MAGNETIC FIELD
Magnetism, like electricity, is invisible – but its effects can be seen. Iron-containing substances such as iron filings are attracted to an ordinary bar magnet, and they line up to indicate the direction of the invisible "lines of force" of the magnetic field. An electric current also creates a magnetic field. With no current in the wire, the filings lie randomly on the card. Switch the current on, tap the card, and the filings line up to reveal a circular magnetic field around the wire.

AMPÈRE'S ACHIEVEMENT

Ampère developed the science of electrodynamics. He proved that the strength of the magnetic field around a wire, shown by the amount of the compass needle's deflection, rises with increasing current, and decreases with the distance away from the wire. Ampère extended Oersted's work, but he could not see a clear relationship between the needle's movements and the position of the wire. Then he realized that the direction in which the needle settled depended on the earth's magnetic field as well as the magnetic field produced by the current. He devised a way of neutralizing the earth's magnetic field and found that the needle then settled in the direction of the magnetic field produced by the current and not with the earth's north-south magnetic field. Ampère also found that two parallel electric currents had an effect on each other. If the currents run in the same direction, they attract each other; if they run in opposite directions, they repel each other. To commemorate Ampère's achievements, the modern unit of current – the ampere (shortened to "amp") – was named after him.

André-Marie Ampère

Thumb points in the direction of movement

First finger points in the direction of the magnetic field

Second finger indicates flow of current

THE LEFT-HAND RULE

When an electric current crosses a magnetic field, then the magnetic field, the current, and the force on the current – and thus the movement of the wire carrying the current, if it can move (p. 284) – are all in different directions. A current-carrying wire or other conductor in a magnetic field tries to move according to this handy rule: With the thumb and first two fingers of the left hand at right angles to each other, the first finger shows the direction of the magnetic field (points from the north pole to the south pole of the magnet); the second finger shows the flow of the electric current (points from positive to negative); and the thumb shows the movement of the wire.

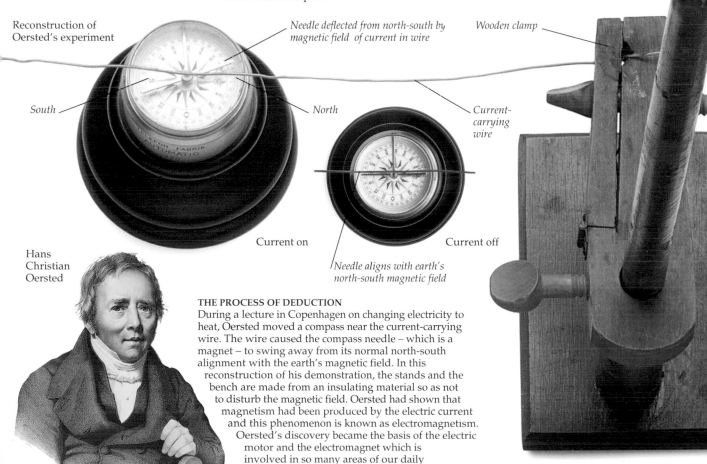

Reconstruction of Oersted's experiment

Needle deflected from north-south by magnetic field of current in wire

Wooden clamp

South

North

Current-carrying wire

Current on

Current off

Hans Christian Oersted

Needle aligns with earth's north-south magnetic field

THE PROCESS OF DEDUCTION

During a lecture in Copenhagen on changing electricity to heat, Oersted moved a compass near the current-carrying wire. The wire caused the compass needle – which is a magnet – to swing away from its normal north-south alignment with the earth's magnetic field. In this reconstruction of his demonstration, the stands and the bench are made from an insulating material so as not to disturb the magnetic field. Oersted had shown that magnetism had been produced by the electric current and this phenomenon is known as electromagnetism. Oersted's discovery became the basis of the electric motor and the electromagnet which is involved in so many areas of our daily lives from the telephone to the starting of a car.

Plates of copper and zinc soldered back-to-back and cemented into wooden trough

Electromagnets

THE DISCOVERY OF a magnetic field around a current-carrying wire, and the fact that a coil of wire had a greater magnetic effect than a single turn, led to a fascinating new gadget that made lecture audiences gasp with surprise. In 1825 William Sturgeon (1783-1850) wound a coil of wire around an iron rod and built one of the first electromagnets. An electromagnet differs from the usual permanent magnet – its magnetism can be turned on and off. It usually consists of insulated electrical wire wound around a piece of iron, known as the core. Switch on the current, and the magnetic field around the wire makes the core behave like a magnet. It attracts iron-containing substances in the usual way. Switch off the electricity, and the magnetism disappears. Sturgeon built the electromagnets as demonstration models for his lectures.

ELECTROMAGNETIC CHAIR
A chair was a convenient base for this great horseshoe electromagnet of Michael Faraday (p. 280). It was used to investigate the effects of magnetism.

Electromagnet with current off

Positive terminal to source of current

Negative terminal to source of current

Horseshoe-shaped core of soft iron

Wire connecting the two coils

Copper wire insulated with lacquer

With current off, there is no magnetism

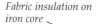

Fabric insulation on iron core

Coil of wire

Sturgeon's electromagnet

Iron core

End connected to battery

End connected to battery

STURGEON'S ELECTROMAGNET
Sturgeon was a craftsman and instrument maker who published catalogues of his electromagnetic apparatus (left). He enjoyed the practical "how-to" side of science, but had less concern for theories about why things happened. His electromagnet (above) depended on current passing through a coil of wire, to create an appreciable magnetic field. In his time, wires were made bare and uninsulated. (Later electromagnets had insulated wire.) He insulated the iron core to stop the electricity passing straight along it instead. The turns of the coil were also spaced apart, to prevent the current jumping straight from one to the next where they touched – short circuiting.

INVISIBLE LIFTING POWER
This modern electromagnet demonstrates its strength by attracting a loose pile of iron filings when the current is switched on. In a bar-shaped electromagnet, one end of the core becomes the north pole and the other is the south pole, depending on the current's direction of flow. This horseshoe-shaped core has two coils for a stronger magnetic field between its ends (bringing the poles closer together makes the magnet more powerful). Sturgeon made an initial discovery that soft iron was a good metal for the core, since it became magnetized more easily than steel. In the early days, there were races to build the biggest electromagnets and lift the heaviest weights. By the late 1820s electromagnets in Europe could lift around 11 lb (5 kg). In the United States, Joseph Henry realized that more turns in the coil produced a stronger magnetic field (up to a limit). It is said that he made insulated wire by wrapping bare wire with strips of silk from his wife's clothes. He could then pack more turns of wire into a smaller space, without the risk of short-circuit. The greater the current, the more powerful was the magnetic field. Henry's large electromagnet (above right) lifted about 750 lb (340 kg).

Iron filings

Electromagnet with current on

Positive terminal to source of current

Negative terminal to source of current

Horseshoe-shaped core of soft iron

Wire connecting the two coils

Copper wire insulated with lacquer

Force of magnetic field overcomes gravity and lifts iron filings

Henry's electromagnet

Nonmagnetic stand

Iron core

Several layers of insulated wire

Zinc plate

Copper plate

Wooden base

JOSPEH HENRY
Henry (1797-1978) was an engineer whose inventive genius led him to improve electromagnets, for example by wrapping a second coil of wire around the first. In this small electromagnet (left), the two metal plates of copper and zinc were immersed in a jar of dilute acid. This formed a voltaic cell that produced the electric current.
The wire was wrapped in insulating fabric, so that the coil's turns could be close together for a stronger magnetic field. Henry also developed an early form of telegraph in 1831, although others made fame and fortune from it (pp. 302-303), and some of his work with electromagnetism induction paralleled that of Faraday.

HENRY'S LIFTING RIG
This type of apparatus was used to measure the lifting power of electromagnets made to different designs, from various metals, and with different numbers and arrangements of windings.

ELECTROMAGNETS AT WORK
The lifting power of modern electromagnets is used to separate iron-containing, or ferrous, metals from other materials at the junkyard before recycling.

Electromagnets at work

Since the time of Sturgeon and Henry, electromagnets have been central components in electrical machines. Their power to attract and hold iron-containing materials, for example, when sorting out steel cans from aluminum ones at the recycling center, is not their only use. An electromagnet is a convenient way of turning electrical energy into rotary motion, using the forces of magnetic attraction and repulsion in electric motors. The reverse occurs in generators. Electricity is converted into push-pull movements by electromagnetic relays and solenoids. The movements operate mechanical devices, such as telegraph receivers. Electro-magentism is also used in electrical transformers and to manipulate atoms in particle accelerators.

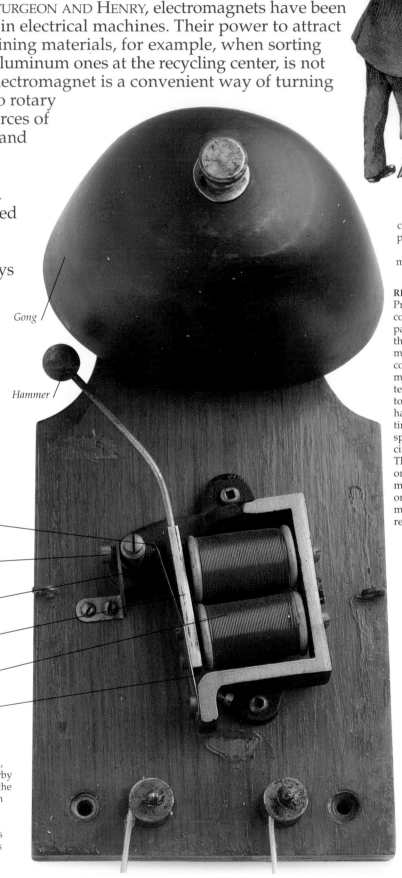

Gong

Hammer

Contact points

Contact-adjusting brass screw

Steel contact spring

Soft iron armature

Electromagnet

Spring mounting for armature

SAVING SIGHT
A finely controlled electromagnet could remove iron-containing foreign particles from the tissues of the eye. It pulled fragments straight out, minimizing the risk of further damage.

RINGING A BELL
Pressing the button of this doorbell completes a circuit in which the current passes into one terminal of the doorbell, then through the coils of the electromagnets, along the springy steel contact, into the brass screw and its mounting, and out through the other terminal. As the armature is pulled towards the electromagnets, the hammer hits the gong. At the same time, a gap opens between the contact spring and the screw, which breaks the circuit and switches off the electricity. The magnetism disappears, the spring on which the armature is mounted moves the armature back into its original position, the contacts touch and make the circuit again. The process is repeated until the button is released.

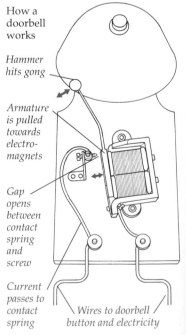

How a doorbell works

Hammer hits gong

Armature is pulled towards electro-magnets

Gap opens between contact spring and screw

Current passes to contact spring

Wires to doorbell button and electricity

THE DOORBELL
When the current is switched on, the electromagnet attracts a nearby piece of iron. The movement of the iron, known as the armature, can be used to switch on a separate electrical circuit. In this doorbell the armature also switches off its own circuit. Huge rows of relays are still the basis for some telephone exchanges.

Brass ink bath

Tape drive roller

Clockwork motor

Return spring

Pivot rotates and feeds
paper past inking wheel

Terminals

Iron bar

Galvanometer for
testing purposes

Clockwork
winding
key

Tape emerges
from drawer
containing paper reel

Message-sending key

Electromagnet

GETTING THE MESSAGE

The telegraphic receiver printed the dots and
dashes of Morse code on to paper tape. The tape was
pulled by a roller driven by the clockwork motor. As an electric
current flowed along the telegraph line, it energized the twin electromagnets.
These attracted the iron bar, operating a system of levers which pressed the tape
against an inking wheel. When the current ceased, the return spring pulled the tape
away from the inking wheel. The tape moved at a constant speed. A short burst of
current inked a short line – the "dot;" a pulse three times as long made the "dash."

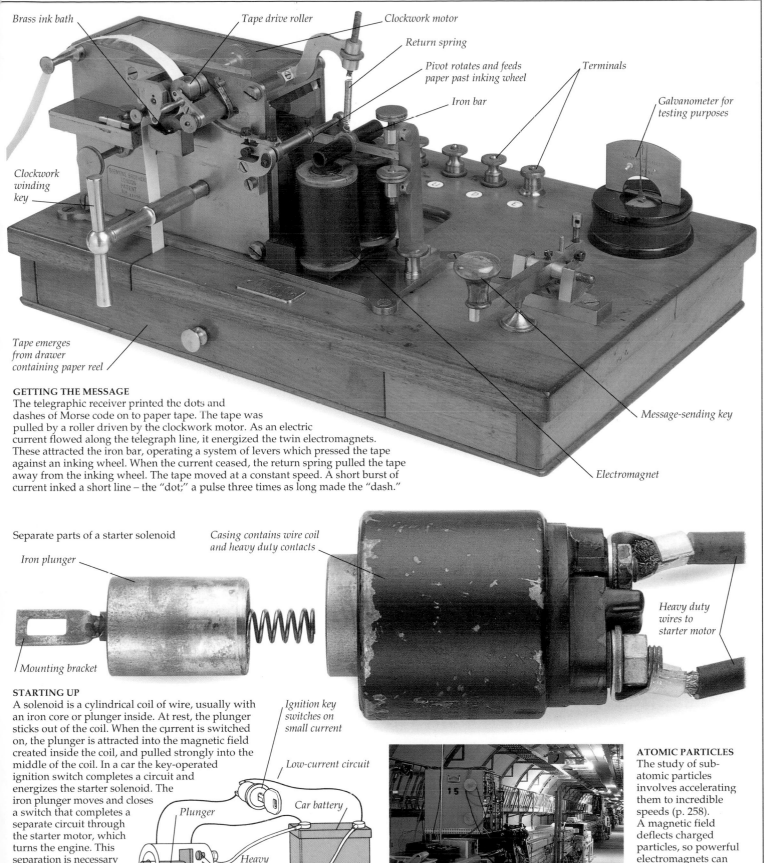

Separate parts of a starter solenoid

Casing contains wire coil
and heavy duty contacts

Iron plunger

Heavy duty
wires to
starter motor

Mounting bracket

STARTING UP

A solenoid is a cylindrical coil of wire, usually with
an iron core or plunger inside. At rest, the plunger
sticks out of the coil. When the current is switched
on, the plunger is attracted into the magnetic field
created inside the coil, and pulled strongly into the
middle of the coil. In a car the key-operated
ignition switch completes a circuit and
energizes the starter solenoid. The
iron plunger moves and closes
a switch that completes a
separate circuit through
the starter motor, which
turns the engine. This
separation is necessary
because a starter
motor draws a high
current from the car's
battery which would
otherwise deliver a
shock to the driver.

Ignition key
switches on
small current

Low-current circuit

Plunger

Car battery

Heavy
duty contacts

Motor is
activated

Starter
solenoid is
energized

Starter motor receives high current

ATOMIC PARTICLES

The study of sub-
atomic particles
involves accelerating
them to incredible
speeds (p. 258).
A magnetic field
deflects charged
particles, so powerful
electromagnets can
be adjusted to control,
bend, and focus their
paths. These long,
square electromagnets
on the left are at a
nuclear research
center near Geneva
in Switzerland.

Discoveries using electricity

HUMPHRY DAVY
In 1807 Davy (1778-1829) made pure potassium by electrolysis. With a bigger electric current he made pure sodium. He helped popularise science, demonstrating such wonders as the intense light of an arc lamp (p. 278)

IN 1800 A FEW WEEKS AFTER VOLTA announced his electricity-making pile (p. 262), William Nicholson (1753-1815) and Anthony Carlisle (1768-1840) were experimenting with their own version. They noticed bubbles appearing in a drop of water on top of the pile. They then passed the electric current through a bowl of water. Bubbles of gas appeared around the two metal contacts where they dipped into the water. The bubbles around one contact were hydrogen, and the others were oxygen. The electric current had produced a chemical reaction, splitting water into its two elements. This was electrolysis. Soon other substances were being investigated. Humphry Davy brought electrolysis to prominence when he used it to make pure potassium and sodium for the first time. Today's uses include electroplating, refining pure copper, extracting aluminum from its treated natural ores, and making substances such as chlorine.

VOLTAMETER
This modern demonstration apparatus shows how gases are produced by electrolysis. A replica of the original glass apparatus is shown on p. 250. Faraday named it a "volta electrometer" because the gas collected was proportional to the quantity of electricity made by a voltaic pile.

Rising bubbles of hydrogen gas

Negative electrode (cathode)

Battery as source of current

Current-carrying wires

Potash melted by current

Connecting wire

Watertight rubber plug

MAKING PURE POTASSIUM FOR THE FIRST TIME
Pure potassium is a soft, silvery-white metal. It does not occur on its own in nature, because it combines so readily with other substances to form compounds. One is potash (potassium carbonate), found in the ashes of burned plants. This is an ingredient in certain types of glass. Davy passed a large current through molten potash in a metal pot, and pure potassium collected around the negative contact. He named the new substance potassium after its source. In the same way he prepared sodium from soda (sodium carbonate). Davy's successor at the Royal Institution, Michael Faraday, also studied electrolysis. Two laws of electrolysis are named after him.

Potassium reacts with air so must be sealed

To electricity supply

Pure potassium in a sealed glass tube

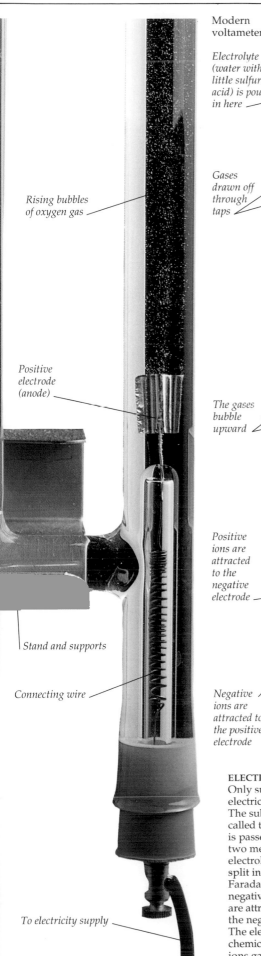

Rising bubbles of oxygen gas

Positive electrode (anode)

Stand and supports

Connecting wire

To electricity supply

Modern voltameter

Electrolyte (water with a little sulfuric acid) is poured in here

Gases drawn off through taps

The gases bubble upward

Positive ions are attracted to the negative electrode

Negative ions are attracted to the positive electrode

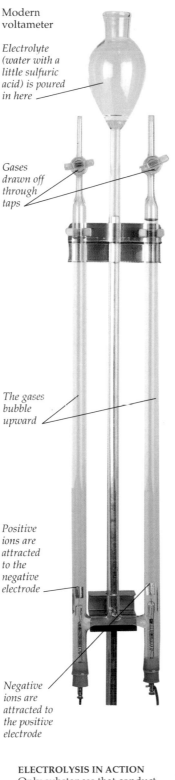

Electroplating

In this process, an object receives a coating of a metal by electrolysis. The object to be plated is connected to the negative terminal of a battery or similar electricity supply so that it acts as the negative electrode (cathode). It is left for a time in a solution containing a compound of the metal that will form the plating. For example, an object to be plated with copper is put into copper sulfate solution. This solution is the electrolyte. In it, the copper exists as positively charged ions. When the electric current flows, these ions are attracted to the negative electrode – the object. They settle evenly on its surface.

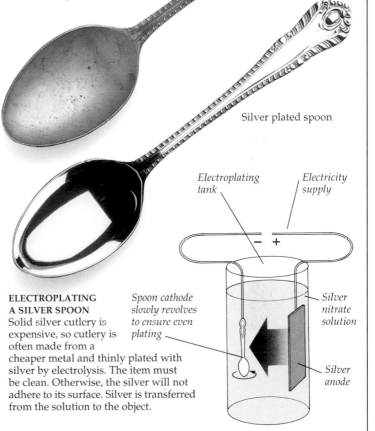

Nickel spoon

Silver plated spoon

ELECTROPLATING A SILVER SPOON
Solid silver cutlery is expensive, so cutlery is often made from a cheaper metal and thinly plated with silver by electrolysis. The item must be clean. Otherwise, the silver will not adhere to its surface. Silver is transferred from the solution to the object.

Electroplating tank

Electricity supply

Spoon cathode slowly revolves to ensure even plating

Silver nitrate solution

Silver anode

ELECTROLYSIS IN ACTION
Only substances that conduct electricity can be electrolyzed. The substance to be split is called the electrolyte. Electricity is passed through it between two metal electrodes. In an electrolyte, the molecules are split into substances that Faraday called positive and negative ions. The positive ions are attracted to the cathode and the negative ions to the anode. The electrical energy causes chemical reactions in which the ions gain or lose electrons.

RUST-RESISTANT CARS
Steel vehicle bodies can be electroplated with a thin layer of a metal such as zinc to protect them from rust. The car body (the cathode) is electrified, and the zinc (the anode) is drawn from the solution to cover every nook and cranny.

Electricity from magnetism

FATHER OF ELECTRICITY
Michael Faraday (1791-1867) studied many areas of science, including the effects of intense magnetism on light. This phenomenon led him to ideas that were to form the foundation of electromagnetic field theory (p. 28, p. 176).

W HEN AN ELECTRIC GUITARIST plucks a string in a vast stadium, the metal string is almost silent. However, its vibrations are detected by an electromagnetic pickup, boosted by the amplifiers, and this fills the stadium with sound. The guitar's pickup is one of the hundreds of electric devices, including generators and transformers, that rely on electromagnetic induction – manipulating magnetism to make electricity. The principle was demonstrated in 1831 by Michael Faraday in Britain and by Joseph Henry in the United States. In electromagnetic induction, a varying or moving magnetic field produces an electromotive force (EMF) in a nearby conductor, and thus an electric current if the conductor is part of a circuit (p. 20). The current flows only while the magnetic field varies.

Magnet

Coil

First coil connected to battery

Galvanometer

MAGNET AND COIL
A wire can be subjected to a changing magnetic field by moving a nearby permanent magnet (above), or the changing magnetic field may come from an electromagnet (above right). In one of Faraday's experiments, a rod-shaped permanent magnet was thrust in and out of a coil of wire. The magnet was surrounded by invisible "lines of magnetic force," as might be traced out in iron filings. If the magnet is still, there is no change in the magnetic field, and no current flows. When the magnet moves, its lines of force cross the wire and so induce a current, which can be detected by the galvanometer. The idea of "lines of magnetic force" was one of many proposed by Faraday.

Swing of pointer indicates induced current

Thumb shows the direction of motion

First finger points in the direction of magnetic field

Second finger points in the direction of the EMF

RIGHT-HAND RULE
This useful rule helps work out the direction of the induced current. It relates the direction of the magnetic field (north to south), the direction of movement in a generator, and the EMF or current (positive to negative). The direction of movement in an electric motor is shown by the left-hand rule (p. 273).

This painting shows Faraday at Britain's Royal Institution in 1856. He gave many lectures that helped to popularize science among the general public. His rational approach to developing theories, and analyzing the results, is still admired.

FARADAY'S INDUCTION RING

Faraday investigated the effects of electromagnetic induction using this equipment (left). One wire is wound in a coil around part of an iron ring, with ends to connect to the terminals of a battery. A separate wire is wound around another part of the ring – it does not touch the first wire. Its ends are connected to a galvanometer. When the first coil is connected to the battery, a magnetic field builds up almost instantaneously around it, and in the iron ring. As the magnetic field forms, it induces a current in the second coil, which shows as a sudden swing of the galvanometer pointer. In a split second the magnetic field has formed and becomes steady, so current no longer flows. If the first coil is disconnected from the battery, the magnetic field collapses, again inducing a pulse of electric current in the second coil, but in the other direction.

RECORDKEEPING

An entry in Faraday's notebook, dated 29 August 1831, shows his sketch of the induction ring apparatus. Faraday always kept careful scientific records.

Galvanometer shows existence of current

Second coil connected to galvanometer

Soft iron ring

Cups to hold mercury to improve electric connections

Terminals

Fabric insulation

CONTINUOUS MOVEMENT

This 1870s model of a disc generator demonstrates one of Faraday's experiments of 1831. An EMF (voltage) is induced in the copper disc when it is rotated in the magnetic field between the poles of the electromagnet. Spring contacts on the edge of the disc and the axle connect to terminals on the base. If a galvanometer is connected to these terminals, the circuit will be completed and a current will flow.

Axle

Electromagnet creates strong magnetic field

Copper strip bent into spiral shape

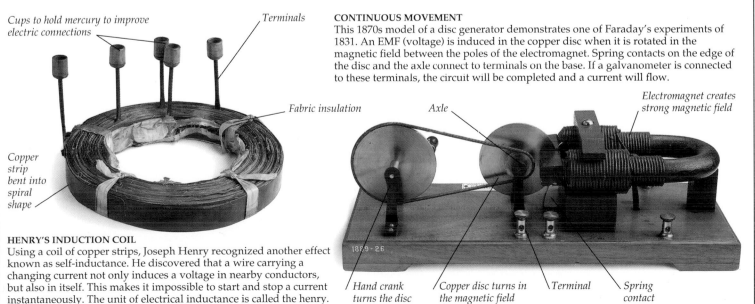

HENRY'S INDUCTION COIL

Using a coil of copper strips, Joseph Henry recognized another effect known as self-inductance. He discovered that a wire carrying a changing current not only induces a voltage in nearby conductors, but also in itself. This makes it impossible to start and stop a current instantaneously. The unit of electrical inductance is called the henry.

Hand crank turns the disc

Copper disc turns in the magnetic field

Terminal

Spring contact

Magneto-electric machines

THE RESEARCHES of Henry, Faraday, and others in the 1830s were followed gradually by practical machines that converted mechanical energy to electrical energy. These machines were known as magneto-electric machines. Later they used electro-magnets and came to be called generators or dynamos. The earliest uses were as demonstration models and for medical treatment. Electroplating was the earliest serious application in 1844, followed by lighthouse illumination. It was not until the 1880s that innovations in design led to their use for electric lighting.

CLARKE'S MACHINE
Edward Clarke, a London instrument maker, designed an efficient magneto-electric machine where turning the handle rotated coils of wire, not a large magnet as in Pixii's machine (right). Clarke's machine was used in the treatment of rheumatism and headaches.

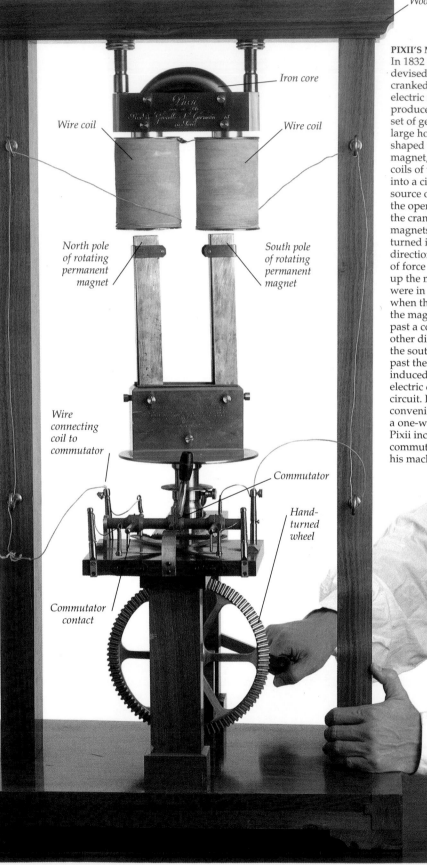

Wooden frame

Iron core

Wire coil

Wire coil

North pole of rotating permanent magnet

South pole of rotating permanent magnet

Wire connecting coil to commutator

Commutator

Hand-turned wheel

Commutator contact

PIXII'S MACHINE
In 1832 Hippolyte Pixii devised a hand-cranked "magneto-electric machine" to produce electricity. A set of gears turned a large horseshoe-shaped permanent magnet, close to two coils of wire linked into a circuit. The source of energy was the operator turning the crank. The magnets were always turned in the same direction, but the lines of force which made up the magnetic field were in one direction when the north pole of the magnet moved past a coil and in the other direction when the south pole moved past the coil. This induced an alternating electric current in the circuit. For the convenience of having a one-way current, Pixii incorporated a commutator on his machine.

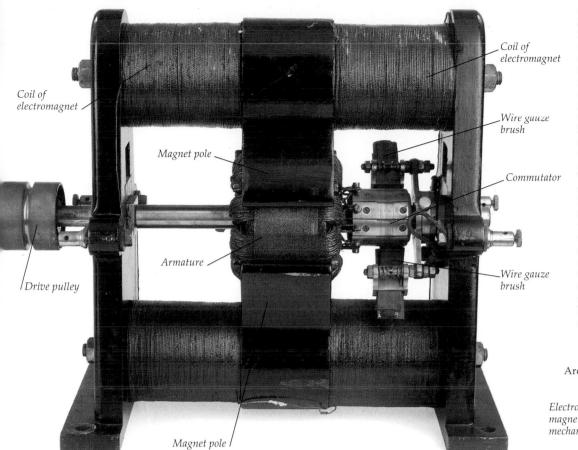

Coil of
electromagnet

Coil of
electromagnet

Magnet pole

Armature

Drive pulley

Wire gauze
brush

Commutator

Wire gauze
brush

Magnet pole

GRAMME DYNAMO

In about 1870 Belgian inventor Z. T. Gramme devised a dynamo that generated enough electric current, flowing sufficiently steadily, to be useful for large-scale applications such as illuminating factories by carbon arc lights (below). The rotating part of the dynamo, bearing the coils of wire, is known as the armature. Gramme's dynamos were steam-driven and, unlike their predecessors, did not overheat in continuous operation. The Gramme dynamo produced a one-way, or direct, current (DC). It incorporated a commutator – segments of copper which rotated with the armature and caused the current to flow in one direction only. Gauze brushes rubbing against the commutator picked up the current. The dynamo was expensive to maintain because the commutator and brush contacts became worn by pressure and the sparks that flew between them.

Arc lamp

Electro–
magnetic
mechanism

WERNER SIEMENS

The German Siemens family made many contributions to electrical engineering. Werner von Siemens (1816-1892) designed a dynamo (1866) which used opposing electromagnets to produce a magnetic field around the armature, rather than around a permanent magnet.

Carbon rods for lighting

An early use for dynamo-generated electricity was arc lighting. The arc is a "continuous spark" between carbon rods – carbon being a good conductor. Arc lamps threw intense light, but they were inefficient, unpredictable, and needed constant attention. Even so, they were installed in public buildings, lighthouses, and used for street lighting.

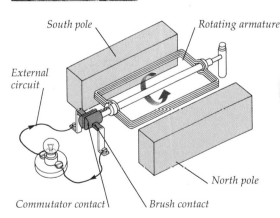

South pole

Rotating armature

External
circuit

Commutator contact

Brush contact

North pole

HOW THE DYNAMO WORKS

A coil of wire (the armature) is rotated between the poles of permanent magnets. As one side of the coil travels past the north pole, it cuts the lines of magnetic force, and a current is induced. The coil moves on and the current dies away. Then it approaches the south pole, inducing a current in the opposite direction. The coil is attached to the commutator, which causes the current on the external circuit to flow in the same direction all the time.

HOW THE ARC WORKS

The electric current passes through the pointed tips of the rods as they touch. It heats them so much that the carbon vaporizes. As the rods are drawn apart, the vapor will carry the current across the small gap, glowing intensely as it does so. Davy and Faraday demonstrated arcs at their lectures.

PUBLIC LIGHTING

In an arc lamp, the gap between the carbon rods is critical. It needs regular adjustment because the gap widens as the carbon vaporizes. A mechanism operated by electromagnets controls the upper carbon rod to keep the necessary gap.

19th-century lighthouses at La Hève, France, which used arc lamps

Carbon rod

Gap
where
white
light is
produced

Carbon rod

Making things move

In 1821, the year after Oersted's discovery of a connection between electricity and magnetism, Michael Faraday devised a simple apparatus in which a current-carrying wire rotated around a magnetic pole. It was the first electric motor, although it was too crude to have any practical use. During the 1830s many types of primitive electric motors were built, and some were used to drive machines. The American engineer Thomas Davenport used them to turn a drill and lathe, but they were inefficient and expensive, partly because the source of electricity to drive them was a battery. By the 1870s dynamos were able to provide a cheaper source of electricity, and engineers had learned that when a dynamo operated in reverse and was supplied with electrical current, it made an efficient motor. The commercial use of motors grew, especially traction motors to drive trains.

Metal support arm carries current

Wire to battery

CONTINUOUS MOTION

In Faraday's "electro-magnetic rotation apparatus" electric current produced continuous movement. A stiff wire was suspended from a flexible one so that it could move freely. The lower part of the stiff wire was placed near one pole of a permanent magnet. The end of the wire dipped into a dish of mercury (a metal that is liquid at normal room temperatures). The mercury allowed the end of the wire to move and, being a metal, it also conducted electricity. When a current flowed through the wire, this produced a magnetic field around it. The field interacted with the magnetic field around the magnet, and the wire began to move around it. The liquid mercury allowed the wire to rotate around the magnet, while still maintaining the circuit and permitting the current to flow.

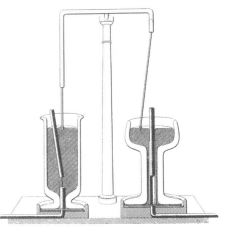

ELECTROMAGNETIC ROTATIONS

In a drawing of one of Faraday's versions, a wire rotated around a magnet (right), while in another (left), the magnet rotated around a fixed wire.

BARLOW'S WHEEL

In this apparatus, devised by Peter Barlow (1776-1862) in 1823, a star-shaped metal wheel was free to rotate on an axle, within the magnetic field of a horseshoe magnet. Current flowing from a battery through the wheel set up a magnetic field around it, and so the points of the star near the horseshoe magnet moved. The points of the wheel dipped into a mercury bath below, to maintain the circuit while allowing the wheel to move.

Rotating conductor

Bar magnet

Liquid mercury

Glass dish

Wire to battery

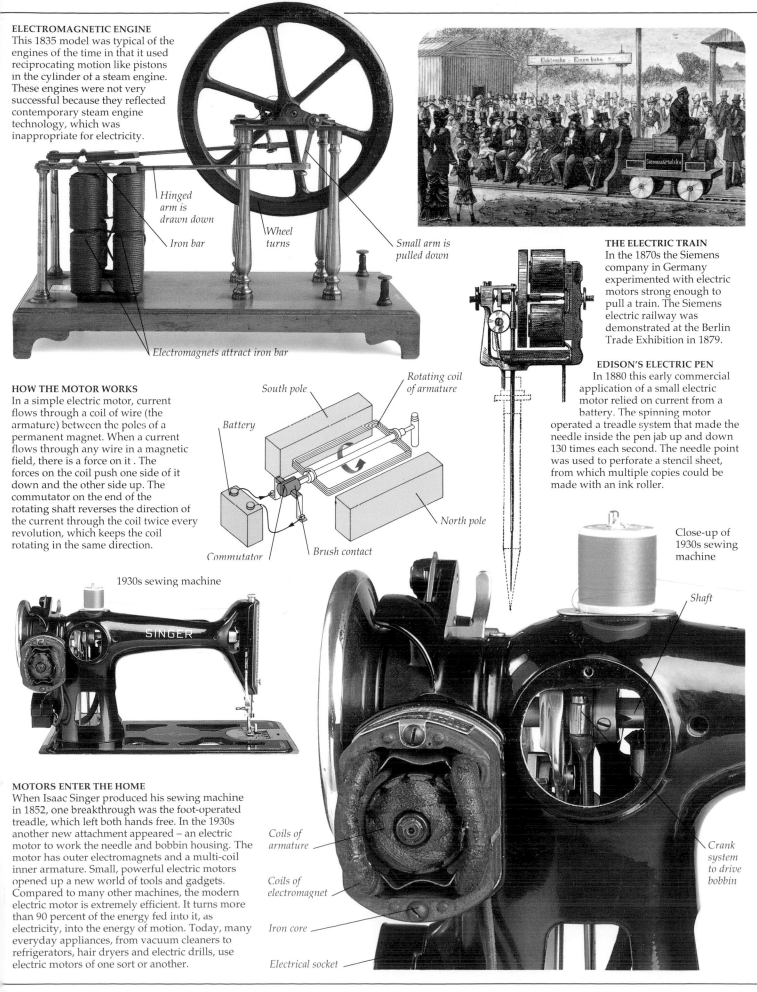

ELECTROMAGNETIC ENGINE
This 1835 model was typical of the engines of the time in that it used reciprocating motion like pistons in the cylinder of a steam engine. These engines were not very successful because they reflected contemporary steam engine technology, which was inappropriate for electricity.

Hinged arm is drawn down

Iron bar

Wheel turns

Small arm is pulled down

Electromagnets attract iron bar

THE ELECTRIC TRAIN
In the 1870s the Siemens company in Germany experimented with electric motors strong enough to pull a train. The Siemens electric railway was demonstrated at the Berlin Trade Exhibition in 1879.

EDISON'S ELECTRIC PEN
In 1880 this early commercial application of a small electric motor relied on current from a battery. The spinning motor operated a treadle system that made the needle inside the pen jab up and down 130 times each second. The needle point was used to perforate a stencil sheet, from which multiple copies could be made with an ink roller.

HOW THE MOTOR WORKS
In a simple electric motor, current flows through a coil of wire (the armature) between the poles of a permanent magnet. When a current flows through any wire in a magnetic field, there is a force on it . The forces on the coil push one side of it down and the other side up. The commutator on the end of the rotating shaft reverses the direction of the current through the coil twice every revolution, which keeps the coil rotating in the same direction.

South pole

Rotating coil of armature

Battery

North pole

Commutator

Brush contact

1930s sewing machine

Close-up of 1930s sewing machine

Shaft

MOTORS ENTER THE HOME
When Isaac Singer produced his sewing machine in 1852, one breakthrough was the foot-operated treadle, which left both hands free. In the 1930s another new attachment appeared – an electric motor to work the needle and bobbin housing. The motor has outer electromagnets and a multi-coil inner armature. Small, powerful electric motors opened up a new world of tools and gadgets. Compared to many other machines, the modern electric motor is extremely efficient. It turns more than 90 percent of the energy fed into it, as electricity, into the energy of motion. Today, many everyday appliances, from vacuum cleaners to refrigerators, hair dryers and electric drills, use electric motors of one sort or another.

Coils of armature

Coils of electromagnet

Iron core

Electrical socket

Crank system to drive bobbin

Manipulating electricity

MICHAEL FARADAY'S INDUCTION RING, with two electrically separate coils, was in effect the first transformer. A transformer can alter the voltage of an electricity supply by having a different number of turns in each coil. Sending electricity long distances through power cables is more efficient at high voltages than at low ones. Transformers boost voltage for transmission, then reduce it at the other end for everyday use. As a transformer works by electromagnetic induction and requires a varying magnetic field, it cannot work with direct current (DC). It operates using alternating current (AC) which rises to a peak flowing one way, fades, and rises again in the reverse direction.

Terminal of coil B

Twine

Terminal of coil B

FARADAY'S RING
This soft iron ring, wound around with coils of copper wire separated by twine and calico, was used by Faraday in his discovery of electromagnetic induction (p. 280). Faraday found that electric current in the coil he marked A (below) induced an electric current in coil B (above) although the wires did not touch. This ring was the first transformer, though it was not used as such because Faraday did not have alternating current. He used the direct current from a battery.

Iron ring

Terminal of coil A

Terminal of coil A

Copper wire

Calico covering formerly marked with the letter A

Slip rings

South pole

Brush contact

First half turn of armature

Current flows one way

North pole

Brush contact

Second half turn of armature

South pole

Current flows the other way

AC GENERATOR
AC is produced by the alternator, a type of generator. Unlike a DC dynamo (p. 37), it lacks a commutator to reverse the connections in the circuit. Instead, brushes press continuously on slip rings. As the armature rotates, the induced current flows one way for half a turn (as a part of the coil passes the North pole), then flows the other way for the other half-turn (as it passes the South pole). Speed of rotation determines how quickly the current reverses.

North pole

CHARLES STEINMETZ
Steinmetz (1865-1923) studied in Germany and moved to the United States in 1889, where he worked as an electrical engineer. From the 1890s he studied the behavior of alternating current circuits and developed the theory that allowed engineers to design AC circuits and devices. With scientists such as Tesla (opposite page), he helped to make AC a practical proposition for households.

Nikola Tesla

Tesla (1856-1943), who was born in Croatia of Serbian parents, emigrated to the United States in 1884. He worked briefly for Thomas Edison. Several years earlier Tesla had realized how he could build an AC motor that would not need a commutator. In 1888 he built his first "induction motor." This was a major factor in the widespread adoption of AC supplies. The induction motor is probably the most widely used type of electric motor. Tesla also invented a type of transformer, the Tesla coil, which works at very high frequencies and produces enormous voltages.

INDUCTION MOTOR
The induction motor has no brushes or commutators. It uses a "rotating magnetic field," made by rapidly feeding carefully timed alternating currents to a series of outer windings – the stator – to produce a magnetic field pattern which rotates. The inner set of windings on the shaft is the rotor. The stator's magnetic field induces a current in the rotor, and this becomes an electromagnet too. As the stator's magnetic field pattern rotates, it "drags" the rotor with it.

Stator winding

READING IN A THUNDERSTORM
Tesla imagined that one day even the power of lightning bolts could be harnessed. This photograph shows him reading at his high-voltage research laboratory in the United States in 1899, surrounded by giant sparks and bolts of electricity.

Brass frame

Rotor

Wooden base

Rotor shaft

Rods form part of brass frame

Connection to AC electricity supply

STEPPING UP OR DOWN
The change of voltage in a transformer depends on the number of turns in the two coils, called the primary and secondary windings. If the secondary has more turns than the primary, voltage is increased (stepped up). If it has fewer, voltage is decreased (stepped down). There is no magical gain – as voltage rises, current falls, keeping the overall electrical energy the same.

Step-up transformer

Primary windings to electricity source

Secondary windings connected to high voltage lines

Step-down transformer

Primary windings to electricity source

Secondary windings connected to load – electric motors

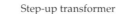

TRANSFORMERS IN INDUSTRY
The generators at a modern power station do not produce electricity at sufficently high voltage for efficient transmission. Their voltage is increased by step-up transformers for efficient long-distance transmission.

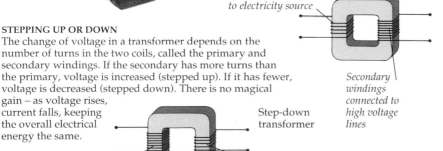

Early electricity supplies

STEAM ENGINES
James Watt (1736-1819) was a Scottish engineer who made important improvements to the steam engine, thereby helping to stimulate the Industrial Revolution. The unit of power, the watt, is named after him. In electricity, the number of watts is obtained by multiplying volts by amps.

THROUGHOUT THE 19TH CENTURY visionaries attempted to put electricity to practical use and even replace steam power, but with no results apart from electroplating, some instances of arc lighting and a few small models. In the 1860s efficient generators such as steam turbines were developed, and electricity became available on a wider scale. In the 1880s the rocketing demand for incandescent lamps provided the stimulus for electricity distribution networks. At first, all electricity was generated at the place where it was to be used. This remained the case for a long while until the first central generating stations were built and took over from the small, isolated units.

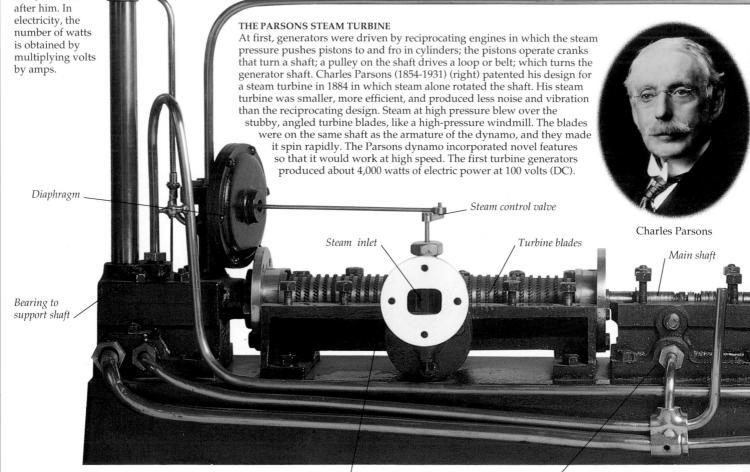

Pipe from governor to diaphragm

THE PARSONS STEAM TURBINE
At first, generators were driven by reciprocating engines in which the steam pressure pushes pistons to and fro in cylinders; the pistons operate cranks that turn a shaft; a pulley on the shaft drives a loop or belt; which turns the generator shaft. Charles Parsons (1854-1931) (right) patented his design for a steam turbine in 1884 in which steam alone rotated the shaft. His steam turbine was smaller, more efficient, and produced less noise and vibration than the reciprocating design. Steam at high pressure blew over the stubby, angled turbine blades, like a high-pressure windmill. The blades were on the same shaft as the armature of the dynamo, and they made it spin rapidly. The Parsons dynamo incorporated novel features so that it would work at high speed. The first turbine generators produced about 4,000 watts of electric power at 100 volts (DC).

Charles Parsons

Diaphragm

Steam control valve

Steam inlet

Turbine blades

Main shaft

Bearing to support shaft

Strong casing (cutaway)

Bearing to support shaft

Electromagnet produces magnetic field

ELECTRICITY FROM STEAM
Inside a steam generator, steam at high pressure is fed through a central inlet into the turbine section, which consists of a spinning shaft inside a strong casing. Half the steam flows in each direction. It rushes through an array of alternate moving turbine blades, which it pushes around, and fixed guide vanes, which guide it in the most efficient way. As steam progresses, its pressure drops but the Parsons turbine distributes this drop in pressure along the blades. The long shaft has a 15-coil armature and commutator mounted near one end. The magnetic field around the armature is produced by the field coils – electromagnets on a horseshoe-shaped iron core.

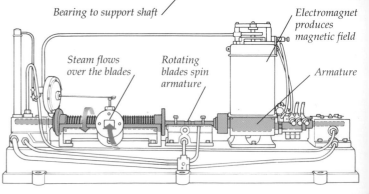

Steam flows over the blades

Rotating blades spin armature

Armature

How the steam turbine works

Electricity to the people

Thomas Edison (1847-1931) began his career as a telegrapher on North American railroads. He turned to inventing, developing things that people might want which he could patent and sell. His first money-maker, in 1870, was an improved stock ticker. This device communicated stock and share prices telegraphically between offices in New York's financial area. There followed a string of inventions and improvements to other people's inventions. Edison was a central figure in the move towards large-scale distribution of electricity to factories, offices, and homes. One of his commercial aims was to break the monopoly of the gas companies, which he considered unfair.

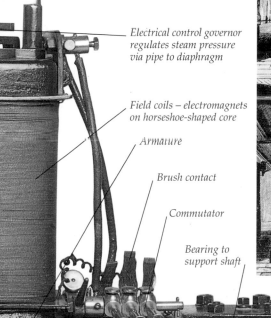

Thomas Edison

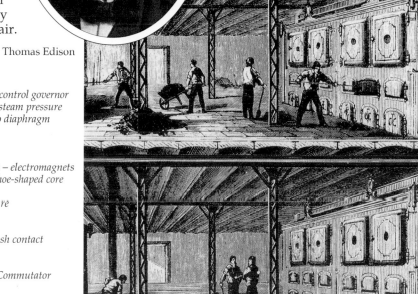

Electrical control governor regulates steam pressure via pipe to diaphragm

Field coils – electromagnets on horseshoe-shaped core

Armature

Brush contact

Commutator

Bearing to support shaft

PEARL STREET PLANT
In 1882 Edison and his colleagues fitted steam boilers and improved dynamos into a building on Pearl Street, New York, shown here in this stylized engraving. He had cables installed to distribute the current to the surrounding city district south of Wall Street. Edison manufactured light bulbs and all the other components needed to make it easy for people to equip their homes for electric lighting.

HORSE-DRAWN POWER
The early Parsons turbine generators could be moved by means of a horse-drawn cart to the required site. Their uses were varied. Some were used to provide temporary electric lighting. In 1886 this practical Parson's turbine was used to provide the electric light for ice skating after dark in the northeast of England when a local pond froze.

CITY LIGHTS
Before incandescent lamps, some city streets were lit by electric arc lamps, as in this New York scene of 1879. But the light was unpleasantly glaring and unreliable, so gas was used for most street lighting.

The power station

AN ELECTRICITY SUPPLY is regarded as a major requirement for a modern society. In the late 19th century electricity-generating power stations were being installed in many of the world's large cities, although it was some decades before the suburbs, and then the rural areas, received supplies. Today, electricity is such a familiar and convenient form of energy that it is simply called "power" – a word with its own scientific meaning (the rate at which energy is used). The majority of modern power stations use turbines to turn generators. These turbines are turned by running water in hydroelectric power stations, or by steam obtained from water boiled by the heat from burning coal, oil, nuclear fuel, or some other source. Less-developed areas may obtain their electricity from local generators.

BIGGER AND BETTER
This model shows the planned Deptford Central Station of the London Electricity Supply Corporation. The engineer who designed it, Sebastian Ferranti (1864-1930), believed it would be more economical to build large power stations outside cities where land was cheap, and to transmit the power at high voltage to substations near the users. Unfortunately, he was ahead of his time. Bureaucracy and technical problems kept the station from being completed. The machines on the right-hand side were installed and supplied power. The enormous ones on the left were never finished.

Flat copper coils

Feedpipes

Check valve

Flywheel

Connecting rod to crank shaft

POWER FOR NEW YORK
Great power stations, like this Edison Company station in New York, were often built on riverbanks or coastlines. The coal to fire the boilers could be delivered by barge, and river or sea water supplied the cooling requirements. Electricity changed people's lives, but smoke belched from the chimneys and soot settled over the neighborhood.

DISTRIBUTION NETWORK
A typical power station generator produces alternating current at 25,000 volts. This is stepped up to hundreds of thousands of volts to reduce the energy loss during long-distance transmission. A main substation step-down transformer (p. 287) reduces the voltage for the local area. Smaller substation transformers reduce it further for distribution to offices and homes.

Power station

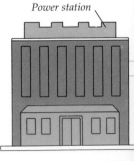

Looking to the future

The production of electricity is using up nonrenewable sources – coal, oil, and gas. Energy sources that will not run out are now under investigation: solar power, tides, wind, super-heated water gushing from the Earth (geothermal energy), and inflammable gases from "bio-digestors" of rotting plant and animal matter. Nuclear fuel is another option. Each method has its advantages and disadvantages.

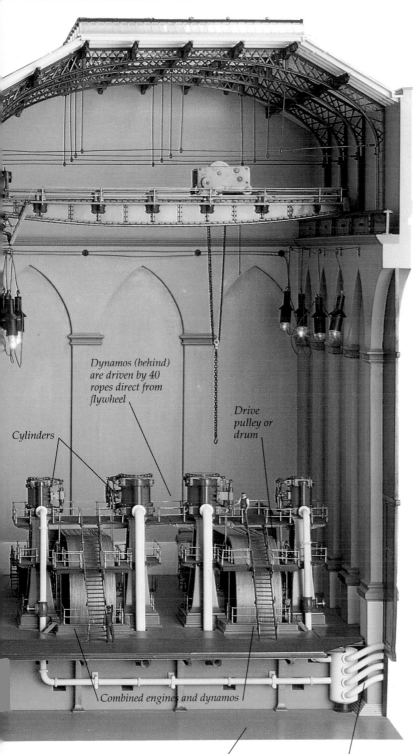

Cylinders

Dynamos (behind) are driven by 40 ropes direct from flywheel

Drive pulley or drum

Combined engines and dynamos

Thick concrete floor to support heavy machinery *Feedpipes from boiler*

POWER FROM THE SUN
People are now turning to nature's energy source for electric power. This solar power complex in the Mojave Desert in the US generates electricity from rows of computer-controlled mirrors. The mirrors track the sun, and reflect and focus its rays on to tubes containing a special oil. The oil is used to boil water to drive turbines.

HYDROELECTRIC POWER
Glen Canyon dam on the Colorado River in the United States channels running water through great turbines, which turn generators. In countries with sufficient rainfall and plentiful fast rivers, such as New Zealand, hydroelectric stations generate most of the total electricity needs.

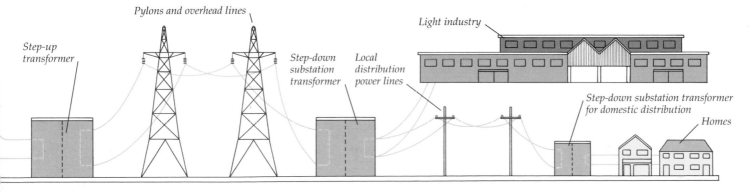

Step-up transformer

Pylons and overhead lines

Step-down substation transformer

Local distribution power lines

Light industry

Step-down substation transformer for domestic distribution

Homes

Electricity in the home

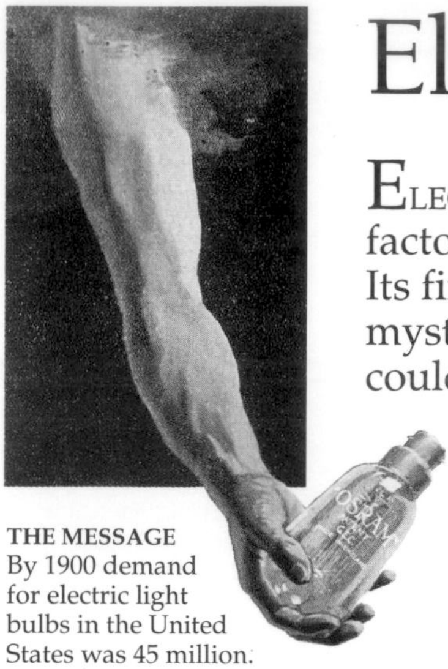

ELECTRICITY WAS FIRST WIRED from power stations into homes, offices, and factories in the 1880s, in big cities such as New York, London, and Paris. Its first major use was for lighting – and it seemed both miraculous and mysterious. Instead of fiddling with gaslights, oil lamps, and candles, users could turn night into day at the flick of a switch. In 1882 Thomas Edison's factories made 100,000 light bulbs; but because of the years it took to lay cables and establish electricity locally, electric light was not easily available until the 1930s. The new power was dangerously invisible. A wire looked the same whether it was carrying a current or not. Early users were warned of the new dangers, though electricity was still safer than the naked flames of candles and gas.

THE MESSAGE
By 1900 demand for electric light bulbs in the United States was 45 million.

Early electric meter

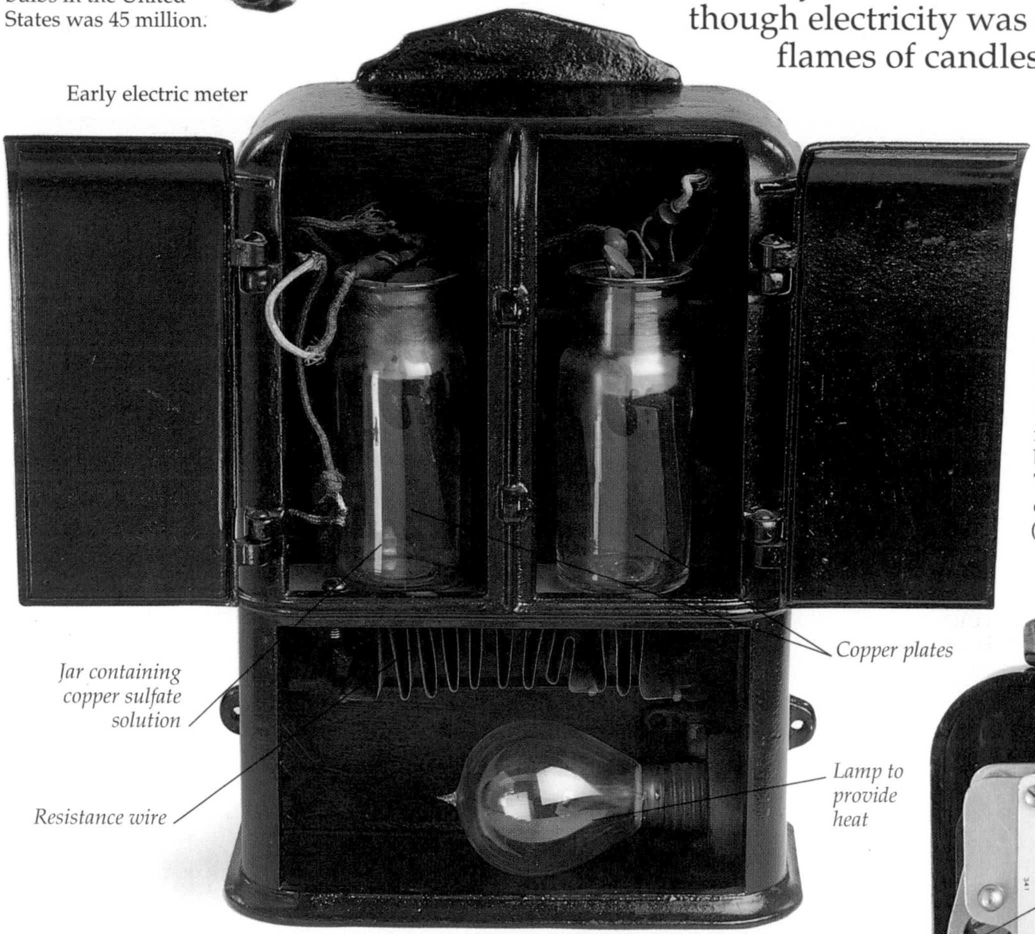

ELECTRICTY METERS
An early meter (left), pioneered by Thomas Edison, used electrolysis to measure the electricity used. The current passed through copper sulfate solution in the jars. The passage of the electric current caused the copper to dissolve on the plate and be deposited on the other. The change in weight of the plates was proportional to the electricity used. The wavy resistance wire and the lamp below prevented the solution from freezing in winter. By the 1930s the meter (below) had a spinning plate moved by induction, geared to a series of dials. These showed the amount of electrical energy used, measured in kilowatt-hours (1,000 watts of power for one hour of time).

1930s meter

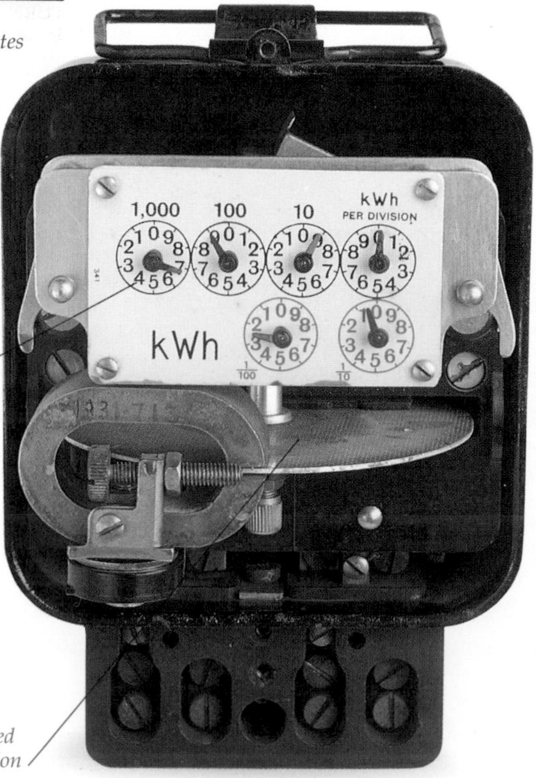

Copper plates

Jar containing copper sulfate solution

Resistance wire

Lamp to provide heat

Dials showing kilowatt hours

READING THE METER
Officials from electricity companies were soon visiting consumers on a regular basis to check the electricity meter. The meter reader switched off the supply, removed the copper plate, replaced it with a new one, and took the plate away for weighing. In this way companies figured out how much the consumer should pay.

Spinning plate moved by induction

Electric lamps

Around 1880 light bulbs were developed by Edison, Joseph Swan (1828-1914), and others. These bulbs were called filament or incandescent bulbs, because of the way they worked. Electricity flowed through a thin piece of carbon with high resistance – the filament. This became so hot that it glowed white, or incandesced. If the filament glowed, oxygen in the air would combine with it and quickly burn it away, so air was sucked out of the bulb, to create a partial vacuum around the filament.

Modern light bulb

THE FILAMENT LAMP
The modern light bulb works on the same principle as the Edison-Swan versions, but the materials have changed. The filaments made of tungsten can now withstand very high temperatures. The filament may be 20 in (50 cm) long, but is coiled tightly to take up little space. An inert gas such as argon, to reduce melting of the tungsten, has replaced the vacuum.

Bulb fits into ceramic safety socket

Wires that carry electricity to and from filament

Filament support

Inert gas such as argon

Hard metal (tungsten) filament

FLUORESCENCE
The French scientist Antoine Becquerel (1852-1908) used fluorescent light in his discovery of radioactivity. This type of light works when a substance gives off light after being stimulated by other rays, such as invisible ultraviolet (UV) light. However, practical fluorescent lamps were not in use until the 1950s.

Edison screw-in bulb

Contact metal end

Metal screw fitting

Carbonized bamboo filament

Wires carrying electricity to and from filament

Partial vacuum within bulb

TURNING ON THE LIGHT
This early electric switch has the metal components in a ceramic body. Two metal arms are sprung so they flick quickly from one position to another. When the switch is turned on, the arms slot into U-shaped springy contacts, so completing the electric circuit. This must happen fast, and the contacts must be good, or the electricity could spark across any gaps and cause damage.

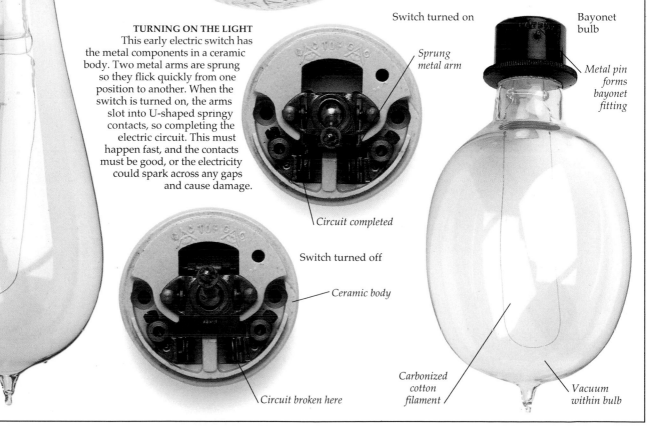

Switch turned on

Sprung metal arm

Circuit completed

Switch turned off

Ceramic body

Circuit broken here

Bayonet bulb

Metal pin forms bayonet fitting

Carbonized cotton filament

Vacuum within bulb

Electrical appliances

AS SOON AS ELECTRICITY was available in houses, people began to think up new uses for it. Although the early 20th century saw the invention and design of "labor-saving" appliances to make domestic life easier, the electric iron was the only appliance commonly found in the home, along with electric lights. Most early appliances used electricity's ability to generate heat in appliances like curling irons. When electric motors came into wide use in the 1900s, electricity could be converted into movement. The range of appliances grew to include small heaters, food blenders, and hair dryers. However, the large appliances, such as the vacuum cleaner, were still only found in more affluent homes.

ELECTRIC COOKING
Electric cooking in the 19th century offered freedom from the smoke, burning coals, and hot ashes of the traditional stove. Hot plates could be switched on and off and temperatures adjusted to give the cook greater control.

Arc jumps here

Carbon rod

Insulated wire

Wooden handle

Connection for electric cord

Heavy cast-iron base

SMOOTHING IRON
The first electric irons used a high-temperature electric spark for a heat source. This was an arc, jumping between carbon rods. The rods burned away, so they had to be manually slid together when the electricity was turned off, to maintain the correct gap between them. Like the carbon arc lights, which used the same principle, this method of changing electricity into heat was unsafe and unreliable. In 1883 the safety iron was patented in the United States. It replaced the carbon rods with a heating element.

Individual fuses   *Indicator light*

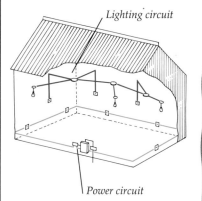

Lighting circuit

Power circuit

THE HOUSE CIRCUITS
Most modern houses have different electric circuits serving different needs. A main service line leads to a central distribution panel. Separate branch circuits go to wall outlets and lighting fixtures. A heavy-duty circuit serves the kitchen and its appliances. These lines carry 120 volts. Some equipment, such as water pumps, ranges, and dryers, require special circuits with 240 volts.

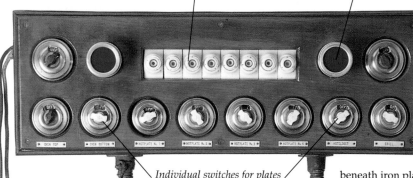

Individual switches for plates

Wires carrying power to switchboard and range

Wires from switchboard to range encased in corrugated metal

Iron plate

High-resistance wire inside insulated cast-iron case

ELECTRIC RANGE
In this 1900 range, coils of high-resistance wire were placed beneath iron plates. The wire became hot as electricity flowed through it, and the heat passed to the plate. Insulating materials were necessary to prevent electricity from flowing from the wire to the plate.

Copper reflecting dish

Wire safety grill

ELECTRIC KETTLE
Water and electricity are a dangerous combination, since water is an electricity conductor. The first electric kettles had a separate compartment for the element beneath the water. The element heated the container itself but most heat passed into the air. The Swan electric kettle of 1921 was the first with a fully insulated, waterproof heating element in the water.

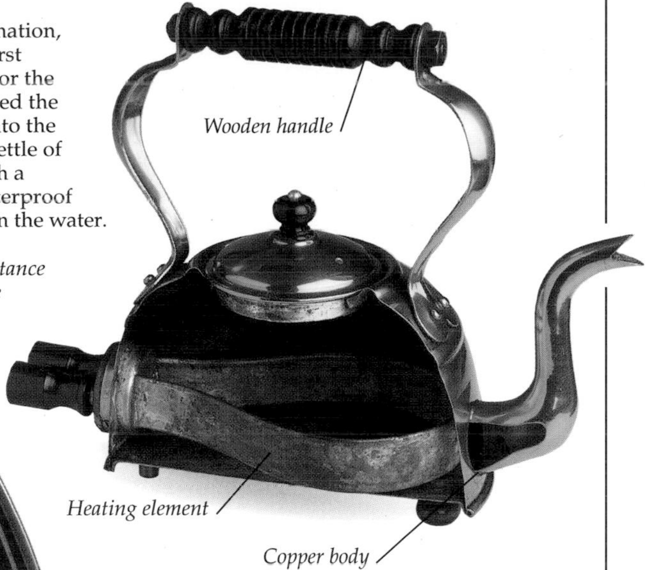

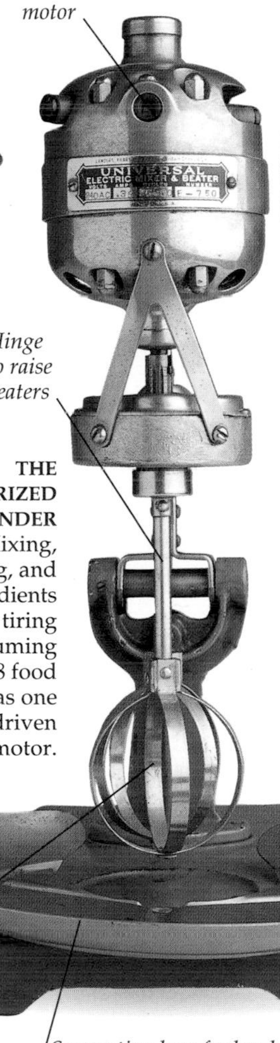

Wooden handle

High-resistance coiled wire

Heating element

Copper body

Electric motor

Hinge to raise beaters

THE MOTORIZED BLENDER
Mixing, whisking, and beating ingredients by hand is a tiring and time-consuming process. This 1918 food beater and mixer was one of the earliest to be driven by a small electric motor.

THE ELECTRIC PERCOLATOR
One of chief advantages of an electrical appliance is that it can be moved around and used wherever there is a socket to plug it in. This 1912 coffee maker is plugged in to an electric light socket.

Whisks

Supporting base for bowl

Current-carrying wire

ELECTRIC HEATER
The coiled, high-resistance heating element in this 1930s portable heater glows a comforting red as electricity is pushed through it. The copper dish reflects the radiant heat. The types of wires used here show the principle of resistance; the high resistance wire is used as the heating source because it glows hot, while the insulated connecting wires that carry current stay cool and safe to the touch

Electricity and medicine

THE WATERY SOLUTION OF CHEMICALS in living tissue makes a moderately good electrical conductor. Galvani noted the responses of dissected frog nerves and muscles to discharges from an electrostatic machine (p. 262), and many scientists detected electricity by the shocks it gave them. The body's own "electrical signals" are very small, measured in microvolts, and travel along nerves, sometimes at great speed. They detect, coordinate, and control, especially in the sense organs, brain, and muscles. If increasingly powerful electrical pulses are fed into the body, they cause tingling and then pain; they can send muscles into uncontrolled spasm, burn, render unconscious, and kill. However, doctors have discovered that, used carefully, electricity can diagnose, heal, and cure. Today, electrically heated scalpels slice and then seal small blood vessels to reduce bleeding during operations. Controlled currents passing through tissue can relieve pain. Delicate surgery can be performed with electric laser scalpels.

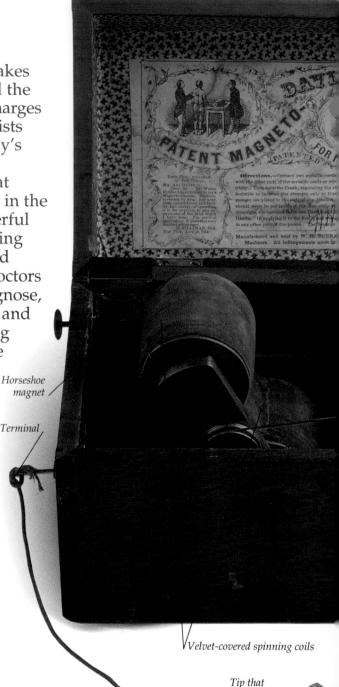

Horseshoe magnet

Terminal

Velvet-covered spinning coils

Tip that touches skin

A CURIOUS TREATMENT
This electro-medical machine of the 1850s had a handle and series of gear wheels which whirled coils of wire next to a horseshoe magnet, to generate electric current in the coils. A simple switch mechanism used this current and the self-inductance of the coils to produce a series of high-voltage pulses which caused the electric shock. The operator held the metal applicators by their insulating wooden handles, and applied the tips to the skin of the patient (below), so the pulses traveled through the tissues to treat rheumatism, headaches, and aching joints. When it was discharged through the patient's tissues, the shock often made the muscles contract uncontrollably.

EXECUTION
Movie villains sometimes meet their end in a dazzling flash of electricity. The reality is the electric chair, and the accidental electrocutions which occur each year in factories, offices, and homes as a result of carelessness.

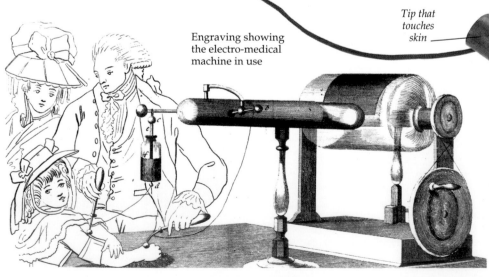

Engraving showing the electro-medical machine in use

SUBDUING ANIMALS
In the 19th century electricity was sometimes used for controlling vicious horses. A generator was operated by the driver to deliver a shock via a wire in the rein and the metal bit into the horse's mouth.

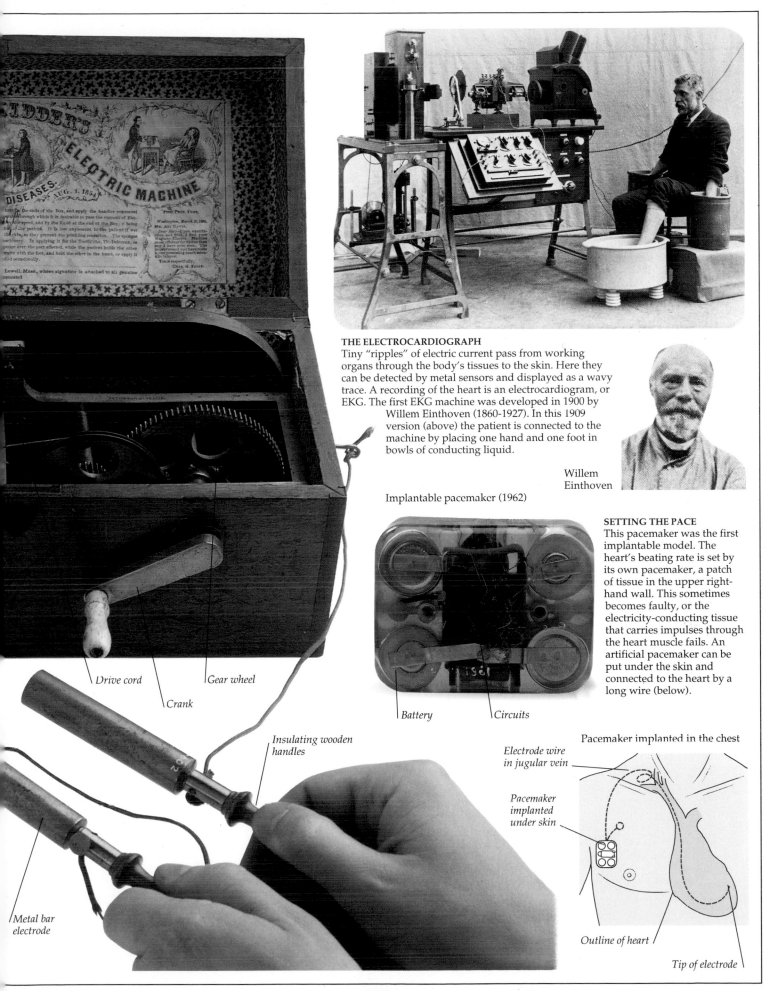

THE ELECTROCARDIOGRAPH

Tiny "ripples" of electric current pass from working organs through the body's tissues to the skin. Here they can be detected by metal sensors and displayed as a wavy trace. A recording of the heart is an electrocardiogram, or EKG. The first EKG machine was developed in 1900 by Willem Einthoven (1860-1927). In this 1909 version (above) the patient is connected to the machine by placing one hand and one foot in bowls of conducting liquid.

Willem Einthoven

Implantable pacemaker (1962)

SETTING THE PACE

This pacemaker was the first implantable model. The heart's beating rate is set by its own pacemaker, a patch of tissue in the upper right-hand wall. This sometimes becomes faulty, or the electricity-conducting tissue that carries impulses through the heart muscle fails. An artificial pacemaker can be put under the skin and connected to the heart by a long wire (below).

Battery

Circuits

Drive cord

Gear wheel

Crank

Insulating wooden handles

Metal bar electrode

Pacemaker implanted in the chest

Electrode wire in jugular vein

Pacemaker implanted under skin

Outline of heart

Tip of electrode

Heat, pressure, and light

Electricity can be produced directly from heat, pressure, and light. When heat is applied to one of the junctions of two conductors, so that the two junctions are at different temperatures, an electrical potential is generated; this is thermoelectricity. In the piezoelectric effect, an electrical potential is generated between opposite faces of crystals made from substances such as quartz, when the crystals are compressed – in simple terms, when the crystal is squeezed or stretched. In the photoelectric effect, light rays cause certain substances to give up electrons and produce an electric charge or current. In the photovoltaic effect, light produces an electric potential between layers of different substances, so current flows in a circuit without need for an electricity source.

THOMAS SEEBECK
In the 1820s German scientist Thomas Seebeck (1770-1831) studied the effects of heat on conductors. This "Seebeck effect" is now known as thermoelectricity. There have been many attempts at using thermoelectricity. Its main use today is for thermometers (below right).

THE SEEBECK EFFECT
In a circuit of two metal strips joined at their ends, Seebeck heated the junction at one end and saw a compass needle between the strips swing. Seebeck thought the heat was creating magnetism. In fact, an electric current was generated when the junctions were at different temperatures, and the magnetic field it produced deflected the compass needle. The Seebeck effect is effective only with certain conductors. Seebeck obtained his best results with the dissimilar conductors bismuth and antimony. The same effect can be produced using iron and copper. The "opposite" is the Peltier effect, named after French scientist Jean Peltier (1785-1845). A temperature difference is produced between the junctions when an electric current from a battery flows around the circuit.

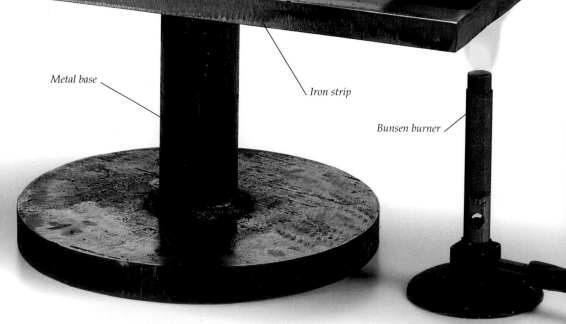

Reconstruction of Seebeck's experiment

Copper strip

Current flows around circuit

Junction at room temperature

Deflected compass needle

Junction being heated

Metal base

Iron strip

Bunsen burner

MAKING A THERMOCOUPLE
One application of the Seebeck effect is the type of thermometer based on a thermocouple (opposite). Here the probe of the thermocouple is being made from a wire of platinum joined by welding to a wire of platinum-rhodium alloy.

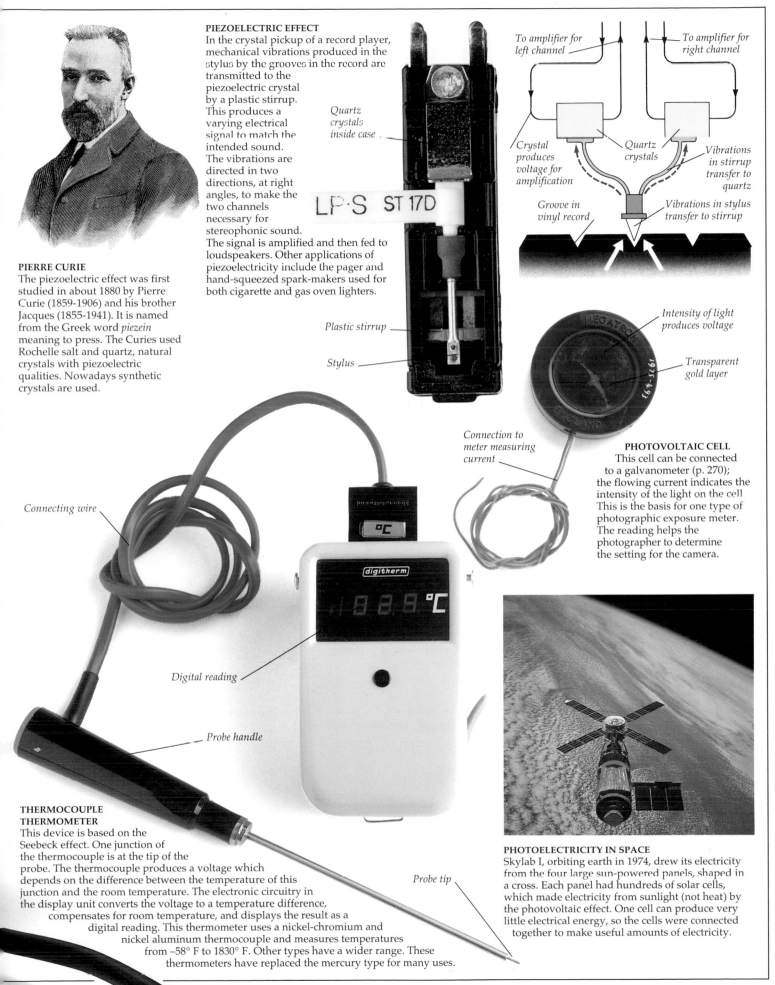

PIEZOELECTRIC EFFECT

In the crystal pickup of a record player, mechanical vibrations produced in the stylus by the grooves in the record are transmitted to the piezoelectric crystal by a plastic stirrup. This produces a varying electrical signal to match the intended sound. The vibrations are directed in two directions, at right angles, to make the two channels necessary for stereophonic sound. The signal is amplified and then fed to loudspeakers. Other applications of piezoelectricity include the pager and hand-squeezed spark-makers used for both cigarette and gas oven lighters.

Quartz crystals inside case

Plastic stirrup

Stylus

LP·S ST 17D

To amplifier for left channel

To amplifier for right channel

Crystal produces voltage for amplification

Quartz crystals

Vibrations in stirrup transfer to quartz

Groove in vinyl record

Vibrations in stylus transfer to stirrup

PIERRE CURIE

The piezoelectric effect was first studied in about 1880 by Pierre Curie (1859-1906) and his brother Jacques (1855-1941). It is named from the Greek word *piezein* meaning to press. The Curies used Rochelle salt and quartz, natural crystals with piezoelectric qualities. Nowadays synthetic crystals are used.

Intensity of light produces voltage

Transparent gold layer

Connection to meter measuring current

PHOTOVOLTAIC CELL

This cell can be connected to a galvanometer (p. 270); the flowing current indicates the intensity of the light on the cell. This is the basis for one type of photographic exposure meter. The reading helps the photographer to determine the setting for the camera.

Connecting wire

Digital reading

digitherm

Probe handle

THERMOCOUPLE THERMOMETER

This device is based on the Seebeck effect. One junction of the thermocouple is at the tip of the probe. The thermocouple produces a voltage which depends on the difference between the temperature of this junction and the room temperature. The electronic circuitry in the display unit converts the voltage to a temperature difference, compensates for room temperature, and displays the result as a digital reading. This thermometer uses a nickel-chromium and nickel aluminum thermocouple and measures temperatures from –58° F to 1830° F. Other types have a wider range. These thermometers have replaced the mercury type for many uses.

Probe tip

PHOTOELECTRICITY IN SPACE

Skylab I, orbiting earth in 1974, drew its electricity from the four large sun-powered panels, shaped in a cross. Each panel had hundreds of solar cells, which made electricity from sunlight (not heat) by the photovoltaic effect. One cell can produce very little electrical energy, so the cells were connected together to make useful amounts of electricity.

Investigating cathode rays

It was known in the 18th century that a gas at low pressure inside a tube could be made to glow by passing a discharge from an electrostatic machine through it. In the latter part of the 19th century new electrical apparatus enabled scientists to study the effect more thoroughly. For instance, improved vacuum pumps allowed the air pressure inside the tubes to be reduced. At very low pressures the glow disappeared and was replaced by invisible rays which came from the cathode or negative terminal. This made the glass of the tube containing the gas glow green where the rays struck it. In 1883, Edison had noticed that particles seemed to be given off from the negative ends of the filaments of his electric light bulbs. The British scientist William Crookes was one of the discoverers of these "cathode rays." Later, J. J. Thomson extended this work with insights that led to the new science of atomic physics and to the discovery of the structure of the atom by Ernest Rutherford (1871-1937) and his team. The cathode ray tube became the basis for the television set and radar equipment.

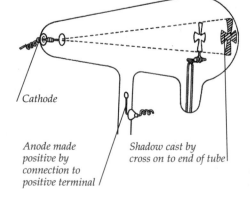

Replica of Crookes's tube

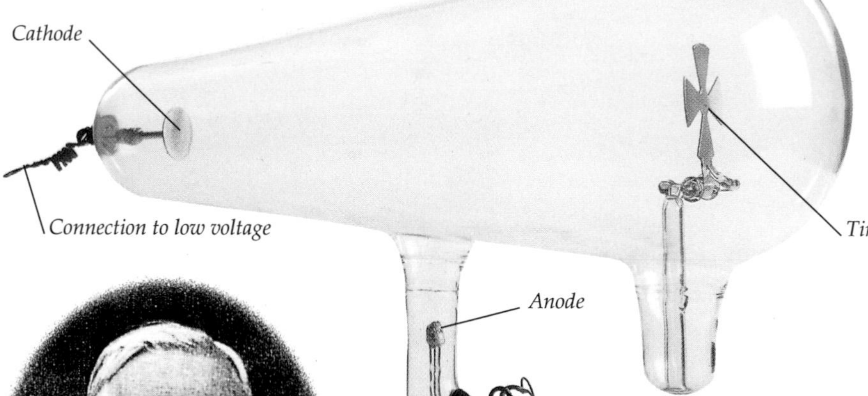

Cathode

Connection to low voltage

Anode

Connection to high voltage

Tin Maltese cross

Shadow cast by cross

WILLIAM CROOKES
An accomplished experimenter, Crookes (1832-1919) helped to found the science of spectroscopy and discovered thallium.

CROOKES'S EXPERIMENT
In the original apparatus (above) the electrons that formed the cathode rays were produced by a complex interaction between the cathode and the residual gas in the tube. In Crookes's famous experiment in 1887, a small metal cross was put in the path of the rays coming from the cathode. The cross cast a shadow on the glass screen beyond. This demonstrated that rays came from the cathode, and that they traveled in straight lines – just as a flashlight shining light rays onto the cross shape would cast a shadow behind it.

Crookes's Maltese cross experiment

Cathode

Anode made positive by connection to positive terminal

Shadow cast by cross on to end of tube

Front view of modern apparatus

Thomson's tube

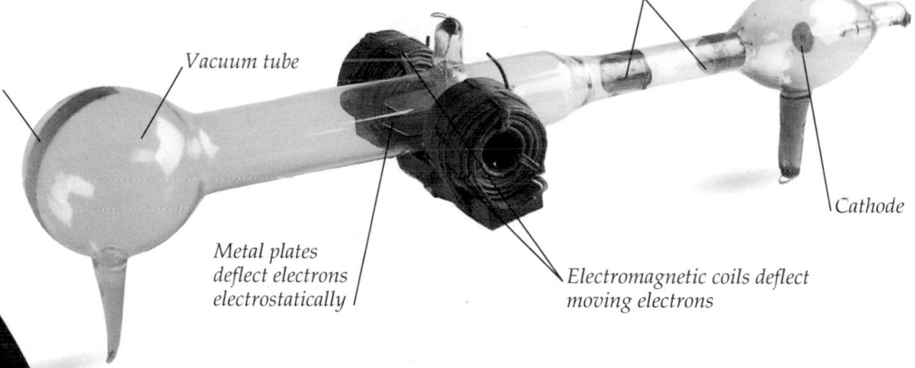

Anodes

Calibrations to show deflection

Vacuum tube

Cathode

Metal plates deflect electrons electrostatically

Electromagnetic coils deflect moving electrons

THE DISCOVERY OF THE ELECTRON
Joseph John Thomson (1856-1940) is credited with identifying the first subatomic particle, now called the electron, in 1897. Thomson knew that cathode rays could be "bent" or deflected by a magnetic field. He devised an experiment to measure the ratio of the charge carried by particles, which he believed made up cathode rays, to their mass. This involved balancing two separate forces on the particles, one produced by the magnetic field of the current flowing in a pair of coils, and the other by the electric field between two metal plates. Thomson explained his results by suggesting that cathode rays consisted of particles which carried an electric charge. This charge was equal to the charge carried by the hydrogen ions involved in the electrolysis. This proved that there was a particle even smaller than the hydrogen atom. He called it the electron (p. 175).

J. J. Thomson

Fleming's tube

FLEMING'S TUBE
The Fleming tube, also called the thermionic valve or an electron tube, was patented in 1904. It was designed to detect the faint signals transmitted by Marconi's recently invented radio sets (p. 307) . A triode developed by Lee De Forest in 1906 was able to amplify radio signals. The cathode (negative electrode) was a hot wire that gave off electrons. These were attracted across the vacuum in the tube to the anode (positive electrode), but could not go the other way. Connected to an alternating voltage, the device thus allowed current to pass in one direction as a series of pulses. Through this capacity to amplify feeble electric signals, the vacuum tube became the key to the development of all electronic machines.

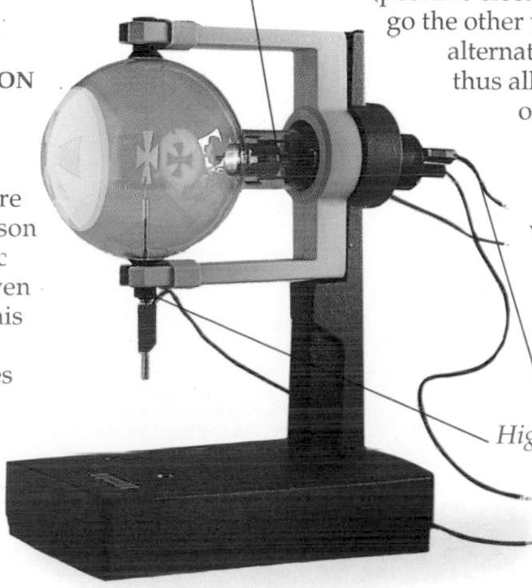

Vacuum tube

Anode

Hot filament acts as cathode

Supporting frame

Heated wire

MODERN DEMONSTRATION
In modern apparatus electrons are produced more easily in larger quantity from a heated wire – the effect noticed by Edison and now called thermionic emission. The anode is given a high positive voltage. This attracts the electrons from the cathode and accelerates them. The electrons strike a fluorescent layer on the inside of the glass causing it to glow brightly – much more brightly than the plain glass of the original tubes.

Low-voltage supply

High-voltage supply

Terminal for electricity supply

301

Communicating with electricity

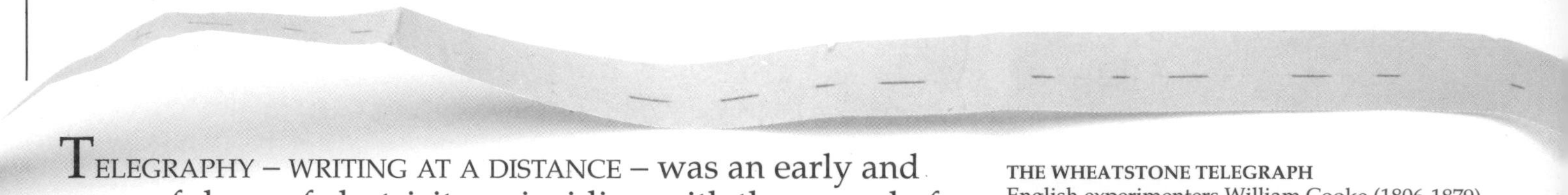

TELEGRAPHY – WRITING AT A DISTANCE – was an early and successful use of electricity, coinciding with the spread of railroads in Europe and North America. Telegraph wires or lines were laid alongside the railroad tracks, where they were easy to check and maintain. The discoveries about the connection between electricity and magnetism had led several people to develop the idea of sending pulses of current in coded form from one place to another. A simple on-off switch completed the circuit and allowed current to flow from the sender. This was read in a code of dots and dashes. Although it took several years for the electric telegraph to be accepted, the era of fast communication had begun.

THE WHEATSTONE TELEGRAPH
English experimenters William Cooke (1806-1879) and Charles Wheatstone (1802-1875) demonstrated a telegraph in England in 1837. At first people were suspicious of the electric wires passing over their land. Wheatstone used the deflections of a needle to spell out letters, in a code of swings to the left and right. The needle was moved by the magnetic field produced by the current through coils of wire inside the case. Twisting the handle one way connected the positive terminal of the battery into the circuit and the negative one to ground, sending a current in one direction, making the needle of the receiving instrument deflect one way. Turning the handle the other way connected the negative terminal of the battery, making the needle deflect the other way.

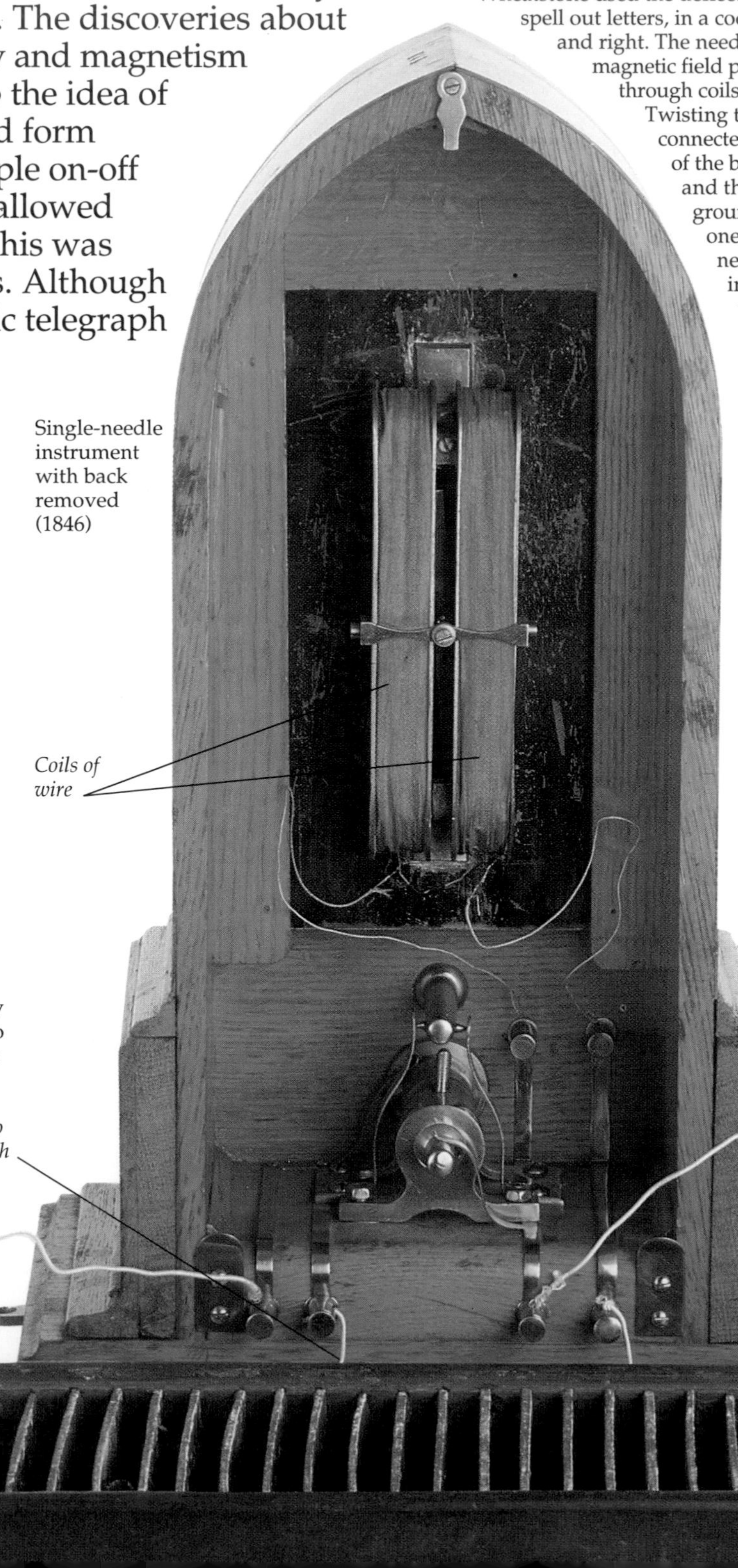

Single-needle instrument with back removed (1846)

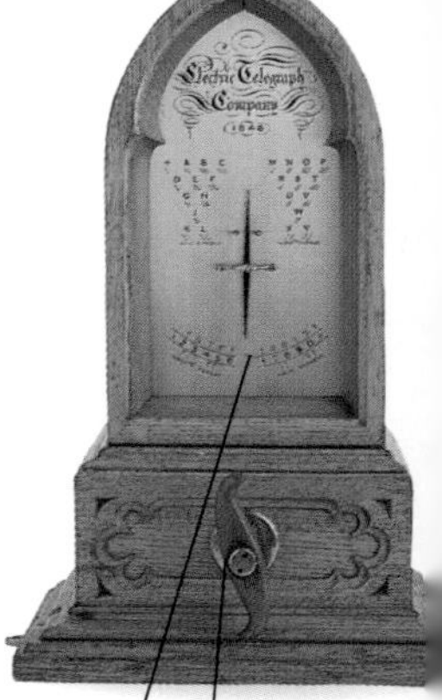

Coils of wire

THE TRAIN IS COMING
Along a copper wire, the signal travels at nearly the speed of light, making telegraphy an almost instant method of sending messages. It was used extensively for signalling on the railroads. This operator listens to the clicking code through earphones; the batteries are on the floor under his desk.

Wires to telegraph

Trough battery   *Wire to battery*

Operating handle

Magnetic needle that acts as pointer

A .−	J .−−−	S ...	2 ..−−−
B −...	K −.−	T −	3 ...−−
C −.−.	L .−..	U ..−	4 ....−
D −..	M −−	V ...−	5 .....
E .	N −.	W .−−	6 −....
F ..−.	O −−−	X −..−	7 −−...
G −−.	P .−−.	Y −.−−	8 −−−..
H	Q −−.−	Z −−..	9 −−−−.
I ..	R .−.	1 .−−−−	0 −−−−−

Modern Morse code alphabet

The "father of the telegraph"

American Samuel Morse (1791-1872) began his career as a professional portrait painter. The idea for a telegraph came to him in 1832 when he saw an electromagnet on a ship while returning from a European tour. He gave up painting and began to investigate electromagnetism. By 1837 he had devised electromagnetic transmitters and receivers, and the first version of the code of dots and dashes that took his name and eventually became used worldwide. Morse's first permanent telegraph line, spanning 37 miles (60 km) between Baltimore and Washington, opened on 24 May 1844 with Morse's message, "What hath God wrought!"

Samuel Morse

DOTS AND DASHES
Morse's early designs for a receiver used an electromagnet and a stylus that pressed a groove into a moving paper strip. Later, there was an inking device (p. 277) for writing dots and dashes. Trained telegraphers listened to the receiver's clicks or a sounding device, decoded the message from these, and wrote it down.

Morse tapes received on the Great Eastern when it was laying the 1865 Atlantic cable

Battery

Relay

Transformer

Electromagnets

Coherer

WIRELESS RECEIVER
An advance on telegraphy, based on electromagnetic waves, was the wireless telegraph. This was made possible by the early experiments of Heinrich Hertz and the practical efforts of Guglielmo Marconi. This wireless receiver was the same as the telegraphy receivers in that it used Morse code, but instead of a connection to a land line, it had a radio receiver which used a coherer. The coherer contains filings that increase in conductivity when they are subjected to radio waves. The link between the radio signal and the sounder circuit is made by the relay, which uses electromagnets (pp. 30-31). It passes the on-off pattern of the received current to a new, more powerful circuit.

Wire to battery

LONG-DISTANCE BUSINESS
Telegraph lines spread across the land. Their real importance was appreciated by businesses where investments and information could be received quickly. These wealthy businessmen no doubt await the 19th-century version of the latest stock market figures.

Talking with electricity

SOUND WAVES DO NOT TRAVEL VERY FAR or very fast in air. As the telegraph system became established for sending messages in coded form, several inventors pursued the idea of using the complex pattern of sound waves from the voice to produce a corresponding pattern of electric signals. These could be sent along a wire much farther, and faster, than sound waves in the air. At the other end, the electric signals would be converted back to sound, to recreate the original speech. A receiver and transmitter at each end allowed both callers to speak and listen. Bell, Edison, and others succeeded in making such devices, which became known as telephones. Telegraphs retained their role of sending relatively simple messages.

ALEXANDER GRAHAM BELL
Born in Scotland, Alexander Graham Bell (1847-1922) emigrated to the United States in 1871, where he became an outstanding figure in the education of the deaf. He found that different voice tones could vary the electrical signals flowing in a wire, by the process of electro-magnetic induction. He also realized that a varying signal could vibrate a flat sheet, or diaphragm, and produce sound waves. The principle of the telephone was born.

Terminals

INSIDE A BELL TELEPHONE
The "candlestick" design (1878) came about due to the mistaken belief that a longer permanent magnet would be stronger than a short one. The same design (below) could function as a mouthpiece (the sound detector or microphone) or earpiece (the sound producer). Sound waves vibrate an iron diaphragm varying the magnetic field of the bar magnet, which produces varying currents in the coil by electromagnetic induction. The principle of the earpiece design changed little from Bell's time until the 1970s, though improved materials allowed the permanent magnet inside the earpiece to be smaller. It is Edison's carbon microphone that is used for the typical mouthpiece.

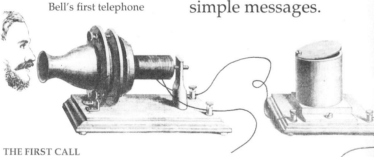

Bell's first telephone

THE FIRST CALL
With advice from Joseph Henry (p. 275), Bell and his assistant, Thomas Watson, constructed early versions of the telephone. Sound waves from the speaker's voice funnelled into a chamber, where they vibrated a flat sheet of thin iron, the diaphragm. This disturbed the magnetic field of a permanent magnet, around which was wrapped a current-carrying coil connected to an external battery. The magnetic field induced varying electrical signals in the circuit, which was completed through a grounded connection.

The two-part telephone in use

Signal-carrying wire

Permanent bar magnet

Wooden casing

Coil of wire

Diaphragm

OPERATOR SERVICE
Only a few years after the first telephones were demonstrated, exchanges were being set up in major cities. The caller's plug had to be inserted into the correct socket. This is Croydon Exchange, near London, which opened in 1884.

Funnel for sound waves

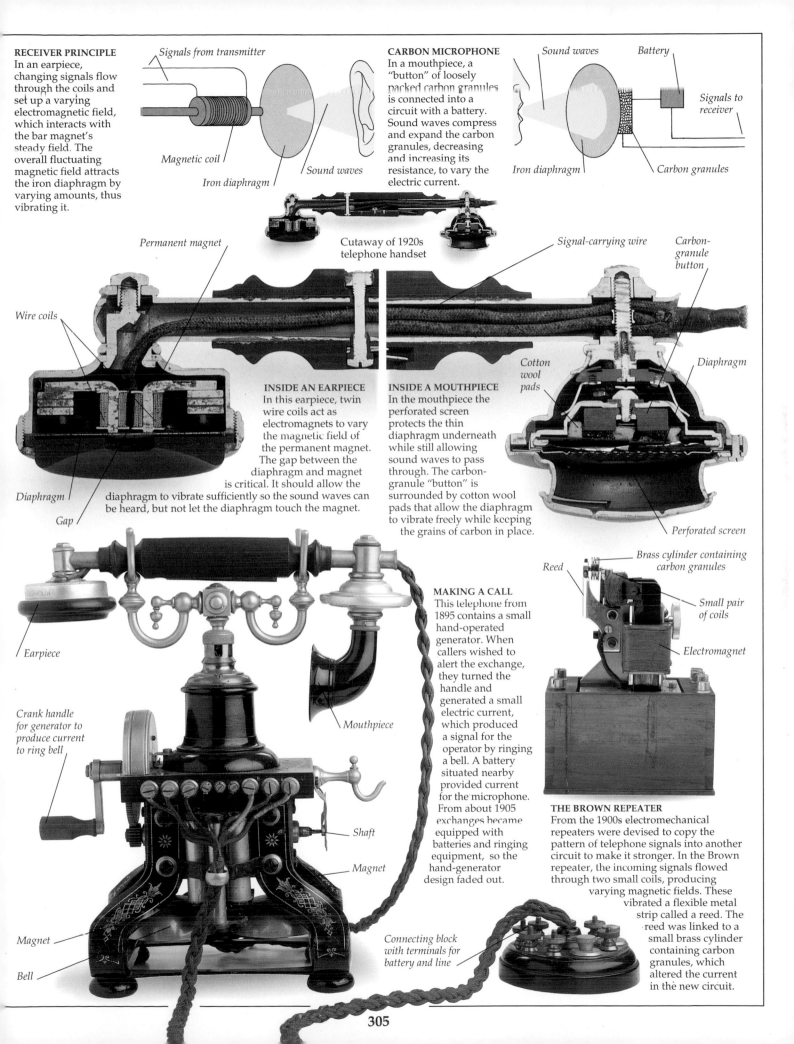

RECEIVER PRINCIPLE
In an earpiece, changing signals flow through the coils and set up a varying electromagnetic field, which interacts with the bar magnet's steady field. The overall fluctuating magnetic field attracts the iron diaphragm by varying amounts, thus vibrating it.

Signals from transmitter

Magnetic coil

Iron diaphragm

Sound waves

CARBON MICROPHONE
In a mouthpiece, a "button" of loosely packed carbon granules is connected into a circuit with a battery. Sound waves compress and expand the carbon granules, decreasing and increasing its resistance, to vary the electric current.

Sound waves

Battery

Signals to receiver

Iron diaphragm

Carbon granules

Cutaway of 1920s telephone handset

Permanent magnet

Wire coils

Diaphragm

Gap

Signal-carrying wire

Carbon-granule button

Cotton wool pads

Diaphragm

Perforated screen

INSIDE AN EARPIECE
In this earpiece, twin wire coils act as electromagnets to vary the magnetic field of the permanent magnet. The gap between the diaphragm and magnet is critical. It should allow the diaphragm to vibrate sufficiently so the sound waves can be heard, but not let the diaphragm touch the magnet.

INSIDE A MOUTHPIECE
In the mouthpiece the perforated screen protects the thin diaphragm underneath while still allowing sound waves to pass through. The carbon-granule "button" is surrounded by cotton wool pads that allow the diaphragm to vibrate freely while keeping the grains of carbon in place.

Earpiece

Crank handle for generator to produce current to ring bell

Magnet

Bell

Mouthpiece

Shaft

Magnet

Connecting block with terminals for battery and line

MAKING A CALL
This telephone from 1895 contains a small hand-operated generator. When callers wished to alert the exchange, they turned the handle and generated a small electric current, which produced a signal for the operator by ringing a bell. A battery situated nearby provided current for the microphone. From about 1905 exchanges became equipped with batteries and ringing equipment, so the hand-generator design faded out.

Reed

Brass cylinder containing carbon granules

Small pair of coils

Electromagnet

THE BROWN REPEATER
From the 1900s electromechanical repeaters were devised to copy the pattern of telephone signals into another circuit to make it stronger. In the Brown repeater, the incoming signals flowed through two small coils, producing varying magnetic fields. These vibrated a flexible metal strip called a reed. The reed was linked to a small brass cylinder containing carbon granules, which altered the current in the new circuit.

Communicating without wires

JAMES CLERK MAXWELL (1831-1879) developed the findings of Faraday and other scientists, using concepts such as magnetic lines of force, and reduced the phenomena of electricity and magnetism to a group of four mathematical equations. One prediction from these equations was that an oscillating electric charge would send out "waves" of electromagnetic energy from its source. A series of experiments by Heinrich Hertz (1857-1894) in the 1880s demonstrated that these waves existed, and that they could be detected at a distance. Further work by Guglielmo Marconi (1874-1937) in the 1890s resulted in radio telegraphy, the sending of messages without wires.

JAMES CLERK MAXWELL
Scottish-born Maxwell predicted the existence of radio waves before they were demonstrated by Hertz (below). He showed that an oscillating electric charge would produce a varying electromagnetic field, which would transmit at a speed that turned out to be equal to the speed of light. From this, he suggested that light rays were electro-magnetic waves.

HERTZ'S EXPERIMENTS
Hertz demonstrated the existence of radio waves in the late 1880s. He used a device called an induction coil to produce a high voltage. One of his early transmitters consisted of two tiny coils with a spark gap. The rapidly oscillating current in the sparks between the ends of the coils produced radio waves. To detect the waves, Hertz used a receiver consisting of two rods with a spark gap as the receiving antenna. A spark jumped the gap where the waves were picked up. Hertz showed that these signals had all the properties of electromagnetic waves. They could be focused by curved reflectors, and a grid of parallel wires placed in their path showed they were polarized.

Heinrich Hertz

Transmitter

Receiver

Spark appeared between coils

Induction coil produced high voltage

Polarizing screen

Radio waves

Plane reflector

Replica of Hertz's equipment

Two coils and spark gap

Reflector

Polarizing screen

GUGLIELMO MARCONI

Marconi began radio experiments on his family's estate near Bologna, Italy. He devised arrangements of long wires and metal plates to send and receive the waves. These were the first antennas. His first radio message across the Atlantic, from Cornwall in England to Newfoundland on December 12, 1901, was Morse code for the letter S. It established the viability of radio for long-distance communication. Here, Marconi (left) shows some of his equipment to visitors in 1920.

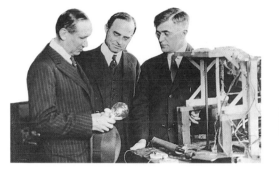

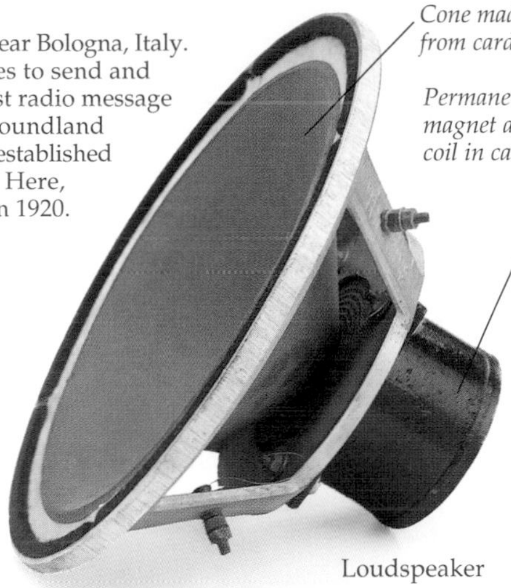

Cone made from cardboard

Permanent magnet and coil in casing

Loudspeaker

How a loudspeaker works

Cylindrical magnet produces strong magnetic field

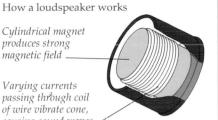

Varying currents passing through coil of wire vibrate cone, causing sound waves

ELECTRICITY INTO SOUND ENERGY

Headphones were used to listen to the first radio sets. Loudspeakers were then developed so that several people could listen at once. Loudspeakers needed radios with better detectors and amplifiers. This became possible when the triode valve was devised in 1906 by Lee De Forest (1873-1961) since the valve could amplify weak signals. The loudspeaker has a strong permanent magnet shaped like a cylinder. A coil of wire fits between the poles of the magnet within the strong magnetic field, and is attached to the cardboard cone. The varying electric currents pass through the coil making it move to and fro. As the coil moves, the cone moves, making sound waves that correspond to the varying electric currents.

PAPAL AUDIENCE

From the 1920s radio broadcasts became used for spreading news and for entertainment. Pope Pius XI (reigned 1922-1939) listens to a musical broadcast on his headphones.

Antenna

RADIO RECEIVER

This state-of-the-art radio dates from 1925 and shows that large multi-wound antennas were required to gather the energy represented by radio waves. Each stage of circuitry in the receiver had to be individually tuned to the radio station.

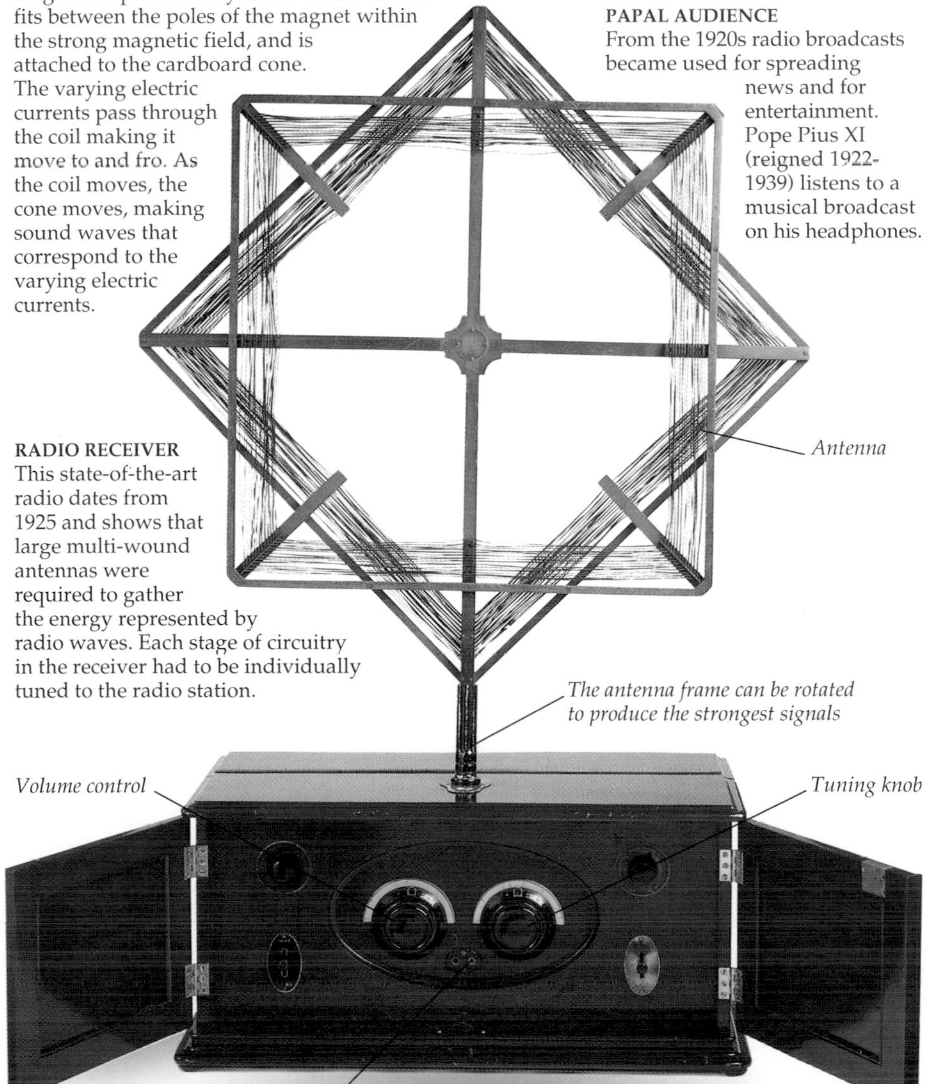

The antenna frame can be rotated to produce the strongest signals

Volume control

Tuning knob

Receiver in curved reflector

Rods pick up radio waves

Headphone socket

Television and the future

IN THE AREA OF COMMUNICATION, there was another great aim for researchers and inventors. This was the wireless transmission not only of sounds, but of images too – television. Several systems were tried for turning patterns of light into electric signals in the camera, transmitting and receiving the signals as radio waves, and displaying the received signals as a moving image for the viewer. A version of the vacuum tube, the cathode ray tube (CRT), became established as the image-displaying unit. This device was yet another stage in the two centuries of research, manipulation, and utilization of electricity – a form of energy that has become master and servant, indispensible and central to modern scientific thought.

INSIDE A 1930S TV SET
Many of the major electrical components described in this book, or their descendants, are contained in this electric machine. The transformer and associated components produce high voltages which drive electrons in beams from the cathode, through the anodes and towards the screen. The screen has a special coating so that it fluoresces white when the electrons hit it. Variable capacitors and other items tune the set to receive signals from different transmitters.

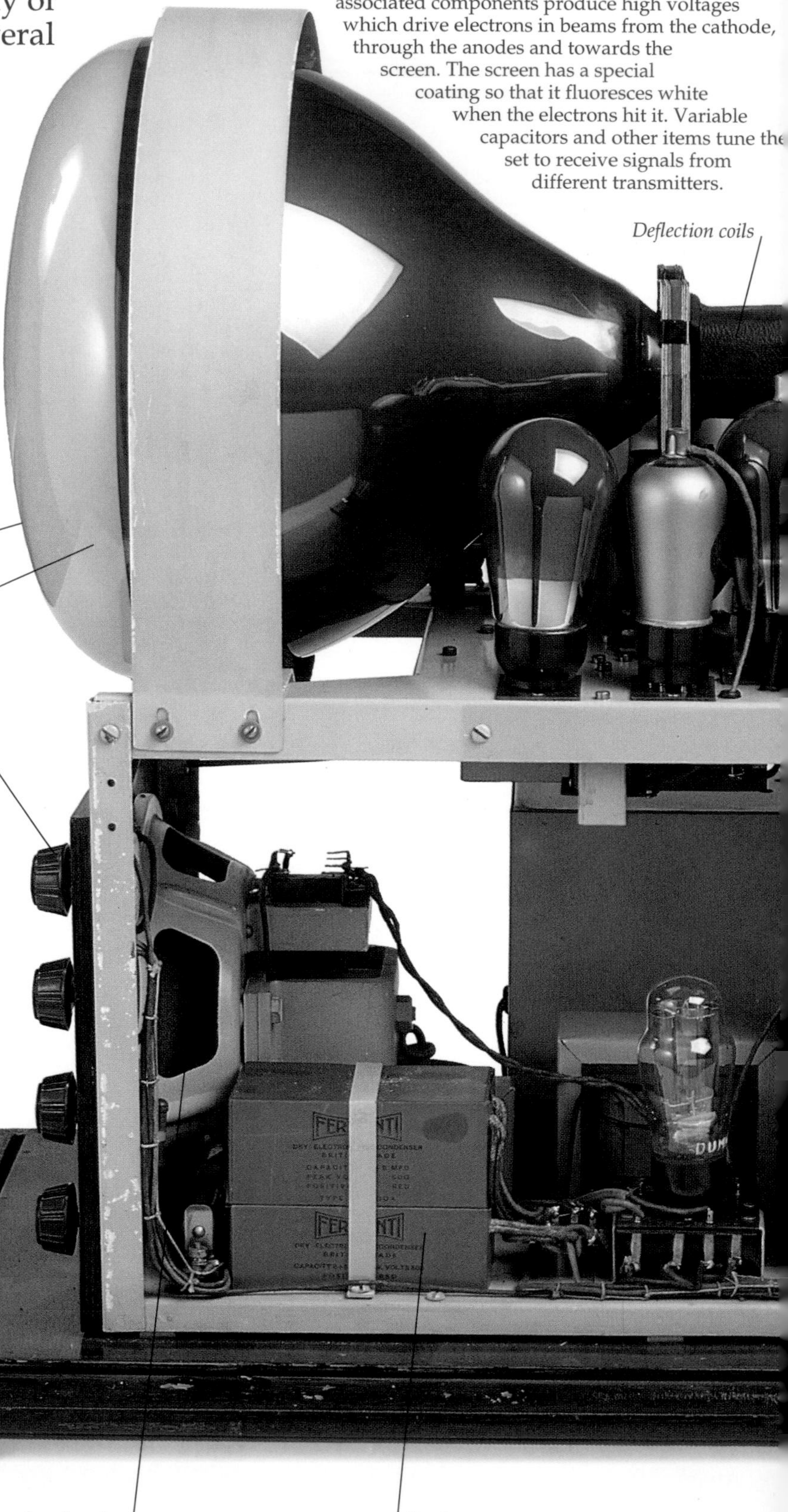

Deflection coils

Screen

Cathode ray tube

Control knobs

BAIRD'S MECHANICAL SCANNER
The television transmission equipment devised in the 1920s by John Logie Baird (1888-1946) was built using various bits of scrap metal and electrical components. Central was the Nipkow disc, a fast-spinning disc with holes arranged in a spiral. As the disc turned, each hole traced a curved line and exposed part of the scene behind. A photoelectric cell (p. 299) transformed the light intensity of each part of the line into electric signals, and sent them to the receiver. Baird's 1926 version produced a 30-line image which was renewed 10 times each second. This electromechanical system was replaced by a purely electrical one (opposite).

Loudspeaker

Condenser

HOW THE TELEVISION WORKS

In the black-and-white television, electrons are produced at the cathode and are accelerated towards the positive electrode, the anode. They pass through holes in the anode, and are focused by the magnetic field produced by focusing coils to produce a spot on the screen. These pairs of focusing coils, one pair arranged vertically and the other horizontally, create fields which deflect the electron beam. The fields are varied so the beam sweeps across the screen, jumps back, sweeps an adjacent line, and so on to cover the screen. At the same time, the intensity of the beam is varied by a signal applied to another electrode near the cathode. When the beam is stronger, it makes the screen glow more brightly at the spot it hits. Each second, 30 complete pictures or frames are produced. The human eye cannot follow the rapid movement of the electron beam and perceives a smoothly changing picture.

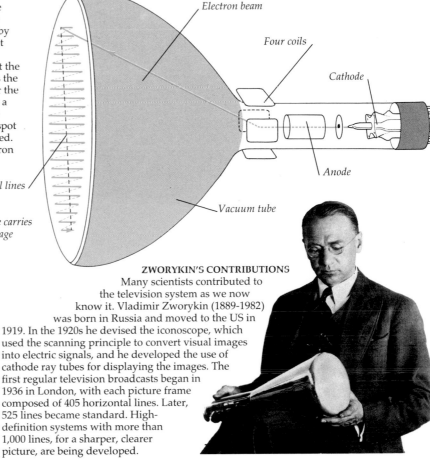

Electron beam

Four coils

Cathode

Anode

Vacuum tube

Scanned horizontal lines

Focusing coil

Electron gun

Insulated wire carries very high voltage

ZWORYKIN'S CONTRIBUTIONS
Many scientists contributed to the television system as we now know it. Vladimir Zworykin (1889-1982) was born in Russia and moved to the US in 1919. In the 1920s he devised the iconoscope, which used the scanning principle to convert visual images into electric signals, and he developed the use of cathode ray tubes for displaying the images. The first regular television broadcasts began in 1936 in London, with each picture frame composed of 405 horizontal lines. Later, 525 lines became standard. High-definition systems with more than 1,000 lines, for a sharper, clearer picture, are being developed.

The electronic age

An understanding of the behavior and nature of electrons lead to electronic components such as the valve. This was an enormous breakthrough in electrical technology but it relied on heat, wasting lots of energy, and it was relatively fragile. During the late 1940s the first transistors were developed. Transistors were used for similar purposes as valves, and soon replaced them for many applications. In the 1960s techniques were introduced to etch whole networks of components on to a thin wafer or "chip" of silicon, to make integrated circuits.

DIODE VALVE
The experimental Fleming diodes of 1904 were the forerunners of other types of vacuum tube, the triode and pentode, with more electrodes. Valves could use small electric signals and control the current through the valve, and could thus amplify the radio signal.

TRANSISTOR
Like valves, transistors could amplify electric signals and manipulate currents and voltages in various ways. But they were smaller, more efficient, more robust, and eventually cheaper than valves.

SILICON CHIP
A tiny wafer of silicon has circuits containing hundreds of transistors and other electrical components.

Wafer of silicon

Resistor

Transformer

Late 19th-century carpenter's plane

Bronze-Age axe head

Universal joint, 1935

BUDDING

Model of Greek water mill

Gyroscopic globe

18th-century apparatus demonstrating the lifting power of the pulley

Toothed gear-wheel
from a calendar
clock c. AD 500

A spinning
gyroscope

FORCE &
MOTION

Screw
threads

Twin-cylinder
aircraft engine

PATENT. N3157

The first
lawn-mower c.1830

A pendulum clock
designed by Galileo
Galilei, built in 1883

The world in motion

THE WORLD AROUND US is never still. In the towns, cars and trucks move along the streets. Above the countryside, aircraft fly through the sky. Obviously, such machines are driven by their engines. Their engines are complex machines that produce a force – a push or a pull – to drive the vehicle along. But how do machines produce their power and how do forces produce movements? And what about the movement of natural objects and phenomena? Why do winds blow and rivers flow? Why do the sun and the moon move across the sky? Are all moving objects pulled or pushed along by forces? These questions have been asked for thousands of years. Ancient Greek thinkers such as Aristotle thought they had the answers, but later scientists proved them wrong. Over the centuries scientists such as Galileo, Newton, and Einstein have investigated the world around us and discovered that it is a far more wonderful and mysterious place than even Aristotle imagined.

Flames and smoke rise into the air from a raging forest fire

THE FOUR ELEMENTS
Aristotle, who was born in northern Greece in 384 BC and died in 322 BC, studied with Plato and later taught Alexander the Great. From his study of the natural world he concluded that there were four basic forms of matter, called elements: solid earth, fluid water, gaseous air, and hot fire. He believed that if they were left to themselves, the elements would move to their natural places: air bubbles rise through water; fire rises through air; earth sinks through water. Forces were produced by elements striving to find their natural places. It was air and fire struggling to rise through the earth that produced earthquakes and volcanoes.

The earth's crust is torn apart as a volcano releases fire and gas from below the ground

Water cascades down a rockface in the Atlas Mountains in Morocco

Banks of cloud are sent flying across the sky by strong winds

THE CRYSTAL SPHERES
This statue represents Atlas, the legendary Greek Titan, holding up the earth on his shoulders. The question of how the earth, the sun, and the planets are supported and what causes them to move across the skies has troubled thinkers since ancient times. In his book *Meteorology*, Aristotle explained that water, air, and fire form spherical shells around the earth. Above these was a set of transparent spheres that held the stars and planets as they revolved. The spheres were thought to be made of a rigid, clear material like crystal, which was not subject to the laws that govern the behavior of the earthly elements. This was why the stars and planets could move without a force acting on them. On earth an object could move only if it was acted upon by a force. The movement would stop if this force was removed.

Assyrian sculpture c. 650 BC
showing soldiers carried by
mule-drawn chariot

Greek athletes
throwing discus
and javelin

Persian archer shooting an arrow

Greek trireme powered
by oarsmen or sails

GREATER FORCE

The Greeks knew that humans were
weak in comparison to the natural
forces that can be seen all around us.
They looked for ways of increasing
human power and of harnessing the
forces of nature. These are tasks that
can be performed by simple machines.
Machines are devices that magnify
forces or allow forces to be used in
new ways. The chariot wheel and the
axle allow a horse to carry a larger
number of people. The bow can shoot an
arrow farther than a javelin can be thrown.
The sailing ship harnesses the wind and
makes it possible to travel farther and faster.

Ramps and wedges

How did the Ancient Egyptians raise huge blocks of stone to build the pyramids? Surprisingly, the answer is that they used machines – not complicated ones with wheels and gears and shafts, but machines so simple that they don't even look like machines. All machines deal with forces, increasing the usefulness of forces. Some machines transmit forces from one place to another. Others magnify forces, so that a small effort can produce a large effect. No one is sure exactly how the Egyptians moved the huge stone blocks to build the pyramids, but they must have used a simple machine – probably the ramp, or inclined plane. They may have built ramps from the ground around the rising pyramid and dragged the blocks up the slope. This was easier than lifting the blocks straight up – the force needed to drag a block along a perfectly smooth slope is less than the weight of the block. However, it must be dragged farther to achieve the same lift.

THE ZIG-ZAG ROUTE
A winding mountain road is a simple machine that makes it easier for vehicles to travel up a slope by turning back and forth across the mountainside.

Spiral ramp

PYRAMID BUILDING
A spiral ramp winds its way around a pyramid, like a road winding up a mountain. A spiral ramp is longer and more gradual than a ramp going directly up the side of the pyramid. This means that less effort is needed to lift the building blocks. Of course, the blocks have to be dragged much farther, around the pyramid many times, to reach the top.

THE ADVANTAGE OF MACHINES
On the far right, four workers struggle to lift a stone block directly into position. Meanwhile, assuming that there is no frictional force, a single worker can accomplish the same task by dragging the block up a ramp. Although the load is the same in each case, the effort required is less using the ramp. It has allowed a small effort force (the pull of a single worker) to overcome a larger load force (the weight of the stone). The ramp is said to give a "mechanical advantage" since it magnifies the effort force. This perfectly smooth ramp allows one worker to accomplish what it normally takes four workers to do, so the mechanical advantage is four. The reason for this is that the ramp is four times as long as its height, and the single worker is having to drag his load four times as far. Increasing the distance moved reduces the effort needed, but the task will take longer to complete.

Wedge-shaped blade

BRONZE AGE AXE HEAD
The inclined plane appears in many guises. The most common form is as a wedge. An axe is a sharp wedge fitted to a handle. While the ramp allows a weight to be raised, the axe head allows a small force – swinging the axe – to produce a strong cutting or splitting force as the blade moves between the two surfaces being split apart. A doorstop works in the same way, forcing the floor and the door apart and jamming the door in position. The cutting blades of knives and scissors are also wedges, forcing apart the material being cut.

Load

Effort applied up the ramp

Ramp

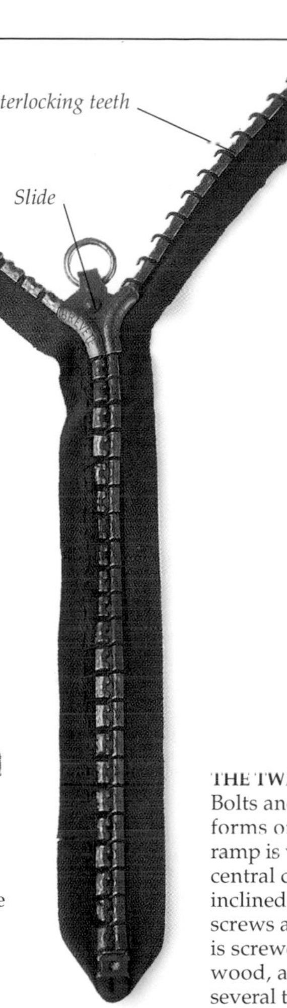

ZIPPING UP

The zipper fastener, like this early French design, exploits the inclined plane to join and separate two rows of interlocking teeth. The zipper's slide contains wedges that detach the teeth and force them apart when opening the zipper. Other wedges force the teeth back together when the zipper is being closed, causing them to lock shut. The wedges convert the small effort needed to move the slide into the strong force needed to mesh and separate the teeth.

Interlocking teeth

Slide

Bolt to hold blade

Blade with wedge-shaped tip

THE CARPENTER'S PLANE

The blade of a carpenter's plane is wedge-shaped. The blade cuts into the wood and lifts the surface above it with a large force, enabling even the toughest woods to be smoothed. The farmer's plough works in a similar way, dragging a wedge-shaped blade through the ground to cut and turn the earth.

Screw

Bolt

THE TWISTING FORCE

Bolts and screws are disguised forms of the inclined plane. The ramp is wrapped around a central cylinder. Like all inclined planes, bolts and screws alter forces. When it is screwed into a piece of wood, a screw rotates several times in order to move forward a short distance. Hence it pulls into the wood with a greater force than is used to turn it.

Effort

Downward motion produces sideways force, splitting wood apart

Wedge

Log

SPLITTING WOOD

A wedge can split wood because it converts a downward movement into a sideways force that splits the wood apart. Because the wood is forced apart by only a small amount when the wedge moves down by a large amount, the forces involved are not equal. The sideways force is much more powerful than the force needed to push the wedge into the wood.

Effort applied vertically

Load

Wheels and axles

THE WHEEL IS A VERY ANCIENT INVENTION and a very useful one, with more uses than just transportation. When it revolves around a central axle, the wheel becomes a machine that can transmit and magnify forces. As in any machine, a small force moving a large distance can produce a large force moving a small distance. If a wheel is turned by a small force at its rim, a larger force will be generated at the axle. Waterwheels and capstans are obvious examples, but there are many others, such as a round door handle or a water faucet.

POTTER'S WHEEL
This 1822 picture shows an Indian potter pushing a wheel around with his foot to produce a turning force at the axle, where the clay is being worked.

HARD AT WORK
Early industry relied upon a few simple machines, such as levers, pulleys, and wheels. This medieval painting shows a man-powered treadmill in the shape of a wheel being used to lift building materials up a tower under construction.

WATER POWER
This waterwheel was in use in the early 19th century to provide power to drive machinery in a cotton mill in Lancashire, England. The wheel was 62 ft (19 m) across and produced the same power as 150 horses. Vertical waterwheels proved better than horizontal ones because they could be built larger and could therefore generate more power.

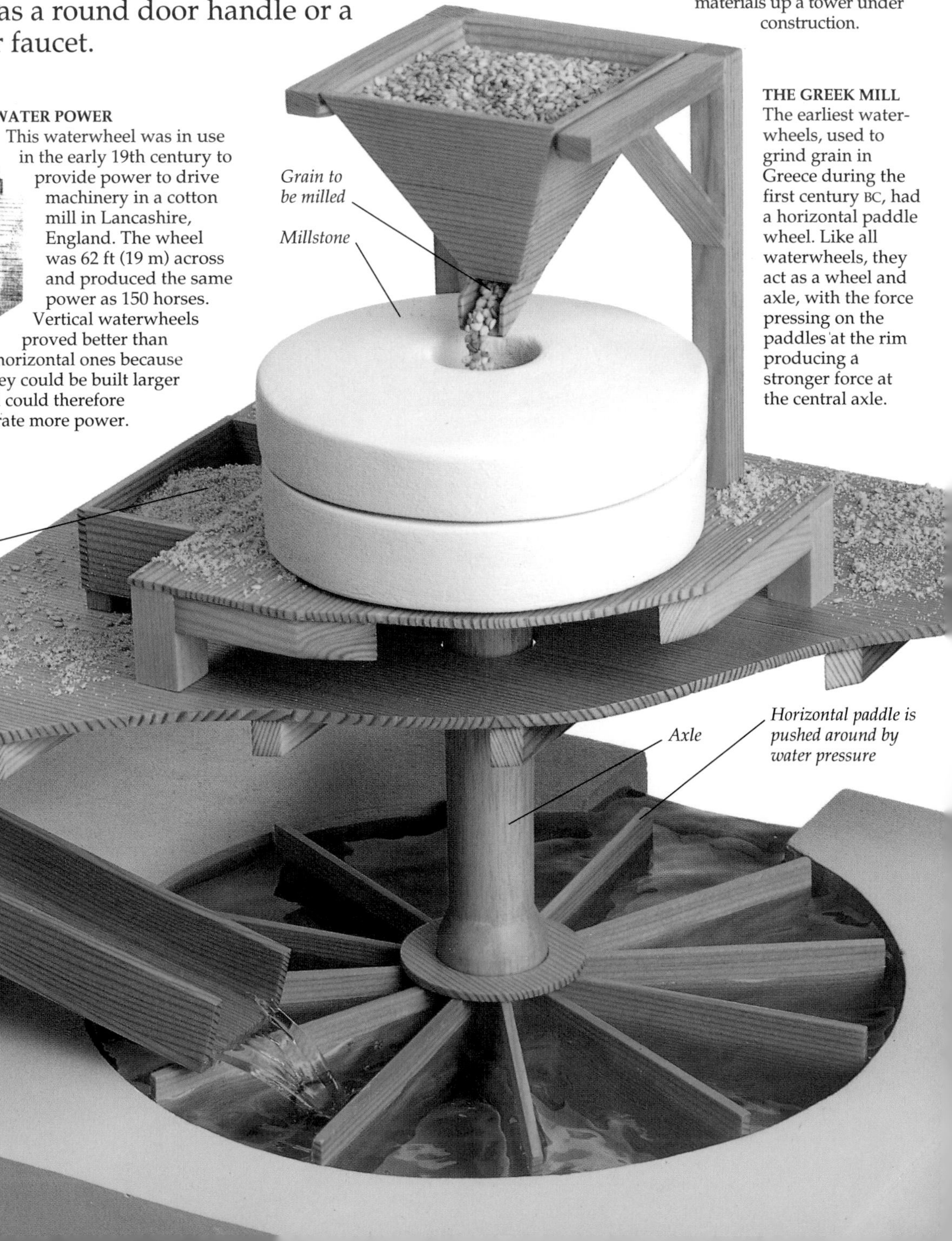

THE GREEK MILL
The earliest water-wheels, used to grind grain in Greece during the first century BC, had a horizontal paddle wheel. Like all waterwheels, they act as a wheel and axle, with the force pressing on the paddles at the rim producing a stronger force at the central axle.

Grain to be milled

Millstone

Milled flour

Water supply

Axle

Horizontal paddle is pushed around by water pressure

HAUL AWAY

The capstan was used for many centuries to haul up the anchor of a ship. Turned by sailors pushing on the long arms, the capstan acts as a wheel and axle, magnifying the turning force. The anchor is lifted by a rope or chain winding around the central axle. The arms on this 1820 capstan can be removed so that it takes up less room on deck when not in use. A ratchet in the base of the capstan prevents it from turning back and allowing the anchor to fall.

Arm on which pressure is applied

Rope is hauled in

Ratchet mechanism

Central axle

THE CAPSTAN ON LAND
The capstan, or windlass, can also be used to move loads on land. This 19th-century watercolor shows a horse-driven windlass being used to haul up coal from an underground mine by means of ropes that run over pulleys at the top of the shaft.

Rolling along

The most common use of the wheel is not as a machine, but as a means of reducing the effect of friction, the dragging force between surfaces. As a wheel rolls along, each point along the wheel's rim touches the ground and then rises up, rather than dragging. This makes it easier to move heavy loads over rough surfaces.

SOLID WHEELS
The wheels on this chariot from 2,500 BC, found painted on a stone in the tomb of the kings of Ur in Iraq, are clearly made from two separate planks joined together. Being mounted on axles, wheels remain in position under the load and they are therefore more convenient to use than rollers.

THE SEMI-SOLID WHEEL
In order to reduce weight, heavy solid wooden wheels could be made lighter by cutting out sections and leaving a crossbar, as this picture of an early Brazilian carriage shows. The spoked wheel developed from wheels like these.

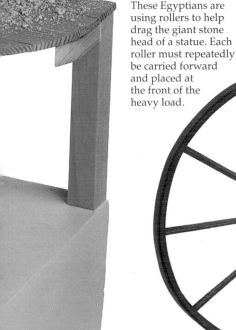

BEFORE THE WHEEL
These Egyptians are using rollers to help drag the giant stone head of a statue. Each roller must repeatedly be carried forward and placed at the front of the heavy load.

Saddle

Spoked wheels

THE HOBBY HORSE
In 1817 the German Baron Karl von Drais produced the forerunner of the bicycle. Like this English version, it consisted of a wooden beam set above two spoked wooden wheels in line. The rider sat astride the saddle, pushing the ground with alternate feet, turning the front wheel to steer. Apart from the true horse, this was the fastest thing on the roads at the time, reaching speeds of up to 10 mph (16 km/h).

Archimedes' screw

THE FIRST MECHANIC
Archimedes lived from about 287 BC to about 212 BC in the Greek colony of Syracuse on the island of Sicily.

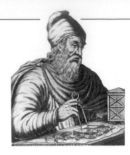

ARCHIMEDES WAS ONE OF THE GREATEST engineers and inventors in ancient Greece. He was the first person to make a scientific study of simple machines, and he used his knowledge to build many different machines. His name is associated with the lifting screw, a simple machine in which an inclinded plane is wrapped around a shaft inside a tube. Turning the screw causes the inclined plane to act as a wedge that lifts a portion of water. The effort needed to lift the load is reduced, but the screw has to be turned many times to raise the water a short distance. It also takes longer than raising water vertically by hand.

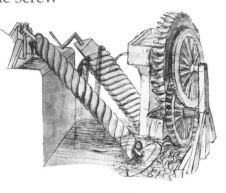

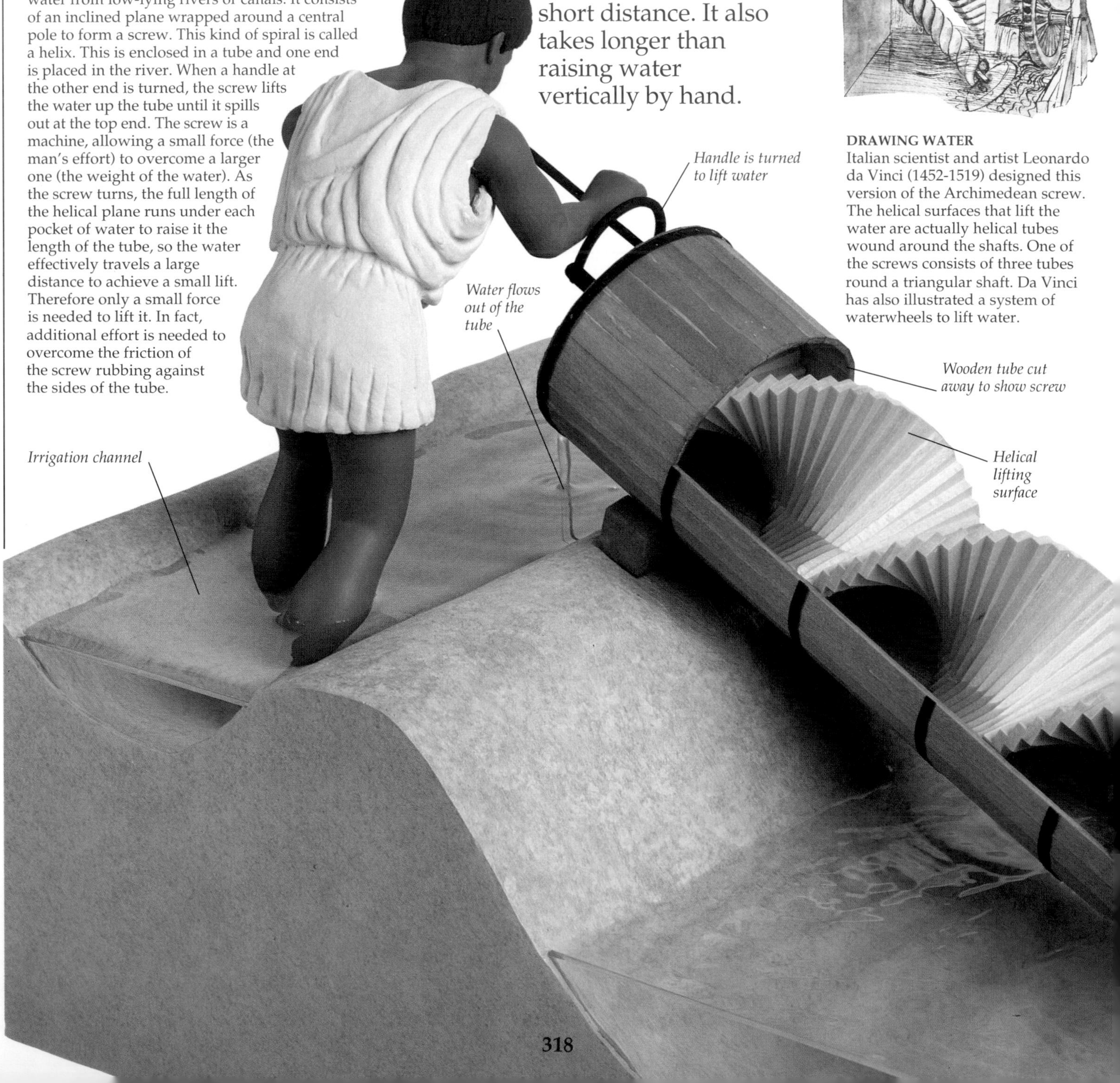

DRAWING WATER
Italian scientist and artist Leonardo da Vinci (1452-1519) designed this version of the Archimedean screw. The helical surfaces that lift the water are actually helical tubes wound around the shafts. One of the screws consists of three tubes round a triangular shaft. Da Vinci has also illustrated a system of waterwheels to lift water.

RUNNING UPHILL
The Archimedean screw is a device for raising water from low-lying rivers or canals. It consists of an inclined plane wrapped around a central pole to form a screw. This kind of spiral is called a helix. This is enclosed in a tube and one end is placed in the river. When a handle at the other end is turned, the screw lifts the water up the tube until it spills out at the top end. The screw is a machine, allowing a small force (the man's effort) to overcome a larger one (the weight of the water). As the screw turns, the full length of the helical plane runs under each pocket of water to raise it the length of the tube, so the water effectively travels a large distance to achieve a small lift. Therefore only a small force is needed to lift it. In fact, additional effort is needed to overcome the friction of the screw rubbing against the sides of the tube.

Handle is turned to lift water
Water flows out of the tube
Wooden tube cut away to show screw
Helical lifting surface
Irrigation channel

RAISING GRAIN
The Archimedean screw finds a place today on the farm. When a combine harvester has cut the crop and separated the grain from the chaff (the straw and the husks), a rotating screw, or auger, carries the grain up a tube. It then flows out of the top into a waiting truck. Similar augers are used in bakeries and factories to move flour and other fine powders that behave rather like liquids.

Ratchet

Handle   *Auger bit*

THE MINER'S ROCK-DRILL
This kind of drill is also called an auger and it is used to drill a hole and remove the loose material. This particular drill is used to cut holes in rock so that explosives can be inserted. As the drill is turned, its double-bladed cutting tip bites into the rock and earth, breaking away small pieces. This waste material is carried out of the deepening hole along the grooves of the drill bit, in the same way that water is lifted up the Archimedean screw. Large augers are used to make holes in soft ground to insert the foundations for tall buildings.

CURLING SWARF
When a drill bit cuts through soft metal, the waste metal, or swarf, that the drill cuts out takes the form of a helix. This demonstrates the similarity between the Archimedean screw, the auger, and the spiral staircase. The stairs are more accurately called a "helical staircase."

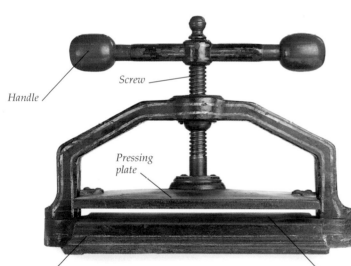

Handle

Screw

Pressing plate

Base plate

PRESSING DOWN
An early use for the screw was in the simple printing press. A screw was used to force down a plate that pressed a sheet of paper on to a tray of inked metal letters, or type. The small force needed to turn the handle produces a far greater force pressing down on the paper. This press was used for making copies of letters. Similar presses were also used to stamp coins out of soft metals.

Paper inserted here

Helical swarf   Drill bit

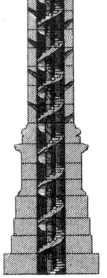

Water source

Fixing post holds the tube in place

Sharpened drill tip

TAKING THE LONG WAY AROUND
Walking up a spiral staircase from the bottom to the top is easier than climbing the same height up a vertical ladder, even though the distance walked is much greater. This is because the slope of the winding stairs is far less steep. This is similar to Archimedes' screw, which winds around and around in order to raise the water a small distance.

Floating and sinking

The GREEK SCIENTIST Archimedes is best known for his "Principle." This explains why some objects float and some objects sink in liquids. Objects that are full of air, such as a hollow ball, are good floaters. But it is not just air-filled objects that float. Many solid objects, such as apples, also float. Archimedes' first insight was that all floating objects are supported by an upward force, called buoyancy, or upthrust. The upthrust is caused by the liquid pressing against the floating object. The upthrust can be felt if a table tennis ball is pushed under water. This is the force that makes things float. Archimedes' second insight was that the force of the upthrust on an object depends on how much liquid the object pushes aside, or displaces. If an object displaces enough liquid, it experiences an upthrust strong enough to support its weight, and the object floats. After many experiments, Archimedes discovered that the amount of upthrust on a floating object is equal to the weight of the liquid it displaces. This is called Archimedes' Principle.

Spring balance

Apple being weighed

1 WEIGHING
An object that will float – in this case an apple – is weighed on a spring balance and its weight is recorded.

2 FLOATING AND BALANCING
Two identical beakers are then placed in the pans of an accurate set of scales (right). The two beakers are filled to the brim with water and the scales are seen to balance. The apple is now lowered into the right-hand beaker until it floats. The water that overflows is carefully caught. When the apple has settled, it is found that the scales are still balanced.

Testing the theory
This three-part experiment puts Archimedes' principle to the test by comparing the weight of a floating object with the weight of the liquid that it displaces. The principle that the upthrust on an object is equal to the weight of liquid that it displaces also applies to objects that do not float, but in these cases the upthrust is less than the weight of the object, which therefore sinks. Archimedes realized that a sinking object displaces a volume of liquid equal to its own volume, and he used this fact to help King Hieron find out whether his crown was pure gold.

Beaker full of water

Scale pan

FLOATING BALLS
Three balls of the same size – a table tennis ball (left), a rubber squash ball (center), and a hardwood ball (right) – float in water. Each ball sinks until it displaces enough water to produce an upthrust equal to its weight. The table tennis ball is light and so sinks little. The hardwood ball weighs the most. It sinks until it is almost underwater.

UNDER THE WAVES
A submarine, such as this 1881 Russian model, submerges because it takes water into its tanks. This increases the weight of the boat and, since the upthrust is unchanged, the submarine sinks. To make it rise, water is pumped out of the tanks.

Arm of weighing balance

"EUREKA!"
Archimedes is said to have discovered his Principle on seeing the water rise as he got into his bath. King Hieron had asked him to find out whether the King's new crown was pure gold, without damaging it. At the palace he lowered the crown into a jug of water and noted how far the water rose. He then did the same with a piece of pure gold of the same weight and the water rose by less, proving that the crown contained another, less dense metal.

FLOATING ON AIR
Albert and Gaston Tissandier, French aeronauts, made a trial run in their rigid airship, or dirigible, in 1883. The airship was filled with hydrogen gas, which is less dense than air, so the upthrust of the air on the airship was greater than the ship's weight.

HOT AIR
The hot air inside a balloon is less dense than the colder air that surrounds it. The balloon will stay aloft as long as the air inside it is kept warm.

Spring balance

Full beaker with apple floating in it

3 WEIGHING THE WATER
When the water that overflowed from the beaker is weighed (right), this displaced water is found to weigh precisely the same as the apple. The reason that the scales still balance is that the apple has displaced exactly the weight of water that compensates for the addition of the weight of the apple to the pan. Because the apple floats, the upthrust must be equal to the weight of the apple. The spring balance has shown this to be the same as the weight of the water displaced. So Archimedes was right – the size of the upthrust on the apple equals the weight of the water displaced.

Water being weighed

MEASURING DENSITY
The hydrometer is an instrument used to measure the density of liquids. It is used in the brewing industry, for example, to measure the density of alcoholic drinks. The instrument consists of a glass tube that floats upright, sinking deeply into less dense liquids such as denatured alcohol (below) and floating high in dense liquids such as glycerin (far right).

Hydrometer in glycerin

Hydrometer in denatured alcohol

Hydrometer in water

Scale pan

STAYING BUOYANT
Bony fishes have an air-filled sac, called a swim bladder, inside their bodies. The pressure of the air in the swim bladder is adjusted to maintain buoyancy at different depths of water. By compressing the air in the bladder, the fish can sink down in the water.

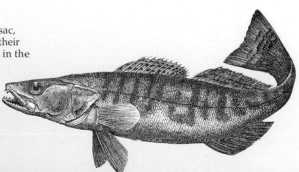

Levers

A LEVER IS A simple machine. It consists of a rigid bar which can turn around a fixed point, called the fulcrum. A crowbar is a kind of lever, and it is used as a force magnifier to lift heavy weights by using smaller forces. The load, at one end of the bar, is overcome by a smaller force, the effort, applied at the other end. Such a lever is said to have a positive "mechanical advantage." To achieve this, the lever must obey the rule that applies to all force magnifiers: the effort must move a greater distance than the load. To raise a heavy rock, the effort applied at the end of the bar must move farther than the rock rises.

Studying levers

This apparatus was made during the 1700s to show the action of the lever. The lever is the horizontal beam resting upon, or held down by, the fulcrum at the top of the upright on the left. The "load" consists of a weight hung below the lever, and the "effort" force is provided by another weight hanging over the upper pulley. The positions of the load and effort can be changed to demonstrate the three different classes of lever.

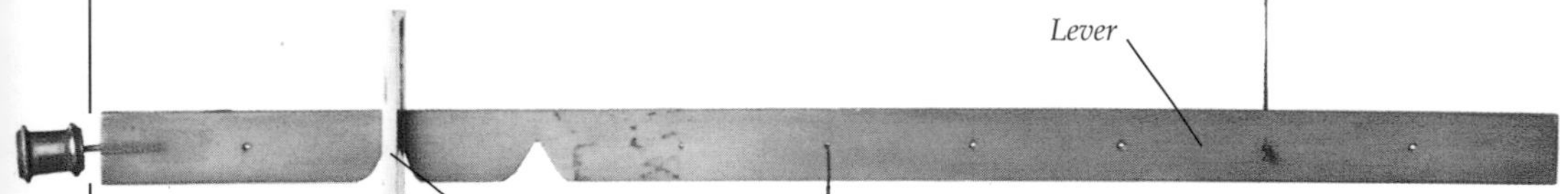

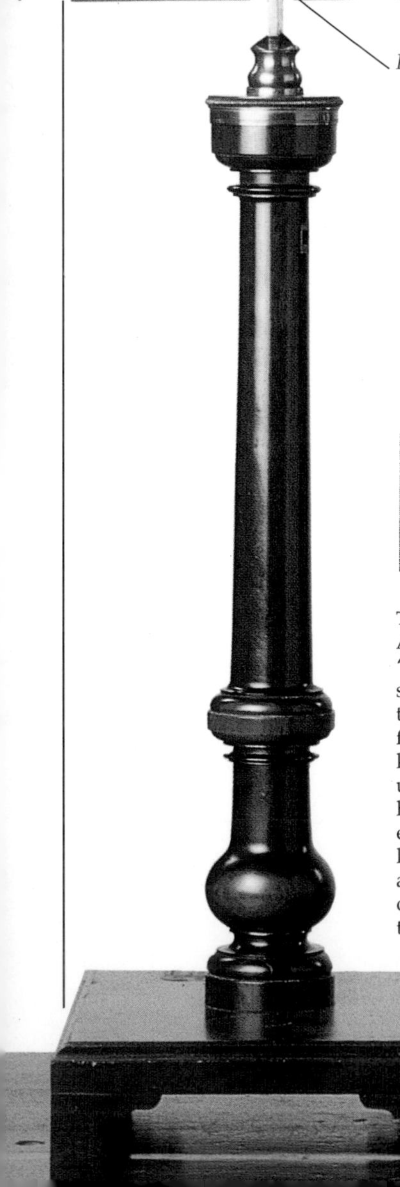

Effort

Lever

Fulcrum

Load

CLASS 2 LEVER
In a class 2 lever, the load lies between the fulcrum and the effort force. This kind of lever is always a force magnifier, having a good mechanical advantage. In the setup shown here, the two small weights over the pulley are the effort, and the larger load hangs below the center of the lever. Since the load is twice the size of the effort that is supporting it, the mechanical advantage is two.

Effort

Fulcrum

Load

THE CROWBAR – A CLASS 1 LEVER
After a study of levers, Archimedes boasted "Give me a long enough lever and a place to stand, and I will move the earth." Of course, to operate his lever he would have needed a fulcrum, and the artist of this old drawing has kindly provided a conical rock. Archimedes is using a crowbar, a typical class 1 lever, which has the fulcrum between the load and the effort. For greatest mechanical advantage, the load (the earth) must be close to the fulcrum and the lever must be long. During his study of levers, Archimedes discovered the "law of the lever": for balance, the effort multiplied by its distance from the fulcrum must equal the load multiplied by its distance from the fulcrum.

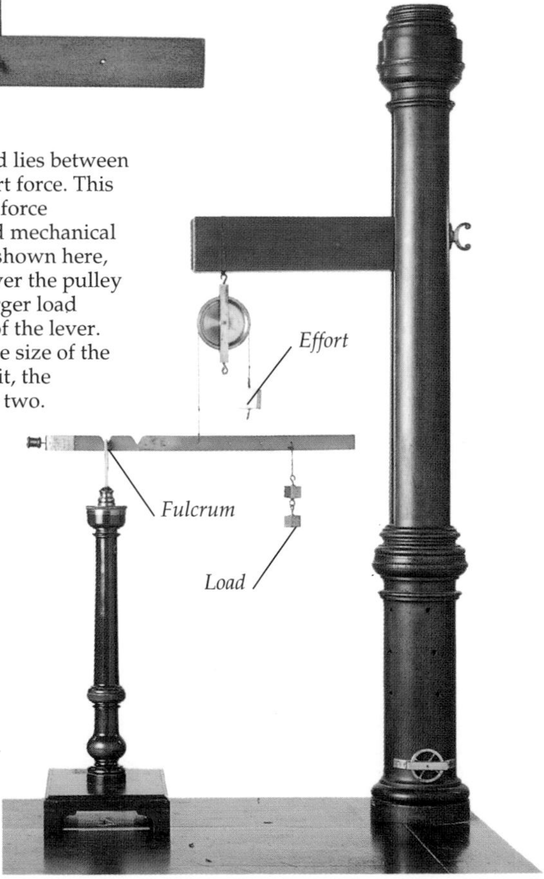

CLASS 3 LEVER
In a class 3 lever, the effort is applied between the fulcrum and the load. Such a lever is a force reducer, since the effort (the single large weight) is greater than the load (the two small weights), and its mechanical advantage is therefore less than one. In this case the effort is pulling up against the fulcrum rather than resting on top of it. The human arm is a class 3 lever with the elbow as the fulcrum.

SWEET AND STRONG

These 19th-century sugar nippers are a pair of class 1 levers joined in the middle. Each arm turns around the central hinge or fulcrum. The effort is applied to the ends held in the hand. The load consists of a lump of sugar between the cutting blades. These nippers were used to break off chunks from a sugar loaf for cooking or to sweeten coffee or tea. Modern scissors work in the same way.

ROCK-A-BYE BABY

A seesaw is a class 1 lever with a central fulcrum. It is designed to balance and to produce no mechanical advantage. Children of equal weights should therefore sit at the ends of the seesaw, but if the weights are unequal, the heavier child should sit nearer to the fulcrum.

Load

THE LEVER AT WAR

The trebuchet, a medieval war machine for hurling large rocks, used a class 1 lever. When the heavy weight at one end is dropped, it levers the longer arm swiftly around and launches a rock from the rope bag at the other end of it.

Fulcrum

Effort

Effort

Fulcrum

CRACKING FORCE

Nutcrackers are a pair of class 2 levers sharing a fulcrum at one end. The effort is applied at the ends of the levers, or arms, squeezing the nut held in the middle, which is the load. Class 2 levers can be powerful force magnifiers – in this case enabling the effort of a hand to crack the toughest nut.

Load

ON THE FIDDLE

As the giant pincer of the fiddler crab is a class 3 lever, the muscle that pulls the pincer shut has to be extremely strong to produce the force that the crab needs.

A MEAL OF RICE AND FISH

Chopsticks are class 3 levers and are therefore force reducers. They do not grip the food strongly, but they are able to magnify movements. Small motions of the fingers are converted into longer, though weaker, movements at the tips of the chopsticks.

AGE-OLD DESIGN

As this medieval painting shows, the design of the wheel barrow has not changed in centuries, as it is ideal for moving heavy loads by hand. It is a class 2 lever, with the load being placed between the effort and the fulcrum. Lifting the handles with a light effort raises a heavy load closer to the fulcrum, which is the axle of the wheel on which the barrow rolls.

A TOOL FROM ANCIENT ROME

These bronze Roman scissors, once used for cutting cloth, are a pair of class 3 levers. The blades turn about the hinge at one end, and the user squeezes the blades together in the middle. The load is the resistance of the cloth. These scissors require a greater effort than modern ones, but they are still used by sheep shearers, as the blades open wide to take in the thick fleece.

Fulcrum *Effort* *Load*

Hoist away

ACCORDING TO LEGEND, King Hieron of Syracuse once challenged Archimedes to drag a large ship up the beach singlehandedly. Archimedes studied the problem and decided upon the best machine for the task – a pulley. A pulley is a machine in which a rope passes back and forth over one or more grooved wheels. One end of the rope is attached to the load and the other end is pulled in order to move or lift the load. Simple pulleys have only one wheel. These pulleys change the direction in which a force acts, but they do not magnify forces. Compound pulleys – pulleys with more than one wheel – are able to magnify forces. Archimedes attached to the ship a compound pulley, composed of many pulley wheels, and he was able to drag the ship up the shore without help. Like the ramp and the lever, the pulley allows a small effort to overcome a large load because the effort moves through a greater distance than the load. In a pulley system comprising two wheels, the effort will move twice as far as the load, giving a mechanical advantage of two, but friction and the weight of the pulleys reduce the advantage.

Load, including weight of the lower pulley

Effort

THE POWER OF THE PULLEY
Making use of the same effort, different pulley systems will support different loads. On the right is a simple pulley in which the weights on both ends of the string are equal. There is no force magnification. The compound pulley system on the left consists of two triple wheels with the string passing over all six wheels. Using this system, the load is much greater than the weight that is lifting it. This system magnifies the lifting force by six times (assuming that there is no friction), although this is not immediately apparent since the weight of the lower pulley must be considered as part of the load. The middle pulleys magnify the lifting force by four and two times. The theoretical mechanical advantage of a pulley system – how much the system magnifies a force – is the same as the number of strands of rope supporting the lower wheel. This advantage is gained at the price of having to pull the end of the rope farther than the load rises.

THE PULLEY AT WAR
A medieval bowman loads his crossbow by winding a handle attached to a double pulley that pulls back the string. A crossbow bolt could pierce armor, but to achieve this power the string had to be under great tension, and a large force was therefore needed to load it.

THE PULLEY AT WORK
Five men pull a rope that passes over a simple pulley, raising a weight, which is then allowed to drop on to a pile, driving it into the ground. The pulley makes the work lighter since it is easier to pull a rope down than to lift a weight up.

Rotating cabin mounted on steel rollers

145-ton counterweight

100-foot-long hull

FLOATING CRANE

Seen here as a cutaway model, this crane was built in 1886 for use at the Tilbury Docks on the River Thames near London. The crane has a lifting capacity of 60 tons and is mounted on a floating platform. The tubular steel boom, strengthened by a wrought iron framework, is 92 ft (28 m) long and rests on a 26 ft (8 m) diameter circle of steel rollers. The rollers are supported on an iron cylinder built into the hull. The crane's lifting tackle consists of a compound pulley system through which the cable runs. The cable is raised and lowered by a hoisting drum powered by a two-cylinder engine. Inside the cabin, the weight of the boom and the load is counterbalanced by a wrought iron truck weighing 145 tons. This counterbalance truck runs on rails and can be moved back and forth to achieve the best balance.

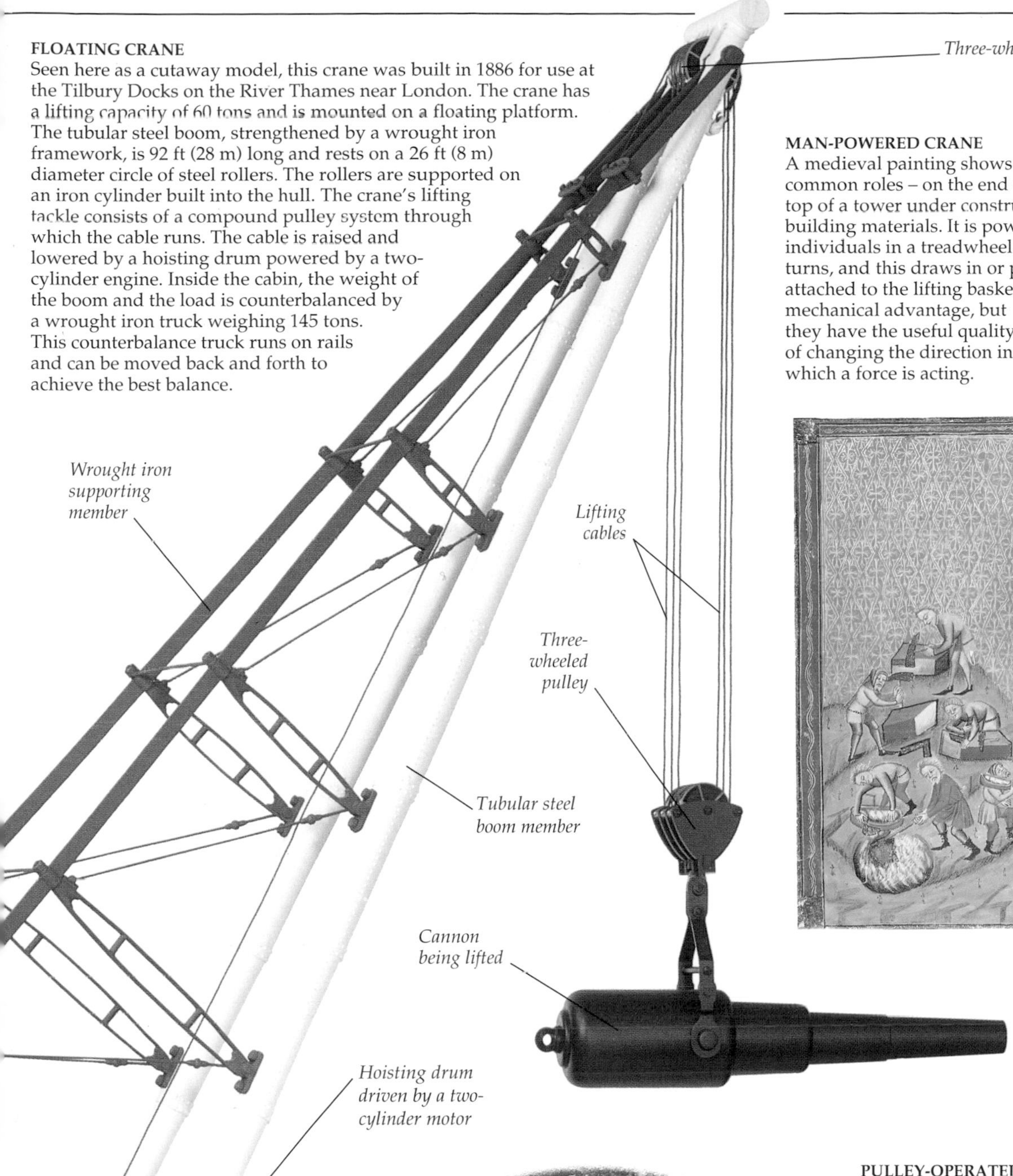

Three-wheeled pulley

Wrought iron supporting member

Lifting cables

Three-wheeled pulley

Tubular steel boom member

Cannon being lifted

Hoisting drum driven by a two-cylinder motor

MAN-POWERED CRANE

A medieval painting shows a single pulley in one of its most common roles – on the end of a simple crane. The crane, at the top of a tower under construction, is being used to raise building materials. It is powered by two unfortunate individuals in a treadwheel. As they walk, the treadwheel turns, and this draws in or plays out the rope, which is attached to the lifting basket. Single pulleys do not offer a mechanical advantage, but they have the useful quality of changing the direction in which a force is acting.

ARCHIMEDES REVISITED

In a scene from the movie *Fitzcarraldo*, this ship is being dragged up a steep slope in the Andes Mountains in South America using an elaborate system of pulleys. The ship's own power is being used to haul on the cables. This scene echoes the story of Archimedes' accomplishment at Syracuse when he moved a ship singlehandedly.

PULLEY-OPERATED ELEVATOR

A 19th-century design for a water-powered elevator shows pulleys being used in two ways. A strong cable runs from the roof of the elevator car, up over a pulley wheel and down to another pulley wheel. This is attached to a piston that slides up and down in a tube. The piston is driven from above and below by the pressure of water in the tube. A rope passing around a second pair of pulley wheels enables the lift attendant to turn a valve at the base of the shaft, directing water into the top or bottom of the tube, pushing the piston down or up to raise or lower the elevator car.

Getting into gear

GEARS ARE PAIRS of interlocking toothed wheels that transmit force and motion in machines. The four basic kinds of gears are rack and pinion, spur, bevel, and worm gears. In a pair of gear wheels, the smaller wheel turns more quickly than the larger one, and this difference in speed produces a difference in the force transmitted; the larger wheel turns with a greater force. Gears can therefore be used to increase or decrease a force, and to change the speed of a rotation, as well as its direction.

Inter-locking teeth

SPUR GEAR
The spur gear consists of two interlocking toothed wheels in the same plane. The gears above are fragments of an ancient calendar instrument, dating from around AD 500, which probably showed the positions of the sun and moon on a dial.

WORM GEAR
The worm gear is a shaft encircled by a screw thread, into which a toothed wheel fits. It can produce a strong force, and it is often used on musical instruments, such as the guitar and double bass, to tighten the strings.

CHANGING DIRECTION
The ancient Romans used wooden bevel-type gears like these in water mills, to change the direction of rotation from horizontal to vertical.

BEVEL GEARS
Bevel gears consist of two toothed wheels that mesh at an angle, altering the direction of the rotation. If the two wheels have different numbers of teeth, they also alter speed and force. For instance, if the big wheel has twice as many teeth, it rotates with half the speed and twice the force of the small wheel.

RACK AND PINION
The rack and pinion gear consists of a toothed wheel, the pinion, which meshes with a toothed sliding rack. It converts a rotary motion into a straight line motion. In this apparatus, moving the diagonal bar up and down raises each plunger in turn to pump out air from below. Rack and pinion gears are also used in the steering systems of some cars to connect the steering column to the front wheels.

BUDDING'S BLADE-RUNNER
Edwin Budding made this, the first lawn mower, in 1830. A series of spur gears connects the main roller to the knife blades, rotating them at 12 times the speed of the roller. A lever operates the clutch to disconnect the gears so that the mower can be moved without the blades being turned.

Clutch lever

Roller

Intermediate gear wheels

Blades

Gear wheel to turn the blades

STEAM-POWERED GEARS
Richard Trevithick, from Cornwall in England, designed and built the very first steam locomotive in 1803. This is the original drawing of his improved version, built in 1805. In both engines the back-and-forth motion of the piston was made to turn the wheels by an arrangement of spur gears. His first locomotive was tested at a coal mine in South Wales, where it hauled five wagons and 70 men a distance of 9 miles (15 km) at a speed of nearly 5 mph (8 km/h).

Driving gear wheel

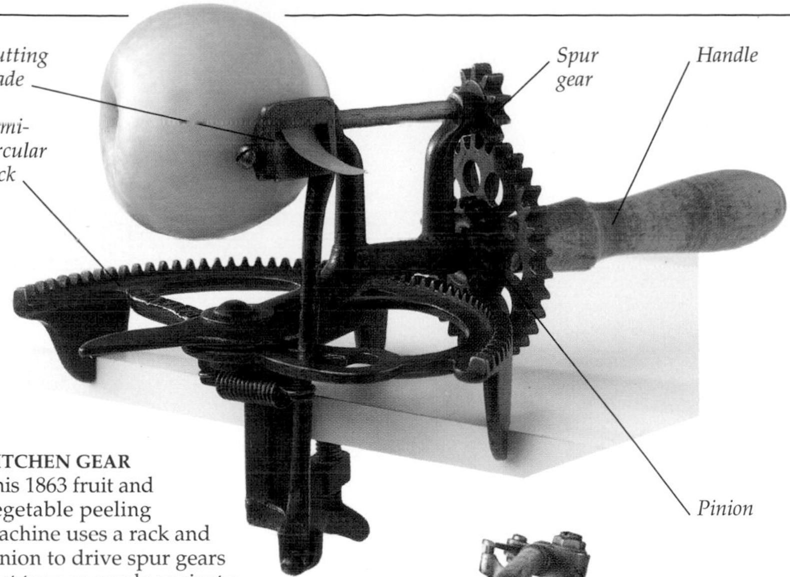

Cutting
blade

Semi-
circular
rack

Spur
gear

Handle

KITCHEN GEAR
This 1863 fruit and
vegetable peeling
machine uses a rack and
pinion to drive spur gears
that turn an apple against a
cutting blade. As the handle
is pushed around the semicircular
base, the peel is removed from the
apple in a single sweep.

Pinion

JAMES WATT
The great British engineer
James Watt (1736-1819)
developed the first
efficient steam engine,
one of the driving forces
behind the Industrial
Revolution. His engines
made use of a kind of
spur gear called a
sun-and-planet (or
epicyclic) gear, which
turned the up-and-
down motion of the
engine piston into a
rotary motion to drive
an axle. The gears
consist of a small
"planet" gear that
revolves around a larger
"sun" gear wheel (see also
p. 22, p. 288).

THE GEARED "FACILE" BICYCLE
Early bicycles often had a very large front wheel, so that a single
turn of the pedals would carry the rider a long way. The large
wheel also gave a smoother ride. One bicycle introduced
in the 1870s had a front wheel 5 ft (1.5 m) tall and a
back wheel only two-fifths as large.
Unfortunately, these bicycles
were dangerous to ride – if the
bicycle stopped suddenly, the
rider was thrown over the
handlebars. This Facile bicycle,
produced in 1888, was safer
because there was less difference in
the size of the two wheels. The
pedals are connected to the front
wheel by sun-and-planet gearing,
converting the up-and-down
movement of the pedals into
rotation of the wheel.

Pedal driving
planet gear, which runs
around the central sun gear
to turn the wheel axle

Complex machines

Sᴍᴘʟᴇ ᴍᴀᴄʜɪɴᴇs ᴀʀᴇ the building blocks of complex machines. Even the most complex of machines is made up of levers, gears, pulleys, screws, wheels, and axles. These simple machines are connected together in many ingenious ways to produce printing presses, cars, dental drills, photocopiers, food processors, and so on. The parts of many complex machines are linked by series of gears (gear trains), levers, belts, chains, and transmission shafts. Cranks and cams are also useful, converting a turning motion into a back-and-forth motion – to drive the needle up and down in a sewing machine, for example.

THE MIGHTY MACHINE
Actor Charlie Chaplin feels like a small cog in a large machine in the film *Modern Times*. Many industrial machines dwarf the people that operate them.

Knob to wind up mainspring

Balance wheel driven by hairspring

MACHINERY ON THE FARM
An early steam engine drives a threshing machine by means of a belt drive. Sheaves of wheat are forked into the thresher at the top. Sacks are filled with grain at the front of the machine, and the threshed straw is passed up the elevator at the far end.

KEEPING TIME
A mechanical clock, like this early 1900s pocket watch, consists mainly of trains of gearwheels. One train connects the mainspring to a hairspring which spins a balance wheel back and forth at a regular rate. Another series of gears moves the hands round the clockface at a rate dictated by the vibrations of the hairspring.

INSIDE A 1904 AUTOMOBILE
A complex machine, such as a car, can be understood by dividing it up into groups of related parts called systems. The power to drive the car is provided by the engine. The drive train carries the power from the engine to the driving wheels. It consists of clutch, gearbox, universal joint, drive shaft, differential, and half axles. The braking system slows the car down when necessary. It consists of levers and brake drums, connected by various rods. The steering system enables the driver to turn corners. It consists of the steering wheel and linkages to the front wheels. The cooling system keeps the engine at the correct temperature. Its main part is the radiator. The exhaust system takes the waste gases away from the engine through the muffler.

Gearbox controls the speed of the wheels in relation to the speed of the engine

Suspension spring

Half axle

Battery

Differential allows wheels to turn at different rates when cornering

Hand brake

Universal joint

Exhaust pipe

Muffler

Drive shaft

Brake drum

Chassis

Brake rod

Gear lever

Steering wheel

THE MATHEMATICAL MACHINE

The earliest automatic calculator was assembled in 1832 by the English mathematician and engineer Charles Babbage. It consisted of nearly 2,000 levers, cams, and gears, and was one of the finest examples of precision engineering of the time. Called the Difference Engine, the device represented numbers by the teeth on the numerous gearwheels. To make a calculation a handle was turned to drive the first column of gears in a connected series. Babbage also designed a bigger machine consisting of 4,000 parts and weighing 3 tons. Difference Engine No. 2 was finally built by engineers at London's Science Museum in 1991, proving that Babbage's complex design ideas really did work.

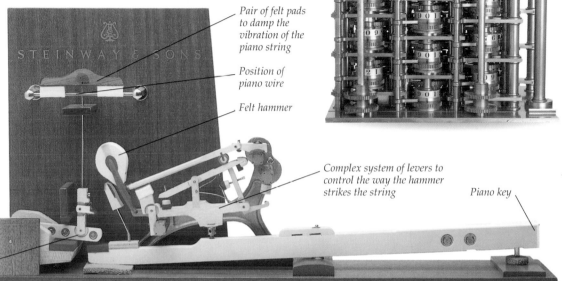

THE WRITER'S FRIEND

This early manual typewriter contains a system of levers that converts a small movement of the fingers on the keys into a long, fast movement of the type bar, which presses an inked ribbon against the paper. On the tip of each type bar there is a lowercase letter and a capital letter. Pressing the "shift" key selects capital letters. Most typewriters have at least five levers between the key and the type bar.

Pair of felt pads to damp the vibration of the piano string

Position of piano wire

Felt hammer

Complex system of levers to control the way the hammer strikes the string

Piano key

Lever to raise damping pads

INSIDE A PIANO

Each key in a piano is linked to a complex system of levers that cause a felt-tipped hammer to strike a taut wire when the key is pressed. The levers, called the action, magnify the movements of the keys so that the pianist is able to play quickly and to produce notes of different loudness. A system of damping pads, operated by the piano key and by foot pedals, enables the player to control the duration, or length, of each note.

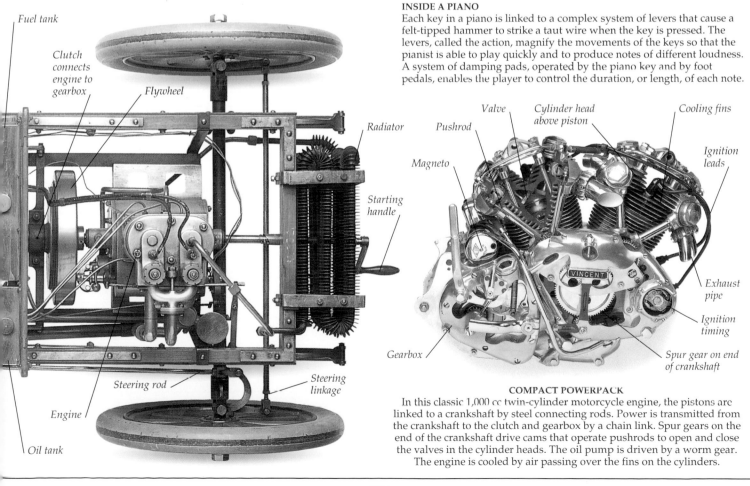

Fuel tank

Clutch connects engine to gearbox

Flywheel

Radiator

Starting handle

Steering rod

Steering linkage

Engine

Oil tank

Gearbox

Valve

Pushrod

Magneto

Cylinder head above piston

Cooling fins

Ignition leads

Exhaust pipe

Ignition timing

Spur gear on end of crankshaft

COMPACT POWERPACK

In this classic 1,000 cc twin-cylinder motorcycle engine, the pistons are linked to a crankshaft by steel connecting rods. Power is transmitted from the crankshaft to the clutch and gearbox by a chain link. Spur gears on the end of the crankshaft drive cams that operate pushrods to open and close the valves in the cylinder heads. The oil pump is driven by a worm gear. The engine is cooled by air passing over the fins on the cylinders.

Galileo's science of motion

FOR MORE THAN 1,500 years after Archimedes, science in Europe made little progress. However, new ideas gradually appeared, particularly during the Renaissance, a period of great intellectual activity in Europe from the 1300s to the 1600s. The most important scientist of the late Renaissance was the Italian Galileo Galilei, who was born at Pisa in 1564. He studied the ideas of Archimedes, particularly the use of mathematics to solve physical problems. His study of Archimedes' Principle led him to conclude that all objects would fall at the same speed. This idea was contrary to the teachings of Aristotle, and to prove his point Galileo undertook a series of experiments. His belief in the importance of the experimental approach marks Galileo as one of the first modern scientists and his mathematical description of the way objects fall is still valid today. In 1592 Galileo obtained a post at the University of Padua where he made many discoveries in astronomy using the newly developed telescope. These discoveries conflicted with the teachings of the Roman Catholic Church, and in 1633 Galileo was tried by the Inquisition and forced to deny his findings. He died under house arrest in 1642.

ARISTOTLE DISPROVED (*left*)
According to some stories, Galileo dropped two weights from the top of the leaning tower of Pisa to test his ideas about falling bodies. Aristotle had believed that a heavier weight would hit the ground first, but Galileo found that the two weights hit the ground at about the same time.

IN A VACUUM (*right*)
In this replica of an 18th-century experiment, all the air has been pumped out of the glass tube so that there is no resistance to a falling object. A feather and a golden coin are then released one after the other, and they are found to accelerate at precisely the same rate, as the distances between successive images show.

FALLING SLOWLY
This 19th-century painting shows Galileo demonstrating his ideas by rolling balls down a slope. He reasoned that they would behave in the same way as falling objects – only more slowly. He was able to measure the time they took to fall and found that "the spaces passed over in natural motion are in proportion to the squares of the times."

Release mechanism open to allow feather to fall

Release mechanism open to allow the coin to fall

GALILEO'S TRIAL
In 1630 Galileo wrote a book supporting the theory of Polish astronomer Nicolaus Copernicus, who said that the planets, including the earth, revolved around the sun. Galileo was called before the Inquisition to explain why he was questioning traditional beliefs. He was forced to declare that the earth is the immovable center of the universe.

SANDS OF TIME
In a sandtimer, fine sand runs down through a narrow hole between two bulbs. Used to show when a fixed period of time has elapsed, it is inadequate for measuring short time intervals.

Timing experiments

It was difficult for Galileo to measure short time intervals in his experiments. The very first clock, the sundial, was obviously unsuitable for measuring short time periods. Other simple clocks, such as a sandtimer or candle clock, were also unsuitable for precise scientific work. Mechanical clocks of the time were crude. They were regulated by a small bar that rocked back and forth, and they were inaccurate. Some early mechanical clocks had no dial, but struck a bell each hour. Others had a dial, but with only a single hour hand. Galileo used the human pulse as a simple clock, or measured the amount of water escaping from a jar or funnel to indicate amounts of time. Indeed, the Egyptian water clock was one of the earliest kinds of clock. Galileo did in fact design an accurate pendulum clock but it was not built in his lifetime.

SIMPLE WATER CLOCK
Galileo may have used a device like this to time his experiments on rolling balls. When a ball is released, the finger is raised from the tube, allowing the water to flow, and when the ball passes a certain point the finger is replaced and the flow of water is stopped. The amount of water collected in the bottle gives a good indication of the time taken.

PENDULUM CLOCK
When he was a young man, Galileo observed that a pendulum always took the same time to swing back and forth. Putting this observation into practice, he later designed a clock that operated on this principle. One of his pupils drew this diagram of the internal workings of the clock, but it was not actually built until the 19th century (p. 352).

The science of the cannonball

SCIENCE AT WAR
Early on it was realized that if the path of an arrow or cannonball could be calculated accurately, weapons of war would be more effective. The science of ballistics was invented to study this problem.

GALILEO'S STUDIES OF moving objects brought many insights. He recognized that any force, even a small one, could set an object in motion. In practice, friction prevents objects from being moved by small forces, but if there were no friction, the smallest push or pull would start an object moving. Furthermore, Galileo recognised that once an object was moving it would keep moving until a force halted it. No force was needed to keep an object moving, contrary to Aristotle's teachings that an object would cease to move if the force ceased to act upon it. Galileo went on to study projectiles – objects that are thrown into the air and travel up and along before falling down. A spear, arrow, or cannonball hurled into the air is a projectile. He found that projectiles were moving in two ways at the same time: they were moving forward at a constant speed and moving up and down with a changing speed. The resulting path was a combination of the two motions. Galileo tested his idea by projecting a small ball from the edge of a table and marking the spot where the ball landed. The path of a projectile, he discovered, was a curve called a "parabola." Galileo had solved a problem that had puzzled kings and warriors ever since gunpowder was invented: how to calculate the flight path of a cannonball.

ARISTOTLE'S FLIGHT PATH
According to Aristotle, the path of any projectile consisted of two straight lines, as seen in this 1561 print. Here a cannonball is shown traveling in a straight line from the cannon and then dropping straight down. Aristotle thought that an object could undertake only one motion at a time.

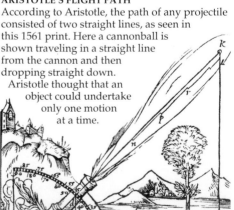

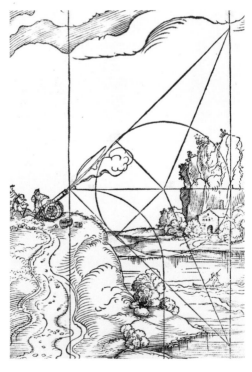

A CIRCULAR PATH
Using a geometrical construction, the artist of this 1547 print drew the path of a cannonball as a circular arc. The ball was thought to begin moving along a straight line, then to move in the arc of a circle, and finally to fall straight down.

COMBINED MOTION
On an apparatus designed to show Galileo's projectile experiment, a ball runs down the curved slope at the top left and is projected from the end of the slope. The ball leaves the slope with a certain horizontal speed, and this is maintained as it falls. This is why the horizontal distances between the images of the falling ball are all equal. The downward, falling motion of the ball is unaffected by the horizontal motion. The increasing vertical distances between the images show that the ball is speeding up, or accelerating, in the normal way for a falling object. The combination of a steady horizontal speed and an accelerating downward motion produces the curved parabolic path. If the ball is projected slightly upward, like a cannonball, its path is a combination of a steady horizontal motion and a changing up-and-down vertical motion.

Curved slope

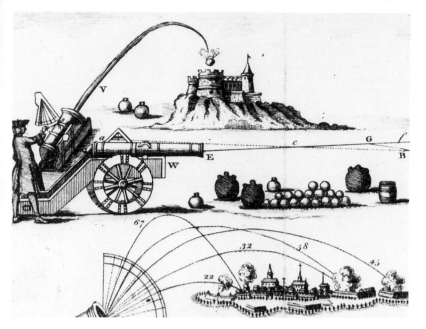

SCIENTIFIC BOMBARDMENT
The paths of the cannonballs in this 18th-century print are shown as parabolas – the correct curve, as Galileo proved. The drawing shows that the maximum range is achieved when the cannon is elevated to 45°. Even today, gunners use computations similar to these to calculate the elevation and direction of artillery fire. Every factor that might affect the flight of the shell is taken into account: distance to target, wind, temperature, air pressure, and even the spin of the earth.

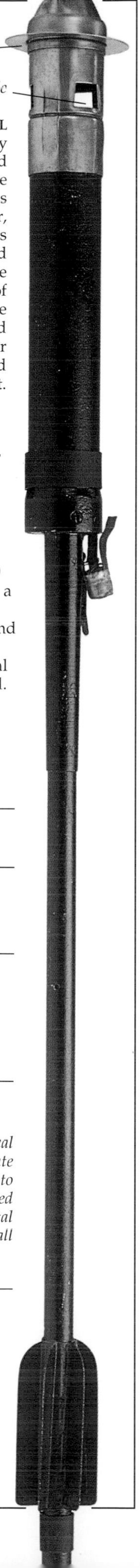

Ring around nose cone

Whistle

BALLISTIC MAIL
Rockets were used to carry messages during World War I (1914-1918). The body of the rocket was packed with gunpowder, which launched it on its way. The nose contained the message and a whistle which shrieked to warn of the rocket's approach. The size of the flange around the nose altered the air resistance and controlled the length of the flight.

THE BALLISTIC ROCKET
A German V2 rocket from World War II (1939-1945) takes off. These rockets carried an explosive warhead and had a range of about 190 miles (300 km), reaching a height of about 60 miles (100 km) under power and then falling freely in a parabolic curve at several times the speed of sound.

End of slope

Constant horizontal speed

Increasing vertical distances indicate acceleration due to gravity, unaffected by the horizontal motion of the ball

Newton's clockwork universe

ISAAC NEWTON, BORN IN 1642, just a few months after the death of Galileo, was one of the greatest scientists of all time. In the words of the poet Alexander Pope, "Nature, and Nature's Laws lay hid in Night: God said Let Newton be! and All was Light." Isaac Newton extended Galileo's work, admitting himself that "If I have seen further it is by standing on the shoulders of giants" – paying a compliment to Galileo and others who made the discoveries on which he was able to build. Newton's achievement was to bring together the significant discoveries made up until his time and to combine them into a unified picture of the universe. According to Newton, the universe ran like a clockwork machine governed by a few simple laws. Like Galileo, Newton realized that mathematics was the language of science, and he formulated these universal laws of motion and gravitation mathematically. They describe how objects move when they are acted upon by forces.

Moon

Earth

Disc indicating
time around
the globe

Sun

EARLY LIFE
Isaac Newton was born in the manor house at Woolsthorpe in Lincolnshire, England. His father had died two months earlier, and when Isaac was three his mother remarried. Isaac was then brought up by his grandmother. A quiet, lonely child, he was not interested in the family farm, so in 1661 was sent to study at nearby Cambridge University. During 1665 and 1666, while spending time back at the family home, Newton made many of his most important discoveries.

TRINITY COLLEGE, CAMBRIDGE
In 1669 Newton was appointed Professor of Mathematics at Cambridge, and he remained there until after the publication of his great work, the *Principia*, in 1687. His rooms at Trinity College (below) are situated at the front right of this picture, and he probably had a small laboratory in the gardens outside his rooms.

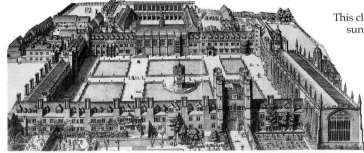

THE CLOCKWORK UNIVERSE
This clockwork model of the solar system, with the sun in the center orbited by the earth and the moon, was built in about 1712 by John Rowley of London. It is called an orrery after the fourth Earl of Orrery, for whom it was made, and it reflects Newton's view of the universe as a giant machine. The orrery shows the earth's changing position throughout the year. In the Newtonian view, if the position and velocity of every particle in the universe and the size and direction of the forces acting upon them were known, all the future positions and movements of all the particles could be calculated using his laws.

Pointer indicating the earth's progress through the signs of the zodiac in the course of a year

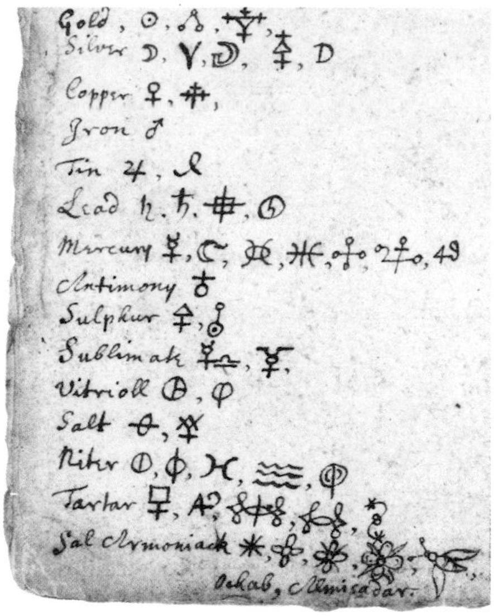

AN ECCENTRIC MAN

In 1701 Newton resigned his position at Cambridge when he was elected as a Member of Parliament. By this time, Newton had become secretive and argumentative, quarrelling with many of his scientific colleagues, and his interests had widened to include such fields as religion and alchemy, as this page from his notebook shows. In 1705 Newton was honored with a knighthood, and after his death in 1727 he was buried in London's Westminster Abbey.

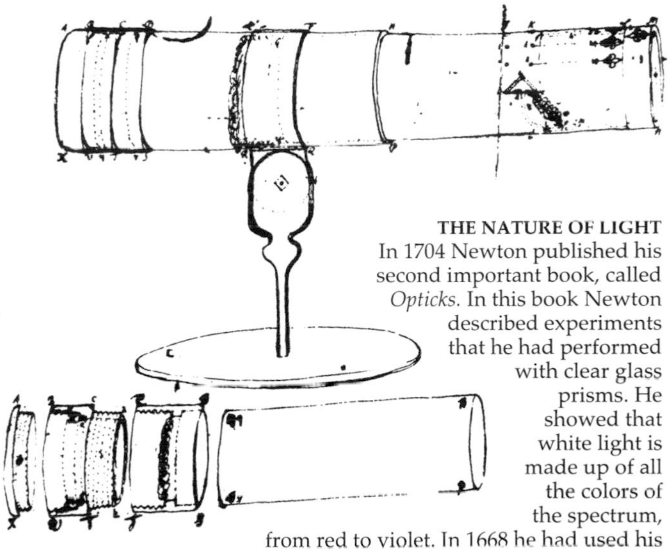

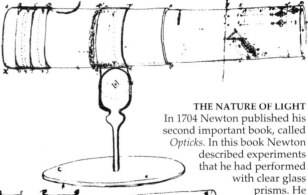

THE NATURE OF LIGHT

In 1704 Newton published his second important book, called *Opticks*. In this book Newton described experiments that he had performed with clear glass prisms. He showed that white light is made up of all the colors of the spectrum, from red to violet. In 1668 he had used his research to design an improved telescope. At this time all telescopes used curved pieces of glass, called lenses, but these produced blurred images with colored edges. Newton's telescope, sketched here in his notebook, used a curved mirror to focus light, and it did not produce unwanted colors.

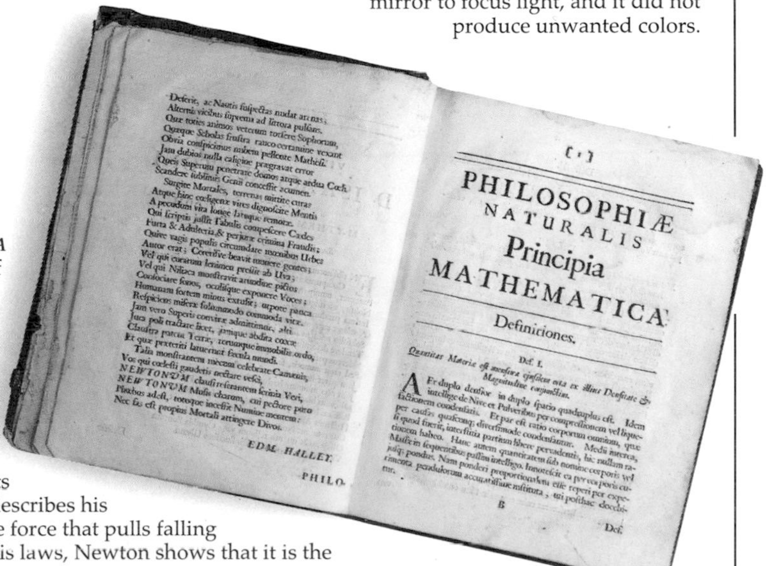

THE *PRINCIPIA*

This is the title page of Newton's most important book, the *Principia*. Newton was following in Galileo's footsteps by explaining the world mathematically. The first part of the *Principia* explains that three basic laws govern the way in which objects move. Newton then describes his theory of gravity, the force that pulls falling objects down. Using his laws, Newton shows that it is the force of gravity that keeps the planets moving in orbits round the sun. Finally, Newton uses his laws to predict that the earth must be a a slightly flattened sphere and that comets orbit the sun in elongated oval-shaped paths. These predictions were later shown to be true.

Winding handle to turn the orrery

PHILOSOPHIÆ
NATURALIS
Principia
MATHEMATICA

Definiciones.

Newton's Laws in action

NEWTON'S FIRST LAW states that if an object is not being pushed or pulled by a force, it will either stay still or keep moving in a straight line at a steady speed. It might be obvious that a stationary object will not move until a force acts on it, but it is less obvious that a moving object can continue to move without the help of a force. The tendency of an object to remain moving in a straight line at constant speed or to remain stationary is called inertia. Newton's Second Law defines what happens when a force acts on an object – the object accelerates in the direction in which the force is acting. A force acting on a stationary object starts it moving. A force acting on a moving object will speed it up, slow it down, or change the direction in which it is moving. The Third Law states that if an object is pushed or pulled, it will push or pull to an equal extent in the opposite direction. For example, if a bulldozer pushes against a wall, the wall will exert an equal and opposite force on the bulldozer.

FREE FALL
Falling objects, such as parachutists when they jump from a plane, accelerate because they are pulled downward by a force – gravity. If the effects of air resistance are ignored, the speed at which a freely falling object travels will increase by 32 ft/sec (9.8 m/sec) for every second that it is falling. Known as g, this is the acceleration due to gravity. In practice, at a certain speed the upward force of air resistance equals the downward force of gravity and at this speed, called terminal velocity, an object ceases to accelerate. From then on it will fall at a constant speed.

FARMYARD ACTION
All of Newton's Laws are illustrated by a horse pulling a cart. When the cart is stationary, the horse must strain to apply a force in order to move it. For the cart to move, the horse's force must overcome the inertia of the cart and the frictional forces that prevent the cart from moving. Once there is an overall forward pull, the cart will accelerate forward, obeying the Second Law. The horse can then relax, reducing its pull until it matches the frictional drag of the cart. There is then no overall force acting and the cart will move forward at a constant speed, as the First Law predicts. According to the Third Law, the force applied by the horse that acts upon the cart will at all times be matched by an equal and opposite force applied by the cart and acting upon the horse.

Load

Frictional force acts to prevent the wheel from turning

SIGNS OF THE SHAKING EARTH
This ancient Chinese earthquake detector relies upon the inertia of a central pendulum, attached to a system of levers, to cause a ball to fall from a dragon's jaws into the mouth of a waiting frog when the bowl is shaken.

INTO SPACE

The takeoff of a rocket illustrates several points about Newton's Laws. The rocket engine shows the Third Law in action; the force with which the hot gases are blasted from the combustion chamber produces a reaction force on the rocket. This force lifts and accelerates the rocket, as the Second Law leads us to expect. The exact formulation of the Second Law shows that the acceleration produced depends upon the mass of the rocket. The smaller the mass, the greater the acceleration. For this reason, the rate of acceleration increases as the rocket's fuel is burnt up.

UNDER PRESSURE

The straining face of a weightlifter shows that large forces can be involved even when nothing is moving. According to Newton's Third Law, the force with which the athlete lifts the weight produces an equal downward force on his arms. The weight of the bar is transmitted down through his legs, and presses downward on the floor. The floor presses upward with an equal force. The force pressing down must equal the upward force. If the floor pushed less strongly, then the athlete would fall through it. If it pushed more strongly, then he would fly into the air.

PULL AWAY

Rowers make use of Newton's Third Law. When pulling on an oar, a rower pushes water backward. The backward force on the water produces an equal and opposite force which moves the boat forward. An added advantage is gained because the oar is a lever; a short pull by the rower produces a longer movement at the other end of the oar.

UNDERWATER JET

A squid propels itself through the water using jet propulsion. It squirts water backward in order to move forward. According to Newton's Third Law, the force of the expelled water is balanced by a force that propels the animal forward. Jet and rocket engines work in the same way.

Forces are transmitted in both directions through the shafts

The horse's muscles apply a forward force to accelerate the load

Gravity: the long-range force

THE FORCE THAT MAKES OBJECTS FALL to the ground is also the force that keeps the planets in their orbits around the sun. Isaac Newton was the first person to realize this. The ancient Greeks thought that objects fell because they were seeking their natural places, and that the planets were moved by invisible crystal spheres. Even Johannes Kepler, who showed in 1609 that the planets moved in elliptical, or slightly oval-shaped, orbits, thought that they were being supported by an invisible framework. In 1687 Newton proved in his book *Principia* that the planets orbit around the sun because there is a long-range force – gravity – attracting them toward the sun. He was also able to show that the force of gravity between the sun and a planet depends on the distance between the two. A planet twice as far from the sun as another will experience only one-quarter of the force; if it is three times as far away, the force will be one-ninth, and so on. Newton also showed that the force of gravitational attraction between two objects depends on their masses. The greater the mass of the objects, the greater the force pulling them together.

COMETS
Isaac Newton showed that comets were objects in elongated elliptical orbits around the sun. Their paths were therefore predictable, like those of the planets. Edmond Halley, who paid for the publication of Newton's book *Principia*, used Newton's ideas to predict that a comet seen in 1531, 1607, and 1682 would return in 1758. When the comet appeared on schedule, it became known as Halley's comet.

THE SUN'S FAMILY
This early 19th-century orrery shows the planets of our solar system. The planetary orbits are shown as being circular although they are actually very slightly oval. Neptune, whose orbit lies outside the orbits of Saturn and Uranus, is not shown, as it was not discovered until 1846. Pluto, the outermost planet of our solar system, was not discovered until 1930.

THE MOMENT OF DISCOVERY
Newton is said to have realized the wider importance of gravity in 1666 when he saw an apple fall from a tree in his garden. In the words of one of his contemporaries, "It came into his thought that the power of gravity (which brought the apple from the tree to the ground) was not limited to a certain distance from the earth but that this power must extend much further than is usually thought. Why not as high as the moon, said he to himself, and if so that must influence her motion. Whereupon he fell a-calculating what would be the effect."

THE MOON AND THE APPLE
Newton calculated the force needed to keep the moon in a circular orbit around the earth, and compared this with the force that accelerated the apple downward. After allowing for the fact that the moon is much farther from the earth and has a greater mass, he found that the two forces were the same. The circular motion of the moon and the fall of the apple were the results of the same force – gravity.

Uranus

Earth   *Sun*   *Mercury*

Jupiter

Venus

THE UNIVERSE OF COPERNICUS

Polish astronomer Nicolaus Copernicus (1473-1543) put forward the idea that the planets orbit around the sun and not the earth. His vision of the solar system is shown in this print. In 1514 Copernicus outlined his ideas in a pamphlet and sent it to a few scholars, but he hesitated to publish more widely, fearing the anger of the Church. It is said that the first printed copy of his book, *On the Revolutions of the Celestial Spheres,* was brought to him on his deathbed.

JOHANNES KEPLER (1571-1630)

German mathematician and astronomer Johannes Kepler discovered the laws of planetary motion by studying the orbit of Mars. His studies led him to declare that the planets moved in slightly elongated elliptical orbits, and not in circles as Copernicus had supposed. Kepler also discovered that there was a relationship between the speed of a planet's movement and its distance from the sun, each planet moving fastest as it passes closest to the sun. Isaac Newton provided the theoretical explanation for Kepler's discoveries (see also p. 77).

Drawing pencil

Winding handle to operate the device

Mars

Central ring

Ellipses drawn by the ellipsograph

Saturn

DRAWING AN ELLIPSE

The path of a planet orbiting the Sun is not a perfect circle, but an ellipse, an oval shape like the ones drawn by this piece of apparatus. The device is called an ellipsograph and it was made in 1817 by John Farey of London. An ellipse is a combination of two circular motions. The drawing pencil is fixed in position in the central ring, which then revolves. At the same time, the ring itself is carried round in a circle and the pencil traces the combination of these two paths. The simplest way to draw an ellipse is by tying the ends of a piece of thin string to two tacks and then sticking the tacks into a sheet of cardboard so that the string is loose. When a pencil is placed against the string so that it pulls the string tight, the path that the pencil will trace as it moves around is an ellipse. An ellipse has two focuses – the tacks in this case. The orbit of a planet has the sun as one of the focuses of the ellipse around which it travels. Each planet travels fastest when it is closest to the sun and slowest when it is furthest away.

PULLING THE WATER

The rise and fall of the tides is caused by gravity. The oceans on the side of the earth nearest to the moon are pulled outward by the force of the moon's gravity, creating a high tide. At the same time a high tide occurs on the opposite side of the earth because the moon's gravity is less there and the water bulges away. The sun has a smaller effect on the planet's water, but when the moon and the sun are in line, at the new or full moon, their forces combine to produce extremely high and low "spring" tides. When they are at right angles, less extreme "neap" tides occur.

Weight and mass

AN ASTRONAUT STANDING ON the moon weighs only one-sixth as much as on earth. This is because the weight of an object is due to the downward force of gravity acting upon it. The force of gravity on the surface of a planet depends upon the mass of the planet and its size. Gravity on the surface of the moon is only one-sixth as strong as gravity on earth. Jupiter's surface gravity is 2.64 times that of the earth, so an object would weigh 2.64 times as much there. An object's mass, on the other hand, is the amount of material that it contains, and this remains constant. Mass is a measure of an object's resistance to being accelerated by a force. The same force would be needed to roll a bowling ball on Jupiter as is needed on Earth.

MEASURING MASS
A balance, like this Roman steelyard from Pompeii, really measures mass rather than weight. Since the force of gravity is the same at both ends of the beam, which acts as a lever, the measurement that it gives would be the same here or on the moon. It does not depend upon gravity. The small mass (confusingly called a "weight") is moved to the left until it balances with the object whose mass is being measured. This mass is shown by the scale along the beam.

Fulcrum

Beam with scale

Weight

Scale pan

Grapes whose mass is being measured

TWO-PAN BALANCE
This money changer's balance, made in 1653, was used for valuing coins of pure gold. A coin of unknown value is placed in one pan, and its value in other currencies can be found by balancing it against fixed weights from the box below, which represent coins from other countries.

Unknown coin

Standard weight

SCALES OF JUSTICE
The balance has been used since ancient times. This scene from an Egyptian papyrus shows the jackal-headed god, Anubis (left) weighing the heart of Princess Nesitanebtashru (right) on the Day of Judgment. Her heart, in an urn on the right-hand pan, is being balanced against the goddess of truth and righteousness on the left-hand pan.

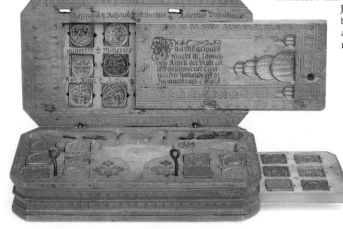

LOCAL STANDARDS
The need to weigh precious metals accurately has led people in many countries to develop their own systems of fixed, or standard, weights. On the right are some examples of weights from around the world.

Assyrian lion

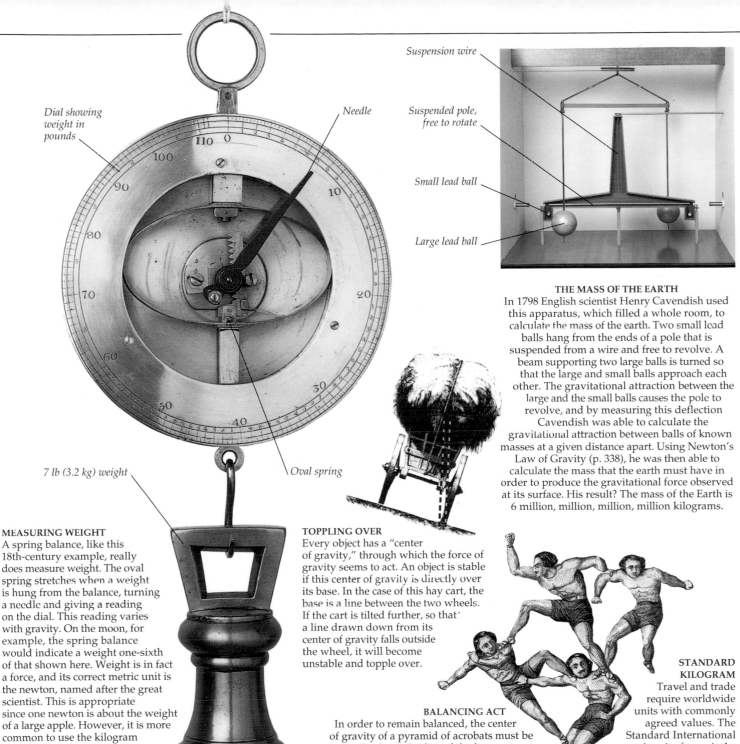

Dial showing weight in pounds

Needle

110 0
100
90 10
80
70 20
60 30
50 40

Suspension wire

Suspended pole, free to rotate

Small lead ball

Large lead ball

7 lb (3.2 kg) weight

Oval spring

THE MASS OF THE EARTH

In 1798 English scientist Henry Cavendish used this apparatus, which filled a whole room, to calculate the mass of the earth. Two small lead balls hang from the ends of a pole that is suspended from a wire and free to revolve. A beam supporting two large balls is turned so that the large and small balls approach each other. The gravitational attraction between the large and the small balls causes the pole to revolve, and by measuring this deflection Cavendish was able to calculate the gravitational attraction between balls of known masses at a given distance apart. Using Newton's Law of Gravity (p. 338), he was then able to calculate the mass that the earth must have in order to produce the gravitational force observed at its surface. His result? The mass of the Earth is 6 million, million, million, million kilograms.

MEASURING WEIGHT

A spring balance, like this 18th-century example, really does measure weight. The oval spring stretches when a weight is hung from the balance, turning a needle and giving a reading on the dial. This reading varies with gravity. On the moon, for example, the spring balance would indicate a weight one-sixth of that shown here. Weight is in fact a force, and its correct metric unit is the newton, named after the great scientist. This is appropriate since one newton is about the weight of a large apple. However, it is more common to use the kilogram weight, the weight of one kilogram mass in earth's gravity, as the metric unit of weight.

TOPPLING OVER

Every object has a "center of gravity," through which the force of gravity seems to act. An object is stable if this center of gravity is directly over its base. In the case of this hay cart, the base is a line between the two wheels. If the cart is tilted further, so that a line drawn down from its center of gravity falls outside the wheel, it will become unstable and topple over.

BALANCING ACT

In order to remain balanced, the center of gravity of a pyramid of acrobats must be precisely above the feet of the lowest person. If the pyramid starts to topple, the acrobats must lean away from the fall, moving their center of gravity back to the stable position.

STANDARD KILOGRAM

Travel and trade require worldwide units with commonly agreed values. The Standard International metric unit of mass is the kilogram, like the one below. Mass and volume are connected, because one liter of pure water weighs precisely 1 kg (2.2 lb).

Chinese jade

Siamese dragon

Ashanti warrior

Burmese elephant

Standard kilogram

Collisions

I MAGINE A TRUCK SPEEDING ALONG A ROAD. A car pulls out in front of the truck, and a collision looks likely. The driver applies the brakes but only just manages to slow the truck down in time. This is because the momentum of the truck carries it forward. The greater the speed of the truck, the more momentum it has and the harder it is to stop quickly. Furthermore, the heavier the truck's load, the harder it is to stop. The momentum of any moving object depends on both its speed and its mass. The effects of a collision can often be predicted by calculating the momentum of the objects involved, owing to the fact that when objects collide, their total momentum is unchanged by the collision, provided that no other forces are acting. This is called the Law of Conservation of Momentum, and it applies to all moving objects. Unless other forces act, the momentum of the truck will not change. In practice, frictional forces tend to reduce an object's momentum. The brakes that slow the truck down work in this way.

HOT METAL
The blacksmith's anvil is so massive that it is hardly moved by the blows from the hammer. Instead, the momentum of the hammer is absorbed by the hot metal of the horseshoe, which is beaten into shape.

CONSERVATION OF MOMENTUM
The total momentum of colliding objects is the same before and after the collision. In the picture above, a white billiard ball collides from the left with a row of stationary red balls, and stops dead at the left-hand end of the row. A single yellow ball moves away from the right-hand end of the row. The momentum of the white ball has passed, unchanged, right through the row of reds and into the yellow ball. Since the yellow ball has exactly the same mass as the white, it accelerates to exactly the same speed that the white ball was traveling before the collision. If the yellow had twice the mass of the white, it would move away at half the speed.

Incoming white ball collides with first red ball

Momentum passes through the red balls, which remain stationary

AT AN ANGLE (*left*)
Momentum has a direction, as well as a size. If two billiard balls collide off-center, they rebound at an angle. However, the total momentum is still the same before and after the collision. Before the collision the momentum was carried by the single white ball moving directly toward the stationary yellow ball at a certain speed. After the collision the momentum is shared between the white ball and the yellow ball, and both balls now move more slowly than the original speed. Although neither ball is now moving directly to the right, each ball has some momentum towards the right and the total rightward momentum remains the same as before the collision.

A DESTRUCTIVE COLLISION

A heavy steel ball being swung on a chain has considerable momentum. When the ball strikes the wall, this momentum is transferred. The wall starts to move, the cement between the bricks is torn apart and the bricks themselves, because they are light, are knocked away.

METEORITE CRATER

The effects of a meteor colliding with the earth are seen at the Barringer crater, a circular depression about 4,000 ft (1,200 m) across, near Winslow, Arizona. The wall surrounding the crater rises 160 ft (50 m) above the plain. Attempts have been made to find the remains of a large meteorite under the soil, but only small pieces have been found. Large meteorites generally disintegrate when they hit the earth.

TAKING THE STRAIN

Taken at the moment of impact, this photograph shows one side of a golf ball being flattened by the face of the colliding golf club. This illustrates the great forces generated by the swinging club. Because the ball distorts rather than moving away immediately, the club stays in contact with the ball for longer and more power can be transferred to the ball. The club is far heavier than the ball, and, because total momentum is conserved, the ball will move faster after the collision than the club moved before the collision.

Momentum is passed to yellow ball, which accelerates away

BIG GUNS

A British gun in action during World War I recoils as a shell is fired. This is a consequence of Newton's Third Law (p. 336); the force propelling the shell forward is matched by an equal and opposite reaction force which drives the gun backward. The momentum of a recoiling gun is equal and opposite to the momentum of the shell, producing a total momentum of zero – the same as before firing. Since the mass of the gun is so much larger than the mass of the shell, the shell moves forward with a far greater speed than the gun moves back.

SUBATOMIC COLLISIONS

In this photograph of a collision between subatomic particles in a bubble chamber, a kaon particle (yellow) has entered at the bottom and collided with a proton to produce pions (orange and mauve tracks). An invisible lambda particle is also created, and its mass can be calculated using the laws that describe the collisions of particles.

Friction

GALILEO AND NEWTON realized that everyday experience makes it difficult to understand force and motion. People are used to seeing moving objects slow down and stop when the force pushing them is removed. Galileo and Newton said that this is because there is usually a force – called friction – acting to slow moving objects. Remove friction, they said, and moving objects would continue to move without being pushed. For instance, a stone skidding across a frozen pond travels an enormous distance because there is little friction between the stone and the icy lake surface. (This is because a thin layer of water keeps the stone and the ice apart.) Friction is the force that opposes the movement of objects sliding over each other. Friction occurs because no surface is perfectly smooth, however flat it may appear. All surfaces consist of tiny "hills and valleys," and where the microscopic peaks on the two surfaces come in contact they can weld together, making it difficult for one surface to slide over the other. Friction increases as the pressure between the two surfaces increases. The heavier an object, the greater the number of peaks that come in contact and the greater the number of tiny welds. This makes heavier objects harder to slide.

ELECTRICITY BY FRICTION

Early electrical machines produced electricity by rubbing a rotating glass plate with a leather or silk pad. Francis Hauksbee, maker of scientific apparatus and unofficial Curator of Experiments at the Royal Society in London, made one of the first frictional electrical machines in about 1710. This machine has four fixed pads that press against a circular glass plate. When the plate is spun, an electrical charge is created. This charge is carried away by four wire-tipped arms, and it builds up on the surface of the tube. The electricity can be discharged at a chosen voltage by adjusting the gap across which it must spark.

Friction pad

Glass plate

Tube to store charge

Adjusting knob to regulate voltage

Wire-tipped arm

Handle to rotate glass plate

Mouthpiece

Firestick

Point at which friction creates heat

Leather thong

Wooden firestick made and used by the Inuit people of the Arctic

HEAT FROM FRICTION

Rubbing two sticks together is a very ancient way of making fire. The Inuit firestick is more sophisticated: a leather thong is wound around the upright stick, and when this is pulled back and forth the stick spins at high speed. The end of the stick becomes hot and ignites the tinder. In the same way, when a match is struck, friction causes the chemicals in the match head to ignite. Friction also heats up the pads and discs in a car's braking system and causes the Space Shuttle to heat up as it reenters the earth's atmosphere from space.

HOUSE OF CARDS

Without friction, a house of cards would collapse. Friction between the cards keeps them in place so long as they are at a steep angle. The same is true of a ladder. The angle at which the cards or the ladder will begin to slip is determined by the "limiting friction," or the maximum friction that can occur between the touching surfaces. In 1781 the French physicist Charles de Coulomb found that the limiting friction did not depend upon the area in contact, only on the materials involved and the pressure between the surfaces. Coulomb introduced the term "coefficient of friction" to describe a value that indicates the frictional force of a particular surface under standard conditions. Slippery substances have a low coefficient of friction.

UNDER THE MICROSCOPE

This is the surface of a piece of paper, magnified 100 times by a powerful microscope. Although the paper looks smooth to the naked eye, the microscope reveals the small-scale roughness that causes friction. When one surface is pressing against another, the pressure on the points of contact can be immense, creating bonds between the surfaces. Friction, a resistance to motion, is caused by these bonds.

FLOATING ON AIR

This is the first hovercraft ever built, making its first public appearance in 1959. The hovercraft was invented by British engineer Christopher Cockerell. In 1955, in an attempt to design a boat that would slide over water as easily as a skate slides over ice, Cockerell thought of using a cushion of air under pressure to hold the boat away from the water and so reduce friction. His idea proved so successful that hovercraft are now used in many parts of the world for crossing calm waters at high speed.

Ball bearings in a race   *Oil*

Ball bearing

ROLLING AND SLIDING

Ball bearings reduce friction by rolling rather than dragging across a surface, in the same way that a wheel reduces the friction of a load being moved over a surface. When held in a cage, or race, ball bearings allow a wheel to turn freely on an axle passing through the inner ring. Lubricants such as oil and grease are also used in machines to reduce friction. They form a thin layer between moving surfaces, preventing them from rubbing together.

STREAMLINING

An object moving through a liquid or gas also experiences friction which causes drag, slowing the object down. To reduce this drag, ships, submarines, racing cars, and aircraft are all streamlined – shaped so that water or air will flow smoothly over their surfaces when they are moving at speed. Such craft are often tapered to a point at the back. Dolphins, fish, and sharks are well streamlined and glide through water with ease.

Energy

WHEN ISAAC NEWTON FORMULATED his Laws of Motion in 1687, he did not mention energy. English scientist Thomas Young first used the word in its scientific sense, 80 years after the death of Newton. According to Young, a moving object has energy because it can be made to do work – anything that can do work has energy. A moving object could, for example, drag a small cart along. Today we call the energy of a moving object "kinetic energy." Scottish engineer William Rankine coined the term "potential energy," half a century after Young, to describe the energy possessed by a raised weight. A raised weight can do work; if allowed to fall down, the weight can hammer a pile into the ground. In 1847 English scientist James Joule showed that heat was a form of energy, too. The steam engine, invented by English engineer Thomas Newcomen in 1712, was a device for using heat to do work. Joule discovered that the amount of potential or kinetic energy needed to produce a unit of heat was always the same. This discovery led to the Law of Conservation of Energy, one of the most important laws in science.

ENERGY PIONEER
James Prescott Joule (1818-1889) was born in Salford, England. Joule studied the heating effect of an electric current and realized that heat was energy. A unit of energy was named after him (see also p. 30, p. 270).

JOULE'S EXPERIMENT
This apparatus was used by James Joule to measure the mechanical equivalent of heat. The falling weight turned a paddle wheel in a container of water, and the water became slightly warmer. Joule then compared the work done by the falling weight with the heat produced. By using different weights and letting them fall different heights, Joule found that the same amount of work always produced the same amount of heat.

Cord / Pulley

Paddle wheel in water with thermometer

Falling weight

Scale

ENERGY QUALITY
This is a model of a fairground steam engine built in 1934 by John Fowler of Leeds, England, to run an electricity generator. Electricity is a high-quality form of energy. It can easily be converted into other forms of energy, so it is very versatile. Low-quality energy, such as sound or waste heat, cannot easily be changed into other forms and is less useful. Whenever energy is transformed the amount of low-quality energy always increases, though the total amount of energy remains constant. Steam engines, for instance, always produce useless waste heat. This is why a perpetual motion machine cannot be built – such machines always lose useful energy in the form of waste heat, principally because of friction.

ENERGY TRANSFORMATIONS
Energy can take many different forms – kinetic, potential, electrical, heat, sound, light, chemical – and they are all interchangeable. Chemical energy can be changed into heat by burning a fuel. Heat can produce kinetic energy in an engine. Kinetic energy can be changed into electrical energy by a generator. An electric bulb produces light. An electric range produces heat. A radio emits sound energy and a fan converts electrical energy to kinetic energy. During these transformations the total amount of energy after the change is the same as the amount before the change. Energy cannot be destroyed or created. This is called the Law of Conservation of Energy.

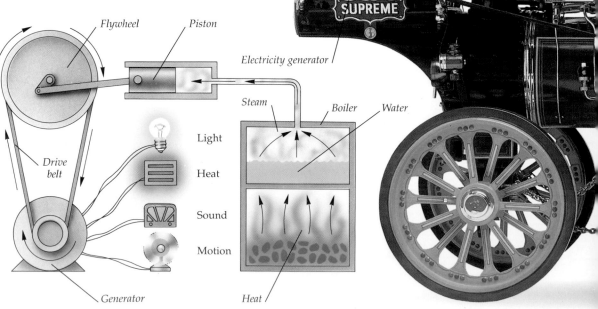

Flywheel

Piston

Electricity generator

Steam

Boiler

Water

Light

Heat

Sound

Motion

Drive belt

Generator

Heat

A. DEAKIN & S...

SUPREME

ROLLER COASTER

As a roller coaster car rushes up and down, its energy changes from kinetic to potential and back again. Kinetic energy is greatest when the car is going at its greatest speed. The car has maximum potential energy when it is at its highest point.

THE WIND OF CHANGE

This wind farm near Palm Springs, California, converts the kinetic energy of the wind into electrical energy. Wind and waves are created by the heat of the sun – their energy is a form of solar energy. The rate at which energy reaches the earth in the form of sunlight is more than 12,000 times greater than the rate at which humans consume fuel. Although solar energy is spread out and difficult to collect, it can provide a clean, safe, and renewable source of energy to replace the use of fossil fuels and nuclear power.

ENGINE POWER

The energy held in fuels such as gasoline is called chemical energy. Engines such as this twin-cylinder aircraft engine convert the chemical energy to kinetic energy, plus waste heat and sound. The power of an engine is a measure of the energy it converts in a given time. A high-power engine is one that can convert energy quickly. A unit used to measure power is the watt (or joule per second), named after Scottish engineer James Watt, who produced the first efficient steam engine in 1776.

Spark plug

Carburetor

Cylinder head

Propeller

Flywheel

IS, MODERN AMUSEMENTS

Drive belt

LIGHT AND SOUND

The busy fairground is an energy-packed place. Electricity, the most versatile form of energy, drives almost all of the machines, being converted into motion and heat, bright lights and music. The people, too, are driven by energy – chemical energy from their food.

Combined forces

Most objects have more than one force acting on them. For instance, a yacht sailing across the sea has the force of the wind on its sails. Resistance forces of the air and water act to slow down any motion. In addition, the weight of the yacht pulls down, while the buoyancy force of the water lifts the boat. There is also a force produced by the heavy keel of the yacht that prevents it from tipping. The combined effect of all these forces is called the resultant – the single force that has the same effect as many forces acting on an object. In many situations the forces cancel each other out and the resultant is zero, meaning that no overall force is acting and that the object is moving at a constant speed or it is stationary. An object whose speed is not changing is said to be in a state of equilibrium.

AIR FORCE
Fighter aircraft are acted on by several forces. Gravity pulls them downward; the wings provide a lifting force; air resistance produces a drag, or slowing, force; and the engine provides a forward thrust. The pilot must balance the aircraft's weight, thrust, lift, and drag to produce the correct overall resultant force in the required direction.

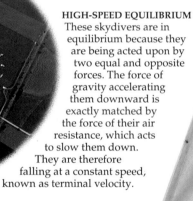

HIGH-SPEED EQUILIBRIUM
These skydivers are in equilibrium because they are being acted upon by two equal and opposite forces. The force of gravity accelerating them downward is exactly matched by the force of their air resistance, which acts to slow them down. They are therefore falling at a constant speed, known as terminal velocity.

ON THE HIGH SEAS
A yacht can sail in many directions, and not only in the direction that the wind is blowing. This versatility is achieved by moving the sail around to catch the force of the wind at different angles. The force of the wind acting on the sails is transferred to the yacht through the mast. Some of this force will be in directions other than forward, and the keel helps to counteract the sideways component of this force. The pressure of the water against the keel prevents the yacht from moving sideways. To find the resultant of these two forces, or any other pair of forces, geometry is needed, because the effect of a force depends upon its direction as well as its size. If two forces acting on an object are represented by the sides of a parallelogram (with the angle between them representing their relative directions and the lengths of the lines representing the sizes of the two forces) then the resultant force acting on the object is represented by the diagonal of the parallelogram (below). This useful diagram is called the parallelogram of forces.

Parallelogram of forces

Force on yacht from the effect of wind on the sails

Resultant force on yacht

Force on yacht from the effect of water against the keel

Pressure of water against the keel produces a sideways force on the yacht, preventing it from slipping sideways

THE SCIENCE OF STATICS
The science of statics studies the forces acting on objects that are at rest. The earliest investigation into statics was made by Archimedes in ancient Greece. Architects use statics to understand the forces acting on buildings. The weight of the roof and upper walls of this cathedral is enormous, and the lower walls must be thick to bear the load. Flying buttresses support the walls and spread the load.

Wind acts on the sails to produce a force

BRIDGE BUILDING
Bridge builders use statics to calculate the loads that will be supported by the bridge. The forces tending to bend the bridge and make it collapse must never exceed the forces tending to keep the bridge straight. In a suspension bridge the load is borne by flexible cables, which are in turn supported by towers at each end. These towers are built to withstand extremely strong forces. Since this kind of bridge can tend to sway in strong winds, the road is often stiffened with a beam or a girder shaped like a hollow box.

PRESSING DOWN
In this human pyramid, the weight of each person is spread to the two people below who are linked to each other, thus forming a stack of triangles.

THE STRONG TRIANGLE
The triangle is often used in buildings, bridges, and towers because of its strong rigid shape. A structure made of beams connected together in triangles cannot be twisted or collapsed without deforming the beams. The triangle is the only geometric shape with this property. The 984-ft (300-m) Eiffel Tower in Paris, built in 1889, is made almost entirely of triangles. The wide base supports almost 8,000 tons of iron and steel.

THE BUCKYBALL
This newly found carbon molecule is now known as buckminsterfullerene because its molecules resemble the geodesic domes designed by the American inventor, Buckminster Fuller. The molecules, nicknamed buckyballs, each consist of 60 carbon atoms forming pentagons and hexagons (5- and 6-sided figures). Each atom is held in place by the combined forces from its neighboring atoms, producing a very stable structure.

The weight of the yacht acts downward on the water

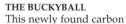

Pressure of water on the rudder produces a force to turn the yacht

Upthrust due to weight of displaced water acts upwards on the yacht

Pressure and flow

IF TWO PEOPLE OF THE SAME WEIGHT walk on deep snow, one wearing ordinary shoes and one wearing snowshoes, the person wearing the ordinary shoes will sink deeper than the other. In both cases the weight on the snow is the same, but the snowshoes spread the weight over a larger area. The force under a snowshoe is less concentrated than that under an ordinary shoe. This shows the importance of pressure, or force per unit area. In many situations it is pressure rather than force that matters. A thumbtack has a large head to spread the force of the thumb, but a sharp point to concentrate the force on to a tiny area, producing great pressure. A sharp knife cuts well because the force of the cut is concentrated into the small area of the cutting edge. Liquids and gases exert pressure; any object that is put in a liquid has pressure on its sides. The pressure is caused by the weight of the fluid above it.

POND WALKER
A bird walks across the delicate leaf of a water plant. The bird's long toes are splayed to spread its weight, reducing the pressure on the leaf. This prevents the bird from sinking or breaking through the leaf.

THE MAGDEBURG SPHERES
In 1654 Otto von Guericke, mayor of the German town of Magdeburg, performed a spectacular demonstration of the air's pressure. He made two round cups of copper that fitted together to form a hollow ball. When the air inside the ball was pumped out, the air pressing on the outside held the two cups together so firmly that it was impossible to pull them apart, even by hanging heavy weights from the lower cup. When the air was allowed back into the ball, returning the inside pressure to normal, the two cups simply fell apart.

MEASURING AIR PRESSURE
Air pressure is measured by using a barometer. The mercury barometer, like this example, was invented in 1643 by Galileo's pupil Evangelista Torricelli (1608-1647). A tube, sealed at one end, is filled with mercury and then turned upside down in a small bulb of mercury. The mercury in the tube falls until its weight is supported by the pressure of the air on the surface of the mercury in the bulb. Air pressure can therefore be determined by measuring the height of the column of mercury. Mercury is used because it is extremely dense and the supported column is of a manageable height.

BLAISE PASCAL (1623-1662)
Frenchman Blaise Pascal packed three careers into his short life: scientist, mathematician, and religious thinker. When he was 19 years old he made the first successful calculating machine to help his father with his business accounts. In 1646 he made a mercury barometer and later demonstrated that it measured air pressure, by showing that the mercury level fell as the barometer was carried up a mountain. He concentrated on mathematics after an intense religious experience in 1654. A unit of pressure, the pascal, is named after him.

Air supply

Window of strengthened glass

UNDER THE SEA
The pressure in any liquid depends on the liquid's depth; the greater the depth, the greater the pressure. A diver in deep water must be able to survive great pressures, so diving helmets are thick and strong. Pressure also depends on the density of the liquid; mercury exerts more pressure than a less dense liquid such as water.

Diving helmet from the early 19th century

Small weight

Large weight

Liquid

PASCAL'S PRINCIPLE
Pascal's Principle states that in a liquid or gas at rest, the pressure is transmitted equally in all directions. Many kinds of hydraulic devices, such as the car jack, work on this principle. As this engraving shows, a small weight pressing on a narrow column of liquid is able to support a large weight on a wide column connected to it. The pressure in both columns is the same, but as the large column has a greater area it produces a larger total force.

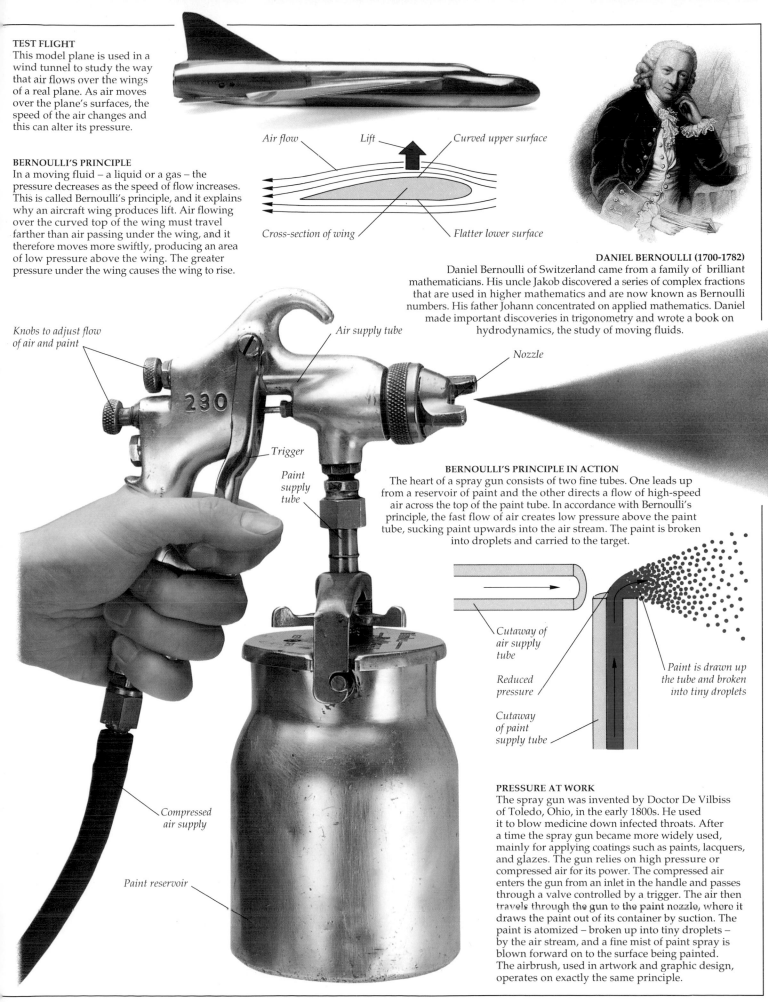

TEST FLIGHT
This model plane is used in a wind tunnel to study the way that air flows over the wings of a real plane. As air moves over the plane's surfaces, the speed of the air changes and this can alter its pressure.

BERNOULLI'S PRINCIPLE
In a moving fluid – a liquid or a gas – the pressure decreases as the speed of flow increases. This is called Bernoulli's principle, and it explains why an aircraft wing produces lift. Air flowing over the curved top of the wing must travel farther than air passing under the wing, and it therefore moves more swiftly, producing an area of low pressure above the wing. The greater pressure under the wing causes the wing to rise.

Air flow

Lift

Curved upper surface

Cross-section of wing

Flatter lower surface

DANIEL BERNOULLI (1700-1782)
Daniel Bernoulli of Switzerland came from a family of brilliant mathematicians. His uncle Jakob discovered a series of complex fractions that are used in higher mathematics and are now known as Bernoulli numbers. His father Johann concentrated on applied mathematics. Daniel made important discoveries in trigonometry and wrote a book on hydrodynamics, the study of moving fluids.

Knobs to adjust flow of air and paint

Air supply tube

Nozzle

Trigger

Paint supply tube

Compressed air supply

Paint reservoir

BERNOULLI'S PRINCIPLE IN ACTION
The heart of a spray gun consists of two fine tubes. One leads up from a reservoir of paint and the other directs a flow of high-speed air across the top of the paint tube. In accordance with Bernoulli's principle, the fast flow of air creates low pressure above the paint tube, sucking paint upwards into the air stream. The paint is broken into droplets and carried to the target.

Cutaway of air supply tube

Reduced pressure

Cutaway of paint supply tube

Paint is drawn up the tube and broken into tiny droplets

PRESSURE AT WORK
The spray gun was invented by Doctor De Vilbiss of Toledo, Ohio, in the early 1800s. He used it to blow medicine down infected throats. After a time the spray gun became more widely used, mainly for applying coatings such as paints, lacquers, and glazes. The gun relies on high pressure or compressed air for its power. The compressed air enters the gun from an inlet in the handle and passes through a valve controlled by a trigger. The air then travels through the gun to the paint nozzle, where it draws the paint out of its container by suction. The paint is atomized – broken up into tiny droplets – by the air stream, and a fine mist of paint spray is blown forward on to the surface being painted. The airbrush, used in artwork and graphic design, operates on exactly the same principle.

Back and forth

WHEN A WEIGHT IS HUNG FROM A SPRING and given a slight downward push, it will dance up and down. Movements like this, in which an object moves repeatedly back and forth, are called oscillations or vibrations. When a weight is hung from a string and pushed to one side, it will swing from side to side in a regular way. This, too, is an oscillation, and this simple device – called a pendulum – provides a method of timekeeping because its oscillations are very regular. The number of times that a particular pendulum swings each second – called its frequency – is always the same, provided the swing is small. Legend has it that Galileo noticed this one morning while sitting in church. During a boring sermon, his attention turned to a lamp that was swinging from the ceiling at the end of a long rope. The lamp seemed to be taking the same time to make each swing, but like all good scientists Galileo needed exact data. He timed the swings using his own pulse as a clock, an experiment that could be conducted without attracting attention. He was able to confirm his initial impression and later designed a clock which made use of a pendulum.

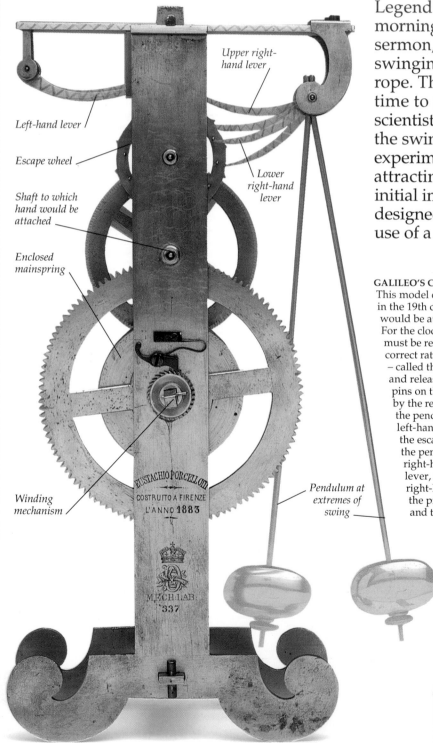

Upper right-hand lever

Left-hand lever

Escape wheel

Shaft to which hand would be attached

Enclosed mainspring

Lower right-hand lever

Winding mechanism

Pendulum at extremes of swing

EUSTACHIO PORCELLOTTI

COSTRUITO A FIRENZE

L'ANNO 1883

MECH·LAB· 337

GALILEO'S CLOCK – A DOUBLE EXPOSURE

This model of Galileo's clock was made in Italy in the 19th century. A shaft, to which a hand would be attached, is driven by a large spring. For the clock to work, the power of this spring must be released slowly and at exactly the correct rate. To achieve this, the top gear wheel – called the escape wheel – is regularly held and released by levers that fit into teeth and pins on the wheel. The levers are operated by the regular swing of the pendulum. As the pendulum swings outward, the left-hand lever drops down, stopping the escape wheel from turning. When the pendulum swings in, the upper right-hand lever lifts the left-hand lever, releasing the wheel. The lower right-hand lever is pushed down by the pins on the escape wheel as it turns, and this keeps the pendulum swinging.

A side view of Galileo's clock

BEATING TIME

A metronome is a device used to help musicians keep a regular pace or beat. The beat is adjusted by moving a weight up or down the swinging arm. This changes the effective length of the pendulum and therefore its frequency.

Christian Huygens
(1629-1695)

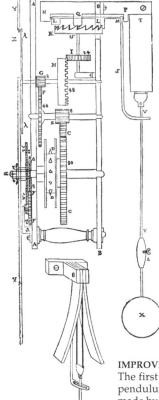

Knife-edged pivot

MEASURING GRAVITY

This piece of equipment, packed with all its accessories in a strong box for safe transport, is called an invariable pendulum. At one end of the pendulum is a knife-edged pivot on which it swings, and at the other end is a heavy weight. The rate at which a pendulum swings changes with its length and with the force of gravity. Since this "invariable" pendulum has a fixed length, its rate of swing can be used to determine the force of gravity at different places around the globe. Gravity decreases with the distance from the center of the earth, so the pendulum can be used to determine the shape of the planet, which is slightly flattened at the North and South Poles.

Between 1828 and 1840 this particular pendulum was taken to the South Atlantic, the Euphrates River in Iraq, and Antarctica.

THE SPINNING EARTH

Léon Foucault (p. 127) is best known for using a pendulum to demonstrate the rotation of the earth. In 1851 he suspended a very large iron ball by a long steel wire from the center of the dome of the Pantheon in Paris. When the pendulum was first released it swung along a line marked on the floor beneath it, but after several hours the pendulum appeared to have changed direction. In fact, Foucault's pendulum was still swinging in the same direction – it was the earth below the pendulum that had turned.

Léon Foucault
(1819-1868)

Fixed heavy weight

IMPROVED ACCURACY

The first practical pendulum clock was made by Dutch scientist Christian Huygens in 1657. These drawings are taken from his book *Horologium Oscillatorium* of 1673. His design used a short pendulum and a weight to drive the hands. An endless chain or rope provided the drive, even when the clock was being wound. This arrangement is still used today in "grandfather" clocks. The lower drawing shows the curved, or "cycloidal," cheeks between which the pendulum swung for greater accuracy.

THE BALANCE SPRING

In 1675 Huygens made a watch regulated by an oscillating spring, called a balance spring or hairspring. Many clocks and watches have since used this mechanism. This model shows how the mechanism works. One end of the hairspring is fixed and the other end is attached to the center of the balance wheel. The spring alternately winds and unwinds, spinning the wheel back and forth. The rate of the oscillations can be adjusted by altering the tension in the spring, or by turning the cylindrical screws around the balance wheel.

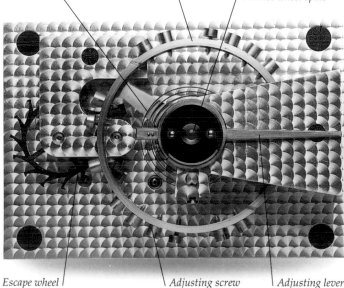

Hairspring *Balance wheel* *Ruby bearing on which balance wheel spins*

Escape wheel *Adjusting screw* *Adjusting lever*

Giant vibrations

SOLDIERS NEVER MARCH IN STEP across a bridge. This is because any bridge will vibrate slightly as the soldiers cross, and if the rhythm of the vibrations matches the rhythm of the soldier's steps, the marching could shake the bridge to pieces. Anything that can vibrate – a swing, a pendulum, or a tuning fork – has its own natural rhythm, or natural frequency. This is the number of vibrations that the object makes each second when it vibrates. If an object is given a single push, it will start to vibrate at its natural frequency, but the vibrations will die down unless it is given regular pushes or pulls. A child's swing will gradually stop swinging if left alone, but if it is pushed with the correct rhythm it can be made to rise higher and higher. This happens when the frequency of the pushes is the same as the natural frequency of the swing. Increasing the size – or amplitude – of a vibration by regular pushes is called resonance. A bridge will resonate and may even be destroyed if the rhythm of the marching soldiers' steps is the same as the natural frequency of the bridge.

HIGHER AND HIGHER
For a swing to go high, it must be pushed at the beginning of each swing. The frequency of the pushes must match the natural frequency of the swing. Pushing with any other rhythm will slow the swing down.

MUSICAL RESONANCE
The sound box of a violin or other stringed musical instrument increases the sound of each vibrating string by resonance. Bowing the string causes it to vibrate, producing a sound. These vibrations start the bridge vibrating, and this in turn spreads the vibrations to the whole body, since the front and back are connected by a post. This amplifies the sound. The violin is built so that its sound box resonates to a wide range of notes, amplifying them all equally.

WIND INSTRUMENTS
In woodwind instruments, such as the Pan pipes (above) and the fife (right), a column of air vibrates in a tube. The air in each tube of the Pan pipes vibrates strongly at only one fundamental frequency, which depends on the length of the tube; the longer the tube, the lower the resonant frequency. In the fife, the frequency of the vibration is altered by covering holes to change the effective length of the tube.

VIBRATING STRINGS
The simplest way that a stretched string can vibrate is shown below. The middle of the string moves strongly back and forth. This point of maximum movement is called an antinode. The points of minimum movements, called nodes, are at the ends of the string. This vibration produces a note called the fundamental. However, strings can also vibrate in more complicated ways. The other vibrations are called harmonics. The first harmonic occurs when a string vibrates in two halves, with a node at its center. The frequency of this vibration is twice that of the fundamental. Other harmonics occur when the string vibrates in three, four, or more sections. Strings, therefore, resonate with more than one frequency, although the fundamental frequency is always the strongest. Vibrating columns of air, which are created in the tubes of instruments such as flutes and organs, show the same behavior, producing a fundamental note and a series of harmonics.

Vibrating string

BAFFLING THE ECHOES

Concert halls are designed to suppress unwanted resonances. In a badly designed hall, sound waves of certain frequencies can be repeatedly reflected back and forth between the walls and the ceiling, producing an amplification of certain musical notes. Particular notes might sound quiet in some parts of the hall and very loud in others. In this hall, geometrical shapes called "baffles" have been hung from the ceiling to absorb unwanted echoes.

NUCLEAR RESONANCE

The technique of nuclear magnetic resonance (NMR) uses the fact that the nuclei of some atoms behave like small magnets. In an oscillating magnetic field, these nuclear magnets vibrate back and forth, and since the frequency at which a nucleus absorbs the maximum energy is its natural frequency, NMR can be used to identify the composition of chemical compounds (above). NMR can also be used in a scanner as an alternative to X-rays. By passing a radio wave over a patient's body and noting where energy is absorbed by resonance between the waves and the nuclei in the body, a computer can create a picture of the patient's internal organs.

EXPLODING WINEGLASS

Resonance occurs because energy is transferred to the vibrating object, building up and increasing the amplitude, or size, of the vibration. In some situations, the energy transferred can be destructive. A wineglass can be exploded by a sound wave if the frequency of the sound wave matches the natural frequency of the glass. The natural vibrations of a wineglass are of high frequency or pitch. This can be demonstrated by running a wet finger rapidly around the rim of the glass, producing a ringing note. If a singer now sings this note loudly, the glass resonates with the sound. The size of these vibrations can be enough to break the glass apart. This transfer of energy during resonance plays an important part in the tuning of a radio or a television. In both cases the tuning circuit consists of components in which electric current flows back and forth. The frequency at which the current oscillates can be varied to match the frequency of the signal being received by the aerial. This sets up resonance in the circuit, enabling it to absorb the maximum energy from the aerial signal, and this produces the clearest picture or sound.

Antinode

TACOMA NARROWS COLLAPSE

During a storm in November 1940, the bridge over the Tacoma Narrows in Washington State began to twist back and forth so violently that it finally collapsed, only four months after it was opened. The very strong wind just happened to set up a twisting motion at the natural frequency of the 2,800-ft (860-m) bridge.

Node

Making waves

ENERGY IS NOT ONLY continually changing form – it is also continually moving from one place to another. One way this occurs is through wave motion. When a stone is dropped into a pond, at first only the moving stone has energy. But after a while, a leaf on the far side of the pond will bob up and down as the ripples reach it. Now the leaf has energy, too. The ripples have transported some of the stone's energy across the pond. Water waves or ripples are just one kind of wave. They are called transverse waves because, while the waves move outward from their source, the individual water particles move up and down only at right angles to the wave's direction. Another kind of wave is called the longitudinal wave. In these waves the particles move back and forth in the same direction as the wave. Sound waves are of this type.

ENERGY RAMPANT
The enormous energy of a huge ocean wave comes from the wind blowing across large stretches of sea. The surfer uses this energy to accelerate and drive the board.

A TRANSVERSE WAVE
Like a water wave, the wave traveling down a rope is a transverse wave. Each particle in turn is pulled up or down by the movement of its left-hand neighbor as the wave moves from left to right. In a longitudinal wave, particles knock each other along in the direction that the wave is traveling.

DEFINING A WAVE
The distance between successive wave ripples is called the wavelength. The number of waves passing any point each second is called the frequency. The size of the up-and-down movement is called the amplitude.

ADDING WAVES
This 18th-century apparatus shows the effect of combining two waves – an effect called "interference." A row of brass rods are cut to different lengths so that their tops form a wave shape. A wooden template in the form of another wave is slid underneath the rods. The tops of the rods now trace the combination of the two waves. Where the crests of the waves are above each other, the waves reinforce each other and the amplitude of the combined wave is greater than either of the two original waves. When the crest of one wave aligns with the trough of the other, the waves cancel each other out, producing a flat region where there is no wave activity.

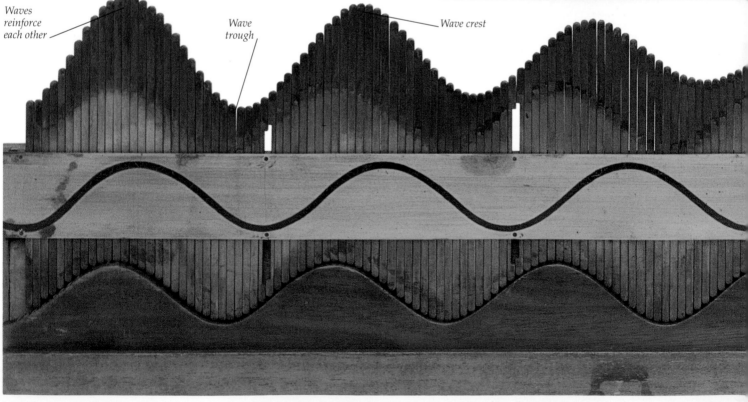

Waves reinforce each other

Wave trough

Wave crest

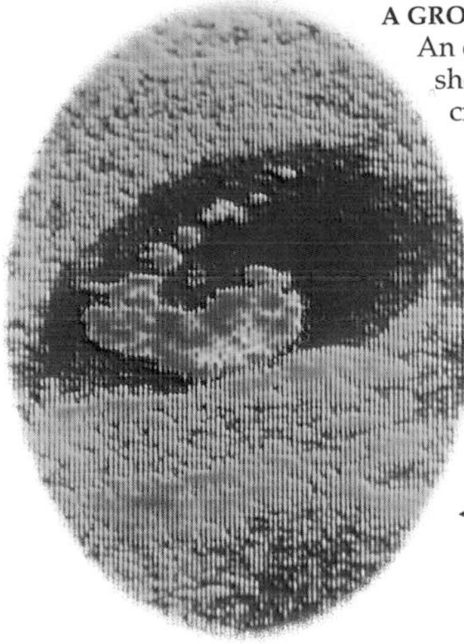

A GROWING BABY

An eight-week-old baby inside the womb is shown in orange and yellow in this image created by ultrasound – sound waves with frequencies so high that they cannot be heard by humans. Audible sounds have frequencies of between 20 and 20,000 vibrations per second, while ultrasounds have frequencies above 20,000 vibrations per second. The ultrasound waves are reflected at the boundaries between different kinds of tissue, such as muscle and bone. In an ultrasound scanner, a computer uses information about the reflected waves to create a picture of the growing baby.

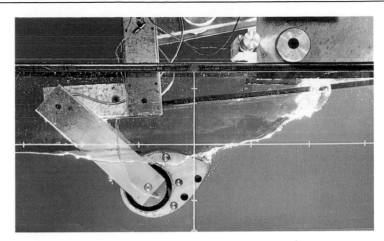

CLEAN ENERGY FROM THE SEA

The power of ocean waves offers a rich source of energy. This working model of "Salter's duck," being tested in a wave tank, absorbs a high proportion of each wave's energy and converts it into electricity. The up-and-down motion of the water, as a wave passes through from right to left, causes the oval-shaped "duck," designed by British scientist Professor Stephen Salter, to nod up and down. This turns a dynamo inside it and generates electricity.

SEEING WITH SOUND

Bats can "see" in the dark by using ultrasound. They emit short bursts, or clicks, of high-frequency sound waves. The waves bounce off trees and flying insects and produce an echo that the bat can hear. The shorter the time between a click and its echo, the closer the insect. As the bat approaches its target it emits more frequent clicks, allowing it to locate the insect with ever greater accuracy.

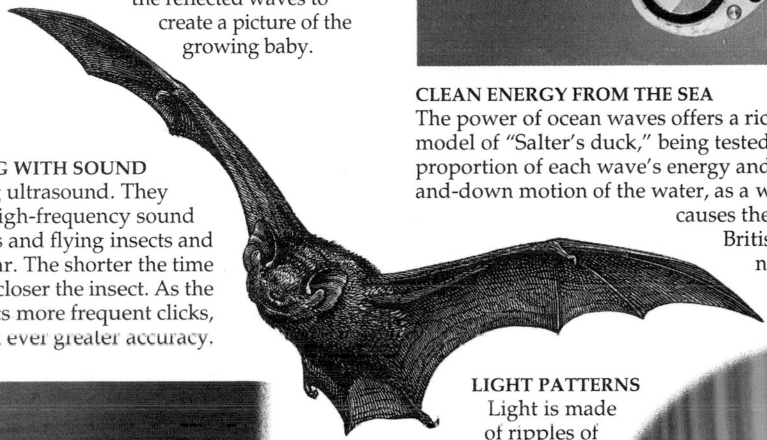

LIGHT PATTERNS

Light is made of ripples of electricity and magnetism called electromagnetic waves. This pattern of colored bands is caused by interference between light waves being reflected from the front of a film of soap and light waves being reflected back inside the film. This produces bands of light at different wavelengths and therefore of different colors.

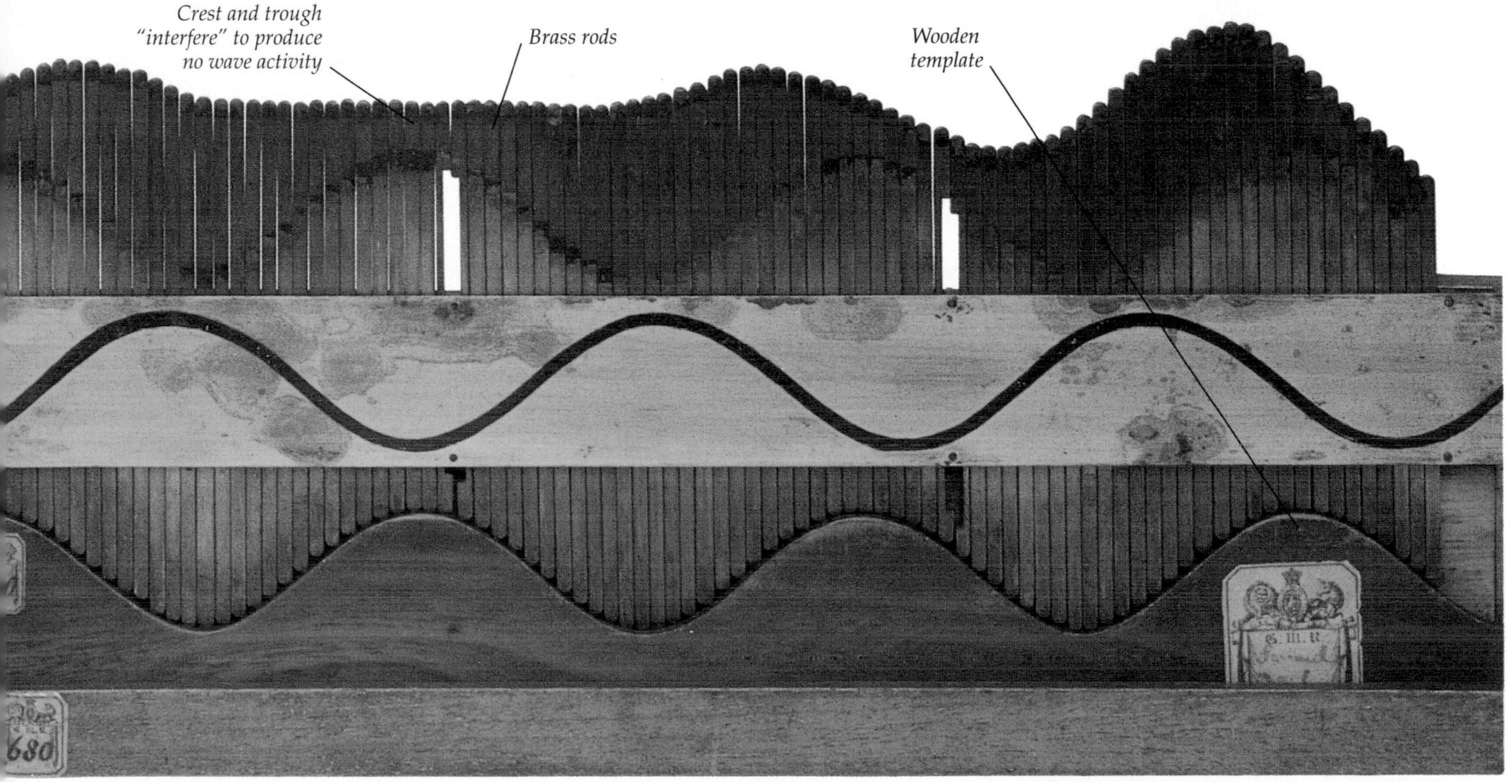

Crest and trough "interfere" to produce no wave activity

Brass rods

Wooden template

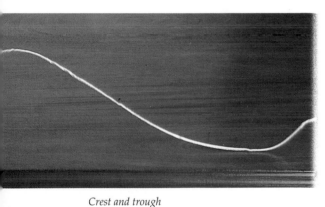

Around in circles

IF A BUCKET OF WATER IS SWUNG in a circle on the end of a rope, the water will not spill out if the bucket is moving fast enough. This is because the water is trying to continue in a straight line and therefore pushes against the bucket that is pulling it around in a circle. This tendency to continue moving in a straight line appears to produce a force acting away from the center. This illusory force is sometimes referred to as centrifugal force. The real force acting towards the center of the circle to keep the bucket moving in a circular path is called centripetal force. It is provided by the rope. Without this force, the bucket would fly off in a straight line. The faster the bucket is swung, the greater the centripetal force needed to prevent it from flying off.

Sack of seed

Handle to spin plate

Spinning plate

Arm to push the seed around

SEED SCATTERER
This late 19th-century seed scatterer shows centrifugal force at work. Seeds from the bag at the top fall on to a plate that is being turned by the handle. Arms on the spinning plate push the seeds round, but centrifugal force pushes the seeds away from the center to the edge of the plate where they fly off in straight lines. Centrifugal forces arise because moving objects always attempt to continue traveling in a straight line. This quality is called inertia. Any object moving in a circle is continuously being forced to change direction. The inertia of the object resists this change and seems to produce a force that acts away from the center.

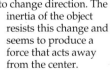

DAVID AND GOLIATH
This stone carving illustrates the Biblical Old Testament story in which David slays Goliath with a stone from his sling. The sling provides a centripetal force to restrain the stone while it is accelerated around. When one end of the sling is released, the moving stone flies off in a straight line, propelled by centrifugal force.

UP AND OVER

As a trick cyclist loops the loop, the pressure of the track against his tires provides the centripetal force to pull him around in a circle. As he goes over the top, gravity is pulling him down, but his tendency to travel on in a straight line (so-called centrifugal force) keeps the bicycle pressed outwards against the track. To complete a loop safely, the rider must be going fast, so he needs a long ramp down which to gain speed.

CENTRIFUGAL GOVERNOR

In the 18th century this device was used to control the gap between the millstones in a windmill. The turning sails drove a rope that spun the governor around. Centrifugal force caused the two weights to be thrown out, raising the boss at the bottom, which was attached to one of the millstones. Similar governors were used on steam engines to control the flow of steam and keep the engine speed constant.

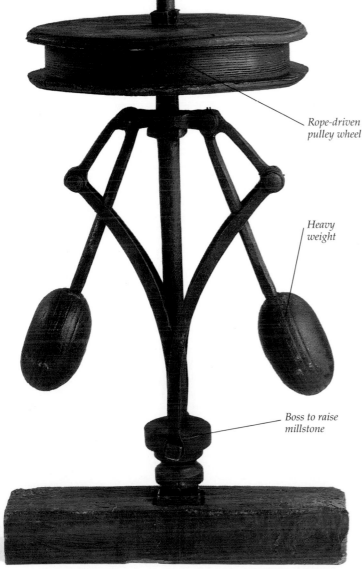

Rope-driven pulley wheel

Heavy weight

Boss to raise millstone

Bowl for unseparated milk

Supply tap

Separator mechanism

Outlet for milk

Outlet for cream

Driving gear operated by handle on back

THE CENTRIFUGE

This 1930s cream separator works by spinning the milk very rapidly. The heavier part of the milk is spun away from the center with a greater force than the cream, which is less dense, and the two parts can therefore be separated. A similar kind of centrifuge is used in laboratories to separate the heavier red cells from the lighter plasma in blood.

AROUND THE BEND

A racing motorcyclist leans into a tight corner to counteract the tendency of the bike to continue traveling forward in a straight line. The grip of the tires on the track provides a centripetal force toward the center of the turn. Steeply banked corners provide additional centripetal force and make turning at speed easier and safer.

FLOATING IN SPACE

An astronaut "walking" in space appears to have no forces acting on him. In fact he is continuously falling towards the earth under the influence of gravity. However, at the same time, his forward momentum produces a tendency to continue in a straight line, and the overall result is that he travels in a circular orbit around the earth. If his speed were to increase, he would fly off into space.

Spiraling in

A FAN OR CLOTHES DRYER continues to spin after its power is turned off. This is because, like all moving objects, a spinning object has momentum, but in this case it is momentum in a circle rather than straight-line momentum. A spinning object is said to have "angular momentum" and, like linear momentum, this increases with speed and with mass. Surprisingly, angular momentum also depends upon the shape and size of the object. For example, if two wheels have the same mass but different diameters, the larger wheel will have the greater angular momentum when rotating. Like linear momentum, angular momentum is conserved; it does not change unless a force acts upon the object. One effect of the conservation of momentum is that changes in the shape of a spinning object will change its speed of rotation. It is for this reason that when the arms of a spinning ice skater are pulled in to the body, reducing the skater's diameter, the speed at which the skater spins increases. If the speed remained the same, angular momentum would have been lost rather than conserved.

SPINNING SKATER
An ice skater shows the conservation of angular momentum in action. The speed of rotation increases as the skater's arms are pulled in to the body.

DOWN THE PLUGHOLE
A whirlpool, or vortex, can occur spontaneously wherever a fluid (a gas or a liquid) flows through a hole. It is a very efficient form of flow. As the fluid spirals in to the center it speeds up, conserving its angular momentum. The whirlpool above occurs at a reservoir in France, but the same kind of vortex can be seen whenever water flows out of a bathtub or a sink. In theory, the earth's rotation should cause water to spiral in a counterclockwise direction in the northern hemisphere and in a clockwise direction in the southern hemisphere, but in practice the direction depends upon other factors, like the initial direction in which the water is moving.

Ball in position 2

WATERSPOUT
A waterspout occurs when a tornado passes over a body of water. The wind speeds up as it spirals in toward an area of low pressure at the center, and it acts like an inverted whirlpool, sucking water and spray up into the air. Water spouts are usually between 15 and 33 ft (5–10 m) across and can be up to 330 ft (100 m) high. The weather conditions that produce them are most common in tropical regions.

IN A WHIRL

Together, four superimposed images taken at equal time intervals reveal how a spiral motion speeds up. When the small ball, which is attached by a string to the central pole, is swung around, the string winds around the central rod and causes the ball to follow a spiral path. As the ball approaches the center the radius of its path decreases, and so the ball moves faster, since its angular momentum must be conserved. In the first time interval the ball has traveled from position 1 to position 2 – approximately one third of a circle. In the last time interval it has traveled from 3 to 4 – almost half a circle. Several different shapes of spiral are found in nature. This one is called Archimedes' Spiral, after its discoverer.

Ball in position 3

Spiral track

Ball in position 1

Ball in position 4

FUNNEL OF DESTRUCTION

A tornado, or twister, in which winds spiral into the center and speed up as they do so, is the most destructive type of storm known. The worst tornado on record occurred on March 18th, 1925. In three hours it tore a 220-mile (350-km) path through the states of Missouri, Illinois, and Indiana, killing 689 people, injuring almost 3,000 more, hurling cars into the air, and demolishing buildings.

THE RED SPOT

The spirals that are seen in weather systems are due to the fact that the earth is spinning. This causes winds to move in spirals rather than straight lines – the tornado is an extreme case of this. The famous Red Spot on Jupiter is a giant spiral storm that has been raging for more than 300 years. Winds spiral upward from the lower atmosphere and then spread out. The area of the storm is three times larger than the earth – about 24,000 miles (38,500 km) long by 7,000 miles (11,000 km) wide.

SPIRAL ELECTRON

A single electron moving through a magnetic field flies in a spiral path. As the electron loses energy, the magnetic field has a steadily greater influence on the electron, causing it to curl more and more tightly. The track is revealed in an apparatus called a bubble chamber, in which the particle leaves a trail of minute bubbles.

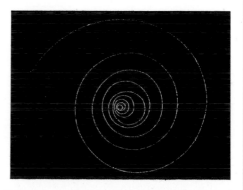

Spinning tops

A SPINNING TOP is a fascinating toy. It can be made to balance on the end of a pencil, and if the pencil is moved the spinning top remains pointing in the same direction. This happens because the top has angular momentum (p. 360), and this momentum does not change unless a force acts on the spinning top - angular momentum is always conserved. Spinning tops , or their more sophisticated cousins called gyroscopes, are used in compasses because they resist changes to the axis of their spin. When a spinning top slows down, it leans to one side. Gravity is pulling the spinning top down, but it does not fall. Instead it slowly circles around its balance point. The spinning object converts the vertical force of gravity into a horizontal motion. This is known as precession.

THE GYROSCOPE
This 19th-century gyroscope is a piece of precision engineering. It consists of a wheel-shaped rotor on an axle that is mounted inside a metal ring. The rotor is set spinning by winding a string around the axle and then giving it a strong pull. This gyroscope has been suspended upright from a string attached to its base. One would expect it to simply fall and hang upside down, but in fact the spinning gyroscope precesses – it leans at an angle and swings around in a horizontal circle.

Rotor

Axle

Ring

JAPANESE TOPS
An old Japanese print shows children playing with spinning tops, seeing who can keep a top going the longest. A top is set spinning by pulling a string wrapped around its axle. Once it is spinning fast, a top is amazingly stable. Tops will right themselves if knocked and can even be made to balance on the edge of a knife.

MECHANICAL TIGHTROPE WALKER
Demonstrating the properties of the gyroscope, this 19th-century apparatus balances on a stretched string. The ring holding the spinning rotor is attached to a pole with a ball at each end, like that used by a circus high-wire walker. If the device tilts in one direction, the gyroscope swings the other way and the balancing pole corrects the tilt. The term "gyroscope" was first used by Léon Foucault (p. 353) in 1852.

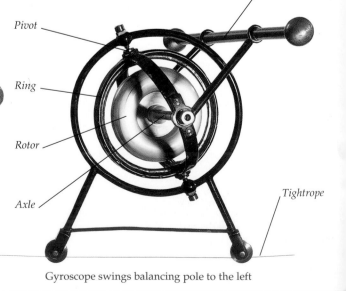

Balancing pole

Pivot

Ring

Rotor

Axle

Tightrope

Apparatus starts to tilt to the right

Gyroscope swings balancing pole to the left

DEFYING GRAVITY

The explanation of the gyroscope's strange behavior involves complicated mathematics and the use of Newton's Laws (p. 336). According to these laws, any force acting upon a spinning object will cause it to move at right angles to the force. The force of gravity acts downward and therefore causes the gyroscope to move around horizontally.

THE BICYCLE AS A GYROSCOPE

The spinning wheels of a bicycle act as gyroscopes and help to keep the bike upright. Like all gyroscopes, the wheels tend to remain spinning in the same plane, giving the bicycle stability. A well-designed bike can be steered by leaning to one side, without touching the handlebars. The sideways force produced by leaning is converted into a turning force as the wheels precess. This makes the bicycle easier to handle.

Tip of axis of rotation, which travels in a circle as the globe precesses

Globe

THE EARTH AS A GYROSCOPE

The axis of the spinning earth is remarkably stable but our planet does precess very slightly, as shown by this 19th-century model. The earth takes 25,800 years for each circular wobble. This precession is largely caused by the gravitational pull of the sun and moon on the earth's equatorial bulge. It is thought that the tilting of the earth's axis in relation to the sun may be one of the causes of the Ice Ages.

Hollow conical base resting on pointed support

GYROSCOPES FOR STABILIZATION

The sights on the top of this early 20th-century ship's navigational sighting device are mounted on a frame that is stabilized by a gyroscope. Because of their ability to remain stable, gyroscopes have even been used to stabilize oceangoing ships. The Italian liner *Conte di Savois*, built in 1933, had three giant gyroscopes fitted as stabilizers. Each one was 13 ft (4 m) across and weighed more than 100 tons. Such large stabilizers were found to be too unwieldy, but smaller gyroscopes are still used to control the movements of stabilizing fins. These project from the hulls of ships to counteract the effects of the rolling seas.

Sights

Plate mounted on gyroscope frame

Gyroscope rotor

GYROSCOPES FOR GUIDANCE

This piece of equipment is a gyrocompass. It was used to guide a World War II V2 rocket during the powered section of its flight, after which the rocket went into ballistic flight (p. 333). Inside a gyrocompass, a spinning gyroscope maintains a constant orientation. The gyrocompass was invented by American engineer Elmer Sperry, and was first used in the US Navy ship *Delaware* in 1911.

Gyroscope

Handle to spin rotor

Weight to hold gyroscope vertical

The ultimate speed limit

IN 1905 GERMAN SCIENTIST ALBERT EINSTEIN published a revolutionary new theory. It was called the Special Theory of Relativity and it dealt with the effects of high-speed motion. Einstein realized that when objects approach the speed of light – about 186,000 miles/second – common sense is an unreliable guide. If two cars are heading toward each other, and each is traveling at 100 mph, an observer in one of the cars would see the other car approaching at 200 mph. That is common sense. But if one of the cars is replaced by a beam of light, common sense would suggest that an observer in the car would see the light approaching at a speed that is 100 mph faster than 186,000 miles/second. Strangely, the light actually approaches at its usual speed. In fact, as Einstein realized, whatever speed an observer travels, the light always approaches at the same speed. How is this possible? After much thought, Einstein showed that for the speed of light to be always the same, distances must shrink and time must slow down at near-light speeds. Einstein also showed that matter can be transformed into energy and that the mass of an object increases with speed. This makes it increasingly difficult to accelerate objects as they approach near-light speeds. In fact, nothing can travel faster than the speed of light and only electro-magnetic waves, such as light, can travel that fast. It is the ultimate speed limit.

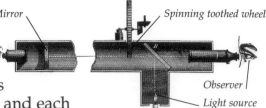

Mirror   Spinning toothed wheel

Observer

Light source

THE SPEED OF LIGHT
The speed of light is 186,000 miles (300,000 kilometers) per second – 10,000 times faster than the fastest rocket. At this speed, a rocket could travel around the world seven times in one second. The first reliable measurement of the speed of light was made by French scientist Armand Fizeau (1819-1896) in 1849. He directed light at a distant mirror and measured its time of travel by spinning a toothed wheel in the path of the beam. The beam departed through a gap in the toothed wheel and was blocked by the following tooth. Knowing the speed of revolution of the wheel, Fizeau could calculate the time of travel of the beam and hence its speed.

Albert Michelson (1852-1931)

Edward Morley (1838-1923)

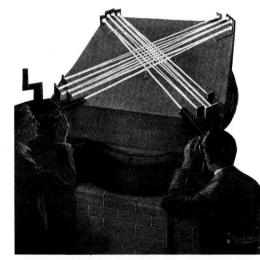

MICHELSON-MORLEY EXPERIMENT
In 1887 American physicists Albert Michelson and Edward Morley carried out an experiment. A beam of light was split into two parts moving at right angles to each other and then brought together again. The experiment produced an unexpected result: the speed of light was the same whether the beam was traveling in the same direction as the earth's motion or at right angles to it. Michelson and Morley had found that the speed of the earth's motion did not affect the speed of the light beam. This fact is central to the theory of relativity: the speed of light remains the same for all observers, no matter how fast they are moving.

IT IS TIME ITSELF THAT CHANGES

Two rockets are traveling past the earth, at a fixed distance apart, at almost the speed of light. A flash of light is sent from one ship to the other. To the astronauts aboard the rockets, the light is seen to travel in a straight line between them. However, since the rockets are moving forward at high speed, to an observer on the earth the light beam appears to follow a diagonal path. This diagonal path is clearly longer than the direct distance between the rockets. Since the speed of light is constant, the passage of the light beam between the rockets must therefore seem to take longer when seen from earth. Although the observers on the rockets and on the earth have witnessed the same event, they make different judgements about the time taken. In other words, time does not pass at the same rate for all observers. If the rockets were passing the earth at 90 percent of the speed of light, the earth-bound observer would see the beam take 2.3 times longer to cross than would the crew of the rocket. This also means that the observer on the earth is aging 2.3 times as fast as the astronauts.

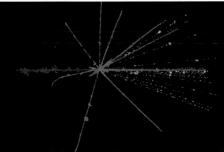

ALBERT EINSTEIN

As a young man, Albert Einstein (1879-1955) was thought to be rather dull. One of his school reports read, "He will never amount to anything." Yet he proved to be a scientific genius. Einstein's ideas about forces and motion were so revolutionary that many people, including members of the scientific community, could not believe them. In 1905 he published his Special Theory of Relativity, describing how objects behave when traveling at near-light speed. In 1916 he published the General Theory of Relativity, which extended his ideas. He received the Nobel Prize for Physics in 1921. He emigrated to the USA in 1933 to avoid persecution by the Nazis.

PROVING EINSTEIN RIGHT

Many experiments have proved Einstein's amazing ideas to be correct. In 1971 very sensitive "atomic" clocks were carried around the world in high-speed aircraft and then compared with clocks left on the ground. The clocks that had traveled at high speed were found to have slowed down by 0.0000001 seconds – enough to prove Einstein correct. Cosmic rays provide another proof. These high-speed particles reach the earth's atmosphere from space and normally exist for only a brief time. But because they are traveling at such high speeds, time slows down for them and some can survive for long enough to be detected within the Earth's atmosphere.

Einstein's gravity

ARTHUR EDDINGTON (1882-1944)
The English astronomer and mathematician Arthur Eddington led the expedition to Príncipe, in the Atlantic, that confirmed Einstein's radical new ideas about gravity.

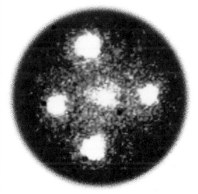

EINSTEIN'S CROSS
This image shows the effect of gravity on light. The central spot is a relatively close quasar, or starlike object. The four surrounding spots are images of a distant quasar behind the near one. The nearby quasar acts like a giant lens, bending the light from the far one and producing four images. Einstein predicted this gravitational lens effect in 1936.

"LIGHT CAUGHT BENDING" screamed a newspaper headline in 1919. The event being reported was an expedition led by English astronomer Arthur Eddington to the island of Príncipe, off the west coast of Africa. The purpose of the expedition was to measure the position of stars during an eclipse of the sun. Albert Einstein had predicted that light from the stars would be affected by the sun's gravity. According to Einstein, space acts as if it were a stretched rubber sheet. When a heavy object is placed on the sheet it creates a dip or hollow. A small ball rolled across the sheet will be affected by the dip and will roll towards the heavy object. This is the way that gravity acts, according to Einstein. If a light beam travels across the sheet, it too will follow the curves of the sheet, and the beam will be bent. Eddington had observed the stars' light rays being bent by the sun's gravity, and overnight Einstein became famous. His theory of gravity, which he called the General Theory of Relativity, became the talk of the scientific community. Einstein's theory was even able to explain the fact that Mercury's orbit around the sun twists a little each year. Newton's theory of gravity could not explain why this happens, but Einstein's theory could. This convinced most scientists that Einstein's view of gravity was correct.

The rubber sheet of space-time is distorted by the presence of a massive object

Path of passing comet

Sun

RUBBER-SHEET GRAVITY
Of course Einstein did not suggest that there really was a rubber sheet stretched through space. However, his work showed that there was something called "space-time" which acted like a rubber sheet. Space-time is difficult to visualize: it is a combination of space and time. Einstein had to use complicated mathematics to explain the properties of space-time. This model shows an object, perhaps a comet, passing the sun in a curved path. Newton would have explained the curved path by saying that there is a force – gravity – which is attracting the object to the sun. Einstein, on the other hand, said that the object's path is curved because the sun distorts space and time around it.

THE BLACK HOLE

A black hole is like a very small, very heavy ball on the "rubber sheet" of space-time, creating a deep narrow dent into which nearby objects fall. The gravity is so strong that once something has been attracted toward the black hole, it can never escape from it. Not even light can escape from black holes – that is why they appear black. This picture is an artist's impression of a black hole with a giant blue star in the background. A stream of gas is being pulled from the atmosphere of the blue star by the immense gravity of the black hole. As the gas spirals into the black hole, it forms a flat disc that heats up and emits X-rays, creating the central white region.

BLACK HOLE EXPLORER

English physicist Stephen Hawking is Professor of Mathematics at Cambridge University, the post once held by Isaac Newton. Confined to a wheelchair for many years because of a muscular disease, Hawking has worked to combine Einstein's theory of gravity with quantum physics, which explains the structure of atoms. Quantum theory describes how random chance plays a part in the events of the subatomic world, an idea that Einstein was never able to accept. Disputing the role of chance, Einstein once said, "I shall never believe that God plays dice with the world." To this Hawking replies that "God not only plays dice, he throws them where they can't be seen." Hawking has discovered that the strong gravity around a black hole can produce particles of matter. He has also used Einstein's theories to explore the very early history of the universe (see also p. 189).

SPACEWARPS

Gravitational waves are ripples in space-time, similar to ripples traveling across a rubber sheet. Einstein's theory suggests that cataclysmic events in space, such as the explosions of stars, might produce these waves. Gravitational wave detectors, like the one here, consist of large blocks of metal. The experimenters use lasers to look for inexplicable shudders in the metal, caused by one of these waves. So far, no such waves have been detected, despite a 20-year search.

Comet's path is bent into a curve by the distortion of space and time produced by the sun's mass

The fundamental forces

THE FASTEST OBJECTS ON EARTH
are the tiny particles used in
experiments to investigate subatomic particles and forces.
Inside giant machines called
accelerators, these particles
reach speeds approaching the
speed of light, and then smash
together with far greater energy
than any natural collision on earth.
The collision creates a shower of
new particles which explode in a starburst of
fragments. Inside an accelerator the particles reach
speeds of more than 99.99 percent of the speed of
light. At these speeds, the effects predicted by
Einstein's Special Theory of Relativity can be
observed. Careful measurements show that particles
called muons, which normally only live for about two
millionths of a second, have their lifetimes extended by 20 times
inside an accelerator, as predicted by Einstein's theory. The mass
of the moving particles is also seen to increase as the speed rises.
Einstein said that matter and energy are interchangeable, and
new particles are indeed created from the energy of the speeding
particles. Scientists can identify these particles and study the
forces acting on them. Forces unknown in everyday life are
found at work between the particles that make up the atomic
nucleus. These are the strong nuclear force and the weak
nuclear force. It is now possible to see that there are just a few
basic forces acting in the universe – electromagnetic forces,
gravitational forces, and the strong and weak nuclear forces.
All other forces are derived from these fundamental forces.

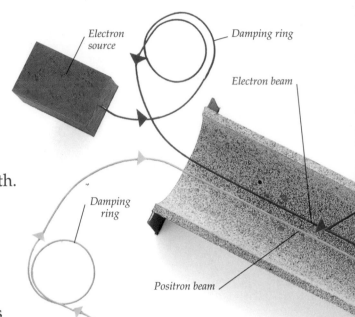

Electron source

Damping ring

Electron beam

Damping ring

Positron beam

INSIDE AN
ACCELERATOR
In this schematic model of the
Stanford Linear Accelerator, electrons
(red) and positively charged electrons, called
positrons (yellow), are accelerated along the
straight 2-mile (3-km) tube and then steered into a
head-on collision. An electron source fires bunches
of electrons down the track via the damping ring.
The damping ring squeezes the electron bursts
into short pulses. About halfway along the track,
some electrons are diverted to a target, where they
create positrons. These positrons are injected into
the head of the accelerator tube and are fired
down the tube with the electrons. Magnets guide
the beams to the final collision, which is studied
inside the massive 1,600-ton particle detector.

THE ELECTROMAGNETIC FORCE
The electromagnetic force is one of the
fundamental forces and is responsible for
binding atoms together to form molecules.
Every aspect of life depends on this
force. Electromagnetic forces hold
the molecules of the body
together and maintain the
structure of all physical
objects. The chemical
reactions that release
energy from food and
make it possible for
muscles to do work are
rearrangements of
electrical charges in
atoms and molecules, as
is the process of burning.
Electromagnetic forces
are driving this train
along its single track.

ELECTROMAGNETISM
This electric motor was made in
1840 by the English physicist
Charles Wheatstone (1802-
1875). It demonstrates that
a flowing electric current
produces a magnetic
field. Equally, a magnet
can produce electricity in a
wire. Electricity and
magnetism are two
different aspects of a
single force called
electromagnetism.

Iron rotor

*Electricity
flows through
coil of wire
around iron
bar, creating
magnetic field*

THE STRENGTH OF THE FORCES

The energy that powers the sun comes from the fusion of atomic nuclei. The sun would cease to shine without the forces that hold nuclei together. The strong nuclear force is the strongest of all the forces – 100 times as strong as the electromagnetic force. However, the strong force has a very short range. Its influence is only ever felt within the atomic nucleus. The weak force, too, is felt only within the nucleus. It is 100,000 million times weaker than the electromagnetic force. The force of gravity is the weakest of all; it is around a million million million million million million times weaker than the weak nuclear force. However, it is a long range force and can be felt across the universe.

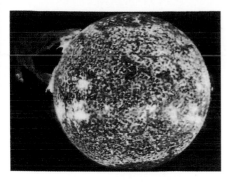

ABDUS SALAM

Pakistani physicist Abdus Salam is known for his work on the fundamental forces. In 1979 he was the first from his country to receive a Nobel Prize. With Americans Sheldon Glashow and Steven Weinberg he proved that the electromagnetic force and the weak nuclear force were variations of a single underlying "superforce," called the electroweak force. His ideas were verified experimentally in 1973 at CERN (*Conseil Européen pour la Recherche Nucléaire*), in Geneva, Switzerland. Scientists are now investigating the possibility that all the fundamental forces are variations of a single force.

Positron source

Arc-bending magnets

Focusing magnets

Focusing magnets

Arc-bending magnets

Particle collision detector

THE STRAIGHTEST LINE

At the Stanford Linear Accelerator, in California, electromagnetic forces are used to speed particles along a track. The track is so straight that its supports have to be of different heights to allow for the curvature of the Earth. The straight-line arrangement at Stanford is unusual; most large accelerators are circular. The Stanford accelerator was used to discover the psi particle and to measure the lifetime of a particle called the Z^0 (Z zero), which helps carry the weak nuclear force.

PARTICLE COLLISION

This is an artifically colored photograph showing the tracks of subatomic particles colliding. It was produced at CERN, the European particle physics laboratory. The complex tangle of tracks can be analyzed by computers to reveal the forces at work. Modern theories suggest that all the fundamental forces are "carried" by particles that flit between other particles. The strong nuclear force is carried by particles called "gluons," the weak force by the Z and W particles, electromagnetism by the photon, and gravity by a particle called the graviton.

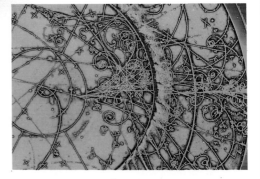

Index

Acknowledgments

Dorling Kindersley would like to thank:

CHEMISTRY
John Becklake, Chris Berridge, Roger Bridgman, Stewart Emmens, Stephen Fougler, Graeme Fyffe, Ian Carter and Science Museum Library Staff, Brian Gilliam and object handling team, Derek Hudson, Douglas Millard, Sue Mossman, Derek Robinson, Robert Sharp, Peter Stephens, Kenneth Waterman, and Anthony Wilson for advice and help with the provision of objects for photography at the Science Musuem; Frances Halpin for technical advice and help with the laboratory experiments; Evelyn Richards, laboratory technician at Harris CTC, London; Deborah Rhodes for page make-up; Neil Ardley for advice in the early stages; Susanne Haines for the calligraphy on pages 28–29; Karl Adamson, Dave King and Colin Keates for photography; Parker Pen UK Ltd for the pen on page 52; Johnson Mathey for the catalytic converter; Boots Co. for the water softener; Ed Evans at the Coal Research Establishment, British Coal Corporation for technical advice. **DTP Manager:** Joanna Figg-Latham; **Illustrations:** John Woodcock; **Index:** Jane Parker; **Project editor:** Charyn Jones; **Art editor:** Heather McCarry; **Designer:** Marianna Papachrysanthou; **Production:** Louise Daly; **Managing editor:** Josephine Buchanan; **Senior art editor:** Thomas Keenes; **Picture research:** Deborah Pownall, Catherine O'Rourke; **Special photography:** Clive Streeter; **Editorial consultant:** Peter Morris, Science Museum, London; **US editor:** Charles A. Wills; **US consultant:** Professor Peter W. Morgan, Teachers College, Columbia University

ELECTRICITY
Fred Archer, Brian Bowers, Roger Bridgman, Janet Carding, Eryl Davies, Robert Excell, Graeme Fyffe, Derek Hudson, Dr Ghislaine Lawrence, Barry Marshall and the staff of the Museum Workshop, Douglas Millard, Victoria Smith, Peter Stephens, Peter Tomlinson, Kenneth Waterman, Anthony Wilson, and David Woodcock for advice and help with the provision of objects for photography at the Science Musuem; Dave Mancini at Nortech and Peter Griffiths for the model making; Deborah Rhodes for page make-up, Peter Cooling for computer artwork; Robert Husle for standing in for Michael Faraday and Humphry Davy; Karl Adamson and Tim Ridley for assis-tance with the photography; Jack Challoner for help in the initial stages of the book; Susannah Steel for proofreading. **Picture Research:** Deborah Pownall and Catherine O'Rourke; **Illustrations:** Kuo Kang Chen; **Index:** Jane Parker; **Project editor:** Charyn Jones; **Senior art editor:** Neville Graham; **Design assistant:** Marianna Papachrysanthou; **DTP manager:** Joanna Figg-Latham; **Production:** Eunice Paterson; **Managing editor:** Josephine Buchanan; **Special photography:** Charyn Jones; **Editorial consultant:** Neil Brown, Science Museum, London; **US editor:** Charles A. Wills; **US consultant:** Harvey B. Loomis

ENERGY
John Becklake, Roger Bridgman, Neil Brown, Robert Bud, Clive Bunyan, Ian Carter, Robert Excell, Peter Fitzgerald, Graeme Fyffe, Mike Harding, Emma Hedderwick, Kevin Johnson, John Liffen, Peter Mann, Robert McWilliam, Steve Preston, Fiona Reid, Stephen Roberts, Derek Robinson, John Robinson, Ken Shirt, Victoria Smith, Peter Stephens, Ken Waterman, Jane Wess, Anthony Wilson, David Woodcock, and Michael Wright for advice and help with the provision of objects for photography at the Science Museum; Peter Griffiths for model making; Deborah Rhodes for page make-up; Karl Adamson, Paul Bricknell, Jane Burton and Kim Taylor, Dave King, Tim Ridley, and Jerry Young for additional photog-raphy; the British Museum for pho-tographing the central image on pages 134–135; Solar Economy, Winchester, United Kingdom, for providing the cutaway solar panel on page 187; Peter Wilson, the Ministry of Agriculture, Norwich, for the loan of the calorimeter on page 179. **Illustrations:** John Woodcock; **Cartography:** Roger Bullen, James Mills-Hicks; **Index:** Jane Parker; **Project editor:** Stephanie Jackson; **Art editor:** Gurinder Purewall; **Designer:** Marianna Papachrysanthou; **Production:** Eunice Paterson; **Managing editor:** Josephine Buchana; **Senior art editor:** Thomas Keenes; **Picture research:** Deborah Pownall, Catherine O'Rourke; **Special photography:** Clive Streeter; **Editorial consultant:** Brian Bowers, Science Museum, London; **US editor:** Charles A. Wills; **US consultant** Professor Warren Yasso, Teachers College, Columbia University

FORCE & MOTION
John Becklake, Neil Brown, Anna Bunney, Helen Dowling, Stewart Emmens, Sam Evans, Peter Fitzgerald, Graeme Fyffe, Ben Gammon, Alex Hayward, Jane Insley, Kevin Johnson, John Liffen, Barry Marshall and the staff of the Science Museum Workshop, Robert McWilliam, Douglas Millard, Alan Morton, Andrew Nahum, Cathy Needham, Keith Packer, David Ray and his staff, Fiona Reid, Francesca Riccini, John Robinson, Ken Shirt, Jane Smith, Victoria Smith, John Smith, Peter Stephens, Peter Tomlinson, Denys Vaughan, Tony Vincent, Jane Wess, David Woodcock and Michael Wright for advice and help with the provision of objects for photography; Reg Grant and Jack Challoner for help in the initial stages of the book; David Donkin and Peter Griffiths for the model making; Deborah Rhodes for page makeup; Karl Adamson for assistance with the photography; Susannah Steel and Stephanie Jackson for proofreading. **Picture research:** Deborah Pownall and Catherine O'Rourke; **Illustrations:** Janos Marffy and John Woodcock; **Index:** Jane Parker; **Project editor:** Ian Whitelaw; **Art editor:** Brian Rust; **Design assistant:** Marianna Papachrysanthou; **DTP manager:** Joanna Figg-Latham; **Production:** Eunice Paterson; **Managing editor:** Josephine Buchanan; **Senior art editor:** Neville Graham; **Special photography:** Clive Streeter; **Editorial consultant:** Anthony Wilson, Science Museum, London; **US editor:** Charles A. Wills; **US consultant:** Harvey B. Loomis

LIGHT
Jane Wess of the Science Museum for checking the text; Fred Archer, Tim Boon, Brian Bowers, Roger Bridgman, Neil Brown, Robert Bud, Sue Cackett, Ian Carter, Ann Carter, Tony Clarke, Helen Dowling, Stewart Emmens, Robert Excell, Graeme Fyffe, Colin Harding, Derek Hudson, Stephanie Millard, Kate Morris, David Ray and his staff, Derek Robinson, Victoria Smith, Peter Stephens, Peter Tomlinson, Tony Vincent, Anthony Wilson, and David Woodcock for advice and help with the provision of objects for photography at the Science Museum; Peter Griffiths for model making; Deborah Rhodes for page makeup; Jane Bull for design assistance; Susannah Steel for edi-torial assistance; Karl Adamson and Jonathan Buckley for addition-al photography and assistance; Jack Challoner and Neil Ardley for con-sulting on the text; Fiona Spence of De Beers for the loan of cubic zirco-nias; British Telecom for the provi-sion of fiber optics; Stephen Herbert for the loan of the magic lantern; Lester Smith for the loan of the magic lantern burner; Phil Farrand for allowing photography of the solar car; Mike Bartley for the loan of the shadow theater. **Picture research:** Deborah Pownall and Catherine O'Rourke; **Illustrations:** Kuo Kang Chen, Janos Marffy, Alistair Wardle, and John Woodcock; **Index:** Jane Parker; **Project editor:** Stephanie Jackson; **Designer:** Gurinder Purewall; **Design assistant:** Marianna Papachrysanthou; **DTP manager:** Joanna Figg-Latham; **Production:** Eunice Paterson; **Managing editor:** Josephine Buchanan; **Senior art editor:** Neville Graham; **Special photography:** Dave King; **US editor:** Charles A. Wills; **US consultant:** Harvey B. Loomis

MATTER
John Becklake, Chris Berridge, Tim Boon, Roger Bridgman, Neil Brown, Robert Bud, Sue Cackett, Ann Carter, Ann de Caires, Helen Dowling, Stewart Emmens, Robert Excell, Stephen Foulger, Graeme Fyffe, Derek Hudson, Kevin Johnson, Sarah Leonard, Steve Long, Stephanie Millard, Peter Morris, Keith Parker, David Ray and his staff, Anthony Richards, Derek Robinson, Victoria Smith, Peter Stephens, Laura Taylor, Peter Tomlinson, Denys Vaughan, Nicole Weisz, and Anthony Wilson for the help with the provision of objects for photography; Jane Bull for design guidance; Deborah Rhodes for page makeup; Debra Clapson for editorial assistance; Marianna Papachrysanthou for design assis-tance; Neil Ardley for synopsis development; Stephen Pollock-Hill at Nazeing glassworks for his expertise; Jane Burton, Jane Dickins, Paul Hammond, and Fiona Spence of De Beers for pro-viding props. **Picture research:** Deborah Pownall and Catherine O'Rourke; **Illustrations:** John Woodcock; **Index:** Jane Parker; **Project editor:** Sharon Lucas; **Designer:** Heather McCarry; **DTP manager:** Joanna Figg-Latham; **Production:** Eunice Paterson; **Managing editor:** Josephine Buchanan; **Senior art editor:** Neville Graham; **Special photography:** Dave King; **Editorial consultant:** Alan Morton, Science Museum, London; **Special consultant:** Jack Challoner; **US editor:** Charles A. Wills; **US consultant:** Harvey B. Loomis